TimeOut

Las Vegas

timeout.com/lasvegas

Penguin Books

PENGUIN BOOKS

Published by the Penguin Group
Penguin Books Ltd, 80 Strand, London WC2R ORL, England
Penguin Books USA Inc., 375 Hudson Street, New York, New York 10014, USA
Penguin Books Australia Ltd, Ringwood, Victoria, Australia
Penguin Books Canada Ltd, 10 Alcorn Avenue, Toronto, Ontario, Canada M4V 3B2
Penguin Books (NZ) Ltd, 182-190 Wairau Road, Auckland 10, New Zealand

Penguin Books Ltd, Registered Offices: Harmondsworth, Middlesex, England

First published 1998
Second edition 2000
Third edition 2001
10 9 8 7 6 5 4 3 2 1

Copyright © Time Out Group Ltd, 1998, 2000, 2001
All rights reserved

Colour reprographics by Icon, Crown House, 56-58 Southwark Street, London SE1
and Precise Litho, 34-35 Great Sutton Street, London EC1
Printed and bound by Cayfosa-Quebecor, Ctra. de Caldes, Km 3 08 130 Sta, Perpètua de Mogoda, Barcelona, Spain

Edited and designed by
Time Out Guides Limited
Universal House
251 Tottenham Court Road
London W1T 7AB
Tel + 44 (020) 7813 3000
Fax + 44 (020) 7813 6001
Email guides@timeout.com
www.timeout.com

Editorial

Editor Sophie Blacksell
Copy Editors Christi Daugherty, Kevin Ebbutt,
Cath Phillips, Nicholas Royle
Consultant Editor James P Reza
Senior Listings Editor Anne Kellogg
Deputy Listings Editor Michael Toole
Proofreader Angela Jameson
Indexer Marion Moisy

Editorial Director Peter Fiennes
Series Editor Ruth Jarvis
Deputy Series Editor Jonathan Cox
Guides Co-ordinator Jenny Noden

Design

Group Art Director John Oakey
Art Editor Mandy Martin
Senior Designer Scott Moore
Designers Benjamin de Lotz, Lucy Grant, Kate Vincent-Smith
Picture Editor Kerri Miles
Deputy Picture Editor Olivia Duncan-Jones
Scanning & Imaging Dan Conway
Ad make-up Glen Impey

Advertising

Group Commercial Director Lesley Gill
Sales Director Mark Phillips
International Sales Co-ordinator Ross Canadé
Advertising Director, North American Guides Liz Howell
(1-808 732 4661/1-888 333 5776 US only)
Advertising in the US co-ordinated by *Time Out New York*
Alison Tocci (Publisher), Tom Oesau (Advertising Production
Manager), Maggie Puddu (Assistant to the Publisher)

Administration

Publisher Tony Elliott
Managing Director Mike Hardwick
Group Financial Director Kevin Ellis
Marketing Director Christine Cort
Marketing Manager Mandy Martinez
Group General Manager Nichola Coulthard
Production Manager Mark Lamond
Production Controller Samantha Furniss
Accountant Sarah Bostock

Features in this guide were written and researched by:
Introduction James P Reza. **History** Deke Castleman. **Las Vegas Today** Gregory Crosby. **Architecture** Geoff Schumacher,
Frances Anderton. **Gambling** Deke Castleman (*Vegas on the cheap: Gambling, Vegas on the cheap: Slot clubs* David
Stratton). **Accommodation** David Stratton. **Sightseeing Introduction** James P Reza. **Casinos** David Hofstede, David Stratton.
The Strip James P Reza (*Vegas on the cheap: Casino freebies* David Stratton). **Off-Strip** James P Reza. **Downtown** James P
Reza. **The Rest of the City** James P Reza (*Art attack* Gregory Crosby). **Restaurants & Buffets** John Curtas, David Stratton
(*Caffeine fix* Geoff Carter). **Bars** Geoff Carter. **Shops & Services** Anne Kellogg. **By Season** Renée LiButti. **Children** Renée
LiButti. **Casino Entertainment** David Stratton (*Las Vegas legends: Frank Sinatra* Gregory Crosby; *Vegas on the cheap:
Entertainment* David Stratton). **Film** Gregory Crosby (*Celluloid city* Geoff Carter). **Nightlife: Adult** James P Reza. **Nightlife:
Dance Clubs** Geoff Carter. **Nightlife: Gay & Lesbian** Anne Davis Mulford (*Las Vegas legends: Liberace* James P Reza).
Nightlife: Music Geoff Carter. **Performing Arts** Gregory Crosby. **Sport & Fitness** David Hofstede. **Weddings** Renée LiButti.
Getting Started Sophie Blacksell, Cath Phillips. **Day Trips** Sophie Blacksell, Cath Phillips. **Into Nevada** Deke Castleman (*The
big bang* Sophie Blacksell; *The Burning Man Festival* Bruce van Dyke). **Into Arizona** Sophie Blacksell. **Into California** Frances
Anderton. **Into Utah** Sophie Blacksell, Cath Phillips. **Getting Around** Anne Kellogg, James P Reza. **Resources A-Z** David
Hofstede (Business, Media) Anne Kellogg, James P Reza. **Further Reference** James P Reza, Nicholas Royle.

The Editor would like to thank:
David Aboderin, Emily, Penny and Simon Blacksell, Bruce Brossman at Grand Canyon Lodges, Portia Clarke, Heather Curry at
the Regional Transportation Commission of Southern Nevada, Jenny Dack, Will Fulford-Jones, Sarah Guy, Simon Jones, the
Las Vegas Convention & Visitors Authority, Stacey Linklater, Colleen Reid at Budget Suites, Megan Riley, Jessica Slama at
the Aladdin Resort & Casino, Celeste Wilson at Alamo and all contributors to previous editions of the guide, whose work
formed the basis for this edition.

The editor stayed at Budget Suites (1-800 752 1501). Car hire was provided by Alamo Rent A Car (UK 08705 994000/
US 1-800 327 9633/www.goalamo.com).

Maps by JS Graphics, 17 Beadles Lane, Old Oxted, Surrey RH8 9JG.

Photography by Paul Avis except: page 28, 183, 185, 229, 236 LVCVA; page 9, 10, 13, 217, 220, 233, 259 Associated
Press; page iii, 3, 5, 19, 22, 25, 50, 56, 64, 79, 82, 91 (bottom), 105, 106, 107, 115 (bottom), 116, 122, 127, 189, 190,
224, 225 Amanda Edwards; page 178 Jeffrey Green; page 193 Jim Porto; page 17, 256 Las Vegas News Bureau; page 255
Corbis; page 263, 264, 265 Grand Canyon National Park Lodges; page 268 AOT/Chris Coe.

The following pictures were provided by the featured establishments: page 15, 47, 194, 198, 200, 204, 205, 223, 251,
270, 278, 279.

Contents

Introduction

Since its raucous, romanticised days as the Rat Pack's mob-ruled playground, Las Vegas has willingly played both the darling and devil of popular culture. It is among a handful of cities whose name instantly evokes vivid imagery: drunken revelry along neon-soaked sidewalks littered with forlorn gambling addicts and temptresses for hire. Such die-hard stereotypes are challenged by the reality of the new Vegas, where world-class (and often class-defining) shopping, dining and entertainment jostle for attention with the sins of the past.

To visitors and new residents, Las Vegas is either a refreshing look into the future or a frustrating reminder of a reckless past. To optimists it is a microcosm of America one hundred years ago and one hundred years from now; a place of freedom and opportunity where even the biggest of dreams may be realised. According to cultural pundit Kurt Andersen, it is the 'Detroit of the 21st Century'; a poster child of middle-class globalisation where the marginalised and the mainstream meet and become fast friends. Visitors sip cheap liquor from plastic pint glasses while window shopping for $1,000 dresses. And ain't life grand?

The city seems to revel in its own newness. Where once only cactus stood, wide, curving boulevards lead to pricey mansions and golf courses carved out of the Mojave Desert. Saplings stand as uncertain sentries for middle-class homes built in a furious 90-day flash. And ever more opulent themed resorts welcome punters before the paint has a chance to dry, throwing their doors wide to throngs of tourists, eager to see the magic and artistry that has been created to separate them from their money.

Such accelerated growth presents its own challenges in a city where the infrastructure has never had time to catch up. Meanwhile, the Strip has blossomed into a fascinating cultural playground, with museums and galleries springing up amid the other glittering attractions. The result is that more and more well-heeled locals are now spending time on the Strip – just like in the old days – blurring the lines between visitor and local.

Despite the city's growth-induced instability, its magnetism is inescapable. Depending upon your perspective, the Vegas vortex can either be the last salvation or the last temptation. And it is this inability truly to identify Las Vegas that remains the city's ultimate allure. To paraphrase a cliché about the weather: if you don't like Las Vegas, wait a short while; it will be a different city the next time you look. *James P Reza*

ABOUT THE TIME OUT CITY GUIDES

The *Time Out Las Vegas Guide* is one of an expanding series of Time Out City Guides, now numbering over 35, produced by the people behind London and New York's successful listings magazines. Our guides are all written and updated by resident experts who have striven to provide you with all the most up-to-date information you'll need to explore the city or read up on its background, whether you're a local or a first-time visitor.

THE LOWDOWN ON THE LISTINGS

Above all, we've tried to make this book as useful as possible. Addresses, telephone numbers, websites, transport information, opening times, admission prices and credit card details have all been included in the listings. And, as far as possible, we've given details of facilities, services and events, all checked and correct as we went to press. However, owners and managers can change their arrangements at any time, and they often do. Before you go out of your way, we'd advise you to telephone and check opening times, ticket prices and other particulars. While every effort has been made to ensure the accuracy of the information contained in this guide, the publishers cannot accept responsibility for any errors it may contain.

PRICES AND PAYMENT

We have noted where venues such as shops, hotels, restaurants, museums and so on accept the following credit cards: American Express (AmEx), Diners Club (DC), Discover (Disc), MasterCard (MC) and Visa (V). Many will also accept travellers' cheques, along with other credit cards (Carte Blanche, for example).

Since the '50s and '60s, Las Vegas has been famous for its bargain prices, but over the past decade, the cost of visiting Las Vegas has increased while the great deals people used to rave about have become harder to find.

However, while the era of vacationing in Las Vegas on 25 cents a day is long gone, casinos must still be competitive to attract customers. During your stay, you should be able to find all manner of attractive promotions and keep expenses to a minimum, while having a good time. Throughout this guide, look out for our **Vegas on the cheap** features, with handy tips on how to get more bang for your buck. While you're in town, pick up a copy of the *Las Vegas Review-Journal*. Its Friday 'Neon' section has information about slot clubs, restaurant deals and show ticket discounts. For a more detailed listing, get hold of the *Las Vegas Advisor* from **Huntington Press** (3687 Procyon Avenue, Las Vegas, NV 89103; 1-800 244 2224). This 12-page monthly newsletter employs a team of researchers to test out the best and cheapest that the casinos have to offer.

The prices we've supplied should be treated as guidelines, not gospel. If prices vary wildly from those we've quoted, please write and let us know. We aim to give the best and most up-to-date advice, so we always want to know if you've been badly treated or overcharged.

THE LIE OF THE LAND
To make the book (and the city) easier to navigate, we have divided Las Vegas into areas and assigned each one its own chapter in our Sightseeing section starting on page 63. Although these area designations are a

There is an online version of this guide, as well as weekly events listings for over 35 international cities, at www.timeout.com.

simplification of Las Vegas's geography and are not official names seen on signposts, we hope they will help you to understand the city's layout and to find its most interesting sights. For consistency, the same areas are used in addresses throughout the guide. We've also included cross-streets, zip codes for those venues you might want to write to and website addresses wherever possible. Finally, there's a series of fully indexed colour maps at the back of the guide, starting on page 307. For further orientation information, *see p64*.

TELEPHONE NUMBERS
The area code for Las Vegas is 702. All telephone numbers listed in this guide take this code unless otherwise stated. For more on telephones and codes, *see p295*.

ESSENTIAL INFORMATION
For all the practical information you might need for visiting Las Vegas, including visa and customs information, advice on facilities and access for the disabled, emergency telephone numbers, useful websites and the lowdown on the local transport network, turn to the **Directory** chapter at the back of the guide. It starts on page 281.

MAPS
Wherever possible, a map reference is provided for every venue listed in the guide, indicating the page and grid reference at which it can be found on our street maps. These fully indexed colour maps are located at the back of the book (*see pp307-316*) and include Trips Out of Town, Day Trips, Central Las Vegas, Downtown, Las Vegas Areas, CAT Bus Routes, and The Strip (north and south).

LET US KNOW WHAT YOU THINK
We hope you enjoy the *Time Out Las Vegas Guide*, and we'd like to know what you think of it. We welcome tips for places that you consider we should include in future editions and take note of your criticism of our choices. There's a reader's reply card at the back of this book for your feedback, or you can email us at lasvegasguide@timeout.com.

HACKETT

b u n g y

L A S V E G A S

why
live on
the edge
when you can
jump

810 Circus Circus Drive
Las Vegas, Nevada 89109

Phone: 702.385.4321
Fax: 702.734.7581

www.aj-hackett.com Email: vegas@aj-hackett.com

In Context

History

From a desolate desert town to the fastest growing major city in America – in under a century.

Around 25,000 years ago, the large valley that Las Vegas inhabits – and which is quickly filling up with casinos, amusement parks and suburbs – was partially underwater. It was the tail-end of the last ice age. Glaciers were retreating from the mountains that surround the Las Vegas Valley and the glacial run-off fed a great lake, 20 miles (32 kilometres) across and thousands of feet deep. The great lake's outlet was a river, known now as the Las Vegas Wash, larger than anything that remains in the western United States today, even though it flowed for only 40 miles (64 kilometres). At its mouth, the Wash was swallowed, with barely a ripple, by a monster waterway, the same waterway that had been carving the Grand Canyon for a couple of hundred million years, on and off. Where Downtown and the Strip now shine was the deepest part of the lake.

According to archaeological evidence, Paleo-Indians lived in caves near the shoreline of the lake, which shrank as the climate changed gradually from cold and wet to warm and dry.

The first Las Vegans shared the tule marsh at the edge of the lake with prehistoric horses, giant ground sloths, American camels and massive condors, and they hunted other big Pleistocene mammals, such as woolly mammoth, bison, mastodon and caribou, as early as 13,000 BC. Paleontologists have uncovered prehistoric hearths, fluted arrowheads and spear points, primitive stone tools and charred animal bones. Beyond these finds, little is known about the area's earliest inhabitants, but from around 5,000 years ago, a clearer picture of the local prehistoric people starts to emerge.

Hunter-foragers known as Archaic Indians introduced an Indian culture that evolved over the next 4,000 years. The area they occupied was by then desert, even though plentiful spring water bubbled up to the surface and flowed down Las Vegas Wash (now a creek) to the canyon-carving Colorado River. They lived and travelled in small bands, used the *atlatl* (an arrow launcher), hunted bighorn sheep and desert tortoise, harvested screw-bean mesquite and cholla fruit, and built rock shelters.

But it wasn't until the first centuries AD that there were signs of civilisation in and around Nevada's southern desert. The native Anasazi resided in pit houses (holes in the ground, topped with brush roofs) and lived basically. Still, by around AD 500, they had evolved into an organised people: hunting with bows and arrows; making pottery and mining salt. In addition, the Anasazi had started to trade with their neighbours and had refined their building techniques so that their dwellings now had adobe walls. Three hundred years later, the Anasazi were cultivating beans and corn in irrigated fields, living in huge 100-room pueblos, fashioning artistic pots and baskets and mining turquoise. An Anasazi village in Las Vegas Valley is the first known prehistoric architecture in Nevada.

Mysteriously, however, the Anasazi people disappeared from the area around 1150. No one is sure exactly why, but theories have included disease, drought, overpopulation and warring with neighbours. A large Anasazi village was discovered in 1924, parts of which are now preserved and commemorated at the Lost City Museum in Overton, 45 miles (72 kilometres) north-east of Las Vegas (see p249).

Southern Paiutes, a tribe of hunter-foragers more like the Archaic Indians than the Anasazi, claimed the abandoned territory, but they never regained the advanced elements of their predecessors' society. For the next 700 years, the Paiute remained semi-nomadic: they established base camps of movable 'wickiups' (similar to teepees), cultivated squash and corn at the springs and creeks, and travelled seasonally to hunt and harvest wild foods, such as pine nuts, screw beans, tules, rabbit, deer and sheep. A frequent stopover on their travels was the Big Spring, the centre of a lush riparian habitat and still the largest area of undeveloped land in the city (see p121).

MEXICANS AND MORMONS

The Paiute were the folk who greeted the earliest European explorers and settlers in the mid-19th century. The first white men to enter the region that is now Las Vegas were Mexican traders, travelling along the Old Spanish Trail blazed by Franciscan friars to connect Spanish-Catholic missions scattered between New Mexico and the California coast.

Then in 1830, a mere three decades before the American Civil War, one Antonio Armijo set out from Santa Fe to trade goods along the trail. An experienced scout in his party, Rafael Rivera, discovered a short cut, by way of the

Big Spring, and became the first non-native to set foot on the land. He named the area Las Vegas, meaning 'the meadows'. Just 75 years later it would become the beginnings of the city we know today.

> **'By 1845 Las Vegas was a popular camping spot, thanks to Big Spring, the only fresh water within a day's march.'**

By the time John C Fremont, legendary surveyor and cartographer for the Army Topographical Corps (whose name lives on as the main street in Downtown Las Vegas), passed through Las Vegas Valley in 1845, the Old Spanish Trail had become the most travelled route through the South-west. Las Vegas by then was a popular camping spot, thanks to Big Spring, the only fresh water within a day's march. Latter-day Saints, who had settled at the shore of the Great Salt Lake a few hundred miles north-east, passed through Las Vegas regularly on their way to Los Angeles, and by the early 1850s, Mormon pioneer parties, wagon trains and mail carriers travelling between central Utah and southern California overnighted at Big Spring so frequently that Church elders decided to colonise the area.

In 1855, a party of Mormon missionaries was dispatched from Salt Lake City to establish a community at Las Vegas that would serve the travellers on the trail and convert the Paiute. The missionaries erected a fort, dug irrigation ditches, cultivated crops and managed to befriend some Indians. But the rigours of domesticating a vast desert took their toll on the settlers. The climate proved unbearably inhospitable. Crops failed and rations were meagre. Timber had to be hauled from the nearest mountainsides, 20 miles (32 kilometres) away. And the isolation further sapped morale.

The mission might have succeeded had the colonists not located deposits of lead nearby. This discovery attracted miners from Salt Lake City, whose needs for food, lumber and shelter taxed the colonists' already inadequate supplies to breaking point. Despite the miners' vociferous objections, the colonists petitioned Salt Lake City to be recalled, and the mission was finally abandoned in 1858. A small remnant of the Mormon fort survives; it is the oldest standing structure in Las Vegas today, 50 years older than any other (pictured p6; see also p123).

OD GASS AND HELEN STEWART

Soon after the Mormons abandoned Las Vegas, prospectors picked up where the lead miners left off and discovered that the ore averaged a rich $650 per ton in silver. A small mining boomtown mushroomed in the desert around Big Spring. Miners who arrived too late to get in on the excitement fanned out from the settlement and discovered gold along the Colorado River, about 50 miles (80 kilometres) south-west of the Meadows.

One of the gold seekers, Octavius Decatur Gass, saw a better opportunity in homesteading the well-watered valley. In 1865, he and his family appropriated the Mormon fort, using the lumber to build a ranch house and utility shop. Gass dug irrigation canals, planted grains, vegetables and fruit trees, and ran cattle on a ranch known as Las Vegas Ranch. Over the next ten years, Gass expanded his land and water holdings, assumed civil duties such as justice of the peace and territorial legislator, and helped other homesteaders get established in Las Vegas.

But in the mid-1870s, Gass was in financial trouble and took a loan from Archibald Stewart, a wealthy Scottish rancher from Pioche, another mining boomtown 100 miles (160 kilometres) north. When Gass couldn't repay the loan, Stewart foreclosed and took Las Vegas Ranch. He worked and successfully expanded the property until 1884, when he had an argument with a ranch hand from a neighbouring spread and was shot dead. Stewart's wife, Helen, managed the ranch for the next 20 years, buying up more acreage, making a tidy living in the livestock business and running a resort for nearby ranchers and a campground for travellers on the Mormon Trail.

LONG TRAIN COMING

In 1903, the San Pedro, Los Angeles and Salt Lake Railroad arrived, planning a right-of-way that would run through the heart of the ranch. Thanks to its strategic location and plentiful water, Las Vegas had already been designated as a division point for crew changes, a service stop for through trains and an eventual site for maintenance shops. Ready to retire, Mrs Stewart sold all but ten acres of her 2,000-acre (810-hectare) shootin' match for $55,000, and deeded the other ten acres to the Las Vegas Paiute (*see p123*), who'd been reduced to living on the edge of town, dependent on government largesse. For this and other civic-minded deeds, Helen Stewart is considered the First Lady of Las Vegas to this day.

In preparation for the sale of her land to the railroad, Helen Stewart hired JT McWilliams to survey her property. McWilliams discovered and immediately claimed 80 untitled acres (32 hectares) just west of the big ranch. McWilliams planned a town site and began selling lots to a steadfast group of Las Vegas 'sooners' (the earliest speculators on the scene). In late 1904, two railroad construction crews, one from the north-east and the other from the south-west, converged on Las Vegas Valley, and in January 1905, the golden spike was driven into a tie near Jean, Nevada, 23 miles (37 kilometres) to the south of Las Vegas.

McWilliams's settlement, known as Ragtown, was one of a long line of boom towns that had been erupting from the desert floor all across the state of Nevada for the past 50 years. On the day that the first train travelled through Big Spring on its inaugural run between Salt Lake City and Los Angeles, Ragtown's saloons, banks, newspaper office and tent hotels teemed with settlers, speculators, merchants, tradesmen and itinerants. But the San Pedro, Los Angeles and Salt Lake Railroad had other plans for the fledgling settlement. It organised a subsidiary, Las Vegas Land and Water, to build its own town of Las Vegas. Officials laid out the town site, scraped the desert scrub from 40 square blocks, and staked 1,200 lots. The new railroad town received enough national publicity to create a demand for the land; prospective buyers came by train from Los Angeles ($16 return) and Salt Lake City ($20).

GAMBLING ON PROSPERITY

The competition for the prime locations proved so overwhelming that in order to handle the hordes of hopefuls, the railroad scheduled an auction to sell the remaining lots, thereby pitting eager settlers, hoping for jobs with the railroad, against Los Angeles real estate speculators and East Coast investors: all were gambling on the initial prosperity of yet another western railroad boomtown.

The auction was held on 15 May 1905 at the corner of Main and Fremont Streets, on the site of today's Plaza Hotel in the heart of Downtown. The bidding quickly inflated the value of the choice lots to more than double their listed values. The locals, who lived across the tracks in JT McWilliams's Ragtown, grumbled about the railroad tactic of encouraging out-of-town investors to heat up the prices; as one participant observed, 'the auction was a nice clever scheme – the simplest way of giving everyone a fair shake (down)'. When it was over, nearly 1,000 lots had been sold for the grand total of $265,000 dollars, $195,000 more than the railroad had paid for the entire Las Vegas Ranch only three years earlier.

Man-made wonder: **Hoover Dam** made the growth of Las Vegas possible. *See p11.*

Immediately, the proud new property owners searched out the stakes sticking out from the desert sand that marked lot boundaries and erected makeshift shelters. Ragtown residents rolled their possessions over to the new Las Vegas on horse- and ox-drawn wagons; what remained of the first town site burned to the ground four months later and Las Vegas's first building boom followed.

SETTLING IN

The saloons and honky-tonks and cribs were the first to go up in the designated nightlife and red-light district on Block 16, between Ogden and Stewart and First and Second Streets (where Binion's Horseshoe parking lot stands today). Hotels, restaurants, banks and shops were quickly erected along Fremont Street, while railroad and town administrative offices, a school, the post office and two churches surrounded the Downtown core. The company installed the infrastructure: gravel streets and plank sidewalks, water service and sporadic electricity. Houses went up on the residential streets of the eight-block-long and five-block-wide town, with the building supplies arriving daily on the through trains. On New Year's Day 1906, 1,500 pioneers called Las Vegas home.

But the initial boom was shortlived. Barely a year passed before the railroad town managers showed their true colours, concerned first with operating the main line and last with servicing the town. Their refusal to extend water pipes beyond the town site stunted growth and forced the rural dwellers to dig wells and tap into the aquifer. The usual fires, political conflicts and growing pains of a young and remote settlement slowed the influx of new residents, reduced property values and dampened optimism; the heat, dust and isolation contributed to the consensus of discomfort.

A rare bit of good news arrived in 1909, when the Nevada Legislature created Clark, a new county in the south of the state named after William Clark, the chairman of the San Pedro, Los Angeles and Salt Lake Railroad; Las Vegas was installed as its seat. Soon after, the railroad gave the new county seat a boost by building a shop for maintaining the steam locomotives,

Las Vegas legends Bugsy Siegel

Bugsy's was a fire that burned so hot and bright and deadly that its glow is still visible today, more than 50 years later. Glamorised and idolised for more than 50 years, his place in the history of Las Vegas is assured.

Benjamin Siegel was born in 1905, the same year as Las Vegas, on the mean streets of central Brooklyn. By the time he'd turned 18, he was the toughest, meanest and most violent kid in the neighbourhood, known to everyone as a thug. When he was 34, the powerful East Coast bosses dispatched Siegel, with two hand-picked 'assistants', to seize control of the Southern California Mob. Within a year, he had muscled into California's race wire (which sent the results of local horse races across the country), the offshore gambling ships, the Mexican marijuana and heroin trade, and the movie-industry labour unions.

Having conquered Southern California, Bugsy and his henchmen set their sights on southern Nevada. Unfortunately, the story of an unknown charmer (who looked like Warren Beatty) kicking sagebrush in the desert and having a vision of the most luxurious casino-resort of its time, is apocryphal at best. In the early '40s, this well-known enforcer showed up in hokey little Las Vegas and immediately began throwing his weight around, taking pieces of the action and extorting money from those he could control.

The truth is that the Fabulous Flamingo had already been designed, financed and started when Bugsy decided to take on the owner and management. It was the dream and brainchild of Billy Wilkerson, a Hollywood impresario, nightclub owner and resort developer with a bad gambling addiction, who figured that the only way to increase his chances of winning was to own the joint. It was Wilkerson's sensibilities, not Siegel's, that provided the inspiration for the Flamingo.

According to a book by Billy Wilkerson's son, *The Man Who Invented Las Vegas*, Siegel approached Wilkerson and asked to serve as an assistant, in order to learn the business of building a resort, and offered to supply the casino with bosses and dealers in return. Wilkerson agreed, but Siegel quickly showed his true colours and began intimidating, then terrorising, everyone involved. On two occasions Wilkerson was forced to flee to Paris for his life.

Siegel took over the Flamingo, but without Wilkerson's brains behind the operation, things soon got out of control. The stories of construction foul-ups, cost overruns, and Bugsy's increasing irrationality and paranoia are true. It's a testament to the strength of his own will that Bugsy managed to piece together the Flamingo and open it at all.

The Flamingo proved to be a spectacular failure, and ultimately cost Bugsy his life, but along the way, in the short nine or ten months that he ran the show, Ben Siegel managed to rewrite history, claiming the Flamingo as his own vision, and creating a legend that has endured to this day.

passenger coaches and freight cars along the line. When the facility opened in 1911, it created hundreds of jobs and by the time the shop was fully staffed, the population of Las Vegas had doubled to 3,000. Telephone service arrived when the first phone – boasting the number '1', of course – was installed at the cigar counter in the lobby of the Hotel Nevada (now the Golden Gate, the oldest hotel in Las Vegas) at the corner of Main and Fremont Streets. And in 1915, the big town generators began supplying electricity to the residents 24 hours a day.

> ## 'Vegas would have dried up and blown away if it hadn't been for the dam-building project gearing up nearby.'

But it was all downhill for the next 15 years. The railroad found itself losing more and more business to car and truck traffic, with the result that workers were laid off. A nationwide railroad, Union Pacific, bought up the San Pedro, Los Angeles and Salt Lake, relegating it to the status of a small siding on its vast network, shutting down the maintenance shops, eliminating more jobs and driving out residents. It also implemented policies, in particular concerning water delivery, that severely inhibited the town's growth. Las Vegas would have dried up and blown away by the late 1920s if it hadn't been for a monumental federal dam-building project gearing up nearby.

HOOVER DAM

The 1,450-mile (2,333-kilometre) long Colorado River, the principal waterway of the arid Southwest, had been gouging great canyons and watering lush valleys for eons, when the US government became determined to harness the flow in the service of irrigation, electricity, flood control and recreation. In 1907, the federal Bureau of Reclamation began to consider damming the Colorado, and by 1924, the Bureau had narrowed the location for the dam to two canyons east of Las Vegas. In 1930, Congress appropriated the $165 million to build it.

Anticipation of the dam project began to fuel noticeable growth in the railroad town. By the time construction of the dam began in 1931, a long-distance phone service, a federal highway from Salt Lake City to Los Angeles and regularly scheduled airmail and air-passenger services had all arrived in Las Vegas. The population soared to 5,000, with thousands more passing through Las Vegas en route to the Colorado River, which was about to be tamed.

Even today, the building of Hoover Dam is mind-boggling in its immensity. The nearest power plant was 200 miles (322 kilometres) away in southern California, from where wires had to be strung to supply the necessary electricity. Five thousand workers had to be hired and an entire town (Boulder City) built to house them and their families. And, most daunting of all, the mighty Colorado River had to be diverted. It took 16 months to hack four diversion tunnels through the canyon walls before the river could be routed around the construction site. Finally, the great dam itself, one of the man-made wonders of the world, had to be put into place.

Five million buckets of concrete were poured into the dam over a two-year period. When it was completed in 1935, Hoover Dam stood 656 feet (200 metres) wide at its base, 49 feet (15 metres) thick at its crest, 1,358 feet (414 metres) across and 794 feet (242 metres) tall. The diversion tunnels were closed and it took three years to fill Lake Mead, the largest man-made lake in North America: 109 miles (175 kilometres) long, 545 feet (166 metres) deep, impounding 37.4 billion gallons (170 billion litres) of water. The dam's legacy has been monumental, endowing Las Vegas with all the power and water it needed to fulfil its promise.

THE NEW BOOM

Another event occurred in 1931 that had long-lasting implications for Las Vegas: the statewide legalisation of wide-open casino gambling. Backroom illegal gambling had long been the norm for a libertine frontier state such as Nevada, but when the legislators gave it their official blessing (along with easy divorces, no-wait marriages, legal prostitution and championship boxing matches), it began the transformation of Las Vegas from a railroad company town into a casino company town.

Casino operators migrated in droves to the only state in the Union where they could ply their trade without risking arrest and jail, and vice-starved visitors streamed into town to partake in the naughtiness. The bars and casinos moved a block, from the shadows of Ogden Street to the cachet of Fremont Street, and though the ladies of the night remained behind at Block 16, neon lights began brightening the gambling joints along Las Vegas's main street, which would soon come to be known to the world as Glitter Gulch. In addition, Las Vegas enjoyed widespread publicity from the building of the dam: in 1935, 20,000 people (Las Vegas's first real crowd) attended the Hoover Dam dedication ceremony, presided over by popular President Franklin Delano Roosevelt. Word got around that this little town by the dam site was a slice of the authentic Wild West, with its legal casinos, legal prostitution and legal everything else to boot. The temptations of Las Vegas and the attractions of Hoover Dam and Lake Mead filling up behind it, flooded the town with visitors. The prosperity of the early 1940s ushered in new luxury casinos: the El Cortez in Downtown, and the resorts Last Frontier and El Rancho Vegas on the Los Angeles Highway, soon to be known as the Las Vegas Strip. Finally, with the nation preparing for World War II, the federal government took over a million acres north of Las Vegas for use as a training school for military pilots and gunners.

Between 1940 and 1945, the Las Vegas Aerial Gunnery School trained thousands of pilots, navigators, bombers, gunners and other warriors, then shipped them to the front in Europe and the Pacific. The school eventually expanded to three million acres (1.2 million hectares). In 1942, Basic Magnesium, one of the largest metal-processing factories in the country, was built halfway between Las Vegas and Boulder City; at the peak of production, 10,000 workers processed millions of tons of magnesium, a newly developed metal used in the manufacture of flares, bomb casings and airplane components. To house them, other workers built an entire town, Henderson, Las Vegas's first next-door neighbour. During the war years, the local population doubled, from 8,500 in 1940 to 17,000 in 1945.

THE MOB AND THE BOMB

As much as the war benefited Las Vegas, it also benefited organised crime throughout the US, which profited handsomely from the vast black-market in scarce consumer goods. And to the masters of the underworld, Las Vegas, where everything was legal, looked like the Promised Land. Gangsters from all over the country, flush with cash from bootlegging during Prohibition and black market trading during the war, stood poised to invade Nevada with their particular brand of gambling money, management and muscle. All they needed was an advance man to raise a torch and show them the way. Enter Benjamin 'Bugsy' Siegel, tall, handsome, fearless and partnered by the most powerful underworld bosses.

Siegel, in the early 1940s, elbowed into and bowed out of several casinos, until he finally found the one he wanted, the Flamingo. He insinuated himself into the inner management (which, contrary to popular myth, already existed; see p10 **Las Vegas legends: Bugsy Siegel**), then so terrorised the existing team that they fled for their lives, leaving him with the whole unfinished joint. Of course, Bugsy knew nothing about constructing a casino; the

Flamingo eventually went $4 million over budget and cost Siegel his life: he was assassinated in his girlfriend's Beverly Hills mansion in June 1947.

Thus began 20 years of the Italian-Jewish crime syndicate's presence in Las Vegas, and ten years of the biggest hotel-building boom the country had ever seen. Black money from the top bosses of the Mob, along with their fronts, pawns, soldiers and workers, poured in from the underworld power centres of New York, New England, Cleveland, Chicago, Kansas City, New Orleans, Miami and Havana. Between 1951 and 1958, 11 major hotel-casinos opened in Las Vegas, nine on the Strip and two Downtown: all but one were financed by underworld cash. Finally, a full 25 years after gambling was legalised in Nevada, the state and federal governments began to wake up to the questionable histories of the people – considered criminals in every other state in the country – who were in charge of the largest industry in Las Vegas. The war between the police and the gangsters had begun.

'Las Vegans seemed to revel in the notoriety radiating out from the test explosions.'

Then something else happened that cast Las Vegas in a strange light. The federal government needed a vast uninhabited tract of land to perfect its nuclear-weapons technology, and it found the optimal site at the Las Vegas Aerial Gunnery School. A mere 70 miles (113 kilometres) north-west of the city, the Nevada Test Site was the scene of approximately 120 above-ground nuclear test explosions, roughly one a month for ten years (see p256 **The big bang**). The first Nuclear Test Ban treaty in 1962 drove the explosions underground; 600 underground tests have taken place since then, the most recent in 1992. Thousands of guinea-pig soldiers were deployed near Ground Zero of the explosions, purposefully exposed to the shockwaves in order that medical teams might measure the effects of the radiation. A few locals worried which way the wind blew, but most of the 65,000 Las Vegans seemed to revel in the notoriety radiating out from the test explosions. The Las Vegas boosters had a field day, marketing everything from atom burgers to tacky frames of Miss Atomic Blast; in fact, the grand openings of several hotel-casinos were scheduled to coincide with nuclear blasts. People had picnics atop the tallest buildings in town, which afforded a bird's-eye view of the mushroom clouds.

Las Vegas legends Howard Hughes

Howard Hughes is an enigma wrapped in a mystery. His relationship with Las Vegas was brief, but remains the stuff of legend. Hughes (supposedly) spent three years in Las Vegas (he was never seen by a single soul), and in that short period of time, the mysterious recluse changed the foundation, the face and the future of the city.

Like Bugsy Siegel and Las Vegas itself, Howard Hughes was born in 1905, in Houston, Texas, the only child of a fabulously wealthy couple that owned and operated a machine tool manufacturing company. Both his parents died before Hughes came of age, and records show that an attorney, an accountant and a business manager were appointed to take control of young Howard's affairs. From the time he was a teenager, Hughes's handlers spoke and made appearances on his behalf, introducing a life-long parade of surrogates that often called into question the sovereignty, sanity, even the existence of the man himself.

In his early 20s, Hughes moved to Hollywood and began a series of well-publicised exploits that included setting numerous aviation records, bankrolling movies, owning airlines and filmmaking studios, and having a string of high-profile affairs with actresses, dancers and models. In retrospect all his 'achievements' seem stage-managed to a degree that suggests they were dubious at best and outright fabrications at worst.

An unpublished manuscript circulating around Las Vegas, *Searching For Howard Hughes* by Richard Bissett, suggests a new diagnosis to explain Hughes's eccentric and deranged behaviour: Bisset presents compelling evidence that Hughes was autistic. 'Withdrawal from social relations, diminution of motor skills, inability or refusal to communicate, apparent sensory dysfunction, self-absorption and detachment from others, diminishing language skills, constant repetition of odd habits and desires' – these all describe Hughes perfectly and add up to the characteristics of autism. 'As Hughes aged,' Bissett writes, 'it may have been necessary to consider institutionalising him. But being wealthy, the arrangement of having a staff of nurses, all male, attend to him may have been more appropriate'. And it was at that stage of his life, when he was 61 years old, that Howard Hughes and his entourage showed up in Las Vegas.

Holed up securely in his high-rise bunker atop the Desert Inn, Hughes, or whoever was making his business decisions by then, went to work. Hughes Tool Company had just sold its interest in TWA for a half-billion dollars, and either had to spend some of the dosh or give it up in taxes. Hughes decided to see how much a medium-sized American city might cost. In three years, he dropped $300 million, buying up casinos, along with land, media, airlines and mining claims. In one fell swoop, the billionaire financier, according to instant legend, single-handedly transformed Las Vegas from a Mob-controlled den of iniquity to a respectable American city.

Hughes ultimately contributed nothing new to the Las Vegas skyline or its industrial sector during his three-year stint in town, but his presence added an enormous amount of long-needed legitimacy to Las Vegas's tarnished image. For the first time since gambling was legalised in Nevada, bankers and lenders from outside Las Vegas began to finance the building of hotels and casinos, setting the stage for the modern era of huge casino corporations.

Hughes died aboard a rented private jet on its way from the Bahamas to Houston in 1976 at the age of 71. More than 25 years later, researchers and amateur sleuths are still trying to unravel the enigma of this man's life.

THE DIATRIBE

The Mob, the bombs, the gambling and the general Sin Cityness of Las Vegas attracted a lot of heat from the rest of the country, most of it magnified by the media. A steamroller of criticism levelled Las Vegas's reputation as Wild West Central, while the media turned the town into a scandal. Known as the Diatribe, this systematic attack on Las Vegas remains the greatest public castigation of an American city in history. It was so damning it coloured Las Vegas's image for another 30 years.

At the same time, however, people were flocking to Las Vegas, proving the rule that even bad publicity is good publicity. And these pilgrims found that a strange thing happened at the Nevada state line: criminals who crossed it suddenly were accorded the status of legitimate businessmen, while the good citizens of the rest of the country suddenly became naughty boys and girls. These were the glamour years, when you didn't go out in Las Vegas after dark if you weren't wearing a cocktail dress or suit and tie. Crap shooters rolled the bones elbow to elbow with hit men. Mafia pit bosses had the 'power of the pencil' (to hand out free rooms, food and beverages at their discretion), and the comps flowed as easily as the champagne.

During this time Frank Sinatra's Rat Pack – which included Dean Martin, Sammy Davis Jr and Lena Horne, among others – performed in the famous Copa Room at the Sands, then invaded lounges around town (*see p196* **Las Vegas legends: Frank Sinatra**). Joining the likes of Shecky Greene, Buddy Hackett or Louis Prima and Keely Smith on stage, they would treat the audiences to a night they would never forget. The majority of the locals and visitors who were around from the early 1950s through to the mid-1960s still pine for those lost years.

THE HUGHES EFFECT

Enter an elusive billionaire, transferred in the middle of the night on a stretcher from a private train to an ambulance, which delivered him to his floor of suites at the Desert Inn. In 1966, the Howard Hughes roadshow stopped off in Vegas for a three-year engagement. He immediately converted the DI's entire ninth floor into an airtight, light-proof, armed command centre and within months bought the whole joint for $13 million cash. Hughes went on to spend a reported $300 million, snatching up casinos, real estate, an airport, an airline, a television station, and other incidentals. *See p13* **Las Vegas legends: Howard Hughes**.

The publicity generated by Hughes's spending spree turned Las Vegas's reputation around; in addition, his investment stimulated

a second wave of building: between 1968 and 1973, another dozen hotel-casinos opened and tens of thousands more people moved to the city. Hughes paved the way for publicly traded corporations to see the city as a strong long-term investment. When respected companies such as Hilton and Holiday Inn entered the legal gambling business, it marked the end of the Diatribe and the beginning of Las Vegas's coverage on the business pages.

Of course, as anyone who's seen Martin Scorsese's movie *Casino* knows, in reality it took another 15 years for the various government task forces to hound the old gangsters into oblivion. One after another scandals erupted in the so-called 1950s casinos where the Mob was still entrenched. But finally, by the mid-1980s, experts agreed that Las Vegas casinos were as free of Mob involvement as could be detected.

THE NEW LAS VEGAS

In November 1989, a 47-year-old casino chairman called Steve Wynn opened a 3,000-room, $650-million pleasure palace called Mirage in the heart of the Strip. Its size, elegance and price tag stunned the old guard of the gambling business in Las Vegas, where a new major casino-resort hadn't been built for 16 years. But the phenomenal enthusiasm, not to mention the $1-million-a-day profits, with which the public greeted the Mirage galvanised the industry into action. Excalibur, a medieval casino-resort, opened in June 1990, followed by the great pyramid Luxor, the pirate-technic Treasure Island, and the MGM Grand, with 5,005 rooms the world's largest hotel, in 1993. The 1,257-foot (383-metre) tall Stratosphere Tower, the opulent Monte Carlo and the pop-art New York-New York all opened within a nine-month period from April 1996 to January 1997.

Yet another wave of casino construction crested in October 1998 with the grand opening of the $1.6-billion Bellagio, the most expensive hotel ever built, in a sort of Mob-contemporary style. The billion-dollar Mandalay Bay followed close on Bellagio's heels, opening in March 1999, with a New Age hipness and whimsy. A mere two months later, the $1.5-billion Venetian opened (though it took until the end of the year for the behemoth complex to be fully finished); in September 1999, the $760-million Paris debuted, the most highly themed mega-resort of them all, and finally, in August 2000, the new $1.4-billion Aladdin flung open its doors.

The action hasn't just centred on the Strip either; in the last few years neighbourhood casinos have sustained a boom of their own. Recent additions include the upmarket Regent

Can you spot Howard? The **Desert Inn** provided refuge for the elusive billionaire. *See p14.*

Las Vegas (opened July 1999), the ultra-posh Hyatt Regency at Lake Las Vegas (opened December 1999), and the 800-room Suncoast next door to the Regent (December 2000). The Aladdin may have marked the end of this particular wave of ever-more-elaborate construction – for the first time in more than a decade, there are no Strip mega-casinos actually on the drawing board – but new resorts abound (*see p97* **Coming soon...**).

While many major casinos went up, however, others came tumbling down. The building boom of the 1990s was accompanied by the equally spectacular implosion of a number of key Vegas casinos. Between October 1993 and April 1998 the Dunes, the Landmark, the Sands, the Hacienda and the old Aladdin were all blown sky-high. Many locals and old-time visitors mourned the loss of these icons of Vegas history, but many more turned up to watch them bite the dust (*see p23* **Implosion fever**).

21ST-CENTURY VEGAS

Today, Las Vegas is the only city in the world that's home to more than 100,000 hotel rooms: it's past 125,000 and counting. It is home to eighteen of the 21 largest hotels in the world. Upwards of 37 million visitors a

year lose more than $6 billion in Las Vegas casinos. They leave another $6 billion from non-gambling expenses. Many of them check out Sin City once just to see what all the excitement is about, but millions more become regulars, attracted by the agreeable climate, the new mega-resorts, the latest thrill rides and high-tech attractions, the top-notch rooms, food and entertainment and, of course, the chance of instant riches.

In fact, many have relocated to the greatest boomtown in the history of the world. Upwards of 4,000 people move to Southern Nevada every month (though another 2,000 leave). Las Vegas, the largest American city founded in the 20th century, has been the fastest growing major city in the US for more than a decade (though technically its neighbour Henderson now holds that honour), while Mesquite, the border boomtown 90 miles (144 kilometres) north-east, is the country's fastest growing small town. Las Vegas is growing so fast that it's the only city in the US to need two new phone books a year, one in January and one in July, and a new street map every year. It has gone from a desolate railroad town to the glitter capital of the world in a mere nine decades. And there's no end in sight.

Key events

c0-1150 AD Anasazi civilisation develops in the southern Nevada desert.
c1150-1850 Southern Paiute live a semi-nomadic existence in the area.

MEXICANS AND MORMONS
1830 Rafael Rivera discovers a short-cut via Big Spring on the trading route from Santa Fe. He names the area Las Vegas.
1845 The surveyor and cartographer John C Fremont visits the Las Vegas Valley. Big Spring has become a popular camping spot on the well-travelled Old Spanish Trail.
1855-8 Mormon missionaries from Salt Lake City establish a short-lived community at Las Vegas. Lead is discovered in the area.
c1858 Silver ore and gold are discovered in the area, prompting the growth of a small mining boomtown around Big Spring and along the Colorado River.

OD GASS AND HELEN STEWART
1865 The abandoned Mormon Fort is appropriated by Octavius Decatur Gass and developed as Las Vegas Ranch.
mid-1870s Las Vegas Ranch is taken over by Archibald Stewart, who expands the property until his death in 1884.
1884-1903 The ranch is managed and developed by Stewart's widow Helen, who finally sells most of the property to the San Pedro, Los Angeles and Salt Lake Railroad.

LONG TRAIN COMING
1903 JT McWilliams claims 80 acres of untitled land west of the Las Vegas Ranch and sells them as lots of a planned town site, known as Ragtown.
January 1905 Completion of the Salt Lake City to Los Angeles railroad at Jean, Nevada.
15 May 1905 A subsidiary of the railroad company auctions off 1,000 lots for a new town site, across the tracks from Ragtown. Four months later, Ragtown is burned to the ground.

SETTLING IN
1905-1909 The new town of Las Vegas develops with a nightlife district on Block 16 (the heart of today's Downtown).
1909 Las Vegas is made the seat of Clark County, prompting a mini boom in the town.
c1915-30 Union Pacific buys up the San Pedro, Los Angeles and Salt Lake Railroad, causing unemployment and economic decline in Las Vegas.

HOOVER DAM AND THE NEW BOOM
1924 Two canyons east of Las Vegas are chosen as the site of a new project to dam the Colorado River.
1931-5 Construction of the Hoover Dam. Boulder City is built to house the workers.
1931 Gambling is legalised in Nevada, prompting an influx of casino operators into Las Vegas, and the development of Fremont Street as the main nightlife area, known as Glitter Gulch.
1935 President Roosevelt and 20,000 others attend the Hoover Dam dedication ceremony.
1940 US government takes over one million acres of Nevada desert to the north-west of Las Vegas to train soldiers for World War II.
early 1940s Construction of three major casinos: El Cortez in Downtown and El Rancho Las Vegas and the Last Frontier on the Los Angeles Highway (the 'Strip').

THE MOB, THE BOMB AND THE DIATRIBE
1946 Construction of Benjamin 'Bugsy' Siegel's Fabulous Flamingo casino.
1947 Bugsy Siegel shot dead in Beverly Hills. For the next 20 years the Mob dominates gambling and business in Las Vegas.
1951-62 One hundred and twenty-six nuclear bombs are detonated above ground on the Nevada Test Site, north-west of Las Vegas.
1951-8 Eleven major hotel-casinos open in Vegas; ten of them are funded by the Mob.
1960-61 The legendary Rat Pack perform in the Copa Room at the Sands casino.
1962 First Limited Nuclear Test Ban Treaty prohibits atmospheric nuclear explosions.
1962-1992 More than 1,000 nuclear devices detonated at the Nevada Test Site.

THE HUGHES EFFECT
1966 Billionaire Howard Hughes arrives in Las Vegas and takes up residence at the Desert Inn.
1966-73 Hughes's investment in Las Vegas stimulates a building boom and the construction of a dozen new casinos.

THE NEW LAS VEGAS
1989 Steve Wynn opens the Mirage – the first major resort casino to be built in Las Vegas for 16 years.
1990-2000 The success of the Mirage prompts a building boom that sees the construction of 30 new major resort casinos.

Las Vegas Today

How is the iconic city of 20th-century America coping with the challenges of the new millennium?

So much has been written about Las Vegas as a glittering exemplar of myth and metaphor that it's easy to forget that the city is also home to a million and a half souls, a sunbelt metropolis that faces many of the same problems and challenges as other cities in the American Southwest: a transient population, water conservation in a potentially fragile environment, and above all else, uncontrolled urban sprawl. This last characteristic defines Las Vegas as much as gambling or neon do. The constant, barely regulated growth of the city is a boon to the economy (particularly the construction trades), while acting as a curse on the quality of life of the city's residents. Wave after wave of identical stucco-and-Spanish-tile housing developments proceed to the very edge of the Red Rock Canyon Conservation Area, while the urban infrastructure struggles to keep up. The result is traffic as snarled as rush-hour Los Angeles and students packed sardine-like into new schools that are overcrowded before their paint is dry.

One local wag joked that the only other organism that grows as quickly and as incessantly is a cancer cell; it's a comparison that brings to mind writer Edward Abbey's tag for the city of Phoenix: 'the blob that ate Arizona'. While the natural beauty surrounding the Las Vegas valley hasn't been swallowed up yet, the extreme boomtown mentality of the city's history (intensifying to dizzying levels in the past decade) has resulted in a cityscape that often feels completely out of control. Convenience stores squat on every corner and massive master-planned communities flow over once-remote spots, such as the tule springs at Floyd Lamb State Park.

Forget the showgirls or Vegas Vic: the true icon of Las Vegas is the developer, and no one fulfils the role better than casino mogul Steve Wynn, who unofficially started the latest boom era with the opening of his mega-resort, the Mirage, in 1989. In fact, 'casino mogul' is a misnomer: Wynn has no interest in running a resort; his goal is to knock 'em down, set up bigger and better new ones, reap the financial rewards and then sell out to start the cycle all over again. After selling off his Mirage properties to MGM in 2000, Wynn snapped up the struggling Desert Inn. But within weeks of the Desert Inn's 50th anniversary, Wynn closed the venerable resort, announcing that it would be imploded to provide room for some new masterplan (*see p97* **Coming soon…**).

Old-timers, or those with a sense of Vegas's short but glamorous history, might decry such cavalier behaviour. But this is what Las Vegas has always been about, ever since its transformation from a railroad stop into America's pleasuredome. It's a place free from history, a place where novelty reigns supreme, and a place that functions as a microcosm of the American Dream of opportunity, wealth and reinvention. Whatever else Vegas may be, it's a city that cares about making money, first and foremost. As Wynn pointed out, the Desert Inn was losing '30 to 40 thousand dollars a day'. In Vegas, the bottom line routinely trumps any notions of urban cohesion and identity, and this is hardly surprising. After all, Vegas is (on one level, at least) a conjuring trick designed to delight and distract the masses while separating them from their money, a vision dreamed up out of thin air in an otherwise empty desert valley.

'Vegas is a gaudy prototype of the decentralised city of the future.'

The question – and the challenge for those who make Las Vegas their home – is whether or not this philosophy of unimpeded growth in search of a permanent boom is a sound foundation for a community. The traditional idea of 'community' is itself suspect in a town where the population changes from month to month. UNLV art professor and cultural critic Dave Hickey has derided the word, saying 'nobody ever said "community" to me and then gave me permission to do something'. Permission, of course, is what the Strip and, by extension, the city, is all about: permission to eat, drink, gamble, have fun and pursue a dream while making a buck in the process. Hickey posits that, rather than being governed by a restricting sense of community, Vegas is a loose-knit 'society' of like-minded individuals.

There's much to be said in favour of this formulation. In post-industrial America, people are less fettered and more mobile than ever before, establishing economic relationships in a free-floating network that mirrors the world's increasing globalisation. And if Las Vegas is the modern American city taken to the nth degree, then perhaps it can be appreciated as a gaudy prototype of the decentralised city of the future.

But the human need for roots, identity and personal relationships runs deep, even in Las Vegas. Tiny island communities abound in the valley, from the tightly knit adherents of the Mormon faith to small ethnic enclaves to hopeful art lovers looking to create a cultural centre for the city. The tension between life-long Vegas and transient Vegas, between competing visions of community and society,

is part of what makes the city so vibrant, fascinating – and perpetually unfinished.

On the other side of the equation is the city of Las Vegas's flamboyant mayor, Oscar Goodman. If Hickey sees Vegas as the city at the crest of the 21st century, Goodman's vision embodies a resolutely 19th-century urbanism. Goodman, whose previous career as a Mob lawyer bespeaks his old Vegas credentials, has made the renovation and re-development of the city's depressed Downtown his personal project (after he realised that acquiring a National Basketball Association franchise for the city was highly unlikely). The quixotic mayor has tilted at several windmills, including developers and the gaming industry, in his effort to bring all kinds of traditional urban amenities to the city's core: a performing arts centre, a museum, a sports stadium, new restaurants, cafés and high-rise apartments.

So far, Goodman's efforts at revitalisation have met with little success. A large mall and movie theatre complex dubbed Neonopolis languished for months before construction finally (and slowly) began. Even the city's acquisition of a prime piece of empty land from the Union Pacific railroad, located just behind the Plaza Hotel at the end of Fremont Street, has met with little interest from developers.

Some might see Goodman as a relic, looking backwards at an idea of urbanism that's no longer relevant in 21st-century America (and probably never was relevant in Las Vegas). But the tenacious mayor has support from those Las Vegans who strive for community identity as well as a sense of place, and who believe that some degree of permanence is a natural and vital element of any city. Whether those residents will ever outnumber the transient populace, who make Vegas a brief stop in their own economic careers, is, however, unlikely.

The fact remains: Vegas is the ultimate 'destination city'; it is dependent on tourism for its lifeblood, but, at the same time, it transcends mere tourist city status. The sheer scale of the Vegas spectacle sets the city apart from nearly every other destination on the planet. There is no 'season' in Vegas, hence no great divide between the locals and the holiday-making hordes. In fact, the proliferation of 'neighbourhood' casinos, specifically targeting residents, would suggest that the locals are just as ripe for the picking as the tourists. People who visit or relocate here in search of economic opportunity are all united by their eagerness to acquire Vegas's only homegrown product – luck (or at least the illusion thereof).

Is Las Vegas a society of materialist strivers, bound together by a common commitment to unfettered individualism? Or is it really a small

Water, water everywhere…

Confronted by the spectacular fountains at Bellagio – great jets of water that twist and turn above the resort's 22 million-gallon lake – visitors to Las Vegas may be forgiven for forgetting that the city lies in the desert.

In fact, nowadays, water seems to be the new neon on the Strip: tugboats shoot streams of the stuff at New York-New York, gondoliers ferry tourists around the Venetian's fake canals, and hotel guests frolic in the palm-fringed watery playground that surrounds Mandalay Bay. There's even a fake rainstorm inside the Desert Passage shops at the Aladdin. Water is both the latest magical attraction to enrapture visitors, and a vital part of the city's ongoing effort to present itself as a lush, carefree, anything-goes oasis.

Environmentally aware visitors may be appalled by this seeming abuse of a precious resource, but the truth is that the resort industry is not the thirstiest quarter of Las Vegas. According to the Las Vegas Valley Water District, the hotel-casinos only use seven per cent of water in the valley, while residents use a whopping 65 per cent.

Las Vegas is the driest large city in the United States, with an average annual rainfall of just 4.31 inches, yet it has one of the highest per capita rates of water consumption of anywhere in the world at over 300 gallons per day. Of that amount, more then 90 per cent is used outdoors during the summer, when the city's neighbourhoods are a patchwork of manicured green grass glistening from the constant hiss of automatic sprinklers. What's more, the sight of wasted water gushing, unattended, all over the pavements and gutters, is far too common.

Disturbingly, the city also has some of the cheapest water rates in the nation. So far the Water District and the Southern Nevada Water Authority have preferred to encourage water conservation with ad campaigns rather than by raising costs. Residents are offered incentives to switch to desert-friendly 'xeriscaping' in their gardens, resulting in a change in the suburban landscape from lawns to water-efficient succulents and trees. The Water District's Desert Demonstration Gardens (3701 W Alta Drive, North-west Las Vegas; 258 3205) feature hundreds of varieties of plants that thrive in a desert environment, along with detailed information on how to grow them. More recently, there have been signs that the Southern Nevada Water Authority is getting serious: water restrictions were enforced in summer 2001 in an effort to save billions of gallons of water a year by 2010.

Yet, despite these efforts, conflict looms as the valley sends feelers out for water from surrounding rural counties, many of which require irrigation for their agricultural livelihood. Las Vegas is still a desert city with dozens of incongruously green golf courses, and a boomtown mentality that views water as an infinitely renewable resource. Conspicuous consumption may be a defining feature of this improbably successful city, but looking beyond the dancing waters of the Bellagio, such consumption may turn out to be its nemesis.

resort town whose explosive growth over the past decade threatens the little cohesion it once enjoyed, while wrecking its delicate desert surroundings in the process?

The paradox, of course, is that Las Vegas is both of these things. Las Vegas lives up to its stereotypes: the buffets and slots machines, Elvis impersonators and white tigers, instant riches and 24/7 debauchery are all here, larger than life. But Las Vegas is also a city struggling, as if in some glitzy laboratory, with the issues that face all urban centres in the 21st century. It's a city filled with people from all walks of life, drawn here for myriad reasons, pursuing their portion of the American Dream while grappling with American realities. If Las Vegas was once the best and worst aspects of American dynamism writ large, it's entirely possible it will soon embody, for better or worse, the triumph of globalisation in the decades to come.

Architecture

From the sublime to the ridiculous.

Las Vegas in the 21st century is not the place your parents visited in the 1960s or '70s. The kaleidoscope of neon that once was the city's trademark has been replaced by themed resorts approximating ancient Egypt, Renaissance Venice and modern-day Manhattan.

In the post-World War II era, Las Vegas developed its own distinctive style, a dazzlingly vulgar cocktail of expressionist modern architecture and monumental neon signs, illuminating stretches of empty desert on Las Vegas Boulevard. The old Vegas was Mafia-controlled, a world where men still dressed in a coat and tie to gamble, watched by ballgown-clad women. Slot machines were for neophytes and children were not welcome. Those were the days when gambling was illegal in much of the US. Now that you can gamble in 48 of 50 states and corporations control the industry, Vegas has had to reinvent itself. The new Vegas has upped the scale and the sophistication of its hotel-casinos, adding shops and amusements to create huge, themed, entertainment complexes that replicate the walk-through fantasy experiences popularised by Disney.

If the architecture of the old Las Vegas was about vivid abstraction, the architecture of the new Las Vegas is all about replication, and hyper-replication, with casinos themed in the style of any period or any place. The Luxor has a sphinx and a pyramid; New York-New York features Big Apple skyscrapers; Excalibur is a riot of candy-coloured turrets. Popular in the most recent spate of casinos have been attempts to ape European cultural sophistication. Paris-Las Vegas (*pictured*) crashes the Eiffel Tower into the Paris Opera House; the Venetian links the Rialto bridge to the Doges' Palace and Piazza San Marco; while Bellagio evokes its namesake village beside Lake Como.

CITY OF LIGHTS

The main attraction of Vegas buildings used to be their magnificent neon signs, such as the Flamingo's blitzkrieg of blinking and running colours (designed by Paul Rodriguez for Heath & Company, 1976) and the Stardust's classic starbursting beacon (Paul Miller for Ad-Art, 1967). Reliant on electric light for effect, the Strip was a queen of the night, and an uninspiring backdrop by day. Movies and TV shows set in the Las Vegas of the 1970s and '80s always featured dizzying collages and panoramas of the city's neon signs. And it wasn't just on the Strip and Fremont Street that the city shone: budget motels, restaurants and convenience stores all adopted neon flourishes to attract customers.

The oldest and largest sign-making company in Vegas is the Mormon-owned Young Electric Sign Company (YESCO), whose most celebrated designers can be credited with elevating neon signage to an art form to produce some of the city's best-loved images, including Fremont Street's Vegas Vic and Vegas Vickie (designed by Charles Barnard), and Circus Circus's Lucky the Clown (Dan Edwards, 1976). Today, some famous old neon signs, including the Hacienda's Horse and Rider (Brian Leming for YESCO, 1967) and the Flame Restaurant (Hermon Boernge for YESCO, 1961) are on display along Fremont Street as part of the city's growing Neon Museum project (*see p116*).

FORM AND FUNCTION

Although the neon art of old Vegas is now getting some of the recognition it deserves, the emphasis these days is on three-dimensional form, overly elaborate detailing and crowd-drawing attractions. Now the artistry lies in styrofoam statuary, precast mouldings, fake frescoes and faux marble. In the competition for verisimilitude, casino owners have become leading patrons of a new kind of arts and crafts. They are plunging millions into decorative effects, and turning Vegas into a mecca for set designers and artists from all over the world.

Las Vegas used to be seen as exurban and anti-architecture – a linear amusement park of buildings as disposable as last year's Christmas cards, plunked down in the Nevada desert for the enjoyment of weekend trippers. Now it consists of cheek-by-jowl complexes that are small cities in their own right. The highly urbanised Strip has evolved into a quasi-pedestrian environment where crowds ogle the sidewalk attractions. And off-Strip, the success of the new casinos has fuelled a building and population boom, making Las Vegas the fastest-growing metropolis in the US. In 20 years, the population has grown from 200,000 to more than 1.3 million people, spawning infrastructure, housing, schools and the urban problems of 'real' cities.

ENTERTAINMENT ARCHITECTURE

Before the arrival of the infamous Benjamin 'Bugsy' Siegel in the mid-1940s, gambling joints had a hokey Western flavour. Then Siegel arrived from the East Coast via LA's Sunset

Strip and created the Flamingo, an LA Moderne-style tropical paradise. Chic Miami/LA Moderne reigned throughout the glamorous, adults-only, postwar years until 1966, when the irrepressible Jay Sarno opened his instantly sensational, cheeky, pseudo-Roman Caesars Palace. Two years later he opened Circus Circus, the first family-oriented casino on the Strip.

The stakes in the theming game escalated in the late 1980s with the work of Las Vegas casino maverick Steve Wynn. In the early 1970s, Wynn bought and remodelled the Golden Nugget on Fremont Street, creating the first neon-free casino in the original gambling heart of the city, and in 1989 he opened the city's first mega-resort. The South Seas-themed Mirage, melded the upmarket styling of Siegel's Flamingo with the fantasy of Caesars Palace and the mass appeal of Circus Circus. Wynn's Caribbean-inspired Treasure Island, next door to the Mirage, followed in 1993. These two casinos reversed the downward spiral of Las Vegas during the early 1980s; they reinvented the casino as a total 'family destination resort'; they established a trend for free spectacles and attractions in front of privately owned casinos; they helped make the Strip more popular than Fremont Street; and they set in motion a styling contest that shows no sign of abating.

> ## 'Some resorts now integrate hotel, casino and sign in one structure'.

In a bid to outdo Wynn, casino operators have gone for more and more extravagant theming. Furthermore, some resorts, such as New York-New York and the 1993 Luxor – a vast, black glass pyramid complete with a squatting sphinx – have integrated hotel, casino and sign in one structure so the building itself is the sign. With a mini-Grand Central Station, a 150-foot (46-metre) Statue of Liberty and 12 jaunty, one-third real size skyscrapers, New York-New York represented theming at its most fully realised when it opened in early 1997.

But it was swiftly upstaged by the Euro-styled competition that followed: in late 1998, Wynn unveiled the $1.4-billion Bellagio, an Italianate theme park for high-rolling grown-ups. It has 19th-century-style Italian villas on an eight-acre 'Lake Como', an art gallery and lashings of real marble, but the basic trefoil tower is hardly innovative. The most imaginative moments are the glass anemones by sculptor Dale Chihuly on the lobby ceiling, the extravagant conservatory and the dancing fountain display on the lake.

Opposite is the new Paris; it's more tongue-in-cheek than super-tasteful Bellagio, with a half-size Eiffel Tower wedged into its casino, but is no less obsessive in its attention to detail. The designers used Gustav Eiffel's original 1889 drawings as a guide, adapting the structure to meet modern building and fire codes. The structure is welded together rather than riveted like the original, but cosmetic rivets are positioned in appropriate places to emphasise authenticity.

While there's plenty more theming potential to be squeezed out of Europe, some casino owners have looked further east for inspiration; 2000 saw the opening of the new Aladdin, which replaced the 1970s remodel of the 1960s casino. The original building was notable for its porte-cochère and ogee-arched tower, but the highlight of the new resort is the Desert Passage shopping mall that surrounds it. The mall re-creates the atmosphere of a (sanitised) Eastern open-air market, but with shops (and prices) more akin to Fifth Avenue.

On the other side of the street sits Caesars Palace, remodelled and expanded so many times it is now a gigantic hotchpotch whose worst additions are brutish towers with twee pedimented tops. The charms of Caesars Palace are inside, and include the Forum Shops (1993), one of Las Vegas's most stunning themed environments. With Paris, the Venetian and the Desert Passage now offering similar effects, it is hard to imagine the initial impact of this 'Roman' shopping street complete with trompe l'oeil sky, and lighting simulating the transition from dawn to dusk. But it was considered a ground-breaker at the time. It showed casino owners that shopping malls in casino complexes could be money-spinners, and also introduced seriously convincing aged walls and styrofoam sculptures to a city that had been quite happy with cheerfully silly evocation.

Theming doesn't rule everywhere, however. Modern, sleek designs are replacing the some-what cheesy restaurants and lounges of the 1990s. Newer restaurants, such as Picasso at Bellagio (*see p135*) and China Grill at Mandalay Bay (*see p132*), and late-night hotspots such as V-Bar and Jack's Velvet Lounge, both at the Venetian (*see p156-7*), reflect the subdued influences of high-end Los Angeles, New York and London. The fetish of design has taken over Vegas in typically hyperbolic fashion, with internationally noted restaurant designers such as Adam Tihany and Tony Chi name-dropped like mobsters would have been in the old days.

The Venetian is also making a play for architectural respectability. In late 2001, it plans to open a pair of Guggenheim art museums (*see p108*), both designed by

Classic neon on the **Riviera**.

renowned Dutch architect Rem Koolhaas, whose cachet is expected to put Las Vegas on an all-new architectural map. The larger museum, located outside the casino, will be a paean to minimalist design, a vertical container-like space with a six-storey entrance and a ceiling painted with Michelangelo's 'Creation' scene from the Sistine Chapel. The building will be virtually invisible from the Strip, which may disappoint visitors and local marketers, but its location fits Koolhaas's desire that the museum should not compete for attention with the riot of excessive styling that surrounds it.

OLD-STYLE VEGAS

For a whiff of the 1950s and '60s, there's very little left – though the Stardust and the Riviera are worth seeing for their classic neon signs. The one building on the Strip that does give an idea of how post-war Vegas might have been is now rather dowdy but still fab: the lobby of La Concha Motel (2955 Las Vegas Boulevard South) is a zinging, freeform concrete structure built in 1961 by LA architect Paul Williams.

For old Las Vegas in a new package, visit downtown's Fremont Street and marvel at its breathtaking collection of cascading neon signs. In the 1990s, in a bid to stop Downtown's deterioration, the city fathers and Fremont Street casino owners formed an unprecedented partnership and created the Fremont Street Experience (*see p117*). The design, by the Jerde Partnership, involved covering four blocks of the street with a high space-frame vault and pedestrianising the street. The sound and light show that plays on the roof of the vault is architecture at its most kinetic.

NON-RESORT ARCHITECTURE

Times are changing away from the tourist areas as well. Construction in Las Vegas used to be utterly utilitarian – unadorned metal frame and concrete block tract houses and industrial buildings – catering to a predominantly low-income community: wartime military personnel stationed at Nellis Air Force Base, workers servicing the casino industry and retirees. Even the housing for the wealthy, peeked at from

outside walls and fences, has been pretty boring. The exceptions are Lonnie Hammargren's self-made palace of *objets trouvés* (4318 Ridgecrest Drive, East Las Vegas); Luxor architect Veldon Simpson's cartoonish Frank Lloyd Wright-style house (6824 Tomiyasu Lane, East Las Vegas); and Siegfried and Roy's eccentric white mansion (1639 Vegas Drive, North-west Las Vegas).

With the current boom, Las Vegas has also begun to make faltering steps towards creating a public domain. The city first drew attention to itself architecturally in the late 1980s with an ambitious library-building programme led by Charles Hunsberger. He hired top architects to make each of the nine libraries adventurous and unique; the resulting buildings not only enliven the Vegas streetscape, but are also vital loci for the performing arts (*see p224* **Culture shock**).

The libraries reflect an attempt by architects to create, without precedent, a Las Vegas 'high' architecture style. Characterised by earthen

Implosion fever

Las Vegas likes to tear down big hotels almost as much as it likes to put them up. From 1993 to 2000, the 'implosion capital of the world' demolished six Strip resorts, all in dramatic fashion. Large crowds gathered and TV crews posted cameras in multiple locations, turning the highly technical act of levelling a high-rise structure into a spectacle. In most cases, bigger, more colourful hotel-casinos have risen from the ashes.

The first and most visually striking of the implosions took place in October 1993 and was choreographed by casino mogul Steve Wynn, who blew up the **Dunes** to erect his latest masterpiece, Bellagio. The implosion is best remembered for the slow implosion of the distinctive Dunes neon sign. The **Landmark** followed in November 1995. Built in the late 1960s by reclusive billionaire Howard Hughes, although it was never a successful casino, its space-age design was a staple of the Vegas skyline. Footage of its demolition was used in the Tim Burton film *Mars Attacks* and the site was purchased by the Las Vegas Convention & Visitors Authority, which now uses it as a car park.

Then down came the **Sands**: the hip playground of Frank Sinatra's Rat Pack was demolished in November 1996 and replaced by the Venetian. The **Hacienda** bit the dust on New Year's Eve 1996, paving the way for Mandalay Bay; while the **Aladdin**, the wedding

venue of Elvis and Priscilla Presley, was turned to rubble in April 1998, watched by an estimated 20,000 people. The site is now occupied by the newer, bigger Aladdin and the Desert Passage mall.

The most recent implosion – of the **El Rancho** in October 2000 – was the most necessary and least hyped of the bunch. The dilapidated structure had been closed for eight years and was an eyesore, safety hazard and haven for the homeless until it was purchased by Turnberry Associates, who are building pricey high-rise condos next door. Turnberry plan to build a London-themed casino on the El Rancho site.

Opposition to Las Vegas's implosion fever has been meagre. A handful of historical preservationists and some nostalgic long-time employees usually complain to the local media, but no organised protests or court actions have sought to stop the process. There's a collective mindset in Las Vegas that newer is better. This ultra-capitalist city, with so few natives and so many newcomers, has little regard for its heritage: respect for history is something you leave back home in Boston or Chicago.

What's next for Las Vegas implosion fans? Likely candidates include the **Desert Inn**, purchased and closed last year by Steve Wynn, and the **New Frontier**, which is slated for rebirth as a San Francisco-themed resort.

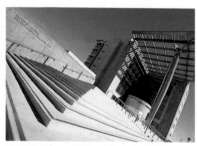

Lloyd D George Federal Courthouse.

forms, variegated concrete and sandy stone, pyramids, cones and dry desert landscaping, this style can be seen as an effort to reflect the spare and harsh Mojave Desert environment. These tendencies can be seen at their most extreme in the 1985 red sandstone Clark County Government Center (500 S Grand Central Parkway) in Downtown by CW Fentress, JH Bradburn & Associates, and in the busy design of the Department of Motor Vehicles office (8250 W Flamingo Road, South-west Las Vegas) by Holmes Sabatini Associates Architects.

Among lively new buildings is the tech-savvy Lied Library (*see p119*) on the UNLV campus. It's an inspiring concrete, steel and glass structure with towering east windows and a massive, inviting lobby. The architectural gem of Downtown is the new Lloyd D George Federal Courthouse (*pictured*; 333 Las Vegas Boulevard South), designed by Dwarsky & Associates of LA, with a keen emphasis on security in the wake of the 1995 Oklahoma City bombing. It has a blast-resistant wall of windows facing Las Vegas Boulevard, and the floors are designed not to collapse in an earthquake or explosion.

Despite growing aspirations, these buildings are still only a few bright points in what largely remains an architectural desert. Non-resort Las Vegas is defined by endless estates of one- and two-storey tract houses, laid out on mile-long blocks. There is little evidence of planning, just an ugly chequerboard of 'leapfrog' development spreading out in all directions.

Las Vegas has less than twice the population of San Francisco but sprawls over 20 times the area. Being close to the centre of town is seen as undesirable in a city whose roads have not yet become permanently gridlocked. Affluent families are moving out in droves to the edges of the valley into residential enclaves built around golf courses and artificial lakes, while on the Strip, high-rise, high-end condos such as Turnberry Place at the north end and Park Towers at the south appeal largely to jetsetters who only come to Vegas for six weeks a year.

However, in recent years there has been a movement to create liveable, downtown dwellings, as well as low-income housing, of which there is very little in fervently free-market Las Vegas. The best example is Tom Hom Group's Campaige Place, an apartment complex just east of Las Vegas Boulevard and Fremont Street. Designed by San Diego architect Rob Wellington Quigley, the colourful, art deco-flavoured building is a stark contrast to the drab motels and casinos that surround it.

As well as simply 'gated' neighbourhoods (walled housing compounds), Las Vegas goes one step further (as usual) with 'masterplanned' communities. These are town-sized swathes of privately owned land on which the management company creates an entire society, complete with housing in several price brackets, business and commercial districts, retirement complexes, schools, parks and hospitals. Residents contract into the community's strict rules and – in theory – settle back to enjoy their suburban utopia.

'Hoover Dam is a marvel of human ingenuity, with some fine art deco touches'.

The most carefully planned community in Vegas is Summerlin. With its abundance of parks, sports fields, tennis courts and trails – not to mention its proximity to Red Rock Canyon — outdoorsy urbanites are hard-pressed to find a better place to settle. But Summerlin is not for those souls who thrive on an independent lifestyle. You want to paint your house green? Forget it! Park a car in the side yard? No way! Let the grass die to conserve water? Dream on. Nevertheless, people are queuing to buy in to what has become the new American Dream. Similar planned communities in the valley include Green Valley, Seven Hills and Anthem, all located in Henderson.

There is one structure – not a building, not in Las Vegas and not designed by an architect – that you cannot miss: the Hoover Dam. Designed by engineer John Savage, built by the Bureau of Reclamation as part of Roosevelt's public works programme and completed in 1935, this monumental dam is a marvel of human ingenuity (and has some fine art deco touches). Though utterly utilitarian, it has all the grandeur and permanence missing from most buildings in Vegas, particularly the absurd, if entertaining, confections parading along the Strip.

> ► For further information about the casinos mentioned here, *see chapter* **Casinos**.

Craps action at the Excalibur.
See p34.

Gambling

The games, the odds and the colour of money.

If life's a gamble, then the casino is one of the few places where you can dance with the devil and live to tell the tale. And where better to dally with Old Nick than in Las Vegas, the undisputed casino capital of the known universe? You'll pay for the pleasure, of course; taking your dollars via the currency exchange known as legalised gambling is the main purpose of this town: what do you think pays for all those lights? But, if you learn a bit about the process and bet within your limits, you'll also have scads of fun. It's even possible to win a few dollars… maybe a few million dollars, either by

studying your brains out and making a career of it (though most wannabe professionals don't last a year), or by getting lucky, or – and this could be the crux – by simply earmarking your gambling budget for entertainment and chalking up reasonable losses to the cost of a little indoor recreation.

HOW CASINOS MAKE MONEY

Before learning the games, it's smart to know the casinos' angle. There are four ways of generating gaming revenue: the house edge, favourable rules, commissions and dumb players.

Gambling tips for beginners

Everyone in the casino is playing a different game, even if they're sitting at the same table. It might appear as if the five players at a blackjack table, for example, are simply trying to get closer to 21 than the dealer without busting. But look closer.

In the first seat is a basic strategy player, playing every hand exactly by the book. In the second seat is a card counter, eyeing the cards like a hawk, doing mental gymnastics to calculate the correlation between the edge and his bet, and trying to spread his chips from minimum to maximum without attracting attention. In the third is a front-end loader, using a variety of strategies to spot the dealer's hole card, which gives him a huge advantage on the hand. In the fourth is a comp hustler, slowing down the game by engaging the dealer in small talk and taking time to play a hand. And in the fifth is a casino novice, who barely knows how to hold his cards, let alone recognise all the games that are being played under his nose.

Here are a few tips to help you avoid sitting in that last seat.

● If you don't have the inclination to memorise the whole basic chart (*see p31* **Blackjack strategy**), at least learn the following five golden rules: stand on 17 to 21, but always hit soft 17; stand on 12 to 16 against the dealer's 2 to 6, but hit on 12 to 16 against the dealer's 7, 8, 9, 10 and ace; always split 8s and aces, but never split 4s and 10s; double down on 10s and 11s against the dealer's 2s to 9s; never take insurance.

● Never play a slot or video poker machine without belonging to the casino's slot club (*see p37* **Vegas on the cheap: Slot clubs**).

● The house edge is the difference between the true odds of an event occurring and the odds used for actual payouts by the casinos. For example, in double-zero roulette, there are 38 possible winning numbers. If the casino paid true odds, it would pay off a winning number at 37 to 1 (for a total of $38, which includes your $1 stake). Instead, the casino pays off a winning number at 35 to 1. To calculate the house edge, imagine placing a $1 bet on every spot in roulette – a total wager of $38. Whatever number wins, you'll be given $36 ($35 plus your $1 stake). That's $2 less than the true odds payout – that $2 went directly into the house's pocket. Now divide the money kept by the house by the total it would have paid on true odds (two divided by 38), and you get a house edge of 5.26 per cent. So the house expects to retain 5.26¢ of every dollar bet at roulette. The house edge varies from game to game and within each game. Casinos love it when gamblers play for hours and hours because the house edge grinds away at every dollar wagered.

● Rules for casino games are structured to favour the house. The best example is blackjack, where the dealer gets to play his hand last. Should a player bust, the dealer wins by default immediately. Even if the dealer ends up busting himself a few seconds later, the player loses and the house wins.

● Commissions are collected by the house in a few table games. In poker, the house serves as dealer, but doesn't play a hand. So to make money from poker, the house takes a percentage of every pot, called the 'rake', or charges players a flat fee of $5 to $7 per half hour of play. In baccarat, the house takes five per cent of all winnings from bank bets.

● Finally, be they drunk, careless, superstitious or ill-informed, dumb gamblers are a boundless source of funds for casinos. That's why free drinks are provided. Alcohol is wonderful for loosening inhibitions (namely the inhibition against losing next month's rent). Thus, although the house edge in blackjack has been calculated at an average of only two per cent, casinos expect a win (or 'hold') of 15 to 20 per cent of the total amount of money brought to the table (the 'drop').

BETTING LIMITS AND TABLE MINIMUMS

At every table game, there's a sign detailing the minimum (and often maximum) allowable bet. At blackjack, it might be $5 to $500. Casinos expect players to bet towards the low end of the limit. This separates players by class, so a guy seeking a speedy $500-a-hand game doesn't have to endure poky play from a tourist betting $5. High-rollers can bet at higher-than-posted limits if the house is willing to 'fade' (cover) them. In roulette, the minimum means the sum total of all bets you place in one round. Hence, if the table has a $5 minimum, five $1 bets satisfies it. But in blackjack, if you play two hands simultaneously, you must bet the minimum on each.

It costs nothing to join, you accrue slot club points as you play, and you can redeem those points for rooms, food, shows, even cash.
● Always ask for comps when you play table games. As soon as you sit down and make a bet, call over a floorman and ask: 'How long do I have to play to get a comp to the buffet?' He'll look at your bet and tell you. Play for as long as he indicates, then collect your free buffet.
● Play slow. You're better off exposing your bankroll to the house edge for 50 hands an hour (at a busy table) than 100 hands an hour (playing one-on-one against the dealer). Similarly, it's better to go for 400 spins an hour (by feeding coins into a slot machine and pulling the handle) than 800 spins an hour (by hitting the spin button like a madman).
● Most 'money management' advice is mathematically unsound. (Quick quiz: when does the size of your bet affect the outcome of a play? Answer: never.) However, some of it is emotionally supportive. For example,

to ensure gambling funds for your whole trip, divide your money into session portions. If you drop one entire session portion quickly, end of session. Don't dig into your remaining bankroll until it's time for the next session.
● Look for coupons everywhere – in funbooks (*see p75* **Vegas on the cheap: Funbooks**), the free magazines handed out by hawkers in front of the casinos. Two-for-one, three-for-two and seven-for-five coupons on even-money bets give you a huge edge over the house at blackjack, craps and the like. A first-card-is-an-ace coupon at blackjack is like money in the bank.
● Keep an eagle eye on your coins, cash and chips. Always make sure back-to-back slot machines have a plastic or metal guard between them to prevent 'reach through' thievery of coin buckets or purses. Watch for 'rail thieves' at the crap table and sneak thieves everywhere.

ETIQUETTE
Before you lay your money down on a table, take note of the minimum-bet requirement, which is posted on a sign, usually in the far left corner. Don't toss out a red ($5) chip on a $100-minimum table, unless you want to look like a fool. Likewise, don't put a quarter into a dollar slot or video poker machine; the coin will pass through the machine and clank, embarrassingly, into the hopper.

Table games have strict rules about when players can touch chips or cards – these exist to discourage cheaters. Many blackjack games are dealt face up and players never touch the cards. As for chips, once you make a bet, never touch them. If you're splitting or doubling down in blackjack, push out a separate pile of new chips but don't touch the original ones. This rule is to discourage 'past posting', a scam by which cheats sneak more chips onto their bet after peeking at their cards.

Similarly, you should only handle dice with one hand. Everyone, from the players to the dealers and the bosses, will get very nervous if you touch them with two hands, or even make a fist around them with one hand so they can't be seen. Blow on them, shake them and turn them so your favourite numbers are up, but don't hide them, not for the briefest moment. That's how dice cheats use sleight of hand to get loaded dice into a game of craps. And if you must kiss them, instead of touching them to your lips, just pantomime the kiss; no one likes shooters to slobber on dice.

You must be 21 to gamble. There are no exceptions to this rule. If you're under 21 and you start winning (or hit a jackpot that requires you to sign federal tax forms), not only will your chips or jackpot be confiscated, you'll be tossed out of the casino faster than you can say, 'But…'.

Most casinos subscribe fiercely to the old tradition that cameras are unwelcome, however, as long as you're discreet or ask permission you can sometimes get away with taking photographs in casinos (particularly at the Excalibur). Though why you'd want to is another matter. Generally, it's better to leave your SLRs and videocams in your room, car or backpack. On the other hand, wherever you go in a casino (except the toilets), you'll be watched by 'eye in the sky' cameras and taped by video recorders in a central surveillance room. Nowhere on earth are civilians under more surveillance than in a casino; make sure you behave accordingly.

MONEY, MONEY, MONEY
To play table games, you'll need chips, though you can usually throw down a bill for your first plays (rules vary from casino to casino). In blackjack, cash can always play, though any winnings will be paid as chips. You can buy chips at the table in a process called a 'buy in' or at the 'cage' (*see p38* **Gambling jargon**). Chips can only be redeemed at the cage.

Chips are like currency in the casino from which they're issued, but due to counterfeiting

Spin that wheel – **roulette** wheels in America generally have two zero slots. *See p37.*

and other problems, casinos rarely honour each others' chips for gambling (unless, like Treasure Island and the Mirage, they're under the same ownership). However, it is sometimes possible to exchange sub-$100 denominations from other casinos for house chips at the cage.

Most modern slot and video poker machines have bill acceptors that change your greenbacks into credits on the machine's credit meter. If you don't want to use the bill acceptor, or if you have a bill that's larger than is accepted by the machine, press the 'Change' button on the machine. That activates a light on top, which summons a roving change person.

LEARNING TO GAMBLE

If you want to study the games further before arriving in Las Vegas, you'll find hundreds of books on gambling, covering everything from baccarat to video poker; for our recommendations, *see p298*. Some of the best are available by mail order from **Huntington Press** (3687 S Procyon Avenue, Las Vegas, NV 89103; 1-800 244 2224 enquiries and credit card orders) and in specialist shops. In the past decade numerous software programs have also been developed to teach you how to play most games, from blackjack to craps, video poker, even roulette and slots. Send for catalogues from the **Gamblers Book Club** bookshop (*see p166*), the **Gambler's General Store** (*see p176*) and **Huntington Press**.

Almost all the large casinos offer free hands-on lessons for most table games, taught by personable, informative and experienced instructors. They take you step by step through the playing procedures and etiquette (but don't expect them to warn you about sucker games and bets; they're paid by the casino, after all). Lessons are usually held in the late morning, when the casino is least busy, and some are followed by open low-minimum 'live' games right afterwards for people who want to celebrate their new-found skills under actual casino conditions. One of the best places to learn is Caesars Palace, where the instructor, Barney Vinson, is a local gambling author and celebrity. *See chapter* **Casinos** for details of which other casinos offer lessons.

When you're ready to join a game in progress, first stand back, watch the action for a while and pick up the game's rhythms and routines (don't stand too long behind a blackjack table before you sit down, however; most bosses will suspect you of 'back counting' the deck in order to slip in a bet at the most advantageous time). Choose a table with the lowest minimum possible, so you're not risking $100, $25 or even $10 a hand at a game you are playing for the first time. Note that the locals and Downtown casinos tend to have lower minimums than those on the Strip – *see chapter* **Casinos** for more details.

Vegas on the cheap Gambling

If you want to make the most of your gaming budget, then it's worth knowing where to play without running the risk of ending up homeless.

Table games, such as blackjack and craps, have higher betting minimums on the Strip than their counterparts in Downtown. In fact, it's practically impossible to find a $1 blackjack table anywhere on the Las Vegas Boulevard South; the exceptions are the **Casino Royale** (*see p107*), the **Sahara** (*see p85*) and **Slots-o-Fun** (*see p109*), however, they usually deal only one table, and it's not always open.

Other spots worth checking out for $1 blackjack include the **Reserve** (777 W Lake Mead Drive, at I-515, Henderson; 558 7000/ www.stationcasinos.com), **Silverton** (3333 Blue Diamond Road, at I-15, South-west Las Vegas; 263 7777/www.silvertonhotel.com) and the **Las Vegas Club** on Fremont Street in Downtown (*see p93*).

Most craps tables on the Strip have betting minimums of $5, with a very small handful offering $3 tables. Downtown casinos routinely offer $1 craps, with the **El Cortez** (*see p93*) and **Las Vegas Club** casinos even offering 25¢ craps.

Other reliable spots for $1 dice tables are the **Sahara** (*see p85*), **Boulder Station** (*see p100*), **Nevada Palace** (5225 Boulder Highway, between Tropicana Avenue & Harmon Avenue, East Las Vegas; 458 8810/www.pcap.com/nvpalace.htm), the **Reserve**, **Silverton** and **Westward Ho** (2900 Las Vegas Boulevard South; 731 2900/www.westwardho.com).

You'll find penny slot machines at various Downtown casinos, such as the **Plaza** (*see p95*), **Gold Spike** (400 Ogden Avenue, at Las Vegas Boulevard, Downtown; 384 8444/www.goldspikehotelcasino.com), **El Cortez** (*see p93*) and **Western Hotel** (899 Fremont Street, Downtown; 384 4620).

TIP TALK

From bellmen to doormen, Vegas is a town that runs on tips. It's the same for casino dealers, who are officially paid little more than the minimum wage. Every shift of dealers combines and divides their tips, which make up the bulk of their pay. Giving tips (or 'tokes', as dealers call them) is smart because a happy dealer is your friend. Dealers can assist players in a number of ways: they can slow down the pace of the game (this is extremely useful when you're playing for comps), create a sociable atmosphere, and even deal a little deeper in the deck, which is critical for card counters.

You can toke the dealer as you leave the table; this will certainly be appreciated, but it won't gain you any help while you're playing. The second method is to toke after a big win – better, because the dealer knows you're thinking of him and could start to help you. But the best way is to place a bet for the dealer alongside your wager. If you win, the toke is paid off at regular odds and the dealer takes it. If you lose, the house wins the toke, but the dealer will still appreciate the thought.

In blackjack, there are two ways to bet for the dealer. You can place a chip outside the line surrounding your wager circle, but if this toke bet wins, it has to be scooped up by the dealer right away. Instead, if you're riding a hot streak, you can place the dealer's toke next to your bet within your wager circle. That way, if you win you can let the toke ride (continue to the next deal), because it's yours until you give it to the dealer. Just tell the dealer the extra bet is a toke. Amazingly however, some dealers

resent it if you let their tokes ride; they aren't immune to a take-the-money-and-run attitude.

Don't bother toking if the dealer is rude, creepy or unco-operative. There is no reason to reward this type of behaviour. In fact, don't even play with such a dealer; instead, get up and move to another table, fast.

The Games

Baccarat

Long viewed as an obscure, weirdly ritualised game for high-rollers, baccarat (pronounced 'bah-cah-rah') is a table game with a small house edge that's especially popular with Asians. Up to 15 players sit around the layout and bet on BANK, PLAYER or TIE. Tuxedo-clad dealers lay out two hands of two cards each, titled PLAYER and BANK. The object is for each hand to total as close to nine as possible. Face cards and tens count as zero and any total over nine is reduced by eliminating the first digit (for instance, 15 is valued as five). Players have no control over whether to 'draw' or 'stand'. Dealers follow a strict set of rules to determine if they must 'hit' either hand with a third card.

If PLAYER or BANK bets win, the house pays off at even money. Since the rules determine that BANK wins slightly more often, the house retains a five per cent commission on all BANK winnings. Even with the commission, the house holds only a 1.17 per cent edge on BANK bets and 1.36 per cent on PLAYER bets.

The **Aladdin**'s luxurious London Club has 30 high-limit tables. *See p69*.

(The TIE bet should be avoided. It pays off at eight to one, giving the house a 14 per cent edge since the true odds are about 9.5 to one.)

The rhythm of baccarat is leisurely and the mood subdued. In fact, it's rarely necessary for players to speak (which might be why the game is so popular with Far Eastern gamblers). Baccarat pits are usually secluded behind velvet ropes to lend an air of exclusivity, but if you can handle the minimum – often $100 – you're welcome to join the action. Casinos catering to low-end gamblers tend to ignore baccarat, but high-end casinos hold it dear for good reason – it's very profitable. The Mirage estimates that about ten per cent of its annual revenue comes from baccarat.

MINI BACCARAT

Mini baccarat is a low-stakes version of baccarat played in the main pit, usually near the blackjack tables. It's a good introduction to the game, since the rules are the same, the bets lower and the pace faster because there are fewer players.

Bingo

It might not be posh, but bingo is a gambling stalwart in Vegas, especially in the neighbourhood casinos. The game is the same as found in church basements all over the world. The house edge is slightly better than the similar keno, though it's hard to pin down since so much depends on the variety of the game and the number of cards being played. The one advantage bingo has over keno is that bingo numbers are called until somebody wins. By contrast, a million keno games can go by without anyone hitting the big jackpot.

Blackjack (21)

Blackjack is by far the most popular table game in the casinos. The reasons are obvious – it's easy to play, there's a basic strategy that slims the house edge to nearly zero, and dozens of books on the market claim the house can be easily beaten with card counting.

You'll hear a lot about card counting. It's a technique whereby a player visually tracks exposed cards and mentally keeps a running total to determine if the deck is positive or negative. In the simplest count, the ten-value cards and aces are valued at –1 and small cards (two to seven) at +1. The eights and nines have no value. If the running total is positive, players have an advantage and should raise their bets. Does it work? Yes, but only if you devote hours and days and weeks of practice to it, develop good camouflage skills so that the house doesn't

Blackjack strategy chart

Dealer's up card										
	2	3	4	5	6	7	8	9	10	A
If you have										
2-8	H	H	H	H	H	H	H	H	H	H
9	H	D	D	D	D	H	H	H	H	H
10	D	D	D	D	D	D	D	D	H	H
11	D	D	D	D	D	D	D	D	D	D
12	H	H	S	S	S	H	H	H	H	H
13-16	S	S	S	S	S	H	H	H	H	H
17-20	S	S	S	S	S	S	S	S	S	S

Dealer's up card										
	2	3	4	5	6	7	8	9	10	A
If you have an ace										
A+2	H	H	D	D	D	H	H	H	H	H
A+3	H	H	D	D	D	H	H	H	H	H
A+4	H	H	D	D	D	H	H	H	H	H
A+5	H	H	D	D	D	H	H	H	H	H
A+6	D	D	D	D	D	H	H	H	H	H
A+7	S	D	D	D	D	S	S	H	H	S
A+8	S	S	S	S	S	S	S	S	S	S
A+9	S	S	S	S	S	S	S	S	S	S

Dealer's up card										
	2	3	4	5	6	7	8	9	10	A
If you have a pair										
2s	Sp	Sp	Sp	Sp	Sp	Sp	H	H	H	H
3s	Sp	Sp	Sp	Sp	Sp	Sp	H	H	H	H
4s	H	H	H	H	H	H	H	H	H	H
5s	D	D	D	D	D	D	D	H	H	H
6s	Sp	Sp	Sp	Sp	Sp	H	H	H	H	H
7s	Sp	Sp	Sp	Sp	Sp	Sp	H	H	H	H
4s	H	H	H	H	H	H	H	H	H	H
8s	Sp	Sp	Sp	Sp	Sp	Sp	Sp	Sp	Sp	Sp
9s	Sp	Sp	Sp	Sp	Sp	S	Sp	Sp	S	S
10s	S	S	S	S	S	S	S	S	S	S
As	Sp	Sp	Sp	Sp	Sp	Sp	Sp	Sp	Sp	Sp

H=hit; **S**=stand; **D**=double down; **Sp**=split.

Players should consider 'surrendering':
● if they have a hard total of 13-16 against the dealer's ace
● if they have a hard total of 14-16 against the dealer's ten
● if they have a hard total of 15-16 against the dealer's nine

know you're counting – you'll be 'backed off' or 'barred' if they think you are – and are very cool under the distractions and pressures of real-time casino play. Counting cards is a gruelling discipline at which most fail, but successful card counters, especially high-stakes players,

Eyes down at Castaways. **Bingo** (*see p31*) is a popular pastime at the locals casinos.

are the legendary gamblers who beat the casinos at their own game. The rest of us should stick to basic strategy. This involves memorising a chart that contains the answer to every decision in blackjack, based on your first two cards and the dealer's up card. Alternatively, you can usually bring the chart to the table and check it as you play, as long as you don't slow down the game.

In blackjack, everyone at the table is dealt two cards after putting up their bets. Single- and double-deck blackjack are dealt from the dealer's hand, while multiple decks are combined and placed in a 'shoe' (*see p38* **Gambling jargon**), from which the dealer pulls cards. All face (picture) cards count as ten and aces can count as one or 11 (a hand that includes an ace is known as a 'soft' hand). Each player competes against the dealer's hand in trying to get as close as possible to a total of 21 without exceeding it (that's called 'busting'). After checking your cards, indicate a 'hit' for each extra card you want. When satisfied with your total, you 'stand'. After all players stand or bust, the dealer reveals and plays his hand, according to fixed rules: they must hit totals of 16 or less, and must stand on 17 or above (the rules can vary if the hand contains an ace; *see p31* **Blackjack strategy chart**). Once they stand or bust, hands are compared and players who beat the dealer are paid off at even money. Ties between the house and player are a 'push' and no money changes hands (dealers indicate a push by knocking gently on the layout). If a player is dealt an ace and a ten-value card, it's considered a 'natural' blackjack and the player is paid off at three to two immediately, unless the dealer also shows an ace or ten, indicating another possible blackjack.

Almost all multi-deck games are dealt face up (except the dealer's second card). In these games, players never touch the cards, but instead indicate hit or stand with hand motions. This reduces the potential for misunderstandings and makes it easier for disputed plays to be reviewed on security videos filmed by an overhead camera. For a hit, players hold one hand palm down just above the felt and brush their fingers toward themselves. For stand, hold the hand the same way, but with fingers straight outward, and move it right and left.

Single- and double-deck games are almost always dealt face down, and players hold their own cards. Hitting is indicated by scratching the cards towards you on the layout, while standing is indicated by sliding the cards face down under the chips.

There are four ways players can alter their bets once the cards have been dealt: 'doubling down'; 'splitting'; 'insurance'; and 'surrender'. Aggressively splitting and doubling down is the secret to winning at basic strategy blackjack, because it gives players the chance to press their bets when they are holding a strong hand.

When a player doubles down, he wagers another bet equal to the original and receives one (and only one) more card. It's the choice move when you've got a total of nine, ten or 11 and the dealer shows a weak card such as a six. You can double down only if you haven't taken a hit. Splitting is an option when players are dealt two cards of the same value. An additional bet equal to the original bet is put out and the cards are split with each played as a separate hand. It's to the player's advantage to be able to double down or split each of the

The best Casinos

For baccarat
The **Mirage** (see p81) has the most elegant baccarat pit, complete with a mini-buffet for players. This is Las Vegas's home of baccarat – if you can fade the minimums.

For bingo
This game is the same everywhere, so play in the largest, brightest, and airiest room, which is at the **Castaways** (see p98).

For blackjack
Binion's Horseshoe (see p93) has the best combination of good rules, the most single-deck games, and the easiest comps for players.

For Caribbean stud
Once again, **Binion's Horseshoe** should be your Caribbean stud joint of choice: it offers low minimums (there's no such thing as a Caribbean stud high-roller!), and the casino's progressive jackpot is usually the highest in town.

For craps
For a third time, **Binion's Horseshoe** has the most tables, with the most rammin' jammin' action, easy comps, and a long reputation as the best crap joint in town.

For keno
The least of all the keno evils might be the **Gold Coast** (see p98) or the **Silverton** (3333

Blue Diamond Road, at I-15, South-west Las Vegas; 263 7777/www.silvertonhotel.com), where the house advantage on the eight-spot tickets is a mere 25%, as opposed to closer to 30% at most other joints.

For Let It Ride
O'Sheas (see p106), which offers the lowest betting minimum, is the best place to play this high-house-edge and high-variance game.

For roulette
The **Monte Carlo** (see p83) is by far the best place to play roulette. The casino is in the heart of the fabulous Strip, the game is in the heart of the fabulous casino, and the wheels have a single zero, which cuts the usual house advantage in half.

For slots
It's hard to escape to any corner of the city where there are none, so you might as well play slot machines at your favourite casino – with your player's club card firmly inserted. Make up your inevitable losses with free rooms, food, and amenities.

For video poker
The locals' casinos in general have the best pay schedules and comp systems; the **Orleans** (see p98) with its new multiplay machines, and **Arizona Charlie's West** (see p98) are the best of the bunch.

post-split hands, though some casinos limit what you can do. Check the chart (see p31) to see when you should double down or split.

'Insurance' is a side bet offered when the dealer has a possible blackjack (ie, is showing an ace or ten-value card). An insurance bet is limited to 50 per cent of the original bet and is lost if the dealer doesn't have blackjack. If he does, insurance pays off at two to one. Despite the warm connotations of the word 'insurance', this is a sucker bet. Unless you're a card counter, there's no reason to take insurance, even if you're holding a natural blackjack.

'Surrender' is an obscure but useful rule that's not in effect everywhere. When it's on, 'surrender' permits players to fold and sacrifice half their bet as long as they haven't played their hand. It's an excellent way to drop out and minimise losses when dealt weak cards. If it is used correctly, surrender increases the player's edge by 0.2 per cent.

Here's another easy rule to help players. Some casinos require dealers to hit a 'soft 17' (an ace plus a six or cards totalling six), while others require them to stand. If possible, play at places that require the dealers to stand on a soft 17 – it shifts the edge about 0.2 per cent to the players' favour.

One final note: though blackjack sets each player's hand against the dealer's, most players view the game as everyone against the dealer. Their goal is to make the dealer bust, which means payoffs for all the players still in the game. These folks don't take kindly to people who play stupidly and split tens or hit a 14 against a dealer's six, especially if the offending party sits in the last seat on the left (known as 'third base'), since they feel those cards should have gone to the dealer. We suggest that you don't sit at third base unless you have a particularly good grasp of the game.

Craps

Fast, furious and enormously confusing, craps is an action-filled dice game that terrifies most novices. Players curse and scream, chips fly across the table and everybody roots for different winning numbers. Fortunes can be won and lost in minutes, which is exactly why craps is worshipped by a subculture of dice players. It's confounding, but by sticking to a few smart bets, players can enjoy a boisterously fun game with a house edge as low as one per cent or less.

THE BASICS

Craps is played on a large table surrounded by a low, padded wall (don't put your glass on it). The game is staffed by one to four casino employees and there's room for 12 to 14 players to belly up. The layout is divided into three sections. The two at each end are identical; in the centre is an area reserved for special wagers known as 'proposition bets'. A game of craps starts with dice being offered to a new 'shooter' by the 'stickman' (the dealer located mid-table who's holding the stick). Each player will be offered the shooter job at some point, though it's common to refuse the dice. The shooter must throw two dice so that they bounce off the far wall of the table.

Basically, players bet on which numbers the shooters will throw and in what order. The shooter must lay a bet before his first throw, and traditionally chooses PASS. Those betting with the shooter are called 'right' bettors, while those betting against the shoot are called 'wrong' bettors.

HOW TO BET

There are four basic wagers known as 'line bets' marked on the layout – PASS, DON'T PASS, COME and DON'T COME (the DON'T bets are for wrong bettors). The shooter's initial throw is called a 'come out roll'. Players bet on the PASS or DON'T PASS lines. If the shooter throws a seven (statistically the most likely roll) or 11 on the come out roll, PASS bettors win at even odds and DON'T PASS bettors lose. If the shooter throws a two or three, DON'T PASS wins and PASS loses. If a 12 is tossed, PASS bettors lose and it's a 'push' (or tie) for DON'T PASS bettors. Rolling a two, three or 12 is known as 'crapping out'. If any other number is thrown (four, five, six, eight, nine, ten), that becomes the 'point'.

Once a point is established, the shooter keeps rolling, attempting to repeat the point before rolling a seven (known as 'sevening out'). Other numbers tossed don't count in this context. PASS and DON'T PASS bets ride until the 'point' is hit or the shooter 'sevens out'. If the shooter hits the 'point', PASS bettors win and DON'T PASS bettors lose. If the shooter tosses a seven, DON'T PASS bettors win, PASS bettors lose and the shooter relinquishes control of the dice. The shortest roll a shooter can have is two throws – by hitting a point on the come out roll followed by a seven (that's when wrong bettors rake in the chips). But if they avoid 'sevening out', the shooter can roll for ever (that's when right bettors rack up big bucks). Every time the 'point' is hit, the game is reset and the next throw is a fresh 'come out roll', although all the side bets – such as COME bets – remain in action.

COME and DON'T COME bets represent an optional second layer of betting that runs concurrently. They are similar to PASS and DON'T PASS bets, with exactly the same set of outcomes – an immediate win, lose or 'push' or the establishment of a 'point' – but can only be made on throws subsequent to the 'come out roll'. For instance, the shooter establishes a point of four; on the next roll you make a COME bet. (Note that you can enter the game with a COME/DON'T COME bet at any time during a hand without having previously made a PASS or DON'T PASS bet.) The next roll is nine, so nine becomes your 'point'. Should that throw have yielded a seven or 11, you would have won immediately, and the DON'T COME bets would have lost. If the throw yielded a two, three or 12, your COME bet would have lost. If a shooter hits their number, the COME bets ride, awaiting a seven or a repeat of their 'point'.

TAKING THE ODDS

If a player sticks to the four 'line' bets outlined above, the house edge is only about 1.4 per cent. But even that tiny amount can be reduced with the use of the 'odds' bet, a wager where the house holds an edge of zero. That's right, these bets are paid off at exactly true odds. They're the only such wagers in the casino, which is probably why the layout of a craps table doesn't mention them at all.

Once a point is established, any player with a 'line' bet can 'back up' that wager with an 'odds' bet. This allows players to increase their bet midstream. In a game with single odds, the maximum 'odds' bet equals the 'line' bet. That alone slashes the house edge from about 1.4 per cent to 0.85 per cent. Some casinos offer double, triple, 10X or even 100X odds, all of which reduce the house edge even further. A few offer different odds on specified points. Anyone making line bets in craps should take at least single odds on every bet made. Attend a lesson to learn how to make the most of this tactic.

THE REST OF THE TABLE

Smart players stick to line and odds bets, but action junkies need more. For them, the table offers another world of wagers, none of which are worthwhile to any right-thinking human. Granted, some bets offer an edge only slightly worse than line bets. But most of the one-roll proposition bets are simply horrific.

For instance, the ANY 7 proposition bet has a stunning house edge of 16.67 per cent, the worst edge of any table game wager apart from the Money Wheel. Don't waste chips on these bogus bets. Instead, stick to right and wrong betting with line bets pressed with odds and you'll get more than enough action. A straightforward odds-effective play is to bet the minimum stake on PASS, the same amount on two COME bets and take odds on both (double or triple, if they're offered and you can afford it).

Keno

Keno ranks as the worst bet in the casino. This lottery offshoot gives the house an intolerable edge of 25 to 40 per cent. You might as well climb to the top of the Stratosphere tower and throw your money into the wind. At least you'll have a nice view.

Like a lottery, keno involves a ticket (or 'blank') containing 80 numbers. Players circle up to 15 or 20 numbers on their blank. When the game starts, 20 numbers are selected at random (ping-pong balls are blown from a 'goose' into a pair of 'arms') and displayed on screens around the casino. If your numbers are picked, you win. If not, you lose. (Get used to the second option.) The greater the proportion of your numbers picked, the higher the payback. Remember that, if by some remote chance you win at keno, you must claim your money before the next game begins or you will forfeit your winnings.

There are many variations for betting keno, but none makes the edge even remotely acceptable. Worst of all, payouts for keno in no way reflect the true odds of your bet, since they're capped at an arbitrary figure. For instance, your chances of selecting nine numbers and hitting all of them are about 1.38 million to 1. Your payout for such a feat? Usually no more than $250,000 on a $2 bet. Here's another fun fact: if by some bizarre chance two players hit the big jackpot at the same time, they have to split the winnings. Amazingly, there are books published that claim to offer a strategy to beat the odds in keno. Ha! The only way to beat the odds in keno is to ignore it.

Money Wheel or Big Six

You have to worry when a casino game is imported from the morally challenged universe of carnivals. That's the case with the Money Wheel, aka Big Six, the grandchild of spin-the-wheel games loved by carnies everywhere. The game is simple. A large, ornate wheel is mounted vertically a few feet above the floor. On it are 54 evenly spaced slots. Two show joker or house symbols; the other 52 are divided into $1, $2, $5, $10 and $20 denominations. There are usually 24 $1 slots and only two $20 slots. A layout in front of the wheel has squares matching those denominations. Players put cash or chips on the squares of their choice, the wheel spins, and when it stops bettors who selected the correct denomination win, with the payoff determined by the dollar value of the winning slot. A $20 symbol pays off at 20 to 1; a $1 symbol pays off at even money. House or joker symbols pay off at 40 to 1. As you might guess, the casino holds a serious edge, ranging from 11 per cent on a bet on the $1 symbol to 25.9 per cent on the joker.

This should be called the Clint Eastwood Wheel. Every time you lay down a bet, the dealer could sneer, 'Are you feeling lucky, punk?' If not, keep your money in your pocket.

Poker

In poker, gamblers bet against each other, not the house. A casino employee only deals and acts as a cashier. The house's income is limited to a percentage taken from each pot, or a seat rental of $5 or $7 per half hour. You'd think the casinos would have figured out a way to grab more of the action by now. Oh wait, that's what slot machines are for, right?

To join a game, just sit in an empty seat and buy in (which usually costs ten times the minimum or maximum bet, depending on the game) with chips or cash. If there's no space, you can put your name on a waiting list. The traditional rules everyone knows are in effect for Vegas poker. The most popular games are Texas Hold 'Em and seven-card stud, but casinos are eagerly experimenting with variations that can be played outside the poker room. In Texas Hold 'Em, each player is given two cards face down, while five common cards are dealt for the table. Players assemble the best five-card hand possible from the seven cards available to them. In seven-card stud, players get two cards face down and one face up, followed by three cards face up and a final card face down. Again, they put together the best possible hand from their own seven cards.

Both of the above games have numerous rounds of betting and raising, so a hefty bankroll is essential. For games with betting limits, posted signs indicate the smallest and largest bet allowable (usually written in the form '$5/$10'). In a limit game, you'll need a bankroll of at least 20 times the maximum bet. There are also pot-limit games, which means raises can go as high as the pot, and no-limit games, in which raises can go as high as the largest bankroll on the table. In all games, no matter what the stakes, players are not allowed to bring more money to the table once a hand is dealt. If a player is 'all in' (meaning all their money is bet) and they can't match a raise, a side pot is formed for those who wish to continue betting. The player who is all in is now limited to playing for the main pot.

Explaining poker strategy here is impossible. Besides the complexities of the game, much of poker is psychological. Reading other players and bluffing is a huge part of the process, which, if you didn't know it already, you'll learn the first time you sit down in a card room. If you're not a seasoned poker player, be very careful of high-stakes games, which can be populated by sharks (sometimes operating in teams). They've learned the primary casino secret – it's easy to take money from amateur gamblers. If you're a novice, stick to low-stakes games, which are straightforward and friendly.

PAI GOW
Pai Gow poker is played with a 53-card deck (a standard deck plus a joker, which is wild). Players get seven cards, which they assemble into a five-card hand and a two-card hand. The five-card hand must score higher than the two-card hand. The object is to beat both the banker's hands. The banker wins all hands that tie. If a player wins only one hand, it's a push. The house or any player can be the banker. Winning hands are paid at even money, minus a five per cent commission. If all this sounds a bit intimidating, don't worry; the dealer will help you arrange your cards in such a way as to maximise your two hands. It only takes observing several hands to get the hang of it.

LET IT RIDE
Let It Ride offers the unusual feature of allowing players to take back two thirds of their wager. Players bet three equal amounts and are dealt three cards face down. Two common cards are dealt, also face down. At this point, players can pull back one of their bets (don't touch your chips, that's the dealer's job). When the first common card is turned over, players can withdraw their second bet. The final common card is then shown and payouts made

according to a fixed schedule, ranging from even money for a pair of tens or better to 1,000 to one for a royal flush. As you might guess, that's way below true odds. For instance, the odds against drawing a flush are 508 to one but the payout is eight to one. Overall, the house holds about a four per cent edge, if players make all the right decisions. The biggest lure of Let It Ride is that players compete against the cards, not each other, making it more appealing to amateurs. Also, there's that ability to withdraw two thirds of the bet, which gives the illusion that your money is lasting longer than in other games. But don't be fooled. The house edge grinds down almost everyone eventually, and since this game is basically five-card stud, it's often a long time between winning hands.

CARIBBEAN STUD
Caribbean stud is a rather dumb game with a house edge of 5.27 per cent, just a hair worse than double-zero roulette. Sitting around a table similar to a blackjack layout, players put out a single ante bet and receive five cards face down. The dealer also gets five cards, though one is dealt face up. At this point, players either fold (and lose their ante) or 'call' by adding a bet that's twice their ante. Everyone then reveals their cards. If the dealer doesn't 'qualify' with at least an ace and king in his hand, all players win even money for their ante and the call bets are returned. Should the dealer's hand qualify, each player's hand is compared against the dealer's. If the player wins, the ante is paid off at even money and the call bet qualifies for a 'bonus' payout based on the hand. Bonus payouts range from even money for a pair to 100 to 1 for a royal flush (most of these payouts are even lower than those found in Let It Ride).

The maximum bonus payout is usually capped somewhere between $5,000 and $60,000, so make sure your bet is no higher than it needs to be to win that amount. For example, if the bonus payout is capped at $5,000, your ante should never be above $25 (this would make your call bet $50 and thus your 100-to-1 payout would hit the $5,000 ceiling exactly). The simple maths? Divide the maximum bonus payout by 200. Your ante should never exceed that amount.

For a side bet of another dollar per hand, Caribbean stud poker also offers players the chance to hit a progressive jackpot with payoffs based on the quality of their hand. A royal flush wins 100 per cent of the jackpot, while a flush gets a mere $50. The fact that jackpots have been known to go up to $5 million will tell you something about how often a royal flush occurs.

Vegas on the cheap Slot clubs

Virtually every casino has a slot club. Its main purpose is to keep track of a customer's slot and video poker play, and to retain customer loyalty by providing rewards in the form of points that can be redeemed for cash or merchandise. Slot clubs have become very popular with players, and the casinos are always coming up with better ways to attract members; many clubs offer introductory gifts such as free buffets, bonus points or other perks to get your name on the dotted line.

Most slot clubs issue members with an ID card, which must be inserted into the slot or video poker machine to allow the machine's computer to track the amount of play. The points awarded by the computer are redeemable for cash, or comps in the casino's restaurants or shows. Slot club members also qualify for discounts in casino shops, reduced room rates, free meals and tickets to events such as slot tournaments, parties and barbecues.

It's hard to recommend one slot club over another because the benefits change frequently. You can get an idea of what the clubs are offering by checking out the *Las Vegas Advisor*, or the Friday edition of the *Review-Journal* newspaper. Some of the better spots for signing up include the **Hard Rock** (*see p90*), which awards $20 of slot play to new members, and **New York-New York** (*see p83*), which gives away a slot tournament entry, taxicab cap, and five free slot pulls for signing up.

A relatively new type of promotion currently offered by **Harrah's** (*see p77*) and the **Stratosphere** (*see p89*) is the loss recovery plan for new slot club members. The new member receives a rebate of the losses incurred during their first hour of play up to a total of $125. The money is sent to the customer's home as a voucher, which must be redeemed on the next visit to Las Vegas.

All it takes to join a slot club is a picture ID, and a few minutes at the casino's slot booth. Some casinos even have roving recruiters who will sign you up at the machine. It doesn't cost anything to join.

Roulette

Despite its popularity in Europe, roulette doesn't have much of a fan club in the US. That's partly due to the calm nature of the game; Americans want action and speed when they gamble, roulette gives them neither. Another reason is a subtle but crucial change in the US version. In Europe, roulette wheels typically have 36 numbered slots and one zero slot. On most American wheels, there are two zero slots (marked as zero and double zero). That change alone nearly doubles the house edge to 5.26 per cent, as compared to 2.7 per cent on single-zero wheels.

Roulette is simple to play. The wheel is mounted horizontally and a matching table layout serves as the betting area. All the numbers are coloured red or black, except the zero and double zero, which are green. Players make their bets on the table, the wheel is spun and a little ball is launched. Betting is halted, the ball comes to rest in a slot, then winners are paid off. To minimise confusion about who made which bet, each player receives specially coloured 'wheel' chips when they buy in (these chips can only be used at the roulette table).

The easiest wager is a straight-up bet, where the player drops a chip on a single number (17

is the most popular, supposedly due to its central location and the fact that James Bond bets it in the movies). If the number is the winner, it's paid off at 35 to 1. You can also make bets on groups of numbers; for example, on lines separating numbers, rows of numbers or in special areas denoting odd or even, red or black and so on. In this way, a single bet covers anywhere from two to 18 numbers. Needless to say, the more numbers the wager covers, the lower the payoff. For instance, betting odd or even pays even money.

The variety of wagers makes roulette an interesting game, especially if you like the languid pace. But bear in mind, the odds are tough. Your best bet is to find a casino with a single-zero wheel – such as the Monte Carlo, Stratosphere and Regent Las Vegas – and try to look elegant while losing.

Slot machines

Slot machines were once shunned, patronised only by the bored wives and girlfriends of gamblers. These days, they're the most popular and profitable part of the entire gambling industry, so much so that some casinos offer nothing but slots and video poker. Novice gamblers prefer slots because there's little to learn and no pressure from dealers or other players. Put in money, pull the handle and in a few seconds, you're either a winner or a loser. Simple. Plus, jackpots can reach millions of dollars. But there is a downside – slots give the house an edge from two to 25 per cent, often making them one of the worst bets in the house. And your chance of hitting a million-dollar jackpot is well, gee, what's the tiniest unit of measurement you can imagine? Your chances are smaller than that. Way smaller.

The basic slot machine accepts a maximum of either two or three coins (some take four or five, some just one, and a new breed of slots now takes up to hundreds of coins, including pennies). Each coin beyond the minimum increases the payout proportionally (twice as much for two coins, triple for three) should a winning combination appear. Sometimes the winnings on the final coin are exponentially higher: always check the pay tables at the top of the machine. Many machines have multiple pay lines. On these machines, an added pay line is activated each time another coin is wagered.

Modern slots usually have a coin counter that displays your credits. Instead of coins crashing into the steel bin, wins are registered as credits. Often, there's a bill changer attached, so players can simply slide in a $20, and $20 of credits appear on the counter. Bets are made by pulling a handle or pressing a button. When finished,

players hit the 'Cash out' button, and coins for all unused credits drop into the bin. The casino provides plastic cups to carry coins to other machines or the cashier. Some of the newest slots are 'coinless'. When you cash out, these machines print a voucher for the amount of money you have won. You redeem the voucher for cash at a change booth or the cage.

All slots fall into two categories: non-progressive (or stand-alone) and progressive. Stand-alone slots have fixed payouts, which are posted on the front of the machine. Progressive slots offer a fixed and a posted payout schedule, as well as the chance to hit a huge jackpot. This jackpot (funded by a percentage of every coin wagered) grows continuously until somebody wins it. A meter above the machines displays a running total of the current jackpot. Many progressive slots are linked to form a system that feeds the jackpot. These machines might be from one carousel in a single casino (with a $1,000 jackpot), or spread across casinos throughout the state (with multi-million dollar jackpots). With hundreds of machines in the system, the jackpot can reach astronomical levels. A Megabucks machine at the former Desert Inn paid almost $35 million in January 2000. Though rare, these payouts are well publicised and make excellent bait.

Gambling jargon

bankroll your total gambling budget; the casino has a bankroll too, but in mathematical terms, it's considered unlimited.

Black Book a list, kept by the State Gaming Control Board, of people legally excluded from any Nevada casino due to a history of cheating or connection to organised crime.

boxman casino executive who acts as the umpire in a game of craps.

buy in exchange cash for casino chips.

cage the main casino cashier, where chips and tokens are converted into cash, credit is established and, usually, foreign currency can be exchanged.

carousel a group of slot machines that are often connected to a joint 'progressive jackpot'.

change colour swap chips for ones of a higher or lower denomination.

check another word for chip.

chip token issued by casinos and used, instead of cash, for table games.

colour up exchanging small denomination chips for larger denomination chips before leaving a table game.

comps short for 'complimentaries'. Comps range from free cocktails to 'RFB' – room, food and beverage. Their value is calculated by the gambler's average bet multiplied by the time spent playing multiplied by the house edge. To qualify for comps, you must be a rated player or belong to a slot club.

credit line amount of credit a gambler is allowed to play with.

drop the total amount of money, including chips, cash and markers, brought to the gaming table.

European wheel a roulette wheel with a single '0' position (which gives players better odds). Most wheels in Vegas have '0' and '00'.

eye in the sky the casino's in-house surveillance system.

George dealer-speak for a good tipper.

grind joint a casino with low table minimums and low-denomination slot machines.

NEW SLOTS

Slot machines are getting increasingly flashy. A few years ago, video machines with oversized screens, multiple games and other gimmicks were all the rage. Today, a whole new generation of slots is being developed. Slot machines are becoming much more interactive and look a lot like video poker; on these slots, you'll be able to make choices about which symbols to hold or discard, based on a certain internal and intuitive logic.

Slot (and video poker) machines now account for upwards of 65 and even 70 per cent of total casino revenues, which means that gambling machines take in nearly twice as much revenue or more as all other casino games combined. Of the $10 billion won by Nevada casinos in fiscal 2000, $6.4 billion – nearly 65 per cent – was from slots and video poker.

Slots are much more fun to play today than they were even ten years ago, when they were still primarily 'one-armed bandits' (derisively referred to by table-game players as the 'idiot pull'). But they still won't line your pockets.

HOW SLOTS WORK

Modern slots are controlled by a computer chip called a random number generator, which continually churns out strings of numbers whether the game is being played or not.

Pulling the handle of a machine (or pressing the spin button) releases the reels and selects one of these randomly generated numbers. Each number corresponds to a certain set of symbols on the reels. That's how the outcome is determined. The force of the pull has nothing to do with where the reels stop.

Since this is computer technology, regulating the payout is a science. By adjusting the random number generator, a slot technician can make a machine 'tighter' (pays out less often) or 'looser' (pays out more often). In the old days, slots often had a built-in edge of 20 or 30 per cent or more. But players flocked to machines with the higher returns. Casinos did the maths and realised it was better to get five per cent of a lot than 30 per cent of nothing, hence, most Vegas slots now return about 95 per cent of the drop (slightly less on nickel machines), leaving the house with a five per cent edge.

Certain casinos boldly advertise 98 or 99 per cent payouts, but read the small print. It's usually 'up to 99 per cent'. That means one machine on the floor might be set at 98 or 99 per cent, if that. Short of running 2,000 to 5,000 plays through similar machines and comparing payouts, there's no way to find out which slots are set tight or loose. Payout percentages are supposedly verified by the state Gaming

---

high-roller big-money gambler who bets a minimum of $100 per hand on a table game, and plays $5 slot machines or $1 multi-play machines.

house advantage, **house edge** *or* **vigorish** the percentage difference (retained by the casino) between the true odds and the actual payout.

juice the ultimate Las Vegas power and influence; who you know.

layout diagram on the playing table that marks the area of the game.

loose used to describe a slot machine that pays out frequently. Casinos compete in claiming that their slots are the loosest in town.

low-roller a gambler who bets almost exclusively at low-minimum slot machines, usually in grind joints.

marker IOUs signed by rated players to obtain chips and paid off with chips or cash.

pit area between the gaming tables reserved for casino employees.

pit boss casino executive who oversees the gambling action from inside the pit.

progressive jackpot the payout on a slot or video poker machine (or group of machines) that increases as each coin is played.

rated player a player whose gambling has been assessed by the casino and is thus eligible for comps.

shill casino employee who plays at empty tables (with house money) to encourage dithering visitors to get down to business.

shoe container for decks of cards from which card games are often dealt.

shooter the player who throws the dice in a game of craps.

slot clubs clubs for slot and video poker machine players. Members accrue points as they play, which can be redeemed against meals, gifts, cash and other perks. *See p37* **Vegas on the cheap: Slot clubs.**

stiff someone who doesn't tip; one of the worst names to be called by dealers, waitresses, bellmen, cab drivers, and others in Las Vegas.

toke a tip for a casino employee, often given in the form of a bet on their behalf.

true odds the real chances of winning on any game as opposed to the money actually paid out by the casino.

whale big-money gambler who is prepared to wager huge amounts (at least $5,000 per hand) at high-stake games.

Lots and lots of **slots** (*see p37*) at McCarran Airport and New York-New York.

Control Board, but they rarely check unless a casino advertises something absurd. The real advantage for the house comes with the constant repetition of slot plays. For instance, a player with $50 starts betting $1 per pull on a quarter machine (via four 25¢ bets per pull). Sometimes the player wins and those winnings are reinvested: the drop might only be $50, but they're giving the casino $240, say, of action every hour. A five per cent edge is substantial enough for a slot machine to retain about $12 an hour (five per cent of $240). That's a hold equal to nearly a quarter of the original bankroll. With a little less luck, that money could vanish even quicker. Over time, even an edge of half of one per cent grinds down players, which is why so many stumble away from machines empty-handed. That and the fact most of the payouts go towards the big (and seldom won) jackpots.

SLOT TIPS

Slot jockeys say non-progressive machines are looser than progressive machines, though payouts are smaller. And non-progressive machines with smaller top payouts are reportedly looser than those with large top payouts. Similarly, among progressive machines, those with smaller jackpots hit more often. Interestingly, the amount of your wager going to the progressive jackpot is an indication of payout frequency. According to one casino executive, if it's less than one per cent, that progressive machine is likely to have more non-jackpot winners. If three to five per cent of every bet goes towards the progressive jackpot, that game is seriously weighted toward fewer, large payouts. Of course, this percentage isn't posted, so you're mostly flying blind.

One belief states that slots placed near doorways and aisles are looser than others. The constant sound of coins dropping is supposed to lure folks into betting a few bucks. One casino exec said house machines (those with the casino's name and logo) are set looser than non-house brand slots. We know one someone who's convinced slots near waitress stations are looser because that yields more tips.

The only recommendation that makes sense is that if you're going to play slots for big money, bet the maximum number of coins on each pull. This way, if lightning strikes and you're a winner, you'll get the biggest payout possible. If you want to lay out a dollar per pull, play four coins in a quarter machine (although $1 and higher machines tend to have higher percentage payouts). Avoid slots in non-casino locations such as the airport and

Having a whale of a time

The highest of the casino high-rollers – players who bet $100,000 or more on a single hand and drop $1 million a visit – are known as 'whales'. They are truly a rare breed, numbering fewer than 250 worldwide and Strip casinos vie aggressively for their patronage. Among them are film star Bruce Willis, basketball player Dennis Rodman, singer Diana Ross, Australian media mogul Kerry Packer, porn king Larry Flynt, Saudi arms dealer Adnan Khashoggi and many businessmen from the Far East, including members of Malaysia's Quek family.

In order to entice the whales to the baccarat, blackjack or roulette tables – the games of choice for big spenders – the Strip casinos will offer free air fares (or even a jet), a fleet of limos, special events tickets, private chefs and butlers, and the most luxurious suites in the resort; in fact, no gesture of goodwill is deemed too extravagant or unreasonable, as long as it's legal – in other words, unlike the old days, casinos will not pimp. The latest piece of strategy is to change Nevada gambling regulations to allow

for the creation of private gaming salons in casinos. The law as it now stands – and has stood since day one – requires all gambling in Nevada casinos to be done in public, which means super high rollers, though they can be segregated in high-limit pits, are still forced to play in view of the hoi polloi, who can stand behind the stanchions and indulge in a spot of whale-watching. The lack of privacy for high rollers in Nevada limits the ability of the poshest casinos, such as MGM Grand, Bellagio and Slots-A-Fun (just kidding), to compete with the fanciest gambling joints in Europe and Asia.

Finally, here's a story told about Kerry Packer. He was playing baccarat in the high-roller pit at the Mirage. An obnoxious player at another table was getting on Packer's nerves, so he went over and asked the player to behave himself. The player jumped up, faced Packer and demanded, 'Do you know who I am? I'm so-and-so, and I'm worth three hundred million!' Packer coolly sized up the player and said, 'I'll flip you for it.'

convenience stores. They have a house edge one step below outright thievery.

Slot machines can only pay out so many coins at a time, so if you hit a monster jackpot, stay put and wait for an attendant. If you walk away, someone else might claim your prize. The attendant will inform you of your tax obligations (US citizens need to fill out IRS paperwork on slot wins of more than $1,200; the tax situation varies for non-nationals).

Video poker

This electronic cousin of live poker enjoys a huge following in Vegas, much of it from hardcore local gamblers. Although a video poker machine resembles a slot machine and is typically located in the slot pit, it is an entirely different beast. Make no mistake: video poker is a game not of chance but of skill. If played perfectly, the house edge can often be flattened to zero or even pushed into the negative, meaning a return to players of over 100 per cent. Casinos can afford to do this because perfect play is the province of only a handful of experts, who use powerful computer programs to work out strategies that are accurate within ten thousandths of a percentage point.

Instead of a slot machine's spinning reels, a video poker screen displays a five-card hand of draw poker. Every deal comes from a freshly shuffled 52-card deck. Buttons allow the player to hold or replace the dealt cards. After the draw, the game pays off according to a payout schedule listed on the screen. A pair of aces might pay at one to one, while a royal flush almost always pays at 4,000 to one. Most basic poker rules are in effect as far as hand rankings go, but the psychological angle is jettisoned. You're playing against a machine that doesn't respond to bluffing, so your hand is all.

There's no way to summarise basic strategy for video poker, partly because it's extremely complex and partly because the game comes in so many varieties. Each has unique characteristics, such as wild cards and bonus options, and consequently different pay tables and different strategies for optimum play. You can buy video poker strategy cards (Huntington Press has a good set), which allow you to make the right decision on every hand; in essence, you're playing computer-perfect strategy.

The basic variation is 'Jacks or Better', which plays most like five-card stud (no wild cards) and pays on pairs of jacks or better. The strategies for Jacks or Better are mostly intuitive for anyone who knows how to play poker, but some rules have to be learned: for example, you never hold a 'kicker' (unpaired or unsuited high card); you never draw to a four-

card inside straight (for example, you hold 3, 4, 6, 7 and you're looking for a 5); and you always go for the royal flush if you hold four of the cards, even if it means sacrificing a pair, flush or straight in the process.

As with slots, you should play the maximum number of coins, as this greatly increases the top payout for a royal flush. Another tip: be sure to play full-payout games as opposed to their partial-payout brethren. The same style of game might pay the same hand differently in different casinos. For instance, in Jacks or Better, the full-payout version pays 9 for 1 on a full house and 6 for 1 on a flush (that's called a '9/6 machine'). On the partial-payout version, it's sliced to 8/5 or even as low as 6/5. The only reason to play a partial-payout version of Jacks or Better is if it's connected to a progressive jackpot or pays off on a pair of tens or better.

However, 8/5 Bonus, with extra payouts for four-of-a-kind, is a different animal. So are Double Bonus, Double Double Bonus and Triple Bonus variations. Then there are Joker Poker and several different varieties of Deuces Wild. Video poker players should consult the books and reports on the market that detail proper play for sample video poker hands. Excellent computer programs also tutor players in video poker strategies. Casinos don't mind if you refer to strategy charts while playing, but draw the line at laptop computers. Since it's impossible to absorb the tactics for all the variations at once, we recommend you study and master strategy for Jacks or Better, then, as you feel more comfortable, move on to the more complex – and financially rewarding – games such as full-pay Deuces Wild and Double Bonus varieties.

The latest rage are multi-play machines, such as Triple Play, Five Play and Ten Play. Here, three, five and ten hands of video poker are dealt at the same time from the same number of decks, requiring three, five, and ten times the maximum bet. Only the bottom-hand cards are displayed, however; the upper hands are face down. When you hold cards from the bottom hand, the held cards appear in the upper hands and when you draw, all the hands' cards are filled in around the held cards.

There's now even a Fifty Play video poker machine. With 50 hands of video poker on a screen, the cards are so small and go by so fast you can only watch the credit tally to see if you're winning. In Spin Poker, when you discard cards, the open spots spin like slot reels. Heads Up Poker, meanwhile, combines live poker with video poker. You're dealt five cards and you bet the hand. The machine responds by calling, raising or folding (the machine sometimes bluffs!). Then you play out the video poker hand, but you still have the live hand to be resolved.

Accommodation

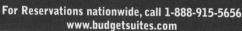

Accommodation

Since you hotel's your playground, where you stay can make a big difference to your experience of Las Vegas. Here's how to find the hotel of your dreams.

Tomb with a view.
Luxor's pyramid. *See p53.*

For the first time in years, the number of guest rooms in Las Vegas will grow only slightly in 2001 – by 3,000, pushing the total to about 127,000. This modest 2.5 per cent increase from two years ago is in stark contrast to the extraordinary growth rate of the late 1990s, when the Strip provided fertile ground for a bumper crop of ever more elaborate hotel-casinos, culminating in the arrival of the Aladdin in summer 2000.

This latest wave of construction, and the numerous expansions and renovations of existing resorts, have each been characterised by two key features: hotel-casinos are becoming more and more luxurious, and they are relying far less on frivolous, Disney-like attractions. The result is a much greater range of hotel choices for the upscale traveller. The newest resorts tempt visitors with large shopping malls, internationally known restaurants, elaborate pool complexes and star-quality entertainment. Spas and health clubs (*see p235*) offering massage, tanning booths and other creature comforts have become hugely popular accompaniments to the standard aerobics classes and weights room.

Of course, the downside to this trend is that room rates have climbed considerably: at the last survey, average weekend room rates were $190, while weeknight room rates had soared nearly 18 per cent to $119. Luckily, there are still (relative) bargains to be found, depending on the property and the season.

WHERE TO STAY

If you want to stay on the Strip, remember it's a 3½-mile (5.6-kilometre) hike from one end to the other. You could spend a lot of time tramping from casino to casino, so consider whether you want to be based at the north, centre or south. The more recent mega-resorts are the most attractive places to stay, but there are also older properties that retain a charm that hints of old Vegas. The cluster of Downtown casino-hotels do a good job with accommodation, although their dining options are more limited than those on the Strip, and non-gambling entertainment is practically non-existent.

Of course, you don't have to stay in a casino. Off the Strip, in the area surrounding the Convention Center, rooms are aimed at the business traveller and are generally

Hotels

For budget travellers
Sahara (see p55); **Stardust** (see p53).

For business travellers
Las Vegas Hilton (see p56); **Venetian** (see p50).

For families
Circus Circus (see p54); **Excalibur** (see p55).

For high rollers
Bellagio (see p47); **Caesars Palace** (see p47); **MGM Grand** (see p53).

For honeymooners
Flamingo (see p52); **Hyatt Regency Lake Las Vegas** (see p58); **Paris-Las Vegas** (see p50); **Regent** (see p58).

For singles
Hard Rock (see p55); **Mandalay Bay** (see p49); **Venetian** (see p50).

For water babies
Mandalay Bay (see p49); **Tropicana** (see p55).

unencumbered by noisy casinos, while out of town, the Regent in Summerlin and the Hyatt at Lake Las Vegas cater for visitors who want to combine casino luxury with easy access to the golf course. Casino rooms offer such good value that the budget accommodation sector is relatively small. In addition to the hostel on page 62, there are any number of fading 1950s motels cluttering up the more unfashionable stretches of Las Vegas Boulevard; their modern counterparts, the chain cheapies (see p54 **Chain gang**), can be found all over town.

WHAT TO EXPECT
Because the majority of casinos continue to use amusement as a means of inducing people into their fleecing pens, their attractions – the thrill rides, virtual-reality dens, magic shows and belt-popping prime-rib buffets – take precedence over guest rooms. As a result, although the newer resorts offer high-class rooms (at high-class rates), most Las Vegas hotel rooms tend to be of the Holiday Inn variety – clean and modern but nothing that would rival a Ritz-Carlton.–

Generally, however, they do a good job and typically provide valet parking, dry cleaning/ laundry service, room service (usually 24

hours), swimming pool, rooms adapted for disabled visitors (except in the older hotels) and no-smoking rooms (an increasing trend – two thirds of Bellagio's rooms are no-smoking). Some hotels offer a shuttle to and from the airport: ask when you book.

You'll find a phone and TV (usually with cable and pay movies) in your room; VCRs, mini-bars and refrigerators are usually only available in suites, though you can always request one (for a charge). Don't overlook the fact that mini-bars and in-room bottled water are often painfully overpriced, so it's a good idea to supply your own.

RATES
Expect to pay (for a double room, per night) from $50 to $75 in a budget hotel, $60 to $150 in a mid-range hotel and from about $180-$225 in a first-class property, plus hotel tax (currently at 11 per cent Downtown and nine per cent elsewhere). However, remember that rates fluctuate hugely as the listings below will indicate. They are typically lower from Sunday to Thursday, when it is easier to find a room, and higher on weekends, during holidays and special events, such as Memorial Day, New Year's Eve and Super Bowl weekend, and during the busiest conventions, such as Comdex and the Consumer Electronics Show (see chapter **Resources A-Z: Business**). Rates vary seasonally, too. From Thanksgiving to Christmas and during January, rooms are usually cheaper and easier to find. The city is busiest in March during Spring Break, when room rates may be driven up considerably.

The price categories in this chapter are meant as general guidelines only; it is important that travellers call ahead to query about rates for specific dates. If price is your main motivation, you may find exceptional bargains – even at the very expensive hotels – during mid-week, off-season times, when $200 rooms often drop below $100, so do not hesitate to try. Bear in mind, too, that the room rates listed below are based on information received from the hotels and are subject to change. For tips on keeping the costs down, see p60 **Vegas on the cheap: Rooms**.

RESERVATIONS
At the time of writing, there were more than 127,000 hotel rooms in Las Vegas, the most in any US city, so you'd imagine it wouldn't be difficult to find a place to sleep. But because of the continuing rise in numbers of tourists (to more than 35 million a year) and weekend visitors from Southern California, hotels can and do sell out. Book in advance as much as possible to ensure the greatest choice. Nearly

all casinos have websites, which offer a booking facility via email. The city also has several reservation agencies, which can advise on the current best deals. Try **Reservations Plus** (2275A Renaissance Drive, between Tropicana & Eastern Avenues, NV 89119; 1-800 805 9528/ fax 795 8767/www.houseol.com), or **Travelscape.com** and **Expedia.com**. The website www.a2zlasvegas.com/rooms/ provides links to other reservation companies and has visitor comments on specific hotels. It is also worth contacting the **Las Vegas Convention & Visitors Authority** (892 0711).

Casino Hotels

The Strip

First class

Bellagio
3600 Las Vegas Boulevard South, at W Flamingo Road, Las Vegas, NV 89109 (reservations 1-888 987 6667/front desk 693 7111/fax 693 8546/ www.bellagio.com). Bus 202, 301, 302. **Rates** single or double $159-$599; suite $300-$1,600. **Credit** AmEx, DC, Disc, MC, V. **Map** p316 A7.
In a city that doesn't know the meaning of restraint, Bellagio is positively demure. One of the first hotels to package luxury at all levels, Bellagio boasts lavishly appointed standard rooms (3,005 in total, including 400 suites and nine luxury villas

reserved for high-rollers), a bustling, attractive casino, a very impressive collection of restaurants, a top-notch spa (*see p235*) – and Prada, too. The hotel's deluxe guest rooms and suites have views of the resort's lake with its effervescent fountain shows, the surrounding mountains and the Las Vegas skyline. The rooms are large enough to accommodate a glass-top table and rattan-style chairs, plus additional wing chairs. Bathrooms have Italian marble floors and surfaces with a soaking tub and shower.
Bellagio is an adult-oriented resort: under-18s are not allowed on the property unless they are staying there. Bellagio's elegant pool terrace, among the most beautiful on the Strip, was inspired by Italian gardens and includes mature pine trees transplanted from the old Dunes golf course that used to occupy the property.
Hotel services *Beauty salon. Business centre. Car rental desk. Concierge. Gym. Pool. Spa. Tour desk.* **Room services** *Dataport. Room service (24hrs). Safe. Turndown. TV: cable/pay movies. Voicemail.*

Caesars Palace
3570 Las Vegas Boulevard South, at W Flamingo Road, Las Vegas, NV 89109 (reservations 1-800 634 6661/front desk 731 7110/fax 731 6636/ www.caesars.com). Bus 202, 301, 302. **Rates** single/double $89-$500; suite $650-$850. **Credit** AmEx, DC, Disc, MC, V. **Map** p316 A7.
Since 1966, Caesars Palace has been the quintessential Vegas pleasure dome and, unlike many of the other themed resorts, its splendidly ridiculous amenities extend from the casino to its rooms and suites, which are among the most luxurious in town. Features include European-style bathrooms (marble

Luxury awaits at the non-gaming **Four Seasons**. *See p58.*

Accommodation

Monte Carlo: Euro-glitz on the Strip.

and tiles, double sink, separate enclosure for the toilet), dressing rooms, velvet chaise longues and platform beds. The even fancier suites have circular beds, private dining rooms, wet bars, in-room saunas, steam rooms and elaborate audio-visual systems. And for its best customers (ie biggest gamblers), Caesars provides ultra-lavish accommodation such as the Via Suites with a lush Italian garden atmosphere and the two-storey Roman and Greek 'fantasy suites'. Caesars also has a magnificent pool and sun deck area, aptly named the Garden of the Gods. A rather ugly, 29-storey tower opened in 1997, adding 1,200 rooms, furnished with Greco-Roman art, sculptures, columns and marble tubs; the tower also has a health spa and meeting rooms. In 2001, construction began on a 4,000-seat Colosseum events centre, 1,500 extra guests rooms and some villas. The Circus Maximus showroom, the tennis courts and two long-time restaurants were lost in the expansion.

Hotel services *Beauty salon. Concierge. Golf course. Gym. Pool. Spa. Tour Desk.* **Room services** *Room service (24hrs). TV: cable/pay movies. Voicemail.*

Mandalay Bay

3950 Las Vegas Boulevard South, between W Tropicana Avenue & Russell Road, Las Vegas, NV 89119 (reservations 1-877 632 7000/front desk 632 7777/fax 632 7011/www.mandalaybay.com).

Bus 301, 302. **Rates** single/double $99-$599; suite $149-$599. **Credit** AmEx, DC, Disc, MC, V. **Map** p316 A9.

Weathered stone idols stand watch throughout this 60-acre tropical-themed luxury property. Mandalay Bay opened in 1999 and is quickly becoming one of the hotspots in town. Except for its garish gold Y-shaped tower, it's hard to believe that Mandalay Bay is from the same stable as Circus Circus and the Excalibur. Given the hotel's heritage, the interior is surprisingly elegant and spacious: a huge and beautiful lobby, high ceilings throughout, great carpets and a casino big enough to host a soccer match make the common areas an unexpected delight. The well appointed standard rooms average 500sq ft (46sq m), while the larger Vista suites command spectacular views of the Strip or the mountains. It's also a haven for beach freaks; the 11-acre water park – probably the best in town – has a lazy river and a wide sandy beach with wave machine, and there's also a full-service spa. But the real draw is the restaurant area, uniquely separated from the hustle and bustle of the casino, and featuring some of the city's highest-profile eateries.

Hotel services *Beauty salon. Business centre. Car rental desk. Gym. Pool. Spa. Tour desk.* **Room services** *Dataport. Room service (24hrs). TV: cable/ pay movies. Voicemail.*

Mirage

3400 Las Vegas Boulevard South, between Spring Mountain & W Flamingo Roads, Las Vegas, NV 89109 (reservations 1-800 347 9000/front desk 791 7444/fax 791 7446/www.themirage.com). Bus 301, 302. **Rates** single/double $79-$400 Mon-Thur, Sun, $159-$399 Fri, Sat; suite $250-$3,000. **Credit** AmEx, DC, Disc, MC, V. **Map** p316 A6.

The Mirage exemplifies the Vegas tendency to focus on dramatic public spaces at the expense of guest rooms. The hotel's 3,055 rooms tend to be identical and unmemorable and, in fact, many had to be remodelled within a year of opening because the closets were too small. The casino's Polynesian-jungle theming is carried into the rooms, which are decorated with tropical colour schemes and have cane furnishings and floor-to-ceiling headboards made from white louvred panels. Some have been redecorated with rather more subtle taupe, beige and peach colour schemes and the bathrooms spruced up with Spanish and Indonesian marble. The pool area comprises a series of blue lagoons, inlets and waterfalls, plus two islands exotically landscaped with various palms and tropical flowers.

Hotel services *Beauty salon. Business centre. Car rental desk. Concierge. Golf course. Gym. Pool. Spa. Tour desk.* **Room services** *Dataport. Room service (24hrs). Safe. Turndown. TV: cable/pay movies. Voicemail.*

Monte Carlo

3770 Las Vegas Boulevard South, at Rue de Monte Carlo, between W Flamingo Road & W Tropicana Avenue, Las Vegas, NV 89109 (reservations 1-800 311 8999/front desk 730 7777/fax 739 7200/

www.monte-carlo.com). Bus 201, 301, 302.
Rates single/double $89-$299 Mon-Thur, $99-$369 Fri-Sun; suite $150-$650. **Credit** AmEx, DC, Disc, MC, V. **Map** p316 A8.

Vegas glitz meets European refinement at the Monte Carlo, where the architecture is laden with stately columns, cascading fountains and Renaissance-style statues, yet resists lapsing into overstated baroque. Most of the hotel's attractions were designed for guests who like to participate: sun worshippers can bask next to six pools (including a wave pool) in a lush garden setting, or take a leisurely raft ride in the Easy River. Next to the pool area are four lit tennis courts and a pro shop for rentals and lessons. The 3,005 rooms (including 220 suites) are tastefully decorated with cherry furniture and turn-of-the-19th-century decor, with brass fixtures, Italian marble and polished granite.

Hotel services *Beauty salon. Business centre. Car rental desk. Gym. Pool. Spa. Tennis courts. Tour desk.* **Room services** *Dataport. Room service (24hrs). TV: cable/pay movies. Voicemail.*

Paris-Las Vegas

3655 Las Vegas Boulevard South, between Harmon Avenue & E Flamingo Road, Las Vegas, NV 89109 (reservations 1-888 266 5687/front desk 946 4222/ fax 946 3830/www.paris-lv.com). Bus 202, 301, 302. **Rates** single/double $89-$369; standard suite $350-$650; 1-bedroom suite $750-$1,250; 2-bedroom suite $979-$1,219. **Credit** AmEx, DC, Disc, MC, V. **Map** p316 A7.

Incredibly, considering how jealously the French guard their cultural heritage, Paris-Las Vegas opened in 1999 with the blessing of its real-life counterpart: the lights on the real Eiffel Tower were even dimmed in honour of the casino opening. One of the most eye-catching of the more recent casino resorts, Paris has a façade that incorporates famed Parisian landmarks. The smallish guest rooms (3,000 in total), decorated in French style, are housed in a 34-storey, mansard-roofed tower that was modelled on Paris's Hotel de Ville. They feature crown mouldings, rich fabrics and a European-style armoire. The spacious marble bathrooms have a large vanity unit, a make-up mirror, linen hand towels and European fixtures. Guests have free access to the on-site Spa by Mandara (*see p235*) and can also make use of the tennis courts and other facilities at Bally's next door.

Hotel services *Beauty salon. Business centre. Car rental desk. Concierge. Gym. Pool. Spa. Tour desk.* **Room services** *Dataport. Room service (24hrs). Safe. TV: cable/pay movies. Voicemail.*

Treasure Island

3300 Las Vegas Boulevard South, at Spring Mountain Road, Las Vegas, NV 89109 (reservations 1-800 944 7444/front desk 894 7111/fax 894 7446/ www.treasureislandlasvegas.com). Bus 203, 301, 302. **Rates** single/double $60-$370; suite $120-$1,000. **Credit** AmEx, DC, Disc, MC, V. **Map** p316 A6.

Strip-side view from the **Venetian**.

Like the Mirage next door, Treasure Island's rooms are housed in a Y-shaped configuration, formed by three coral-coloured, 36-storey towers. The casino's dashing pirate theme is evident in the lobby's flamboyant gold trimmings, black corkscrew pillars and marble floors covered with oriental rugs. The 2,800 guest rooms are decorated with brass fixtures, whitewashed wood furniture, copies of 18th-century nautical paintings and floor-to-ceiling windows, many of which offer views of the lively boulevard below. Hotel amenities include a well equipped spa, a beauty salon, spacious swiming pool area with a long slide (ideal for kids) and cabanas, as well as the inevitable two wedding chapels.

Hotel services *Beauty salon. Business centre. Car rental desk. Concierge. Golf course. Gym. Pool. Spa. Tour desk.* **Room services** *Dataport. Room service (24hrs). Safe. Turndown. TV: cable/pay movies. Voicemail.*

Venetian

3355 Las Vegas Boulevard South, south of Sands Avenue, Las Vegas, NV 89109 (reservations 1-888 283 6423/front desk 414 1000/fax 414 2122/ www.venetian.com). Bus 203, 301, 302. **Rates** suite $109-$499; deluxe suite up to $1,500. **Credit** AmEx, DC, Disc, MC, V. **Map** p316 A6.

After a dismal, partially finished grand opening in 1999, the Venetian quickly recovered. An interesting post-modern pastiche of Venice, Italy, the outdoor re-creations of famous landmarks are stunning, while inside, the ceilings boast beautiful re-creations of Italian masterpieces. Standard guest suites (no 'rooms' here), are much larger than the Vegas norm, averaging 700sq ft (65sq m) and the most comfortable and sumptuously appointed in town (even the telephone in the bathroom has a dataport). From the marble foyer to crown mouldings and wrought-iron railings, few amenities have been omitted.

The hotel is a huge hit with conventioneers, thanks to its own convention facilities and its interior corridors leading to the Sands Expo Center. On the weekends, the Venetian is overrun with the hip and pretty, all angling for dinner reservations at one of the 15 top-notch restaurants or a seat in one of the ultra-swanky bars. The Canal Shoppes shopping promenade is reminiscent of the Forum Shops, but the attractions – Madam Tussaud's, Jack's Velvet Lounge, the twin Guggenheim Museums (scheduled to open autumn 2001) – set the Venetian apart.
Hotel services *Beauty salon. Business centre. Car rental desk. Climbing wall. Concierge. Gym. Pool. Spa.* **Room services** *Dataport. Fax. Mini-bar. Room service (24hrs). Safe. TV: cable/pay movies. Voicemail.*

Mid range

Aladdin

3667 Las Vegas Boulevard South, at Harmon Avenue, Las Vegas, NV 89109 (reservations 1-877 333 9474/front desk 736 0111/fax 785 9600/ www.aladdincasino.com). Bus 301, 302. **Rates** single/double $79-$499; suite $199-$1,500. **Credit** AmEx, DC, Disc, MC, V. **Map** p316 A7.

The original Aladdin was built in the mid-1960s and imploded in 1998 to be replaced in 2000 by a brand

new mega-resort, the most recent to rise on the Strip. Co-owned by London Clubs International, the Aladdin has 2,567 guest rooms, the 7,000-seat Aladdin Theater of the Performing Arts (a holdover from the old hotel) and a 500,000sq ft (46,500sq m) dining, shopping and entertainment complex called Desert Passage located next door.

Guest rooms are decorated in soft pastels and dark wood furnishings, with luxurious marble bathrooms that include separate soaking tubs and showers. They are all equipped with slimline computers with Internet access. Other amenities include a health spa, a 24-hour business centre, convention facilities and the London Club – a separate European-style casino-within-a-casino for high-roller players. A pool terrace on the sixth floor overlooks the Strip.
Hotel services *Business centre. Concierge. Gym. Pool. Spa. Tour desk.* **Room services** *Dataport. Room service (24hrs). Safe. Turndown. TV: cable/pay movies. Voicemail.*

Bally's

3645 Las Vegas Boulevard South, at E Flamingo Road, Las Vegas, NV 89109 (reservations 1-800 634 3434/front desk 739 4111/fax 739 4405/ www.ballyslv.com). Bus 202, 301, 302. **Rates** single/double $59-$400; suite $327-$1,500. **Credit** AmEx, DC, Disc, MC, V. **Map** p316 A7.

In 1980, Bally's (then called the MGM Grand) was the site of the city's worst disaster – a fire swept through the hotel, killing 87 and injuring 700. The tragedy forced Vegas to modernise its safety codes which, at the time, didn't even require smoke alarms. Now fully fire-code compliant, the hotel's 2,814 guest rooms (including 185 suites) are among the largest in town; most have a California-modern feel with

Aladdin, without the lamp.

Flash, brash and colourful. Don't expect to rest at the carnival-themed **Rio**. *See p56.*

overstuffed furniture and mushroom coffee tables, while the predominant colours are subdued teal, mauve and earth tones. The swimming pool area, one of the most appealing in town, features a beautiful palm-fringed sun deck and cabanas with their own refrigerators, TVs, rafts and private phones. **Hotel services** *Beauty salon. Business centre. Car rental desk. Concierge. Gym. Pool. Spa. Tennis courts. Tour desk.* **Room services** *Dataport. Room service (24hrs). Safe. TV: cable/pay movies. Voicemail.*

Flamingo

3555 Las Vegas Boulevard South, at E Flamingo Road, Las Vegas, NV 89109 (reservations 1-800 732 2111/front desk 733 3111/fax 733 3353/ www.flamingolasvegas.com). Bus 202, 301, 302. **Rates** single/double $55-$300; suite $119-$699. **Credit** AmEx, DC, Disc, MC, V. **Map** p316 A7.
This place has changed a lot since Bugsy Siegel built his tropically themed oasis in the desert; all that remains in remembrance of the Chicago-mobster-turned-Vegas-hotelier is a stone pillar and small plaque in the rose garden behind the casino. Over the past ten years the hotel has undergone numerous expansions and renovations. The result is 3,642 rooms in six towers, which surround a pool area reminiscent of Hawaii's Waimea Canyon – 15 acres of tropical plants, waterfalls, streams, gardens, koi ponds and a grove of 2,000 palm trees. Water enthusiasts will find five pools, water slides, jacuzzis and legions of lounge chairs. And in the middle of this mini-paradise is an open-air wedding chapel for those willing to take the ultimate plunge. The tropical theme is carried throughout the hotel,

but the rooms retain a Hilton influence, even though the hotel is no longer part of the Hilton family. Among the health club's numerous services are massage, salt glow and oxygen pep-up, for that post-losing depression.
Hotel services *Beauty salon. Business centre. Car rental desk. Gym. Pool. Spa. Tennis courts. Tour desk.* **Room services** *Dataport. Room service (24hrs). Safe. TV: cable/pay movies. Voicemail.*

Harrah's

3475 Las Vegas Boulevard South, between Sands Avenue & E Flamingo Road, Las Vegas, NV 89109 (reservations 1-800 392 9002/front desk 369 5000/ fax 369 5008/www.harrahsvegas.com). Bus 301, 302. **Rates** single/double $50-$300; suite $90-$500. **Credit** AmEx, DC, Disc, MC, V. **Map** p316 A6.
Since it opened in 1973 as the Holiday Casino, Harrah's has undergone innumerable face-lifts and reinventions. The most recent renovation in 1997 gave the resort a hackneyed 'Carnival around the World' motif and added a 35-storey tower with nearly 1,000 rooms and suites. There are now a total of 2,600 guest rooms; all are bright and festive with light wood furniture, brass lamp fixtures and cheerful drapes and bedspreads. Some rooms have whirlpools. Harrah's is a good option if you want to be in the middle of the Strip action – it's within walking distance of the Mirage, Treasure Island, Caesars Palace and the Venetian.
Hotel services *Beauty salon. Car rental desk. Gym. Pool. Spa. Tour desk.* **Room services** *Dataport. Room service (24hrs). TV: cable/pay movies. Voicemail.*

Imperial Palace

3535 Las Vegas Boulevard South, between Sands Avenue & E Flamingo Road, Las Vegas, NV 89109 (reservations 1-800 634 6441/front desk 731 3311/ fax 735 8328/www.imperialpalace.com). Bus 301, 302. **Rates** *single/double $49-$119; suite $109-$300.* **Credit** AmEx, DC, Disc, MC, V. **Map** p316 A6.

The small, blue-roofed pagoda on the Strip is only the tip of the iceberg in this sprawling 2,700-room complex, which appears to be built in tiers, each one further from the main drag. The hotel carries an oriental theme – the entrance is marked by crystal, jade, bamboo and wood accents, and the cocktail waitresses wear side-split skirts à la Suzie Wong. Standard guest rooms are just that, but lovers and players should try one of the 'luv tub' rooms: an oversized room with a mirror over the bed and still more mirrors surrounding a decadent 300-gallon sunken bath. Other amenities include a wedding chapel, health club and Olympic-sized pool. Some rooms have mini-bars, whirlpools and terraces.

Hotel services *Beauty salon. Business centre. Car rental desk. Gym. Pool. Spa. Tour desk.* **Room services** *Dataport. Room service (24hrs). TV: cable/pay movies.*

Luxor

3900 Las Vegas Boulevard South, between W Tropicana Avenue & Russell Road, Las Vegas, NV 89109 (reservations 1-800 288 1000/front desk 262 4000/fax 262 4404/www.luxor.com). Bus 301, 302. **Rates** *single/double $69-$250 Mon-Fri; $99-$599 Sat, Sun; suite $99-$800.* **Credit** AmEx, DC, Disc, MC, V. **Map** p316 A9.

The 2,427 rooms in the Luxor's glass pyramid are reached by 'inclinators', elevators that rise at a 39° angle, making you feel like you're on an enclosed ski lift. Each room (with rampant Egyptian theming) has a sloping wall and bank of windows with views of the Strip and surrounding mountains, and a door that opens to overlook the pyramid's interior atrium. Note that some views are partially blocked by the recently completed tower just north of the pyramid, which houses another 1,950 rooms. Avoid the pyramid if you like to soak in a bath; most rooms have a shower unit, but no tub. There are several wading pools and date palms growing out of the main swimming pool.

Hotel services *Beauty salon. Business centre. Car rental desk. Gym. Pool. Spa. Tour desk.* **Room services** *Room service (24hrs). Safe. TV: cable/pay movies. Voicemail.*

MGM Grand

3799 Las Vegas Boulevard South, at E Tropicana Avenue, Las Vegas, NV 89109 (reservations 1-800 646 7787/front desk 891 1111/fax 262 4404/ www.mgmgrand.com). Bus 201, 301, 302. **Rates** standard rooms $59-$119; concierge level (incl breakfast) $79-$359; suite $89-$2,500. **Credit** AmEx, DC, Disc, MC, V. **Map** p316 A8.

The 5,005 rooms in the MGM Grand – the world's largest resort hotel – are honeycombed in its four emerald-green towers. They are decorated in four distinct motifs, the best of which are the Hollywood rooms done in two-tone wood, with gold-flecked walls, gilded mouldings and beds backed by mirrors. Of the 750 suites, about half are really oversized guest rooms with a sofa and two TVs; others perch on the 29th floor and are huge, split-level in design and served by one butler and up to 27 telephones. The Mansion, a separate high-roller complex with 30 suites, has replaced some of the Grand Adventures theme park, while the rest of the park is closed to the public. It, too, awaits replacement by more amenities. Other facilities including a resplendent pool area and the luxurious, renovated Grand Spa (*see p235*).

Hotel services *Beauty salon. Business centre. Car rental desk. Gym. Pool. Spa.* **Room services** *Dataport. Room service (24hrs). TV: cable/pay movies. Voicemail.*

New York-New York

3790 Las Vegas Boulevard South, at W Tropicana Avenue, Las Vegas, NV 89109 (reservations 1-800 693 6763/front desk 740 6822/fax 740 6700/ www.nynyhotelcasino.com). Bus 201, 301, 302. **Rates** single/double $59-$289. **Credit** AmEx, DC, Disc, MC, V. **Map** p316 A8.

In a triumph of camouflage, New York-New York's guest rooms are concealed in fairly authentic, scaled-down re-creations of NYC landmarks: the Empire State building, Chrysler building, Century building, CBS building and others. The towers range in height from 29 to 47 storeys (Las Vegas's tallest) and house 6,024 guest rooms in a variety of floorplans and themes. The decor, however, is pretty standardised and doesn't reflect the character of the different towers. Most use warm earth tones, with polished chrome lamps and light wood furniture. The hotel's health club is little more than a workout room and the pool is small by resort standards. Check when you book that the Manhattan Express rollercoaster (*see p104*) doesn't pass your window or you will be continually disturbed by the screams of riders.

Hotel services *Beauty salon. Business centre. Car rental desk. Gym. Pool. Spa. Tour desk.* **Room services** *Dataport. Room service (24hrs). Safe. TV: cable/pay movies. Voicemail.*

Stardust

3000 Las Vegas Boulevard South, at Stardust Drive, between W Sahara Avenue & Desert Inn Road, Las Vegas, NV 89109 (reservations 1-800 824 6033/ front desk 732 6111/fax 732 6257/ www.stardustlv. com). Bus 301, 302. **Rates** motor inn rooms $32-$90; tower rooms $60-$289; suite $142-$329. **Credit** AmEx, Disc, DC, MC, V. **Map** p315 B5.

The Stardust – with its famous starburst neon sign – has exemplified Las Vegas style and flash for more than 40 years. It's an adult playground (albeit rather dowdy now) and remains unencumbered by family attractions. Like many hotels on the Strip, the Stardust's 2,431 guest rooms are split between a newer tower and an older wing. The tower rooms are among the better buys on the Strip, decorated with dark carpets, red and black upholstery, glass

or marble tables and light wicker furniture. The original, motel-like rooms are to be avoided, unless you simply must park your car outside your room. Wayne Newton took over in 2000 as the hotel's permanent entertainment headliner, though when he's on a break, other top entertainers pop in for a week or two. Rounding out the Stardust's amenities are eight bars, two pools and a video games arcade.
Hotel services *Beauty salon. Car rental desk. Pool.* **Room services** *Room service (24hrs). Safe. TV: pay movies. Voicemail.*

Stratosphere

2000 Las Vegas Boulevard South, at St Louis Avenue, between Oakey Boulevard & E Sahara Avenue, Las Vegas, NV 89104 (reservations 1-800 998 6937/front desk 380 7777/fax 383 5334/ www.stratlv.com). Bus 301, 302. **Rates** single/double $49-$259; suite $99-$349. **Credit** AmEx, Disc, DC, MC, V. **Map** p315 C3/4.

Sadly, there are no rooms atop the Stratosphere's imposing 1,149ft (350m) high tower, but you can enjoy the view, nevertheless, in the Top of the World restaurant (*see p132*). The hotel area is located in a conversion of the old mid-rise Vegas World hotel, which occupied the site before the Stratosphere. The rooms in the old tower have been upgraded with new carpets and curtains, art deco paintings, black lacquer furniture, safes and dataports. A $75-million expansion has added a 1,000-room tower (as well as two restaurants and an outdoor events centre), bringing the total number of guest rooms to 2,400. Located on the eighth floor of the new tower is a massive pool and recreation deck. Other additions include a new tour bus lobby, porte-cochère and expanded casino area.
Hotel services *Business centre. Car rental desk. Concierge. Gym. Pool. Tour desk.* **Room services** *Dataport. Room service (24hrs). Safe. Turndown. TV: cable/pay movies. Voicemail.*

Budget

Barbary Coast

3595 Las Vegas Boulevard South, at E Flamingo Road, Las Vegas, NV 89109 (reservations 1-800 634 6755/front desk 737 7111/fax 737 6304/ www.barbarycoastcasino.com). Bus 202, 301, 302. **Rates** single/double $39-$199; suite $200-$400. **Credit** AmEx, DC, Disc, MC, V. **Map** p316 A7.

Don't be dismayed by the drab exterior; inside, the theme is turn-of-the-19th-century San Francisco. The Barbary Coast is very small by Las Vegas standards – only 200 rooms, but if you can get one, you'll be charmed by the Victorian wallpaper and paintings, floral carpets, etched mirrors and white lace curtains. Some even have four-poster brass beds, mini-bars and whirlpools. This place is also home to Drai's, one of the city's most famous supper and after-hours clubs (*see p133*).
Hotel services *Concierge. Tour desk.* **Room services** *Dataport. Room service (24hrs). TV: cable/ pay movies.*

Chain gang

The following hotel and motel chains have branches in Las Vegas, many of them conveniently situated along or near the Strip.

Moderate

Holiday Inn 1-800 465 4329/ www.basshotels.com/holiday-inn
Howard Johnson 1-800 446 4656/ www.hojo.com

Budget

Best Western 1-800 528 1234/www.bestwestern.com
Comfort Inn, Econo Lodge, Quality Inn & Rodeway Inn 1-800 221 2222/ www.comfortinn.com
Days Inn 1-800 325 2525/www.daysinn.com
Motel 6 1-800 466 8356/www.motel6.com
Ramada Inn 1-800 272 6232/www.ramada.com
Super 8 1-800 800 8000/www.super8.com
Travelodge 1-800 578 7878/www.travelodge.com

Circus Circus

2880 Las Vegas Boulevard South, at Circus Circus Drive, between Desert Inn Road & W Sahara Avenue, Las Vegas, NV 89109 (reservations 1-800 634 3450/front desk 734 0410/fax 734 5897/ www.circuscircus-lasvegas.com). Bus 301, 302. **Rates** single/double $39-$250. **Credit** AmEx, DC, Disc, MC, V. **Map** p315 B5.

This is the number-one hotel choice for families visiting Vegas, thanks largely to its free circus acts, carnival midway, arcade games and Adventuredome theme park. It was the first of the classless, 'low-roller' casinos to hit the Strip, and its rooms are still among the cheapest in town. After several expansions, there are now 3,800 rooms and suites, mainly decorated with soft blue carpeting, pastel bedspreads and upholstery, and light wood furniture; the circus theming is restricted to just a few hot-air balloons painted on the walls. The West tower is the newest (built in 1997), while the cheapest (and oldest) rooms are in the motel-like Manor section. Ask for a south-facing room in the Skyrise tower for the best view of the Strip. Other amenities include swimming pools and a 365-space RV park (*see p62*).
Hotel services *Beauty salon. Business centre. Car rental desk. Pool. Tour desk.* **Room services** *Dataport. Room service (24hrs). Safe. TV: cable/ pay movies.*

Excalibur

3850 Las Vegas Boulevard South, at W Tropicana Avenue, Las Vegas, NV 89109 (reservations 1-800 937 7777/front desk 597 7700/fax 597 7040/ www.excalibur-casino.com). Bus 201, 301, 302. **Rates** single/double $49-$309. **Credit** AmEx, DC, Disc, MC, V. **Map** p316 A8.

Behind the white, pink and blue fairytale castle exterior, Excalibur offers you a standard, Y-shaped hotel tower, containing a staggering 4,008 guest rooms. (Excalibur is under the same ownership as Circus Circus, so the body count is all-important.) Mercifully, the medieval knights theming doesn't spill into the rooms, which are decorated in bold reds, blues and greens, with dark wood furniture and wrought-iron fixtures. Among the hotel's amenities are a wedding chapel, beauty salon and two pools. It's more downmarket than some of the other casinos, but a good choice for budget travellers and families and well located, opposite the MGM Grand and New York-New York.

Hotel services *Beauty salon. Car rental desk. Pool. Tour desk.* **Room services** *Dataport. Room service (24hrs). TV: cable/pay movies. Voicemail.*

Riviera

2901 Las Vegas Boulevard South, at Riviera Boulevard, Las Vegas, NV 89109 (reservations 1-800 634 6753/front desk 734 5110/fax 794 9451/ www.theriviera.com). Bus 301, 302. **Rates** single/double $29-$95; suite $125-$600. **Credit** AmEx, DC, Disc, MC, V. **Map** p315 B5.

The Riviera's original tower (nine storeys, 200 rooms) was the first high-rise in town when it opened in 1955. Since then the Riv has expanded to 2,089 guest rooms, the best of which are in the newer Monaco and Monte Carlo towers (15 and 18 storeys respectively). The tower rooms are small but not cramped, and decorated with dark wood furniture and burgundy or teal bedspreads with matching gold-tasselled curtains. About half the rooms have views overlooking the pool, the rest face the surrounding mountains. The rooms in the original nine-storey wing (now the Mediterranean tower) were remodelled in 1996 with light wood furniture and flower-print fabrics. They're closer to the casino action, but the views are dismal (plumbing, air ducts, backs of signs). Hotel amenities include a large pool (flanked on all sides by hotel towers – the sun disappears early), two night-lit tennis courts, a well-equipped health club and a convention centre.

Hotel services *Beauty salon. Business centre. Car rental desk. Gym. Pool. Spa. Tennis courts. Tour desk.* **Room services** *Room service (24hrs). Safe. TV: cable/pay movies. Voicemail.*

Sahara

2535 Las Vegas Boulevard South, at E Sahara Avenue, Las Vegas, NV 89109 (reservations 1-800 634 6666/front desk 737 2111/fax 791 2027/ www.saharahotelandcasino.com). Bus 204, 301, 302. **Rates** single/double $55-$85; suite $200-$600. **Credit** AmEx, DC, Disc, MC, V. **Map** p315 C4.

After several expansions the Sahara has taken on a fresh look. Its famous vertical sign has gone, and new towers, Moroccan-style arches, palm trees and cascading fountains have replaced the original two-storey garden buildings. The renovations have helped revitalise the ageing resort, and made it a popular destination for conventioneers and tour groups. It's also boosted the room count to 1,720, including 63 suites. The renovated and new rooms have a sunny disposition with tan carpeting and drapes and earth-tone upholstery. Hotel amenities include two pools, one with landscaped gardens and a thatched-hut bar.

Hotel services *Beauty salon. Business centre. Car rental desk. Pool. Tour desk.* **Room services** *Dataport. Room service (6am-midnight). TV: cable/pay movies. Voicemail.*

Tropicana

3801 Las Vegas Boulevard South, at E Tropicana Avenue, Las Vegas, NV 89109 (reservations 1-800 468 9494/front desk 739 2222/fax 739 2469/ www.tropicanalv.com). Bus 201, 301, 302. **Rates** single/double $39-$179; suite $109-$1,000. **Credit** AmEx, DC, Disc, MC, V. **Map** p316 A8.

Polynesia in the desert may once have described the Tropicana, but it's all looking rather in need of repair now. The 1,900-plus guest rooms continue the island flavour with colourful prints and wood-and-bamboo furnishings. A water park stretches between the hotel's twin towers with three pools (featuring swim-up blackjack in the summer), a waterslide, five spas, two lagoons, tropical plants, lots of exotic flowers, oh, and some live pink flamingos. Other amenities include a wedding chapel and health club.

Hotel services *Beauty salon. Business centre. Car rental desk. Gym. Pool. Spa. Tour desk.* **Room services** *Dataport. Room service (24hrs). Safe. TV: cable/pay movies. Voicemail.*

Off-Strip

First class

Hard Rock Hotel

4455 Paradise Road, at Harmon Avenue, Las Vegas, NV 89109 (reservations 1-800 473 7625/front desk 693 5000/fax 693 5010/www.hardrockhotel.com). Bus 108. **Rates** single/double $75-$250 Mon-Thur, $145-$300 Fri-Sun; suite from $250. **Credit** AmEx, DC, Disc, MC, V. **Map** p316 C7.

The Hard Rock's Miami-style curving hotel block is surprisingly elegant and tasteful for those expecting rock 'n' roll tat, and is one of the most pleasant places to stay in Las Vegas. It's also pretty intimate by Vegas standards (be sure to book ahead), with only 340 original rooms and suites, and 317 new rooms. The decor is classy and masculine, the TV is extra large and the room service is top notch – acres of linen, vases of fresh flowers, gleaming serving domes and designer cruet, all for an $8 hamburger. Ask for a room overlooking the pool area, which has a sandy beach lagoon, hillside gardens

Get away from it all at the sumptuous **Regent** in Summerlin. *See p58.*

and a row of tent cabanas. Amphibian gamblers will like the swim-up blackjack table. You'll also find spas and whirlpools, a waterslide and rock music piped underwater.

Hotel services *Concierge. Gym. Pool. Spa.*
Room services *Dataport. Room service (24hrs). Voicemail. TV: cable/pay movies.*

Las Vegas Hilton

3000 Paradise Road, between Karen Avenue & Desert Inn Road, Las Vegas, NV 89109 (reservations 1-800 732 7117/front desk 732 5111/ fax 732 5805/www.hilton.com/hotels). Bus 108, 112. **Rates** single/double $55-$359; suite $360-$1,600. **Credit** AmEx, DC, Disc, MC, V. **Map** p31 C5.

Located about a block from the Strip, the 3,000-room Hilton is a favourite with conventioneers (the Convention Center is next door), tour groups and those who like a self-contained resort. The outdoor recreation deck has six tennis courts, a putting green, shuffleboard and a large pool area. The hotel's lobby area is magnificently decorated with tropical colours, Grecian bas-reliefs, crystal chandeliers and neon rainbows. As you would expect of Hilton, the rooms are first-rate, with upholstered easy chairs, marble-top dressing tables and deep closets. Some rooms have mini-bars, terraces, fireplaces and whirlpools. Colours tend towards cool blue and green pastels. One of the Hilton's attractions, Star Trek: The Experience (*see p113*), includes a space-age casino and Quark's Bar & Restaurant, and is one of the most popular must-sees in town. In mid-2001, Sheena Easton signed a long-term contract to headline the resort's Nightclub.

Hotel services *Beauty salon. Business centre. Car rental desk. Gym. Pool. Spa. Tennis courts.*
Room services *Room service (24hrs). Safe. Turndown. TV: cable/pay movies. Voicemail.*

Mid range

Palms

4321 W Flamingo Road, at Valley View Boulevard, Las Vegas, NV 89103 (reservations 1-866 725 6773/www.thepalmslasvegas.com). Bus 202. **Rates** phone for details. **Credit** AmEx, DC, Disc, MC, V. **Map** p311 X3.

Scheduled to open in December 2001, the Palms is an intimate boutique hotel-casino. The 470 guest rooms, housed in a 40-storey tower, are bright and airy and furnished with natural wood desks and armoires, plus luxurious hotel beds. Most rooms have panoramic views of the Las Vegas Strip, and all feature built-in safes and oversized mini-bars. Rounding out the hotel amenities are a spa and beauty salon, a pool area and a 14-screen cinema.

Hotel services *Concierge. Pool. Spa.* **Room services** *Coffeemaker. Dataport. Mini-bar. Room service (24hrs). Safe. TV: pay movies. Voicemail.*

Rio

3700 W Flamingo Road, at Valley View Boulevard, Las Vegas, NV 89103 (reservations 1-800 752 9746/front desk 252 7777/fax 252 8909/ www.playrio.com). Bus 202. **Rates** standard suite $59-$1,000; Masquerade suite $250-$1,500. **Credit** AmEx, DC, MC, V. **Map** p311 X3.

The constantly expanding, carnival-themed Rio is an all-suite property. There are 2,548 suites in all (most are actually oversized rooms), split between its original tower and the 41-storey tower in the Masquerade Village wing – a $200-million shopping, dining, entertainment and gambling complex, which also has wedding chapels and two honeymoon suites. It doesn't really matter which tower you're in: the rooms are practically identical and the views the same, though the original tower retains some two-storey suites with curving staircases and giant bathrooms. Otherwise, you should expect rich colours, tropical prints, smoked-glass tables, velour furnishings in the sitting area and floor-to-ceiling windows for panoramic city views. The pool area gets rave reviews: a sandy beach lies at the edge of a tropical lagoon, complete with waterfalls and three pools. There's also an entertainment gazebo and two sand volleyball courts. The Rio Spa has workout facilities, a steam room and whirlpools.

Hotel services *Beauty salon. Business centre. Concierge. Golf course (1-888 867 3226). Gym. Pool. Spa.* **Room services** *Refrigerator. Room service (24hrs). Safe. TV: cable/pay movies. Voicemail.*

Downtown

Mid range

Golden Nugget
129 Fremont Street, at Casino Center Boulevard, Las Vegas, NV 89101 (reservations 1-800 634 3454/ front desk 385 7111/www.goldennugget.com). Bus 107, 403. **Rates** *single/double $58-$160; suite $275-$375; apartment $500.* **Credit** *AmEx, DC, Disc, MC, V.* **Map** p312 C1.

The 1,800 guest rooms at MGM-Mirage Resorts' Golden Nugget (the only Downtown hotel without a neon sign) include 27 apartments and six penthouse suites, and are among the most luxurious in town. The elegant lobby has sculpted-glass chandeliers, white marble floors and columns, gold and brass accessories and red oriental rugs. In the rooms, you'll find cream carpets and wall coverings, light wood tables and club chairs, tropical print bedspreads and curtains. The misted pool deck is huge, but is surrounded by buildings, so catching rays is limited to a few midday hours. The whirlpool spas are a nice touch, as are the marble swans and bronze sculptures. There's also a health club.

Hotel services *Beauty salon. Business centre. Car rental desk. Gym. Pool. Spa. Tour desk.* **Room services** *Dataport. Room service (24hrs). Safe. Turndown. TV: cable/pay movies.*

The bizarre entrance to **Bally's**. *See p51.*

Budget

El Cortez
600 Fremont Street, between Sixth & Seventh Streets, Las Vegas, NV 89101 (reservations 1-800 634 6703/front desk 385 5200/fax 385 1554/ www.elcortez.net). Bus 107, 113. **Rates** *single/double $27-$40; suite $44.* **Credit** *AmEx, DC, Disc, MC, V.* **Map** p312 D2.

Built in 1941, the El Cortez is the oldest casino-hotel in town and was once owned by Benjamin 'Bugsy' Siegel, who sold his interest when he needed to raise cash for the Flamingo. The south-west wing is the original adobe brick building, and although a 14-storey, 209-room tower has been added since, the original rooms with wooden floors and tile baths remain. El Cortez caters mostly to budget travellers, seniors and die-hard video poker fanatics.

Hotel services *Concierge. Hair salon.* **Room services** *Room service (6am-11pm). TV: pay movies. Voicemail.*

Fremont
200 Fremont Street, at Casino Center Boulevard, Las Vegas, NV 89101 (reservations 1-800 634 6460/ front desk 385 3232/fax 385 6270/ www.fremont casino.com). Bus 108, 205, 207, 401. **Rates** *single/ double $40-$200.* **Credit** *AmEx, DC, Disc, MC, V.* **Map** p312 D1.

Built in 1956, the Fremont Hotel was Downtown's first carpet joint (as opposed to Wild West-driven sawdust joints). Today, its block-long neon sign helps light up the Fremont Street Experience. Like its sister hotel, the California, it features a tropical island motif – which is appropriate, since it caters to a large contingent of Hawaiian tourists. The hotel's 450 guest rooms (including 23 suites) are modern and comfortable and feature floral patterns in hues of emerald and burgundy. However, there is no swimming pool.

Room services *Room service (6am-10am). Safe. TV: pay movies.*

Golden Gate Hotel
1 Fremont Street, at Main Street, Las Vegas, NV 89101 (reservations 1-800 426 1906/front desk 385 1906). Bus 108, 205, 207, 401. **Rates** *(incl breakfast) single/double $39 Mon-Thur, Sun; $55 Fri, Sat.* **Credit** *AmEx, Disc, DC, MC, V.* **Map** p312 C1.

For a glimpse of Las Vegas before it became a high-tech spectacle, go to the Golden Gate Hotel in Downtown. Built in 1906 as the Hotel Nevada at the corner of Fremont and Main Streets, it is the city's oldest hotel building and a reminder of Vegas's frontier heritage, before reality became virtual and hype replaced history. The hotel was renamed Sal Sagev ('Las Vegas' spelled backwards) in the 1930s and became the Golden Gate in 1955, when a group of San Francisco investors took over. They opened the casino and introduced the city to the shrimp cocktail – a tasty little treat that's still served in the Golden Gate's Bay City Diner. While the Golden

Gate has modernised to keep up with the times, it still manages to retain much of its historic charm. Many of the original guest rooms remain, though they've been updated with air-conditioning, private baths, cable TV, coffeemakers, voicemail and even dataports. The weekend rates have been bumped up, but the mahogany doors, plaster walls and tiled bathroom floors are a reminder of the joint's more basic past. Room rates include breakfast and a complimentary newspaper.
Room services *TV: cable. Voicemail.*

The rest of the city

First class

Hyatt Regency Lake Las Vegas

1600 Lake Las Vegas Parkway, Henderson, NV 89109 (reservations 1-800 554 9288/ front desk 567 1234/fax 567 6067/http://lakelas vegas.hyatt.com). No bus. **Rates** single/double $175-$245; suite $450-$1,800. **Credit** AmEx, DC, Disc, MC, V.

Hyatt Hotels' first venture into Las Vegas opened in 1999 as a posh, full-service resort that is unlike the Vegas norm. For a start, the resort is nearly 30 minutes' drive from the Strip, in a picturesque, private community near Lake Mead. The major attractions are the water sports, the Jack Nicklaus-designed golf courses and Camp Hyatt, the chain's renowned daycare programme for kids. Other amenities include two restaurants, including a fine dining room, Japanego, modelled on its namesake in La Jolla, California. The 495 guest rooms are large and offer views of either the lake or surrounding mountains. Designs evoke a Moorish ambience through desert colours, accent mouldings and carpet border patterns. If you want to forget you're in Las Vegas, it's ideal; if not, it's too far from the Strip to be convenient.
Hotel services *Babysitting & childcare. Beauty salon. Car rental desk. Concierge. Golf course. Gym. Pool. Spa.* **Room services** *Dataport. Room service (24hrs). Safe. Turndown. TV: cable/pay movies. Voicemail.*

The Regent

221 N Rampart Boulevard, at Summerlin Parkway Las Vegas, NV 89145 (reservations 1-877 869 8777/front desk 869 8777/fax 869 7771/www.resort atsummerlin.com). Bus 207. **Rates** single/double $195-$300; suite $400-$2,100. **Credit** AmEx, DC, Disc, MC, V.

Located in the master-planned residential suburb of Summerlin, about a 25-minute drive from the Strip, the Regent looks out over the Red Rock Canyon Conservation Area and has access to tee times at six nearby golf courses, including TPC at the Canyons across the street. The resort comprises two hotels that operate semi-independently, linked by a casino, shopping and restaurant complex that includes the Italian restaurant Spiedini (*see p148*). The Regent Grand Spa, decorated in Spanish revival style, has

Golden Gate: a Vegas old-timer. *See p57.*

286 rooms and features the state-of-the-art Aquae Sulis spa. The Regent Grand Palms, with 255 rooms is more formal in decor. At press time, financial problems and a possible buy-out mean the resort is facing an uncertain future.
Hotel services *Beauty salon. Business centre. Car rental desk. Concierge. Gym. Pool. Putting green. Spa. Tour desk.* **Room services** *Dataport. Mini-bar. Refrigerator. Room service (24hrs). Safe. Turndown. TV: cable/pay movies/Web with email/VCR. Voicemail.*

Non-casino Hotels

Since casinos subsidise their hotel rooms to provide themselves with a resident pool of gamblers, the non-casino hotels have a hard time competing and may charge slightly higher rates. The price differential, though not as significant as it used to be, buys you a refuge from the madness and a little more individuality. Generally, the closer to the Strip you are, the higher the prices.

The Strip

First class

Four Seasons

3960 Las Vegas Boulevard South, between W Tropicana Avenue & Russell Road, Las Vegas, NV 89119 (reservations 1-888 632 5000/front desk 632 5100/fax 632 5195/www.fourseasons.com). Bus 301, 302. **Rates** single/double $150-$350; suite $350-$950; speciality suite $900-$3,900. **Credit** AmEx, DC, Disc, MC, V. **Map** p316 A9.

The Four Seasons is Las Vegas's first upmarket hotel without gambling facilities. Well, sort of. Admittedly, there's no gaming in the actual hotel,

but it's bang next door to the Mandalay Bay mega-resort – in fact, from the outside, it's hard to tell the two apart – so it's only a step along a corridor to a very large casino. Small by Vegas standards, the Four Seasons' 424 rooms (including 86 suites) are located on floors 35 to 39 of Mandalay Bay's gold tower and accessed by separate elevators. The design of the interior – all golden wood panelling, antique furniture and paintings and huge floral displays – creates an air of understated elegance and exclusivity. You'll almost forget you're in Vegas – until you look out of your window at the Strip stretching away to the north. Rooms are not huge (500sq ft/46sq m), but they're luxurious enough, with all sorts of extras – mini-bar, bathrobes, coffee-maker, shoeshine – that you don't usually get in the hotel-casinos. Guests have their own separate pool within the Mandalay Bay pool complex, complete with lounge chairs and private cabanas, plus a top-class spa and health club (see *p235*). Two restaurants – the Verandah Café (see *p136*) and Charlie Palmer's Steak (see *p139*) – serve excellent food. Plus, you can always nip next door to sample Mandalay Bay's varied dining facilities.
Hotel services *Business centre. Car rental desk. Concierge. Gym. Pool. Spa.* **Room services** *Dataport. Mini-bar. Room service (24hrs). Safe. Turndown (twice daily). TV: cable/pay movies. Voicemail.*

Budget

Algiers Hotel

2845 Las Vegas Boulevard South, at Riviera Drive, Las Vegas, NV 89109 (reservations 1-800 732 3361/front desk 735 3311/www.algiershotel.com). Bus 301, 302. **Rates** *single/double $35-$125; suite $70-$150.* **Credit** *AmEx, Disc, DC, MC, V.* **Map** *p315 B5.*

Built in 1953, the Algiers retains much of the style that characterised Vegas during the Frank-and-Dino Rat Pack days. The motorcourt-style inn is a two-storey garden affair; pink 'bleeding brick' buildings with aqua trim surround a large kidney-shaped pool. Stretch out in a lounge chair under the towering palms and you'll feel like you're back in the Hollywood-high-life oasis of the 1950s. The 105 rooms are clean and well kept, with white panelled walls, light wood furniture, dressing areas and tiled bathrooms. The swag lamps are a reminder of the Algiers' retro polyester heritage. The service is friendly and homey without the hustle of newer establishments, but the hotel lets its neighbours (Stardust, Circus Circus) do the entertaining.
Hotel services *Car rental desk. Pool.*
Room services *TV: cable.*

Glass Pool Inn

4613 Las Vegas Boulevard South, between E Tropicana Avenue & Russell Road, Las Vegas, NV 89119 (reservations 1-800 527 7118/front desk 739 6636). Bus 301, 302. **Rates** *single/double $24-$119.* **Credit** *AmEx, MC, V.* **Map** *p316 A9.*

Opened in 1951, the Glass Pool Inn, at the southern end of the Strip, is famous for its unique, elevated swimming pool with windows. According to the owners – who originally called the motel the Mirage but sold the name to Steve Wynn in 1988 – the pool was built to attract passing motorists, parched and dusty after driving for hours across the desert. The rooms – many with exposed-beam ceilings, plastic dinette-style furniture and tiled baths – are now somewhat run-down and rented mostly to long-term visitors such as construction workers, and people relocating to Vegas. A popular film location, the motel has appeared in *Casino*, *Leaving Las Vegas*, *Indecent Proposal*, the TV series *Vegas* and *Crime Story*, as well as dozens of commercials, documentaries and rock videos.
Hotel services *Pool.* **Room services** *TV: cable/ pay movies.*

Off-Strip

All the following hotels are near the Convention Center and handy for the action on the Strip as well as for delegates visiting a trade show. Some of these hotels cater especially for business people, with fax machines, meeting rooms and other amenities.

Mid range

Alexis Park

375 E Harmon Avenue, between Koval Lane & Paradise Road, Las Vegas, NV 89109 (reservations 1-800 582 2228/front desk 796 3300/fax 706 0766/ www.alexispark.com). Bus 108, 213. **Rates** *1-bedroom suite $99-$139; 1-bedroom loft suite $179-$249; larger suite $350-$1,500.* **Credit** *AmEx, DC, Disc, MC, V.* **Map** *p316 C8.*

The Alexis Park was originally built as a complex of townhouses and apartments and later transformed into an all-suite hotel. It doesn't have a casino, and it is never likely to after airport height restrictions foiled the owner's plans to build a new casino-hotel tower on the site in early 2001. Situated amid lush greenery, streams and waterfalls, the Mediterranean-style villa is a welcome retreat from the concrete and steel behemoths on the Strip. The lobby suggests European elegance with its Spanish tiled floor, overstuffed chairs and French telephones. The 500 suites are available in ten different layouts, with furnishings ranging from Victorian (flower-print ottomans, mahogany dining tables and chairs) to Southwest modern (adobe walls, macramé wall-hangings, club chairs). Some of the larger units (up to 1,200sq ft/112sq m) have fireplaces and jacuzzis, and all units have fridges, mini-bars and VCRs. Recreational facilities include three swimming pools, tennis courts, a putting green and a spa.
Hotel services *Beauty salon. Business centre. Concierge. Gym. Pool. Putting green. Spa. Tour desk.* **Room services** *Mini-bar. Refrigerator. Room service (7am-1am). TV: cable/pay movies. Voicemail.*

Vegas on the cheap Rooms

Some tips to ensure you don't blow your budget on your bed.

● Rates are not as seasonal as in the past, but the weeks between Thanksgiving and Christmas are 'low' periods with better room rates, as are the hottest summer months.

● It's always easier to book a room during the week (arriving on Sunday to Thursday) rather than for Friday and Saturday.

● Always try to book well in advance, and ask for dates that have more favourable rates. The reservation staff know their rates up to a year in advance.

● Avoid holidays such as New Year, Fourth of July, Memorial Day and Labor Day. Steer clear of conventions that dry up the pool of guest rooms. The biggest are Comdex and the Consumer Electronics Show, which force rates to more than double their usual amounts (for dates, see chapter **Resources A-Z: Business**).

● When making reservations, ask about discount rates for auto club members, senior citizens or corporate accounts. If you gamble, ask about a 'casino rate', which is usually 50 per cent below prevailing rates. This rate is frequently made available to slot club members and rated table game players.

● If you arrive in town without a booking, call around the biggest and least fashionable (read older) hotels, which are most likely to have rooms. The **Tropicana** (see p55) and **Circus Circus** (see p54) are good bets.

● Book a room in Downtown, where the rates are often half of those charged by hotels on the Strip.

● Book a room in a 'neighbourhood' hotel, such as the Station properties (**Palace, Boulder, Sunset** and **Texas Stations**), Coast Resorts (**Gold Coast, Orleans, Suncoast**), **Sam's Town** and **Arizona Charlie's**. Although these are often several miles from the Strip or Downtown, the rates are reasonable ($50 to $90) and the rooms are modern and comfortable. For all, see pp98-101.

● Book a room in a motel. There are plenty of local and chain motels from which to choose on the Strip, near Downtown, adjacent to the airport and in the burgeoning Convention Center area. See p54 **Chain gang**.

● Stay at the hostel (see p62). If you're the urban backpacking type, the hostel may be the ticket to a low-rent stay in Vegas. It may not be in the best part of the town, but it's not the worst either.

● Double up in your hotel room. A classic college student tactic is to stay eight deep in a room designed for four. Admittedly, the hotels frown on this practice – and you'll have to make do with just a few keys and one bathroom – but people are rarely found out, especially in the huge resorts containing thousands of rooms.

Carriage House

105 E Harmon Avenue, between Las Vegas Boulevard South & Koval Lane, Las Vegas, NV 89109 (reservations 1-800 221 2301/front desk 798 1020/fax 798 1020 ext 118/www.carriage houselasvegas.com). Bus 213. **Rates** studio (1 or 2 people) $135; 1-bedroom unit (up to 4 people) $165; 2-bedroom unit (up to 6 people) $275. **Credit** AmEx, DC, Disc, MC, V. **Map** p316 B8.

For some reason, the Carriage House is often overlooked by visitors. That's a pity, because the tasteful, moderately priced rooms are among the best buys in town, with luxurious plush carpeting, Midwest tiles, grass-paper wallcoverings and overstuffed sofas and love seats. The relaxing lobby is decorated in cool greys and blues and furnished with country-style sofas and tables. Outside, the tennis court, swimming pool and sun deck are landscaped with pine trees.
Hotel services *Concierge. Basketball court. Pool. Tennis court. Tour desk.* **Room services** *Dataport. Kitchenette. Refrigerator. Safe. TV: cable/pay movies. Voicemail.*

Courtyard by Marriott

3275 Paradise Road, at E Desert Inn Road, Las Vegas, NV 89109 (reservations 1-800 321 2211/ front desk 791 3600/fax 796 7981/ http://courtyard.com/LASCH). Bus 108, 112. **Rates** single/double $109-$119; suite $120-$140. **Credit** AmEx, DC, Disc, MC, V. **Map** p315 C5.

Just across the street from the Convention Center, Courtyard is popular with business travellers because of its readily available fax machines, well equipped meeting rooms, and the large work desks in its 149 rooms. The comfortable lobby is accented by light wood and brass fixtures and has a marble fireplace and club chairs. The rooms, which are decorated in muted tones, range from spartan single-bed quarters to spacious suites with separate living rooms. Some units have outdoor terraces. The cable TV has first-run pay movies and the phones are cordless. After a full day's gambling or doing business, you can relax by the pool or in the pavilion in the pretty courtyard.

Hotel services *Gym. Pool.* **Room services**
Dataport. Room service (4.30-11pm). Turndown.
TV: cable/pay movies. Voicemail.

La Quinta Inn

3970 Paradise Road, at E Flamingo Road,
Las Vegas, NV 89109 (reservations 1-800 777
1700/ front desk 796 9000/fax 796 9000 ext 410/
www.laquinta.com). Bus 108, 202. **Rates** (incl
continental breakfast) single/double $59-$89;
suite $115-$139. **Credit** AmEx, DC, Disc, MC, V.
Map p316 C7.

The Mediterranean-style building with its white
stucco walls, red tile roof and black ironwork, all
surrounded by tall palm trees, is popular with
vacationers as well as conventioneers. The lobby,
which combines Swiss chalet and country farm-
house styles, has exposed-beam ceilings, a tiled
floor, arched windows and leather wing chairs. The
three-storey building contains 269 rooms (many
renovated in 1999), decorated with a French country
flavour, with plush teal carpeting and pastel upholstered furniture. All have coffeemakers; some have
whirlpool tubs. The suites have private balconies,
microwaves, refrigerators and whirlpool tubs. The
courtyard is heavily landscaped with trees, plants
and a picturesque fountain and pool.
Hotel services *Gym. Pool.* **Room services**
Dataport. TV: cable/pay movies. Voicemail.

Residence Inn by Marriott

3225 Paradise Road, at Convention Center Drive,
Las Vegas, NV 89109 (reservations 1-800 331
3131/front desk & fax 796 9300/http://residenceinn.
com/LASNV). Bus 108, 112. **Rates** (incl continental
breakfast) studio $90-$120; townhouse $110-$220.
Credit AmEx, DC, Disc, MC, V. **Map** p315 C5.

Like its stablemate (Courtyard) next door, the
Residence Inn is a hot item during busy conventions,
and its spacious, condo-like units are specifically
designed for guests on extended visits. All the rooms
and suites are tastefully decorated in earth-tone
colour schemes with Danish modern furnishings
and modern art, and have balconies or patios, large
bathrooms and kitchens complete with microwaves
and dishwashers. You can actually relax in the quiet
lobby with its wing chairs and fieldstone fireplace.
Rounding out the hotel amenities are a swimming
pool, three jacuzzis and a grocery shopping service.
Guests can use a nearby fitness centre, and, unlike
most Vegas hotels, pets are allowed.
Hotel services *Pool.* **Room services** *Dataport.*
Kitchen. Refrigerator. Room service (4-10pm).
TV: cable/pay movies. Voicemail.

Downtown

Budget

Victory Hotel-Motel

307 S Main Street, at Bridger Avenue, Las Vegas,
NV 89101 (387 9257). Bus 108, 205, 207.
Rates single/double $24-$35. **No credit cards.**
Map p312 C2.

This whitewashed Mission-style hotel hasn't
changed much since it was built in 1910. The two-
storey building has an upstairs balcony overlooking
the street and a verandah where guests once sat and
watched trains steam into the depot opposite. The
32 rooms are spartan but clean, and surround a modest courtyard. The lobby is equally basic with a TV
set that never turns off, an obscure park bench and
a deer head mounted on a knotty pine wall.
Hotel services *Pool.* **Room services**
TV:cable/pay movies.

Other Accommodation

Extended stay

Budget Suites

3684 Paradise Road, at Twain Avenue, East of
Strip, Las Vegas, NV 89019 (reservations &
information 1-800 752 1501/front desk 699 7000).
Bus 108, 203, 213. **Rates** *Day rate* $49-$129 Mon-
Thur, Sun; $69-$129 Fri, Sat. *Weekly rate* $179.50-
$259. **Credit** AmEx, MC, V. **Map** p316 C6.

Located in various places around the Valley – but
usually within walking distance of the casinos –
every room at these 220- to 300-unit complexes is a
mini-suite with a living room/kitchen, cable TV and
free local phone calls. The buildings are laid out like
large apartment complexes, with two dozen or so
units in each three-storey block. Maid service is
available, but you can save on this extra expense if
you bring your own linen and towels. All Budget
Suites have studios and one-bedroom suites, but
there are also two bedroom set-ups at some locations, including the handily placed 3655 West
Tropicana outpost – a good place from to which to
explore the south end of the Strip. The small pool
areas all have barbecue pits shaded by palm trees,
and there's plenty of parking. Budget Suites are
good places to take children and keep them happy
in the city. They're also popular with people who are
relocating to Las Vegas.
Hotel services *Laundry. Pool.* **Rooms services**
Kitchenette. TV: cable. Turndown.
Branches closest to the Strip: 3655 W Tropicana
Avenue, at Industrial Road, West of Strip (739 1000);
4205 Tropicana Avenue, at Valley View Boulevard,
West of Strip (889 1700); 1500 Stardust Road,
between Las Vegas Boulevard South & Industrial
Road, West of Strip (732 1500).

The Meridian

250 E Flamingo Road, at Koval Lane, East of Strip,
Las Vegas, NV 89109 (735 5949/fax 735 3104).
Bus 202, 301, 302. **Rates** (per month) 1-bedroom
$1,470; 2-bedroom $1,740; 3-bedroom $2,200. **No**
credit cards. Map p316 B7.

You can live like a local at this 685-unit apartment
complex, half a mile east of the Strip, which has 100

units available for short-term rent (by the day, week or month; 30-day advance booking advised). One- and two-bedroom luxury flats come with all the creature comforts: fully equipped kitchens, house- wares, linen, answerphones, washing machines and dryers. The apartments have private balconies and are ensconced inside security gates. There are leisure facilities: two lovely lagoon-style pools and spas, tennis and racquetball courts and a health club. Weekly maid service is available.

Hotel services *Business services. Concierge. Laundry. Pool. Tennis courts.* **Room services** *Dataport. Iron. TV: cable.*

Polo Towers

3745 Las Vegas Boulevard South, between E Harmon & Tropicana Avenues, Las Vegas, NV 89109 (reservations 1-800 935 2233/front desk 261 1000). Bus 301, 302. **Rates** *studio (1 or 2 people) $119 Mon-Thur, Sun; $149 Fri, Sat; 1-bedroom (up to 4 people) $159 Mon-Thur, Sun; $189 Fri, Sat; 2-bedroom (up to 6 people) $259 Mon-Thur, Sun; $289 Fri, Sat.* **Credit** AmEx, DC, Disc, MC, V. **Map** p316 A8.

You and your family can spend days or weeks at this 479-room complex opposite the Holiday Inn. Studio and one-bedroom suites for both business travellers and tourists are decorated in 1980s bach- elor-pad style with their own private balcony, plus refrigerator, VCR, stereo, safe and dataport. One- bedroom flats also have fully equipped kitchens. There's a pool and spa on the roof above the Polo Lounge bar (*see p156*), notable for its kitsch decor and fab view (endless parties of Japanese tourists keep trooping through). Other facilities, such as a fitness centre, are available in the mall at ground level. Note that Polo Towers is a timeshare opera- tion, so sometimes it can be difficult to get a room.

Hotel services *Business services. Concierge. Gym. Laundry. Pool.* **Room services** *Dataport. Iron. Kitchenette. TV: cable.*

Hostel

Las Vegas International Hostel

1208 Las Vegas Boulevard South, between Charleston & Oakey Boulevards, Las Vegas, NV 89104 (385 9955). Bus 301, 302. **Rates** *dormitory $14; private room $28.* **No credit cards.** **Map** p315 C3.

Backpackers take note: this elderly, two-storey brick building is the only hostel in town, and is almost always oversubscribed. Rooms are of the prison-cell variety – four walls and a bed – while the dorms have six beds. All bathrooms are shared; many are in various stages of disrepair so check them out before renting. Guests can use a communal kitchen and a lounge complete with TV, VCR (and tapes), books and magazines. AYH and AAIH members receive a $2 discount per night, making it very good value. The hostel is in rather a seedy location, so take extra care when walking around at night.

Hotel services *TV room. Payphone.*
Room services *No phone.*

RV parks

RVers have diverse ports of call in Las Vegas. Rates are highly competitive, with many sites costing less than $20 a night. All the parks listed below have full hook-ups and accept pets. Reservations are strongly recommended.

Circusland RV Park

500 Circus Circus Drive, at Las Vegas Boulevard South, Las Vegas, NV 89109 (reservations 1-800 634 3450/front desk 794 3757/www.circuscircus- lasvegas.com). Bus 105, 301. **Rates** $15-$19 Mon- Thur, Sun; $17-$21 Fri, Sat; $25-$50 holidays, special events. **Credit** AmEx, Disc, DC, MC, V. **Map** p315 B5.

Just off the Strip next to Circus Circus, this is a family favourite. With the hotel's amusement park just steps away and scores of casinos within easy walking distance, both kids and adults will be kept amused, and you won't have to do much driving once you pull in. The 365-space facility has a handy monorail to the casino and a fenced run for pets, plus a pool, jacuzzi, supply shop and laundry.

KOA Kampground

4315 Boulder Highway, between Desert Inn & E Flamingo Roads, East Las Vegas, NV 89121 (reservations 1-800 562 7782/front desk 451 5527). Bus 107. **Rates** *per night $29.95; per week $180; per month $350.* **Credit** AmEx, Disc, MC, V.

Set up camp here for a day, a week, a month or more. Discounted long-term rates are available at the 240- space facility, which has a shop, showers, pool and jacuzzi. Kids will enjoy the playground, while adults will appreciate the free shuttle to the casinos (it's pretty far from the Strip). It's one of the very few RV parks that also allows tents.

Main Street RV Park

100 Stewart Avenue, at Main Street, Downtown, Las Vegas, NV 89101 (reservations 1-800 634 6505/front desk 388 2602). Bus 106, 107, 208, 214. **Rates** $12. **Credit** AmEx, Disc, DC, MC, V. **Map** p312 C1.

This is a great RV park for Downtown visitors, located an easy two-block walk from the Fremont Street Experience and its ten casinos. The 96-space lot is gated and includes a swimming pool, jacuzzi, showers and laundry.

Silverton

3333 Blue Diamond Road, at Industrial Road, South-west Las Vegas, NV 89139 (reservations 1-800 588 7711/ front desk 263 7777). Bus 303. **Rates** $21 Mon-Thur, Sun; $23 Fri, Sat. **Credit** AmEx, Disc, DC, MC, V.

If you're arriving from California, this is a good place to drop anchor. Just a couple of miles south of the Strip off the I-15, you can settle in before braving the chaos of Las Vegas's traffic and the dollar-hungry casinos. Silverton's 460 spaces are modest, but clean and roomy (60ft by 12ft/18m by 3.6m) and each is cable- and phone-ready. There's a mini-mart, pool, showers, laundry and shuttle to the Silverton casino.

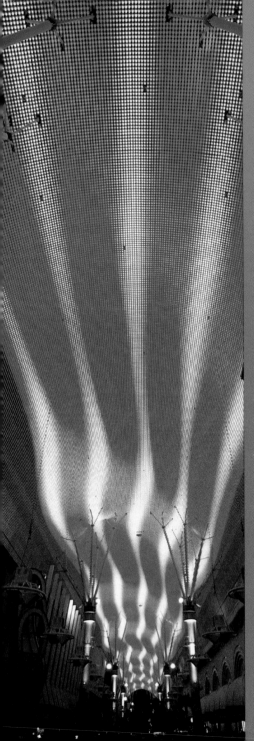

Sightseeing

Introduction

How to make the most of this unique, seductive and exciting city.

Las Vegas remains the largest (some say only) major US city founded in the 20th century – a fact that has only lost some its impact now that we are firmly past all the millennial hype. With its phenomenal growth showing no sign of slowing (some recent surveys put the number of new arrivals at 8,000 per month), the young city, much like a lanky teenager, proudly wears the badge of badly planned spurt growth.

Vegas's development has been influenced by two powerful factors: its location in the American West (and therefore its reliance on and worship of the automobile), and Nevada's formal legalisation of gambling in 1931. A boomtown since its inception, the city has never had time seriously to consider its infrastructure only frantically to fail to keep up with demand. Flanked by the Spring Mountains to the west and the Sheep Mountains to the east, the inhabited Las Vegas valley spreads like spilt batter between them, overflowing to the edges of the foothills. The valley does not reluctantly 'endure' urban sprawl; rather, it is defined by it.

Las Vegas comprises two distinct areas and populations: residents, who typically choose to live in homes away from the resort areas, and tourists, who remain blissfully unaware of the absurdly typical Southwestern city surrounding Downtown and Las Vegas Boulevard.

Servicing these two unique and often disparate populations remains a challenge. At times, more than a quarter of a million non-residents – the population of a largish city – may be visiting, each seeking a good time and a chance to relinquish their responsibilities. This places a strain on an under-realised infrastructure, and

has resulted in decades of concentric rings of suburban development moving further and further away from the central tourist areas.

This developmental pattern, combined with the city's unwavering attachment to the car and aversion to urban housing and public transport, has resulted in a relatively thinly spread populace covering a geographical area 20 times the size of San Francisco with roughly the same number of residents.

ORIENTATION

The Las Vegas valley is divided into quarters by two freeways that cross each other: I-15 coursing north–south through the centre of town on its way from Los Angeles to Salt Lake City, and US 95 (aka I-515), a north–south Canada–Mexico freeway that cuts east–west across the central Las Vegas area before returning to its standard directional path. On a map, these two approximate a twisted pinwheel shape, with its pivot just north-west of Downtown Las Vegas. In 2003, the much-needed Las Vegas Beltway, encircling the valley, should be completed and will connect with these freeways. In mid-2001, much of the beltway is thankfully already accessible to vehicles.

The 'centre' of Las Vegas (and the whole valley), where street numbering starts, is at the junction of Fremont and Main Streets in Downtown. From the Plaza at 1 S Main Street, numbers

Sightseeing

increase as you travel in any direction from this intersection. Streets use an even/odd system, with even-numbered addresses on one side and odd on the other. Main Street eventually ends at its intersection with Las Vegas Boulevard South at the base of the Stratosphere Tower, and everything either east or west of the Main Street/Las Vegas Boulevard artery is tagged accordingly. North/south delineations are more complicated, as they're based on an imaginary line running from the far eastern reaches of Charleston Boulevard, along Fremont Street in Downtown as far as Main Street, and then on to US 95 to the west.

The wide geographic area of metropolitan Las Vegas is made up of four official jurisdictions: Las Vegas, North Las Vegas, Henderson and unincorporated Clark County. Within and overlapping these jurisdictions are a number of 'areas', some with commonly used names, many others without. Their sheer physical size seems to call for a naming system of some type, but one hesitates to term them 'neighbourhoods' as they often lack any distinctive identity. Some are easily recognisable, while others blend in with the surrounding stucco.

ATTRACTIONS

For years, Las Vegas was known as an adult amusement park – a fantasy world of gambling halls, stage shows, topless revues and cocktail lounges – where daring visitors were free to pursue the decadence of their choice, 24 hours a day. But times change and so has Sin City. In an effort to legitimise itself as a widely appealing tourist destination, Las Vegas has evolved, mainly since 1989, into an oversized fairground with an orgy of sights and sounds that vary from the sublime to the exotic, from the outrageous to the bewildering.

No longer confined to smoke-filled casinos, visitors can pass the time dining in a plethora of five-star restaurants, sipping ten-dollar Martinis in cosmopolitan cocktail lounges, or watching free pirate battles, volcanic eruptions and dancing water ballets. They can ride one of several rollercoasters, cruise a Venetian canal, bungee jump or leave offerings at a Brahma shrine. They can marvel at soaring replicas of New York skyscrapers, enjoy the view from the top of a half-sized Eiffel Tower or splash around in a fun-packed water park. They can even spend hours pondering a Picasso, poring over rock 'n' roll memorabilia or examining artefacts in two outposts of the vaunted Guggenheim Museum.

Most of the new generation of attractions are either part of, or built into, the city's hotel-casinos. The casinos themselves are reviewed in detail in the **Casinos** chapter, but casino

Sightseeing

Don't miss ▸ Attractions

Bellagio fountain show
Beautiful, and free to watch. See p105.

Bellagio Gallery of Fine Art
High art comes to Las Vegas. See p106.

Eiffel Tower
A great view from the top. See p106.

Elvis-A-Rama Museum
The King still reigns supreme. See p113.

Fremont Street Experience
Downtown's saviour. See p117.

Gameworks
Video games galore. See p105.

Guggenheim Museums
The big openings of 2001. See p108.

High Roller & Big Shot
Say goodbye to your lunch. See p111.

Liberace Museum
Sequin central. See p120.

Manhattan Express
Say goodbye to your dinner. See p104.

Star Trek: the Experience
The final frontier. See p113.

Treasure Island pirate battle
Watery antics on the Strip. See p106.

Wet 'n Wild
The best place to cool off. See p234.

attractions worthy of a visit in their own right are reviewed in the appropriate area chapter (**The Strip**, **Off-Strip**, **Downtown** or **The Rest of the City**), where we also include non-casino attractions, sights and diversions.

Although Las Vegas Boulevard South remains the focus of tourist interest in the city, you should also venture away from the Strip. Downtown will appeal to visitors looking for a trace of old Vegas, while other areas represent the residential side of the city that most tourists never see. What's more, some of Las Vegas's smaller institutions offer enlightening and unique exhibitions and displays, especially when it comes to the history of Southern Nevada. Exploring these attractions can be a good way to detox from a marathon gambling session or a busy convention. In any case, take the time to explore.

Trips and tours

Tour operators do a brisk business in Las Vegas, with most of the trips taking tourists to nearby mountains, lakes and wilderness areas. Only a few offer tours of the city, and none of the casino resorts explores its own property (so you can forget about being taken behind the scenes at a casino). Most tour outfits provide pick-up from and return to your hotel. It's also worth checking the 'Neon' section of Friday's *Review-Journal*.

Adventure Photo Tours

Information 889 8687/www.adventurephoto tours.com. **Credit** AmEx, Disc, MC, V.
Take a guided full- or half-day photo safari to wilderness spots such as Red Rock Canyon ($75 per adult, $56.25 per child for a four-hour tour), the Spring Mountains, the Goodsprings Valley ghost mines, Valley of Fire State Park, El Dorado Canyon and the Logan Wash.

Casino Travel & Tours

Information 1-800 835 5160/www.casino travel.com. **Credit** AmEx, Disc, MC, V.
This outfit offers professionally guided tours around the city, plus excursions to the Hoover Dam, Grand Canyon West, Red Rock Canyon, Spring Mountain Ranch and Lake Mead. It can arrange reservations at local golf courses and tickets for most shows, and has a small fleet of chauffeur-driven limos, sedans and buses. Finally, it's also a full-service travel agency and a booking agent for most of the other tour operators in town. There are branches at Aladdin's, Bally's, Excalibur, the MGM Grand, Mandalay Bay, New York-New York and Paris.

Desert Eco-Tours

Information 647 4685/www.lvrj.com/ communitylink/zoo. **Rates** *Half-day tour* (minimum two people) $129 per person. *Full-day tour* $179 per person. **Credit** AmEx, MC, V.
If you're a hiker, backpacker or rock hound, check out these jeep tours into nearby wilderness areas, run by the Southern Nevada Zoo. The naturalist-led tours are conducted year round.

Drive-Yourself Tours

Information 565 8761/www.driveyourselftours. com. **Rates** *City tour map & tape* $14.95. **Credit** AmEx, Disc, MC, V.
Perhaps the most interesting city tour is this 90-minute audio tape and road map that directs visitors on a self-guided tour. Points of interest include the obvious tourist landmarks, but you'll also visit several hidden gems that even local residents may not know about. Other tours cover the Hoover Dam and Red Rock Canyon.

Gray Line Tours

Information 384 1234/www.pcap.com/ grayline.htm. **Rates** *City tour* $25 per person. *Night tour* $28 per person. **Credit** AmEx, Disc, MC, V.
This venerable tour operator will take you on a 2.5-hour tour by day or night that includes the Strip, the Fremont Street Experience and wedding chapel row.

Helicopter & aeroplane tours

City helicopter tours are increasingly criticised by Vegas residents due to safety and noise concerns. Grand Canyon flyovers are also under fire for the damage they cause to the environment. Consider carefully before you book one of these tours.

Papillon Grand Canyon Helicopters

Information 1-800 528 2418/736 7243/ www.papillon.com. **Credit** AmEx, Disc, MC, V.
Papillon offers only three basic flights – a 12-minute Strip Tour ($68), a Grand Canyon flyover and the Grand Canyon Champagne Brunch ($317) – but its showmanship is tops. All helicopters have state-of-the-art sound systems and patented viewing windows.

Scenic Airlines

Information 1-800 634 6801/638 3300/ www.scenic.com. **Credit** AmEx, Disc, MC, V.
Scenic Airlines flies to various national parks in the Southwest, including the Grand Canyon ($244 per person for an eight-hour tour), Bryce Canyon and Monument Valley.

Sundance Helicopters

Information 1-800 653 1881/736 0606/ www.helicoptours.com. **Credit** AmEx, Disc, MC, V.
With 17 tours on offer, Southern Nevada's best-regarded – and largest – helicopter operator has a flight for everyone. Experience the neon jungle from the air on the city tour ($72); take a quick jaunt over the Spring Mountains to the Pahrump Winery; or choose from four Grand Canyon flights.

Casinos

From new hotspots to old favourites, we bring you the pick of Vegas's casinos.

Las Vegas has undergone more than its fair share of evolutions. In the 1930s and '40s it was an ersatz Old West outpost with saloons and dirt highways, just like much of the rest of the Southwest; in the 1950s, the dude ranches and motor courts gave way to Miami-modern resorts and the city emerged as a gangsters-meet-Hollywood-elite oasis. This trend continued until the 1970s, when the uninspiring polyester era put a stranglehold on truly creative casino development.

In the late 1980s and through the '90s, casino operators discovered the value of 'theming' their resorts. A tropical forest, fantasy castle, Gotham skyline and other architectural marvels helped fuel an unprecedented period of growth in Las Vegas – a decade-long expansion that is only now showing signs of peaking. Most recently, resorts have taken to creating replicas of other cities to attract visitors. **Paris-Las Vegas** sprouted a half-sized Eiffel Tower to help re-create the City of Lights, and tourists can enjoy an ersatz Venice, complete with canals and gondolas, at the **Venetian**.

Casino attractions have also evolved. There are still the circus acts and midway games at **Circus Circus**, the moat and drawbridge at **Excalibur** and the exploding volcano at **Mirage**, but there are also increasing signs that the casino resorts are moving towards embracing a rediscovered adulthood.

The **MGM Grand**, for instance, has (at least for the moment) scrapped its Grand Adventures theme park in favour of more 'useful' space for hotel rooms, convention halls and (you guessed it) more gambling. The **Luxor** has already removed many of its original Egyptian design elements, including the indoor River Nile that encircled the casino and the talking camels that assaulted guests at the entrance. And, although **Treasure Island** vows to never sink its pirate battle, it has ditched its elaborate games arcade in order to install a new restaurant/nightclub.

Casino bosses have also discovered that visitors are willing to spend money outside the gambling hall, so the trend has been to add expensive shops, international restaurants, stylish bars and high-quality entertainment to the mix of attractions. You can expect all the benefits of first-class accommodation to be standard issue at the newer casinos, and among the upgrades at older properties. In fact, it's now possible to spend a whole vacation in Las Vegas, with a full slate of activities, and (heaven forbid!) never gamble.

Whatever gingerbread surrounds it, however, the heart of a resort is still the casino floor. Depending on the time of day or night, the action can be hot and furious as slot players shovel coins into machines and craps players whoop it up in the dice pit. The scene is set to the distinctive soundtrack of clinking glasses,

Binion's Horseshoe. *See p94.*

rattling chips, tinkling coins and the electronic arpeggios of slot machines. At the height of the action, players may feel like they're in the midst of a prison riot. This has long been the formula for success, and so shall it continue.

WHAT'S NEW?

Although recent indications suggest the Vegas casino building boom has slowed down, construction crews haven't upped stakes and moved to California. Several Strip casinos have expanded their facilities, and off-Strip and locals casinos continue to rise (*see p97* **Coming soon…**). The **Aladdin** and the **Suncoast** opened in 2000, to be followed by the **Palms** on West Flamingo Road, and the **Resort at Green Valley Ranch** in 2001. In mid 2001, the **Stratosphere** completed work on a 1,000-room tower, two new restaurants and a 3,600-seat outdoor events centre; the **Orleans** expanded its casino facilities and began work on a 600-room hotel tower; and **Caesars Palace** started an expansion that will add a 4,000-seat Colosseum events centre and 1,500 new guest rooms. And casino visionary Steve Wynn sits on the historic Desert Inn property, with talk of huge, well-laid plans emerging.

As other states, notably California, expand the availability of gambling, it will be interesting to see how Vegas will keep more than 36 million visitors flocking to the desert resort. The casinos will continue to evolve, but exactly what fuels the next surge in growth is up to the casino moguls and visionaries. And they play their cards close to their chests.

ADVICE AND ETIQUETTE

There is little casino etiquette to worry about. Common sense, common courtesy (and perhaps a knowledge of common law) should see you through. Whatever you wear will be fine, from shorts to a dinner jacket, though you may want to carry a sweater – it may be 110°F (43°C) outside, but the air-con will be deliberately chilly to dissuade you from leaving.

ORIENTATION

This chapter is divided into four casino categories. **The Strip** is ruled by Disney-esque and increasingly sophisticated mega-resorts. There are also a few casinos that are 'Strip-like' in terms of size, decor and theming, but actually lie a few blocks away. These **off-Strip** properties include the Rio, Gold Coast, Palms and Orleans (to the west) and the Hard Rock and Las Vegas Hilton (to the east). **Downtown** is more of a jamboree where carny-like casino hawkers virtually snatch in passers-by, and the gambling is down and dirty. More subdued in design and atmosphere are the **locals casinos**, which are targeted mainly at residents,

although their friendly atmosphere, budget rates and unique amenities make them attractive to visitors, too.

LISTINGS INFORMATION

The address we've given for each casino is its main entrance; the place to arrive whether you're on foot or driving. Here you'll find valet parking and directions to the self-parking garages, which are usually around the back. In some cases, the casino also has another entrance at the side or back, which is particularly useful if you don't want to be constantly driving up and down the often traffic-choked Strip. To clarify this information, we've listed which streets have access to valet parking and self-parking.

We've indicated which attractions – bars, restaurants, shows and so forth – are reviewed in more detail elsewhere in the guide, and we've also provided specific gambling information at the end of each casino review. This indicates which table games the casino offers, including more unusual games such as Pai Gow Tiles and Spanish 21; the minimum and maximum betting limits for baccarat, mini baccarat and blackjack; and the principal odds for craps (with variations where they are known to us). Remember that limits do fluctuate and minimum bets tend to be higher on the Strip, and in the evening, at weekends and during special events. For roulette, we've said if a casino offers a wheel with only a single-zero slot (which offers better odds for the gambler). Note that nearly all casinos offer keno and a sports book; they are all open 24 hours, and have ATMs and multilingual dealers.

For gambling tips and information on the various games, *see chapter* **Gambling**. For information on casino accommodation and other facilities, *see chapter* **Accommodation**.

Caesars Palace. *See p72.*

The Strip

Most casinos in Las Vegas are on the three-and-a-half-mile (5.6-kilometre) stretch of Las Vegas Boulevard South – aka the Strip. Furthest south, you'll find the **Mandalay Bay** (and the adjoining **Four Seasons** hotel) and the **Luxor**. These are followed by four large casinos at the corners of the Tropicana Avenue/Strip intersection: the **Tropicana**, **Excalibur**, **New York-New York** and the **MGM Grand**.

The centre of the Strip has the biggest cluster of hotel-casinos: the **Monte Carlo**, the new **Aladdin** and **Paris-Las Vegas** are followed to the north by **Bally's** (adjoining Paris), **Bellagio**, the **Barbary Coast** and **Caesars Palace** – all of which occupy the intersection with Flamingo Road. After them comes the **Flamingo**, the **Imperial Palace**, **Harrah's** and the **Venetian**. Opposite the Venetian is the **Mirage** and its neighbour **Treasure Island**.

At the north end (above Spring Mountain Road), you'll find the **Stardust**, **Circus Circus**, the **Riviera** and, a long block further north, the **Sahara**. The **Stratosphere**, although still on Las Vegas Boulevard South, is not officially on the Strip and sits in a no-man's land between the top of the Strip and Downtown. For sights and attractions on Las Vegas Boulevard South, *see chapter* **The Strip**.

Aladdin

3667 Las Vegas Boulevard South, at Harmon Avenue (736 0111/London Club 785 5790/www. aladdincasino.com). Bus 301, 302/self-parking & valet parking Harmon Avenue. **Map** p316 A7.

Since it opened in summer 2000, the new Aladdin has struggled to find its market niche. Thanks to several design flaws, the route into the massive, split-level casino is not very obvious from the Strip, although in mid-2001 hotel officials announced architectural changes that would make the property more customer-friendly. The hotel maintains one of the highest room-rate averages on the Strip, but the shortage of casino customers left the resort with severe financial difficulties at press time. In keeping with the original hotel's Arabian Nights theme, the Aladdin's design elements include a phoenix from one of Sinbad the Sailor's tales, giant winged horses guarding the sports book, a two-storey replica of Scheherazade's Palace and the signature Aladdin's lamp. The focus of hotel amenities is the adjoining Desert Passage complex (*see p162*), a meandering collection of 130 shops and 21 restaurants, nightclubs and lounges set against backdrops ranging from a Tangiers marketplace to a North African harbour front.

Despite its limitations, the 100,000sq ft (9,300sq m) multi-tiered casino is one of the most impressive on the Strip. Gambling options include 87 table games,

2,800 slot machines, a live keno lounge and a race and sports book. Well-heeled players frequent the London Club, a luxurious European-style casino overlooking the main casino floor and developed by London Clubs International. The salon features 30 high-limit tables including blackjack, roulette and baccarat and 100 high-denomination slot machines. Although the London Club is currently open to all, an expected change in Nevada gaming regulations would allow the Aladdin to convert it into a private casino for exclusive guests. That change isn't expected before summer 2002.

Entertainment

In 2002, a production show (*Lumiere*) is planned for a new purpose-built venue that will also double as a high-tech nightclub, but for the moment virtually all of the Aladdin's entertainment is presented in the 7,000-seat Theater for the Performing Arts (*see p219*). In addition to headliners, the Theater hosts touring Broadway shows such as *Fosse* and *Les Miserables*. The Desert Passage houses the New York-based Blue Note Jazz Club (*see p222*), which showcases international jazz and blues artists.

Eating & drinking

Among many choices in the Aladdin and the Desert Passage, you may feast on innovative and superlative Cajun and Creole cooking at the Commander's Palace (*see p131*) – an outpost of the original New Orleans eatery. Other dining options include tasty country Italian cuisine at Bice; aged steaks, vintage wines and premium cigars at the Macanudo Steakhouse & Club; and the world's finest caviar at Beluga, which features a turn-of-the-19th-century wharf bar motif.

Gambling

Baccarat ($100-$15,000); mini baccarat ($25-$15,000); blackjack ($5-$10,000); Caribbean Stud; Casino War; craps (2x); Let It Ride; poker; Pai Gow Poker; Pai Gow Tiles; roulette (single & double zero).

Bally's

3645 Las Vegas Boulevard South, at E Flamingo Road (739 4111/www.ballyslv.com). Bus 202, 301, 302/self-parking & valet parking Las Vegas Boulevard South or E Flamingo Road. **Map** p316 A7.

Originally opened as the MGM Grand in 1973, Bally's was built by Kirk Kerkorian, who had constructed the International Hotel (now the Las Vegas Hilton) four years earlier. In its original incarnation, the movie-themed resort offered an enticing combination of old Hollywood class and new Vegas flash. That kind of elegance remains inside the resort today, but outside is another story. Chasing the Las Vegas trend of building properties right up to the street, Bally's installed a tacky $14-million incongruency: a moving sidewalk, surrounded by a series of futuristic, colour-changing neon hoops and columns, palm trees and cascading fountains. This was followed by a huge, electronic sign flanking the Strip. So much for subtlety.

Inside, the casino is one large, rectangular space, a luxurious and inviting atmosphere of soft lighting and art deco accents. Not surprisingly, the machine

Sightseeing

Vegas on the cheap Promotions

The casinos are always trying to outdo each other with bigger and better schemes to attract new players and keep regular gamblers loyal. Cashing in on casino promotions is a good way to make your dollars last that little bit longer, as long as you're proficient at the game you're playing. Always understand what you are trying to win and how much it might cost to do so.

Some casinos, including the **Tropicana** (see p87) and **Four Queens** (see p93), offer free spins on a giant slot machine as a tool to tempt you into the casino. The top prize could be a car or a huge lump sum of cash, though nearly everyone leaves with some kind of meaningless trinket. The **Coast Resort** casinos (see p99 and p100) frequently offer logo jackets with every minimum jackpot, while **El Cortez** (see p94)

and **Las Vegas Club** (see p93) provide a free dinner for two, for every slot jackpot of $200 or more. **Sam's Town** (see p100) even gives away a house each March in a draw based on every four-of-a-kind or 200-coin slot machine payout.

Also popular, especially with locals, is the pay cheque-cashing promotion, in which cheque-cashers receive a free spin on a slot machine, wheel of fortune or video poker machine. The top prize at the **Gold Coast** (see p99) is $250,000, but most 'winners' end up with drink tickets, a roll of nickels or a T-shirt.

Promotions come and go quickly: to find out about them, check with the casino's promotion desk, ask someone in the casino marketing department or read the visitor magazines such as *Tourguide*, *Today in Las Vegas*, *Showbiz* and *What's On*.

selection includes all the latest creations from leading gaming-machine maker Bally Manufacturing, including laserdisc versions of craps, roulette and blackjack – these are excellent practice tools for getting comfortable with the games before heading to the actual tables. The buy-ins at the tables are lower than you might expect, though most of Bally's players wager far more than the minimum. The sports book, located on the lower level, is as classy and technically advanced as those in Bellagio and the Las Vegas Hilton, but it's rarely crowded. At the back of the casino (so a bit of a trek) is a free monorail to the MGM Grand (departures every five minutes, 9am-1am daily). An indoor walkway connects Bally's to the Paris resort next door.

Entertainment

A salute to the classic Hollywood spectacle, *Jubilee!* (see p197) is the ultimate old-time Las Vegas production show, and the only holdover from the property's days as the MGM Grand – where else can you watch the *Titanic* sink twice nightly, and not have to hear Celine Dion sing about it? Headliners of an earlier Vegas era, such as Paul Anka, George Carlin and Englebert Humperdinck, alternate with *Jubilee!* in the 1,035-seat Jubilee Theater. The Celebrity Showroom shut down in 1999, to make room for the promenade mall leading to Paris.

Eating & drinking

Dining options include the Big Kitchen buffet (see p152); Chang of Las Vegas for good Chinese cuisine; Seasons, for continental cuisine and Al Dente, whose Italian specialities are popular with local diners. The highlight, however, is Bally's Sterling Brunch (see p152), which features such luxury items as caviar, fresh sushi, lobsters, oysters and champagne.

Gambling

Baccarat ($100-$5,000); mini baccarat ($5-$5,000); blackjack ($5-$5,000); Caribbean Stud; Casino War; craps (3x on 4&10, 4x on 5&9, 5x on 6&8); Let It Ride; Pai Gow Poker; roulette (single & double zero); Spanish 21. Gambling lessons.

Bellagio

3600 Las Vegas Boulevard South, at W Flamingo Road (1-888 488 7111/693 7111/www.bellagio.com). Bus 202, 301, 302/self-parking Las Vegas Boulevard South/valet parking Las Vegas Boulevard South or Flamingo Road. **Map** p316 A7.

Once the crown jewel of Mirage Resorts, Bellagio is now a gem in the MGM Mirage tiara – the result of a buy-out that saw Mirage Resorts become part of MGM. Set on the site of the old Dunes hotel and golf course, Bellagio features Tuscan-style architecture, a high-end art gallery, upscale shopping promenade and designer restaurants. Most of the hotel's shops and restaurants overlook an eight-acre lake facing the Strip, inspired by Lake Como in Italy. During the afternoon and evening, the lake comes alive with a dazzling fountain ballet (see p105) that sends streams of water hundreds of feet into the air, choreographed to music by composers as diverse as Strauss and Copland. The tree-lined sidewalk assures plenty of vantage points; other good viewpoints are from the lakefront restaurants or the top of the Eiffel Tower (at Paris casino) across the street. Enhancing Bellagio's charm further is the Bellagio Botanical Garden behind the hotel lobby, a huge, glass-roofed greenhouse of exotic flowers and plants, and the Gallery of Fine Art (see p106), a first in Las Vegas. Having sold off much of its own collection, the gallery now holds temporary shows, featuring works from high-profile private collections.

The lake at **Bellagio**. So lovely you could almost be in Italy. *See p71.*

The quality of art on offer will surprise visitors expecting Disney-like spectacles rather than high culture.

Bellagio is geared to well-heeled adult guests; in fact, it's downright child-unfriendly – under-18s and strollers are turned away, unless they're accompanied by adults who are guests of the hotel. During the shooting of the *Ocean's 11* remake, Julia Roberts, George Clooney and other members of the star-studded cast stayed in Bellagio's private mansions. The rooms are among the most expensive on the Strip and most of the dining facilities are high-end. Shops along the Via Bellagio (*see p163*), a walking version of Rodeo Drive, are dominated by designer names, from Armani through Chanel to Tiffany.

The casino is luxurious if rather vulgar; the upholstery, carpets and striped canopies above the tables are a clash of colours and patterns. Still, it offers all the usual games including blackjack, roulette, craps, keno and baccarat, plus not-so-usual games such as Pai Gow Poker, Caribbean Stud and Let it Ride. Celebs such as Drew Barrymore (playing $5 blackjack) and Dennis Rodman have been known to play here. As you might expect, table limits are higher than at most Strip properties: minimums are often $25-$50 and it's difficult to find a $5 blackjack game – maybe they opened one just for Drew. The race and sports book is one of the most comfortable in town: the low-slung seats have special headrests to help relax your spine.

Entertainment

An international cast of synchronised swimmers, divers, acrobats, aerialists and characters charm audiences in Cirque du Soleil's *O* (*see p198*), a water-based production from the famed Canadian circus, which also stages *Mystère* at Treasure Island. Like its cousin down the street, the show is highly visual and often borders on the surreal. For more laidback entertainment, check out the Fontana Lounge (*see p201*), which sometimes features good swing bands.

Eating & drinking

Along with Mandalay Bay, Bellagio took the 1990s Vegas trend for celebrity chef restaurants to a whole new level, and now offers a matchless array of high-end eateries. For the finest French and Italian cuisine, dine in style at Le Cirque (*see p133*) and the neighbouring Osteria del Circo (*see p137*), both overseen by chef Sirio Maccioni. Sample the regional cuisines of France and Spain at Julian Serrano's Picasso restaurant (*see p135*) or enjoy the casual Mediterranean ambience of Todd English's Olives (*see p135*). Other top choices include Prime (a superior steakhouse; *see p139*) and Noodles (an elegant pan-Asian noodle kitchen; *see p140*). Seafood lovers should head for the award-winning delicacies at Aqua (*see p138*), while those with extravagant tastes can savour caviar, champagne and smoked salmon in the Petrossian Bar. The pricey Bellagio Buffet (*see p152*) is one of highest-calibre spreads in town. If that's not enough, there's also Jasmine for Chinese food and Shintaro, a teppan and sushi bar.

Gambling

Baccarat ($100-$15,000); mini baccarat ($25-$15,000); blackjack ($5-$10,000); Caribbean Stud; Casino War; craps (2x); Let It Ride; poker; Pai Gow Poker; Pai Gow Tiles; roulette (single & double zero).

Caesars Palace

3570 Las Vegas Boulevard South, at W Flamingo Road (731 7110/www.caesars.com). Bus 202, 301, 302/self-parking & valet parking Las Vegas Boulevard South or Industrial Road. **Map** p316 A7.
This opulent, Roman-themed fantasy palace epitomises the uniquely Las Vegan vision of luxury for the masses in a kitsch, no-holds-barred rendition untrammelled by any sense of irony. 'All that Caesar could, you have and can do,' wrote Ralph Waldo Emerson, and this feeling of unbounded potential embraces you from the moment you approach the signature entrance fountains. They've been the

backdrop for countless films, the site of the infamous near-fatal motorcycle jump by Evel Knievel in 1969 (three years after the hotel opened), and witnessed a successful jump by Evel's son Robbie in 1989. Others have since developed bigger and more expensive properties, but there is a timeless glamour to Caesars that is unmatched in Las Vegas or anywhere else, OTT though it may be.

Painstakingly crafted Italian marble abounds, in statuary, temples, heroic arches and ornate pediments. The Italian cypresses lining the property's rolling driveways are perfectly manicured, as are the buffed gladiators and centurions who greet guests as they arrive. And speaking of buffed, check out the rather tough-looking cocktail waitresses in togas. Key to Caesars' continued appeal is the Forum Shops mall (see p162), a pioneering and much imitated combination of high-end boutiques, popular chain stores, famous artificial sky and statues that come to life. Techies should try the Race for Atlantis ride: an IMAX 3-D motion simulator (see p108). Empires must expand or fall: in the late 1990s, the Forum Shops doubled in size, and the addition of the ugly 29-storey Palace Tower brought the total number of rooms to 2,500. The resort also has a fantastic pool area, a health spa and fitness facility, restaurants, a hip, new bar, Shadow, and the football-field-sized Palace Ballroom. Coming soon is a 4,000-seat Colosseum arena, plus an additional 1,500 extra guest rooms.

For gambling, few casinos offer the limits or the atmosphere of Caesars. On the main floor, the limits are generally as high as the Roman columns and when there's a big boxing match in town, they can go sky-high. The sports book is one of the highest-energy spots to watch live competition on big-screen TVs and accepts some of the highest bets. You get a good view of the baccarat pit, an intimate nook where wagers of $100,000 per hand are not uncommon. And for the boldest of slot players, the $500 machine – with a $1-million jackpot – uses gold-plated tokens. (The machine itself only pays a jackpot of two $500 coins, so if the $1-million jackpot is won, the machine locks and an attendant pays the gambler.) The high-limit slots are in the Palace Casino, near the main entrance; the blackjack pits and slots in the Forum Casino offer lower limits.

Entertainment

The hotel's Circus Maximus showroom once hosted the biggest names in entertainment – Julio Iglesias, David Copperfield, the Beach Boys, Natalie Cole, to name but a few. The showroom was closed in spring 2001 to make way for the construction of the new, 4,000-seat Colosseum, which will host a production starring Celine Dion beginning in 2003. Also scrapped as part of the expansion was the Omnimax movie theatre. That leaves the overhyped Magical Empire dinner show (see p195); billed as an underground labyrinth where soothsayers and conjurers perform while patrons dine, it's really just an overpriced dinner accompanied by below-average trickery from amateur magicians. However, the casino

still has three of the better lounges in the city, including the famous floating Cleopatra's Barge (see p201). Another bar, Shadow (see p157), featuring scantily clad dancers shaking their stuff behind a light screen, opened in mid-2001. Caesars Palace is also the place to watch high-profile boxing matches; for details, see p233 **Ringside**.

Eating & drinking

Two of Caesars' most famous restaurants – Palace Court and Bacchanal – were closed to make way for the Colosseum expansion. To help fill the culinary void, Caesars opened a Polynesian/Asian restaurant called 808, an outgrowth of two popular restaurants in the Hawaiian Islands. The Empress Court and Hyakumi Japanese restaurant/sushi bar survived the cull and collectively carve up the Orient between them, while La Piazza foodcourt and the Palatium Buffet (see p154) take care of the lower end. One of the most pleasant places to dine is Italian restaurant Terrazza, overlooking Caesars' pool area (see p137). There are more culinary delights in the Forum Shops, where the pick of the bunch include Bertolini's for good-quality Italian (see p136); Wolfgang Puck's pioneering Spago (see p136) and flamboyant Chinois restaurants (see p135); the Palm steakhouse (see p139); and Caviarteria (see p138). Other options include the Cheesecake Factory (see p130) and Planet Hollywood, while the Stage Deli (see p144 **Lunch stops**) is good for lunch.

Gambling

Baccarat ($100-$15,000); mini baccarat ($20-$10,000); blackjack ($5-$3,000); Caribbean Stud; Casino War; craps (3x 4&10, 4x 5&9, 5x 6&8); Let It Ride; Pai Gow Poker; Pai Gow Tiles; roulette (single zero & double zero); Spanish 21. Gambling lessons. Games designed for sight- & hearing-impaired players.

Circus Circus

2880 Las Vegas Boulevard South, at Circus Circus Drive, between Desert Inn Road & W Sahara Avenue (734 0410/www.circuscircus-lasvegas.com). Bus 301, 302/self-parking Industrial Road/valet parking Las Vegas Boulevard South or Industrial Road. **Map** p315 B5.

In the Las Vegas of the 1970s and 1980s, Circus Circus was the only family entertainment in town. Parents dropped off their kids under the big top, and then dashed away to lose their inheritance in the casino. As other resorts dismantle their family-friendly experiments of the 1990s, Circus Circus once again finds itself at the head of the class. The circus theme pervades every aspect of the place, though recent changes and additions have cut back on the glaring pinks and yellows. Traditionalists need not fear, however – the place is still a noisy carnival of cotton-candy colours, as surreal as a Fellini movie in its medley of clowns, carousels and crass commercialism. Adventuredome (see p110), an indoor amusement park under a giant pink dome, houses numerous rides and rollercoasters, a re-creation of a Pueblo Indian cliff dwelling and several mechanical dinosaurs. It almost makes sense when you see it.

Sightseeing

Vegas on the cheap Funbooks

Funbooks are a good source of freebies. They usually contain match-play coupons, two-for-one vouchers, plus discounts on food, drinks, shows, souvenirs, car rentals, beauty shops and virtually anything else you can find in a casino.

The best funbook **vouchers** are the ones that offer free or two-for-one deals, especially when they can be redeemed in a restaurant or showroom. Unfortunately, these coupons have become few and far between in recent times, and you're more likely to receive free souvenirs of the key ring, playing cards or trinket variety.

Match-play coupons can be used like money – but only in conjunction with the real thing. For instance, if you have a $5 coupon, you can combine it with your $5 bet for a total bet of $10 on, say, blackjack. If you win, you're paid even money on the $10; if you lose, you've only lost $5. Not a bad deal.

Most of the casinos in town have funbooks, and they are free for the taking from the slot club or promotion booth. Some hotels also produce special funbooks for their guests, which can usually be obtained at the front desk. The hotel funbooks frequently offer the best deals. Otherwise, visitor centres just outside Las Vegas give away funbooks especially for tourists (you'll need out-of-state identification to get one).

Some of the better funbooks in town include **Circus Circus** ($1 blackjack side bet, $5 for $10 bets on craps and roulette; see p73); **Hard Rock** ($10 for $20 bet on any game, free shot glass; see p90); the **Orleans** ($5 slot/video poker bonus, free drink tickets, Mardi Gras necklace; see p99); **Sahara** ($40 for $50 chips, baseball cap, $2 for $3 bet on blackjack; see p85); **Terrible's Casino** (4100 Paradise Road; 733 7000; $25 for $50 bet on any game).

There are three full-sized casinos dispersed throughout the resort, connected by walkways and a monorail; a total of 107,000sq ft (9,950sq m), each offering the same gaming options (and some rather long walks). The circus acts are visible from the main original casino, while the race book is located near the back of the resort, in the Skyways Tower area. Wherever you play, it may take all day to find someone risking more than $10: Circus Circus is low-roller heaven, and a dollar or two will be enough to get you started at most tables. For non-gaming entertainment, the casino mezzanine features a video arcade, free circus acts and plenty of funfair-style sugary sweets.

'Classy' was never an adjective that came to mind when describing Circus Circus – Howard Hughes complained that it brought 'the poor, dirty, shoddy side of circus life' to the Strip. That said, the lobby, bedecked in royal purples and golds, and drawing its inspiration from 19th-century European circuses rather than American big-top extravaganzas, is unexpectedly beautiful. Of course, a place where you stand on a revolving platform pumping tokens into a clown-face slot machine while trapeze artists fly overhead can only be so refined. After building the upscale Mandalay Bay, Circus Circus Enterprises changed its name in 1999 to Mandalay Resort Group to reflect its changed and more upmarket image.

Entertainment

There's no showroom at Circus Circus, but there's seating inside the casino for the free (though rather less-than-spectacular) circus acts on the mezzanine. Acrobats, trapeze artists and magicians perform every 30 minutes from 11am to midnight.

Eating & drinking

The Steak House (see p140) is a quiet enclave under the big top, serving mesquite-grilled steaks, aged for 21 days, that live up to their billing. You'll also find first-rate Mexican food in the cantina-like Blue Iguana on the mezzanine level. The Circus Circus Buffet (see p153) serves over 10,000 people a day – and at times it seems as if they're all in line in front of you. A $9.5-million renovation spruced up the setting, but the food's still mediocre at best. Head to the Pink Pony coffee shop for a taste of Vegas kitsch or relive Hunter S Thompson's drug-induced panic attack at the surreal Horse-A-Round Bar (see p156).

Gambling

Mini baccarat ($5-$5,000); blackjack ($2-$5,000); Caribbean Stud; Casino War; craps (10x); Let It Ride; Pai Gow Poker; poker; roulette (double zero). Gambling lessons.

Excalibur

3850 Las Vegas Boulevard South, at W Tropicana Avenue (597 7777/www.excalibur-casino.com). Bus 201, 301, 302/self-parking & valet parking W Tropicana Avenue. Map p316 A8.

The Excalibur resort is a perfect illustration of the accelerated evolutionary curve in Las Vegas. Built all the way back in the Year of Our Lord 1990, the property already seems like a throwback to yesterday's Las Vegas. The towering spires of its Bavarian castle façade now seem almost quaint, especially when compared to the more inventive and detailed architecture of New York-New York on the other side of the Strip. By any other standard, the resort is still quite charming. The bright red, blue and gold

The candy-coloured turrets of **Excalibur**. *See p75.*

spires of the castle are beautifully illuminated at night, though they look a little prefabricated by day. Make sure you use the main entrance, on the moving sidewalk that leads from the Strip through the always-open drawbridge. The paths on each side wind though trees as thick as Sherwood Forest, and you could get lost in there for days.

Inside, the casino and common areas are often crowded but never uncomfortably so. The medieval theme is well developed through special slots, tournaments and promotions. It's especially fun to visit around Christmas, when light displays and a visit from Santa Claus enliven the Medieval Village Shoppes. For adults travelling with children, the resort is as family-friendly as Circus Circus, and not quite as noisy. On the Fantasy Faire Midway, carnival games offering stuffed animal prizes pitch for those last few quarters that escaped the slots. If you play 'guess your weight' with the friendly barker, be warned that the giant set of scales will display your weight across the midway.

Neon knights slay neon dragons in the 100,000sq ft (9,300sq m) casino, one of the few in town where photography is allowed. Visitors are surrounded by images of playing-card kings and queens, but the table games are affordable for any commoner. Ten-cent slot and video poker machines – hard to find in Las Vegas – join the more common 5¢, 25¢ and $1 varieties. When you're done throwing coins in machines, toss a few in the moat for good luck – they'll be donated to local charities.

Entertainment

Tournament of Kings (*see p195*), with armour-clad knights on horseback squaring off against the forces of evil, is one of the few dinner shows left in Las Vegas. Stand-up comics perform in *Catch A Rising Star* in the lounge (*see p202*). Wandering minstrels and other period acts perform throughout the day outside the Medieval Village Shoppes.

Eating & drinking

There are five restaurants in Excalibur, the best of which is Sir Galahad's Prime Rib House, where huge portions of beef are cooked to order and served with Yorkshire pudding; before going in, check out the replica of the resort, built to scale in chocolate. You'll find reasonable steaks at the Steakhouse at Camelot, and decent pasta at Regale Italian Eatery.

Gambling

Mini baccarat ($5-$100); blackjack ($3-$2,000); Caribbean Stud; Casino War; craps (2x); Let It Ride; poker; Pai Gow Poker; roulette (single & double zero). Gambling lessons.

Flamingo

3555 Las Vegas Boulevard South, at E Flamingo Road (733 3333/www.flamingolasvegas.com). Bus 202, 301, 302/self-parking & valet parking Las Vegas Boulevard South or Audrie Street.
Map p316 A7.

Half a century ago, when Benjamin 'Bugsy' Siegel opened the 'Fabulous Flamingo' in the middle of nowhere, every employee including the janitors wore tuxedos. Today, the Strip site of the Flamingo is one of the busiest intersections in the world, while the hotel itself has evolved into a lavish resort with a 15-acre tropical water playground. Although the dress code has been greatly relaxed – only the resort's penguins wear black tie – the hotel is still very stylish. And it has one of the most memorable neon creations in the city: pulsing pink and orange flowers and flamingos along the entire front of the building. After a series of 'seamless' expansions, the resort now has 3,642 rooms. In the original, Siegel incorporated a maze of underground tunnels in which to seek refuge from surprise visitors. Today, he could pick his hiding spots among lavish tower suites and lush gardens with meandering streams that provide a haven for ducks, swans, penguins and flamingos. Amenities include five pools, four tennis courts, a health club and lots of upscale shops. The interior is filled with white marble walkways and mirrored glass and decorated with ersatz flora; check out the three banyans at the buffet entrance.

The casino area, accented by bright pinks, yellows and tangerines, offers you a real chance to survive: craps and blackjack minimums are a reasonable $3, and there are several newer games with simple rules, such as Casino War. It's tougher to come out ahead in the slot area, which contains 2,100 machines, none considered especially loose. The last renovation did cost $130 million, after all. The casino conducts numerous slot tournaments, but they're not for the squeamish – entry fees average $2,000. You'll also find a lively card room, a keno parlour and a race and sports book.

Entertainment

The long-running *Great Radio City Spectacular* featuring the Rockettes was recently replaced by the Broadway-style musical, *Men Are From Mars, Women Are From Venus*. Also playing is *Bill Acosta's Lasting Impressions* (*see p194*), which defected from the Luxor in early 2001. In the intimate Bugsy Celebrity Theater, the Second City comedy troupe (*see p202*) set up shop in spring 2001. Their shows feature skits, songs and hilarious comedy schtick. Rounding out the entertainment is *Bottoms Up*, an afternoon burlesque show with plenty of comedy and cleavage.

Eating & drinking

The Flamingo has a clutch of top-end international restaurants, with top-end international prices to match. Chinese cuisine is served against a background of carved teak at the Peking Market; you'll find succulent steaks and sushi at Hamada of Japan (*see p148*); and Alta Villa serves posh Italian. For a quick, low-cost bite, try Bugsy's Deli – and avoid the buffet and coffeeshop if possible.

Gambling

Mini baccarat ($5-$3,000); blackjack ($3-$3,000); Caribbean Stud; craps (3x 4&10, 4x 5&9, 5x 6&8); Let It Ride; Pai Gow Poker; roulette (double zero).

Harrah's

3475 Las Vegas Boulevard South, between Sands Avenue & E Flamingo Road (369 5000/www.harrahs lv.com). Bus 301, 302/self-parking & valet parking Koval Road. **Map** p316 A6.

Just across the Strip from the Roman splendour of Caesars Palace and the South Seas-styled Mirage is Harrah's. Opened in 1973, and once called the Holiday Casino, Harrah's has seen many changes over the years. For a long time, Harrah's main building looked like a giant Mississippi riverboat, complete with a promenade deck and twin red smokestacks. But a renovation in 1997 (costing $200 million) torpedoed the paddlewheeler theme and replaced it with a worldwide carnival motif: in other words, insipid murals of festivals, bright colours, mirrors and a dark glass façade that fronts the Strip. Entertainers and musicians wander through the Carnaval Court, a festive patio area at the front entrance of the casino punctuated by fountains, shops, foliage and a diaphanous canvas cover that's supported by a maypole.

There's a wide selection of table games, including Caribbean Stud, Let It Ride and Casino War. Most blackjack games are dealt from the shoe, but higher limits – at least $25 minimum – are dealt from hand-held decks. Occasionally the gracious pit bosses will bring in the European single-zero roulette wheel for high-rollers. For lively action, take a seat in the compact poker room, while the race and sports book offers booths and table seating, with tableside food and drink service contributing to a sports-pub atmosphere. The casino area has been expanded by a third, but one place once located at the north Strip entrance, has been removed. This was a mistake. The loose festive feel of the place, accentuated by low limits and dealers who jazzed it up like carnival barkers, can never be replaced.

Entertainment

Contemporary singer Clint Holmes performs live in a blockbuster show, *Takin' It Uptown* (*see p197*), in the main showroom. Top comics play the Improv (*see p202*), the hotel's comedy club, and owner Budd Friedman sometimes drops by. There's more laughs with Mac King's *Comedy Magic Show*, which blends King's sleight of hand with visual gags. Following the trend towards more adult-style entertainment, Harrah's debuted a topless revue, *Skintight* (*see p194*), in autumn 2000. For more spontaneous fun, catch a band at La Playa (*see p201*), one of the city's few indoor-outdoor bars.

Eating & drinking

The Range Steak House is impressive, with towering mahogany pillars, copper accents and a great view of the Strip through floor-to-ceiling windows. There are also Asian and Italian restaurants. For cheaper eats, the Fresh Market Square Buffet is good (*see p153*), but be selective if you visit the 24-hour Garden Cafe coffeeshop. For a quick snack, you'll do better at walk-up coffee bar Club Cappuccino.

Gambling

Baccarat ($20-$10,000); mini baccarat ($20-$5,000); blackjack ($5-$5,000); Caribbean Stud; craps (2x); Let It Ride; poker; Pai Gow Poker; Pai Gow Tiles; roulette (double zero). Gambling lessons.

Luxor

3900 Las Vegas Boulevard South, between W Tropicana Avenue & Russell Road (262 4400/ www.luxor.com). Bus 301, 302/self-parking & valet parking Reno Avenue. **Map** p316 A9.

The stark shape of the Luxor's black glass pyramid, identifiable from planes cruising at 30,000ft (9,100m); the high-intensity beam shooting skywards from its apex, supposedly visible from 200 miles (350km) away (smog levels permitting); and, of course, the ten-storey replica of the Sphinx that squats at its entrance are all designed as giant billboards to lure the crowds. Some are disappointed – the Luxor is regarded as a 'warehouse' casino with little atmosphere to back up its impressive exterior.

However, there's no denying that the $650-million resort is perfectly suited to its desert setting and to the modern vision of Las Vegas.

Like most properties on the Strip, the Luxor undergoes frequent (and expensive) changes. During the most recent $300-million renovation, nearly 2,000 rooms were added. The latest addition is an exterior lighting system that illuminates the resort's signature pyramid: before, the black structure used to disappear against the night sky – not a good idea if the outside of your building is its main selling point. However, all these changes won't satisfy superstitious Asian gamblers, who reputedly dislike the Luxor for being, basically, a tomb. Inside, the pyramid shape remains evident – a relief for those who prefer the interior of a building to bear some relation to its exterior, a rare commodity in this town. 'Inclinators', high-gradient elevators, take guests to their rooms, which are accessed from internal balconies (from where more than one bankrupted gambler has launched a suicide dive). The casino area takes up pretty much the entire ground floor; the buffet is down below, and shopping and entertainment are on an attractive, albeit un-Egyptian mezzanine. Luxor remains a family-friendly resort, but doesn't pursue the adolescent market like its cousins, Excalibur and Circus Circus. State-of-the-art attractions include a 3-D IMAX cinema (see p103), one of the best games arcades in the city and a full-scale reproduction of Tutankhamen's tomb, which contains an inventory of glittering handcrafted Egyptian artefacts (see p104).

The massive casino area, decorated with hieroglyphics and ancient artefacts, is filled with the latest high-tech slot and video poker machines. Five-dollar minimums are the norm at the blackjack and crap tables. For poker players, the card room on weekend nights offers lively action that Cleopatra herself would appreciate.

Entertainment
The edgy, unusual, New York-based *Blue Man Group* (see p197) has had huge success since opening at the Luxor in early 2000. The Las Vegas show is the largest and most elaborate of all the Blue Man productions, and continues to thrive. Adult entertainment in the form of a topless revue, *Midnight Fantasy*, takes the stage in the evening (see p193). There's also hip nightspot Ra (see p212), which is popular with European clubbers.

Eating & drinking
The Pharaoh's Pheast Buffet offers made-to-order cooking stations, and above-average tastes. You'll also find excellent Asian and Polynesian cuisine at Papyrus. If you're successful in the casino, consider dining at the very upmarket and pricey Isis (see p131), the Luxor Steakhouse or the five-star Sacred Sea restaurant.

Gambling
Baccarat ($100-$15,000); mini baccarat ($5-$3,000); blackjack ($5-$5,000); Caribbean Stud; Casino War; craps (2x); poker; Pai Gow Poker; Pai Gow Tiles; roulette (single & double zero). Gambling lessons.

The ever-fabulous **Flamingo**. *See p76.*

Mandalay Bay
3950 Las Vegas Boulevard South, between W Tropicana Avenue & Russell Road (632 7777/ www.mandalaybay.com). Bus 301, 302/self-parking & valet parking Hacienda Avenue. **Map** p316 A9.
Surf's up and it's always high tide at Mandalay Bay. At the heart of the resort is an 11-acre tropical water park that features a sandy beach with its own wave-making machine. If you're timid with the white water, there are two other pools, a lazy river ride and a jogging track set among lush green foliage and fountains. Occupying the old Hacienda site and for now the southernmost casino-hotel on the Strip, the hotel's gold Y-shaped tower is a striking addition to the Vegas skyline, visible from practically everywhere – it looks particularly resplendent in the

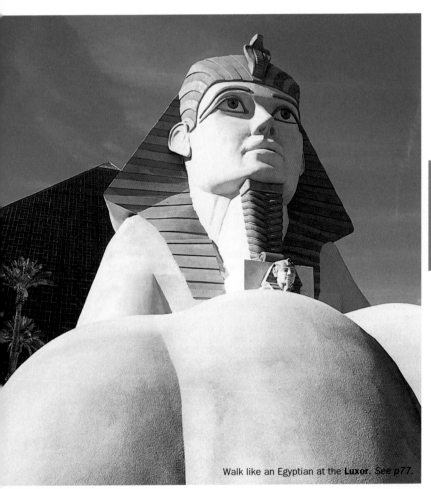

Walk like an Egyptian at the **Luxor**. *See p77.*

afternoon sun. The interior is pretty impressive, too: the South Seas theme has resulted in island-style architecture, a spacious lobby, plenty of foliage and water features, and a generally classy air. A public corridor off the lobby leads to the very upmarket Four Seasons hotel, which shares the same site but is a separate concern (*see p58*).

The resort also boasts the Mandalay Bay Shark Reef, a huge walk-through aquarium with dozens of sharks (*see p104*), two wedding chapels and a large health spa open to non-guests (for a fee). In 2002, 1.8 million sq ft (167,400sq m) of convention space will open, making Mandalay Bay a true one-stop location for many travellers. The only disappointment is the scant number of shops. A huge shopping mall between the Luxor and Mandalay Bay has remained

partially built for several years; the latest plans for this on-off project suggest it will be completed by the end of 2002.

The 135,000sq ft (12,500sq m) casino is airier and more spacious than many. It has 2,400 machines, including the new nickel slots that take up to 45 and 90 coins, such as Chairman of the Board and Reel 'Em In, but you have to hunt for the better video poker machines. Table games (122 of them) include blackjack, roulette, craps, Let It Ride, Caribbean Stud, Pai Gow Poker and mini baccarat. You'll also find a poker room – fast becoming a rarity on the Strip – where you can get your fix of seven-card stud, Texas Hold 'Em and Omaha Hold 'Em. The race and sports book has 17 large screens and enough seating for nearly 300 sports fans.

The signature lion guards the entrance to the vast, green **MGM Grand**.

Entertainment

Though short on shopping, Mandalay makes up for the deficit with its outstanding dining and entertainment choices. In spring 2001 the resort debuted its first production show, *Storm* (*see p199*), which combines cutting-edge music and choreography into an MTV-type show played without a curtain. The 12,000-seat Events Center (*see p221*) hosts superstar concerts with artists ranging from Blues Traveler to the Three Tenors, as well as major sporting events, such as heavyweight title bouts (*see p233* **Ringside**). There are live bands most nights in the Coral Reef Lounge (*see p200*), next to the casino floor, and in the milder months, concerts are often held on the outdoor island stage on the beach. Ultra-hip party people flock to China Grill on Wednesdays for club night Dragon (*see p212*) and the Rumjungle bar is crammed practically every night (*see p157 and p212*). Also on site is an outpost of the renowned House of Blues (*see p219*), which plays host to every form of music (from Moby to metal) in what may be the best concert venue in town.

Eating & drinking

Mandalay Bay is unusual in placing many of its restaurants together in a separate 'restaurant row' away from the casino – so you can drop in for a meal and not even see a slot machine (the self-parking garage leads straight to the restaurant area). It has also made a point of luring celebrity chefs from places like New York and San Francisco. Among them, Charlie Palmer set up shop in a vast designer version of his New York bistro, Aureole (*see p131*), which boasts one of the premier wine lists in the country (and a four-storey wine tower to boot). Another dining icon, Wolfgang Puck, is represented by Trattoria del Lupo (*see p137*), which serves

traditional Italian favourites in California-chic surroundings, and chefs Susan Feniger and Mary Sue Milliken – from TV show *Too Hot Tamales* – present modish California-inspired Mexican dishes at the pleasantly funky Border Grill (*see p138*). Other options include China Grill (Asian), Shanghai Lilly's (Chinese) and Red Square (*see p156*), a Moscow-inspired joint offering caviar, vodka and whispers of the pending revolution.

Gambling

Baccarat ($100-$15,000); mini baccarat ($25-$15,000); blackjack ($5-$15,000); Caribbean Stud; craps (2x); Let It Ride; poker; Pai Gow Poker; Pai Gow Tiles; roulette (single & double zero).

MGM Grand

3799 Las Vegas Boulevard South, at E Tropicana Avenue (891 1111/www.mgmgrand.com). Bus 201, 301, 302/self-parking Las Vegas Boulevard South or Koval Avenue/valet parking E Tropicana Avenue. **Map** *p316 A8.*

Kirk Kerkorian's MGM Grand, the world's largest resort hotel with over 5,000 rooms, made something of a business blunder when in 1993 it set out to appeal to the family market. Since then it has scrapped its Wizard of Oz theme, dismantled its animatronic Oz attraction, removed the cartoony lion's-mouth entrance (largely because it was a big turn-off for superstitious Asian gamblers) and closed down its outdoor, family-oriented Grand Adventures theme park (probably for good) to build more hotel rooms and a convention centre. The final nail in the 'family values' coffin occurred in the summer of 2001, when the hotel opened *La Femme*, a topless show directly inspired by the famed Crazy Horse burlesque in Paris, France. A 70ft (21m) bronze sculpture of a lion now presides over the Tropicana intersection, and there are real lions on view in the small but popular Lion Habitat (*see p104*). The MGM is spread out over 114 acres: pay close attention to the signs or you will get lost. Looking for an elevator? There are 93 on the property. The casino area alone is the size of four football fields, while the valet parking area is wider than the San Diego Freeway.

Now billed as 'The City of Entertainment', the MGM has four gaming areas – Entertainment, Hollywood, Monte Carlo and Sports – where you'll find all the games, including Spanish 21, a version of blackjack with more strategy options but fewer ten-value cards. Table minimums can go down to $5 on weekdays, but most are higher; in the Monte Carlo pit you'll find $25 minimums, $10,000 maximums – and single-zero roulette. The decor throughout is glittery and glitzy, with rainbow-patterned carpets, mirrored emblems and metallic stars: sort of Busby Berkeley on valium. There's also a large race and sports book with floor-to-ceiling screens and a very lively poker room, one of the best in town. As for slots, there are 3,700 of them, ranging from a nickel to $500. A monorail connects the MGM Grand to Bally's further north.

Entertainment

The hotel's production show, *EFX*, saw a radical change when Tommy Tune left in early 2001, and was replaced by rocker Rick Springfield. The new show, *EFX Alive!* (*see p197*) was altered to fit Springfield's guitar-pounding style and seems to be popular with the Generation-X audience. The intimate Hollywood Theater (*see p199*) is a good room for seeing the likes of Jay Leno, Penn & Teller or Randy Travis, while the 16,000-seat Grand Garden Arena (*see p221*) often hosts mega-concerts by Elton John, Billy Joel, the Rolling Stones and Madonna, as well as sporting events like the PRCA rodeo and boxing matches (*see p233* **Ringside**). Nightclub Studio 54 (*see p213*), modelled on the famous 1970s New York disco, is a big success, while *La Femme* (*see p193*) revue near the Studio Walk offers high-class adult entertainment.

Eating & drinking

It's almost worth getting lost in the MGM for the sake of the excellent Southwestern cuisine at Mark Miller's Coyote Café (*see p138*) and the nationally acclaimed seafood at Emeril Lagasse's New Orleans Fish House (*see p131*). The Brown Derby (*see p139*), a re-creation of the popular 1920s Hollywood eatery, offers a good Sunday brunch and still serves the signature Cobb salad and grapefruit cake from the original menu. For a hip blend of food and fun (at a price), Olio! (*see p137*) features a 40ft (12m) long antipasto bar, space-age gelato console and Italian specialities. The adjoining lounge is great for a late-night drink, and the private viewing room features food and the TV show *The Sopranos* on Sunday nights. Other entertaining eating options include the Wolfgang Puck Café for pizza, or the Rainforest Café for a fun family meal complete with a fake jungle backdrop and real parrots.

Gambling

Baccarat ($100-$15,000); mini baccarat ($25-$15,000); blackjack ($5-$10,000); Caribbean Stud; Casino War; craps (2x; 3x 6&8); Let It Ride; Pai Gow Poker; Pai Gow Tiles; roulette (single zero & double zero); Spanish 21. Gambling lessons.

Mirage

3400 Las Vegas Boulevard South, between Spring Mountain & W Flamingo Roads (791 7111/www. themirage.com). Bus 301, 302/self-parking Spring Mountain Road/valet parking Las Vegas Boulevard South. **Map** p316 A6.

Steve Wynn's tropical-themed hotel set the industry standard for modern mega-resorts when it opened in 1989. Now owned by MGM Mirage Resorts, the Mirage has become a haven for high-rollers, but it's also a major draw for those without a private jet. Even if you never drop a quarter into a slot, there's plenty to do. And many of the resort's attractions are free, among them the famous erupting volcano on the Strip; the tropical atrium just inside the front entrance filled with 60ft (18m) palm trees, waterfalls and lush foliage; and the huge fish tank behind the hotel reservation desk. Avoid, however, the Dolphin Habitat – not worth the money – and the not-so-secret Secret Garden; you can see Siegfried & Roy's white tigers for free in a glass-encased habitat in the casino. (For both, *see p107.*)

Despite its huge size, the $730-million resort is surprisingly easy to navigate, partly because the gaming areas are broken up into a conglomeration of Polynesian-styled villages, each with its own thatched roof – though note that it can get very busy, especially at weekends. There are nearly 100 blackjack tables, most dealt from six-deck shoes. As you would expect, minimums are high: $5 for 21 and roulette, $25 for mini baccarat, $100 for baccarat. Unless you have deep pockets, it's probably better to consider the pit area as visual rather than interactive entertainment. You can find a good game of poker at any hour of the day, and since many players are tourists, the action (both low- and high-limit) is good. You'll also find some alternative table games, such as Let It Ride and Casino War.

For a break, check out the high-limit slots. If you're polite, and it's not too busy, an attendant will show you around, and perhaps offer you some fresh, sliced fruit, normally reserved for players who insert $100 tokens, five at a time. The Red, White & Blue slot offers a $1-million jackpot – though, like the machine at Caesars Palace, only the first $1,000 is paid out in gold coins – two of them.

Entertainment

The overpriced and overhyped *Siegfried & Roy* show (*see p197*) boasts elaborate pyrotechnics and special effects, but the spontaneity seems to be gone – let's face it, Siegfried's not getting any younger. During dark periods, headliner acts such as Paul Anka often play S&R's showroom. Another high-profile act is the acclaimed impersonator Danny Gans (*see p195*), who moved to his own purpose-built theatre at the Mirage, after a short stint at the Stratosphere and a

Sightseeing

Night-time dazzle: **New York-New York, Monte Carlo** and **Paris-Las Vegas**. *See pp83-4.*

long one at the Rio. In addition, you can hear light jazz and reggae in the Lagoon Saloon (*see p201*) or classic melodies and torch songs by a lone pianist in the Baccarat Bar (which, along with the Sports Bar, is the best place to play 'Can that really be his wife?'). There's no cover at either.

Eating & drinking

Top-class (and top-priced) restaurants include Renoir (*see p135*), where you'll find superb French cuisine and walls decorated with fine art; Samba Grill where you'll find tangy Brazilian selections; and Kokomo's, a popular spot for classic steaks and seafood. For more reasonable family dining, try the ever-popular California Pizza Kitchen (*see p138*). The Mirage Buffet (*see p154*) is probably the best buffet in town for vegetarians, and also has some delicious desserts; we highly recommend the tasty bread pudding.

Gambling

Baccarat ($100-$15,000); mini baccarat ($25-$15,000); blackjack ($5-$10,000); Caribbean Stud; Casino War; craps (3x 6&8); Let It Ride; poker; Pai Gow Poker; Pai Gow Tiles; roulette (single zero & double zero); Spanish 21.

Monte Carlo

3770 Las Vegas Boulevard South, at Rue de Monte Carlo, between W Flamingo Road & W Tropicana Avenue (730 7777/www.monte-carlo.com). Bus 201, 301, 302/self-parking & valet parking Rue de Monte Carlo. **Map** p316 A8.

This $344-million joint venture between Mirage Resorts and Circus Circus Enterprises (as was) went from conception to completion in just 15 months, and has proved to be one of the most appealing entries in the mid- to high-end resort market. The twin archway entrances, adorned by classical statuary and majestic fountains, have had flashbulbs popping since the hotel first opened in 1996. This being Las Vegas, one half-expects the statues to break into song, but such theatrics would not be appropriate for a resort modelled on the Place du Casino in Monaco.

The resort's *Lifestyles of the Rich and Famous* theme is perfectly captured in the resplendent lobby area, so authentically European that Americans may expect to be asked for a passport. A lavish, glittering crystal chandelier hangs from a dome in the centre, surrounded by imported marble and tiny white lights tracing geometric patterns in the ceiling. Perfume is subtly pumped into the casino to offset the more colourful odour of the tourists who walk over to the Monte Carlo from the MGM Grand in soaring summer temperatures.

There's an abundant selection of $5 blackjack tables, plenty of 5¢ opportunities among the 2,200 slot machines and the atmosphere is bright and casual. But it's the smaller touches that players may appreciate most, such as chairs with backs instead of stools at every machine, wider walkways through the casino and the European-style single-zero roulette wheel. The Monte Carlo attracts brisk traffic from neighbouring casinos, but the tables never

seem crowded. Players stand a better chance of landing a one-on-one blackjack game with the dealer here than at most Strip mega-resorts. Despite its adult posture, the Monte Carlo is actually one of the more kid-friendly resorts; it has a huge video arcade, a wave pool and lazy river, and a fast-food court with burgers, hot dogs and ice-cream. However, the monorail to Bellagio will only allow riders under 18 if they are registered Bellagio guests.

Entertainment

Magician Lance Burton – actually one of the more innovative magicians in town – disappears six nights a week in the appropriately named Lance Burton Theatre (*see p195*). The Victorian-style showroom was designed specifically for its headliner, and its plush seating will delight Las Vegas show veterans who are used to being packed like sardines at long tables arranged perpendicular to the stage.

Eating & drinking

André Rochat, the man who in 1979 opened Las Vegas's first laudable French restaurant, brings his culinary act to the Strip at André's, the Monte Carlo's marquee eaterie (*see p145*). Besides the de rigueur buffet and coffeeshop, other dining options include the trattoria-style Market City Caffe, and the Dragon Noodle Company, which features a speciality tea bar and four types of Asian cuisine. Blackstone's Steak House and the Monte Carlo Pub & Brewery (*see p156*) are also worth a visit.

Gambling

Baccarat ($25-$15,000); mini baccarat ($10-$5,000); blackjack ($5-$5,000); Caribbean Stud; craps (2x); poker; Pai Gow Poker; Pai Gow Tiles; roulette (single & double zero). Gambling lessons (poker).

New York-New York

3790 Las Vegas Boulevard South, at W Tropicana Avenue (740 6969/www.nynyhotelcasino.com). Bus 201, 301, 302/self-parking Las Vegas Boulevard South or W Tropicana Avenue/valet parking W Tropicana Avenue. **Map** p316 A8.

How fitting: 'the city that never sleeps' comes to the city that really never sleeps. Built for $460 million by MGM Grand and Primadonna Resorts and opened in January 1997, New York-New York is Las Vegas-style theming at its most extreme – there isn't a more colourful, eye-catching building in the city. It's been called the 'largest piece of pop art in the world', and its dozen towers, one-third real-size copies of the Empire State building, Chrysler building et al, are magnificently rendered. A 150ft (46m) replica of the Statue of Liberty looms over the intersection of Tropicana and the Strip, and a mini- Brooklyn Bridge serves as a walkway to the Strip entrance. Above them all the Manhattan Express rollercoaster (*see p104*) twists, turns and rolls, with a 144ft (44m) dive past the hotel's valet entrance.

Inside, you'll find every New York cliché, from a fake subway station to graffitied mail boxes. The steaming manhole covers in the Village Eateries area are a particularly clever touch. The slot club is cheekily named the New York-New York Slot Exchange and the cashiers cages are in (where else?) the Financial District. The attention to detail is amazing and will keep you amused, although the layout is rather chaotic: the casino may be a homage to the Big Apple, but the real Manhattan is far easier to navigate.

The 84,000sq ft (7,800sq m) casino area is modelled on Central Park, with street lamps, a footbridge over a winding stream and fake trees in autumnal colours. It's pleasant and picturesque, and you don't have to worry about muggers (though a hot dealer will take your money just as fast). But everything's more expensive in NYC, and the tuxedo-backed chairs at the gaming tables set the right tone. Minimums for blackjack (practically all six-deck shoes) are $5 and $10, $5 for craps and $1 for roulette. There's also a terrific variety of slot machines – one of the best on the Strip – in all the usual denominations.

Upstairs, the Coney Island Emporium (see p103) mixes Daytona-style interactive driving simulators with low-tech carnival games. It's one of the only arcades in town with real personality: ghoulish kids will love the 'electric' chair. Carny hawkers wear straw hats, garters, vests and striped shirts, and you can hear the screams from the riders starting their journey on the Manhattan Express rollercoaster. Finally, you can watch sports or play games at the new ESPN Zone (see p104), which opened along the Boardwalk north of the casino in summer 2001.

Entertainment

Michael Flatley's Lord of the Dance (see p198) is performed five nights a week, without Michael Flatley, which is either good or bad depending on your point of view. It's a scaled-down production, but it still has plenty of toe-tapping energy. Comedienne Rita Rudner performs in her own Cabaret showroom, two duelling pianists entertain lively crowds at the Bar at Times Square (see p200) and, if you're lucky, you'll find a decent swing band in the Empire Bar (see p222).

Eating & drinking

Contemporary Italian dining is offered at Il Fornaio (see p140 **Caffeine fix**), a chic and popular restaurant and bakery next to the Central Park bridge. There's also Gallagher's Steakhouse (see p139) and Chinese restaurant Chin-Chin. Pop into America (see p130) if only to gawk at the huge, 3-D map of the States hanging from the ceiling. Mexican specialities are served at Gonzalez y Gonzalez. The food at the Village Eateries ranges from New York deli sandwiches to pizza and Mexican: it isn't bad, but what's really delicious is the faux Greenwich Village setting: a jumble of brownstone façades, fire escapes and street signs.

Gambling

Mini baccarat ($10-$5,000); blackjack ($5-$5,000); Caribbean Stud; Casino War; craps (2x); Let It Ride; Pai Gow Poker; roulette (double zero). Gambling lessons.

Paris-Las Vegas

3655 Las Vegas Boulevard South, between Harmon Avenue & E Flamingo Road (946 7000/www.paris-lv.com). Bus 202, 301, 302/self-parking & valet parking Las Vegas Boulevard South or Audrie Street. Map p316 A7.

Opened in September 1999 by casino giant Park Place Entertainment (owner of Bally's, Hilton and Caesars Palace), Paris Las Vegas welcomes guests into a shrunken version of the French capital, which, bizarrely, was fully endorsed by French government officials. There's an exact, half-sized replica of the Eiffel Tower, built using Gustave Eiffel's original plans, an Arc de Triomphe with the same statues as the original, and copies of famous buildings, including the Opera, the Louvre and Hotel de Ville. Ascend 46 storeys in a lift to the top of the Eiffel Tower (see p106) for a stunning view of the Strip. The authenticity even extends to parking valets yelling 'allez allez' to one another and casino employees muttering 'bonjour' to guests.

Three of the four Eiffel Tower's legs plunge into the casino itself, which is smaller, noisier and more crowded than most. The 100 table games and more than 2,000 slot machines are budget-friendly, meaning you'll find $5 blackjack and craps tables and 25¢ slot machines. Hot slots include Monopoly, Wheel of Fortune, Let's Make a Deal and Reel 'Em In. The race and sports book has large-screen TVs and 'pari-mutuel' betting on horse racing from throughout the country. As you might expect, the theming is rampant, from the Monet-style floral carpet and Metro-like wrought-iron canopies above the table games to the security guards in gendarme uniforms. Check out the original LeRoy Neiman paintings on the walls. The bartender at Gaston's will tell the tale of the French capital's history. The restaurants and shops are clustered at the back of the casino amid a fantasy Paris streetscape with cobblestone pathways and old-fashioned streetlamps (see p163). Bicycle-riding bakers deliver fresh bread to the resort's restaurants. There's also a walkway to Bally's next door and a high-quality spa (open to non-guests) on site.

Entertainment

The hotel's attempt at a production show, *Notre Dame De Paris*, was short-lived, so stage entertainment has been delegated to headliners such as Bobbie Vinton, Kevin James and Natalie Cole. In Le Cabaret Lounge you can rock to Euro bands under a huge tree draped with hundreds of sparkling lights and surrounded by a Left Bank street scene. For a more intimate encounter, try Napoleon's (see p156), a clubby cigar and pipe lounge with good French wine. At the weekend, it transforms into Vamp, a high-octane dance club (see p213).

Eating & drinking

When Paris opened, the number of French restaurants in Las Vegas nearly doubled. The best option is Mon Ami Gabi, which enjoys a unique Strip-side open-air terrace and serves up some classic bistro food (see p135). The casino's signature restaurant,

the Eiffel Tower Restaurant (*see p133*), is perched 11 storeys above the Strip and offers a great view to accompany its high-class French cuisine. In keeping with the French theme, the casino's 24-hour fast-food restaurant is a boulangerie, selling bread baked on the premises, while the steakhouse is a French rotisserie. Le Village Buffet (*see p154*), although one of the most expensive buffets in town, is worth it: where else will you find duck, venison, coq au vin and bouillabaisse?

Gambling
Baccarat ($100-$15,000); mini baccarat ($25-$5,000); blackjack ($5-$10,000); Caribbean Stud; Casino War; craps (3x, 4x, 5x); Let It Ride; Pai Gow Poker; Pai Gow Tiles; roulette (single & double zero); Spanish 21.

Riviera
2901 Las Vegas Boulevard South, at Riviera Boulevard (734 5110/www.theriviera.com). Bus 301, 302/self-parking Riviera Boulevard or Paradise Road/valet parking Las Vegas Boulevard South. **Map** p315 B5.

When the hotel opened in 1955, its nine-storey tower was Las Vegas's first high-rise. Orson Welles and Marlene Dietrich appeared in the showroom and tuxedoed patrons passed the shoe at the baccarat tables like James Bond in *Dr No*. Today, as pitchmen hand out leaflets to lure low-rollers inside with the promise of a free T-shirt, the name no longer seems appropriate. The beachfront-style architecture always suggested Florida more than St Tropez, but now the side of the building is covered with a

multi-coloured neon collage that sparkles and pops like a fireworks display – impressive, yes, but hardly sophisticated. Like the now-defunct Dunes and Sands hotel-casinos, the Riviera's glory days belong to the past. Several expansions over a ten-year period have resulted in a lack of cohesion; guests will need a map to find the right elevator to their room.

The underwater theme of the Riv's once-popular *Splash!* show is carried into the area outside the showroom, which is awash in blue-green hues, mermaid statues and seashell-patterned carpeting. The rest of the gaming area is an L-shaped expanse of red and gold with an elevated lounge and bar in the centre (your best bet for a meeting place that everyone can find). Minimum wagers at the tables are not as low as the surroundings would suggest: $5 blackjack in a $2 setting. The lowest limits and nickel slots are found in a part of the casino dubbed Nickel Town, which these days is actually a better name for the whole resort. Outside, near the underground valet entrance off the Strip, is a rear-view sculpture of the hotel's *Crazy Girls* cast, their exposed derrières immortalised in bronze. Passers-by like to rub the sculpture's bums for good luck.

Entertainment
More than any other resort in town, the Riviera depends on live entertainment for its business. Two shows a night are performed in each of the four showrooms: *Splash!* (*see p199*) is the headliner, though its canned music, hip-hop choreography and motorcyclists don't match up to the high-tech glamour of more recent shows. *Crazy Girls* (*see p193*) bills itself as the most risqué show on the Strip – you won't actually see any more skin here than at other showgirl extravaganzas, but the presentation is more overt. *An Evening at La Cage* (*see p194*) is probably the best of the drag shows in town, while the Riviera Comedy Club (*see p202*) presents stand-up comics and other performers. It's also worth stopping for a drink at Le Bistro Lounge (*see p201*).

Eating & drinking
Seafood is a speciality at both Ristorante Italiano and Kristofer's Steak House, though the specials at Kady's coffee shop are much better bargains. Rik'Shaw serves Cantonese favourites, and the World's Fare Buffet offers a fine selection of international cuisine: watch for special deals combining the buffet and one of the Riviera's shows. The Mardi Gras foodcourt houses seven fast-food joints, and Nickel Town has the cheapest snacks on the Strip (*see p151* **Vegas on the cheap: Food and drink**).

Gambling
Mini baccarat ($5-$2,000); blackjack ($5-$2,000); Caribbean Stud; craps (2x); Let It Ride; poker; Pai Gow Poker; roulette (single & double zero); Spanish 21. Gambling lessons.

Sahara
2535 Las Vegas Boulevard South, at E Sahara Avenue (737 2111/www.saharahotelandcasino.com). Bus 204, 301, 302/self-parking & valet parking Las Vegas Boulevard South or Paradise Road. **Map** p315 C4.

Built in 1952, the Sahara thrived in the early days of Las Vegas, but has faced difficult times trying to compete with the growth of the mega-resorts at the south end of the Strip. But, while its north Strip location is a bit removed, the revamped Sahara comes across as both passably lavish and affordable to locals and middle-income tourists. The main entrance has been relocated to Las Vegas Boulevard to give the Sahara more of a Strip presence – and a commanding presence it is. The long-famous camel statues have gone the way of the hotel's original 35¢ hot fudge sundaes, replaced by a new $4.6-million porte-cochère topped by a Moroccan-style dome. The camels have been recaptured on a video display in the hotel's 190ft (58m) high minaret-topped electric marquee, where they watch over an expanded Moroccan-themed casino.

There are single-deck, double-deck and shoe blackjack games with $1 minimum limits – the cheapest on the Strip. Minimum bets at the crap tables are a reasonable $3. Low-limit Texas Hold 'Em and seven-card stud games are spread daily in the new card room, and $22 tournaments are held at 7pm on weekdays. The slots include all the latest high-tech machines and are touted as the 'loosest on the Strip' – not that this really means anything.

If you're looking for fast action away from the green felt, check out Speedworld (*see p111*), the hotel's $15-million indoor racing car simulation. All the thrill of driving a high-performance motor, but there's no chance you'll get killed – unlike the scenario in the crap pit. There's also Speed: The Ride (*see p110*), which twists around the lobby and porte-cochère and zooms through a loop facing the Strip.

Entertainment

The Sahara Theater is home to magician Steve Wyrick (*see p197*), who puts on a world class show, while the Congo Room (*see p199*) stages *The Rat Pack is Back*, a popular retro-themed musical reminiscent of the Frank, Dino and Sammy days. (Trivia quiz: who opened the Congo Room in 1952? Ray Bolger, the scarecrow from *The Wizard of Oz*.) Comedian Michael Holly (*see p202*) takes to the stage in the afternoon.

Eating & drinking

Options range from the 'gourmet' Sahara Steakhouse to the buffet on the second floor, where the prices are very palatable, but the taste is typical buffet fare. The food is much better at Mexican restaurant Paco's Hideaway. The Caravan coffee-shop offers graveyard specials and has a tacky kneeling camel sculpture by the front entrance.

Gambling

Blackjack ($1-$500); Caribbean Stud; craps (5x); Let It Ride; poker; Pai Gow Poker; roulette (double zero); Spanish 21. Gambling lessons.

Stardust

3000 Las Vegas Boulevard South, at Stardust Drive, between W Sahara Avenue & Desert Inn Road (732 6213/www.stardustlv.com). Bus 301, 302/self-parking & valet parking Las Vegas Boulevard South or Industrial Road. **Map p315 B5.**

The Stardust, the north Strip hotel behind that world-famous 20-storey sign, is the resort on which the film *Casino* was based and where the disastrous *Showgirls* was shot. But don't worry, you needn't fear running into any Mob characters or (God forbid) Elizabeth Berkley in a gold lamé party dress. What you will find is a delightful mix of locals and tourists who love action. During four decades of operation, the Stardust has built a loyal following of players. There are no family-oriented attractions here. Despite a $100-million expansion and remodelling in 1991, much of the resort, decorated in maudlin azures and aquamarines, still has the dank and dark feeling of an old-time gambling joint.

Treasure Island. *See p87.*

The casino pit is loaded with tables and slots. There are 44 blackjack tables offering double-deck or shoe action from $5 to $2,000. Crap players like the modest minimums and spirited action, and baccarat players play up to $5,000 a hand. Among the new games is progressive Pai Gow Poker, which offers five jackpots for hands ranging from four of a kind to five aces including a joker. The card room is a lot smaller than it was a generation ago, but the room still offers sprightly action, generally at weekends. There are nearly 2,000 slot machines of all varieties, and the slot club offers straightforward cash instead of prizes or gimmicks. The sports book is a mecca for football fans, and hosts sports-oriented radio shows throughout the week.

Entertainment

The long-running *Enter the Night* closed at the end of 1999; 'Mr Las Vegas', Wayne Newton (*see p199*), took over the headline slot in early 2000 and performs at various times throughout the year. In his absence, the Stardust often books old-time rock groups such as the Dixie Cups and Shirrells, or big-band orchestras that entertain the over-50s with swing-era dance music. House bands play in the old-style Starlight Lounge (*see p201*); it's a fun place to hang out or to kick up your heels on the dancefloor.

Eating & drinking

Toucan Harry's coffeeshop offers a diverse menu including Chinese cuisine, and most of the offerings aren't bad. If you're not concerned about cholesterol levels, try William B's Steakhouse, Tony Roma's for ribs or Tres Lobos for innovative Mexican dishes. The new Coco Palms does a much better job than the previous Warehouse Buffet, which was thankfully jettisoned in 1999.

Gambling

Baccarat ($100-$10,000); mini baccarat ($25-$5,000); blackjack ($5-$2,000); Caribbean Stud; craps (2x); Let It Ride; poker; Pai Gow Poker; roulette (double zero). Gambling lessons.

Treasure Island

3300 Las Vegas Boulevard South, at Spring Mountain Road (894 7111/www.treasureislandlas vegas.com). Bus 203, 301, 302/self-parking & valet parking Las Vegas Boulevard South or Spring Mountain Road. **Map** p316 A6.

The pirate-themed resort fronts the Strip with a replica of an 18th-century sea village surrounded by rock cliffs, shrubs, palm trees and nautical artefacts, all perched atop Buccaneer Bay, a blue-water lagoon. Two fully rigged ships – a pirate galleon and a British frigate – play out a mock sea battle every 90 minutes beginning at 4pm. A bit smaller and more intimate than the neighbouring Mirage, the interior of Treasure Island is decorated with bas-relief art on the ceilings, overflowing treasure chests on the walls and black carpets decorated with jewels, gold doubloons and rope chains. In the crowded casino, you'll find all the usual games, as well as a race and sports book – but you're the one who's likely to be plundered. As at the Mirage, the table limits are high and

six-deck shoes are the rule, but the video poker – and, by association, the slots – are not known to have good payback percentages.

Entertainment

Cirque du Soleil's *Mystère* (*see p198*) is still one of the best shows in town. It's pricey at about 90 bucks a go, but worth it to see 70 international acrobats, actors and clowns put on a performance at times winsome, more often captivating, and occasionally jaw-dropping. For more low-key and lower-priced entertainment, try the Cabaret, a new piano bar near the front valet entrance, where sexy songstresses specialise in moody melodies.

Eating & drinking

Posh pirate eatery the Buccaneer Bay Club (*see p131*) offers a great (and costly) view of the pirate battle out front – though you can't hear the show too well. You can feast on Chinese specialities at Madame Ching's and northern Italian cuisine in Francesco's. For more reasonably priced cuisine, the Steak House offers tasty mesquite-prepared selections. The buffet and the Lookout Café aren't bad either, and the new Kahunaville themed restaurant and nightclub looks set to become a hotspot. If you're desperate, there's a Starbucks kiosk.

Gambling

Baccarat ($100-$15,000); mini baccarat ($25-$10,000); blackjack ($3-$5,000); Caribbean Stud; Casino War; craps (2x 4&10, 5&9; 3x 6&8); Let It Ride; Pai Gow Poker; Pai Gow Tiles; roulette (double zero); Spanish 21.

Tropicana

3801 Las Vegas Boulevard South, at E Tropicana Avenue (739 2222/www.tropicana.lasvegas.com). Bus 201, 301, 302/self-parking & valet parking Las Vegas Boulevard South, E Tropicana Avenue or Reno Avenue. **Map** p316 A8.

With the exception of the desolate New Frontier Hotel further north, the Tropicana earns the dubious distinction of being the Strip property most in need of a top-to-bottom face-lift – or a just-start-over implosion. The resort once dubbed the 'Tiffany of the Strip' has abandoned its original Polynesian theme, but forgot to replace it with anything else. Most areas of the casino are fairly generic, and not particularly attractive.

The first sight to greet visitors passing through the front door of the Tropicana is a huge canopy ceiling made of leaded stained glass and mirrors. It's a work of art worthy of a symphony hall or an opera house, but blends with absolutely nothing else on the property. And don't think you'll be able to see the dealer's hole card in one of the mirrored panels: the casino is wise to such tricks.

Between the twin hotel towers are five acres of gardens, waterfalls and lagoons in the pool area, and one of only two swim-up blackjack games in town. Players sit half-submerged in the pool, hitting and splitting waterproof cards. Don't worry about getting your cash wet: when you reach the table, the dealer will insert the bills into a money dryer. The

Wildlife Walk, an enclosed bridge that connects the casino to the Island Tower, is home to tufted-eared marmosets, African tortoises and enough exotic macaws and cockatoos to stock a tropical zoo. The Casino Legends Hall of Fame (*see p103*), featuring artefacts from Las Vegas's gambling history, is worth a look: admission is $4, but coupons to get in free are in all the hotel casino giveaway publications.

The swim-up blackjack is really the one special gaming aspect at the property. Otherwise, there's the usual variety of games, though not quite as many video poker machines as at other places, and some of the slots are showing their age. In short, the Trop isn't as high-roller as it used to be. A tiny, dingy sports book is located at the back of the casino, at the bottom of a stairway, apparently hidden as if the hotel were embarrassed by it. It should be.

Entertainment
Folies Bergère (*see p197*), the longest-running production show in America, has been a mainstay at the Tropicana's Tiffany Theatre for three decades. This popular musical tribute to the Parisian cabaret, featuring can-can dancers, showgirls and speciality acts, hasn't changed much down the years, but its consistency is part of its charm. In the afternoons, the theatre hosts the *Illusionary Magic of Rick Thomas*, a fun, moderately priced show. The Comedy Stop (*see p202*) features a rotating bill of comics, with a no-smoking show early on.

Eating & drinking
Mizuno's, a Japanese steakhouse, is the most acclaimed of the Tropicana's seven restaurants. Steaks, Gulf shrimp and Australian lobster are served tableside, teppan-yaki style. Other dining options include Golden Dynasty (Chinese), Ristorante de Martino (Italian) and exotic specialities (including ostrich) at Savanna.

Gambling
Baccarat ($100-$15,000); mini baccarat ($25-$5,000); blackjack ($5-$3,000); Caribbean Stud; craps (3x); Let It Ride; Pai Gow Poker; Pai Gow Tiles; roulette (double zero). Gambling lessons.

Venetian
3355 Las Vegas Boulevard South, just south of Sands Avenue; also accessible from Sands Avenue (414 1000/www.venetian.com). Bus 203, 301, 302/ self-parking & valet parking Las Vegas Boulevard South or Harmon Avenue. **Map** *p316 A6.*

Unlike the tongue-in-cheek pastiche of, say, New York-New York, this reproduction of Venice in the middle of the desert is quite convincing. Owner Sheldon Adelson has tried to re-create the real Venice, with accurate duplicates of the Doge's Palace, Rialto Bridge, Campanile and other landmarks. The wooden gondolas are authentic – as are the black and white swans swimming around them.

The exterior is certainly a showstopper, and the interior's not bad, either. You enter a grand lobby and hall with a ceiling covered in gilt and hand-painted frescoes. Lavishly decorated with marble floors, plush furniture and glimmering lamps that create the feeling of afternoon sunlight, the Venetian is perhaps the most ornate of the newer casinos on the Las Vegas Strip.

The Grand Canal Shoppes (*see p162*) – a themed shopping complex with flowing canals, arched bridges, fake house fronts and a simulated sky – lies one floor above the casino. Head for St Mark's Square if you want a gondola ride (*see p107*). The strolling minstrels in carnival costumes, who lapse into Verdi at the slightest prodding, are fun, but some may feel the retail selection compares poorly with the Forum Shops. Madame Tussaud's Celebrity Encounter (*see p108*) has more than a hundred reproductions of celebs in various settings, including perky versions of Whoopi Goldberg, Brad Pitt, Jerry Springer and Oprah Winfrey in the Hollywood VIP party. The big openings of 2001 are the resort's two new Guggenheim Museums (*see p108*), which look set to turn Vegas into a high-culture destination. The larger Guggenheim is housed in a purpose-built space on the Strip, designed by Dutch architect Rem Koolhaas, while inside the resort is a smaller space devoted to works from the Guggenheim and the St Petersburg Hermitage. The smart Canyon Ranch Spa (*see p235*), the largest health and fitness facility in Nevada, offers massage, movement therapy, Pilates studios, a beauty salon, healthfood café and a climbing wall. The resort also connects to the recently expanded Sands Expo & Convention Centre, owned by Adelson, who is creator of the Comdex computer show; the Venetian is banking on pulling in a lot of business from Las Vegas's growing convention market.

In the casino itself, the 122 table games include blackjack, craps, Caribbean Stud, Let It Ride and Pai Gow, as well as a James Bond-friendly, single-zero roulette wheel, of which there are only a handful in all Nevada. The casino's 2,500 slot machines are weighted toward reel games, with a large mix of $1 machines. For the player with pull, there are some high-denomination machines – $5, $25 and $100 – in the casino's high-limit salon, which also includes a baccarat pit and 12 table games where you can play blackjack for $50,000 a hand.

This is only the first phase of the Venetian. The owners' ambitious (some would say overly ambitious) plan is to create a second resort, with more casino space and another 3,000 hotel rooms. No firm date for ground-breaking has yet been set.

Entertainment
The performance venue C2K has four levels of seating for 1,400 spectators for shows by Melinda: The First Lady of Magic (*see p195*), impersonator André-Philippe Gagnon, and various headliners. Once the performers have finished, C2K doubles as a popular nightclub (*see p211*). It has hosted world-class electronica DJs in the past, but its status is always on and off, so phone to check first. Live DJs can also be found in the ultra-hip Jack's Velvet Lounge (*see p156*) and at the chicly modernist V Bar (*see p157*), a New York-style lounge with Eames seating and top-shelf liquour.

Venetian: a casino fit for a Doge. *See p88.*

Eating & drinking

The Venetian is at the forefront of the Vegas trend of importing tried-and-tested eateries from other cities. Its eclectic collection of excellent upscale restaurants includes the likes of Joachim Splichal's Pinot Brasserie (French; *see p135*); Emeril Lagasse's superlative Delmonico steakhouse (*see p139*); Wolfgang Puck's Postrio (*see p135*); Stephen Pyle's Star Canyon (new Texas cuisine; *see p138*); Royal Star, an authentic Cantonese restaurant serving superb dim sum (*see p132*); and Il Canaletto, the quintessential Venetian ristorante (*see p137*). You can enjoy the unique interior at Lutece (French; *see p135*) or the canalside setting of Zefferino (*see p137*). And if that's not enough, Warner Brothers has debuted a new dining concept here called WB Stage 16 (*see p132*). Fashioned like a studio soundstage, it features several amazingly themed dining rooms.

Gambling

Baccarat ($50-$15,000); mini baccarat ($25-$10,000); blackjack ($10-$10,000); Caribbean Stud; Casino War; craps (2x, 3x 6&8); Let It Ride; poker; Pai Gow Poker; Pai Gow Tiles; roulette (single & double zero).

Stratosphere Area

Stratosphere

2000 Las Vegas Boulevard South, at St Louis Avenue, between Charleston Boulevard & Sahara Avenue (380 7777/www.stratlv.com). Bus 301, 302/ self-parking & valet parking Las Vegas Boulevard South. **Map** p315 C3/4.

Las Vegans still recall, with a mix of fascination and horror, the legendary Vegas World. From its inexplicable outer space theme, featuring a giant plastic astronaut crawling along the building, to its grammatically incorrect sign reading 'Gambling At It's Best', Vegas World topped local polls every year as the tackiest hotel-casino ever conceived. When flamboyant owner Bob Stupak ran short of money trying to build the city's tallest tower, he sold the property to Grand Casinos of Minnesota and Mississippi. In 1996, the tower was finally completed and Vegas World was incorporated into the Stratosphere. The 1,149ft (350m) tower is every bit the tourist attraction that Stupak intended, but the attached resort seems like an afterthought.

If the views from the observation decks (indoor and outdoor) near the top of the Stratosphere's 12-storey pod don't get the adrenalin pumping enough for you, ride the world's highest rollercoaster, High Roller, which makes three clockwise rotations around the top of the tower, banking at an angle of 32°. A second ride, Big Shot, propels passengers straight up 160ft (49m) to the very tip of the tower and then drops them back to the launching pad. (For both thrill rides, *see p111*.)

The casino area is spacious and comfortable, if somewhat generic – a World's Fair theme was toyed with and then abandoned altogether. The layout approximates a series of attached circles, which looks good, but complicates an attempt to plot a straight course from one end to the other. The emphasis is on liberal machines and table game gimmicks to improve the player's odds. The

Stratosphere advertises a 98% return on more than 150 dollar slots, a 100% return on some of its video poker machines and 100x odds on craps, as well as single-zero roulette and double-exposure blackjack (in which both the dealer's cards are dealt face up).

Long beset by financial problems, the property's economic status has finally stabilised (Carl Icahn, a renowned corporate bargain hunter, now owns it, along with locals casino Arizona Charlie's; *see p98*), but its north Strip location remains a liability. The Stratosphere borders one of the more dangerous areas of Las Vegas, and can be inconvenient for tourists to reach without a car – hence the free shuttle bus to and from the Strip.

Entertainment

American Superstars (*see p194*), a celebrity impersonation show, plays in the Broadway Showroom. Drop-dead impersonations of Ricky Martin have recently joined regulars Madonna and Charlie Daniels. The Showroom occasionally hosts headline entertainers such as Paul Revere and the Raiders. More headline entertainment and special events will be showcased in the new 3,700-seat Outdoor Events Center. The afternoon show, *Viva Las Vegas*, is a fun way to kill time or beat the heat.

Eating & drinking

At 832ft (253m), the revolving Top of the World restaurant and lounge (*see p132*) is the ultimate room with a view in Las Vegas, and the food – the speciality is an ice-cream and chocolate dessert in the shape of the Stratosphere Tower – isn't half bad. Those with a fear of heights can stay on terra firma and opt for tasty American and continental specialities at Lucky's Café, an Italian dinner at the Tower of Pasta, or a burger and milkshake at Roxy's, a 1950s-themed diner. In autumn 2001, the Montana Steakhouse was due to be replaced with a new Tex-Mex and oyster bar restaurant, and the buffet was set to expand.

Gambling

Mini baccarat ($5-$2,000); blackjack ($5-$3,000); Caribbean Stud; craps (10x); Let It Ride; Pai Gow Poker; roulette (single & double zero). Gambling lessons (craps, poker).

Off-Strip

For details of sights and attractions to the east and west of Las Vegas Boulevard South, *see chapter* **Off-Strip**.

East of Strip

Hard Rock

4455 Paradise Road, at Harmon Avenue (693 5000/ www.hardrockhotel.com). Bus 108/self-parking Paradise Road/valet parking Harmon Avenue.
Map p316 C7.

'This is not your father's Vegas any more,' proclaimed a cocky newcomer called the Hard Rock Hotel, and when Sheryl Crow opened the showroom in 1994, nobody disagreed. London entrepreneur Peter Morton's first resort venture has proved to be an unqualified winner. The town's only rock 'n' roll-themed casino sports Grateful Dead lyrics on the crap tables, Sex Pistols lyrics on the blackjack tables and roulette tables in the shape of pianos. Players bet with $5 Red Hot Chili Peppers 'Give it Away' chips, $25 Jimi Hendrix chips and $100 Tom Petty chips. Punk rocker Sid Vicious urges you to line up three Anarchy bars on his slot machine, while the Hendrix 'Purple Haze' machines have handles shaped like Fender guitar necks. Instead of a neon sign, a single 90ft (27m) Fender Stratocaster jutting out from the roof of the porte-cochère beckons visitors inside. Changing displays of rock memorabilia – from one of Elvis's jumpsuits to Elton John's jewel-encrusted piano to Paul Oakenfold's turntables – are dispersed throughout the casino, and classic and modern rock music is piped at loud, though not ear-splitting, volume.

A 1990s beast it may be, and several casinos have opened since, but this is still a hip, young and popular gambling den and one of the top party places in town. Design standards are high both outside – the 11-storey hotel curves gently around a sandy

Stratosphere tower: don't look down. See p89.

Is that a 90ft Fender Stratocaster in your pocket...? Welcome to the **Hard Rock**. *See p90.*

beach and pool – and in. A 1998 expansion doubled the room capacity and added a number of restaurants and a spa, but no space to the casino, which remains small by Vegas standards: only 800 slot and video poker machines and 76 tables. The main floor is one big circle, with an outer hardwood walkway around the gaming area and an elevated bar in the centre. Choosing to forego casino expansion might come back to haunt the Hard Rock in the face of ever-growing crowds, but does ensure an intimate atmosphere for the casino's beautiful clientele.

The action may be a little subdued during the day, but it starts warming up at 10pm and by midnight the place is packed. This is the best joint in town for celeb-spotting; after any big Vegas event, this is where the rich and famous gather to lose some of their inflated salaries. And just like in the Vegas glory days, the craps tables can get loud and crowded when someone is on a roll.

Dealers are encouraged to be friendly and enthusiastic; some will even give you a high-five if you hit a natural blackjack, a stunt that would give the pit boss a heart attack at another casino. And just like in the Vegas glory days, the craps tables can get loud and crowded when someone is on a roll.

Entertainment
The Hard Rock's 1,400-seat theatre, the Joint (*see p219*), has busted any Vegas showroom stigma by drawing artists from all musical disciplines: Blur, the Rolling Stones, Fatboy Slim and David Gray have all played here. It provides a rare chance to see big-name bands in a venue this small, but you'll pay for the privilege (from $20 up to a whopping $250). The acoustics are great, the folding chairs aren't. After hours, the crowd pours into Baby's (*see p211*), a trendy underground nightclub with luminescent walls, a bar surrounded by a moat and a giant retro saltwater aquarium that looks like it was shipped in from a swinging bachelor pad.

Eating & drinking
Mortoni's (*see p143*) serves northern Italian specialities, and turns the volume down on the music for the sake of atmosphere. Other restaurants include AJ's Steakhouse (*see p145*), a Rat Pack era-style meat and potatoes place; Nobu (*see p143*), the celebrity sushi hotspot; and the Pink Taco (*see p143*), a funky Mexican cantina with a name that always induces snickers from the fratboys at UNLV. Mr Lucky's 24/7 coffeeshop (*see p142*) has an innovative selection of pizzas and sandwiches; if you want to feel like an insider, order the steak and shrimp special for $5.95 that isn't on the menu, and save room for the scrumptious blueberry cobbler dessert. For excellent people-watching opportunities, hang out at the Viva Las Vegas Lounge (more commonly known as the Sidebar) on the edge of the casino (*see p158*). The Hard Rock Café (*see p142*), located in a separate building across the parking lot from the hotel – and indeed a separate concern – is nothing to write home about.

Gambling
Baccarat ($100-$5,000); mini baccarat ($5-$2,000); blackjack ($5-$2,000); Caribbean Stud; craps (2x); Let It Ride; Pai Gow Poker; roulette (double zero).

Las Vegas Hilton

3000 Paradise Road, between Karen Avenue & E Desert Inn Road (732 5111/www.lvhilton.com). Bus 108, 112/self-parking Paradise Road or Joe W Brown Drive/valet parking Paradise Road. **Map** p315 C5.

The Las Vegas Hilton was the first resort in the world to reach the size of a small city. The objective was to have everything – gaming, food, shopping, activities – under one roof, so guests would never have to leave. There's a feeling of tremendous space, as one might expect, but the casino's well laid out, so that it never seems overwhelming or unmanageable. On entering, you're greeted by a statue of Elvis Presley, commemorating his 837 consecutive sold-out performances in the showroom from 1969 to 1977. Those were the glory days of the Hilton resort, which has struggled to find an identity ever since.

It's succeeded – up to a point – with the opening of the the Space Quest Casino, a starship-like chamber west of the lobby. It has $5 tables, roulette and sci-fi slot machines that offer the singular experience of starting the game by passing your hand though a laser beam. Star Trek: The Experience (*see p113*), a themed entertainment complex is also housed here, which has led to some problems: the Nevada Gaming Commission fined the Hilton for the number of children who were in the casino, either coming or going from the 23rd century. Access to the attraction has been rerouted, but the hotel is still hypersensitive about under-21s. A visit is a must for families, but walk the kids briskly out or risk the wrath of Khan-like security personnel.

The Hilton was also the place where James Bond battled Blofeld in *Diamonds Are Forever* and Demi Moore blew on Robert Redford's dice in the film *Indecent Proposal*. Although Redford's $100,000 bets would be little unusual, this is still a high-roller haven, where class divisions are more conspicuous than at most casinos. The baccarat pit and high-limit tables are detached from the main gaming area, and the Platinum Plus slot machines, $5 and up per pull, also have their own space. High limits dominate the main floor as well: $5 is the minimum at any table, and the $100 tables are jumping year-round. They'll bring out a single-zero roulette wheel if you agree to bet $25-plus per spin. Sports bettors still flock to the Hilton's 400-seat Super Book, though newer books like the one at Mandalay Bay are now luring upscale sports fans away with more plush accommodations. Posted explanations on how to bet on various sports are helpful to novices.

Entertainment

In the absence of a permanent show, the Hilton Theater (*see p199*) has become a regular stop for the top touring stars of country music, such as Jo Dee Messina, Alabama and Brooks and Dunn. In mid-2001, it announced its intention to return to a series of headline performers, including Sheena Easton, who has also signed a long-term contract to appear at the Hilton Nightclub (*see p199*). The Nightclub, so billed to avoid the negative connotation of 'lounge' (that is, a place full of middle-aged has-beens nodding to grandiose ballads) generally features high-energy shows that draw high-energy crowds, but the $10 cover charge is a bit steep.

Eating & drinking

The very French bistro Le Montrachet serves entrées that change with the season, accompanied by offerings from its extensive wine cellar. For excitement while you dine, try Benihana Village (*see p143*), where chefs perform rapid knife tricks as they slice and dice. Also in a Japanese Village setting is the more upscale Garden of the Dragon. There are several other restaurants as well, none more fun than the futuristic Quark's Bar & Restaurant, which is located in Star Trek: The Experience.

Gambling

Baccarat ($100-$15,000); mini baccarat ($10-$5,000); blackjack ($5-$10,000); Caribbean Stud; Casino War; craps (3x, 4x & 5x); Let it Ride; Pai Gow Poker; Pai Gow Tiles; roulette (double zero; single zero on request).

West of Strip

Palms

4321 W Flamingo Road, at Valley View Boulevard (1-866 942 7770/942 7777/www.thepalmslasvegas). Bus 202/self-parking Fiesta Road, Flamingo Road, Arville Street or Valley View Boulevard/valet parking Flamingo Road. **Map** p311 X3.

Scheduled to open in December 2001, the Palms is the brainchild of George Maloof, who built the Fiesta casino in North Las Vegas before selling it to the Station Casinos chain. He's also the owner of the Sacramento Kings NBA basketball team. Maloof describes his casino-hotel as a 'boutique' resort: with only 470 guest rooms, the resort plans to entice tourists staying at nearby hotels (the Rio and Gold Coast are across the street) as well as drawing on the locals market. The resort has a 14-screen cinema complex, an IMAX and a tropical pool area with bamboo cabanas, dining terraces and poolside bar service. The pool is overlooked by a three-storey spa.

The 95,000sq ft (8,800sq m) casino will include 2,400 slot machines, 55 table games, a bingo room, keno parlour and a race and sports book.

Entertainment

At the heart of the Palms is a 1,200-seat, three-level entertainment venue that can double as a nightclub or concert hall. The club will have an aquatic theme with fountains, pools and water curtains used throughout. In addition to hosting headliner concerts, the venue will feature lounge and nightclub entertainment with DJ-driven music.

Eating & drinking

In keeping with its boutique status, the Palms will offer high-end dining choices, including a penthouse-level French restaurant from André Rochat (the creator of André's in Downtown; *see p145*). Diners will also be able to try the Little Buddha Café, a local rendition of the famed Buddha Bar in Paris, and the award-winning Nine Steakhouse from Chicago.

Rio

3700 W Flamingo Road, at Valley View Boulevard (252 7777/www.playrio.com). Bus 202/self-parking & valet parking W Flamingo Road, Valley View Boulevard or Viking Street. **Map** p311 X3.

The Rio has the unique distinction of being the only Vegas resort to appeal to both tourists and locals in equal measure. However, the hotel has taken a few public relations hits in recent years, for doubling the ticket price of former showroom headliner Danny Gans despite the entertainer's public objections (he has since absconded to the Mirage), and then annexing a residential community's golf course, and then threatening to ban residents from playing there.

Close to extinction in its first few years of operation, the pink and blue Brazilian-themed hotel has since been in perpetual growth for a decade, adding another tower of rooms or more space to the casino every year. The Rio changed most recently and dramatically in 1997 with the opening of Masquerade Village, a $200-million tower capped by the VooDoo Lounge and anchored by two floors of fashion-oriented shops. This is where the *Masquerade Show* (*see p113*), the Rio's much touted free attraction, takes place: for a fee, a few guests can even don costumes and masks and join dancers, musicians and aerialists on floats suspended from a ceiling track.

The casino pit is huge, and the predominant colours in betting circles are green and black – for $25 and $100 chips. At weekends, it's hard to find even a $5-minimum blackjack table. Smaller-stakes gamblers should aim for the lower-limit tables in the outlying areas of the casino, or better yet, walk across the street to the Gold Coast. Poker is offered, but it's a tough room filled with locals, joined, on occasion, by *Hustler* publisher Larry Flynt in his gold wheelchair. A shuttle bus runs between the Rio and the Strip from 9am to 1am daily.

Entertainment

The Scintas (see p198), a family act that has become one of Las Vegas's most popular shows among locals, has finally moved off the lounge circuit and into a main room at the Rio. The music and comedy show plays nightly in the Copacabana Showroom, while the Samba Theatre plays host to a diverse roster of headliners, including Smokey Robinson, magicians Penn & Teller and comic Jeff Foxworthy. The house show *De La Guarda*, a unique high-energy performance, closed in 2001; a replacement has not yet been found. Club Rio (*see p211*) is popular with ageing party people and conventioneers; the Mambo Lounge is classy and comfortable, though the quality of headliners varies; but for chutzpah, the VooDoo Lounge is the only place to go (*see p158*). Forty floors up in a glass elevator (it's numbered 51 because numbers 40 to 49 aren't used, in deference to the Asian superstition about the number four), it works hard not to be upstaged by its own view with animal-skin patterned booths, live music, lurid cocktails and bottle-juggling bartenders. Rumours suggest that a Vegas version of Hollywood's Viper Room may make its way to the Rio in the near future.

Eating & drinking

The Rio's eating options include Jean-Louis Palladin's Napa (French; *see p141*), once considered one of the best restaurants in town. There are two other gourmet rooms, plus eight less formal spots and two buffets: the state-of-the-art Carnival World Buffet (*see p152*) and the Village Seafood Buffet (*see p154*), served nightly. Buzio's is another fishy favourite, especially among local visitors. The VooDoo Lounge, meanwhile, serves average Cajun-Creole food.

Gambling

Baccarat ($100-$10,000); mini baccarat ($100-$10,000); blackjack ($5-$10,000); Caribbean Stud; Casino War; craps (2x on 4&10; 3x on 5&9; 5x on 6&8); Let It Ride; Pai Gow Poker; Pai Gow Tiles; roulette (single & double zero).

Downtown

People were gambling in Downtown Las Vegas as early as 1906, just one year after the land auction that gave birth to the city, and certainly long before the Strip was even a twinkle in Bugsy Siegel's eye. In the early years of the 20th century, railroad workers, ranchers and frontier tradesmen all gathered in rustic gambling halls around Fremont Street and Main Street to try their luck at games of chance. The Downtown casinos prospered throughout the next three decades, but in subsequent years they failed to match the booming activity of their upstart relations further south. Nowadays, if you're looking for a whiff of the old days, head for Downtown where the casinos offer fewer side attractions to distract from the serious business of gambling.

If you're in town just to gamble, it's worth remembering that the house rules at Downtown casinos are often more flexible than on the Strip, permitting very high or (at **Binion's Horseshoe**) no limits on some tables. At the **Las Vegas Club**'s blackjack tables, for example, it's legal to double down on any of the first two or three cards, split and resplit aces and split any pair any time you choose. If you draw six cards without busting, the hand is an automatic winner. Minimum bets in the Downtown casinos also tend to be lower than on the Strip, making it a good place for beginners or low-rollers to polish their skills.

Below we've listed the most interesting casinos in Downtown Las Vegas; others worth visiting include the **Four Queens** (202 Fremont Street, at Third Street; 385 4011/www.four queens.com) and the **Las Vegas Club** (18 Fremont Street, at Main Street; 385 1664/www.vegasclubcasino.net).

For details of sights and attractions in the Downtown area, *see chapter* **Downtown**.

Sightseeing

The glittering **Golden Nugget** adds a touch of class to Downtown. *See p95.*

Binion's Horseshoe

128 Fremont Street, at Casino Center Boulevard (382 1600/www.binions.com). Bus 107, 403/self-parking Ogden Avenue, Casino Center Boulevard or Stewart Avenue/valet parking Ogden Avenue or Casino Center Boulevard. **Map** p312 D1.

There are no rollercoasters or costumed cartoon characters here. Instead, you will find savvy, rene-gade dealers – the best anywhere with a deck or a crap stick in their hands. The Horseshoe was found-ed by famed gambling pioneer Benny Binion, and everything about it, from the whorehouse-velvet wallpaper to the dark mahogany furnishings, tells you this is a gambling joint. In the 21 pit, there are 50 or so single-deck games, most with $5 minimums, and 14 crap tables, with 50¢ or $1 minimums. The standard maximum bet is $25,000 (though only min-imum-bet signs are posted at the tables), which is higher than in any other casino in Las Vegas – but the house will play for more. The only restriction: your first bet is your highest bet. In the late 1980s, a gambler tested Binion's standing offer by betting $1 million on the pass line – and won.

Since Binion's acquired the Mint Casino next door in 1988, the property has been divided into East and West sections. The East is the original Binion's; the West is lighter, more modern and more comfortable, though it doesn't have as much personality. There are 1,200 slots, with denominations ranging from a nickel to $100. Binion's Bonanza $1 progressive, offering up to a $15,000 jackpot on a two-coin bet, is very popular. Monthly slot tournaments each offer a $50,000 prize. The large race book occupies a former lounge in the West Horseshoe; the sports book is in a separate part of the casino. Sadly, Binion's only tourist attraction – its display of a million dollars in cash, which had been on show for nearly 50 years – was sold to a private collector in January 2000.

Entertainment

The Horseshoe is most famous for hosting the world's biggest poker tournament, the annual World Series of Poker (*see p183*), which rewards the cham-pion with a $1-million prize. There's a gallery area where 'railbirds' can watch the action: most inter-esting are the side games where the players use real dollars, not chips, often risking tens of thousands on one hand. If you wish to join in the poker action in a low-limit game, beware: some of the best and most ornery players in the world make Binion's poker room their home.

Eating & drinking

Gee Joon offers some of the best Chinese food in Downtown and Binion's Ranch Steak House on the 24th floor provides a good cut and a great view. If you get killed at the tables, don't worry – you can still fill your plate with an excellent breakfast for a mere $2.75 in the coffeeshop in the basement. The lunch counter in the East Horseshoe is a Las Vegas institution, serving a legendary ham and bean soup with cornbread, and a real roast turkey sandwich.

Gambling

Mini baccarat ($5-$10,000); blackjack ($2-$25,000); craps (10x); Let It Ride; roulette (single zero & double zero); Spanish 21.

El Cortez

600 Fremont Street, between Sixth & Seventh Streets (385 5200/www.elcortez.net). Bus 107, 113/self-parking Ogden Avenue/valet parking Sixth Street. **Map** p312 D2.

Built in 1941, the El Cortez is the oldest unchanged hotel-casino in town (the Golden Gate – *see p57* – may be the oldest hotel building, but it didn't open as a casino until 1955). Benjamin 'Bugsy' Siegel had a share in El Cortez, but sold it to raise cash to build the Flamingo, and it is now owned by gambling pioneer Jackie Gaughan. The air is redolent with stale perspiration and smoke, and the carpet is so worn by the Runyonesque characters constantly shuffling along it that it's generally assumed that Gaughan has never changed it. In fact, he does so every five or six years, and once announced it in a full-page ad in the local newspaper.

Situated on the slightly more squalid fringe of Downtown, the El Cortez is a bit of a walk from the safety of the Fremont Street Experience, so you might want to take a taxi there at night. But once you're there, the glass doors will open to a safely patrolled den of low-limit action. The El Cortez is the place to go if you're short on cash and high on hope. There are plenty of penny and nickel video poker and keno machines, and lots of $2 single-deck black-jack games in the pit. Craps and roulette also offer cheap entertainment: the minimums (among the lowest in town) are 25¢ for both, and tapped-out gamblers can also try to win big in the keno lounge on 40¢ tickets. Twice a year, the casino hosts a social security number lottery: if your number (nine digits, in the right order) is drawn out of the pot, you win $50,000.

Entertainment
Aside from the occasional sight of owner Jackie Gaughan ambling through the casino with his poodle, Charlie, there is none. Rumour has it that Charlie knows how to push the elevator button for the penthouse where he and Jackie reside. One floor above the casino, the barber and beauty shop is a good place to get to know the colourful regulars – which should qualify as entertainment.

Eating & drinking
The filling stations here may be functional, but they do have a downbeat charm. There's Roberta's Café, whose circular booths and kelly-green and hot-pink decor – which matches the cocktail waitresses' retro uniforms – scream Tarantino; the Emerald Room coffeeshop, unrivalled for local colour and its myriad late-night specials; Charlotte's Ice Cream Shop, for hot dogs, hamburgers, pizza and, of course, icecream; and a snack bar.

Gambling
Blackjack ($2-$500); craps (10x); keno; Let It Ride; roulette (double zero).

Fitzgeralds
301 Fremont Street, at Third Street (388 2400/ www.fitzgeralds.com). Bus 107, 403/self-parking Third Street or Carson Avenue/valet parking Third Street. **Map** p312 D1.

Formerly known as the Sundance and once the tallest building in the entire state, the casino was bought by the Fitzgeralds Group in the 1980s. A giant statue of Lucky the leprechaun welcomes visitors to the Fitz and bids good luck to all who enter. The interior of the Fitz (as it's known among locals) used to be a festival of Irish green, where St Patrick's Day was celebrated year-round. The Irish theming was downplayed in the early 1990s, but of late the property seems to have re-embraced its

Emerald Isle heritage, and shamrocks and other Irish symbols are back in abundance – including a chunk of the real Blarney Stone, located opposite the Limerick Steakhouse.

The casino action is strictly low-roller, appropriate to the Fitz's clientele of retirees on package deals and junket tourists chasing funbook giveaways. Some of the $5 blackjack tables deal single-deck – good for those trying to master basic strategy. The three-card poker table game usually draws a crowd (same rules as poker: the object is to make your best three-card hand and beat the dealer), while the $1 crap and 50¢ roulette tables bustle with beginners learning the games without losing a bundle. A good variety of slot machines offer players the prospect of 'Dublin' their jackpot (that's their pun, not ours).

Restaurants and additional casino space occupy the floor above. This used to be a no-smoking zone, but now the only place in the Fitz still off-limits to cigarettes is the McDonald's on the main floor. The spacious booths in the keno lounge are a comfortable place to relax and risk a few dollars, and the outside porch behind the second-floor bar is the only place to get an above-ground view of the Fremont Street Experience.

Entertainment
The First Floor Stage at ground level is a small embarrassment of a lounge, amounting to little more than a raised platform in a particularly dormant corner of the casino.

Eating & drinking
The Shamrock Café serves breakfast, lunch and dinner around the clock. Molly's Buffet is located right next door. The Limerick Steak House offers the usual steakhouse menu at moderate prices. And you can cool off with a fruity concoction at the Lucky Daiquiri Bar.

Gambling
Blackjack ($5-$1,000); craps (2x), Let It Ride; poker; roulette (double zero).

Golden Nugget
129 Fremont Street, at Casino Center Boulevard (385 7111/www.goldennugget.com). Bus 107, 403/ self-parking First Street/valet parking Casino Center Boulevard. **Map** p312 C1.

There's the rest of Downtown, and there's the Golden Nugget. A fixture on the flashiest street in the world since 1946, the Nugget was made over from top to bottom by Steve Wynn in 1987, and now draws attention away from the surrounding neon landscape with its refreshing lack of ostentation. The huge neon sign is gone and the exterior is now lined with a series of tasteful white-gold awnings. The motif is carried inside, with awnings outlined in tiny lights over the gaming areas, and white latticework and gold everywhere. Even the elevators and payphones look gold-plated. Near the elevators, inside a glass case, sits a collection of Alaskan gold nuggets, as well as the world's largest gold nugget, known as the 'Hand of Faith', discovered in Australia in 1980; it's valued at $1 million.

The Nugget's doorman and elegant marble lobby may seem out of place on Fremont Street, but the low table minimums are appropriate. You'll find $3 craps and a selection of nickel machines. Check out the 25¢ zodiac slots – there's one machine for each astrological sign – a cheap but irresistible ploy that plays on the gambler's superstitious nature. As in most casinos, there's a segregated baccarat pit for players with larger bankrolls, but you'll also find $10-minimum blackjack tables, which make the Golden Nugget the mid-level player's best chance to experience life inside a high-roller haven. The sports book is more of a sports boutique: small but plush and comfortable.

Entertainment

After years of dormancy and short-lived production shows, mainroom entertainment has finally returned to the Golden Nugget courtesy of veteran comedian David Brenner, whose nightly shows in the hotel's Theatre Ballroom have played to solid turnouts. The $39 ticket price – a throwback in the era of *O* and *Siegfried & Roy* – may have something to do with his success.

Eating & drinking

The Golden Nugget's Buffet (*see p152*) is one of the best in town, and certainly beats its more upscale competitors hands down when it comes to value for money. The seating area is small, however, so be prepared to take a ticket and wait for at least half an hour for your foody fix. Other good dining options include northern Italian specialities at Stefano's, Cantonese cuisine and mesquite-grilled steaks at Lillie Langtry's, and tasty pizzas at the California Pizza Kitchen. The city's nicest Starbucks outlet is also on site (*see p141* **Caffeine fix**).

Gambling

Mini baccarat ($10-$5,000); blackjack ($5-$5,000); Caribbean Stud; Casino War; craps (2x); Let It Ride; Pai Gow Poker; roulette (double-zero).

Jackie Gaughan's Plaza

1 Main Street, at Fremont Street (386 2110/ www.plazahotelcasino.com). Bus 108, 207/self-parking & valet parking Main Street. **Map** p312 C1.
Ignored by most guidebooks, Jackie Gaughan's Plaza is a marvellous, old-styled caravanserai casino anchored by a bus station and the now defunct train depot. On the corner of Main and Fremont Streets at the heart of the Fremont Street Experience, it's a bit grimy and smoky, but has a lot to offer in the way of colourful Vegas atmosphere and value, 1970s style.

The recently revamped ground-level casino area teems with 1,200 slot machines, including 40 penny machines next to the snack bar. Longtime Vegas visitors will regret the loss of several old-style poker machines, which have been replaced by 900 new themed machines, such as the popular *I Dream of Jeannie* and *Addams Family* models. In the pit, cautious gamblers can play $1 craps or $5 blackjack. Seven-card stud, Texas Hold 'Em and Omaha Hold 'Em poker are played daily in the card room, where

limits are low and the players more gentlemanly than some of the sharks in higher-action games on the Strip. There is also a pan game (a variation of gin rummy) – the only one in Downtown. But if you really want to gamble on the cheap, the keno lounge is your best bet. The Plaza is the only place in the US that offers double keno (simultaneous action on two boards), and with games starting at 40¢, it's a bargain, despite the ridiculous odds.

Entertainment

Hot Trix is an adult revue hosted by veteran comic Pete Barbutti, and featuring the Naked Angels, who aren't really naked. The magic show *Houdini Lives Again* plays in the afternoon in the main showroom. Also check out The Sunspots at the Omaha Lounge. Dressed like ushers at a 1970s Vegas wedding and crooning like half-drunk revellers at a karaoke bar in a bad section of Manila, they have a sizeable local following and are well worth the no-drink minimum.

Eating & drinking

For a quick meal or late-night special, sink into a red leatherette booth at the casino-level Plaza Diner. For a classier menu and a better view, dine one floor up at the Center Stage restaurant. And don't leave without trying a Vienna beef hot dog, a 50¢ shrimp cocktail or a cheap ice-cream at the snack bar.

Gambling

Mini baccarat ($5-$2,000); blackjack ($5-$2,000); craps (10x); Let It Ride; poker; Pai Gow poker; roulette (double zero).

Main Street Station

200 N Main Street, at Stewart Avenue (387 1896/ www.mainstreetcasino.com). Bus 107, 403/self-parking & valet parking Main Street. **Map** p312 C1.
From the moment construction began on Main Street Station in 1990, the hotel-casino (not to be confused with the other Station casinos in town, which are under different ownership) suffered the most tumultuous history of any Downtown property. There were signs of financial difficulty within months of the August 1991 grand opening, and bankruptcy was imminent by December. It closed in June 1992, less than ten months after opening. In 1996, new owner Boyd Gaming and a prominent advertising campaign started to bring in customers, and today the resort has finally left its troubles behind. It is now celebrated as the Golden Nugget's only Downtown rival in understated elegance (or elegance of any kind, for that matter).

The location remains a liability – Main Street Station (two blocks north of the western end of Fremont Street) is not even visible from the FSE mall – but those who find it are in for a treat, as this is one of the most attractive places in Downtown. The Victorian design is accentuated by antiques, stained glass, bronze, marble, bas-reliefs and one-of-a-kind artefacts, including a carved oak fireplace from Preswick Castle in Scotland and a set of doors from an old London bank. A piece of the Berlin Wall is on display in one of the men's restrooms, though no one is quite sure why.

Coming soon...

Much has been made of the Las Vegas building boom of the late 1990s, a thrust of construction that resulted in Bellagio, Mandalay Bay, the Venetian, Paris Las Vegas and the Hyatt Regency at Lake Las Vegas all opening within a few months of each other. That boom crested with the opening of the Aladdin in August 2000, and things have settled down considerably since then. Two other properties – the Suncoast in Summerlin (see p100) and Terrible's Casino on Paradise Road – celebrated millennial openings, but for the first time in years, no new Strip resorts set up shop in 2001. Moreover, there are none planned for 2002 or 2003 either.

It would be foolish to imagine, however, that the casino bosses have called it day as far as large-scale casino construction is concerned: talk of other new resorts are being tossed about all the time; existing properties – such as the Aladdin and the Venetian – are seemingly always expanding and remodelling; proposals for two themed properties on the Strip are moving relentlessly through the planning process, while two new off-Strip resorts are scheduled to open in the last quarter of 2001.

Most prominent of these is the **Palms** (see p92), due to open in December 2001 directly across the street from the Rio and the Gold Coast. Billed as a 'boutique' resort, the Palms will rely on an attractive mix of restaurants, nightclubs, a locals-style casino, cinema complex and childcare centre to draw in the punters. Much further from the Strip, the **Resort at Green Valley Ranch** is partially owned by the Station Casinos chain, so is likely to be geared towards a local customer base, with inexpensive restaurants and a video poker machine-filled casino. With only 200 guest rooms, the Resort is primarily aimed at the Green Valley market.

Back on the Strip, Turnberry Associates are planning a London-themed resort for the site of the El Rancho hotel, with a 44-storey, 2,050-room hotel tower, and a 90,000-square foot (8,400-square metre) casino. The company, which is building high-end condominiums across Paradise Road from the Las Vegas Hilton, bought the El Rancho site for $45 million in May 2000, and imploded the casino in October (see p23

Implosion fever), to ensure that its condo buyers wouldn't have to look out on the run-down site. Instead, if all goes according to plan, the lucky residents will enjoy a picture-postcard view of London's favourite tourist sights: Big Ben, the Tower of London, Tower Bridge and Buckingham Palace reproduced in all their glory but without the bad weather. And, proving that not even royal traditions are inviolable in the city of imitation, outdoor entertainment at the new resort will include a tribute to the Changing of the Guard. No firm date to start construction has been set, but Turnberry – a well bankrolled developer, is actively searching for gaming-experienced partners for the venture.

Meanwhile, a group of California investors has proposed building an Asian-themed, 600-room hotel on ten acres near the Vacation Village hotel-casino at the extreme south end of the Strip. Plans submitted to the county planning department indicate a $104-million Dynasty Forbidden City hotel, which would include a four-storey hotel tower with a U-shaped parking garage wrapped around it like – you guessed it – the Great Wall of China. At press time, no construction dates had been set for this Far Eastern extravaganza.

More intriguing than both these projects, however, is the mooted remake of the old Desert Inn, which was closed shortly after it was purchased by casino mogul Steve Wynn in 2000. Thus far, Wynn has only divulged sketchy plans for a 52-storey resort with up to 2,500 all-suite rooms and a central lake. But that's just a sliver of the 220-acre canvas occupied by the venerable Desert Inn resort and golf course. Ultimately, according to sources, Wynn intends to gut the course and erect up to four resorts, as well as commercial and retail complexes and residential condominiums. If the project proceeds in this manner, it will be akin to the Studio City complex in Southern California, emerging as a self-contained live-work-resort area right on the Las Vegas Strip. With the Fashion Show Mall expanding across the street, there has been talk of Wynn also getting involved in that scheme, furthering his vision of the northern end of the Strip as a bustling multi-use area quite different from the themed mega-resorts further south. Final plans for the site were due to be announced in autumn 2001.

There's a good selection of slot and video poker machines, three-card poker and low limits at the tables; $3 blackjack dominates and the crap tables offer 20x odds. An illuminated sign over the roulette area depicts a single-zero wheel, which is wrong since the actual wheel contains both the single zero and the double zero. On the first level above the ground floor there's a covered pedestrian overpass that leads to Main Street's sister property, the California Club, another attractive and often overlooked Downtown resort.

Entertainment
A jazz/swing trio billed as the Rhythm and Brews performs inside the Triple 7 Brew Pub.

Eating & drinking
The Triple 7 Brew Pub (*see p159*) has excellent sandwiches, Downtown's only sushi bar and a fascinating collection of unusual artefacts. The Garden Court Buffet (*see p154*), featuring a wood-fired pizza oven, is marvellous. Even without the food, the room itself, a sort of antique conservatory with brass and illuminated design elements, is worth a visit.

Gambling
Blackjack ($3-$1,000); craps (20x); Let It Ride; Pai Gow Poker; roulette (double zero); Spanish 21 (at the California Club).

Locals Casinos

Most people who live in Las Vegas gamble, whether they'll admit to it or not. Ask them where the machines are paying, and they'll probably steer you to one of the so-called locals casinos – those located away from the Strip and Downtown areas. This isn't another gamblers' superstition. The locals casinos really do deliver better payouts on video poker, and probably on slots, too. Of course, you've still got to find the right machine at the right time – that's why they call it gambling.

The divide between tourist and local hangouts seems to widen every year, since Las Vegas residents are less inclined to fight the traffic in the resort corridors. There used to be resistance to building casinos near residential neighbourhoods, but gambling has lost so much of its sinister reputation that casinos are now welcomed into most (though not all) areas like any other commercial venture. Residents use them as convenient places to meet for lunch or on social occasions.

Some casinos have movie theatres (the Station chain, Orleans; *see chapter* **Film**) and bowling alleys (Castaways, Sam's Town, Gold Coast, Orleans, Santa Fe; *see chapter* **Sport & Fitness**) that also draw a strong local following; some even have dedicated childcare facilities where parents can stash the kids in safety while they play, eat, drink or catch a flick (*see chapter* **Children**).

The Gold Coast and its sister casino, the Orleans, the Station casinos, the two branches of Arizona Charlie's and the Fiesta are the busiest gambling dens in town. Most of the locals casinos are scattered around the city, but the Castaways, Arizona Charlie's East, Boulder Station and Sam's Town are relatively near one another, in what is known locally as the **Boulder Strip**. The Fiesta, Texas Station and Santa Fe Station all lie along North Rancho Drive, on what is called the **Rancho Strip**.

If you're in town to see the fabulous Las Vegas of the tourist brochures, you won't find it in the neighbourhood casinos, which are attractive, clean and marginally themed, but hardly as lavish as the mega-resorts that have made the city world-famous. The popularity of these casinos derives from other attributes: there's plenty of parking, both valet- and self-; it's easier to get in and out, without dealing with the gridlock of the Strip; the food, especially at the buffets, is generally good and inexpensive; the video poker is positive and there's plenty of hand-held blackjack. What's more the locals casinos offer easy comps through the liberal slot clubs and rating systems; and they promote extensively to the surrounding zip codes with coupons, drawings, two-for-ones and assorted freebies.

Arizona Charlie's
740 S Decatur Boulevard, at Alta Drive, South-west Las Vegas (258 5200/www.azcharlies. com). Bus 103, 207/ self-parking & valet parking S Decatur Boulevard.
A no-frills bunkhouse for serious players, the original Arizona Charlie's on Decatur is long on action and short on atmosphere. The theme is the Yukon gold rush, though you won't notice much of it – the interior design here consists of little more than a floor and a ceiling and row after row of machines. There's $2 double-deck blackjack, $1 roulette, poker (seven-card stud and hold 'em), bingo and a plain but spacious sports book. China Charlie's has replaced the more popular Chin's for Chinese food; the Yukon Grille is a good steak and chop house and the Sourdough Café's bargain steak-and-eggs special will set you back just $2.49. The Naughty Ladies Saloon (*see p201*), once the exclusive home of the resort's Western Dance show, now plays host to a rotating line-up of the city's veteran lounge performers, including the likes of Checkmates and the Jerry Tiffe Band.

In 2000, Arizona Charlie's opened a second branch on the Boulder Strip. It features the same selection of restaurants plus the Wild West Buffet, and a slightly larger casino. The Palace Grand Lounge showcases live music, with billings that are heavy on country and western.
Branch: Arizona Charlie's East, 4575 S Boulder Highway, between E Flamingo Road & E Twain Avenue, East Las Vegas (951 9100).

Sunset Station. *See p101.*

always take top honours in the *Las Vegas Review-Journal*'s 'Best of Vegas' survey. Banks of no-smoking machines were a good idea; putting them next to the smoking machines was not. There's occasional $2 blackjack and $1 roulette for low-rollers, one of the city's bigger bingo rooms and a large bowling alley (*see p229*). Two lounges and an intimate showroom churn out country, jazz and swing music. For food, choose between the Cortez Room – a mid-priced steakhouse – and the Mediterranean Room, which serves seafood and Italian cuisine. Service is a bit slow, but the breadsticks are always hot. There's also a buffet and 24-hour coffeeshop. The Gold Coast is next to the Rio, and there are shuttle buses to both from the Strip.

Orleans

4500 W Tropicana Avenue, at Arville Street, Southwest Las Vegas (365 7111/www.orleanscasino.com). Bus 201/self-parking & valet parking W Tropicana Avenue, Cameron Street or Arville Street.

This trim, bright casino off the main drag is a big hit with locals, and worth a visit for its easy parking, easy navigation, good gaming returns and some great lounge acts. However, despite painstaking attention to detail – French Quarter-style latticework, hand-carved door frames and ceiling trim – the overall feel is closer to an aircraft hangar than the jazz-soused intimacy of Bourbon Street. Still, the high ceilings do make an airy (and less smoky) change from the oppressive, chandeliered norm.

The casino offers lively, low-limit action: the poker room is one of the best in town, with 'bad-beat jackpots' (awarded to the player who loses with a very big hand) that sometimes top $40,000, and tournaments daily, at noon and 7pm. The Orleans has a local reputation for loose slots, although it moved out some of the best video poker machines in 2001 to make room for new multiplay versions. Even louder than the slot machines, though, are the sports fans in the casino book, especially on weekends and Monday nights during football season.

You might hope to find some great jazz in the 999-seat Orleans Showroom but, in fact, country and classic rock are the usual fare. Prices are reasonable and the intimate feel and good acoustics give ageing performers such as Jerry Lewis and the Everly Brothers a perfect setting to recapture a bit of their lost magic. A 'Best of Broadway' series of shows will be staged in the showroom from December 2001. For a Dixieland sound, try Bourbon Street Cabaret (*see p200*). You'll also hear some great zydeco at the small stage next to the Piano Bar. The Century Orleans 12 Cinema (*see p203*) has 12 huge screens, great sound and stadium-style seating, and there's also a 70-lane bowling alley on site (*see p229*). Six different restaurants prepare everything from beef to Las Vegas-style jambalaya. However, for good food and a quiet atmosphere, your only choices are Vito's (Italian delicacies) and the Canal Street Grille. Don't forget to try a grilled frankfurter at Terrible's (it's a locals' favourite).

Castaways

2800 Fremont Street, between E Charleston Boulevard & Sahara Avenue, East Las Vegas (385 9123). Bus 107, 206/self-parking Fremont Street or Atlantic Street/valet parking Fremont Street.

The granddaddy of all locals casinos, the Castaways has been in operation since 1954 under its original name of the Showboat. In 2000, dwindling crowds inspired a top-to-bottom makeover. With a new identity, the Castaways is out to recapture its former prominence on the Boulder Strip.

The bright, festive casino has 25¢ table-top video poker machines with a clear view of the lounge, and blackjack tables that do not allow mid-deck entry by new players – a counter-measure against card counting. The 1,200-seat Bingo Gardens is the largest facility of its kind in town, and one of the nicest looking. The 24-hour, 106-lane bowling centre is the largest in the US, and plays host to several professional tournaments (*see p231*). Dining choices include the San Brisas Buffet, which features hamburgers cooked to order, the Prime Cut Steakhouse, and the Blue Marlin restaurant, serving Spanish-style seafood and Mexican specialities, including a special salsa cart that offers 14 varieties of salsa served tableside.

Gold Coast

4000 W Flamingo Road, at Valley View Boulevard, West of Strip (367 7111/www.goldcoastcasino.com). Bus 202/self-parking & valet parking Valley View Boulevard, Flamingo Road or Wynn Road.
Map p311 X3.

In 1984, the Barbary Coast took its act off the Strip and begat the Gold Coast. Like most sequels, it is bigger – 100,000sq ft (9,300sq m) of casino space, compared with 30,000sq ft (2,790sq m) at the Barbary – and relies on the same formula for success. The Barbary's Victorian trappings and San Francisco ambience have been maintained, though not with the same attention to detail. Locals love the machine selection and the slot club, both of which

Sam's Town

5111 Boulder Highway, at Flamingo Road, East Las Vegas (456 7777/www.samstownlv.com). Bus 107, 201, 202/self-parking & valet parking Boulder Highway, Flamingo Road or Nellis Boulevard.

Opened in 1979, Sam's Town remained a low-key, Western-themed gambling hall for 15 years until the 1990s, when several expansions and makeovers transformed the property into a cowboy theme park. The casino has the same low-limit tables and machines as before, but now it's big enough to drive cattle through. Take the escalator downstairs for 24-hour bowling (*see p229*) or head upstairs for a free Texas two-step lesson in the dance hall. The lounge offers country music from up-and-coming bands.

An enclosed atrium, with real trees and a waterfall, houses shops, restaurants and the Sunset Stampede water and laser show, complete with animatronic animals and a booming Western soundtrack; it's presented four times daily. In December, the holiday light display in the courtyard is the most beautiful in Las Vegas, and definitely worth a visit. The most recent renovation, completed in 2000, has added a new, expanded buffet on the first floor and an 18-screen movie theatre with stadium seating. Sam's Town Live (*see p200*), a 1,100-seat concert and banquet hall, showcases pop, country and rock stars.

Suncoast

9090 Alta Drive, at Rampart Avenue, North-west Las Vegas (636 7111/www.suncoastcasino.com). Bus 207/self-parking & valet parking Alta Drive & Rampart Avenue.

The latest of the Coast casinos opened in late 2000 in the upmarket Summerlin area, 20 miles (32km) west of the Strip. The resort enjoys a beautiful out-of-town location, and is within a chip shot of four major golf courses. Some of the guest rooms, in fact, overlook the Badlands course (*see p231*) and the TPC at The Canyons. Like the other Coast properties (Gold Coast, Barbary Coast and the Orleans), the Suncoast's casino floor is large and player-friendly, with plenty of machines, bingo, a race and sports book, and a progressive slot club that plies regular players with comps and perks. Designed in similar fashion to the Gold Coast, the Suncoast is a Mediterranean-style, low-rise building with a red tile roof and adobe-like walls. The 440 good-sized rooms and suites are contained in a ten-storey tower and are decorated in Southwestern earth tones.

Entertainment at the Suncoast is focused on the Showroom, which stages oldie rock bands, such as The Lettermen, Little River Band and Average White Band. As a contrast, a taste of Vegas-style popular band music is provided by singer Vincent Falcone and his 20-piece orchestra. The Suncoast has a standard all-you-can-eat buffet and coffeeshop, but you'd be better off dining upstairs at Primo's, which serves good-quality steaks, seafood and lamb specialities. Another decent spot is Don Miguel's, a Mexican restaurant offering tasty and innovative specialities from south of the border.

Station Casinos

The phenomenal success of the railroad station-themed Palace Station led the suburban Station Casinos chain (www.stationcasinos.com) to open three sister properties, all of which are bigger and slightly fancier (the Las Vegas version of Monopoly features all four of them as the railroad properties). Station Casinos is now the proud owner of nine hyper-popular casinos and a tenth is on its way, off I-215 in Green Valley (*see p97* **Coming soon…**).

In the past decade, the Station chain has picked up a total of more than 125 'Best of Las Vegas' awards from the *Las Vegas Review-Journal*. It's also beloved by Las Vegans for its slot club. You can earn points in one of the casinos and redeem them in any of the others; no other locals chain can claim that perk.

Boulder Station

4111 Boulder Highway, at E Desert Inn Road, East Las Vegas (432 7777/www.boulderstation.com). Bus 107, 112/self-parking & valet parking Boulder Highway.

Families with small children flock to Boulder Station for its 11-screen Regal Cinema (*see p204*) and for Kids Quest (*see p190*), a huge indoor play area that can entertain toddlers through to 12-year-olds. The play area for adults is pretty big, too – there's plenty of elbow room in the casino, one of the largest in town, and it features all the usual games plus a few of the more cutting-edge machines. Dark wood and stained glass provide a posher-than-usual setting for locals. The Railhead lounge (*see p201*) is really a mini-showroom; the sights and sounds inside are usually open to the casino, but a black curtain drops for shows featuring more prominent performers. John Waite's occasional concerts at Boulder Station are always a hot ticket.

Fiesta

2400 N Rancho Drive, between Lake Mead Boulevard & Carey Avenue, North Las Vegas (631 7000/ www.fiestacasinohotel.com). Bus 106, 211/self-parking Rancho Drive, Lake Mead Boulevard or Carey Avenue/valet parking Lake Mead Boulevard.

The 'ultimate' locals joint – so called because Las Vegans travel from all over the city to play and eat here. The Fiesta, recently acquired by the Station Casinos chain, bills itself as 'the Royal Flush Capital of the World' and for good reason: although some claim the machines have tightened up since Station Casinos took over, the Fiesta still offers some of the best video poker on the planet. The machines are packed so tightly into the casino that aisles and walkways can be uncomfortably narrow, but locals will brave the squeeze for the chance to line up a winning hand. The slot club is known for once-a-week triple-point days and no-hassle food comps, even to the Festival Buffet (*see p153*), which features an excellent barbecue. The Fiesta also has a 'drive-up sports-betting window', where you don't even have to get out of your car to place a bet on an upcoming game. There are only 100 rooms and few guest amenities, but as well as the buffet, there's Garduno's Mexican restaurant (see p149) and the San Francisco Steakhouse.

In November 1999, the Fiesta unveiled a stunning $26-million casino annexe called Spin City, which added a fast-food court plus Garduno's Margarita Factory & Blue Agave Oyster Bar, with 300 types of margarita and the most extensive selection of tequilas in town. But the centrepiece is Roxy's Pipe Organ Pizzeria, serving Regina's Pizza (famous in Boston since the 1920s) and featuring a 1927 Kimball organ. The organ, which occupies a three-storey back wall of Roxy's, has 3,000 pipes, horns and fluted tubes. At 5pm on selected days it fills the big pizzeria with every sound known to man. In 2001, Roxy's underwent a $400,000 makeover, transforming the day-time pizzeria into a night-time lounge. Don't miss the Fiesta.

Palace Station

2411 W Sahara Avenue, at Rancho Drive, West of Strip (367 2411/www.palacestation.com). Bus 204, 401/self-parking & valet parking W Sahara Avenue, Rancho Drive or Teddy Drive. **Map** p311 X2.

Once known as the Bingo Palace, this is the flagship property of the Station chain. Local Las Vegans love it, despite the too-smoky, no-frills atmosphere. However, customer service has plummeted of late; long, slow-moving lines at the cashier's cages and a shortage of casino floormen and change girls have even the most loyal Station patrons grumbling. The tables offer $1 blackjack and 50¢ roulette.

Amid the 2,200 gaming machines are six restaurants of varying quality: the Feast Buffet (see p153) no longer ranks among the best in town, but the Pasta Palace serves good Italian fare at very reasonable prices. The Trax Nightclub features a variety of high-energy music, plus the occasional live jazz band. It also sometimes morphs into Laugh Trax, a good comedy club (see p202).

Santa Fe Station

4949 N Rancho Drive, at US 95 (junction 90A), North-west Las Vegas (658 4900/www.santafe casino.com). Bus 106/self-parking & valet parking N Rancho Drive or Lone Mountain Road.

Santa Fe Station opened in 1991, as one of the earliest, and still the furthest out, of the locals casinos. It has 200 rooms and a smallish casino, with low-limit table games, low-hold video poker, a 450-seat bingo room, and a wide variety of slot machines – for which the Station casinos are famous. There's also a 60-lane bowling alley on site (see p229) and a professional ice-skating arena (see p232).

Its four restaurants include two upper-end dining choices – the Taos Steakhouse, serving prime cuts and Tex-Mex specialities, and Capri, featuring seafood and Italian dishes. There is also a coffeeshop and a buffet on site with rear seats that overlook the ice-skating rink.

Sunset Station

1301 W Sunset Road, at Stephanie Street, Henderson (547 7777/www.sunsetstation.com). Bus 212, 217, 402/self-parking & valet parking Stephanie Street, W Sunset Road, Marks Street or Warm Springs Road.

Opened in 1997, Sunset Station is now the most satisfying and successful manifestation of the Station chain's winning formula. It's big, colourful, friendly, fancy, but not too fancy, and offers an excellent assortment of table and electronic games. It is also one of the first casinos in town to debut new slot machines, such as the *Austin Powers* and *I Dream of Jeannie* progressive games. The Spanish-style architecture of the exterior, the lobby and the shopping and restaurant areas is rendered in surprisingly fine detail. However, finding landmarks inside the low-ceilinged, labyrinthine gaming area can be a challenge, and as a result, it's easy to get lost.

Don't miss the gaudy Gaudi Bar (see p160) in the centre, or the buffet; the queues start early for lunch and dinner, but the food is worth it. The Sonoma Steakhouse has earned honours in national publications for its beefy choices, but if your food budget is limited there's also Fatburger, a fine fast-food joint (see p130), and a Krispy Kreme doughnut shop. As at Boulder Station, the Sunset's enclosed lounge occasionally draws big-name performers, and there's a great 13-screen Regal Cinema (see p204) and a Kids Quest childcare centre (see p190). Sunset Station can also be a convenient stop on the way back into town after a visit to Boulder City or the Hoover Dam.

Texas Station

2101 Texas Star Lane, at N Rancho Drive, between Lake Mead Boulevard & Vegas Drive, North Las Vegas (631 1000/www.texasstation.com). Bus 106, 208/self-parking N Rancho Drive/valet parking Lake Mead Boulevard or N Rancho Drive. **Map** p311 X1.

Everything's bigger in Texas, or so they say, and you'll believe it after walking the length of this 90,000sq ft (8,370sq m) casino, past the impressive variety of machines for which all Station casinos are renowned. The Lone Star theme is picked up in the miniature oil wells that rhythmically pump over the slot carousels; the red-fringed dance hall-girl attire of the cocktail waitresses; and in the poker room, where the game of choice is, of course, Texas Hold 'Em. Country music, as well as the popular 1980s cover band Love Shack, are featured in the Armadillo Lounge (see p200), and visitors are invited to take to the stage every Thursday evening for karaoke. The 3,000-seat South Padre Amphitheater presents country stars as well as some non-title boxing matches (see p233 **Ringside**). There's a Kids Quest (see p190), an 18-screen Regal Cinema (see p204) on the north side of the casino and a full complement of restaurants, from Italian and Chinese to steaks and seafood, and a Texas-sized buffet with a Texas chilli serving station. As you enter from either side of the building, note the historical plaque next to the doors: 'On this site in 1897, nothing happened'.

The Strip

Huge casinos, streetside spectacle, thrill rides and even a couple of museums: Las Vegas Boulevard South is where it all happens.

Ever since mobster Bugsy Siegel opened his Flamingo Hotel in 1946 on a spot far from the developed areas of town (the closest resort then was the original El Rancho, on the south-west corner of the Strip and Sahara Avenue), the Strip has been an oasis of decadence in the desert, luring travellers with its gaudy imagery and irresistible temptations. You won't find 'the Strip' in any street index – it's not an official designation, but a universally used nickname for the nearly four-mile (6.4 kilometre) stretch of Las Vegas Boulevard South that runs from Sahara Avenue in the north to the 'Welcome to fabulous Las Vegas' sign in the south. The following description runs south to north.

Russell Road to Tropicana Avenue

Map p316 A9-A8

The few remaining tiny motor inns of the 1950s and '60s, replete with neon signs far flashier than the hotels themselves, are near Russell

Road. To the east is the **Little Chapel of the West**, a part of the Old Frontier Hotel and site of many celebrity weddings (*see p239* **Celebrity splicings**). The chapel has been moved several times, most recently from the front lawn of the old Hacienda casino, which was imploded on New Year's Eve 1996, to its new site just south of the **Glass Pool Inn** (*see p59*) – notable for its above-ground swimming pool with giant glass portholes in the sides, and the site of many movie scenes. The Glass Pool Inn used to be called the Mirage, until that name was sold to casino magnate Steve Wynn to be used for his mega-resort further north.

Across from the Glass Pool is the former Hacienda site, now home to both the **Mandalay Bay** (*see p78*), a South Seas-themed mega-resort, and the subdued, non-gaming **Four Seasons** – the first Las Vegas hotel to win the coveted five-diamond award (*see p58*). At Mandalay Bay, don't miss the new **Shark Reef** aquarium (*see p104*) or the excellent selection of restaurants. Just south of the resort, the **Bali Hai Golf Club** (*see p231*) continues the Pacific

Miss Liberty welcomes you to... Las Vegas. *See p103.*

Vegas on the cheap Casino freebies

Sightseeing in Vegas begins at – where else? – the casinos, which have a long tradition of creating attractions to entice patrons. Some are more exciting than others, but the following are all free and worth a look.

Circus acts
Circus Circus. *See p109.*
Check out the bizarre goings-on in the casino with the big top.

Fountain show
Bellagio. *See p105.*
The city's best free attraction is created by 1,200 water cannons in Bellagio's lake.

Dragon battle
Excalibur. *See p103.*
Merlin shows that pesky dragon who's really the boss around here.

Lion Habitat
MGM Grand. *See p103.*
Get up close to the MGM lions and their cubs.

Masquerade Show
Rio. *See p113.*
Aerial acrobatics, gliding floats and plenty of pzazz, just off the Strip.

Pirate battle
Treasure Island. *See p106.*
Dramatic pyrotechnics and hammy theatrics make this one of the best of the Strip-side spectacles.

Volcano eruption
Mirage. *See p106.*
Watch this mini volcano spew fire and smoke onto the waterfalls and over the surrounding lagoon.

Sightseeing

island theme, while to the north is a partially constructed retail mall, due to open in late 2002. Next up is the unmistakable pyramid of **Luxor** (*see p77*), with its trademark laser lights flitting up the sides and a dramatic beacon shooting into the sky. Inside you'll find an **IMAX Theater** (*see below*), a state-of-the-art games arcade, the **Search for the Obelisk** ride (*see p104*) and a pretty authentic recreation of Tutankhamen's burial chamber in **King Tut's Tomb & Museum** (*see p104*).

At the intersection with Tropicana Avenue, you are within easy walking distance of more hotel rooms than in the whole of San Francisco. On the south-east corner are the white towers of the **Tropicana** (*see p87*). The old boy on the block, the Trop was built in 1957 and it shows, but you may want to pop in to visit the **Casino Legends Hall of Fame** (*see below*), a homage to past entertainers and casino moguls. Across Tropicana to the north is the **MGM Grand** (*see p80*) – the largest hotel on the planet, with its signature lion – the world's largest bronze sculpture – standing guard above the entrance. There are more big cats to be found inside the resort, lurking in the **Lion Habitat** (*see p104*).

To the north-west is **New York-New York** (*see p83*), where the Statue of Liberty replica is hosed down by mock fire boats and the **Manhattan Express** rollercoaster swoops overhead (*see p104*). Head inside for family fun at the **Coney Island Emporium** (*see below*). Across a walkway sits the medieval-themed **Excalibur** (*see p75*), which was built in 1990 but is already starting to show its age. King

Arthur's Vegas-style court performs every 30 minutes from 10am to 10pm daily inside this fairytale castle, while outside, a fire-breathing dragon does battle with Merlin the Magician, but frankly, it's all rather tame.

Around the Tropicana intersection the seething crowds spill onto street corners and squeeze through the pedestrian overpasses.

Casino Legends Hall of Fame
Tropicana, 3801 Las Vegas Boulevard South, at E Tropicana Avenue (739 5444). Bus 201, 301, 302. **Open** 7am-9pm daily. **Admission** $4; $3 concessions; under-18s must be accompanied. **No credit cards.**
The Hall of Fame has hundreds of photos, documents and audio and video displays covering the Mob's involvement in Vegas, old-time stage acts and hotel implosions. Although there is an entry fee, you can usually find free admission coupons in tourist magazines or inside the Tropicana casino.

Coney Island Emporium
New York-New York, 3790 Las Vegas Boulevard South, at W Tropicana Avenue (736 4100). Bus 201, 301, 302. **Open** 8.30am-2am daily.
This arcade and family amusement centre recreates the atmosphere of the original Coney Island. It has over 200 video and midway games, Bumper Cabs, a prize counter and lots of sticky cotton candy.

IMAX Theater
Luxor, 3900 Las Vegas Boulevard South, between W Tropicana Avenue & Russell Road (262 4000). Bus 201, 301, 302. **Open** 9am-midnight daily. **Tickets** $8.95 single feature; $13.50 double feature. **Credit** AmEx, DC, Disc, MC, V.

Since the closing of the Caesars Palace Omnimax, the Luxor's IMAX is the only game in town when it comes to overwhelming movies. The facility is impressive, with a huge screen and a monster sound system. It shows the documentaries formerly booked by Caesars, as well as more hokey features.

In Search of the Obelisk
Luxor, 3900 Las Vegas Boulevard South, between W Tropicana Avenue & Russell Road (262 4000).
Bus 201, 301, 302. **Open** 9am-11pm daily.
Tickets $7. **Credit** AmEx, Disc, MC, V.
One of Vegas's better motion-simulators takes the audience on a *Raiders of the Lost Ark*-style action adventure through the Luxor archeological dig. Realistic, but too long to be thoroughly enjoyable.

King Tut's Tomb & Museum
Luxor, 3900 Las Vegas Boulevard South, between W Tropicana Avenue & Russell Road (262 4000).
Bus 201, 301, 302. **Open** 9am-11pm daily.
Admission $5. **Credit** AmEx, DC, Disc, MC, V.
Worth a visit for the full-size re-creation of Tutankhamen's burial chamber and his golden throne and sarcophagus – hand-crafted by Egyptian artisans in historically correct materials.

Lion Habitat
MGM Grand, 3799 Las Vegas Boulevard South, at E Tropicana Avenue (891 7777). Bus 201, 301, 302.
Open 24hrs daily. **Admission** free.
Not to be outdone by the Mirage's white tigers (*see p106*), the MGM is proud of its own pride of 'display' lions. The habitat is distressingly small for the animals, but the glass walls mean you can get a close-up view of the cubs and adult lions – up to five at any one time may be lurking among the foliage. Admission is free, but if you want your photo taken with Simba it will cost 20 bucks.

Manhattan Express
New York-New York, 3790 Las Vegas Boulevard South, at W Tropicana Avenue (740 6969). Bus 201, 301, 302. **Open** 10.30am-10.30pm Mon-Thur, Sun; 10.30am-midnight Fri, Sat. **Tickets** $10.50.
No credit cards.
Gotham never saw anything like this – a roller-coaster soaring around skyscrapers and Miss Liberty. The Manhattan Express twists, loops and dives at breakneck speeds, and features the first ever 'heartline roll', which creates the sensation a pilot feels when going through a barrel roll in an aeroplane. Try hard to smile in the last section – this is where the photos are taken.

Shark Reef
Mandalay Bay, 3950 Las Vegas Boulevard South, at Russell Road (632 4555). Bus 201, 301, 302.
Open 10am-10pm daily. **Admission** $13.95; $9.95 concessions; free under-5s. **Credit** AmEx, Disc, MC, V.
Nearly two million gallons of water course through this exhibit's four separate areas. A 'walk-through' aquarium, the Shark Reef is filled with 100 species

of underwater life, including rays, jellyfish, eels, and, of course, eleven varieties of sharks. A perfect complement to the South Seas-themed Mandalay Bay, the Shark Reef is an unexpected gem in a city lacking in the educational entertainment department.

Tropicana Avenue to Harmon Avenue

Map p316 A8
A pleasant pedestrian boardwalk that morphs into a replica Brooklyn Bridge leads north on the eastern side of New York-New York as far as the **ESPN Zone** restaurant and sports bar (*see below*). As you walk, note the old-fashioned Pepsi and Pete sign on the wall of a replica brownstone building, in direct competition with the Times Square-style giant neon Coke bottle on the **Showcase Mall** across the street. Vegas has become the latest battleground in the so-called cola wars, and the stakes are enormous. Coke reportedly pays the MGM $1 million each year for sponsorship rights and exclusivity at the hotel, while Pepsi has a similar arrangement at New York-New York. Also in the Showcase Mall is **M&M World** and **GameWorks**, a huge games arcade with the world's tallest indoor climbing wall (for both, *see p105*). Further on, you'll find night-time dance action at **Club Utopia** (*see p212*) and excellent fast food at **Fatburger** (*see p130*). These are followed by the pink and mauve **Polo Towers** hotel (*see p62*), at the top of which is the fine **Polo Lounge** (*see p156*), perfect for a quiet cocktail and a great view of Las Vegas Boulevard.

Due west are the fountains of the glamorous **Monte Carlo** (*see p83*), flanked on the south by a Vegas landmark and favourite of the locals, a petrol station with a neon sign offering gamblers 'free aspirin and tender sympathy', and on the north by the tired façade of the **Holiday Inn Boardwalk** casino, which is rumoured to be one of the next places in town up for implosion. (The hokey fairground rides facing the Strip are for show only.) On the east side the block ends at the **Harley-Davidson Café** (*see p131*), which comes complete with an oversized motorcycle protruding from the front of the building, while across the street the former Country Star restaurant has been transformed into **Seven**, a trendy restaurant and DJ lounge (*see p211*).

ESPN Zone
New York-New York, 3790 Las Vegas Boulevard South, at W Tropicana Avenue (933 3776). Bus 201, 301, 302. **Open** 11am-midnight Mon-Thur; 11am-4am Fri; 8am-4am Sat; 8am-11pm Sun.
Credit AmEx, Disc, MC, V.

Replacing one themed restaurant (Motown Cafe) with another (ESPN Zone) may not seem like a smart plan, unless you know that ESPN Zone is rapidly becoming the most popular themed entertainment chain in America. A family-friendly, hyper-sized combination of a restaurant, sports bar and games arcade, ESPN Zone offers decent American food, big-screen sports and a games room all in one place.

GameWorks

Showcase Mall, 3785 Las Vegas Boulevard South, between E Tropicana & Harmon Avenues (432 4263). Bus 301, 302. **Open** 10am-1am Mon-Thur, Sun; 10am-2am Fri, Sat. **Admission** free. *Arcade games* $20 1hr game pass; $27 3hr game pass; or pay for individual games. **Credit** AmEx, Disc, MC, V.
If you'd rather shove quarters into a video game than a slot machine, GameWorks is for you. The brainchild of Steven Spielberg, this huge madhouse is the ultimate arcade and a good place for trying out the latest video game creations (50¢-$5). There are more than 250 arcade games, all the latest video games, a billiards lounge, two restaurants, a coffee bar and a 75ft (23m) high indoor rock climbing wall – the world's tallest. Attendants help climbers with helmets and rigging, and collect fees ($10). There's sometimes live music on Fridays and Saturdays.

M&M World

Showcase Mall, 3769 Las Vegas Boulevard South, between E Tropicana & Harmon Avenues (740 2525). **Open** 10am-midnight Mon-Thur, Sun; 10am-1am Fri, Sat. **Credit** MC, V.
This is a four-level chocolate lover's paradise. Check out M&M Academy, an interactive entertainment attraction showing visitors how these chocolate candies earn their trademark. The attraction includes a 3-D movie, and 'graduates' get a diploma.

Harmon Avenue to Flamingo Road

Map p316 A7

The new **Aladdin** (*see p69*), which opened in summer 2000, stands to the east of the Harmon Avenue intersection, engulfing the original **Aladdin Theater for the Performing Arts** (*see p219*) with new construction. The most prominent feature here is the front façade, which leads directly into the **Desert Passage** shopping mall (*see p162*) and the adjoining **Blue Note Jazz Club** (*see p222*). This intersection is also the proposed (but disputed) site for a new Vegas attraction: a 500-foot (152.4-metre) high-tech observation wheel, larger than the London Eye.

The west side of the Strip is unspectacular, though: a helipad for airborne city tours, a strip mall of T-shirt shops and the time-share **Jockey Club**, which looked horribly out of place even when it was built in the 1970s.

Bellagio's dancing fountains.

To the north of the Aladdin is the spectacular (but small) **Paris-Las Vegas**, with its half-scale **Eiffel Tower** (*see p106*), spot-on architectural replicas, grand fountains and **Mon Ami Gabi** – a popular street-side brasserie (*see p135*). A little skip north brings you to the original 'Four Corners' at Flamingo Road. On the south-west corner, at **Bally's** (*see p69*), a blazing new animated sign adds to the existing bizarre light-and-water tunnels. To the north sits the wedged-in **Barbary Coast** (3595 Las Vegas Boulevard South; 737 7111/1-888 227 2279), the home of **Drai's** supper club (*see p133*).

Across to the south is the drama of **Bellagio** (*see p71*) – whose large replica of Lake Como comes alive every afternoon and night with an impressive **fountain show**. Every 30 minutes during the day (3-8pm Mon-Fri; noon-8pm Sat, Sun) and every 15 minutes in the evening (8pm-midnight daily), the eight-acre (3.2-hectare) lake becomes the site of incredible fountain displays choreographed to music ranging from Pavarotti to Sinatra. The 1,200 water 'cannons', arranged in lines and circles, shoot water that dances and sways to the music, and reaches as high as 240 feet (73 metres). The best seats are in the Bellagio restaurants, but you also get a great view from the pavements out front, which have alcoves and trees but, unfortunately, no benches. The top of the Eiffel Tower at Paris, opposite, is also a fine viewing point. Inside Bellagio, don't miss the **Gallery of Fine Art** (*see p106*) or the glass-domed **Botanical Gardens**, which lie beyond the lobby and are home to thousands of exotic plants and flowers.

The opulent and ever expanding **Caesars Palace** (*see p72*) commands attention with its striking blue-white lighting and huge fountains. Outside Caesars, just to the north of the main fountain (the one that Evel Knievel's son vaulted with his motorcycle in 1989) is a small open-air **Brahma shrine**, where visitors worship and leave offerings of fruit and flowers in exchange for luck. It's a tranquil place to pause while walking along the Strip.

Bellagio Gallery of Fine Art

Bellagio, 3600 Las Vegas Boulevard South, at W Flamingo Road (693 7722/www.bellagiolasvegas. com). Bus 202, 301, 302. **Open** 8am-11pm daily (children admitted 9-11am daily). **Admission** $12. **Credit** AmEx, Disc, MC, V.

Following the sale of Mirage Resorts to the MGM, former owner Steve Wynn took much of this gallery's art collection with him. Thinking that a private art collection was a silly way to hold capital, MGM sold most of what was left. Luckily the company has kept the gallery alive by curating some exceptional exhibitions, including masterworks from the Washington, DC-based Phillips Collection and the impressive private collection of Steve Martin. There's a large giftshop next to the gallery.

Eiffel Tower

Paris, 3655 Las Vegas Boulevard South, between Harmon Avenue & E Flamingo Road (946 7000). Bus 202, 301, 302. **Open** 9am-1am daily. **Tickets** $8; $6 concessions; free under-5s. **Credit** AmEx, Disc, MC, V.

OK, so it's only half the size of the real Eiffel Tower in Paris, but the Vegas version gives visitors a great view of the Strip and the surrounding mountains. You take a lift to the 46-storey observation deck – go at dusk to watch the Strip suddenly light up as if someone's flicked a switch.

Flamingo to Spring Mountain Road

Map p316 A7-A6

Just north of the Barbary Coast, the **Flamingo** (*see p76*) features some of Las Vegas's best remaining and most oft-photographed neon. The casino is on the same spot as Bugsy Siegel's Flamingo, although nothing of the original property remains. In its place are lush grounds and winding pathways that take you past penguins, Chilean flamingos, Mandarin ducks and koi fish swimming in ponds under three-storey high waterfalls. If it weren't for the tennis courts, pool and spa, it would almost look like a wildlife habitat.

The smaller **O'Sheas** (3355 Las Vegas Boulevard South; 697 2711) and the right-up-to-the-asphalt oriental-looking **Imperial Palace** (*see p52*) follow. It's worth seeking

Battling the Brits at **Treasure Island**.

out the palace's impressive **Auto Collection** (*see p108*), secreted in the parking garage at the back of the hotel. Across the street is the romanesque arch leading to the Roman-themed **Forum Shops** at Caesars Palace (*see p162*). Here, under an ever-changing 'sky', animated statues come to life every hour for a bizarre seven-minute revel with dancing water and laser lights. Nearby, the **Atlantis** attraction atop an aquarium by Virgin Records offers an unintentionally hilarious lights and special effects drama every hour on the hour. Better than either, however, are the **Race for Atlantis** ride (*see p108*) and the **Cinema Ride** (*see p107*), both located below the shops at either end of the mall.

Immediately to the north begins the block-long tropical paradise created by the **Mirage** (*see p81*) and **Treasure Island** (*see p87*), whose façade and pirate ships are straight from the Robert Louis Stevenson handbook. In 1989, the Mirage introduced the first large-scale free spectacle to Las Vegas: an erupting 54-foot (16-metre) **volcano**, next door to the Strip. Even though the volcano is rather small, lacks a cinder dome and looks more like a granite wall, the ten-minute spectacle (every 15 minutes; 8pm-midnight daily) – spewing fire and a piña colada scent into the palm trees, waterfalls and lagoon – is worth a look.

Inside the Mirage, you can see Siegfried & Roy's white tigers looking bored in a glass-enclosed compound, have a cocktail inside a tropical rainforest and view pygmy sharks and multicoloured fish in a large aquarium behind the registration desk. For a closer look at the illusionists' exotic pets visit the **Secret Garden** and the **Dolphin Habitat** (*see p107*).

Treasure Island fronts the Strip with a replica of an 18th-century sea village set on a blue-water lagoon, and surrounded by rock cliffs, palm trees and nautical artifacts. The focus of attention however are the two fully rigged ships – a pirate galleon and a British frigate that enact a mock **battle** every 90 minutes (4-11.30pm daily). The show fills the pavement to capacity with onlookers who stare slack-jawed at the cannons blazing, masts toppling, powder kegs exploding and stunt actors leaping into the lagoon as the Brits' ship sinks beneath the waves.

Back on the east side, **Harrah's** (*see p77*) sports a tired 'carnival' look that sinks into the background of the surrounding overkill. Further on, inside the **Casino Royale**, you'll find **Denny's** restaurant, where a 24-hour parade of hungry Las Vegas characters chows down on greasy food. Past this is the ghost of the Rat Pack – the site of the famed Sands casino, now replaced by another imposing Euro-mimic, the **Venetian** (*see p88*), where the painfully hip stare out over the Strip from the balcony of **Jack's Velvet Lounge** (*see p156*), and singing **gondoliers** transport embarrassed tourists along the resort's faux canals (*see below*).

Venetian: enjoy an 'O sole mio' moment.

The Venetian is also the home of the high-profile, high-art **Guggenheim-Las Vegas** and **Guggenheim-Hermitage** museums (*see p108*), which opened in autumn 2001. Steve Wynn may have shocked Vegas when he included an art gallery in the Bellagio, but Sheldon Adelson shocked the entire world when it was announced in late 2000 that the Guggenheim museum would bring not one but two museums to the city. Designed by architect Rem Koolhaas, they are evidence of Vegas's new cultural credibility. As light relief from all this high art and good taste, the Venetian also houses an outpost of **Madame Tussaud's** (*see p108*).

Beyond the Venetian are a series of strip malls and the old Vagabond Inn. Don't bother trying, as many do, to see the pirate battle at Treasure Island from here: six lanes of noisy traffic will frustrate you.

Cinema Ride

The Forum Shops, Caesars Palace, 3500 Las Vegas Boulevard South, between W Flamingo & Spring Mountain Roads (369 4008). Bus 301, 302. **Open** 11am-11pm Mon-Thur, Sun; 11am-midnight Fri, Sat. **Tickets** $8-$16. **Credit** AmEx, Disc, MC, V.
Hold on to your toga during this wild 3-D experience. There are six different motion-simulator cinema rides to choose from, including exploring the ocean's depths in a submarine, riding a runaway rollercoaster and taking an intergalactic flight.

Dolphin Habitat & Secret Garden

Mirage, 3400 Las Vegas Boulevard South, between W Spring Mountain & Flamingo Roads (791 7111). Bus 203, 301, 302. **Open** 11am-3.30pm Mon-Thur; 10am-5.30pm Fri-Sun. *Secret Garden closed Wed.* **Admission** $10 Mon, Tue, Thur-Sun; $5 Wed; free under-10s. **Credit** AmEx, DC, Disc, MC, V.
Flipper in the desert? Anything is possible in Las Vegas, where seven bottlenosed dolphins swim in a special habitat behind the Mirage hotel. You can watch the antics from above and below water level and even join the dolphins for a game of catch.

Adjacent to the Dolphin Habitat is the Secret Garden, a small but attractive zoo, with plenty of vegetation and Asian-themed architecture. The best part is getting close to the big-ticket animals: white tigers, white lions, Bengal tigers, an Indian elephant, a panther and a snow leopard.

Gondola rides

Grand Canal Shoppes, Venetian, 3355 Las Vegas Boulevard South, south of Sands Avenue (414 1000). Bus 203, 301, 302. **Open** 10am-11pm Mon-Thur; 10am-midnight Fri, Sat. **Tickets** $10; $5 concessions. **No credit cards.**
Purchase your tickets at St Mark's Square, then take a gondola ride through canals that weave between replica Venetian architecture. The wooden gondolas are authentic, the singing gondoliers are tuneful, but the backdrop of tourists gawking at you will dampen any hope of a romantic moment.

Sightseeing

Guggenheim-Hermitage/ Hermitage-Guggenheim Museum

Venetian, 3355 Las Vegas Boulevard South, at Sands Avenue (414 2440/1-888 283 6423). Bus 301, 302. **Open** 10am-11pm daily. **Admission** $15. **Credit** AmEx, Disc, MC, V.

A truly intimate space (by Vegas standards) and tiny – at 7,660 sq ft (728 sq m) compared to its big brother next door, this museum is a joint project between the Hermitage museum in St Petersburg and the Guggenheim – both names are used to illustrate the co-operation between the two institutions. The opening exhibition features 40 works of Impressionism, post-Impressionism and early Modernism drawn equally from both institutions' holdings.

Guggenheim-Las Vegas

Venetian, 3355 Las Vegas Boulevard South, at Spring Mountain Road (414 2440/1-888 283 6423). Bus 301, 302. **Open** 9am-10pm daily. **Admission** $15. **Credit** AmEx, Disc, MC, V.

The main Guggenheim museum is wedged between the Venetian and its parking garage. Its first exhibition (in late 2001) is 'The Art of the Motorcycle' with an installation designed by Frank Gehry. This will be followed by a variety of shows, ranging from design, fashion and architecture exhibitions to comprehensive presentations of multi-media, video and technology-based art. Ain't Vegas great?

Imperial Palace Auto Collection

Imperial Palace, 3535 Las Vegas Boulevard South, between Sands Avenue & Flamingo Road (731 3311). Bus 301, 302. **Open** 9.30am-11.30pm daily. **Admission** free (with entry pass from the casino).

You don't need to be a car freak to appreciate the classic and historic vehicles here. If you can find the museum in the parking garage, you'll discover about 200 rare and speciality cars (part of a rotating collection of 750, all of which are for sale). Among them are Hitler's 1936 Mercedes, JFK's 1962 Lincoln and vehicles that once belonged to Al Capone, WC Fields and such Las Vegas icons as Howard Hughes and Elvis Presley. Among the vintage classics are a 1947 Tucker (one of just 51 manufactured), a 1910 Thomas Flyer and a room full of Duesenbergs.

Madame Tussaud's Celebrity Encounter

Venetian, 3355 Las Vegas Boulevard South, south of Sands Avenue (367 1847). Bus 203, 301, 302. **Open** 10am-10pm daily. **Admission** $12.50; $10-$10.75 concessions; free under-4s. **Credit** AmEx, Disc, MC, V.

Opened in mid-1999, this is the first US incarnation of London's top tourist trap with more than 100 wax celebs in various settings. In the Hollywood VIP party, you'll see perky versions of Whoopi Goldberg, Brad Pitt, Jerry Springer and Oprah Winfrey. Other settings feature sports figures (Babe Ruth, Joe Montana, Muhammad Ali), rock stars (Elton John, Tina Turner, James Brown) and Las Vegas legends (Tom Jones, Frank Sinatra, Bugsy).

Race for Atlantis

The Forum Shops, Caesars Palace, 3500 Las Vegas Boulevard South, between W Flamingo & Spring Mountain Roads (733 9000). Bus 301, 302. **Open** 10am-11pm Mon-Thur, Sun; 10am-midnight Fri, Sat. **Tickets** $10; $7-$9 concessions. **Credit** AmEx, Disc, MC, V.

On this 3-D IMAX ride visitors take part in a visually stunning chariot race through the legendary kingdom of Atlantis. Some visitors, however, may find that the build-up to the ride and the hyper-themed setting is better than the action itself.

Spring Mountain Road to Convention Center Drive

Map p315 B6-B5

By 2003, the **Fashion Show Mall** on the west side (*see p163*) will nearly double in size to include the city's first Nordstrom fashion store. The Strip-facing façade will be remodelled with a huge 'cloud' to shade pedestrians and a screen to broadcast fashion shows and other events from inside the mall. Until then, however, expect some disruption caused by the extensive building work. Further along is the **New Frontier** (3120 Las Vegas Boulevard South; 794 8200), formerly the site of the longest labour strike in US history, but currently under new ownership and contract. If financing can be sorted out, it is likely that this dowdy property will bite the dust in the near future to be replaced by a San Francisco-themed casino.

Due east is the shuttered high-roller palace **Desert Inn Casino & Country Club**. Once the home of Howard Hughes, it was purchased by Steve Wynn following his sale of Mirage Resorts in 2000. Since then, the property has taken on a mythical status that's almost on a par with Willie Wonka's Chocolate Factory. Wynn has bought up most – if not all – of the country club homes surrounding the Desert Inn's golf course; huge trenches are being dug and pipes are being laid around the perimeter of the property, but work is being carried out in an atmosphere of cloak-and-dagger secrecy. Wynn has made public part of his plans for a Vegas version of Los Angeles's Century City – a massive hotel-office-residential-entertainment compound right on the Strip – but nothing concrete has been announced and curiosity is killing the locals (*see p97* **Coming soon…**).

From the Desert Inn you pass almost unknowingly over the **Desert Inn Super Arterial**, an east–west expressway bypassing both the Strip (by tunnelling under) and I-15 (by flying over). To the east is the **Guardian Angel Cathedral** (336 Guardian Angel Way; 735 5241), a Catholic church set back from the

Over-the-top? Nah. The **Riviera** makes its presence felt on the Strip.

Strip. The themed stained-glass windows here are one of the few places where you can still see old Vegas icons such as the Landmark Hotel.

Across from the Cathedral is the purple hue of the **Stardust** (*see p86*), whose dramatic neon and fibre-optic sign is perhaps the most impressive in the city. The east side of the Strip, which continues with a series of malls, is notable only for its fast-food outlets and a Starbucks with plenty of outdoor seating.

Convention Center Drive to Sahara Avenue

Map p315 B5-C4

A cluster of development greets the visitor north-east of here, with a tacky-looking two-storey shopping mall giving way to the small **Silver City** casino (2000 Las Vegas Boulevard South; 366 0900). Don't look now, but San Francisco developer Luke Brugnara, owner of both the Silver City and the shopping mall, also has plans for a San Francisco-themed resort. Hopefully, any such plans will not interfere with the squat 1970s rotunda-styled **Peppermill's Fireside Lounge** next door (*see p156*) – one of the best places in the city for late-night food and romantic relaxation. Next to the Peppermill is **La Concha Motel** (2955 Las Vegas Boulevard South; 735 1255), a funky building-as-sign development whose lobby is made up of a series of exaggerated arches.

It's back to the big neon at the 1955 **Riviera** (*see p85*), whose façade and sign very nearly constitute overkill, even by Vegas standards; don't miss the life-sized bronze statues of the Crazy Girls' derrières, just in front of the casino. Gamblers rub 'em for good luck. Across the

street is **Westward Ho!** (2900 Las Vegas Boulevard South; 731 2900) and the neon umbrellas of **Slots-o-Fun** (2880 Las Vegas Boulevard South; 734 0410). This was the place where Vegas's New Year's Eve crowds first became so large that they spilled out into the street, way back in the early 1990s. Since then, New Year has become such a mob party in Vegas that the whole of the Strip is now closed to traffic for the evening (*see p186*).

The Lucky the Clown sign of the original family fun palace, **Circus Circus** (*see p73*), still leers cheerfully over the Strip, and has been upgraded with a fibre-optic reader board. Nothing can compare with the hotel's night-into-day porte-cochère. The casino under the pink concrete big top has free circus acts every 25 minutes (11am-midnight daily) high above the casino floor, best seen from the **Horse-Around Bar** (*see p156*), immortalised in Hunter S Thompson's *Fear and Loathing in Las Vegas*. Although the cramped space and shabby decor lessen the spectacle, it's a surreal experience watching a trapeze artist in spangled tights fly overhead. While Mom and Pop gamble away the rent money, the kids can whoop it up at **Adventuredome**, the resort's popular theme park (*see p110*). Adrenaline junkies, meanwhile, may like to know that **AJ Hackett Bungy** (*see p231*) is located next door.

Recovering your equilibrium, continue across Riviera Boulevard to the **Candlelight Wedding Chapel**, which is open 24 hours for those romantic emergencies. Also here is a small-scale shopping mall, anchored by the **Algiers Hotel** (*see p59*), one of the few old-time small motels remaining on the Strip; its 'bleeding brick' walls and kidney-shaped swimming pool are still intact.

Run away to **Circus Circus** for family fun under the big top. *See p109.*

Heading north of here, on the west side is a Travelodge motel, followed by a shopping mall with a gift shop selling – as the sign proudly proclaims – 'hats, belts, cactus'. There's also a gas station and an Arby's fast-food joint, behind which is the **Guinness World of Records Museum** (*see below*). Then it's empty wasteland right up to the corner of Sahara Avenue and the site of the original El Rancho Vegas, built in 1941 and later destroyed by fire. Once regarded as the most expensive piece of undeveloped property in Nevada, the land has lost value since development reached the south end of the Strip.

The east side finishes brightly, however. The decaying eyesore of the second El Rancho was recently bought and imploded by Turnberry Associates, who are building four towers of pricey condominiums to the east. and are considering building a new hotel-casino or additional condominiums on the former El Rancho site. Next come the aqua attractions of **Wet 'n Wild** (*see p236*), a fantastic (and fantastically popular) water park with some great tubes and slides. The park sidles up to the revamped **Sahara** (*see p85*), where animated camels on a new fibre-optic sign usher value-conscious customers into the resort's bright new porte-cochère, and thrill seekers flock to **Speedworld** (*see p111*) and **Speed: The Ride** (*see below*). According to most residents, the Strip begins and ends right here.

Adventuredome

Circus Circus, 2880 Las Vegas Boulevard South, at Circus Circus Drive, between Desert Inn Road & W Sahara Avenue (794 3912). Bus 301, 302. **Open** 10am-6pm Mon-Thur; 10am-midnight Fri, Sat; 10am-8pm Sun. **Admission** *Unlimited rides* $16.95; $12.95 concessions. *Individual rides* $2-$5. **Credit** AmEx, DC, Disc, MC, V.

This is one of the most popular kids' spots in town, especially with teens. The five-acre (2ha) park, climate-controlled under a pink plastic dome, is a scene Fred Flintstone would love: waterfalls, faux mountains and animated spitting dinosaurs stuck in fake tar pits. The rides are good, though hardly of the white-knuckle variety; the best is the double-loop, double-corkscrew rollercoaster ($5), but it lasts only a minute and a half. The Rim Runner is a tame but fun log-flume ride that will get you soaked. Also popular is playing laser tag ($5) in the Lazer Blast Arena. Tots will like the bumper cars, Ferris wheel and other small rides, as well as new attractions such as a wall for climbing and an obstacle course for creative crawling.

Guinness World of Records Museum

2780 Las Vegas Boulevard South, between Circus Circus Drive & W Sahara Avenue (792 3766). Bus 301, 302. **Open** 9am-6pm daily. **Admission** $6; $4-$5 concessions; free under-5s. **Credit** AmEx, Disc, MC, V.

Displays, replicas and videos highlight some of the world's most meaningless records. How about the tallest, fattest, oldest or most married man? Or the most tattooed woman? They're all here, revelling in their forgettability. The Vegas computer databank is fun, though, for some quirky facts about Sin City.

Speed: The Ride

Sahara, 2535 Las Vegas Boulevard South, at E Sahara Avenue (734 7223). Bus 204, 301, 302. **Open** 10am-10pm Mon-Thur, Sun; 10am-midnight Fri, Sat. **Tickets** $6. **Credit** AmEx, Disc, MC, V.

Though it may look like one, Speed is not a rollercoaster by definition. That's because it doesn't have a lift hill, nor does it run by gravity. Instead, it's driven by the force of magnetic impellers that rush it from zero to oh-my-god in three seconds. Riders shoot out from the Sahara Hotel into a tunnel drop, only to re-emerge directly into a vertical loop and up a 23-storey tower at 70mph (118kph). And then they do it all again – backwards.

Speedworld

Sahara, 2535 Las Vegas Boulevard South, at E Sahara Avenue (737 2750). Bus 204, 301, 302. **Open** *Summer* 10am-11pm Mon-Thur, Sun; 10am-midnight Fri, Sat. *Winter* 10am-10pm Mon-Thur, Sun; 10am-11pm Fri, Sat. **Admission** free; individual rides prices vary. **Credit** AmEx, Disc, MC, V.

A variety of virtual racing thrills, prime among them Virtual Reality Racing: eight people, eight minutes, eight bucks each. Alternatively, there's a 3-D 'motion theater': 3-D, three minutes and three bucks for a passenger's-eye race simulation. Everything is the highest of high-tech.

Stratosphere area

Map p315 C4-C3

Facing north at the corner of Sahara Avenue and the Strip, you can hear the screams emanating from the top of the **Stratosphere** (*see p89*). A look up will show you why: at the top of the tallest building in the state of Nevada is the **Big Shot** (*see below*), a ride that propels the daring vertically up to the tip of the needle of the tower – enough to make anyone scream.

Building the tower was certainly enough to make Bob Stupak scream; the former owner of the old Vegas World (which once occupied the Stratosphere site) suffered a series of financial and construction setbacks that forced him to do anything he could – including selling his stake in the property – to get the tower completed. The completed Stratosphere still suffers from a poor location (on the edge of the down-at-heel 'Naked City' area), but recently its new owners finished the second hotel tower and an events arena, hoping to get more people to stay on once they've been to the top of the tower.

North from Sahara the unmissable **Holy Cow** casino and microbrewery (*see p156*) to the east and **Coffeemania** Internet café (*see p140* **Caffeine fix**), the only one in the city if you need to check your e-mail. Across from here is the must-stop **Bonanza**, which claims to be the world's largest gift shop and sells a vast array of cheap and tacky souvenirs of all kinds (*see p176*). Approaching the Stratosphere, the east side has the **Holiday House Motel** (2211 Las Vegas Boulevard South; 732 2468), a holdover from the old days, notable for its wacky animated neon sign and Palm Springs-like motor court design.

The Stratosphere is where Main Street and Paradise Road cross Las Vegas Boulevard and turn into each other by way of St Louis Avenue. Beyond here, at the intersection of Oakey

Boulevard, is **White Cross Drugs** (*see p178*), which has one of the few remaining drugstore food counters in the city. Further down is the 24-hour **Odyssey Records** (*see p178*), a good spot to pick up free newspapers and city guides, and east is the two-storey white building of the **Olympic Garden** topless club (*see p208*). Just east on Oakey Boulevard, behind the Arco gas station, is **Luv-It Frozen Custard**, a Vegas stalwart offering rich desserts from a drive-up window. Further east is one of the older, posh neighbourhoods in the city, which is filled with modest, well-kept, single-storey, ranch-style homes with circular driveways.

Just beyond Oakey is the 'Gateway to Downtown' (you'll need to imagine the planned archway): here Fourth Street veers left, leading you, one-way, right to the heart of Downtown. The two-storey **Tod Motor Motel** (1508 Las Vegas Boulevard South; 477 0022) on the west side and the **Little White Wedding Chapel** on the east (*see p239*), where Joan Collins and Jon Bon Jovi were married (not to each other), lure you closer to Charleston Boulevard. You'll pass **Thai Town** (a small shopping centre with a Thai grocer, restaurant and atmospheric cocktail lounge; *see p158*) and **Talk of The Town** adult bookstore (*see p209*). On the west side is the **Las Vegas International Hostel**, which is the city's only backpacker hostel (*see p62*). At Charleston Boulevard, the Stratosphere area ends, and you enter Downtown and the Gateway District. The best view of this area is from I-95 to the west, from where you can see landmarks such as the **Holsum Bakery** on West Charleston and the architecturally striking **Clark County Government Center** (500 S Grand Central Parkway; 455 4011).

High Roller & Big Shot

Stratosphere, 2000 Las Vegas Boulevard South, at St Louis Avenue, between Oakey Boulevard & E Sahara Avenue (380 7777). Bus 301, 302. **Open** 10am-1am Mon-Thur, Sun; 10am-2am Fri, Sat. **Tickets** (incl admission to the Stratosphere Tower) $9 High Roller; $10 Big Shot; $14 both rides. **Credit** AmEx, DC, Disc, MC, V.

If you're afraid of heights, stay well away from the 1,150ft (350m) high Stratosphere Tower. Those with cast-iron stomachs can try the High Roller roller-coaster that circles above the observation deck in a series of tight twists and rolls. Because of the space limitations, don't expect high speeds; you may, however, experience vertigo or even a nosebleed. More invigorating is the Big Shot, also open-air, which rockets you 160ft (49m) up the tower's spindle under a force of 4Gs; at the top you experience a stomach-lurching moment of weightlessness and float off your seat before free-falling back to the launch pad. If your eyes aren't scrunched up in fear, you get a magnificent view of the city from the top.

Off-Strip

Drawn to the Strip but not wanting to pay its steep real estate prices, hotels and attractions have developed just to the east and west of the famed boulevard.

East of Strip

The most obvious area of encroachment is Paradise Road (also known as the Convention Corridor), which flanks the Strip to the east. It has been the site of development since 1969, when the Landmark and the International casinos opened just south of Sahara Avenue. The International is now (and has long been) the **Las Vegas Hilton** (*see p92*); its showroom has staged everyone from Elvis Presley to the cast of *Cats*, and the Nightclub currently hosts Sheena Easton on a long-term contract (*see p199*). Also in the Hilton is the amazing **Star Trek: The Experience** (*see p113*), a combined live-action, motion-simulator thrill ride. West of the Hilton is **Turnberry Place**, a swanky four-tower, high-rise condo development, where many Vegas luminaries have already purchased pricey homes; Madison Towers further north is similar, but slightly less costly. Behind the Hilton is the exclusive enclave of the **Las Vegas Country Club**, while south on Paradise is the Arco service station that appeared (in its former incarnation as a Shell gas station) in the James Bond film *Diamonds Are Forever* – the Hilton itself was the film's Whyte House Hotel.

From the south end of the Hilton stretching all the way across Desert Inn Road is the **Las Vegas Convention Center** – the largest convention facility in the world (*see p286*). Even if you aren't attending a convention or trade show here, stop in at the helpful **Las Vegas Convention & Visitors' Authority** office (*see p296*) at the top of the main entrance drive, for a huge selection of brochures and visitor magazines. On the west side is a car park – not the most respectful way to treat the former site of the Landmark.

South of here is a huge bar and nightclub, the **Beach** (*see p211*), a favourite conventioneers' haunt, followed by a few business hotels. A skip west on Convention Center Drive is the **Flyaway** (*see p113*) indoor skydiving centre, where people too scared to jump out of a plane can jump into the slipstream of a giant jet engine instead. Further south on Paradise Road are a few of the once-coveted country-club homes lining the Desert Inn Country Club golf course. Most of them have been bought and torn

down by Steve Wynn, the Desert Inn's new owner, in preparation for his latest development (*see p97* **Coming soon…**).

Just past Twain Avenue begins a high-density collection of restaurants known as Restaurant Row. The **Hughes Center** office towers are to the west, followed by university student fave **Gordon Biersch** microbrewery (*see p142* and *p158*). To the east you'll find delicious Southwestern food at **Z'Tejas** (*see p143*) and a strip mall housing **Marrakech** (*see p144*), a Moroccan restaurant where seating is on floor pillows and belly dancers entertain the diners. At the junction with Flamingo Road, Restaurant Row really takes shape: in the north-west corner a new branch of **Piero's** (opening late 2001; *see p143*) competes with **Cozymel's** (*see p143*), **Lawry's: The Prime Rib** (*see p145*), and the new location of **Hamada of Japan** (*see p148*). To the south-east, the long-struggling Continental Hotel, has finally been replaced with **Terrible's** (4100 Paradise Road; 733 7000), a small, locals-style, slot machine-driven hotel-casino.

Further south, the junction of Harmon Avenue is the centre of hipster attractions. The giant guitar sign of the **Hard Rock Café** (*see p142*) may be striking, but you should head straight for the Miami Beach-styled **Hard Rock Hotel** to the north-west (*see p90*). Yes, we know music memorabilia can get a bit tired unless you're a rock 'n' roll trainspotter, but the Hard Rock's collection is impressive. Classic memorabilia from the likes of Hendrix, Gaye, Presley (a fabulous white jumpsuit) and the Beatles is supplemented by pieces from more contemporary icons such as the Red Hot Chili Peppers, Paul Oakenfold, Courtney Love and Madonna. Michael Hutchence donated his guitar to the Hard Rock after playing at the **Joint** (*see p219*) a couple of months before his death. There's also some interesting old Vegas paraphernalia – neon signs, showroom menus – in **Mr Lucky's** restaurant (*see p142*).

Beckoning further south is the Gay Triangle, home to gay-oriented bars, clubs, cafés and shops (*see chapter* **Nightlife: Gay & Lesbian**), followed by the vast expanse of **McCarran International Airport** (*see p282*). To the east, meanwhile, are the delights of the **University District** (*see p119*).

Flyaway

200 Convention Center Drive, between Las Vegas
Boulevard South & Paradise Road (731 4768).
Bus 301, 302. **Open** 10am-7pm daily. **Rates** $45.
Credit AmEx, MC, V. **Map** p315 B5.
Skydiving without an aeroplane? Well, sort of: you
can free-fall in one of only three skydiving simulators in the world, an indoor 21ft (6.5m) vertical wind
tunnel that generates air speeds of up to 115mph
(185kph). After 15 minutes of instruction, you get 15
minutes of flying time shared with five others. Your
experience is, of course, videotaped for you to buy.

Star Trek: The Experience

Las Vegas Hilton, 3000 Paradise Road, between
Karen Avenue & E Desert Inn Road (732 5111).
Bus 108, 112. **Open** 11am-11pm daily.
Admission $24.99. **Credit** AmEx, DC, Disc, MC, V.
Map p315 C5.
This space-age attraction promises to 'boldly go
where no entertainment experience has gone before'.
Although your trip includes a stunning 'beaming' to
the bridge of the Starship Enterprise and a ride in a
virtual shuttle, most of your time is spent looking at
costumes, props and weaponry from every Trek
incarnation. Unusually tall Ferengi and unusually
friendly Klingons roam through the Experience,
happy to pose for photos and chat about their last
trip through the Gamma Quadrant. There's also
the Spacequest casino, which uses dozens of TV
monitors disguised as portholes in order to create
the illusion that you're orbiting Earth. If you're not
interested in throwing your money away on 24th-
century slot machines, at least step into Quark's Bar
& Restaurant for some out-of-this-world exotic
drinks. Big surprise – the management also found
room for a couple of souvenir shops.

West of Strip

Between Las Vegas Boulevard South and
Valley View Boulevard, the west of Strip
corridor is bisected by the roaring thrust of the
I-15. Wedged next to it and running parallel,
Industrial Road is a good, low-traffic alternative
to the Strip, with many access roads along the
way. However, it would be a mistake only to
use this road as a useful short cut, since among
the industrial businesses and strip clubs, just
behind the Fashion Show Mall, you'll also find
the unmissable **Elvis-A-Rama Museum**.

Overpasses at Tropicana, Flamingo or
Sahara take you across I-15 to Valley View
Boulevard, but note that Valley View is not
continuous between Tropicana and Flamingo.
The intersections at Flamingo Road and
Sahara Avenue are the focus of development
in this area of town. At the Flamingo Road
intersection, you'll find a trio of casino-hotels:
you can go bowling at the **Gold Coast** (*see*
p99); check out developments at the new
Palms (opening December 2001; *see p92*);

and pop into the flamboyant **Rio** (*see p93*)
for the free **Masquerade Show**, which takes
place in the casino's Masquerade Village every
two hours from noon to 10pm daily. It's a kind
of Mardi Gras parade in the sky, in which floats
glide high above the floor to an orchestration
of music and dance.

Beyond the Rio, Gold Coast and Palms,
Valley View continues north through a semi-
residential, semi-industrial district. An easterly
turn at Sahara leads past small strip-malls ad
infinitum (as well as **Montesano's Deli &**
Restaurant; *see p148*) until reaching the
train-themed casino **Palace Station** (*see*
p101), just before I-15. Families may also
want to check out **Scandia** (*see p190*), a
small sports and games complex, south of
Palace Station on Rancho Drive.

Elvis-A-Rama Museum

3401 S Industrial Road, at Desert Inn Road (309
7200/www.insidervlv.com). Bus 203, 301, 302.
Open 10am-6pm daily. **Admission** $9.95. **Credit**
AmEx, MC, V. **Map** p315 A5.
Does Las Vegas idolise Elvis, or did Elvis idolise
Vegas? Investigate for yourself at this shrine to one
of the city's most enduring icons. The museum has
the largest collection of 'Elvibilia' this side of
Graceland – $3 million worth, including cars, a racy
handwritten letter, a boat, a gold lamé suit and *the*
blue suede shoes. There's also a jam-packed gift
shop, and a 15-minute tribute show by an Elvis
impersonator every couple of hours. You can even
get married here.

'Beam me up' at **Star Trek:**
The Experience.

Downtown

It may be hard to tear yourself away from the grandiose theming of the Strip, but for visitors who want a taste of old Vegas, a trip to Downtown is a must.

In 1905, officials of the San Pedro, Salt Lake and Los Angeles Railroad perched on a wooden platform where Jackie Gaughan's Plaza casino now stands and auctioned 1,200 lots to settlers and speculators, jump-starting the rapid-fire, haphazard development that continues to characterise Las Vegas to this day. Believe it or not, today's bustling city of casinos, chain restaurants and chi-chi communities evolved from what was, less than one hundred years ago, merely a dusty tent city centred on Main and Fremont Streets.

Since the 1900s, Downtown has gone through several transformations. First, it was the city's centre of commerce (department stores Sears and JC Penney's had downtown branches until the late 1970s), and by the 1930s, the area was bustling with gamblers and entertainers. The Apache hotel (now the site of Binion's Horseshoe), opened in 1932 as the first major hotel in Las Vegas, with one hundred rooms on three storeys, and at the Meadows Casino, 13-year-old Frances Gumm performed with her sisters, three years before changing her name to Judy Garland.

Though Downtown prospered throughout the next three decades, it could not match the booming activity a few miles south on the Strip. The availability of land on Las Vegas Boulevard made possible the construction of huge resorts, while Fremont Street, surrounded on all sides by the city it had helped to create, had no room to grow. As the city spread out further in the 1980s and '90s, Downtown suffered increasing deterioration.

Still, as Mayor Oscar Goodman is so fond of reminding his citizens, today there are more cranes working in Downtown than anywhere else in the Las Vegas valley – a remarkable fact when you consider the rapid development taking place all over the city. And with the mayor's persistence, the future of the greater Downtown area looks more hopeful than it has in decades. Goodman, a champion of new urbanism, is using his political power and popularity to push ahead with an agenda that will develop office space, upmarket shops, housing, performing arts facilities and public spaces throughout Downtown.

In the early 1990s, things didn't look so good. With the majority of resort development

happening at the south end of the Strip, Downtown desperately needed a gimmick to encourage visitors. Spearheaded by Steve Wynn, then owner of the Golden Nugget, Downtown hoteliers sought answers through various redevelopment proposals, before finally settling on the **Fremont Street Experience**. Opened in December 1995, the Experience pedestrianised a five-block section of Fremont Street and covered it with a canopy of colour, sound and light to create a pedestrian-friendly gambling mall that brought a piece of futuristic dazzle to the city's heart (*see p117*).

Although the Experience has brought some stability to Downtown and has succeeded in keeping the tourist numbers up, old-time Las Vegans complain that it has destroyed much of the street's character and freedom in the process; the area that was once a public street is now a private 'park' owned indirectly by the participating hotels. Still, Downtown manages to retain an old-school Vegas appeal that even the high-tech efforts of the programmed lightshow can't dispel. While the rest of Las Vegas becomes increasingly upmarket and Disneylike, Downtown has kept some of the spirit of what Las Vegas used to be: Sin City, a playground for adults. In other words, keep your pirate ship battles and pass the dice.

Moreover, the concentrated assemblage of lights and neon tubing on Fremont, between Fourth Street and Main Street, remains without peer in the world. 'Glitter Gulch', as it has been known since the 1940s, is home to many of Vegas's iconic symbols including Vegas Vic (*pictured p115*) and Vegas Vickie.

The revitalisation of Downtown away from Fremont Street has been a hot issue for nearly a decade, and since 2000, several projects have broken ground. (The most prominent is the pedestrianised **Lewis Street Corridor**; *see p117*.) Talk of more office space, shops, mixed-use residential buildings, a cultural centre and a sports arena to fill the remaining land induces both dreamy eyes and frustrated responses from locals. Many, however, are pushing for and participating in the redevelopment of the so-called **Gateway District** (*see p118*), a section of Downtown south of Fremont Street and north of Charleston Boulevard. Moreover, thanks to Goodman, the city now owns an 61-acre plot in the triangle of mostly empty land west of the Plaza Hotel (bound by Charleston Boulevard, US 95 and I-15), where a county government office building already stands. It is on this plot of prime real estate that Mayor Goodman is now focusing his vision of a liveable, workable Downtown area.

GETTING THERE

To reach Downtown from the Strip, catch bus 301 or the evening express 302. If you're driving, head north on the I-15, then east on US 93/95 and take the Casino Center Exit (which is faster), or simply drive north on the Strip and Fourth Street (which is more interesting). The public and casino parking garages are safe, and free with validation (you must stamp your parking ticket in a machine inside the casino). After sunset, however, it is not advisable to wander too far beyond the safety of the Fremont Street pedestrian mall.

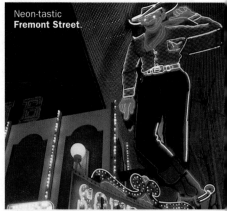

Neon-tastic
Fremont Street.

Fremont Street & around

Fremont Street, once the geographic, cultural and commercial centre of Las Vegas, has, in recent years, almost become a caricature of its former self. As the light-and-sound shows of the **Fremont Street Experience** start, busloads of camera-toting tourists disgorge themselves under the canopy, where they stand, head back, mouths agape, marvelling at the hourly spectacle. When the light show is over, they promptly board the bus and head back to the Strip, as if Downtown was just another single-attraction tour-bus stop. For other visitors, however, visiting Fremont Street can be a delightful trip into Vegas past.

Standing near the FSE canopy at the intersection with Fourth Street, surrounded by the incomparable dazzle of 50 miles of neon tubing, you are within easy walking distance of all the major casinos in Downtown. On the south side, **Fitzgeralds**' Irish style leads the way (*see p95*), followed by the billowing **Four Queens**' sign (*see p93*) and the white and gold **Golden Nugget** (*see p95*), the most attractive hotel-casino in the whole of Downtown. **Vegas Vic**, the neon cowboy, still waves atop the long-closed Pioneer Club (*pictured*), while across First Street is the red-brick **Golden Gate** (*see p57*), the city's oldest hotel; don't miss the retro Bay City Diner inside, which still serves a 99¢ shrimp cocktail in a classic tulip glass.

On the northside, meanwhile, is the partially completed hulk of **Neonopolis**, an upmarket retail and restaurant mall that has floundered in various stages of development since its construction was announced in 1997. Currently, it is slated for completion in 2003 – about three years behind schedule – but it might just as

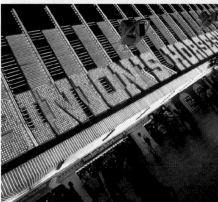

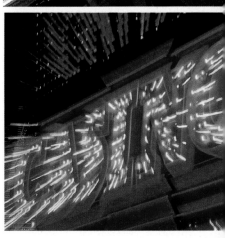

The **Fremont Street Experience** in full razzle-dazzle mode. *See p117.*

easily disappear, as the nearby NASCAR-themed Race Rock restaurant did in early 2001. Beyond this are the **Fremont** (opposite the Four Queens; 385 3232), the glorious neon of **Binion's Horseshoe** (*see p94*), and the **Girls of Glitter Gulch** (*see p207*), a strip club that opted to retain the classic Vegas Vickie neon sign already in place. At the far west end of Fremont Street stands **Jackie Gaughan's Plaza** (*see p96*), where it all began.

Walking east along Fremont Street from its intersection with Fourth Street leads you away from the Fremont Street Experience canopy. The street remains pedestrian-only until you reach Las Vegas Boulevard, and is worth walking along to see the **Neon Museum** (229 5366), a small but growing outdoor collection of classic Las Vegas neon signs, restored and placed atop poles. The Hacienda Horse and Rider sign is the centrepiece of the museum, but the smaller Aladdin's Lamp, Flame Restaurant, Chief Hotel Court, and Andy Anderson Dairy signs are all beautiful examples of neon art. Interpretive plaques

accompany each display. Across Fourth Street you'll also see perhaps the only sparkling neon 7-11 convenience store sign in the world.

Continue along Fremont to the **El Cortez** casino (*see p94*), a must-visit, if only for a taste of old Vegas and its denizens. In the **Metropolitan Police Department** building directly to the south, topless dancers (clothed!) and blackjack dealers wait in the same line in order to obtain background checks for sheriff's department work cards.

Further east, beyond the FSE's controlling influence, Fremont Street gets seedy, littered with low-rent hotels and drug dealers. Still, this makes a great night drive to see the vintage neon signs of the many old motels; just remember to lock your car doors. On the north side at Seventh Street, look for the notable 1960s-mod **City Center Motel**, followed by the **Fergusons Motel** and the kitschy motor court of the **Gables**.

Back to Las Vegas Boulevard and heading north from Fremont takes you to Stewart Avenue and the half-moon-shaped **City Hall**

(400 Stewart Avenue; 229 6011). Heading west on Stewart Avenue will take you past the original federal courthouse building (now the **Downtown Post Office** and the **Downtown Transportation Center** (the terminus for CAT buses and trolleys; *see p282*). Both are slated for relocation in the near future, with Mayor Goodman and the city government first in line to convert the buildings when they become available. Goodman plans to transform the three-acre site into a plaza of museums, colleges and public spaces.

Further along, Stewart leads straight into the 19th century-styled **Main Street Station** (*see p96*) – an unpretentious gem of a casino, chock-full of antiques and fronted by restored railroad carriages once owned by Buffalo Bill, Annie Oakley and Theodore Roosevelt. A left on Main leads past Jackie Gaughan's Plaza to the **Greyhound bus depot** (*see p282*).

Further on, you will pass the **Gamblers General Store** (*see p176*) and the tiny 1951 **El Sombrero Café** (*see p146*), the city's oldest Mexican restaurant, which lies on the edge of the Gateway District.

Fremont Street Experience

Fremont Street, between Las Vegas Boulevard South & Main Street. Bus 107, 301. **Shows** hourly from dusk daily. **Map** p312 C/D1.

This five-block pedestrian mall, covered by a 90ft (27m) high, white metal lattice space frame was supposed to be Downtown's saviour, by attracting tourists who had forsaken Vegas's roots in favour of the glitzy Strip resorts. Certainly, the canopy's computer-programmed light-and-sound shows are worth seeing, but it's open for debate whether they have added to or detracted from Fremont Street's singular seedy beauty.

There are about four different seven-minute shows, featuring images from streaking jets and tumbling dice to boot-scooting country dancers, all accompanied by classic pop tunes. It can be a bit awkward to watch as the images are directly overhead; the best place to stand is right in the middle, directly outside the entrance to Binion's Horseshoe.

Aladdin's missing **neon lamp**. See p116.

The most welcome addition to the Experience in recent times has been the periodic staging of free concerts featuring local bands and nearly forgotten groups from the 1960s and '70s.

From Fremont Street to Charleston Boulevard

Heading south on Las Vegas Boulevard from Fremont Street takes you into the heart of the Downtown business district. At Bridger Avenue to the west is the old **Foley Federal Building**, while the stunning new **Lloyd D George Federal Courthouse** (333 Las Vegas Boulevard South), which opened in July 2000, is across the street. Just south at Lewis Avenue, Goodman's vision of a pedestrian-friendly environment is beginning to take shape: a $1.82-million federal grant and $101,000 from the city will create the **Lewis Street Corridor**, a pedestrian avenue between Fourth Street and Las Vegas Boulevard, with trees, benches and perhaps even a waterfall. Already at Fourth Street and Lewis is **City Centre Place**, a six-storey building that will house the first class-A office space in Downtown in decades, while at Clark Avenue is the historical **Fifth Street School**, which opened as the Las Vegas Grammar School in 1936. The school served the city until the 1960s, when it was converted into a courthouse; it now houses city offices and university classrooms.

Two streets east, at Seventh Street and Bridger, lies the sprawling campus of the **Las Vegas Academy of International Studies & Performing Arts** (315 S Seventh Street). The campus was the original site of the city's first high school, which has since relocated to the far eastern end of the valley. While today's prison-like US schools are designed with student control in mind, this open campus spreads itself over two blocks. Check out the three-storey art deco main building facing Seventh Street, and the separate performance centre on Eighth, complete with sunken orchestra pit. Slated for destruction, the campus was saved by the intervention of several prominent Nevada citizens who graduated from the original high school, and turned it into a public high school for the performing arts.

A little further south on Seventh Street before Charleston Avenue, is **'Lawyers' Row'**, a collection of attractive, early 20th-century plaster-walled and wood-floored bungalows, which have been purchased and restored by ad agencies, graphic arts studios and, of course, attorneys. Although most of residential Las Vegas is unimaginatively cast in the same faux-Mediterranean stucco form,

Sightseeing

Only in Vegas...

the area around Sixth, Seventh, Eighth and Ninth Streets, south from Bridger Avenue to Oakey Boulevard, is an example of architectural diversity and small-town homeliness; well-kept single-storey homes with large yards and wide driveways are typical. In addition to the Lawyers' Row homes from the 1900s, south of Charleston you will pass 1940s bungalows, followed by 1950s and 1960s dwellings.

Heading east on Charleston Boulevard, meanwhile, takes you towards the **Huntridge District**, one of Las Vegas's few distinctive residential neighbourhoods. At Maryland Parkway – it isn't named 13th Street due to superstition – stop in at the old-fashioned **Huntridge Drug Store Restaurant** (*see p144* **Lunch stops**) for a taste of authentic old Vegas. Next door, is the **Huntridge Performing Arts Theatre**, a 1943 art deco institution that was built to serve the surrounding neighbourhood. The building may be architecturally dull, but take a look at the integrated tall neon sign and imagine the gracefully curved marquee board lit up with the names of the stars who attended premières here: Frank Sinatra, Jerry Lewis, Marlene Dietrich. It was resurrected in the mid 1990s by the dedicated efforts of Huntridge neighbourhood alumnus and businessman Richard Lenz, and is now used primarily as the city's main all-ages performance centre and concert hall (*see p221*).

The Gateway District

Loosely bordered by Charleston Boulevard, Las Vegas Boulevard, Carson Avenue and Main Street, the artsy Gateway District takes its name from the **Gateway Motel**, which sits at Charleston and Las Vegas Boulevards. The district is struggling to become the cultural centre that Las Vegas has always lacked, and is home to several businesses that fall into the loose category of 'cultural retail'.

On Charleston at Casino Center sits the centrepiece of the district: the **Arts Factory**, a block-long, two-storey 1940s building filled with studios and shops for photography, art, architecture, music and other creative businesses. Set up by photographer Wes Isbutt in 1997, the Arts Factory's aim was to establish a community of creative forces, both commercial and non-profit, that would energise each other and centralise the incipient arts scene. These ambitious ideals have suffered a number of setbacks in the last few years. Nevada's premier arts group, the Nevada Institute for Contemporary Art (NICA), moved its offices into the Arts Factory in 1999, only to disintegrate shortly afterwards, while many of the non-profit gallery spaces have been taken over by private enterprises. Still, the fact that the Factory exists at all provides a focus for the creative development of the district.

Fourth Street, the one-way thoroughfare from the Strip into Downtown, bustles north of Charleston Boulevard, with locals flocking to **Doña Maria's** Mexican restaurant and **Chicago Joe's** Italian restaurant, a Vegas classic (for both, *see p146*). And, to the west on Main Street, the **Attic** (*see p171*), a huge two-storey vintage clothing, furniture and appliance store, keeps the scene alive.

Arts Factory

101 E Charleston Boulevard, between Main Street & Casino Center Boulevard (676 1111/www.thearts factory.com). Bus 113, 206. **Open** varies.
Map p312 C3.
Any visitor interested in the local art scene should consider the Arts Factory an excellent first stop. It houses the city's foremost non-profit gallery (the Contemporary Arts Collective), along with the best commercial galleries, plus architecture and graphic design firms and individual artists' studios, not to mention the Nevada Arts Council offices (486 3700).

Continuing its mission as the only artist-run, non-commercial, high-calibre gallery in town, the **CAC Gallery** (suite 102; 382 3886/http://contemporary. artscollective.org/) walks the fine line between an edgy, grass-roots aesthetic and academic polish (many of its members are associated with UNLV) with great success. Also of note is the **George L Sturman Fine Arts Gallery** (suite 204; 384 2615), which features connoisseur George Sturman's collection of drawings and prints by artists such as David Hockney, Franz Kline and Claes Oldenberg, plus some wonderful pieces of African folk art and Disney animation. Other galleries worth visiting here include the **M(9) Atelier** (suite 108; 845 7907) and the **Sunrise Gallery** (suite 101; 477 7705).

The Rest of the City

Get behind the wheel, get off the Strip and explore the 'other' Las Vegas.

Using the following overview as a general field guide, a visitor should be able to take a tour of those parts of Las Vegas that few tourists see. For this, a car is a must; doing it by bus, though possible, would be prohibitively time-consuming. Remember, however, that the entire Las Vegas valley is rapidly filling with new housing development, so construction delays and detours are possible; allow plenty of time to travel from one area to another.

The areas in this chapter are arranged clockwise, starting with the **University District**, closest to the Strip, and finishing with the city of **Henderson**, in the south-east.

University District

Bounded roughly by Flamingo Road, Paradise Road, Tropicana Avenue and Eastern Avenue, the University District is a reassuring enclave of normality just a skip away from the Strip. Businesses stick mostly to Maryland Parkway, while the rest of the area is filled with apartments. Although interest is focused around the **University of Las Vegas-Nevada** or **UNLV** (4505 S Maryland Parkway; 895 3011), the entire area has plenty to offer visitors.

On the south-west corner of Flamingo and Maryland you'll find the **Mediterranean Café & Market** (*see p149*) and its adjacent **Hookah Lounge** (*see p160*), a hip, intimate, Bedouin-styled cocktail bar that offers authentic hookahs for smoking. Across the way is the used/vintage clothing superstore **Buffalo Exchange** (*see p171*), plus more ethnic eateries and savvy clothing outlets. The striking architecture of the **Clark County Library & Performing Arts Center** (*see p226*) is just to the east.

The UNLV campus starts further west along Maryland Parkway, where the stunning **Lied Library** (895 3531/www.library.nevada.edu). and a beautiful desert garden (open to visitors) compete for attention. Art-lovers should check out the **Barrick Museum** and the **Donna Beam Fine Arts Gallery** on campus (*see p120*), both of which have exhibitions by student and professional artists. The Barrick Museum also houses a permanent natural history exhibition. Meanwhile, on the east side, two shopping centres filled with cafés, pizza joints, bars, music stores (check out **Big B's**; *see p178*) and copyshops line the road all the way to Tropicana Avenue. Any one of these places provides a great opportunity to tune into the youth culture of Las Vegas: you'll find nightclubs, poetry readings, live music – and the natives are usually friendly.

And, in case you were forgetting you're in Vegas at this point, nearby on Tropicana is the gloriously kitsch **Liberace Museum** (*see p120*), where tearful old ladies and reverential staff relive the performer's glory days.

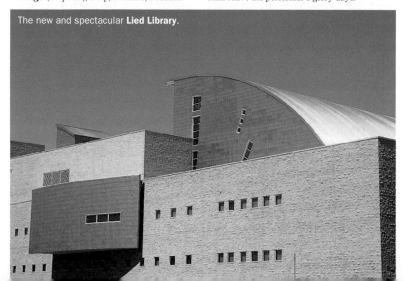

The new and spectacular **Lied Library**.

Liberace Museum

Liberace Plaza, 1775 E Tropicana Avenue, between Maryland Parkway & Spencer Street (798 5595). Bus 201. **Open** 10am-5pm Mon-Sat; 1-5pm Sun. **Admission** $8; $3.50-$5 concessions; free seniors, 6-12s. **Credit** AmEx, Disc, MC, V. **Map** p311 Y3.

Unless you have a pathological aversion to camp, don't miss this place. A testament to Las Vegas's dedication to ersatz, it's like a costume jewellery boutique run wild: on display are Mr Showmanship's rhinestones, stage jewellery, sequinned jackets, hotpants and a genuine, mirrored Rolls-Royce. About 15 of his finest antique pianos are also displayed here. In an age when Las Vegas is trying to be everything but itself, this shrine to excess and bad taste is a kitschy reminder of the city's heritage. *See also p217* **Las Vegas legends: Liberace**.

UNLV Barrick Museum

4505 S Maryland Parkway, between E Flamingo Road & Tropicana Avenue (895 3381). Bus 109, 201, 202. **Open** 8am-4.45pm Mon-Fri; 10am-2pm Sat. **Admission** free. **Map** p311 Y3.

Technically UNLV's natural history museum, the Barrick contains some fine permanent displays on ancient and modern Vegas history, including a wonderful collection of folk art masks. It has also become one of the city's finest art exhibition spaces. Several excellent shows have graced its front rooms, drawing from the best of UNLV's art faculty and regional sources. A must for any gallery crawl; call for details of current exhibitions.

UNLV Donna Beam Fine Arts Gallery

Alta Ham Fine Arts Building, 4505 S Maryland Parkway, between E Flamingo Road & Tropicana Avenue (895 3893). Bus 109, 201, 202. **Open** 9am-5pm Mon-Fri; 10am-2pm Sat. **Admission** free. **Map** p311 Y3.

A wide range of intriguing and well-curated student and professional work, from MFA candidates to painters such as Peter Alexander and Karen Carson, is shown at this gallery on the UNLV campus. It's one of the airiest exhibition spaces in town, with an upstairs gallery overlooking the main floor.

South-west Las Vegas

South-west Las Vegas is one of the older, more established suburbs of the city, and easily accessible by travelling west on Tropicana Avenue. Most of the area is unremarkable in the sense that, like much of Vegas, it is made up of middle-class suburban homes surrounded by strip malls. Along Tropicana beyond the I-15, you'll pass two **Budget Suites** hotels (*see p61*) before reaching the **Orleans** (*see p99*), a locals joint, notable for its movie theatres (*see p203*). Further west, about half as far as the mountains, are the ultra-posh residential developments of **Spanish Trail** and **Spanish**

Hills. Many of Las Vegas's most notable residents live behind the walls of these pricey, immaculate communities and, though you can't get inside, you can gaze longingly at the dramatic elevations and landscaping provided for the city's elite. Continuing beyond the Spanish Hills, Tropicana leads into the planned communities of **Siena** (an age-restricted community) and the southernmost reaches of **Summerlin**. Heading north at Rainbow will lead you through one of the city's older neighbourhoods, **Spring Valley**, though you won't see the modest homes unless you turn off.

North-west Las Vegas

Continuing north on Rainbow Boulevard eventually leads to Sahara Avenue. In the mid-1980s, this intersection was dark and nearly empty, save for the 7-11 on the south-east corner, but today, it is surrounded by residential and heavy commercial development. An east turn here will lead past countless car dealerships and chain restaurants, eventually reaching the **Sahara-Decatur Pavilions**, at the intersection of Decatur Boulevard. Here, four corners of development offer a full day's eating and shopping. Most notable is the north-east side, with food ranging from Mexican at **Baja Fresh** (4760 W Sahara Avenue; 878 7772) to Persian at **Habib's** (*see p149*), and shops that include **Borders Books & Coffee** (*see p166*), the **Tower-Good Guys-Wow!** superstore (*see p167*). A short northerly drive on Decatur leads to Westland Fair shopping centre, where you'll find **Globe Salon** (*see p177*), and a 24-hour **Wal-Mart Superstore** (opening in 2002).

Heading west on Sahara, meanwhile, beyond Buffalo Drive, you'll pass **Rosemary's** (*see p147*), consistently voted the one of the best restaurants in the city and the ever-popular **Jazzed Café** (*see p148*), located in a shopping centre at Durango Drive. Durango Drive also marks the beginning of the **Lakes** neighbourhood, where you'll find the eclectic **Mermaid Café** (*see p222*), **Marché Bacchus** (*see p173*) – a perfect lunch stop on the lake – and lakeside homes with boating and fishing. Note that although the Lakes area is for the most part accessible by car, facilities are for residents only. However, it's worth heading out this far to admire the architectural beauty of the **Sahara West Library** (*see p224* **Culture shock**) and the exhibitions at the adjoining **Las Vegas Art Museum** (*see p122*). The neighbouring **Village Square** has some pleasant shopping and dining outlets and a good cinema (*see p204*). At the far western reaches of Sahara Avenue, nestled at the base of the mountains, lies the **Red Rock Country Club** (2466 Grassy Spring Place; 304 5600), a Scottsdale-inspired desert golf community seemingly a galaxy away from the Strip. The new I-215 beltway intersects Sahara here.

Heading north from Sahara on Durango to Charleston Boulevard and then turning west towards the mountains will lead you to the southern edge of clean and somewhat snobby **Summerlin**, the best-selling corporate-planned community in the nation. The community incorporates housing (ranging from $60,000 condos to multimillion-dollar homes), schools, parks, churches and businesses to create a regular prefab life. The infrastructure is magnificent, but the overall *Truman Show* effect is somewhat disconcerting.

At Rampart Boulevard, development has transformed what were just empty acres in the late 1990s into a bustling commercial area. Just north on Rampart are the dual resorts of the **Suncoast** (*see p100*) and **Regent Las Vegas** (*see p58*), surrounded by the green, manicured fairways of several major golf courses (*see p233*). Further west at Charleston's intersection with Town Center Drive, plans are being laid for the Summerlin Town Center, a high-density cluster of shopping, business and residential properties designed to re-create a traditional small-town atmosphere. From here, it is a mere ten minutes' drive west to reach beautiful and wild **Red Rock Canyon National Conservation Area** (*see p250*).

For a taste of old north-west Las Vegas, travel east along Sahara back towards the centre of town as far as Rancho Road. A north turn here will lead you past the **Scotch 80s** – a swanky neighbourhood of large-lot homes built mostly in the 1950s and 1960s, bordered by Rancho Drive, Oakey and Charleston Boulevards and I-15. This is where Mayor Oscar Goodman resides; entertainer Shecky Greene once lived here, too, as did Nevada's first African-American neurosurgeon, Dr Frederick Boulware. The 80-acre enclave is a mere dice throw from Downtown, yet its quiet, winding labyrinth of tree-lined streets secrete ranch-style estates and one-acre homesites with tennis courts. The gardens are beautifully tended and surprisingly lush, a holdover from the old days when a supply of underground water made the area almost swampy. To the west of the Scotch 80s are the **McNeil Estates**, a middle-class neighbourhood where young professionals are joining more established residents in a bid to restore the charming 1950s homes. Turn along Charleston to the west to reach the Charleston Heights Art Center, housing one of the **City of Las Vegas Galleries** (*see p122*), or continue north to the corner of Rancho and

Alta Drive, where you'll find **Rancho Circle**, perhaps the most exclusive old district in the city: BB King once lived here; Bob Stupak and Phyllis McGuire still do.

Loosely bordered by US 95, Valley View Boulevard and Alta Drive is the largest area of undeveloped land in the central city. The 180-acre **Las Vegas Springs Preserve** (aka Big Springs) is where legendary Old West explorers Kit Carson and John Fremont parked their horses in the mid-1800s (*see p7*). Huge cottonwoods and natural scrub fill the area, surrounding an early 19th-century well house, and wild animals – including coyotes and foxes – roam behind the freeway fencing. The land is owned and administered by the Las Vegas Valley Water District and has survived both fire and the threat of being paved over in the name of freeway expansion. Thanks to a bit of foresight, the land is currently in the process of being restored and prepared for a 2005 opening as the 'Central Park of Las Vegas', just in time for the city's centennial; it will include nature trails, interpretive exhibits, wetlands and more.

Continuing north on Rancho and passing under US 95 will take you through some of the city's oldest districts. The primarily African-American area of West Las Vegas spreads out north-east from Bonanza Road. Here you'll find the shuttered **Moulin Rouge** (900 W Bonanza Road), Las Vegas's first interracial casino. In the bad old days, Las Vegas hotels forced African-American entertainers to flee the Strip after showtime. Black performers (Sammy Davis Jr and Nat King Cole among them) sought refuge at the Moulin Rouge – once disparagingly called 'the Mississippi of the West' – generating a short-lived, but legendary stint of daring after-hours performances that also drew Frank Sinatra and other white Strip players to the hotel-casino. It was at the Rouge in 1960 that strip casino bosses signed an agreement ending the city's racial segregation. Plans to revive this historic landmark have fallen flat, though more are now in the pipeline.

Also here, east of Rancho Drive, is **Binion Ranch**, the property of the legendary gambling and ranching family who own the **Horseshoe** casino in Downtown (*see p94*). Family patriarch Benny Binion once lived in this long-boarded-up, two-storey block-and-timber ranch house and, as recently as the 1990s, horses and cattle were still kept on the property. Although the death did not occur here, Lonnie 'Ted' Binion's murder in 1998, has invested the ranch with even greater historical significance.

To the west of Rancho Drive are Twin Lakes and **Lorenzi Park**, whose attractive ponds were once spring-fed. The park has various sports facilities and is also the site of the

Sightseeing

Liberace Museum: kitsch heaven. *See p120.*

Nevada State Museum & Historical
Society (*see below*), with worthwhile displays
on the history of the region. Further north,
a west turn at Vegas Drive leads past the
Southern Nevada Zoological Park (*see
p123*) to the palatial home of master illusionists
Siegfried and Roy. It's on the north side, and
certainly quite gracious, though you can't see
much. Look for the white adobe walls and the
wrought-iron gate bearing the initials S and R.
Tiger Woods-wannabes can try out their skills
at the good-value **Las Vegas Golf Club** (*see
p233*), just across the road, while budding
Schumachers might want to try the **Las Vegas
Mini Gran Prix** (401 N Rainbow Boulevard;
259 7000), where you can race against friends
or against the clock on the four go-kart tracks
($4.50 a ride or five rides for $20).

Rancho Road continues in a north-westerly
direction past **North Las Vegas Airport**
and the **Texas Station** (*see p101*), **Fiesta**
(*see p100*) and **Santa Fe Station** casinos
(*see p101*), en route to the outdoor attractions
of **Floyd Lamb State Park** (*see p252*) and
Mount Charleston (*see p251*).

City of Las Vegas Galleries

*Charleston Heights Art Center, 800 S Brush Street,
between W Charleston Boulevard & Evergreen
Avenues (229 6388). Bus 206.* **Open** 1-9pm Mon,
Thur; 10am-9pm Tue, Wed; 10am-6pm Fri; 9am-5pm
Sat; 1-5pm Sun. **Admission** free. **Credit** AmEx,
Disc, MC, V.
The cultural affairs division of the city's Department
of Parks & Leisure organises exhibitions of a con-
sistently high quality at its two galleries, one at the
CHAC and one at the Reed Whipple (*see p123*).
Formerly a branch library, the CHAC has been

transformed into a neighbourhood arts centre with
a small gallery that has been put to excellent use,
showing both regional and local artists. It's a bit off
the beaten path, but usually worth the effort.

Las Vegas Art Museum

*Sahara West Library, 9600 W Sahara Avenue,
between S Fort Apache Road & Grand Canyon Drive
(360 8000). Bus 204.* **Open** 10am-5pm Tue-Sat;
1-5pm Sun. **Admission** $5; $3 concessions.
Credit AmEx, Disc, MC, V.
Ensconced in a fabulous museum space attached to
the Sahara West Library, the LVAM aims to make
a quantum leap from its former identity showing
'watercolour-league' artists to become the city's
premier visual arts organisation. Despite some
exhibitions of questionable quality, the museum has
slowly raised its profile, featuring exhibits of minor
works by Marc Chagall and Salvador Dalí and
pieces by glass sculptor Dale Chihuly. The LVAM
is now an exhibition partner of the Smithsonian in
Washington, DC, meaning it will receive some of the
Smithsonian's travelling exhibits.

Nevada State Museum &
Historical Society

*Lorenzi Park, 700 Twin Lakes Drive, at Washington
Avenue (486 5205). Bus 108, 204.* **Open** 9am-5pm
daily. **Admission** $2; free under-18s. **No credit
cards. Map** p311 X1.
Located not far from Downtown, the Nevada State
Museum has permanent exhibits on the natural and
anthropological history of the region, from the
ancient Paiute Indians to 19th-century pioneers to
the men and women of the Nellis Gunnery School in
World War II. The standout exhibit tells the story
of Bugsy Siegel's Flamingo, complete with interactive recordings of Bugsy (played by an actor) threatening business partners with bodily harm.

Southern Nevada Zoological Park

1775 N Rancho Drive, between Vegas Drive & Lake Mead Boulevard (648 5955). Bus 106, 208, 209. **Open** 9am-4pm daily. **Admission** $6.50; $4.50 concessions; free under-2s. **Credit** AmEx, MC, V. **Map** p311 X1.

This will never be confused with the Bronx or San Diego zoos, but it contains an interesting collection of reptiles and birds indigenous to the state of Nevada, as well as a variety of endangered cats and the last family of Barbary apes in the US. The park also has a coati exhibit (a racoon-like animal), botanical displays of endangered palms and rare bamboos, and a children's petting zoo.

North Las Vegas

After suffering years of public opinion that placed it as a grimy little sister to Las Vegas, North Las Vegas – a city unto itself – has experienced a limited renaissance, a result of the tremendous growth in the valley as a whole. New homes and shops have sprung up to fill previously undeveloped land north of Craig Road (between Rancho Road and I-15) to create an area known as the 'Golden Triangle', an area of new development that's on a par with the pricier north-west. In reality, the shiny new Golden Triangle area seems somewhat removed from most of North Las Vegas, a working-class city that grew from the **Nellis Air Force Base** to the north-east, especially since the areas are physically separated by the interstate.

North Las Vegas is home to the majority of the ethnic population of the valley, as well as the main campus of the **Community College of Southern Nevada** (which has a great planetarium; *see p124*). African-American, Asian and Mexican residents have moved in as Anglos have moved out, turning North Las Vegas into a melting pot of ethnicities, with business signs often printed in native languages. The older area, largely untouched by redevelopment, carries with it more of the historical and urban flavour generally associated with modern cities that Las Vegas proper seems to lack. (It's not particularly dangerous, but you'd be wise to take the usual urban precautions.)

A good way to reach these areas is to turn off either US 95 or Rancho Road at Craig Road, heading east. A southward turn at Las Vegas Boulevard North, leading back towards Downtown, will take you past **Jerry's Nugget** casino (1821 Las Vegas Boulevard North; 399 3000), numerous ethnic eateries, the historic public **Forest Lawn Cemetery** – the only one of its kind in the city – and the original Las Vegas **Paiute Indian Reservation** (1 Paiute Drive, at Main Street; 386 3926). Now surrounded

by metropolitan Las Vegas, this small reservation represents the original ten acres deeded to the Paiute by Helen Stewart back in the 1900s (*see p8*). Stop in at the **Paiute Tribal Smoke Shop** (*see p176*). There is a much larger reservation at Snow Mountain, north-west of the city, which incorporates the **Las Vegas Paiute Golf Club** (*see p231*).

On the northern edge of Downtown are a cluster of historical and cultural attractions that merit a visit before you speed on south. They include the architecturally interesting **Las Vegas Library** and **Lied Discovery Children's Museum** (*see below*), the Reed Whipple Cultural Center (which houses one of the **City of Las Vegas Galleries**; *see below*), **Cashman Field** sports ground and convention centre (*see p230*) and the **Las Vegas Natural History Museum** (*see below*). This is also the area where Mormon missionaries first settled in the mid-19th century, a fact that is remembered at the recently restored **Old Las Vegas Mormon Fort Historic Park** (*see p124*).

City of Las Vegas Galleries

Reed Whipple Cultural Center, 821 Las Vegas Boulevard North, between Washington Street & Bonanza Road (229 6211). Bus 113. **Open** 1-9pm Mon, Thur; 10am-9pm Tue, Wed; 10am-6pm Fri; 9am-5pm Sat; 1-5pm Sun. **Admission** free. **Credit** AmEx, Disc, MC, V. **Map** p312 D1.

The second of the Department of Parks & Leisure's two galleries is older and far larger than the Charleston Heights Arts Center (*see p122*), and is easily accessible from Downtown. Exhibitions are generally good quality, but the Reed Whipple lacks the CHAC's intimacy.

Las Vegas Natural History Museum

900 Las Vegas Boulevard North, at Washington Avenue (384 3466). Bus 113, 208. **Open** 9am-4pm daily. **Admission** $5.50; $3.50-$4.50 concessions; free under-4s. **Credit** AmEx, Disc, MC, V. **Map** p312 E1.

The Marine Life Room features small sharks in a large tank, the Wild Nevada Room has exhibits on the flora and fauna of Nevada and the Young Scientist Center is full of interactive displays. But the big draw are five, huge, roaring, robotic dinosaurs, including a vast Tyrannosaurus Rex. Combine a visit here with a trip to the nearby Lied Discovery Children's Museum and you have a perfect family excursion away from the arcades.

Lied Discovery Children's Museum

Las Vegas Library, 833 Las Vegas Boulevard North, between Washington Avenue & Bonanza Road (382 5437). Bus 113. **Open** 10am-5pm Tue-Sun. **Admission** $6; $5 concessions; free under-1s. **Credit** MC, V. **Map** p312 D1.

A stimulating interactive museum, similar to the famed Exploratorium in San Francisco, the Lied features dozens of scientific exhibits that make the viewer a part of the demonstration. Don't be put off by the name, as this is the sort of place many adults would visit by themselves if they thought they could get away with it. Good fun, and infinitely more edifying than Circus Circus's Adventuredome.

Old Las Vegas Mormon Fort Historic Park

500 E Washington Avenue, at Las Vegas Boulevard North (486 3511). Bus 403. **Open** 8am-4.30pm daily. **Admission** $2; $1 concessions; free under-6s. **No credit cards. Map** p311 Y2.

Built by Mormon missionaries in 1855, then abandoned to become part of the Las Vegas Ranch, this is Vegas's pioneer settling site, the oldest Euro-American structure in the state, and an example of what the area was like before the railroad. Though only remnants of the original structure remain, restoration and reconstruction has brought the compound back to life, and history guides are on hand to answer any questions you may have about this intriguing site.

The Planetarium

Community College of Southern Nevada, 3200 E Cheyenne Avenue, between Las Vegas Boulevard North & Van Der Meer Street (651 4759). Bus 110. **Shows** 3.30pm, 8.30pm Fri, Sat. **Admission** $4; $2.50 concessions. **Credit** AmEx, Disc, MC, V.

Star-gazers will enjoy interesting and educational movies and presentations in a small cinema with a 360° screen. After the last performance, you can scan the sky through the planetarium's telescopes (weather permitting).

The **Latter Day Saints Temple** at night.

East Las Vegas

East Las Vegas is a large, older section of town, once characterised by ugly quick-build housing tracts and trailer parks, but again unable (and probably unwilling) to avoid the incursion of new development. At the far eastern end of the valley is Frenchman's Mountain (more commonly known as **Sunrise Mountain**), which in the 1960s and '70s was where the independently minded rich would forgo spots in the Scotch 80s to build desert-style homes with backyard pools and panoramic views of the city. Following this lead, most new housing development has been focused on and around Sunrise Mountain. Also of note is the **Latter Day Saints Temple** (827 N Temple View Drive, off Bonanza Drive; 452 5011), near the eastern end of Charleston Boulevard, at the foot of the mountain. Non-Mormon visitors are not allowed inside, but it is a sight to behold, especially when lit up at night.

Heading west on Charleston towards Downtown, you'll pass the down-at-heel **Charleston Plaza** on your left – an inauspicious home for **Tinoco's Bistro** (1756 E Charleston Boulevard; 678 6811),

which serves an eclectic European and Latin American menu to the Downtown suits – followed by the Huntridge neighbourhood on your right. Turn south at Maryland Parkway, past the **Bishop Gorman Catholic High School** (1801 S Maryland Parkway; 732 1945), to reach the University District. At the corner of Sahara Avenue, you're within walking distance of the old **Commercial Center**, featuring numerous ethnic restaurants, groceries, plus some boutique shops; further south is the popular **Boulevard Mall** (*see p163*).

Alternatively, instead of travelling south on Maryland Parkway towards the University District, follow Fremont Street away from Downtown to the south-east. At 2504 E Fremont Street is the **Green Shack** restaurant, now closed, despite being listed on the National Register of Historic Places. In continuous operation from the 1930s until July 1999, the Green Shack restaurant evokes decades of memories: construction workers building Hoover Dam stopped by here; the politicos and powerful lunched here; newspaper reporters held down bar stools here; even Bugsy Siegel ate in the place. But history is yesterday and, in Vegas, yesterday is long gone. The building is a sad and empty shell awaiting an unknown future. A little further on is the former Showboat casino, now remodelled and updated as the **Castaways** (*see p99*); it's worth a stop for its enormous bowling alley.

South of Sahara Avenue, Fremont Street becomes Boulder Highway, along which you'll find a handful of locals casinos, including the recently opened **Arizona Charlie's East** (*see p98*). Catch a movie at **Boulder Station** (*see p100*), and if you're in town in December, don't miss the Christmas lights at **Sam's Town** (*see p100*). Continue south-east down Boulder Highway to reach Henderson, Boulder City and the Hoover Dam.

Green Valley & Henderson

A tale of two cities within two cities is the history of Henderson and Green Valley. Founded in 1941 as a company town housing employees of the then-new Basic Magnesium plant, Henderson naturally developed a reputation as an industrial town. This reputation was well deserved; in the 1980s the town generated over half of Nevada's industrial output and Las Vegas residents joked about the 'Henderson Cloud', a foul-smelling haze that lingered over the city, attacking the nose of anyone venturing along Boulder Highway towards Lake Mead.

The haze cleared when smokestack scrubbers were installed in the area's factories, but the industrial nature of Henderson could not be so easily expunged. This was proven in 1988 when an earth-shaking ammonium perchlorate (an ingredient in rocket fuel) explosion at the now-relocated Pepcon plant levelled two factories and shattered windows across the valley.

Today, Henderson proper is an interesting town, with an original downtown, a couple of food and toy factories that are open to the public (*see p126*), and two of the newest and most dynamic suburban developments in Southern Nevada. **Lake Las Vegas** is an impressive high-dollar resort community with hotels, golf courses and residential properties surrounding a vast man-made lake that empties into Lake Mead. The development is set in a striking desert environment of various elevations and homes start at a chilly half-million dollars; opulent, but somewhat obscene, at least for environmentalists. The first hotel – the **Hyatt Regency** (*see p58*) – opened in December 1999, offering an excellent, romantic alternative to the Strip, as well as golfing on a Jack Nicklaus-designed course. Also worth a look if you're in Henderson is the **Clark County Heritage Museum** (*see below*). It's

quite a long way from town, but handy for combining with an excursion to the Hoover Dam and Boulder City further to the south-east.

Green Valley, to the north-west of Henderson, was the valley's first masterplanned community. Separated by US 95 from the rest of Henderson, Green Valley, like Summerlin, is home to a massive corporate development of homes in all price ranges, plus shops, schools, parks and more. To reach the area, take Sunset Road west from Boulder Highway to the intersection of Green Valley Parkway.

Green Valley residents have developed a local and perhaps deserved reputation for snobbishness – at one point they fought unsuccessfully for independence from low-rent Henderson. So many Green Valley dwellers hail from Southern California that it is often referred to as 'Little LA'; some have even taken to wearing shirts emblazoned with 'Green Valley 89014', a pretentious take on the TV series, *Beverly Hills 90210*. On the other hand, the inhabitants of Green Valley participate in and provide financial support for numerous cultural activities in their neighbourhood. Ethnic eateries, creative businesses and community cultural events survive and thrive here, creating a sense of community synergy of which others in the metropolis are undoubtedly envious.

Visit the **Green Valley Town Center**, a mall and plaza on the north-west corner of Sunset at Green Valley Parkway, for a perfect example of the area's community focus. Or explore the area surrounding the **Galleria Mall** (*see p163*) further east on Sunset Road. Near here is **Sunset Station**, a neighbourhood casino with a fabulous, Gaudi-inspired bar (*see p160*). Heading west on Sunset leads past Wayne Newton's home, at the south-west corner of Russell Road, and the huge **Sunset Park**, at Eastern Avenue, eventually returning you, once again, to the inescapable lure of the Strip.

Clark County Heritage Museum

1830 S Boulder Highway, between Horizon Drive & Wagon Wheel Avenue (455 7955). Bus 107. **Open** 9am-4.30pm daily. **Admission** $1.50; $1 concessions; free under-3s. **Credit** MC, V.

Long before Las Vegas was a resort mecca, it was just another Western railroad town. Here you'll find an assortment of exhibits relating to Southern Nevada's past: a re-created city street featuring historic area homes with period furnishings, a 'timeline' mural, and a 1918 Union Pacific steam engine.

Henderson factory tours

If you think your vacation's over because you've run out of gambling money, think again. Henderson has factories – in lieu of themed casinos or mega-resorts – that you can tour for

Art attack

As art critic and Las Vegan Dave Hickey observed, aesthetically, Las Vegas is a rather Catholic town; the icons of worship to the twin gods of the American Dream (money and the 'freedom' to be whatever you want to be) are writ large in the cavalcade of spectacles that parade past the visitor's dazzled eye. To be an artist in such an environment can be daunting – and enormously challenging and liberating. While it has not spawned any movements or schools, Las Vegas has attracted a rich diversity of visual artists, including Rita Deanin Abbey, Mary Warner, Robert Beckmann, Jose Bellver, Jim Stanford, Kathleen Nathan, Jack Hallberg, Merilee Horrt and dozens of others.

Unfortunately, a corresponding gallery scene to support and nurture these artists hasn't been as forthcoming. The downtown two-storey **Arts Factory** (see p118), once home to diverse and promising non-profit and commercial galleries, has of late become more of an office park filled with photography studios and graphic arts agencies. While Vegas remains a great place to live and produce art, thanks to its proximity to Los Angeles and its lower cost of living, it has yet to become a place that attracts visitors looking to discover and buy local artwork.

There was a time when the Vegas culturati could blame the lack of a viable art scene on the benign neglect of local arts by the casino and resort industry. But that was before the pioneering effort of Steve Wynn's **Bellagio Gallery of Fine Art** (see p106) proved that fine art could be another lucrative visitor attraction on the Strip. Even after Wynn sold off his properties to MGM, admirably, the new

owners kept and expanded the Bellagio's mini-museum, with shows from the Phillips Collection and sure-fire, sexy exhibitions such as the private art collection of Steve Martin (a rare confluence of Hollywood and good taste). Not to be outdone, Sheldon Adelson's Venetian lured the **Guggenheim** into creating a satellite exhibition space alongside its property, along with (of all things) a small space devoted to works from the Hermitage (for both, see p108). These three arenas ensure that fine art, from old masters to contemporary artists, is set to be the 'next big thing' on the Strip. What's more, they represent the fulfilment of the local population's dream that a big, cosmopolitan city should have a substantial art museum.

So, now that art with a capital 'A' is established as part of Vegas's crazy mosaic of attractions, will there be a corresponding growth in the local art scene? Don't bet on it: Vegas is a fickle environment where today's hot property becomes yesterday's news all too quickly. With luck, however, the buzz created by these galleries may draw attention to the admirably tenacious group of photographers, painters, sculptors, and video artists who depend on the city for their living as well as their inspiration.

In the meantime, visitors seeking fine art away from the Strip, should head for the following galleries: **City of Las Vegas Galleries** (see p122 and p123); the **Contemporary Arts Collective** (Arts Factory; see p118); **George L Sturman Fine Arts Gallery** (Arts Factory; see p118); **Las Vegas Art Museum** (see p122); and the **UNLV Donna Beam Fine Arts Gallery** (see p120).

Sightseeing

free. They're not the most fascinating places on the planet, but you do get plenty of free goodies. Both factories are best visited during the week.

Ethel M Chocolates

2 Cactus Garden Drive, at Sunset Way & Mountain Vista Street (433 2500/433 2665). Bus 217. **Open** Factory shop *8.30am-7pm daily. Tours 8.30am-5pm daily.* **Admission** free. **Credit** AmEx, Disc, MC, V.
If you're a sweet-eater, Ethel M's is definitely for you. The M stands for Mars, as in Forrest Mars, chocolate bar-creator extraordinaire. Ethel M Chocolates are named after his mother and produced exclusively in this factory. Try to visit on weekday mornings, when you can watch the chocolates being made, then sample some of the mouth-watering butter creams,

truffles, caramels or nut clusters. Next door is a cactus garden that's rich with 300 species of cacti, succulents and desert plants.

Ron Lee's World of Clowns Factory & Tour

330 Carousel Parkway, at Warm Springs & Gibson Roads (434 1700). Bus 217. **Tours** 9am-5pm Mon-Sat. **Admission** free.
If you've ever seen a Hobo Joe clown statue, it was made here, where they produce more than 50,000 ceramic and pewter statuettes every year, including the ubiquitous figurines of Disney and Warner Brothers characters. Take a factory tour to learn how they're made. There's also an authentic Chance carousel here, which kids can ride on for $1 a go.

Eat, Drink, Shop

DON'T GO ON A RIDE, GO ON A MISSION.

See the 24th century first

hand as you interact with the

people and technology of

the Star Trek universe.

Whether you're already a fan

or just looking for the most

unique attraction in town,

Star Trek: The Experience

lives up to its reputation as

a "Best of Vegas" attraction.

STAR TREK
THE EXPERIENCE™
LAS VEGAS HILTON

Restaurants & Buffets

Welcome to one of the world's top dining destinations. Yes, really.

Las Vegas witnessed nothing short of a dining revolution in the 1990s. Kick-started by Wolfgang Puck with the opening of **Spago** in 1992, and carried forward by the likes of Mark Miller (**Coyote Café**, 1994), Emeril Lagasse (**New Orleans Fish House**, 1995) and Jean-Louis Palladin (**Napa**, 1997), the influx of high-calibre celebrity restaurants transformed the city of all-you-can-eat-buffets into a world-class dining destination. Apart from New York and Atlanta, Las Vegas is the only city in the US with more than one five-star restaurant.

Now that the feeding frenzy and the millennium hoopla have passed, Las Vegas is beginning to settle into its seat at the gastronomic top table. No large high-end properties have come online since the Bellagio, Mandalay Bay, Venetian, Paris blitz of 1997-2000, but every one of the restaurants in those properties is alive and thriving. Nor has the recently opened Aladdin with its super-trendy Desert Passage mall had any trouble establishing its eateries, but even there, **Commander's Palace** is a tough table to score on most weekend nights. What's more, the dining-out public, the restaurateurs and the chefs seem more comfortable with one

another, and with the city's remarkable culinary reputation. All of which means you can now eat better in Vegas than in any other resort town in the world.

If you need proof of the city's exalted dining status, look no further than the Venetian. Where else on earth would four celebrity chefs/restaurateurs have the audacity to open world-famous restaurants side by side in the same hotel? You'll find Piero Selvaggio's **Valentino** next door to Joachim Splichal's **Pinot Brasserie**, adjacent to Steven Pyle's **Star Canyon**, which cosies up to Emeril Lagasse's **Delmonico** – probably the best steakhouse (in a crowded category) in all of Las Vegas right now. Added to this line-up is the **Royal Star** Cantonese restaurant, an offshoot of the famous Ocean Star seafood restaurant in Monterey Park, California, plus a supporting cast of quality eateries that will make international gourmets drool in anticipation.

As dramatic and wonderful as the restaurants at the Venetian are, many would rank those at the Bellagio even higher. This ultra-luxurious resort has no less than nine celebrity restaurants, with Julian Serrano's **Picasso** and Sirio Maccioni's **Le Cirque**

Enjoy top-notch Creole cooking at the new **Commander's Palace**. *See p131.*

leading the way. Picasso was recently named the number one restaurant in the US by *Esquire* magazine and awarded five stars by the prestigious Mobil travel guide. Along with Maccioni's **Osteria del Circo**, John-Georges Vongerichten's **Prime**, Michael Mina's **Aqua** and Todd English's **Olives**, this star-studded line-up gives Bellagio probably the strongest collection of high-end restaurants of any hotel in the world.

Not to be outdone, the Mirage can boast the high-class cuisine of Alessandro Stratta at **Renoir** (another Mobil five-star winner), while the other major resorts – in particular Paris, MGM Grand, Mandalay Bay and the Hard Rock – keep the stakes high, with restaurants that combine increasingly sophisticated interior design with top-notch food and service. Add it all together, and you'll see why the term 'hotel dining' has lost its pejorative ring.

The tidal wave of gourmet offerings has also improved the choices off the Strip. **McCormick & Schmick's** brings an astounding (and daily) array of fresh fish and shellfish to its east of Strip location, while neighbourhood restaurants **Rosemary's** and **La Scala** demonstrate the panache and cooking needed to challenge the big hitters in the resorts. Just east of Las Vegas Boulevard, on Paradise Road (between Twain Avenue and Flamingo Road; *see p112*), a burgeoning Restaurant Row is evolving, while in the south-west of the city on Spring Mountain Road you'll find regionally diverse restaurants bringing the food of China, Japan and Vietnam to the uninspiring surroundings of the Chinatown Plaza.

Forget the out-of-date image of Las Vegas as a cow town for rubes or the 'town that taste forgot'. The gourmet sophistication now on offer will overwhelm even the most jaded palates.

ESSENTIAL INFORMATION
Note that although the casinos are open 24 hours a day, their gourmet restaurants usually take last orders between 10.30 and 11.30pm and often don't open for lunch. All casinos have at least a coffeeshop, however, that serves food around the clock. Non-casino restaurants keep surprisingly early hours: several take last orders at 9pm, although 10pm is the norm. Reservations are usually necessary at the fashionable spots, and you should also check dress restrictions.

Most of the famous eateries in the large Strip hotels are in the very expensive category, with dinner for two easily topping $150. But – unlike the Vegas of old – these gourmet outposts are now delivering some fabulous bangs for your buck. We have listed the price range for a typical main course (entrée) at each restaurant

to give you an idea of how much you should expect to spend. Casino restaurants serving food in a particular cuisine are listed under that subheading. The best of the remaining 'gourmet' rooms are listed under 'Casino classics' and typically serve French, Italian and continental standards, plus steak and seafood.

With so many kinds of cuisine and so many world-famous restaurants, the choices facing the Vegas diner have never been more dizzying. We've picked out what we think are the best places, but it's also worth checking out the local papers and free magazines for details of new eateries, as well as money-saving coupons. **Waiters on Wheels** (735 6325) prints the menus of about 50 restaurants across town and can deliver food to your room, for a fee.

The Strip

American & burgers

America
New York-New York, 3790 Las Vegas Boulevard South, at W Tropicana Avenue (740 6451). Bus 201, 301, 302. **Open** 24hrs daily. **Main courses** $10-$18. **Credit** AmEx, DC, Disc, MC, V. **Map** p316 A8.
A huge map of the United States hangs from the ceiling, and each state is marked with a characteristic symbol; Vegas is the brightest. Beneath, the restaurant is large and open, and festooned with old travel posters. The menu features a wide variety of dishes such as a traditional turkey dinner, meatloaf, pastas, salads, burgers, a few seafood choices and all-day breakfast. Great dessert menu, too.

Cheesecake Factory
The Forum Shops, Caesars Palace, 3500 Las Vegas Boulevard South, between Spring Mountain & W Flamingo Roads (792 6888). Bus 202, 301, 302. **Open** 11.15am-11.30pm Mon-Thur, Sun; 11.15am-12.30am Fri, Sat. **Main courses** $12-$23. **Credit** AmEx, DC, Disc, MC, V. **Map** p316 A7.
Just reading the menu here (250-plus items, with 28 specials) will exhaust you, but the kitchen (or is it a factory?) pulls it off on most dishes. Choices range from the mundane (decent meatloaf and mashed potatoes) to the bizarre (Beverly Hills Thai pizza salad). Still, it's constantly jammed. Maybe it's the prices (moderate) or the people-watching (great).

Fatburger
3765 Las Vegas Boulevard South, between W Tropicana & Harmon Avenues (736 4733). Bus 201, 301, 302. **Open** *Restaurant* 10.30am-10pm daily. *Drive-thru* 24hrs daily. **Main courses** $4-$6. **No credit cards. Map** p316 A8.
One of the best fast-food burger chains in the States. Here they make 'em good, with chopped onions and, wait for it, real cheese. The old-time atmosphere

Fatburger: the name says it all. *See p130.*

offers a taste of true Americana, and the milkshakes are definitely worth trying, too.
Branches: throughout the city.

Harley-Davidson Café

3575 Las Vegas Boulevard South, at Harmon Avenue (740 4555). Bus 301, 302. **Open** 11.30am-midnight daily. **Main courses** $8-$22. **Credit** AmEx, DC, Disc, MC, V. **Map** p316 A7.
For those who worship the almighty hog, this hyper-themer is a must. For those who worship good food, look elsewhere.

Cajun & Creole

Commander's Palace

Desert Passage, Aladdin, 3667 Las Vegas Boulevard South, at Harmon Avenue (892 8272). Bus 301, 302. **Open** 11.30am-11pm daily. **Main courses** $10-$29 lunch; $24-$45 dinner. **Credit** AmEx, Disc, MC, V. **Map** p316 A7.
Owned and operated by the Brennan family from New Orleans, Commander's brings Creole cooking to Vegas with a seafood-heavy menu that travels remarkably well to the desert Southwest. Big Easy favourites like tasso shrimp henican, veal chop tchoupitoulas and pecan-crusted Gulf fish are toned down slightly for the conventioneer crowd but without compromising on ingredients and flavour. The bar serves up classic cocktails, and the sizeable, well-selected wine list is priced for maximum enjoyment. To finish, the Commander's Creole bread-pudding soufflé is possibly the best dessert you'll ever eat.

Emeril Lagasse's New Orleans Fish House

MGM Grand, 3799 Las Vegas Boulevard, at E Tropicana Avenue (891 7374). Bus 201, 301, 302.

Open 11am-2.30pm, 5.30-10.30pm daily. **Main courses** $19-$21 lunch; $19-$38 dinner. **Credit** AmEx, DC, Disc, MC, V. **Map** p316 A8.
Emeril Lagasse's fish house features redfish, blackened tuna and Cajun seafood. Six oysters baked and served with an intense, hot and smoky Tasso hollandaise sauce are a delicious appetiser for four or a satisfying meal for one. Can't-miss entrées include the cornmeal-crusted redfish with a spicy (and they mean it) red bean sauce, and the Norris Farms' free-range chicken. The fish of the day is also consistently good. For dessert, we recommend the banana cream pie.

Casino classics

Aureole

Mandalay Bay, 3950 Las Vegas Boulevard South, between W Tropicana Avenue & Russell Road (632 7401). Bus 301, 302. **Open** 5-10.30pm daily. **Set menu** $55. **Credit** AmEx, DC, Disc, MC, V. **Map** p316 A9.
Designed by Adam Tihany, Aureole is vast – as in 340 seats and the world's largest wine vault, holding 9,000 bottles of wine, stretching up four storeys to the ceiling. A two-course set menu might include a seasonal salad tossed in orange shallot vinaigrette or seared sea scallops with crème fraîche potatoes, followed by sautéed Atlantic salmon over crab bread pudding or pan-seared guinea hen with crisp leg roulade. In other words: big-city cuisine that competes with the New York original. Pay extra for a selection from the exquisite dessert menu.

Buccaneer Bay Club

Treasure Island, 3300 Las Vegas Boulevard South, at Spring Mountain Road (894 7223). Bus 203, 301, 302. **Open** 5-10.15pm daily. **Main courses** $20-$40. **Credit** AmEx, DC, Disc, MC, V. **Map** p316 A6.
This upscale eaterie has the best view of the Treasure Island pirate battle, though the sound isn't great and it can be disruptive as crowds dash to the window. The kitchen can impress with unusual fare, such as game, pheasant and buffalo prime rib on occasion – it all depends on who's manning the stoves that night, or month or year – and there's an interesting wine list, too. For dessert, try a soufflé.

Isis

Luxor, 3900 Las Vegas Boulevard South, between W Tropicana Avenue & Russell Road (262 4773). Bus 301, 302. **Open** 5.30-11pm daily. **Main courses** $30-$75. **Credit** AmEx, MC, V. **Map** p316 A9.
This small, round room, with its large, comfortable booths and star-studded blue ceiling, has all the requisites of a romantic restaurant. Food is typical continental/gourmet fare with just enough nouvelle twists to keep it interesting: poached oyster with creamed spinach and Pernod; magret of duck with cassis and ginger or lobster tail en croute with seafood mousse. Not the best of the bunch, but worthwhile if you're staying at the Luxor.

Eat, Drink, Shop

Michael's

Barbary Coast, 3595 Las Vegas Boulevard South, at E Flamingo Road (737 7111). Bus 202, 301, 302.
Open 6-9.30pm daily. **Main courses** $35-$75.
Credit AmEx, DC, Disc, MC, V. **Map** p316 A7.
High-roller heaven that's only worth it if someone else is paying. Stratospheric prices, impossible-to-get reservations and a cool reception to unfamiliar faces make this place a must only for dining obsessives. If you do manage to get in, try the Dover sole, Florida stone crab (in season) or the milk-fed veal chateaubriand.

Top of the World

Stratosphere, 2000 Las Vegas Boulevard South, at St Louis Avenue, between Oakey Boulevard & E Sahara Avenue, Stratosphere Area (380 7711). Bus 301, 302. **Open** 6pm-midnight daily. **Main courses** $22-$70. **Credit** AmEx, DC, Disc, MC, V. **Map** p315 C3/4.
Even if the food (continental) were awful – which it isn't – it would be hard not to adore this revolving restaurant high above Las Vegas. The tables are mounted on a ring around the edge of the circular space, which rotates the full 360° every hour. Despite the ever-changing view, well-trained and eager staff will actually have you paying attention to what's on your plate. Go at dusk and watch the sunset for a sight of Vegas at its most dramatic.

WB Stage 16

Venetian, 3355 Las Vegas Boulevard South, at Sands Avenue (414 1699). Bus 203, 301, 302.
Open 11am-1am daily. **Main courses** $17-$27.
Credit AmEx, Disc, MC, V. **Map** p316 A6.

This is not the Bugs Bunny-themed restaurant one might expect. Warner Brothers has painstakingly re-created sets from movies such as *Batman*, *Casablanca* and the Vegas classic, *Oceans 11* in its dining rooms. The food stands up to the new Vegas culinary scene with an eclectic continental menu, and the upstairs Jack's Velvet Lounge – where starters are served until 2am – is a jewel (*see p156*).

Chinese

China Grill

Mandalay Bay, 3950 Las Vegas Boulevard South, between W Tropicana Avenue & Russell Road (632 7474). Bus 301, 302. **Open** 6-11pm daily. **Main courses** $25-$55. **Credit** AmEx, MC, V. **Map** p316 A9.
New York's China Grill is known for hip, pan-pacific fusion food and avant-garde decor, and this winning formula is replicated in Vegas. Everything from the modish cocktail lounge to the zen bathrooms rates a look, as do the beautiful people that keep the place humming most nights. Steer clear of the overwrought, ingredient-heavy dishes, and stick with simpler items like pot stickers, spring rolls or sweet hoisin spare ribs. Don't miss the killer cocktails whipped up by some of Vegas's best bartenders.

Royal Star

Venetian, 3355 Las Vegas Boulevard South, at Sands Avenue (414 1888). Bus 203, 301, 302. **Open** 11am-11pm daily. **Main courses** $3-$20 lunch; $18-$85 dinner. **Credit** AmEx, Disc, MC, V. **Map** p316 A6.

Dress up for **Drai's**, where you'll find French food and after-hours parties. *See p133.*

California restaurateur Kevin Wu brought his distinctive, upmarket Chinese cuisine to the Venetian in 1999. Open for lunch, tea and dinner, the Royal Star will satisfy those who want an exquisite dim sum snack as well as flash hosts spending an entire evening in the ornate private dining rooms. Classic Cantonese and Mandarin fare is prepared from live seafood kept on the premises. Delicacies such as Shanghai lobster, salt and pepper shrimp and giant stir-fried scallops confirm the Royal Star as the most broad-ranging of Vegas's Chinese restaurants.

French & Mediterranean

Drai's
Barbary Coast, 3595 Las Vegas Boulevard South, at E Flamingo Road (737 0555). Bus 202, 301, 302. **Open** 5-9.30pm daily. *After-hours club* midnight-6am Thur-Sat. **Main courses** $14-$32. **Credit** AmEx, Disc, MC, V. **Map** p316 A7.

Victor Drai's restaurant offers lighter-than-average French cuisine, such as fresh tomato, basil and goat's cheese tart, organic carrot and leek soup, and a tasty vegetarian selection. However, it is the fish, chicken and lamb dishes that keep most customers coming back. Try roast turbot, fast-seared Maine salmon, free-range chicken, or the seven-hour leg of lamb, stewed in red wine. Finish up with hot chocolate soufflé or home-baked cookies. After dinner, you can relax in the adjoining candlelit lounge, which resembles the study of an eccentric millionaire. Lined with plush sofas, leopard prints and bookshelves, it serves pricey cocktails, while a quiet jazz combo plays in one corner. After-hours parties are also held here several times a week (*see p212*). Dress code: smart casual.

Eiffel Tower Restaurant
Paris, 3655 Las Vegas Boulevard South, between Harmon Avenue & E Flamingo Road (948 6937). Bus 202, 301, 302. **Open** 5.30-10pm Mon-Thur, Sun; 5.30-11pm Fri, Sat. **Main courses** $26-$55. **Credit** AmEx, DC, Disc, MC,V. **Map** p316 A7.

The decor is drop-dead gorgeous and the view is spectacular, but the food isn't as good as it should be. That doesn't prevent the Eiffel Tower Restaurant from being all booked up at the weekend. French twists are given to simple fare such as impeccably fresh herb-crusted Pacific snapper, pristine seafood and shellfish and chicken fricassee, and the French pastries are suitably over the top. But at these prices, you'd expect more innovation on the plate. The wine list is broad, deep and obscenely priced: good luck finding a decent bottle under $50.

Le Cirque
Bellagio, 3600 Las Vegas Boulevard South, at W Flamingo Road (693 8100). Bus 202, 301, 302. **Open** 6-11pm daily. **Main courses** $37-$41. **Credit** AmEx, DC, Disc, MC, V. **Map** p316 A7.

Probably the best restaurant in town right now, with an arsenal of eats, both refined and bourgeois, that is creating a new standard of excellence in French

The best Restaurants

For a taste of old Vegas
Battista's Hole in the Wall (Italian; *see p143*); **Bob Taylor's Ranch House** (Steak; *see p150*); **Golden Steer Steakhouse** (Steak; *see p141*); **Hilltop House** (Steak; *see p150*); **Huntridge Drug Store** (Lunch stops; *see p144*); **El Sombrero Café** (Mexican; *see p146*).

For a power lunch
Osteria del Circo (Italian; *see p137*); **Palm** (Steak; *see p139*); **Spago** (Fusion; *see p136*).

For hip & happening eats
Drai's (French; *see p133*); **Olio!** (Italian; *see p137*); **Spago** (Fusion; *see p136*).

For people-watching
AJ's Steakhouse (Steak; *see p145*); **Bertolini's** (Italian; *see p136*); **Mon Ami Gabi** (French; *see p135*); **Nobu** (Japanese; *see p143*); **Olives** (French; *see p135*); **Spago** (Fusion; *see p136*).

For bangs for your buck
Abacus (Chinese; *see p147*); **Huntridge Drug Store** (Lunch stops; *see p144*); **Lotus of Siam** (Thai; *see p150*); **Palm** for lunch (Steak; *see p139*).

For an unforgettable meal
Aqua (Seafood; *see p138*); **Le Cirque** (French; *see p133*); **Commander's Palace** (Cajun & Creole; *see p131*); **Coyote Café** (Southwestern; *see p138*); **Picasso** (French; *see p135*); **Renoir** (French; *see p135*); **Prime** (Steak; *see p139*).

For a great view while you eat
Buccaneer Bay Club (Casino classics; *see p131*); **Eiffel Tower Restaurant** (French; *see p133*); **Top of the World** (Casino classics; *see p132*); **Prime** (Steak; *see p139*).

food. Executive chef Marc Poidevin and pastry chef Patrice Caillot push the envelope nightly with such succulent offerings as 'Black Tie' scallops tied with black truffles, consommé de boeuf with foie gras ravioli, salade mesclun and roasted lobster in a port wine sauce. Follow these with ethereal desserts such as bomboloni (Italian doughnuts filled with vanilla cream) or a dense and warm chocolate fondant with the richest oozing centre imaginable. Dress code: smart (jackets and ties for men).

Eat, Drink, Shop

Lutece

*Venetian, 3355 Las Vegas Boulevard South, at
Sands Avenue (414 2220). Bus 203, 301, 302.*
Open 5.30-11pm daily. **Credit** AmEx, Disc, MC, V. **Map** p316 A6.
Named after the ancient Celtic word for Paris,
Lutece (pronounced 'loo-tess') competes with other
big hitters in town, but sadly remains a notch
below some of the top tables. At these prices –
probably the city's highest – you expect perfection,
but unfortunately, you don't get it. The copper-clad
interior by Morphosis is eye-popping, however, and
if you order smartly you will dine well. Less elaborate offerings like applewood smoked codfish
with white truffle oil, roasted monkfish or braised
leg of duck tend to be the most successful. Dress
code: smart casual.

Mon Ami Gabi

*Paris, 3655 Las Vegas Boulevard South, between
Harmon Avenue & E Flamingo Road (946 7000).
Bus 202, 301, 302.* **Open** 11.30am-3.30pm, 5-11pm
Mon-Fri; 11.30am-3.30pm, 5pm-midnight Sat, Sun.
Main courses $10-$25 lunch; $25-33 dinner.
Credit AmEx, DC, Disc, MC, V. **Map** p316 A7.
Lettuce Entertain You Enterprises runs some of
Chicago's most innovative eateries; in Las Vegas
it's responsible for the Eiffel Tower Restaurant and
Mon Ami Gabi, both of which transcend their roots
with solid French food. However, while the Eiffel
Tower goes for romance and dazzle over innovation, Gabi offers honest renditions of simple bistro
fare. As well as great steak frites and garlicky
escargots, Mon Ami Gabi has portable wine bars,
the best people-watching outside the Forum Shops
and a dead-on decor that echoes the real Paris beautifully. It's also the only restaurant with seating
right on the Strip.

Olives

*Bellagio, 3600 Las Vegas Boulevard South, at
W Flamingo Road (693 8111). Bus 202, 301, 302.*
Open 11am-3pm, 5-11.30pm daily. **Main courses**
$10-$22 lunch; $17-$45 dinner. **Credit** AmEx, DC,
Disc, MC, V. **Map** p316 A7.
Fans of Mediterranean cuisine will love this version
of Todd English's original Boston eaterie. Upscale
and only slightly pretentious (wives of powerful men
often lunch here together), Olives is a European-style
café that offers the best Greek-style salad in town
and irresistible flatbreads. Entrées – such as barbecued yellowfin tuna and Israeli couscous carbonara
– are a delightful exercise in contrast, and the tables
outside overlook Bellagio's lake.

Picasso

*Bellagio, 3600 Las Vegas Boulevard South, at
W Flamingo Road (693 8105). Bus 202, 301, 302.*
Open 6-9.30pm Mon, Tue, Thur-Sun. **Set menus**
$79.50, $89.50. **Credit** AmEx, DC, Disc, MC, V.
Map p316 A7.
Of all the celeb chefs appearing in Vegas in the past
few years, Julien Serrano took the biggest gamble
and has made the biggest splash. He's a permanent

fixture in the kitchen, and his glorious and inventive
Mediterranean/French cooking has the food press
checking their thesauruses for superlatives. Only
two menus are offered nightly: a tasting menu and
a slightly cheaper prix-fixe menu. The food is very
expensive, but surrounded by a stunning display of
Pablo's art, you're guaranteed an incredible evening.

Pinot Brasserie

*Venetian, 3355 Las Vegas Boulevard South, at
Sands Avenue (414 8888). Bus 203, 301, 302.*
Open 11.30am-3pm, 5.30-9.30pm Mon-Thur, Sun;
11.30am-3pm, 5.30-10.30pm Fri, Sat. **Main courses**
$11-$18 lunch; $24-$39 dinner. **Credit** AmEx, DC,
Disc, MC, V. **Map** p316 A6.
Tantalising aromas and the musical chimes of silver
and china provide the backdrop at chef Joachim
Splichal's French bistro. The space is decorated with
imported items, including a wooden French door
façade (from a hotel in Lyon). Sample the lighter
tastes of French cuisine, with pastas, seafood, steak
and wild game, plus a large rotisserie and oyster bar.

Renoir

*Mirage, 3400 Las Vegas Boulevard South, between
Spring Mountain & W Flamingo Roads (791 7223).
Bus 301, 302.* **Open** 6-10.30pm Mon, Tue, Thur-Sun.
Main courses $35-$42. **Credit** AmEx, DC, Disc,
MC, V. **Map** p316 A6.
When the Mirage decided to get serious about its
food in 1999, it plucked chef Alessandro Stratta from
the Phoenician hotel in Scottsdale, Arizona. In nine
months, he'd earned Mobil's coveted five-star award,
with cuisine that is suffused with the tastes of southern France. Stratta manages to be ungimmicky and
creative, with intriguing dishes such as baby lamb
with fricassee of vegetables, and honey- and vine-
gar-braised short ribs with spinach. There's some
decent art in the room as well.

Fusion

Chinois

*The Forum Shops, Caesars Palace, 3570 Las Vegas
Boulevard South, between Spring Mountain & W
Flamingo Roads (737 9700). Bus 301, 302.* **Open**
Café 11.30am-midnight daily. *Restaurant* 6-9.30pm
daily. **Main courses** $10-$15 lunch; $15-$30 dinner.
Credit AmEx, DC, Disc, MC, V. **Map** p316 A7.
More Chinese and less cutting-edge than Chinois in
Santa Monica, this offshoot trumps its namesake
with some drop-dead decor. Asian art and sculpture
are displayed in a vividly coloured, two-storey setting, but the flavours and textures on the plate more
than compete with the walls. Whole fried fish is
never less than perfect and the roasted Shanghai
lobster packs an oily wallop with some serious sea-
sonings. Don't miss the super dim sum and sushi.

Postrio

*Grand Canal Shoppes, Venetian, 3355 Las Vegas
Boulevard South, at Sands Avenue (796 1110). Bus
203, 301, 302.* **Open** 11.30am-11pm Mon-Thur, Sun;

11.30am-midnight Fri, Sat. **Main courses** $9-$30 lunch; $9-$45 dinner. **Credit** AmEx, DC, Disc, MC, V. **Map** p316 A6.

This eaterie from the omnipresent Wolfgang Puck serves up American cuisine with Mediterranean and Asian influences. Specials include gourmet pizzas; grilled quail with spinach and soft egg ravioli; lamb chops with tamarind glaze, shoestring potatoes and peanut sauce; and Chinese-style duck with mango sauce and crispy fried scallion. Yum.

Spago

The Forum Shops, Caesars Palace, 3570 Las Vegas Boulevard South, between Spring Mountain & W Flamingo Roads (369 6300). Bus 301, 302. **Open** *Café* 11am-4pm, 5-11pm daily. *Restaurant* 5-10pm Mon-Thur, Sun; 5-11pm Fri, Sat. **Main courses** $12-$24 lunch; $18-$30 dinner. **Credit** AmEx, DC, Disc, MC, V. **Map** p316 A7.

When Wolfgang Puck opened Spago in the Forum Shops in 1992, he paved the way for the subsequent invasion of 'celebrity chef' restaurants in Vegas. An offshoot of the LA power haunt, Spago is the quintessential melting-pot restaurant, overlaying America's multicultural cuisine with classical French, Italian and Asian techniques and flavours. Spago continues to deliver an inventive menu, excellent service, an interesting wine list and astonishing desserts. As you might expect, it attracts the rich and the beautiful.

Verandah Café

Four Seasons, 3960 Las Vegas Boulevard South, at Four Seasons Drive, between W Tropicana Avenue & Russell Road (632 5309). Bus 301, 302. **Open**

7am-11pm daily. **Main courses** $8-$14 breakfast; $13-$26 lunch; $21-$29 dinner. **Credit** AmEx, Disc, MC, V. **Map** p316 A9.

One of two top-flight restaurants on the ground floor of the Four Seasons, the Verandah serves three meals a day. There's not a slot jangle within earshot as you munch on the sophisticated breads and ponder the intriguing three-course menus. Warm baby chicken galantine with balsamic lentils and pistachio oil might be followed by a trio of Atlantic salmon in blood orange butter, or hot smoked escolar with a french bean salad.

Italian

Bertolini's

The Forum Shops, Caesars Palace, 3570 Las Vegas Boulevard South, between Spring Mountain & W Flamingo Roads (735 4663). Bus 301, 302. **Open** 11am-midnight Mon-Thur, Sun; 11am-1am Fri, Sat. **Main courses** $12-$25. **Credit** AmEx, DC, Disc, MC, V. **Map** p316 A7.

Bertolini's offers solid, consistent and inspiring Italian food under the artificial skies of the Forum Shops. Pastas and pizzas are the safest bet, but getting a table is never easy: this is one of the best spots in town to watch the mall's parade of humanity. There's also a branch in north-west Vegas, with indoor and outdoor seating and a beautiful, full-length hardwood bar – the perfect place to sip a selection from the extensive wine list.

Branch: 9500 W Sahara Avenue, between S Fort Apache Road & S Hualapai Way, South-west Las Vegas (869 1540).

Space-age ice-cream and inflated prices at super-trendy **Olio!**. *See p137.*

Il Canaletto

Venetian, 3355 Las Vegas Boulevard South, at Sands Avenue (733 0070). Bus 203, 301, 302. **Open** 11.30am-11pm Mon-Thur, Sun; 11.30am-midnight Fri, Sat. **Main courses** $11-$30. **Credit** AmEx, DC, MC, V. **Map** p316 A6.

Chef Maurizzo Mazzon – a native Venetian – evokes the north Italian countryside with his menu of fresh seafood, beef, game and poultry, prepared in wood-fired rotisseries and grills. What's more, Canaletto's two-storey architecture and classic decor replicates the best eateries of design-conscious Milan.

Lombardi's Romagna Mia

Desert Passage, Aladdin, 3663 Las Vegas Boulevard South, at Harmon Avenue (731 1755). Bus 301, 302. **Open** 10am-midnight daily. **Main courses** $10-$17 lunch; $14-$29 dinner. **Credit** AmEx, DC, MC, V. **Map** p316 A7.

Ensconced in the Desert Passage mall, Lombardi's Romagna Mia serves Italian food with a Tuscan flair in a casual Mediterranean setting. You can choose from the usual pastas and salads, but we recommend sharing a variety of the tasty starters, such as puréed garbanzo bean soup, buffalo mozzarella and tomato salad and wood-fired pizza. Request patio seating and you'll be rewarded with the sounds of a large fountain and the lively rush of passers-by.

Olio!

MGM Grand, 3799 Las Vegas Boulevard South, at E Tropicana Avenue (891 7775). Bus 201, 301, 302. **Open** 5pm-midnight Mon-Thur, Sun; 5pm-2am Fri, Sat. **Main courses** $10-$45. **Credit** AmEx, DC, MC, V. **Map** p316 A8.

If you're looking for trendy overpriced Italian food in an über-stylish setting, your search is over. Style triumphs over substance at Olio!, but none of the Armani/Prada crowd seem to mind that they're paying top-shelf prices (expect to spend $80 per person) for mid-level cooking. Slurping up the scene as part of the neo-trendy communal bar is a must for the fashion crowd, but families will enjoy the adjacent space-age gelato bar much more for much less money.

Osteria del Circo

Bellagio, 3600 Las Vegas Boulevard South, at W Flamingo Road (693 8150). Bus 202, 301, 302. **Open** 11.30am-2.30pm, 5.30-10pm daily. **Main courses** $10-$26 lunch; $19-$39 dinner. **Credit** AmEx, DC, Disc, MC, V. **Map** p316 A7.

Still the best Italian restaurant in Las Vegas, Osteria del Circo captures the conviviality of the original in New York. Sirio Maccioni and his talented sons came west in 1998 and brought their ultra-fabulous talent for running great restaurants with them. This colourful circus (designed by Adam Tihany) looks out at Bellagio's lake and inwards to a talented kitchen for authentic, imaginative Italian eats like Vegas has never seen.

Terrazza

Caesars Palace, 3500 Las Vegas Boulevard South, at W Flamingo Road (731 7568). Bus 202, 301, 302. **Open** 5.30-10.30pm daily. **Main courses** $17-$36. **Credit** AmEx, DC, Disc, MC, V. **Map** p316 A7.

Terrazza is huge, high-ceilinged and expensive, not to mention gorgeous, comfortable and one of the best Italian restaurants in town. The essences of Mediterranean cuisine – olive oil, capers, olives, rosemary, fennel and garlic – are used with a light hand in extraordinary dishes such as rigatoni alla boscaiola, risotto with spring vegetables, and succulent rack of lamb dusted with pecorino romano cheese. Dining alfresco at the edge of the stunning Caesars pool area is one of the most coveted power lunch spots around.

Trattoria del Lupo

Mandalay Bay, 3950 Las Vegas Boulevard South, between W Tropicana Avenue & Russell Road (740 5522). Bus 301, 302. **Open** 5.30-11pm Mon-Fri; 11.30am-3pm, 5.30-11.30pm Sat, Sun. **Main courses** $8-$15 lunch; $18-$35 dinner. **Credit** AmEx, DC, Disc, MC, V. **Map** p316 A9.

Created by Wolfgang Puck, this spot is a signature eaterie developed especially for Mandalay Bay's 'restaurant row'. Lupo (as it's commonly known) offers a traditional northern Italian atmosphere with a menu to match. Still, this is Puck's place, so expect the hostesses to be beautiful, the wine list to be pricey and the hand-made ravioli to be exquisite. Flexibility and spontaneity are key elements: up to four menus are offered during the day.

Valentino

Venetian, 3355 Las Vegas Boulevard South, at Sands Avenue (414 3000). Bus 203, 301, 302. **Open** 5.30-11pm daily. **Main courses** $15-$20 grille; $40-$60 dinner. **Credit** AmEx, Disc, MC, V. **Map** p316 A6.

High ceilings, sinuous curves and yawning spaces provide the setting for some of the most expensive Italian food in America – and to be blunt, it's not worth it. To add insult to injury, the famous encyclopedia-sized wine list is broad and deep, but lacking in anything drinkable under $50. The service is crisp and perfunctory, but no one, least of all the staff, seems to be enjoying themselves. Order simply – most pastas, medallions of veal, filet mignon, carpaccio or roast quail – and you will dine well at Valentino, if not happily.

Zeffirino

Grand Canal Shoppes, Venetian, 3355 Las Vegas Boulevard South, at Sands Avenue (414 3500). Bus 203, 301, 302. **Open** 11am-midnight daily. **Main courses** $14-$22 lunch; $25-$70 dinner. **Credit** AmEx, MC, V. **Map** p316 A6.

The rumour is that Pope John Paul II has a secret passion for Zeffirino's world-famous pesto. You, too, can find out how good it is at this canalside bistro (but bring your own holy water). With a focus on seafood, the specials might include filet of sole piccola, lobster tail, soups, salads, 'pizzarettes' and pastas. Enhancing the award-winning cooking are imported speciality oils, pastas, spices, tomatoes and other ingredients from Italy.

Mexican & Southwestern

Border Grill

Mandalay Bay, 3950 Las Vegas Boulevard South,
between W Tropicana Avenue & Russell Road (632
7403). Bus 301, 302. **Open** 11.30am-3pm, 5.30-11pm
daily. **Main courses** $12-$16 lunch; $16-$30 dinner.
Credit AmEx, DC, Disc, MC, V. **Map** p316 A9.
Chefs Mary Sue Milliken and Susan Feniger have
come a long way on the strength of their uniquely
updated Yucatan-Mexican recipes. The bright decor,
natural sunlight and potent Margaritas are important components of Border Grill, but the food is the
main draw. From the sautéed rock shrimp to the
sweet, savoury and spicy plantain empanadas, this
is a far cry from stereotypical Mexican food. The
café upstairs has a limited menu (tacos, tamales and
such), while the downstairs restaurant has outside
seating, near Mandalay Bay's tropical pool.

Coyote Café

MGM Grand, 3799 Las Vegas Boulevard South, at
E Tropicana Avenue (891 7349). Bus 201, 301, 302.
Open 8.30am-10.30pm daily. **Main courses** $5-$10
breakfast; $6-$17 lunch, dinner. **Credit** AmEx, DC,
Disc, MC, V. **Map** p316 A8.
Along with Emeril's (*see p131*), this trend-setting
restaurant gives locals a reason to get within a mile
of the MGM Grand. Mark Miller and his crew
impress with their nouvelle Southwestern creations:
chilli-heads and adventurous gourmands should
rejoice. Service tends not to live up to the standards
of other top restaurants, but the ingenuity of the
kitchen usually compensates.

Star Canyon

Grand Canal Shoppes, Venetian, 3355 Las Vegas
Boulevard South, at Sands Avenue (733 5000).
Bus 203, 301, 302. **Open** 11.30am-2.30pm,
5.30-10pm daily. **Main courses** $8-$15 lunch;
$30-$35 dinner. **Credit** AmEx, DC, Disc, MC, V.
Map p316 A6.
Cowboy boots, barbed wire and a ceiling branded
with Texas towns provide the setting for superstar
chef Stephen Pyle's beautiful take on Southwestern
Tex-Mex cuisine. Intriguing dishes such as spicy
rock shrimp taquitos with a punchy guacamole,
tamale tart with savoury egg custard and crab
meat, and a huge multilayered vegetable plate with
wood-roasted corn typify Pyle's approach. Equally
good is the hickory-smoked tenderloin with pepper
zinfandel sauce.

Middle Eastern

Neyla

MGM Grand, 3799 Las Vegas Boulevard South, at
E Tropicana Avenue (736 2100). Bus 201, 301, 302.
Open 5-10.30pm Mon-Thur, Sun; 5-11.30pm Fri, Sat.
Main courses $22-$35. **Credit** AmEx, DC, MC, V.
Map p316 A8.
Thanks to Brendan McGovern at Neyla, Middle
Eastern cuisine no longer means overwarmed

falafel on a plastic tray. A delightfully stylish
restaurant, Neyla blends the classic Arabic lines of
its architecture with a modern mentality, and the
scent of fruit-scented hookahs and charbroiled
shish kebabs fill the air as belly dancers entertain
diners. Nine meat or vegetarian meze selections
(including falafel, houmous and baba ganoush) can
be ordered as a group meal.

Pizza

California Pizza Kitchen

Mirage, 3400 Las Vegas Boulevard South, between
Spring Mountain & W Flamingo Roads (791 7357).
Bus 301, 302. **Open** 11am-midnight Mon-Thur,
Sun; 11am-2am Fri, Sat. **Open** 11am-11pm daily.
Main courses $9-$12. **Credit** AmEx, DC, Disc, MC,
V. **Map** p316 A6.
While the salads, 'gourmet' pizzas and desserts are
usually well prepared, the pastas are simply not
worth the bother. It always seems to be full though;
an hour's wait is quite common.

Seafood

Aqua

Bellagio, 3600 Las Vegas Boulevard South, at
W Flamingo Road (693 8199). Bus 202, 301, 302.
Open 6-11pm daily. **Main courses** $30-$49. **Credit**
AmEx, DC, Disc, MC, V. **Map** p316 A7.
Michael Mina and chef Mark Lo Russo demonstrate
that thrilling seafood can be created 250 miles from
the ocean. Clean lines and a smart casual look (by
designer Tony Chi) provide the perfect backdrop for
seafood that will have even the most avid meat-eater
drooling. Menu delights include miso-glazed Chilean
sea bass, wild turbot with truffle mash potatoes and
Maine lobster pie. Additional eye candy is provided
by a Robert Rauschenberg painting.

Caviarteria

The Forum Shops, Caesars Palace, 3500 Las Vegas
Boulevard South, between Spring Mountain & W
Flamingo Roads (792 8560). Bus 202, 301, 302.
Open 11am-11pm Mon-Thur, Sun; 11am-midnight
Fri, Sat. **Main courses** $12-$20. **Credit** AmEx, DC,
Disc, MC, V. **Map** p316 A7.
New York's purveyor of all things fishy and fine
has come to Las Vegas. Featuring top-quality
caviar, smoked salmon and fine champagnes, this
beautiful small space at the end of the Forum Shops
is only marred by the blaring of the animated
Atlantis show every hour. The Oscietra caviar is
the best buy, the blinis are deliciously light and
sweet, and you really must try the Park Avenue
smoked salmon pastrami sandwich.

Steakhouses

Alan Albert's Steak House

The Plaza Center, 3763 Las Vegas Boulevard South,
between E Harmon & Tropicana Avenues (795

4006). Bus 301, 302. **Open** 5-11.30pm daily.
Main courses $25-$45. **Credit** AmEx, DC, Disc,
MC, V. **Map** p316 A8.
A convenient Strip location opposite the Monte
Carlo and moderate pricing make Alan Albert's a
popular joint for tourists and quite a few locals. Run
and owned by the same group responsible for
Rosewood Grill (*see p140*), this is newer, nicer and
trying harder.

Brown Derby

*MGM Grand, 3799 Las Vegas Boulevard South, at
E Tropicana Avenue (891 7318). Bus 201, 301,
302.* **Open** 5.30-10.30pm Mon-Sat; 9am-2pm, 5.30-
10.30pm Sun. **Main courses** $30-$40 Sun brunch;
$25-$40 dinner. **Credit** AmEx, DC, Disc, MC, V.
Map p316 A8.
The Brown Derby is a huge, Hollywood-themed
steakhouse adjacent to Emeril's (*see p131*) in the
MGM Grand. It's crowded, noisy and expensive,
with food and service a notch below that offered at
other steakhouses. Your best bet is the Sunday
brunch, offering better fare than the usual menu.

Charlie Palmer's Steak

*Four Seasons, 3960 Las Vegas Boulevard South, at
Four Seasons Drive, between W Tropicana Avenue &
Russell Road (632 5123). Bus 301, 302.* **Open** 5.30-
11pm daily. **Main courses** $17-$39. **Credit** AmEx,
Disc, MC, V. **Map** p316 A9.
Every steakhouse chain in America has an outpost
in Vegas, but Charlie Palmer's seems to rise above
the cookie-cutter fray by offering unique twists on
the steak-spuds-seafood genre; try pastramied duck
salad, caramelised onion soup with three cheese
gnocchi, Colorado lamb (two ways) or miso glazed
salmon with roasted apple slaw. And if you go for a
steak, the classic Béarnaise and Cabernet reduction
side sauces are invariably perfect.

Delmonico Steakhouse

*Venetian, 3355 Las Vegas Boulevard South, at
Sands Avenue (414 3737). Bus 202, 301, 302.*
Open 11.30am-1.30pm, 5.30-11pm, daily. **Main
courses** $20-$30 lunch; $28-$40 dinner. **Credit**
AmEx, DC, Disc, MC, V. **Map** p316 A6.
Emeril Lagasse has put his Cajun twist on the genre
with punchy, heavily seasoned selections such as a
Cajun rib-eye and simple but exquisite steaks that
can't be beat. Other favourites include a deliciously
tender lamb shank on a bed of risotto, and a
chateaubriand that melts in your mouth. Seafood
offerings are also strong, with shrimp and crab
given the full and exotic new American/Cajun treatment. If you still have room, try the bread pudding.

Gallagher's

*New York-New York, 3790 Las Vegas Boulevard
South, at W Tropicana Avenue (740 6450).
Bus 201, 301, 302.* **Open** 4-11pm daily. **Main
courses** $24-$35. **Credit** AmEx, DC, Disc, MC, V.
Map p316 A8.
This copy of the real Gallagher's in the real New
York City serves choice (not prime) beef in the ersatz

New York-New York, in the ersatz city of all time.
It's good enough, but there are better steakhouses in
town for the same price.

Palm

*The Forum Shops, Caesars Palace, 3570 Las Vegas
Boulevard South, between Spring Mountain &
W Flamingo Roads (732 7256). Bus 301, 302.*
Open 11.30am-11pm lunch; $17-$40 dinner. **Credit** AmEx, DC, MC, V.
Map p316 A7.
From the bread to the prime steaks, Palm consistently excels, and the huge, slightly charred grilled
lobsters for around $140 make it good for fish-eaters,
too. The service is consistently spot on, and the
improved wine list includes a good selection by the
glass. Only a high noise level and uncomfortable
booths keep a meal here from being close to perfect.

Prime

*Bellagio, 3600 Las Vegas Boulevard South, at
W Flamingo Road (693 8484). Bus 202, 301, 302.*
Open 5-11pm daily. **Main courses** $20-$45. **Credit**
AmEx, DC, Disc, MC, V. **Map** p316 A7.
First-class, superior and pre-eminent pretty much
sum up Jean-Georges Vongerichten's steakhouse.
Chef Kerry Simon turns out sophisticated cuisine in
a striking blue and brown setting with a perfect view
of Bellagio's fountains. There's magic on the plate
too: prime steaks are the highlights, but don't overlook the free-range chicken, seared ahi tuna, wood-
grilled veal chop, ten potato side dishes, plus a
choice of 11 sauces and seven mustards.

Celebs smile down on you at old-style
Italian **Battista's**. *See p143.*

Caffeine fix

How do you expect to survive a 24-hour city without coffee? Nearly every Las Vegas hotel has a coffee stand inside its casino, but Vegas also boasts some unexpectedly fine establishments that offer a civilised cup of coffee in a sedate, non-casino atmosphere. Many of them open early and close late (the Riviera's Jitters is even open 24 hours) – an absolute necessity if you're going to enjoy this nighttime city the way it's meant to be enjoyed.

Café Espresso Roma

4440 S Maryland Parkway, at Harmon Avenue, University District (369 1540). Bus 109. **Open** *9am-1pm daily.* **No credit cards.** **Map** *p311 Y3.*
Essentially a satellite study hall for UNLV across the street, the venerable Roma manages to win you over through sheer personality. The students are friendly and the coffee drinks include the strongest mocha in the University District. Local art, poetry and music events are presented regularly; call ahead to find out what's happening and when.

Coffeemani@ Las Vegas

2417 Las Vegas Boulevard South, at Sahara Avenue, Stratosphere Area (737 5241/ www.coffeemania.ws). Bus 203, 301, 302. **Open** *9am-10pm daily.* **No credit cards.** **Map** *p315 C4.*
Coffeemani@ Las Vegas is a marvel of a place – a friendly, cosy little Internet café on one of the most frenetic streets in the world. The staff are amazingly friendly and the beverages are little short of perfect: they're all good, but we highly recommend the caramel macchiato.

Il Fornaio Bakery

New York-New York, 3790 Las Vegas Boulevard South, at W Tropicana Avenue (740 6403). Bus 201, 301, 302. **Open** *8.30am-10.30pm daily.* **Credit** *AmEx, MC, V.* **Map** *p316 A8.*
Located in a (relatively) quiet corner of the bustling casino, Il Fornaio serves freshly baked breads and pastries, delicious sandwiches, biscotti and some pretty fine coffee. You can even have a conversation without your brains being rattled by the din.

Rosewood Grill

3339 Las Vegas Boulevard South, between Sands Avenue & Flamingo Road (792 9099). Bus 203, 301, 302. **Open** *4.30-11.30pm daily.* **Main courses** *$18-$100.* **Credit** *AmEx, DC, Disc, MC, V.* **Map** *p316 A6.*
Rosewood is known for its huge lobsters and amazingly long, eclectic wine list. Otherwise, this older sibling of Alan Albert's (*see p138*) has the look, feel and service of a tourist food factory.

The Steak House

Circus Circus, 2880 Las Vegas Boulevard South, at Circus Circus Drive, between Desert Inn Road & W Sahara Avenue (794 3767). Bus 301, 302. **Open** *5-11pm Mon-Fri, Sun; 5pm-midnight Sat.* **Main courses** *$17-$46.* **Credit** *AmEx, DC, Disc, MC, V.* **Map** *p315 B5.*
Mesquite-grilled steaks are dished up at prices that are well below those of other beef emporia along the Strip. The strong, musky hardwood imparts a flavour to the meat that is nirvana to some, anathema to others. Maybe because of the good prices, it can be next to impossible to get a table here.

3950

Mandalay Bay, 3950 Las Vegas Boulevard South, between W Tropicana Avenue & Russell Road (632 7414). Bus 301, 302. **Open** *5.30-11pm daily.*
Main courses *$28-$60.* **Credit** *AmEx, Disc, DC, MC, V.* **Map** *p316 A9.*
The flashy design and overstuffed booths at 3950 can't disguise what is essentially an outrageously priced seafood and spud joint, albeit one with just enough fancy flourishes to make you think the food is as cutting-edge as the fabric. High-rollers on comps may enjoy recouping some of their losses here, but those paying with their own money will be left disappointed.

Thai, Vietnamese & pan-Asian

Noodles

Bellagio, 3600 Las Vegas Boulevard South, at W Flamingo Road (693 8131). Bus 202, 301, 302. **Open** *11am-3am daily.* **Main courses** *$10-$15.* **Credit** *AmEx, DC, Disc, MC, V.* **Map** *p316 A7.*
Designed by Tony Chi, Noodles is the epitome of casual modern elegance. Teak panelling and modern fixtures dominate, but do not detract from the delicious pan-Asian dishes. Served chilled, the wickedly hot Korean spicy vegetable noodles send a delightfully confusing sensation to your palate, while the Thai noodle soup and congees are superlative. An absolute gem in service, quality and atmosphere. And the prices are good, too.

Eat, Drink, Shop

Jitters

Riviera, 2901 Las Vegas Boulevard South, at Riviera Boulevard (697 4281). Bus 301, 302. **Open** 24hrs daily. **Credit** AmEx, DC, Disc, MC, V. **Map** p315 B5.

Homegrown café chain Jitters desperately wants to be the next Starbucks – and from the taste of things, it seems it's well on its way, with coffee, pastries, food and service that are largely unexceptional. (The selection of teas is good, however.) The branch at 8441 W Lake Mead Drive (256 1902) is the best of the lot, with patio seating around a natural-rock fountain.
Branches: throughout the city.

Starbucks Coffee

Polo Towers Plaza, 3743 Las Vegas Boulevard South, at Harmon Avenue (739 9780). Bus 301, 302. **Open** 5.30am-10pm Mon-Thur; 5.30am-midnight Fri-Sun. **Credit** AmEx, MC, V. **Map** p316 A8.

All you'd expect from the all-conquering Seattle chain: unremarkable baked goods, bitter house coffees (but admittedly tasty espresso drinks) and a wealth of merchandise, from beans to beakers. The Golden Nugget branch (129 Fremont Street, Downtown, 385 7111) is the best;

it overlooks the Fremont Street Experience and affords an unexpected air of urban sophistication. If you're in a car, the branch at 2530 S Decatur Avenue (248 9166/ 457 3313) offers drive-up service.
Branches: throughout the city.

Tea Planet

Suite 106, Chinatown Plaza, 4355 Spring Mountain Road, between Wynn Road & Arville Street, South-west Las Vegas (889 9989). Bus 203. **Open** 11am-2am daily. **Credit** MC, V.

True to its name, Tea Planet has a veritable global village of teas on its menu – from English to Thai, oolong to coconut. It makes a change from all that coffee-drinking.

Wildflower Café

3818 Meadows Lane, at Valley View Boulevard, North-west Las Vegas (258 1554). Bus 104. **Open** 11am-3pm Mon-Sat. **Credit** AmEx, MC, V.

This casual and friendly café is one of the more popular lunchtime destinations on the west side of town. It never feels harried no matter how many bodies pour in for java and sandwiches, and it's a fine place to enjoy afternoon tea, light lunch or merely a quiet conversation.

West of Strip

American & burgers

In-n-Out Burger

4888 Industrial Road, at W Tropicana Avenue (all locations 1-800 786 1000). Bus 201. **Open** 10.30am-1am Mon-Thur, Sun; 10.30am-1.30am Fri, Sat. **Main courses** $4-$6. **No credit cards.** Map p316 A8.

If you want to taste what made the hamburger famous, this California-based chain delivers the goods. You haven't tasted burger heaven until you've tried the Double Double Cheeseburger here. A classic experience, not to be missed.
Branches: throughout the city.

French & Mediterranean

Napa

Rio, 3700 W Flamingo Road, at Valley View Boulevard (247 7961). Bus 202. **Open** 6-11pm Tue-Sat. **Main courses** $28-$38. **Credit** AmEx, DC, Disc, MC, V. **Map** p311 X3.

The exalted celebrity chef Jean-Louis Palladin who opened Napa in 1993 is rarely in the place any more. His lieutenants do a workmanlike job with a dated menu that remains at the top of the price-

per-entrée ladder, but many Vegas foodies mourn the demise of one of the city's former top restaurants. Still, the Rio's bakery provides delicious breads at every meal, and the Rio Wine Cellar's list is hard to match – more than 240 wines are available by the glass.

Steakhouses

Golden Steer Steakhouse

308 W Sahara Avenue, between Las Vegas Boulevard South & Industrial Road (384 4470). Bus 103, 204. **Open** 5-11.30pm daily. **Main courses** $18-$42. **Credit** AmEx, DC, Disc, MC, V. **Map** p315 B4.

The enormous (and, yes, golden) steer that signposts this steak place also advertises its decor: discreet it is not. Think updated bordello crossed with an Old West saloon and you're almost there. But the decor doesn't detract from steaks that are as classic as they come: large, juicy and perfectly grilled.

East of Strip

Aside from the Strip resorts, the stretch of Paradise Road between Sands Avenue and Flamingo Road boasts the city's highest-density collection of good-quality restaurants.

Eat, Drink, Shop

LA, New York, London and Las Vegas. Welcome to **Nobu**. *See p143.*

American & burgers

Mr Lucky's 24/7

Hard Rock, 4455 Paradise Road, at Harmon Avenue (693 5592). Bus 108. **Open** 24hrs daily. **Main courses** $6-$15. **Credit** AmEx, Disc, MC, V. **Map** p316 C7.

Mr Lucky's draws what is undoubtedly the youngest and hippest crowd in Las Vegas. So distracting is the constant stream of MAWs (models-actresses-whatever) that your eyes will be diverted from some fairly classy food, which in no way resembles the coffeeshop fare in most hotels. Some of the specials here are as good as anything at Mortoni's (the hotel's more formal dining room; *see p143*), and cost half the price. Beyond cool.

Hard Rock Café

4475 Paradise Road, at Harmon Avenue, East of Strip (733 8400). Bus 213. **Open** 11am-midnight Mon-Thur, Sun; 11am-12.30am Fri, Sat. **Main courses** $8-$22. **Credit** AmEx, DC, Disc, MC, V. **Map** p316 C7.

Great people-watching and burgers, along with a 30ft (9m) Gibson guitar out front, make this a must-stop on the tourist trail. Only a distant relation of the neighbouring Hard Rock hotel.

Chinese

PF Chang's China Bistro

4165 Paradise Road, at E Flamingo Road (792 2207). Bus 108, 202. **Open** 11.30am-11pm daily. **Main courses** $8-$13. **Credit** AmEx, DC, Disc, MC, V. **Map** p316 C7.

The high-toned atmosphere and toned-down food make this spot more popular than it deserves to be. A happening bar scene (some nights) and lots of pretty Gen-Xers will help you forget about the badly seasoned pseudo-Sichuan dishes and well-meaning

but often atrocious service. The branch near the Regent in Summerlin is perhaps the best.
Branches: 1095 S Rampart Boulevard, North-west Las Vegas (968 8885). Desert Passage, Aladdin, 3667 Las Vegas Boulevard South (836 0955).

Fusion

Gordon Biersch

Hughes Center, 3987 Paradise Road, at E Flamingo Road (312 5247). Bus 108, 202. **Open** 11.30am-midnight Mon, Sun; 11.30am-2am Tue-Sat. **Main courses** $10-$25. **Credit** AmEx, DC, Disc, MC, V. **Map** p316 C7.

This San Francisco-based brew pub puts out a small list of well-made lagers (no ales) and a highly seasoned and wide-ranging menu that spans the globe: everything from Hawaiian sushi to Italian pastas to grilled meats. Pizzas are generally weak, but salads and rotisserie items are pretty good. It's also got a happening bar scene – *see p158.*

Indian

Gandhi

4080 Paradise Road, at E Flamingo Road (734 0094). Bus 108, 202. **Open** 11am-2.30pm, 5-10.30pm daily. **Main courses** $7-$9 lunch; $10-$12 dinner. **Credit** AmEx, DC, Disc, MC, V. **Map** p316 C7.

Good northern and southern Indian cuisine plus a selection of vegetarian dishes make Gandhi the best Indian (and possibly the best veggie) restaurant in Las Vegas. The elegant dining room is a good alternative to the hotel restaurants. The all-you-can-eat lunch buffet is spicier than at Shalimar.

Shalimar

Citibank Park, 3900 Paradise Road, between Twain Avenue & E Flamingo Road (796 0302). Bus 108, 202. **Open** 11.30am-2.30pm, 5.30-10.30pm daily. **Main courses** $8.50 lunch buffet; $10-$16 dinner. **Credit** AmEx, DC, Disc, MC, V. **Map** p316 C6.

Shalimar is the longest-lived of Vegas's meagre Indian restaurant quota, featuring a bargain all-you-can-eat buffet lunch where you can sample reliable, if uninspiring curries, biryanis, tandooris, kebabs and vegetable dishes. Wash it all down with a drink from the interesting iced tea selection. Comfortable, friendly and almost never crowded.

Italian

Battista's Hole in the Wall

Battista's Shopping Center, 4041 Audrie Street, at E Flamingo Road (732 1424). Bus 202, 301, 302. **Open** 4.30-10.30pm Mon-Thur, Sun; 4.30-11pm Fri, Sat. **Main courses** $17-$34. **Credit** AmEx, DC, Disc, MC, V. **Map** p316 B7.

A genuine hoot across the road from Bally's. The casual Italian (cooking, that is) in a kitsch setting will keep both your eye and palate awake. One-price meals, based on pasta, seafood or veal, include unlimited house wine, which, believe it or not, isn't bad. A strolling accordion player (Gordie) and 'celebrity' photos of everyone from Sinatra to obscure TV acts make a meal here unforgettable.

Mortoni's

Hard Rock, 4455 Paradise Road, at Harmon Avenue (693 5047). Bus 108. **Open** 6-11pm daily. **Main courses** $13-$30. **Credit** AmEx, DC, Disc, MC, V. **Map** p316 C7.

This place offers celebrity-watching at its best, plus some solid Italian cooking. Mortoni's is postmodern and neo-hip, with twice the iron-y of a pound of calf's liver. It looks Danish, cooks Italian and oozes cool. Pictures of the ubiquitous Rat Pack line the walls and some pretty good food fills the huge plates. Pastas tend to be overpriced and unexciting, so it's best to stick with the tasty salads, appetisers and fish specials.

Piero's

3555 Convention Center Drive, at Paradise Road (369 2305). Bus 108. **Open** 5.30-9.30pm daily. **Main courses** $20-$65. **Credit** AmEx, DC, Disc, MC, V. **Map** p315 C5.

Overpriced Italian food in a dark, clubby setting. Big shots and minor celebs flock here thinking this is as good as it gets; big hair and bad jewellery predominate, and that's just the men. But if washed-up crooners and minor politicos are your idea of people-watching, then grab a booth and be prepared to pay for the privilege. In fairness, the osso bucco is not bad and is the sole reason many people visit. Another branch is opening at the end of 2001.

Japanese

Benihana Village

Las Vegas Hilton, 3000 Paradise Road, between Karen Avenue & E Desert Inn Road (732 5821).

Bus 108, 112. **Open** 5-10.30pm daily. **Main courses** $18-$42. **Credit** AmEx, DC, Disc, MC, V. **Map** p315 C5.

If you're after an intimate dinner, forget it. Benihana is all about dramatic, and sometimes humorous, hibachi cooking. Entrées include meat, fish or vegetables, accompanied by rice and Asian veg. Once the ordering is complete, a chef wheels in a cart full of raw ingredients and prepares them with a flourish on the hot-top grill built into the table. It's very popular with groups, so book ahead.

Nobu

Hard Rock, 4455 Paradise Road, at Harmon Avenue (693 5090). Bus 108. **Open** 6-11pm Mon-Thur; 11.45am-2pm, 6-11pm Fri-Sun. **Main courses** $25-$30. **Credit** AmEx, MC, V. **Map** p316 C7.

This restaurant puts a positive slant on the fusion-confusion that is everywhere, with a cuisine that is best described as Japanese-Fusion-Peruvian. The genius behind it is Japanese chef, Nobu Matsuhisa, responsible for such acclaimed celebrity eateries as Matsuhisa in LA, and Nobu in New York and London. You won't find more interesting, fresher or healthier food anywhere, combined into dishes that are startling and ingenious. And for goodness sake, don't forget the raspberry-infused saké.

Mexican & Southwestern

Cozymel's

Hughes Center, 355 Hughes Center Drive, between Koval Lane & Paradise Road (732 4833). Bus 202. **Open** 11am-10pm Mon-Thur, Sun; 11am-midnight Fri, Sat. **Main courses** $5-$21 lunch; $9-$21 dinner. **Credit** AmEx, DC, Disc, MC, V. **Map** p316 C7.

Another franchise Mexican restaurant, albeit an upmarket one, with large open dining areas and kitchen. The seafood specials are usually the best bets, with fajitas, house salad and chicken/pozole soup also well worth a try. Cozymel's crowded bar scene packs them in late in the week.

Pink Taco

Hard Rock, 4455 Paradise Road, at Harmon Avenue (693 5000). Bus 108. **Open** 11am-11pm Mon-Thur, Sun; 11am-1.30am Fri, Sat. **Main courses** $8-$14. **Credit** AmEx, DC, Disc, MC, V. **Map** p316 C7.

Tacho Kneeland of LA's Border Grill has brought his updated Mexican recipes to Las Vegas in a groovily kitsch restaurant that is designed to look like a rundown Mexican watering hole. If you can stop smirking over the double entendres long enough, you'll discover low prices and tasty options on the menu. However, one suspects that the food is secondary to the huge frozen Margaritas and poolside vantage.

Z'Tejas

3824 Paradise Road, between Twain Avenue & Flamingo Road (732 1660). Bus 108. **Open** 11am-

Eat, Drink, Shop

11pm Mon-Thur, Sun; 11am-midnight Fri, Sat. **Main courses** $5-$14 lunch; $8-$19 dinner. **Credit** AmEx, DC, Disc, MC, V. **Map** p316 C6.

Food that is not as bad as it could be, nor as good as it should be, is served in an informally elegant environment. The seared black sesame tuna can be excellent, while the mole sauces are anything but. However, none of this keeps Z'Tejas from being a big hit with both the business lunch crowd and the Margarita maniacs who come later in the week. For an enjoyable time, stick with simpler dishes, such as Jamaican jerk chicken or crunchy fried catfish, and just let the cocktails work their magic. The westside location on Sahara Avenue has an attractive covered patio.
Branch: 9560 W Sahara Avenue, South-west Las Vegas (638 0610).

Middle Eastern

Marrakech

Citibank Park, 3900 Paradise Road, between Twain Avenue & Flamingo Road (737 5611). Bus 108, 203. **Open** 11am-11pm daily. **Set meal** $26.95 for six courses. **Credit** AmEx, DC, Disc, MC, V. **Map** p316 C6.

Sit on the floor, eat with your hands and learn to appreciate the nuances of Moroccan cuisine.

Seafood

McCormick & Schmick's Seafood

335 Hughes Center Drive, at E Flamingo Road (836 9000). Bus 202. **Open** 11am-10pm Mon-Fri;

Lunch stops

Capriotti's Sandwich Shop

324 W Sahara Avenue, between Las Vegas Boulevard South & Industrial Road, West of Strip (474 0229). Bus 203, 301, 302. **Open** 10am-7pm Mon-Sat. **Main courses** $6-$9. **No credit cards. Map** p315 B4.

A place of which the Earl of Sandwich would be proud. Capriotti's stand-out speciality is an awesome turkey sub, made from turkey roasted on the day, on the premises. Try the Bobbie, an entire Thanksgiving dinner, complete with turkey, stuffing, cranberry sauce and mayo on a sub sandwich roll. **Branches**: throughout the city.

Coffee Pub

The Plazas, 3800 W Sahara Avenue, at Paseo Del Prado, North-west Las Vegas (367 1913). Bus 204. **Open** 7.15am-3pm daily. **Main courses** $6-$11. **Credit** AmEx, DC, Disc, MC, V.

Smoothies, sandwiches, soups and breakfasts fill the bill at this daytime-only place. It's big with politicos and bimbos, so the people-watching is great, too.

Huntridge Drug Store Restaurant

1122 E Charleston Boulevard, at Maryland Parkway, Downtown (384 3737). Bus 109, 206. **Open** 8am-6pm Mon-Sat; 9am-1pm Sun. **Main courses** $3-$5. **No credit cards. Map** p312 D3.

Located inside the Huntridge Drug Store and looking exactly as it did 30 years ago, this place serves good, old-fashioned Chinese-American food. Chef/owner Bill Fong turns out some yummy chop suey and chow mein, and there are great burgers, too.

Super subs at **Capriotti's**.

Montesano's Italian Deli

3441 W Sahara Avenue, between Valley View Boulevard & Arville Street, South-west Las Vegas (876 0348). Bus 104, 204. **Open** 10am-8pm Mon-Wed; 10am-10pm Thur-Sat. **Main courses** $5-$18. **Credit** AmEx, MC, V. This family-run New York-style deli/bakery serves up some of Vegas's best bread and southern Italian food. On Saturdays, the crowds line up outside for semolina, cheese breads and scrumptious Italian desserts. Small, informal, cheap and friendly. **Branch**: 4835 W Craig Road, North-west Las Vegas (656 3708).

Stage Deli

The Forum Shops, Caesars Palace, 3500 Las Vegas Boulevard South, at W Flamingo Road (893 4045). Bus 202, 301, 302. **Open** 7.30am-10.30pm Mon-Thur, Sun; 7.30am-11.30pm Fri, Sat. **Main courses** $8-$16. **Credit** AmEx, DC, Disc, MC, V. **Map** p316 A7. A clone of the NYC original, offering huge sandwiches, half-sour pickles, tomatoes, bagels and blintzes. As good as it gets for anyone needing a kosher fix this far from the East Coast.

5-10pm Sat, Sun. **Main courses** $6-$18 lunch; $13-$35 dinner. **Credit** AmEx, DC, Disc, MC, V. **Map** p316 C7.

You can get chicken and steak here, but that's hardly the point at this upmarket seafoody grill. Try the daily selection of oysters so fresh and briny you'll swear you're on the coast. A happy hour features huge platters of top-shelf crab, quesadillas, fish tacos and bar food that are sinfully cheap and shrimply delicious. A limited, expensive wine list and some overcomplicated fusion experiments are the only detractions from an otherwise satisfying operation.

Steakhouses

AJ's Steakhouse

Hard Rock, 4455 Paradise Road, at Harmon Avenue (693 5500). Bus 108. **Open** 6-10pm Mon-Thur, Sun; 6-11pm Fri, Sat. **Main courses** $22-$36. **Credit** AmEx, DC, Disc, MC, V. **Map** p316 C7.

AJ's is so swinging, baby, that you expect Bobby Darin to be draggin' on a fag in the neo-hip lounge or Sammy D to be boppin' the night away with the in-house pianist. For a bygone sense of cool, tuck into a Martini straight from the days of tailfins and bullet bras, followed by a super tender filet smothered in real Béarnaise sauce, and tell those calories to be damned: it's a classic cholestrol fest and a homage to the Vegas of the Rat Pack.

Del Frisco's

Hughes Center, 3925 Paradise Road, between Flamingo Road & Twain Avenue (796 0063). Bus 108, 202. **Open** 5-11pm daily. **Main courses** $26-$50. **Credit** AmEx, Disc, MC, V. **Map** p316 C6.

Big and beefy best describes this brand new steak emporium. As the high-end offshoot of the Lonestar Steakhouse Chain, it serves a simple menu – prime sirloins, bone-in ribeyes, simple seafood and even simpler salads – in a dark, wood-panelled setting. Highlights include crab cake, shrimp remoulade and salad wedge with chunky blue cheese dressing, but beware: the wine list and the à la carte pricing can run your tab up in a hurry.

Lawry's The Prime Rib

Hughes Center, 4043 Howard Hughes Parkway, between Koval Lane & Paradise Road (893 2223). Bus 202. **Open** 5-11pm daily. **Main courses** $25-$32. **Credit** AmEx, DC, Disc, MC, V. **Map** p316 C6.

In one of the most beautiful dining rooms in the city, Lawry's serves one of the most limited menus. You can have anything you want – as long as it's prime rib. Lawry's got started in the 1930s in Beverly Hills, and has been at the pinnacle of America's meat-and-potatoes culture ever since. It still prides itself on doing a few things splendidly well: prime rib (three different cuts carved tableside), whipped potato and a famous spinning house salad that has been made the same way since 1938 with few complaints.

Morton's of Chicago

400 E Flamingo Road, at Paradise Road (893 0703). Bus 108, 202. **Open** 5.30-11pm Mon-Sat; 5.30-10pm Sun. **Main courses** $20-$35. **Credit** AmEx, DC, Disc, MC, V. **Map** p316 C7.

As chains go, this is a good one. Selected dishes are brought to the table before cooking, still wrapped in cellophane – a somewhat contrived, not to say unappetising flourish – and the high prices are a significant downer, but you can dine well on an outstanding house salad with a sinfully rich blue cheese dressing, perfectly cooked sirloin and reliable salmon, swordfish and other seafood dishes. The wine list is lengthy, but severely overpriced. Love the souvenir piggy table lamps, though.

Ruth's Chris Steakhouse

Citibank Park, 3900 Paradise Road, between Twain Avenue & E Flamingo Road (791 7011). Bus 108. **Open** 11am-10.30pm daily. **Main courses** $18-$35. **Credit** AmEx, DC, Disc, MC, V. **Map** p316 C6.

Two health warnings before you come here: too much butter could raise your cholesterol level, while too many à la carte selections could send your blood pressure (not to mention your overdraft) through the roof. Prime steaks are served in an attractive setting, but most aficionados prefer Prime, Charlie Palmer's or Delmonico (for all, *see p139*). **Branch**: Cameron Corner, 4561 W Flamingo Road, South-west Las Vegas (248 7011).

Downtown

Casino classics

Hugo's Cellar

Four Queens, 202 Fremont Street, at Casino Center Boulevard (385 4011). Bus 107, 403. **Open** 5.30-10.30pm daily. **Main courses** $26-$52. **Credit** AmEx, DC, Disc, MC, V. **Map** p312 D1.

An outstanding wine list and a knowledgeable sommelier make Hugo's a must for oenophiles, but the food remains hopelessly mired in the 1970s 'continental' genre, and shows no sign of improving. Stick with a seafood speciality or beef to avoid disappointment. Surprisingly, given the dated food and atmosphere, Hugo's remains popular, making a table hard to come by at weekends or other busy times.

French & Mediterranean

André's

401 S Sixth Street, at Bridger Avenue (385 5016). Bus 113. **Open** 6pm-closing times vary Mon-Sat. Closed July. **Main courses** $26-$56. **Credit** AmEx, DC, Disc, MC, V. **Map** p312 D2.

This Las Vegas institution is very popular with the expense account crowd. Chef/owner André Rochat serves French haute cuisine accompanied by a world-class cellar (though it yields few bargains). The other branch inside the Monte Carlo casino is

Eat, Drink, Shop

You want spaghetti and meatballs? Visit Vegas stalwart **Chicago Joe's**.

open daily and has a large, plush cigar and cognac bar for post-prandial relaxation.
Branch: Monte Carlo, 3770 Las Vegas Boulevard South (730 7955).

Italian

Chicago Joe's
820 S Fourth Street, between Gass Avenue & Hoover Street (382 5637). Bus 206, 408. **Open** 11am-11pm Mon-Fri; 5-10pm Sat. **Main courses** $8-$20. **Credit** AmEx, MC, V. **Map** p312 C2/3.
Come here for some of the best-priced pastas in town. Located in a tiny old brick house, CJ's has been in business for a quarter of a century thanks to the solid southern Italian cooking of its kitchen. No frills, no dinners over $20 and great service in an intimate setting make Joe's a fantastic bargain.

Mexican & Southwestern

Doña Maria's
910 Las Vegas Boulevard South, between Gass Avenue & Charleston Boulevard (382 6538). Bus 206, 301, 302. **Open** 8am-10pm daily. **Main course** $7-$12 lunch; $9-$11 dinner. **Credit** AmEx, DC, Disc, MC, V. **Map** p312 C3.
This loud and boisterous place serves some of Vegas's best Mexican food. The tamales (spicy chopped meat and ground corn, served in a corn husk) are the real draw, but the tortas (sandwiches) and fiery salsas also help keep the place packed, especially at lunchtime. Both branches are very popular with the city's large Mexican community.
Branch: Doña Maria Tamales Restaurant, 3205 N Tenaya Way, North Las Vegas (656 1600).

El Sombrero Café
807 S Main Street, at Gass Avenue (382 9234). Bus 408. **Open** 11am-9pm Mon-Sat. **Main courses** $6-$10.50. **Credit** AmEx, MC, V. **Map** p312 C2.

Vegas's oldest Mexican restaurant (it opened in 1950) is housed in a small, nondescript building on South Main Street, a location in which no restaurant should be able to survive. However, the El Sombrero has thrived by feeding Las Vegans a simple Mexican menu full of fresh fiery salsas, fresh tortillas and a chilli. The food is good, the portions are huge and nothing on the menu tops $10.

Seafood

Second Street Grill
Fremont, 200 Fremont Street, at Casino Center Boulevard (385 6277). Bus 107, 402. **Open** 5-10pm Mon, Thur, Sun; 5-11pm Fri, Sat. **Main courses** $18-$33. **Credit** AmEx, DC, Disc, MC, V. **Map** p312 D1.
The Fremont seems to enjoy its gritty status amid the renovations elsewhere on the street, but that doesn't stop it having an upscale, attractive Pacific Rim seafood restaurant. Ignore the state of the hotel and follow the Hawaiian tourists to some of Vegas's most innovative seafood: the whole fried Thai red snapper is food as both art and architecture. Service and wine could be improved.

The rest of the city

American & burgers

Manhattan of Las Vegas
2600 E Flamingo Road, between Eastern Avenue & Pecos Road, East Las Vegas (737 5000). Bus 202. **Open** 4pm-1am daily. **Main courses** $9.95 lunch; $10-$25 dinner. **Credit** AmEx, DC, Disc, MC, V. **Map** p311 Z3.
If the Rat Pack were intact, this is where they would be today. Plush booths, tuxedoed waiters and lots of pinky rings make this a *Goodfellas* retreat of the first order. The crowd is straight from a casting, and the

food decent enough to keep the limos lined up at the door. Veal is the kitchen's strong suit, with pastas and an excellent Caesar salad not far behind. For dessert, what else but cheesecake or a rich tiramisu?

Tony Roma's 'The Place for Ribs'

620 E Sahara Avenue, at Sixth Street, East Las Vegas (733 9914). Bus 204. **Open** 11am-10pm Mon-Thur, Sun; 11am-11pm Fri, Sat. **Main courses** $7-$15 lunch; $7-$20 dinner. **Credit** AmEx, Disc, MC, V. **Map** p311 Y2.

Ribs done right, and by the US's largest rib franchise at that. The slightly sweet BBQ sauce has a mild pepper bite and the hot sauce lives up to its name. The famous onion ring loaf is huge and satisfying enough for four people. Skip the steak and seafood choices and go straight for the ribs or chicken.
Branch: Best of the West 2040 N Rainbow Boulevard, North-west Las Vegas (638 2100).

Chinese

Abacus

5960 Spring Mountain Road, at Jones Avenue, South-west Las Vegas (221 0456). Bus 102, 203. **Open** 11.30am-10pm daily. **Main courses** $7-$14. **Credit** AmEx, Disc, MC, V.

This peaceful little place is the best thing to happen to Chinese food fans in years, offering the adventurous diner Taiwanese specialities such as scallion pancake, crispy fried tofu, tea-smoked duck and five-flavoured shrimp. Owner Edward Huang knows his audience – usually a mix of locals and Asian tourists – so there's enough standard fare to keep the sweet-and-sour-chicken crowd happy; but his special menu of authentic dishes is where the flavour's at.

Sam Woo BBQ

Chinatown Plaza, 4215 W Spring Mountain Road, at Wynn Road, South-west Las Vegas (368 7628). Bus 203. **Open** 10am-5am daily. **Main courses** $8-$19. **No credit cards.**

This is not a place for vegans or vegetarians, and it's not coy about it either. The window display is a carnivorous collage of barbecued pigs and poultry, displayed with justifiable pride: they're very, very good. For a cholesterol-laden overview of what these cooks can do, try the barbecue combi: sweet pork, caramelised duck breast and a whole chicken (share it or regret it). The seafood's great, too.

French & Mediterranean

Bonjour Casual French Restaurant

8878 S Eastern Ave, Suite 100 between Wigwam & Pebble Road, Henderson (270 2102). Bus 111. **Open** 11am-2pm Tue-Fri, 5.30-10pm Tue-Sun. **Credit** AmEx, Disc, MC, V.

Dinner and a movie anyone? This place makes it easy, because it is located right next to a multiplex in Henderson. Lovers of good food should rejoice, too, since French menu stalwarts are admirably represented here. Avoid the barely passable shrimp

risotto and the Caesar salad, and order instead the onion soup or the woody fricassee of wild mushrooms, followed by roasted chicken or steak frites. The wine list is well chosen.

Pamplemousse

400 E Sahara Avenue, just east of Paradise Road, East Las Vegas (733 2066). Bus 204. **Open** 6pm-closing times vary Tue-Sun. **Main courses** $17-$28. **Credit** AmEx, DC, Disc, MC, V. **Map** p315 C4.

Owned by local Georges LaForge, Pamplemousse has been serving country-style French fare in a rustic setting to Las Vegans, celebrities and visitors for 20 years. Specialities are duck, veal and seafood, while soufflés are the most sought-after dessert. It's popular with performers on the Strip, making it a good place for celebrity-spotting.

Rosemary's

West Sahara Promenade, 8125 W Sahara Avenue, at Cimmaron Road, North-west Las Vegas (869 2251). Bus 204. **Open** 11.30am-2.30pm, 5.30-10.30pm Mon-Fri; 5.30-10.30pm Sat. **Main courses** $11-$20 lunch; $17-$27 dinner. **Credit** AmEx, DC, Disc, MC, V.

Rosemary's is probably the best non-Strip restaurant in Las Vegas. Michael and Wendy Jordan have created a top-shelf experience that gives every celebrity chef a run for their money. Best of all, they deliver the goods at prices that won't leave you groaning. For $100, two people can enjoy a complex array of tasty dishes that are big on flavour, with everything from sweetbreads to roasted halibut given the star treatment. Jordan does his mentor Emeril Lagasse proud with homages to Southern cooking. Don't miss it.

German

Old Heidelberg German Deli & Restaurant

610 E Sahara Avenue, at Sixth Street, East Las Vegas (731 5310). Bus 204. **Open** 11am-8.30pm Mon-Sat. **Main courses** $15-$18. **Credit** AmEx, Disc, MC, V. **Map** p311 Y2.

Hearty German food and scorching Vegas summers would hardly seem to be a match made in heaven, but when the mood strikes, this small storefront will give you a schnitzel fix. Excellent sauerbraten, a good selection of German beers (which do go down nicely on a hot day) and a German delicatessen give this place an unexpected Bavarian charm.

Indian

Dosa Den

Tropicana Plaza, 3430 E Tropicana Avenue, at Pecos Road, East Las Vegas (456 4920). Bus 111, 201. **Open** 11.30-3pm, 5.30-9pm daily. **Main courses** $8-$12. **No credit cards. Map** p311 Z3.

Dosas are huge Indian crêpes, and this modest restaurant turns them out beautifully, along with excellent vegetarian food, soothing yoghurt sauces, piquant spicing and pulse-flour breads that suit Las Vegas's desert climate very well.

Italian

Jazzed Café, Vinoteca & Trattoria

8615 W Sahara Avenue, at Durango Drive, South-west Las Vegas (233 2895). Bus 203. **Open** 6pm-3am Tue-Sun. **Credit** AmEx, Disc, MC, V.

Jazzed opened as a tiny eastside late-night wine and coffee bar, but recently abandoned that locale for a much larger westside location. The chef-owned eaterie features excellent risotto, pasta and salad (all cooked to order) and an international reputation. The new hangout is similarly cluttered with paintings and candles and has acid jazz grooving on the stereo to keep the beautiful people flocking back. The 50-strong, by-the-glass wine menu doesn't hurt, either.

Montesano's Deli & Restaurant

3441 W Sahara Avenue, between Valley View Boulevard & Arville Street, South-west Las Vegas (876 0348). Bus 104, 204. **Open** 10am-8pm Mon-Wed; 10am-10pm Thur-Sat. **Main courses** $8-$22. **Credit** AmEx, MC, V.

Besides making a mean pizza pie, the Montesano family runs a very successful wholesale Italian bakery, producing everything from wedding cookies to tasty cheese bread. Of the gourmet pies, the five-cheese and fresh tomato are favourites, but you can't go wrong with the pasta, gnocchi with pink cream sauce or ziti braciole. The tiramisu, cannoli and Italian cheesecakes are superb.

Nora's Pizza & Subs

Flamingo Verde, 6020 W Flamingo Road, at Jones Boulevard, South-west Las Vegas (873 8990). Bus 102, 202. **Open** 11am-2.30pm, 4.30-10pm daily. **Main courses** $7-$17. **Credit** AmEx, Disc, MC, V.

Informal and very small, this classic Italian family-run pizzeria serves some outstanding pastas as well. Go for the pasta con sarde (ground olives, sardines and fennel) or puttanesca (redolent of strong capers and green olives) to sample some of this town's best pasta at obscenely low prices.

La Scala

Mark I Tower, 1020 Desert Inn Road, between Maryland Parkway & Swenson Avenue, East Las Vegas (699 9980). **Open** 11.30am-2.30pm, 5-11pm daily. **Main courses** $7-$13 lunch; $10-$26 dinner. **Credit** AmEx, Disc, MC, V. **Map** p311 Y3.

Located on the site of the departed, but not lamented Vesuvio's, and unfortunately saddled with its decor, this kitchen pops out some outstanding northern Italian favourites that compete at almost half the price with similar Strip offerings. You can tell from the superior bread that you're in for something special, and if that doesn't do it for you, then the cool artichoke salad (large enough for two), calamari fritti or prosciutto with figs certainly will.

Spiedini

Regent, 221 N Rampart Boulevard, at Summerlin Parkway, North-west Las Vegas (869 8500). Bus 210. **Open** 5-10.30pm daily. **Main courses** $35. **Credit** AmEx, DC, Disc, MC, V.

Gustav Mauler's Spiedini offers diners at the Regent a comfortable mix of old-world charm and modern atmosphere. The menu, a combination of soups and salads, rich pasta and over-the-top meat dishes, serves traditional Italian tastes, while the funky, modernist environment evokes the palette of Giorgio de Chirico. Come dressed like you mean it, and leave room for the tantalising apple tart with vanilla ice-cream.

Japanese

Dragon Sushi

Chinatown Plaza, 4215 W Spring Mountain Road, at Wynn Road, South-west Las Vegas (368 4328). Bus 203. **Open** 11.30am-10.30pm daily. **Main courses** $7-$25. **Credit** AmEx, DC, Disc, MC, V.

At this small local restaurant, friendly staff and a picture-filled menu make sushi and Japanese specialities easy to order, even for the uninitiated. A refreshing addition to Las Vegas's strong contingent of Japanese choices.

Hamada of Japan

598 E Flamingo Road, just east of Paradise Road, East Las Vegas (733 3005). Bus 202. **Open** 5pm-midnight daily. **Main courses** $26. **Credit** AmEx, DC, Disc, MC, V. **Map** p316 C7.

Sushi and hibachi cooking are given the full treatment at Hamada. The chefs slice some of the best toro (tuna) and unagi (freshwater eel) to be found in Las Vegas, and the sushi hand-rolls are interesting and varied. The sushi bar is preferable to the touristy look, feel and quality of the dining rooms and is popular with Japanese visitors – always a good sign. This branch is due to move to a new building on Paradise Road in late 2001; call for the latest information.

Branches: Flamingo, 3555 Las Vegas Boulevard South (737 0031); Polo Towers Plaza, 3743 Las Vegas Boulevard South (736 1984); Regent, 221 North Rampart Boulevard, North-west Las Vegas (869 7777).

Osaka

4205 W Sahara Avenue, between Sixth Street & Maryland Parkway, East Las Vegas (876 4988). Bus 204. **Open** 11.30am-midnight daily. **Main courses** $15-$25. **Credit** AmEx, DC, Disc, MC, V.

Sushi, hibachi cooking and traditional Japanese fare are all done well in Vegas's oldest Japanese restaurant. The newer sister establishment in Summerlin is upscale but comfortable, with a small bar, a large dining room and a teppan (hibachi) grill area – great fun for large groups or gregarious types. The menu combines traditional fare with a fusion twist. The bilingual staff are most helpful at both places.

Branch: Summerhill Plaza, 7511 W Lake Mead Boulevard, North-west Las Vegas (869 9494).

Togoshi Ramen

Twain Center, 855 E Twain Avenue, at Swenson Street, East Las Vegas (737 7003). Bus 203. **Open** 11.30am-11pm daily. **Main courses** $5-$9. **No credit cards. Map** p311 Y3.
Togoshi Ramen is cheap and downscale, but don't let that deter you. Enjoy ramen and udon noodles in various guises at unbelievably low prices; this is fast food the way it should be.

Mexican & Southwestern

Garduno's

Fiesta, 2400 N Rancho Drive, at W Carey Avenue, North Las Vegas (631 6064). Bus 106, 211. **Open** 11am-3pm, 4-10pm daily. **Main courses** $7-$15. **Credit** AmEx, MC, V.
Good cuisine – featuring the chillis, soups and stews of Hatch, New Mexico – a wide variety of salsas and a serious nod to authenticity have made this hugely popular with locals and worth a visit by tourists, despite its off-Strip location.

Lindo Michoacan

2655 E Desert Inn Road, between Eastern Avenue & Pecos-McLeod Road, East Las Vegas (735 6828). Bus 112. **Open** 11am-11pm daily. **Main courses** $10-$18. **Credit** AmEx, DC, Disc, MC, V. **Map** p311 Z3.
Las Vegas's best Mexican, hands down, though the service can be spotty. Usually, authentic Mexican restaurants are harder to find in Vegas than a flat-chested showgirl, but this is the real article: proper Mexican food cooked by a family that takes pride in its native cuisine. True chilli artistry means the *colorado* (red) will blow your head off and yet have you eager to take the next bite. The crème caramel-like flan is pure heaven.

Rigo's Tacos #8

2737 Las Vegas Boulevard North, at 11th Avenue, North Las Vegas (399 1160). Bus 117. **Open** 24hrs daily. **Main courses** $1-$10. **No credit cards.**
For fast Mexican food done right, this is the place. Rigo's brings authentic tortillas, tacos and fried pork burritos to local Mexican-Americans, who appreciate the difference between the real deal and the pathetically franchised. A fantastic salsa bar features freshly made tomato, smoked chilli and green chilli sauces. Gringos are thin on the ground.

Viva Mercado

Green Valley Towne Center, 4500 E Sunset Road, at Green Valley Parkway, Green Valley (435 6200). Bus 212. **Open** 11am-9.30pm Mon-Thur, Sun; 11am-10pm Fri, Sat. **Main courses** $7-$21. **Credit** AmEx, DC, Disc, MC, V.
A solid restaurant that stands out from the crowd by serving authentic Mexican food. Huge burritos, steak asado and lobster or fish tacos are among the specialities. It's locally owned and very popular.

Middle Eastern

Habib's

Sahara Pavilion, 4750 W Sahara Avenue, at Decatur Boulevard, South-west Las Vegas (870 0860). Bus 103, 204. **Open** 11am-3pm, 5-10pm Mon-Sat. **Main courses** $11-$25. **Credit** AmEx, Disc, MC, V.
This bright and open restaurant on the west side of town serves Middle Eastern food that is unequalled in Las Vegas, including houmous, tabouleh, kebabs and dolma (stuffed vine leaves). Try the khoresht fesenjan (chicken stewed with pomegranate seeds and crushed walnuts) – a tasty eye-opener to the wonders of Persian cuisine.

Mediterranean Café & Market

Tiffany Square, 4147 S Maryland Parkway, at E Flamingo Road, University District (731 6030). Bus 109, 202. **Open** 9.30am-9.30pm daily. **Main courses** $6-$18. **Credit** AmEx, DC, Disc, MC, V. **Map** p311 Y3.
Paymon Raouf served the kind of ethnic food that the college crowd adores, long before anyone else thought of doing so. With so many Middle Eastern restaurants now open, the café has kept its favoured place by expanding its dining room and extending its hours. Tasty and cheap falafel, houmous, braised lamb and more are available for lunch and dinner. Don't miss the Hookah Lounge next door (*see p160*).

Long-time favourite **Mediterranean Café**.

Pizza

Anthony & Mario's Broadway Pizzeria

850 S Rancho Drive, at Charleston Boulevard, North-west Las Vegas (259 9002). Bus 206. **Open** 11am-midnight daily. **Main courses** $8-$15. **Credit** AmEx, Disc, MC, V. **Map** p315 A3.

Good thin-crusted New York pizza done right. Small, brightly lit and decorated only by two sports-oriented TVs, A&M's serves quite possibly the best take-out pizza in town at prices that leave plenty of *lire* for feeding the slots. The baked ziti, spaghetti and meatballs, and huge, hot grinders (sandwiches), aren't bad either.

Metro Pizza

Paradise Market Place, 3870 E Flamingo Road, at Sandhill Road, East Las Vegas (458 4769). Bus 202. **Open** 11.30am-10pm daily. **Main courses** $5-$21. **Credit** AmEx, Disc, MC, V. **Map** p311 Z3.

Decent pizza, very popular with locals, who apparently have never tasted the real thing. **Branches**: Renaissance Center West, 4001 S Decatur Boulevard, South-west Las Vegas (362 7896); Renaissance Center East, 1395 E Tropicana Avenue, East of Strip (736 1955).

Northside Nathan's

7531 W Lake Mead Boulevard, at Buffalo Drive, North-west Las Vegas (255 8822). Bus 210. **Open** 11am-10pm Mon-Thur, Sun; 11am-11pm Fri, Sat. **Main courses** $5-$23. **Credit** AmEx, DC, MC, V.

It is nearly impossible to find a decent pizza (or pizzeria) in Vegas, but never fear, Nathan's is here. With its tinted windows, friendly staff, sports memorabilia and giant-screen TV, stepping into Nathan's is like walking into a pizzeria in Detroit.

Salvadorian

Salvadoreño Restaurant

720 Main Street, between Washington Avenue & Bonanza Road, North Las Vegas (385 3600). Bus 108. **Open** 10am-9pm Tue-Sun. **Main courses** $1-$10. **No credit cards.**

Plain but satisfying food – papusas (savoury dumplings), fried plantains, black beans and the like – is served in a friendly setting in an unfriendly part of town. For that reason alone, go for lunch.

Steakhouses

Bob Taylor's Ranch House

6250 Rio Vista Drive, at Ann Road, North Las Vegas (645 1399). No bus. **Open** 11am-10pm Mon-Thur, Sun; 11am -11pm Fri, Sat. **Main courses** $5-$30 lunch; $13-$44 dinner. **Credit** AmEx, DC, Disc, MC, V.

Located just off North Rancho Drive, Bob Taylor's used to be surrounded by empty desert and a few ranches, but now suburban encroachment is closing in. Mesquite grilled steaks, cooked almost inside the ranch-styled dining room, are the speciality of the house. Memorabilia and movie posters line the walls, and a great spur collection is displayed in the bar. A must-visit if you're interested in how Vegas looked before the fake volcanoes and skyscrapers.

Hilltop House

3400 N Rancho Drive, just north of Cheyenne Avenue, North Las Vegas (645 9904). Bus 106. **Open** 5-9.30pm Wed-Sat; 5-8.30pm Sun. **Main courses** $10-$40. **Credit** AmEx, DC, Disc, MC, V.

Walking into this converted home is like entering a time warp. Steaks and chicken are the specialities, at prices way below joints closer to the Strip. Quite bizarrely, frog's legs have also appeared on the specials list. If you crave 1950s nostalgia and a simple steak dinner, this is not a bad place.

Thai & Vietnamese

Komol

Commercial Center, 953 E Sahara Avenue, at Maryland Parkway, East Las Vegas (731 6542). Bus 103, 204. **Open** 11am-10pm Mon-Sat; noon-10pm Sun. **Main courses** $6-$10. **Credit** AmEx, Disc, MC, V. **Map** p311 Y2.

Despite its location in a run-down mall, Komol remains hugely popular with locals for its authentic rendering of Thai cuisine. Specify the degree of heat you would like, and the kitchen will try to comply.

Lotus of Siam

Commercial Center, 953 E Sahara Avenue, at Maryland Parkway, East Las Vegas (735 3033). Bus 103, 204. **Open** 11.30am-2.30pm Mon-Wed; 11.30am-2.30pm, 5.30-9.30pm Thur-Sat. **Main courses** $8.99-$19.99. **Credit** AmEx, Disc, MC, V. **Map** p311 Y2.

Named one of America's best Thai chefs by *Gourmet Magazine*, Saipin Chutima brought her ingenious and intensely flavoured Thai-Issan cuisine to Vegas in 2000. Forget the run-down surroundings, and focus instead on exotic fare like nua nam tok (beef with green onion and chilli lime juice) or grilled sour pork sausages with chillis, ginger and peanuts.

Saigon

Sahara Pavilion, 4251 W Sahara Avenue, at Decatur Boulevard, South-west Las Vegas (362 9978). Bus 103, 204. **Open** 10am-10pm daily. **Main courses** $8-$10. **Credit** AmEx, MC, V.

Stick with Vietnamese items and avoid the Chinese-sounding ones. Saigon truly excels at pho dishes: large, hearty bowls of noodle soup, which are sometimes very hot and spicy, but always full of thick rice noodles and made with deeply flavoured broth. The spicy beef noodle soup is a knockout, as is the spicy beef with vermicelli and vegetables.

Thai BBQ

Bill Plaza, 4180 Jones Boulevard, at W Flamingo Road, South-west Las Vegas (222 0375). Bus 102, 202. **Open** 11am-11pm daily. **Main courses** $8-$15. **Credit** AmEx, Disc, MC, V.

Vegas on the cheap Food and drink

Inexpensive food and drink has been a cornerstone of Las Vegas since its inception. The all-you-can-eat buffets, 99¢ breakfast specials and the free Scotch and soda in the casino are as much a part of Vegas lore as craps, cards and cleavage. Despite the recent onslaught of higher-end restaurants, you can still find enough bargain eats to gorge yourself into oblivion, and as long as you're over 21 and you're gambling, you will be served free drinks in every casino in town.

Note that food and drink – like everything else in Las Vegas – tend to be cheaper in Downtown. For addresses and contact details of the venues listed here, *see* chapter **Casinos**.

Buffets

The least expensive buffets include those at the **Sahara**, **Circus Circus**, **Excalibur**, **Sam's Town**, **Station Casinos** and **Coast Resorts**.

Breakfast

Las Vegas Club The coffeeshop serves a New York steak-and-eggs breakfast for $2.95 11pm-6am daily.
Orleans Nightcrawlers will be glad of the graveyard specials, including a pancake sandwich or a full-blown two-egg breakfast with bacon or sausage, all for $1.95.
Westward Ho (2900 Las Vegas Boulevard South; 731 2900). Grab a cup of coffee for a nickel and a doughnut for 50¢.

Lunch

Golden Gate (1 Fremont Street, Downtown; 385 1906). Don't miss the Bay City Diner's classic 99¢ prawn cocktail.
Riviera Spend 99¢ on foot-long hot dogs or $1.50 on burgers at the Riviera's Nickel Town snack bar.
Westward Ho Tuck into a ¾ lb hotdog served with all the trimmings for 99¢.

Dinner

Gold Coast The Monterey Room serves a 24-hour Texas T-bone special for $7.95 that includes a 16oz steak, mixed green salad, cowboy beans, onion rings, potato wedges, garlic Texas toast and a frosty 12oz draught beer.
Hard Rock Order the $5.95 steak and shrimp special at Mr Lucky's (*see p142*). It's not on the menu, but it's worth every penny.

Drinks

Gold Spike (400 Ogden Avenue, Downtown; 384 8444). A watered-down well drink costs just 50¢.
Las Vegas Club Guzzle beer or cocktails for about a buck and a half.
Riviera The Nickel Town snack bar will charge you 25¢ for lemonade or 50¢ for draught beer.

Also good value and worth a visit are the bars at **Binion's Horseshoe**, **O'Shea's** and the **Imperial Palace**.

Despite a downscale, hard-to-find location, this place gets a steady stream of customers who recognise it as one of the best Thai eateries in town. The friendly and helpful service makes all-comers welcome and the hearty and huge portions of classic dishes will blow your head off. Highlights include papaya salad, excellent satay, stuffed chicken 'Wings of Angel' and rich and spicy beef noodle soup.

Thai Spice

4433 W Flamingo Road, at Arville Street, South-west Las Vegas (362 5308). Bus 202. **Open** 11am-10pm daily. **Main courses** $4-$16. **Credit** AmEx, DC, Disc, MC, V.

A real anomaly among Thai restaurants in Vegas, Thai Spice is larger, brighter, nicer and generally better than the others. A short drive or cab ride from the Strip hotels, it serves excellent versions of favourites such as Thai beef salad, pad thai, tom kha gai (hot and sour chicken soup) and fishcakes. Good accessibility, decor and service make this one of Las Vegas's most popular Thai restaurants.

Buffets

Las Vegas's all-you-can-eat buffets are an institution that should be experienced at least once during your trip. Buffets offer the means to consume a huge volume of food for relatively little money (despite steadily rising prices in recent years). Moreover, the food is generally good, offering variety, if not five-star dining.

The idea of the buffet started in the early 1940s at the original El Rancho Las Vegas. Looking for a way to keep customers in his casino after the late stage show, owner Beldon Katleman dreamed up the 'Midnight Chuck Wagon Buffet – All you can eat for a dollar'. His idea of treating guests to an elaborate feast for a small price was soon copied and expanded by other hotels: why not offer it at breakfast, lunch and dinner, too? And so the Vegas buffet boom was born.

Eat, Drink, Shop

WHAT TO EXPECT

Casino buffets typically serve breakfast, lunch and dinner (in separate sittings), often scrapping breakfast and lunch at weekends in favour of a more expensive all-day brunch (Bally's Sterling Brunch is the out-and-out star in this category). Some locations offer theme buffets featuring a different cuisine on different nights of the week. But, whatever the variations, all Vegas buffets work in the same way: you pay one price at the beginning and then stuff yourself silly.

Modern buffets barely resemble the old chuckwagon smorgasbords. Featuring a variety of carving and cooking stations plus steam tables or kiosks (to ensure food is warm but not dried out), the average dinner buffet has at least 50 food selections ranging from salads and fruit to roast meats, vegetables, potatoes, rolls, coffee and all the desserts imaginable. In addition to standard American fare, many casinos offer international cuisine and speciality barbecue dishes. The best lunch buffets offer nearly the same choices as at dinner but for several dollars less, making them a great bargain.

Buffet prices vary and have edged higher recently, but at most major resorts they run from $5 to $8 per person for breakfast, $7 to $13 for lunch and $10 to $22 for dinner, with cheaper rates for kids. For this you should expect good quality food, especially at the new mega-resorts and the highly competitive locals casinos. Bellagio's dinner buffet, at $22.95 a head, is the most expensive standard buffet in town, but the food is very good. The lunch buffet ($16.95) at Paris is also recommended.

ADVICE AND ETIQUETTE

Buffet etiquette is simple: you can eat as much as you want while you're there, but the casinos disapprove of customers trying to taking food out. Health codes require you to take a new plate every time you return to the buffet; leave your used plates and a small tip on the table to be picked up by the buffet staff.

Finally, if you don't like to wait in queues for your food, a time-tested rule of thumb goes something like this: early for breakfast, late for lunch, and early for dinner. It seems to work.

Casino buffets

Bally's Big Kitchen

Bally's, 3645 Las Vegas Boulevard South, at E Flamingo Road (739 4111). Bus 202, 301, 302. **Buffets** *Breakfast* 7-11am daily. *Lunch* 11am-2.30pm daily. *Dinner* 4.30-10pm daily. **Prices** $10.95 breakfast; $12.95 lunch; $17.95 dinner. **Credit** AmEx, Disc, MC, V. **Map** p316 A7.
From the carpeted and chandeliered dining area to the bountiful food, this is one of the best spreads in town. Diners eat at booths and tables in a split-level

dining room overlooking the Strip. As well as standard buffet fare, there's often leg of lamb, sirloin, crab legs, peeled shrimp and Chinese specialities.

Bally's Sterling Brunch

Bally's, 3645 Las Vegas Boulevard South, at E Flamingo Road (739 4111). Bus 202, 301, 302. **Buffet** *Brunch* 9.30am-2.30pm Sun. **Price** $55. **Credit** AmEx, Disc, MC, V. **Map** p316 A7.
So extraordinary are some of the dishes at Bally's Sterling Brunch and so upmarket is the clientele that even calling it a Vegas buffet seems tawdry and inappropriate. From the fresh smoked Nova salmon with (very good) bagels to caviar with blinis and a cold lamb potato salad with lime vinaigrette, the 20-plus appetisers and scores of entrées are all made in-house, daily. This is Vegas as it used to be: upmarket food, tuxedoed waiters, flowing champagne, all lapped up by swellegantly dressed guys and dolls.

Bellagio Buffet

Bellagio, 3600 Las Vegas Boulevard South, at W Flamingo Road (693 7111). Bus 202, 301, 302. **Buffets** *Breakfast* 7-10.30am daily. *Lunch* 11am-3.30pm daily. *Dinner* 4-10pm daily. **Prices** $10.95 breakfast; $13.95 lunch; $22.95 dinner. **Credit** AmEx, Disc, MC, V. **Map** p316 A7.
The price tops virtually all other Strip buffets, but it's worth it. The tasteful dining room is well laid-out and divided into separate smoking and no-smoking areas. The usual buffet fare is upgraded with offerings such as venison, duck breast, steamed clams, crab legs and desserts made from the freshest ingredients. Note that Bellagio's no under-18s rule also applies to the Buffet.

The Buffet

Golden Nugget, 129 Fremont Street, at Casino Center Boulevard, Downtown (385 7111). Bus 107, 403. **Buffets** *Breakfast* 7-10.30am Mon-Sat. *Brunch* 8am-10pm Sun. *Lunch* 10.30am-3pm Mon-Sat. *Dinner* 4-10pm Mon-Sat. **Prices** $5.75 breakfast; $10.95 brunch; $7.50 lunch; $10.25 dinner. **Credit** AmEx, Disc, DC, MC, V. **Map** p312 C1.
You'll find a touch of class in the Buffet's opulent dining room: marble-top tables, partitioned booths, etched glass and brass fixtures. The offerings are near the top of the Vegas food chain, especially the elaborate salad bar, the cold food stations and the carvery, typically serving turkey and prime rib. Excellent desserts include fresh-baked tarts, cakes, pies and a locally famous bread pudding.

Carnival World Buffet

Rio, 3700 W Flamingo Road, at Valley View Boulevard, West of Strip (252 7777). Bus 202. **Buffets** *Breakfast* 8-10.30am Mon-Fri. *Brunch* 8.30am-3.30pm Sat, Sun. *Lunch* 11am-3.30pm Mon-Fri. *Dinner* 3.30-11pm daily. **Prices** $7.99 breakfast; $15.99 brunch; $10.99 lunch; $14.99 dinner. **Credit** AmEx, Disc, MC, V. **Map** p311 X3.
If you can stand the long queues, you'll be rewarded with fresh and tasty cuisine, served amid fake tropical blooms and palm-fringed display tables. Choose

from Chinese stir-fry, Mexican taco fixings, Japanese sushi and teppan yaki, Italian pasta, a Mongolian grill and fish and chips. There's even a set-up for hot dogs, burgers, fries and milkshakes. Beat the queues by joining the Rio's slot club.

Circus Circus Buffet

Circus Circus, 2880 Las Vegas Boulevard South, at Circus Circus Drive, between Desert Inn Road & W Sahara Avenue (734 0410). Bus 301, 302. **Buffets** *Breakfast* 7-11.30am Mon-Sat. *Brunch* 7am-4pm Sat, Sun. *Lunch* noon-4pm Mon-Sat. *Dinner* 4.30-10pm Mon-Fri; 4.30-11pm Sat. **Prices** $5.49 breakfast; $6.99 brunch; $6.49 lunch; $7.99 dinner. **Credit** AmEx, Disc, MC, V. **Map** p315 B5.

The large pink room with the circus-tent awnings is the busiest buffet on the Strip, serving more than 10,000 people a day. Although the queues are well managed, you'll inevitably have to wait at peak times. Once you're in, the ranks and ranks of stainless steel dispensers inevitably evoke an institutional feel that's not improved by food that's only a shade above a school cafeteria – Salisbury steak, chicken fritters and ravioli with meatballs.

The Feast

Palace Station, 2411 W Sahara Avenue, at Rancho Drive, West of Strip (367 2411). Bus 204, 401. **Buffets** *Breakfast* 7-11am Mon-Fri. *Brunch* 7am-3.30pm Sat, Sun. *Lunch* 11am-3pm Mon-Fri. *Dinner* 4-10pm daily. **Prices** $4.99 breakfast; $9.99 brunch; $6.99 lunch; $8.99 dinner. **Credit** AmEx, Disc, MC, V. **Map** p315 A4.

In the late 1980s, the Feast pioneered the 'action' buffet, at which short-order cooks prepared steaks, omelettes and burgers to order. Today, it's been surpassed by many other buffets, but its salad and dessert bars remain among the largest in the city. Theme nights include T-bone steak on Thursday and New York Strip on Friday.

Festival Buffet

Fiesta, 2400 N Rancho Drive, at Lake Mead Boulevard, North Las Vegas (631 7000). Bus 106, 210. **Buffets** *Breakfast* 8-10am Mon-Fri. *Brunch* 7am-3pm Sat, Sun. *Lunch* 11am-3pm Mon-Fri. *Dinner* 4-10pm daily. **Prices** $1.99 breakfast; $7.99 brunch, dinner; $4.99 lunch. **Credit** AmEx, Disc, MC, V. **Map** p311 X1.

You can rub elbows with the locals at this popular smorgasbord, featuring the best barbecue in town. It's worth the schlepp from the Strip to sample the ribs, ham, turkey, beef, sausage and shredded pork, along with all the fixings. The Wednesday seafood buffet is also a good catch.

Fresh Market Square Buffet

Harrah's, 3475 Las Vegas Boulevard South, between Sands Avenue & E Flamingo Road (369 5000). Bus 301, 302. **Buffets** *Breakfast* 7-11am Mon-Fri. *Brunch* 10am-4pm Sat, Sun. *Lunch* 11.30am-3.30pm Mon-Fri. *Dinner* 4-10pm daily. **Prices** $8.99 breakfast; $14.99 brunch, dinner; $9.99 lunch. **Credit** AmEx, Disc, MC, V. **Map** p316 A6.

Giant celery and cornstalk columns, oversized muffins and replica fruit create a setting straight out of *Alice in Wonderland*. Chefs prepare fajitas and chimichangas at the Mexican station, and fettucine, lasagne and sausages at the Italian station. The American Bounty station serves chicken étouffée, red beans and dirty rice, barbecued ribs, meatloaf and a good seafood selection. Save room for the signature bananas Foster dessert: skillet-heated bananas topped with caramel-rum sauce.

The pretty **Garden Court Buffet** at Main Street Station. *See p154.*

Garden Court Buffet

Main Street Station, 200 N Main Street, at Stewart Avenue, Downtown (387 1896). Bus 207. **Buffets** *Breakfast* 7-10.30am Mon-Fri. *Brunch* 7am-3pm Sat, Sun. *Lunch* 11am-3pm Mon-Fri. *Dinner* 4-10pm daily. **Prices** $5.29 breakfast; $8.99 brunch; $7.49 lunch; $10.29 dinner. **Credit** AmEx, Disc, MC, V. **Map** p312 C1.

With its high ceilings, marble-top counters, used-brick walls and tall windows, this is one of the best-looking buffets in town. Good Chinese and Polynesian specialities cater for Main Street's many Hawaiian tourists, but there's also fresh salsas, a barbecue rotisserie and Southern dishes. Specials include steak on Tuesday and filet and scampi on Thursday.

Mirage Buffet

Mirage, 3400 Las Vegas Boulevard South, between Spring Mountain & W Flamingo Roads (791 7111). Bus 301, 302. **Buffets** *Breakfast* 7-10.45am Mon-Fri. *Brunch* 8am-3pm Sat, Sun. *Lunch* 11am-2.45pm Mon-Fri. *Dinner* 3-10pm Mon-Sat. **Prices** $8.95 breakfast; $14.95 brunch, dinner; $9.95 lunch. **Credit** AmEx, Disc, MC, V. **Map** p316 A6.

This buffet's usually packed, especially on weekends and holidays, but a slot-club member's comp slip will get you to the front of the line. The food is fresh and well prepared with a nod, oddly enough, towards good nutrition; the enormous salad bar is supported by cholesterol-friendly selections such as tabbouleh, Thai beef, Chinese chicken and seafood. There are even sugar- and fat-free cakes and puds.

Palatium Buffet

Caesars Palace, 3570 Las Vegas Boulevard South, at W Flamingo Road (731 7110). Bus 202, 301, 302. **Buffets** *Breakfast* 7.30-11.30am Mon-Fri. *Brunch* 8.30am-3.30pm Sat, Sun. *Lunch* 11.30am-3.30pm Mon-Fri. *Dinner* 4.30-10pm Mon-Sat. **Prices** $9.99 breakfast; $21.99 brunch; $11.99 lunch; $16.99 dinner Mon-Thur; $25 dinner Fri, Sat. **Credit** AmEx, Disc, MC, V. **Map** p316 A7.

This buffet draws in tourists and locals for its Friday and Saturday nights seafood feast. The food is freshly prepared by chefs at open cooking stations, and often includes poached salmon, grilled swordfish, Alaskan crab legs, peeled shrimp and scallops. One lobster is included in the price; additional lobsters cost $12.

Paradise Buffet

Fremont, 200 Fremont Street, at Main Street, Downtown (385 3232). Bus 107, 403. **Buffets** *Breakfast* 7-10.30am Mon-Fri. *Brunch* 7am-3pm Sat, Sun. *Lunch* 11am-3pm Mon-Fri. *Dinner* 4-10pm daily. **Prices** $4.99 breakfast; $8.75 brunch; $6.99 lunch; $9.99 dinner Mon, Wed, Thur, Sat; $14.99 dinner Tue, Fri, Sun. **Credit** AmEx, Disc, MC, V. **Map** p312 D1.

Palm trees, tropical flowers, bird calls, Polynesian music and the splash of waterfalls set the tone for some great seafood on Tuesday, Friday and Sunday nights. Serving tables are decorated with ice sculptures and laden with lobster claws, crab legs, shrimp, oysters, smoked salmon and clams.

Le Village Buffet

Paris, 3355 Las Vegas Boulevard South, between Harmon Avenue & E Flamingo Road (946 7000). Bus 202, 301, 302. **Buffets** *Breakfast* 7.30-11.30am Mon-Sat. *Brunch* 7am-4pm Sun. *Lunch* noon-5.30pm Mon-Sat. *Dinner* 5.30-10.30pm Mon-Thur, Sun; 5.30-11pm Fri, Sat. **Prices** $10.95 breakfast; $21.95 brunch, dinner; $14.95 lunch. **Credit** AmEx, Disc, MC, V. **Map** p316 A7.

This 400-seat buffet has stations representing five French provinces. Dinner entrées include prime rib, venison, crab legs, shrimps in a shallot cream sauce, freshly sautéed salmon, bouillabaisse, wild mushroom bisque and a delicious French onion soup. Save room for the freshly made pastries, breads and desserts including créme brûlée and crêpes.

Village Seafood Buffet

Rio, 3700 W Flamingo Road, at Valley View Boulevard (252 7777). Bus 202. **Buffet** *Dinner* 4-10pm Mon-Thur, Sun; 5-11pm Fri, Sat. **Price** $28.95. **Credit** AmEx, Disc, MC, V. **Map** p311 X3.

Served on the other side of the casino from the Carnival Buffet, this seafood buffet is more expensive than most, but worth it. Specialities include steamed clams, swordfish, calamari, salmon, scallops, shrimp and king crab legs. The Mongolian Seafood Barbecue offers shrimp, scallops, fish or squid.

Non-casino buffets

Also try the lunch buffets at Indian restaurants **Gandhi** and **Shalimar** (for both, *see p142*).

Classic Buffet House

3331 E Tropicana Avenue, between Eastern Avenue & Pecos Road, East Las Vegas (435 2226). Bus 201. **Buffets** *Lunch* 11am-4.30pm daily. *Dinner* 5-9pm daily. **Prices** *Lunch* $6.95; $3.95 under-8s. *Dinner* $8.95; $5.95 under-8s. **Credit** Disc, MC, V. **Map** p311 Z3.

This bright, airy buffet restaurant offers first-rate Chinese and Japanese cuisine at bargain prices. More than 50 dishes are served each day from a possible 200 recipes, including pork curry, kung pao chicken, shrimp with broccoli, and spicy tofu. At dinner, feast on all-you-can-eat shrimp and crab legs.

Makino Todai Restaurant

3965 S Decatur Boulevard, at Flamingo Road, South-west Las Vegas (889 4477). Bus 103, 202. **Buffets** *Lunch* 11.30am-2.30pm daily. *Dinner* 5.30-9pm daily. **Prices** *Lunch* $12.95 Mon-Fri; $13.95 Sat, Sun; $2.50-$6.48 concessions. *Dinner* $20.95 Mon-Thur; $21.95 Fri-Sun; $2.50-$10.98 concessions. **Credit** AmEx, Disc, MC, V.

For the mother of all Japanese buffets, this hyperactive restaurant is unlike any in town. In the sushi section eight chefs busily replenish 40 different kinds of sushi, while elsewhere you can choose from snow-crab legs, green-lip mussels, shrimp salad, chicken teriyaki, clams with ginger and todai roast beef. Children's prices are calculated according to the size (and presumably the appetite) of the child.

Bars

From trendy casino lounges to seedy dives, Sin City keeps serving them up 24 hours a day, seven days a week.

The bars and lounges of Las Vegas serve beer, wine and cocktails around the clock. Many of them haven't shut their doors even once since opening day. In a city where the casinos never close, why should the bars? Heaven forbid everyone sobers up and realises just how much money has been spent.

Most casinos provide free cocktails to gamblers and many offer bottled beers and cocktails to non-players for under a dollar in the hope that they'll forget themselves and start playing. The downside of this is that almost every bar in Las Vegas, from the glitziest casino to the smallest corner dive, is tainted by the sickly glow and clanking din of video poker machines (if you want to play, make it clear to the bartender to ask for a roll of quarters and your drink will be free if you sign a chit). The few bars that don't have poker machines simply couldn't get a gaming licence.

Despite this feature of bar life, it's possible to enjoy a civilised drink – or an uncivilised drunk, if you prefer – all over Vegas. Most of the action takes place on or near the Strip, where the bars and lounges become more like nightclubs with every passing year, complete with live DJs, modish interiors and twentysomethings dressed to impress. The further you go from the Strip, the thinner the tourist mix gets, but, unfortunately, the quality of the experience dips as well. Most drinking establishments beyond the resort corridor are generic neighbourhood bars with very little variety in vibe or decor. There are a few diamonds to be found beyond the mother lode, but they require a bit of digging to unearth.

If you're rather less fussy about where you drink, it may be enough to know that in Vegas you're never far from a **PT's Pub** – known as the McDonald's of bars among locals, owing to their tendency to pop up on every corner. PT's are no-nonsense drink stops, with cheap, American draught beers, seemingly endless happy hours and well-used pool tables and dartboards. A warning to would-be drunk drivers: many of the outposts are frequented by off-duty policemen.

Note that the terms 'lounge' and 'bar' are often used interchangeably. As a rule of thumb, however, lounges tend to be rather more sedate, sometimes with a live band

Horse-A-Round Bar: it's weird. See p156.

playing pop covers or inoffensive jazz. Casino bars worth visiting in their own right are included here, but you should also check out the casino lounges listed in the **Casino Entertainment** chapter. Music and nightclub venues can be found in the **Nightlife** chapter.

It is inevitable that many noteworthy bars will open during the life of this guide; check free newspapers such as *Las Vegas Weekly* and *CityLife* or websites like www.vegas.com for details of the latest openings.

BOOZE AND THE LAW

You have to be 21 to consume or buy alcohol in Nevada, and you'll be required to produce photo identification, even in casinos – it doesn't matter if you look like Methuselah's older brother.

Las Vegas's drunk-driving laws are as harsh and uncompromising as in any major US city, and the Metro Police department doesn't let too many woozy fish swim by. Fortunately, you can easily walk back and forth between bars on the Strip and Fremont Street, and a taxi ride to and from the best off-Strip joints costs little. Cabs are plentiful around the Strip and the bartender will usually ask if you want one.

The Strip

For over-the-top decor and after-hours parties (*see p212*), head for the plush lounge adjoining **Drai's** restaurant (*see p133*) at the Barbary Coast. Or, if you prefer a room with a view, pay $6 to travel up the Stratosphere tower to the **Top of the World Lounge**. (It's free if you make a reservation at the restaurant; *see p132*.)

Holy Cow Café & Brewery

2423 Las Vegas Boulevard South, at Sahara Avenue (732 2697). Bus 205, 301, 302. **Open** 24hrs daily. **Credit** AmEx, Disc, MC, V. **Map** p315 C4.

Vegas's oldest microbrewery is hardly its best. Far superior suds are served up at Gordon Biersch (*see p158*), the Triple 7 (*see p159*) and Barley's (*see p159*), and the bovine motif is obnoxious beyond belief. The Holy Cow's only advantage is its location, halfway between the major Strip hotels and Fremont Street.

Horse-A-Round Bar

Circus Circus, 2880 Las Vegas Boulevard South, at Circus Circus Drive, between Desert Inn Road & W Sahara Avenue (734 0410). Bus 204, 301, 302. **Open** 24hrs daily. **Credit** AmEx, Disc, MC, V. **Map** p315 B5.

Immortalised in Hunter S Thompson's wild Sin City novel *Fear and Loathing in Las Vegas*, Circus Circus's Horse-A-Round Bar represents Las Vegas at its most chilling and sublime. Yes, patrons sit in a slow-turning representation of a carousel; yes, live trapeze artists spin and dive overhead. The experience is largely what you bring to it – either you'll be intrigued (as Thompson's readers were) or terrified (as Thompson was). Either way, you'll get a unique Vegas experience. And the drinks are cheap, too.

Jack's Velvet Lounge

WB Stage 16, Venetian, 3355 Las Vegas Boulevard South, at Sands Avenue (414 1699). Bus 203, 301, 302. **Open** 4.30pm-3am Mon-Thur, Sun; 4.30pm-4am Fri, Sat. **Credit** AmEx, Disc, MC, V. **Map** p316 A6.

Raw wood walls, long curtains and dramatic low lighting give Jack's Velvet Lounge the feel of a movie set, which is presumably what the creators, Warner Brothers, hoped to achieve. Overstuffed couches and a balcony overlooking the Strip add to the cosmopolitan feel. Arrive early for a low-key, laidback atmosphere, because at 10pm the rooms fill to capacity, the music pumps up and the couches are lined with reserved signs. Velvet flirts the line between ultra-cool and affectation. If you're not interested in seeing and being seen, this may not be the place for you, but extroverts have the potential to become legendary here. As this guide went to press, rumours were circulating about another hip design bar at the Venetian, to be located under Jack's Velvet Lounge.

Monte Carlo Pub & Brewery

Monte Carlo, 3770 Las Vegas Boulevard South, at Rue de Monte Carlo, between W Flamingo Road & W Tropicana Avenue (730 7777). Bus 201, 301, 302.

Open 11am-2.30am Mon-Thur, Sun; 11am-3.30am Fri, Sat. **Credit** AmEx, DC, Disc, MC, V. **Map** p316 A8.

Even if you're not an avid beer drinker you'll like the atmosphere: huge copper beer barrels, antique furnishings, live piano entertainment every night and a pleasant outdoor patio that overlooks the lavish pool area. Visitors can even roam the microbrewery's catwalk and gaze down on the brewing process. Six different styles of Monte Carlo-labelled beer are produced, including an IPA, an unfiltered wheat ale, an Irish stout and a rich amber ale. Soak it all up with a choice of delicious brick-oven pizzas, sausage platters, salads and sandwiches.

Napoleon's

Paris, 3655 Las Vegas Boulevard South, between Harmon Avenue & E Flamingo Road (946 7000, ext 66349). Bus 202, 301, 302. **Open** *Bar* 2pm-2am Mon-Thur, Sun; 2-9pm Fri, Sat. *Vamp nightclub* 10pm-4am Fri, Sat. **Admission** *Vamp* $15. **Credit** AmEx, DC, Disc, MC, V. **Map** p316 A7.

Video screens, laser lights and stylish furnishings set the tone, accompanied by a blend of vocal house and retro-remixes from the in-house DJ. The rich clubby atmosphere is intensified by the presence of a cigar and pipe parlour and imported wines and beers. For details of Vamp at Napoleon's, *see p213*.

Peppermill's Fireside Lounge

Peppermill Inn Restaurant, 2985 Las Vegas Boulevard South, at Convention Center Drive (735 7635). Bus 301, 302. **Open** 24hrs daily. **Credit** AmEx, Disc, MC, V. **Map** p315 B5.

This dark lounge, darker than most, is so thoroughly kitsch it can't help but be cool. A giant fire pit anchors the room, with blue flames inexplicably erupting from a pool of water. Waitresses in long, slit dresses serve up outrageous cocktails; the Scorpion requires a glass the size of a fishbowl. The customers tends to keep to themselves or paw up their respective dates, whichever comes naturally.

Polo Lounge

Polo Towers, 3745 Las Vegas Boulevard South, at Harmon Avenue (261 1000). Bus 301, 302. **Open** 8am-2am daily. **Credit** AmEx, V. **Map** p316 A8.

A well kept secret, this tiny lounge boasts occasional entertainment, cheap but reliable drinks, a well mannered and blessedly unhip clientele and the best view of the middle-Strip you'll find, including Bellagio's fountains, minus the Lionel Richie music. In other words, it's a perfect place to escape the crowds, relax and regroup.

Red Square

Mandalay Bay, 3950 Las Vegas Boulevard South, between W Tropicana Avenue & Russell Road (632 7407). Bus 301, 302. **Open** 4.30-11pm Mon-Thur, Sun; 4.30pm-2am Fri, Sat. **Credit** AmEx, DC, MC, V. **Map** p316 A9.

Presided over by a headless, post-Glasnost statue of Lenin, this vodka bar keeps the October Revolution alive all year round. Soviet propaganda posters

Puff away at the **Hookah Lounge**. See p160.

abound and a hundred-odd Polish, Swedish, Russian and other exotic vodkas are served from a bar topped by a solid block of ice. There's beluga and blinis to nibble, plus a functionally trendy menu with a few Russian twists: Bolshevik salmon pizza anyone? Make like Dr Zhivago, put on a muff and venture into the sub-zero vodka locker for the really pricey liquor and you'll also find Lenin's head, frozen in a solid block of ice and looking none too pleased. Go early for the appetisers, late for drinks and easy on the vodka. If you can't have fun at Red Square, comrade, you'd be better off in Minsk.

rumjungle

Mandalay Bay, 3950 Las Vegas Boulevard South, between W Tropicana Avenue & Russell Road (632 7408). Bus 201, 301, 302. **Open** 5.30pm-2am Mon-Thur, Sun; 5.30pm-5am Fri, Sat. **Credit** AmEx, DC, MC, V. **Map** p316 A9.

Cowneck, Kill-Devil or Nelson's Blood, it all amounts to the same thing: that old demon rum. At rumjungle, the signature beverage is the main attraction, which is no small feat in a room that has walls of fire and water. A hundred different brands of rum are served in countless ways; you are limited only by your imagination and your ability to put on a good pirate's slur. Late in the evening, it becomes a very popular nightclub (*see p212*), which means would-be Long John Silvers hoping to sink a few shots should nab their place at the bar as soon it opens at 5.30pm. Dress: smart casual.

Shadow Bar

Caesars Palace, 3750 Las Vegas Boulevard South, at W Flamingo Road (731 7110). Bus 301, 302. **Open** 24hrs daily. **Credit** AmEx, Disc, DC, MC, V. **Map** p316 A7.

Caesars Palace's entry in Vegas's hip-bar sweepstakes is a somewhat unorthodox combination of faux-Roman kitsch, New York cool and any number of topless bars. Girls in body stockings dance behind screens to create the shadows of the bar's name,

bumping and grinding to funk and pop hits in an attempt to take your mind off the high price of the drinks and appetisers. Not to be left out, bartenders flip bottles over their heads and pour drinks in mid air; it's like drinking at the circus. If you've cash to burn, it's a fun way to kill half an hour, but it's not a place to get comfortable. Dress: smart casual.

V Bar

Venetian, 3355 Las Vegas Boulevard South, at Sands Avenue (414 3200). Bus 203, 301, 302. **Open** 4pm-4am daily. **Credit** AmEx, DC, Disc, MC, V. **Map** p316 A6.

While other Las Vegas bars strive to be more, the V Bar succeeds with less: minimal decor, no advertising and a location that's all but hidden near the Venetian's back doors. Don't be fooled though, the V Bar has one of the best top-shelves in town – the selection of Scotches is beyond belief – and a staff that favours style and service over flash and flair. The burden of the latter, then, falls squarely on the V's clientele, a young, attractive and affluent group that can be up to 50% local on select nights. They crowd into the V's modernist booths, sample the new libations (the bartenders mix up something different each week) and put on a show for the lesser mortals peeking in through small slits in the wall-length frosted glass windows. Dress code: smart casual.

Off-Strip

East of Strip

Double Down Saloon

Paradise Plaza, 4640 Paradise Road, between Harmon & Tropicana Avenues (791 5775). Bus 108. **Open** 24hrs daily. **No credit cards. Map** p316 C8.

The hippest bar in Las Vegas is located less than a mile from the Strip. Darkly psychedelic murals cover every surface, TV monitors display 1940s adventure

For drinking yourself into a stupor

The **Double Down Saloon** asks no questions, offers no advice, draws a steady crowd of serious drinkers from all walks of life and serves a mean Martini. And what's more, there's aspirin in the bar's vending machine. See p157.

For finding a friend for the evening

If you can't pick up a willing partner at **Gordon Biersch**, it might be time to reconsider your approach to personal hygiene. See p158.

For a Cosmopolitan that can't be beat

The **Hookah Lounge** serves a Cosmopolitan that's so perfect, it may well have medicinal uses. If not, the hookahs and flavoured tobacco certainly do. See p160.

For a simple pint

The **Crown & Anchor Pub** is close to the Strip, but not so close that some fool will get in your face while you're trying to watch the footie. See p159.

For potential movie-star sightings

The **V Bar** (see p157) and **Jack's Velvet Lounge** (see p156) fill with a Hollywood crowd nearly every night. Wear your best shirt and shoes and act like you've got somewhere better to be.

For the quintessential Vegas experience (good and bad)

The **Shadow Bar** at Caesars Palace has girls dancing to Janet Jackson tunes behind screens, hard-faced gambling types talking business in booths, and a mix of tourists that's as giddy as it is confused. See p157.

serials and the clientele is deliciously mixed: guests of the house have included film director Tim Burton and late LSD guru Dr Timothy Leary. The infamous jukebox cranks out an eclectic mix ranging from British punk to American jazz, and there's a live blues jam every Wednesday. A giant sign over the front door proclaims the Double Down the 'happiest place on Earth' and more than once it's been proved right. Don't leave without trying the house tipple: a sweet, blood-red concoction of mysterious origin, lovingly dubbed 'Ass Juice'.

Gordon Biersch

3987 Paradise Road, at Flamingo Road (312 5247).
Bus 108, 202. **Open** 11.30am-midnight Mon, Sun;
11.30am-2am Tue-Sat. **Credit** AmEx, DC, Disc, MC,
V. **Map** p316 C7.
San Francisco's prize microbrewery is now one of Las Vegas's most popular pick-up joints. It fills to capacity every night with beautiful people drawn by the fine brew, live music (call for times) and an extensive menu, including colourfully named appetisers such as Angry Prawns. Valet parking is available: you'll need it. See also p142.

Viva Las Vegas Lounge

Hard Rock, 4455 Paradise Road, at Harmon Avenue
(693 5000). Bus 108. **Open** 24hrs daily. **Credit**
AmEx, Disc, MC, V. **Map** p316 C7.
The Viva Las Vegas lounge – known as the Sidebar by locals, owing to its location on the side of bustling casino – is fairly lively around the clock, but really jumps on Friday and Saturday nights, when young singles pack the area to overflow. The drinks cost slightly more than they should, but the people-watching more than makes up for it, as do the light-bulb suits worn by the Red Hot Chili Peppers at Woodstock number two, and mounted behind the bar. Despite the location, there's no live music.

West of Strip

VooDoo Lounge

Masquerade Village Tower, Rio, 3700 W Flamingo
Road, at Valley View Boulevard (252 7777).
Bus 104, 202. **Open** 11am-3am daily. *Café* 5-11pm
daily. *Shows* 9pm daily. **Admission** free Mon-Thur,
Sun; $10 Fri, Sat. **Credit** AmEx, DC, Disc, MC, V.
Map p311 X3.
There's a whole lot of gross pretension going on here. After getting a serious up-and-down from the bouncer at the elevator, you are whisked up 40 storeys, where the air is rare, the view is spectacular, silicone-enhanced cleavage abounds and the over-rated psychedelic cocktails go for the price of an entire steak dinner Downtown. To keep things humming, better-than-average bands offer everything from swing to jazz and Brazilian rhythm while the kitchen doles out less-than-great renditions of Cajun and Creole food. Thousands are drawn to the VooDoo to mix with the pretty crowd, but the vibe is empty. Worth a visit for the view, however. Dress code: 11am-5pm no beachwear; 5pm-2am smart casual, no athletic wear.

Downtown

The Bar at Thai Town

Thai Town, 1201 Las Vegas Boulevard South, at
Park Paseo Drive (388 1682). Bus 301, 302. **Open**
24hrs daily. **Credit** MC, V. **Map** p315 C3.
Located directly across the street from the Las Vegas Youth Hostel (see p62), within staggering distance of several other hostels, the Bar at Thai

Eat, Drink, Shop

Town is a fine stop for the legal-age globetrotter. The Far East decor is unobtrusive and a comfortable sofa allows visitors to stretch out a bit as they sample the fine Martinis and menu of delicious Thai appetisers.

Huntridge Tavern

Huntridge Shopping Center, 1116 E Charleston Boulevard, at Maryland Parkway (384 7377). Bus 206. **Open** 24hrs daily. **No credit cards.** **Map** p312 D3.
The Tavern has been serving up booze, brews and attitude for over 30 years. This is everything a dive bar should be: low-estate without being seedy; intriguing without being dangerous. Presumably, the fiftysomethings who warm the stools here go home to their families for an hour or two, every now and again. Get loaded up here, then take in a band at the Huntridge Theater (*see p221*), across the street.

Triple 7 Brew Pub

Main Street Station, 200 N Main Street, at Stewart Avenue (387 1896). Bus 107, 403. **Open** 11am-7am daily. **Credit** AmEx, DC, Disc, MC, V. **Map** p312 C1.
The Triple 7 serves decent beer and bar munchies (the garlic and herb fries are among the best we've had), but the best reason to visit this microbrewery is to gawk at Main Street's multimillion-dollar collection of antiques and rare collectibles. Once they've filled up on the brew, men can stroll to the lavatory and relieve themselves on a portion of the Berlin Wall encased in plastic. Only in Vegas.

The rest of the city

For live music with your beer, check out local rock groups at **Money Plays** and the **Legends Lounge** (for both, *see p221*), or the old-timers' swing band at **Pogo's Tavern** (*see p222*).

Barley's Casino & Brewing Company

Mountain Vista Shopping Center, 4500 E Sunset Road, at Mountain Vista Boulevard, Henderson (458 2739). Bus 212. **Open** 24hrs daily. **Credit** AmEx, DC, Disc, MC, V.
The residents of Henderson have a lot to be grateful for in Barley's. The fair-sized (but not overbearing) casino is packed every night; one of the better Mexican restaurants in town, Casa Mercado's, adjoins the establishment; and the beer is worth writing home about, particularly the Red Rock and Black Mountain lagers and whatever seasonal brew is on tap. There's outdoor seating, too, overlooking a fountain that children run through in summer.

Crown & Anchor Pub

1350 E Tropicana Avenue, at Maryland Parkway, University District (739 8676). Bus 109, 201. **Open** 11am-5am daily. **Credit** AmEx, Disc, MC, V. **Map** p311 Y3.
This 'proper' British-style pub serves up pints of Guinness, Newcastle Brown and Blackthorn cider hand over fist and does an equally brisk trade in cocktails (sample one of the James Bond-themed Martinis). There's standard pub grub and split-level seating to add to the charm, although the loft closes early. What's more, the Crown & Anchor often screens soccer internationals featuring British teams. Appropriately, it's one of the few bars in Las Vegas that actually closes, so check before you go.

Dispensary Lounge

Ocotillo Plaza, 2451 E Tropicana Avenue, at Eastern Avenue, University District (458 6343). Bus 110, 201. **Open** 24hrs daily. **Credit** MC, V. **Map** p311 Z3.
The 1970s live on in this dark, quiet lounge. Drinks are served by waitresses garbed in tight-fitting Spandex, and the retro decor – churning water

Relive the '70s at the dark and dated **Dispensary Lounge**.

wheel, wood fixtures – would fit neatly into a Quentin Tarantino flick. If the background music ever includes a song made after 1980, let us know.

Gaudi Bar
Sunset Station, 1301 W Sunset Road, at Stephanie Street, Henderson (547 7777). Bus 212, 217, 402. **Open** 24hrs daily. **Credit** AmEx, DC, Disc, MC, V.
Located in the middle of a noisy casino, the Gaudi Bar is the most colourful bar in Las Vegas. Drawing (very) freely from Barcelona architect Antonini Gaudí's wild designs, it's bright, psychedelic and pleasantly womblike, with right angles kept to a bare minimum. The cocktails are cheap, service is fast and the crowd is as easygoing as they come.

The Hookah Lounge
The Mediterranean Café, Tiffany Square, 4147 S Maryland Parkway, at E Flamingo Road, University District (731 6030). Bus 109, 202. **Open** 5pm-1am Tue-Thur; 5pm-3am Fri, Sat. **Credit** AmEx, DC, MC, V. **Map** p311 Y3.
Dark, cool and festooned with Mediterranean knick-knacks, the Hookah Lounge is the perfect environment in which to smoke the signature Turkish water pipes for an experience like few others. The smoke from the flavoured tobaccos feels like cool air going into your lungs and comes out as billowy as a cloud. Even non-smokers have been known to partake, and the fact that the Hookah Lounge serves the best Cosmopolitan in town doesn't hurt, either. Deep lounge and jazz beats play into the morning hours, and the crowd, pacified by booze, smoke and atmosphere, can do little but roll their heads and smile utterly contented grins. The Mediterranean Café & Market (*see p149*) is located next door.

JC Woologhan's Irish Pub
Regent, 221 N Rampart Boulevard, at Summerlin Parkway, North-west Las Vegas (869 7725). Bus 211. **Open** 9am-2am daily. **Credit** AmEx, DC, Disc, MC, V.
Supposedly built in Ireland and shipped piece by piece to Vegas, JC Woologhan's is nothing if not a study in verisimilitude: the menu boasts corn beef sandwiches and boxty; the walls are covered with pub knick-knacks; there are authentic ales, ciders and stouts on tap, and Irish party bands such as the Prodigals kick up a racket. Worth checking out if you find yourself in the north-west of town.

Moose McGillycuddy's Pub & Café
4770 S Maryland Parkway, between E Tropicana & Harmon Avenues, University District (798 8337). Bus 108, 213. **Open** 11am-3.30am daily. **Credit** AmEx, DC, MC, V. **Map** p311 Y3.
This chain establishment is quite possibly the most obnoxious but wildly successful college bar in Sin City. Dare to stay past 8pm and you'll be buried in waves of clueless hotel management majors, howling jocks and every blonde airhead within a ten-mile radius. If you're looking to hook up with someone who won't remember you tomorrow – or ever again, for that matter – this is the place to come.

Stunning views from **Jack's Velvet Lounge** at the Venetian. *See p156.*

Sean Patrick's
8255 W Flamingo Road, between Buffalo & Durango Drives, South-west Las Vegas (227 9793). Bus 202. **Open** 24hrs daily. **Credit** AmEx, Disc, MC, V.
Decked out in hardwood and stained glass and festooned with Emerald Isle knick-knacks, this place tries hard to look like a proper pub – perhaps too hard. It's only after you've perused the stew-heavy menu and ordered a pint of Guinness, Murphy's Stout or Caffrey's that Sean Patrick's seems to relax a bit, and when it does, you'll relax right along with it. It's a fine pub to visit if you happen to be in this far-flung neighbourhood.

Boulder City

Backstop Bar
533 Avenue B, at Nevada Highway & Wyoming Street (294 8445). Bus 116. **Open** 8am-1am Mon-Thur; 8am-3.15am Fri, Sat. **No credit cards**.
By dint of its location, the Backstop Bar offers one bonus that no other bar in the area can claim: no gambling. That diversion removed, you can enjoy the rustic ambience, the stuffed buffalo heads peering down from the walls and a few stiff drinks with the friendly citizens of the town that built that dam.

Eat, Drink, Shop

Shops & Services

High-end boutiques and acres of kitschy souvenirs mean you don't have to gamble to spend a small fortune in Las Vegas.

Las Vegas entered the new millennium with something it never had before: world-class shopping that will impress even the most discerning buyer. You'll find everything from high-end designer boutiques from the likes of Gucci and Prada to big-box retailers such as Cost Plus and Wal-Mart. And if it's not in Vegas, someone is planning to bring it here soon. It seems that no sensible retailer can afford to ignore the 35 million tourists and 1.3 million locals in the Vegas market anymore. The upswing of the signature store has sadly led to the decline of the start-up boutique, where choice and free spirit rule the roost. Of course, there are exceptions to the rule – and we point those out – but in general most shops here are chains with more than one branch in the city.

WHERE TO SHOP

Most visitors who shop in Vegas do not stray beyond the impressive casino malls and other major shopping centres on the Strip, where you'll find a host of big name chain stores, plus designer boutiques and independent shops. Elsewhere in Vegas, shopping is focused in the suburban malls where you'll find the usual chain suspects. Harder to locate are the interesting independent stores that make a trip away from the Strip worthwhile. Look closer, though, and you'll find kooky clothes shops, ethnic groceries, well-equipped outdoors shops, esoteric bookshops, not to mention some classic Vegas collectibles.

For shopping at the high-end, stick with the casino malls. A few boutiques are starting to crop up at random locations throughout the valley, but no single neighbourhood can compete with Las Vegas Boulevard South.

SERVICE WITH A SMILE?

Note that retail service in Las Vegas can be unexpectedly inconsistent. Sales staff can be very helpful, but are often standoffish – which is strange considering you may be about to spend a king's ransom in their store: don't take it personally.

Remember that things change quickly in Vegas, so call first if you're heading to a particular shop. And don't forget that sales tax of 7.25 per cent will be added to the label price.

Hitch a ride around the **Desert Passage** mall. *See p162.*

Tiffany & Co and Gucci are just some of the treats in store at **Via Bellagio**. *See p163.*

One-stop shopping

Casino malls

Desert Passage

Aladdin, 3663 Las Vegas Boulevard South, at Harmon Avenue (866 0703/www.desertpassage. com). Bus 301, 302. **Open** 10am-11pm Mon-Thur, Sun; 10am-midnight Fri, Sat. **Map** p316 A7.

This desert-themed mall encircles the Aladdin hotel-casino with a full mile of 130 shops and 21 restaurants to suit any taste or budget. The mall is set up like an ancient market, with separate themed areas – such as the Merchants' Harbor and the Forbidden City – where vendors of similar products are clustered together. Shoppers have a good variety to choose from, including fashions by FCUK, BCBG, Hugo Boss and Bebe, to home decorations from Illuminations and Z Gallerie. There are also stalls offering henna tattoos and the like. Free rickshaws will convey you from shop to shop, and belly dancers, fire-eaters, sword-swallowers and knife-throwers are on hand to entertain those bored with the retail experience.

Forum Shops

Caesars Palace, 3500 Las Vegas Boulevard South, between W Spring Mountain & Flamingo Roads (893 4800). Bus 202, 301, 302. **Open** 10am-11pm Mon-Thur, Sun; 10am-midnight Fri, Sat. **Map** p316 A7.

More than just a mall, the Forum Shops at Caesars Palace is an experience. Costumed staff, faux pillars, the famous ever-changing skies, huge fountains, lush lighting – it's enough to make you believe they really did have chi-chi shopping centres in ancient Rome. In order to encourage more customers into the extremities, there are attractions at either end: statues come to life at one and Atlantis rises from the waves at the other. Mid-range chain outposts such as the Gap, Banana Republic, Guess, Abercrombie & Fitch and Diesel (*see p168*) punctuate a top-rank designer line-up (*see p168* **Shopping by design**). Good gift shops include the sweet centre at FAO Schwarz (*see p180*) and Caesars' own gift shop. The Virgin Megastore (*see p178*) has a quiet upper-storey café, and there are all manner of food stops, from good chain eateries to off-the-scale restaurants.

Grand Canal Shoppes

Venetian, 3355 Las Vegas Boulevard South, just south of Sands Avenue (414 1000/www.venetian. com). Bus 203, 301, 302. **Open** 10am-11pm Mon-Thur, Sun; 10am-midnight Fri, Sat. **Map** p316 A6.

The Grand Canal Shoppes, like the Venetian itself, got off to a turbulent start when it opened in 1999. The idea of a themed shopping mall – winding canals crossed by bridges, singing gondoliers, fake houses and shops, sky-painted ceilings – had been done before. But what initially felt like a second-rate Forum Shops imitator has finally found its place, and its shortcomings have emerged as points of distinction. Walkways are narrow and cramped, but fewer shops and more restaurants in a smaller space gives the impression of an intimate city streetscape. In it, you'll find some decent shops, including Lladro, Movado, Jimmy Choo, Bebe and Ann Taylor; some Forum Shops duplicates, notably those of Banana Republic and Kenneth Cole, actually have better branches here. There's also pleasant late night 'patio' dining to be enjoyed at Taqueria Cañonita and Zefferino (see p137).

Paris Shoppes

*Paris-Las Vegas, 3655 Las Vegas Boulevard South, at Flamingo Road (946 7000/www.paris.com).
Bus 202, 301, 302.* **Open** 10am-11pm daily.
Map p316 A7.

Just about every shop in this small but divine mall is owned and operated by the Paris hotel-casino, and they all come close to the authentic French mark. Les Enfants has a great collection of Eloise, Babar the Elephant and Madeline toys and dolls, plus the casino's own signature pink-ribboned poodle named Fifi. Rumour has it that she will soon be joined by a bulldog called Jacques. La Cave (see p173) has one of the finest wine and champagne selections in town, plus gourmet cheeses, pâtés and foie gras that are flown in fresh from the real Paris every week, while Lenôtre (see p173) is famed for breads and pastries.

Via Bellagio

Bellagio, 3600 Las Vegas Boulevard South, at W Flamingo Road (693 7111/www.bellagiolasvegas.com). Bus 202, 301, 302. **Open** 10am-midnight daily. **Map** p316 A7.

In line with Bellagio's upmarket, adult-only environment, its small shopping mall contains only the smartest of designer names, including Chanel, Tiffany & Company, Giorgio Armani, Gucci, Prada, Hermès and Moschino. If your wallet can't cope, you can at least enjoy this opulent shrine to materialism and the daylight streaming in through the vaulted glass ceilings. Hungry? Try Olives, a Mediterranean bistro overlooking Bellagio's lake (see p135).

Non-casino malls

Boulevard Mall

3528 S Maryland Parkway, between E Desert Inn Road & Twain Avenue, East Las Vegas (732 8949/www.the-boulevard-mall.com). Bus 109, 112, 203, 213. **Open** 10am-9pm Mon-Fri; 10am-8pm Sat; 11am-6pm Sun. **Map** p311 Y3.

The first mall of its type in the city, this is a bastion of the Las Vegas shopping world: centrally located, reasonably priced and loaded with stores of every type. When you're weighed down with bags and nearing collapse, check out the Panorama Café's food court for cheap international cuisine.

Fashion Show Mall

3200 Las Vegas Boulevard South, at W Spring Mountain Road (369 8382/www.thefashionshow.com). Bus 203, 301, 302. **Open** 10am-9pm Mon-Fri; 10am-7pm Sat; noon-6pm Sun. **Map** p316 A/B6.

At the time of writing, the Fashion Show Mall was undergoing a $100-million expansion that will double the size of the property by spring 2003. Although the current line-up is nothing to sneer at – it includes Bullock's, Neiman Marcus, Saks Fifth Avenue and Robinsons May, as well as a Gap, Williams-Sonoma, Bebe and a handful of more humble marques – new arrivals will include Las Vegas's first Nordstrom and Bloomingdale's, a Lord & Taylor and a host of other speciality shops. The mall will have a space-age theme, and a 300ft (9m) screen on Las Vegas Boulevard will broadcast music and fashion shows from inside the mall to passers-by on the Strip.

Galleria at Sunset Mall

1300 Sunset Road, at Stephanie Street, Green Valley (434 0202/www.galleriaatsunset.com). Bus 212, 217. **Open** 10am-9pm Mon-Sat; 11am-6pm Sun.

The Galleria Mall in Green Valley is geared to fit in with its uppercrust surroundings: it's elegant but not ridiculously overpriced and is crammed with yuppified clothing stores. It also houses some excellent gift and stationery shops, including Papyrus, Spencer Gifts and Natural Wonders.

Meadows Mall

4300 Meadows Lane, between Decatur & Valley View Boulevards, North-west Las Vegas (878 4849). Bus 103, 104, 207. **Open** 9am-10pm Mon-Fri; 10am-7pm Sat, Sun. **Map** p311 X1.

A sprawling honeycomb of more than 140 generic chain shops, the Meadows is on a par with the Boulevard Mall in terms of price. Though it was recently given a much-needed remodel and facelift, it is still utilitarian rather than inspirational.

Department stores

Dillard's

Fashion Show Mall, 3200 Las Vegas Boulevard South, at W Spring Mountain Road (733 2008/www.dillards.com). Bus 203, 301, 302. **Open** 10am-9pm Mon-Sat; noon-6pm Sun. **Credit** AmEx, DC, Disc, MC, V. **Map** p316 A/B6.

This is perhaps the American West's equivalent to Marks & Spencer: nice beauty aisles, a good selection of casual and formal women's shoes and a great selection of men's suits at decent prices.
Branches: Boulevard Mall, 3528 S Maryland Parkway, East Las Vegas (734 2111); Galleria at Sunset Mall, 1300 Sunset Road, Green Valley (435 6300); Meadows Mall, 4300 Meadows Lane, North-west Las Vegas (870 2039).

JC Penney

Boulevard Mall, 3528 S Maryland Parkway, between E Desert Inn Road & Twain Avenue, East Las Vegas (735 5131/www.jcpenney.com). Bus 109, 112, 203, 213. **Open** 10am-9pm Mon-Fri; 10am-8pm Sat; 11am-6pm Sun. **Credit** AmEx, Disc, MC, V. **Map** p311 Y3.

This shop is as American as apple pie. You'll find updated classic staples for both men and women. The quality is good and prices are down to earth,

Eat, Drink, Shop

Broadacres Open Air Swap Meet. *See p165.*

with plenty of seasonal sales. This branch has an extensive housewares and decor section and a decent range of watches and jewellery.
Branches: Galleria at Sunset Mall, 1300 Sunset Road, Green Valley (451 4545); Home Store, 771 S Rainbow Road, South-west Las Vegas (870 7727); Meadows Mall, 4400 Meadows Lane, North-west Las Vegas (870 9182).

Macy's

Fashion Show Mall, 3200 Las Vegas Boulevard South, at W Spring Mountain Road (731 5111/ www.macys.com). Bus 203, 301, 302. **Open** 10am-9pm Mon-Sat; noon-6pm Sun. **Credit** AmEx, MC, V. **Map** p316 A/B6.
The king of US department stores. All outlets offer sturdy, good-quality merchandise at reasonable prices, and clothing ranges from classic to trendy. The Spring Mountain Road branch has great home-wares and frequent sales.
Branches: Home Store, 4450 W Spring Mountain Road, South-west Las Vegas (731 5111); Meadows Mall, 4300 Meadows Lane, North-west Las Vegas (258 2100).

Neiman Marcus

Fashion Show Mall, 3200 Las Vegas Boulevard South, at W Spring Mountain Road (731 3636/ www.neimanmarcus.com). Bus 203, 301, 302.
Open 10am-8pm Mon-Fri; 10am-7pm Sat; noon-6pm Sun. **Credit** AmEx, MC, V. **Map** p316 A/B6.
At this upmarket department store, you'll find top-notch merchandise from the world's best designers, including Prada, Escada, Dolce & Gabbana and Chanel. It also has a nice range of accessories, make-up, lingerie and perfumes and, when the Fashion Show mall expansion is complete, there will be an improved housewares selection. For a cheaper version, try the discount outlet at Primm.
Branch: Last Call at Neiman Marcus, 32100 Las Vegas Boulevard South, Primm (874 2100).

Saks Fifth Avenue

Fashion Show Mall, 3200 Las Vegas Boulevard South, at W Spring Mountain Road (733 8300/ www.sacsfifthavenue.com). Bus 203, 301, 302.
Open 10am-8pm Mon-Wed; 10am-9pm Thur, Fri; 10am-7pm Sat; noon-6pm Sun. **Credit** AmEx, DC, Disc, MC, V. **Map** p316 A/B6.
For those with discriminating taste and a heavy-weight bank account, a trip to Saks is like going to church; you have to go once a week to pay homage and get grounded. The men's and women's apparel sections are especially strong. If you've got the taste but not the money, check out Saks's discount shops in Belz Factory Outlet World or the Fashion Outlet of Las Vegas. (For both, *see p165*).

Discount & factory outlets

Wal-Mart (www.walmart.com) is perhaps the definition of one-stop shopping, known for its vast variety and low prices. Check the phone book for details of Vegas's numerous branches.

Belz Factory Outlet World

7400 Las Vegas Boulevard South, at Warm Springs Road (896 5599/www.belz.com). Bus 303. **Open** 10am-9pm Mon-Sat; 10am-6pm Sun. **Credit** varies.
Rather than schlepp through the high-end malls searching for sales and begging for bargains, head south to Belz where savings are a sure bet. Check out Calvin Klein, Saks Fifth Avenue, Nike, Vans, Lenox, Waterford/Wedgwood, Bose and many others. An eclectic food court will keep you energised and a giant carousel should keep the kids content.

Broadacres Open Air Swap Meet

2930 N Las Vegas Boulevard, at Pecos Road, North Las Vegas (642 3777). Bus 111, 113. **Open** 6.30am-6pm Fri-Sun. **No credit cards.**
For almost 25 years, this weekend selling and swapping marketplace has been a Las Vegas classic. Four miles (6.5km) north of Downtown, it offers 40 acres (16ha) of bargains in new and used goods. Pop into the beer garden for a refresher, give the kids a pony ride or sit in the shade and watch the world go by.

Fashion Outlet of Las Vegas

32100 Las Vegas Boulevard South, Primm (874 1400/www.fashionoutletlasvegas.com). **Open** 10am-9pm Mon-Sat, 10am-8pm Sun. **Credit** varies.
Designer labels are all the rage at this enclosed outlet mall 35 miles (56km) south of the Strip (there's a free shuttle bus if you don't have a car). Browse discounted merchandise by Donna Karan, Versace, Kenneth Cole, Guess and many more, then have a bite at a dozen fast-food and table-service eateries.

Sundance Catalog Company Outlet

8800 W Charleston Boulevard, at Rampart Street, Summerlin, North-west Las Vegas (947 4489). Bus 206. **Open** 10am-9pm Mon-Fri; 10am-7pm Sat; noon-5pm Sun. **Credit** AmEx, Disc, MC, V.
Carrying most (if not all) of the items found in Robert Redford's Sundance catalogue, this place feels just like a high-end mall store. Look for a wide, interesting selection of ranch-inspired clothes, furnishings, jewellery and sweets at great prices.

Antiques

Antiques on Casino Center

1228 S Casino Center Boulevard, just north of Charleston Boulevard, Downtown (678 6278/www.antiques4yu.com). **Open** 10am-5pm daily. **Credit** MC, V. **Map** p312 C3.
Owner Cindy Funkhouser has one of the best vintage and antique stores in Las Vegas. It's especially strong on late 1950s and early 1960s pieces, and there's a wide variety of glass, jewellery and toys.

Charleston Antique Shops

2014-26 E Charleston Boulevard, at Eastern Avenue, East Las Vegas (386 0238). Bus 206. **Open** varies. **Credit** varies. **Map** p311 Y2.
Most tourists and even some locals don't know that there are more than two dozen tiny antique shops in converted old houses at the east end of Charleston

Boulevard. You'll find fine china, dolls, desks, postcards, Tiffany lamps, telephones, perfume bottles, mirrors, train sets, clocks and more. Dealers are knowledgeable and approachable.

Red Rooster Antique Mall

307 W Charleston Boulevard, at Martin Luther King Boulevard, North-west Las Vegas (382 5253). Bus 207. **Open** 10am-6pm Mon-Sat; noon-5pm Sun. **Credit** AmEx, MC, V. **Map** p315 B3.
A labyrinth of cluttered rooms and individually run stalls mean dusty magazines hold shelf space next to $100 antique amber bottles. Look carefully and you'll find fab casino memorabilia: ashtrays, gaming chips, matchbooks, postcards and more.

The Sampler Shoppes

6115 W Tropicana Avenue, at Jones Boulevard, South-west Las Vegas (368 1170). Bus 102, 201. **Open** 10am-6pm Mon-Sat; noon-6pm Sat. **Credit** AmEx, Disc, MC, V.
Some 200 dealers display their wares at this indoor mall, a converted grocery store. You'll find books, antiques, collectibles, dolls, furniture, glassware, jewellery, toys and much more. There's also a small café and a British tea shop serving afternoon tea.

Showcase Slots & Antiquities

4305 S Industrial Road, between W Tropicana Avenue & W Flamingo Road, West of Strip (740 5722/www.showcaseslots.com). Bus 202. **Open** 9am-5pm Mon-Sat; 11am-5pm Sun. **Credit** AmEx, DC, Disc, MC, V. **Map** p316 A7.
What could be a more appropriate souvenir of Las Vegas than an antique slot machine? This store behind the Bellagio has machines from the 1930s and 1940s, as well as new slots, old-fashioned Coca-Cola dispensers and Wurlitzer jukeboxes.

Books

The **Tower Records** superstore (*see p178*) offers the most interesting and eclectic selection of new books in the city.

Albion Book Company

Suite G, 2466 E Desert Inn Road, at Eastern Avenue, East Las Vegas (792 9554). Bus 110, 112. **Open** 10am-6pm daily. **Credit** AmEx, Disc, MC, V. **Map** p311 Z3.
The quintessential used-book store, crammed with obscure offbeat editions alongside classic Dickens and Tolstoy. Prices are low and there's an air of comfortable chaos, with plenty of character, both on the shelves and behind the counter.

Barnes & Noble

3860 S Maryland Parkway, between Spencer Street & Flamingo Road, Henderson (734 2900/www.bn.com). Bus 109, 213. **Open** 9am-11pm daily. **Credit** AmEx, DC, Disc, MC, V.
Done up in rich, dark wood accents, B&N seems to have a more relaxed 'go ahead and sit and read a chapter or two of that book you probably won't buy'

attitude than some of its competitors. It's also got a good choice of magazines, periodicals and national papers, but it's a bit thin on international news.
Branches: 567 N Stephanie Street, between Sunset Road & Warm Springs Road, Henderson (434 1533); 2191 N Rainbow Boulevard, at Lake Mead Boulevard, North-west Las Vegas (631 1775).

Borders Books, Music & Café

1445 Sunset Road, at Stephanie Street, Green Valley (433 6222/www.borders.com). Bus 103, 204. **Open** 9am-11pm Mon-Sat; 9am-6pm Sun. **Credit** AmEx, Disc, MC, V.
A hangout for hip intelligentsia, Borders boasts not only a top-notch book selection, but also a small music selection and a café that's perfect for discussions on love, war and the meaning of life. The periodical selection is extensive and worth a browse, as are the video/DVD aisles.
Branches: 2323 S Decatur Boulevard, South-west Las Vegas (258 0999); 2190 N Rainbow Boulevard, at Lake Mead Boulevard, North-west Las Vegas (638 7866).

Dead Poet Books

3874 W Sahara Avenue, at Valley View Boulevard, West of Strip (227 4070). Bus 104, 204. **Open** 10am-6pm Mon-Sat; noon-5pm Sun. **Credit** AmEx, DC, Disc, MC, V. **Map** p311 X2.
A charming hotchpotch of antiquarian books. Specialities include metaphysical cookbooks, military histories and plenty of first editions.

Gamblers Book Club

630 S 11th Street, at Charleston Boulevard, Downtown (382 7555/www.gamblersbook.com). Bus 109, 206. **Open** 9am-5pm Mon-Sat. **Credit** Disc, MC, V. **Map** p312 D3.

If this shop is any indication, gambling is still king, the Mob never left and Disneyland might as well keep its influence in Southern California. Supposedly the largest distributor of gambling books in the world; if it contains words about the games, the legendary figures or Las Vegas, you'll find it here.

Get Booked

Paradise Plaza, 4636 Paradise Road, at Naples Drive, between Harmon & Tropicana Avenues, East of Strip (737 7780). Bus 108, 213. **Open** 10am-midnight Mon-Thur; 10am-2am Fri; noon-2am Sat; noon-midnight Sun. **Credit** AmEx, Disc, MC, V. **Map** p316 C8.
This small shop, selling books, magazines, greetings cards and videos (for rent or sale) is Las Vegas's only gay and lesbian bookstore.

Native Son Bookstore

1301 D Street, between Owens & Washington Avenues, North Las Vegas (647 0101). Bus 214. **Open** noon-7pm daily. **No credit cards.**
Go native with a trip to this excellent African bookstore, which contains plenty of culture-specific literature, along with history books, biographies and fictional brain-candy.

Psychic Eye Bookstores

1000 N Green Valley Parkway, between Lake Mead Drive & Wigwam Parkway, Henderson (451 5777). Bus 111. **Open** 10am-9pm Mon-Fri; 10am-8.30pm Sat; 11am-6pm Sun. **Credit** AmEx, Disc, MC, V.
Incense swirls around the shelves of tarot cards, crystals, astrology charts and books on mysticism. Religious art from India, the Far East and elsewhere lines the walls, while behind a velvet curtain, Madame Fortune Teller reads palms.

Read all about it at the **Gamblers Book Club**.

Branches: 6848 W Charleston Boulevard, North-west Las Vegas (255 4477); 4810 Spring Mountain Road, at Decatur Boulevard, South-west Las Vegas (368 7785).

Readmore Bookstore

Sahara Town Square, 2560 S Maryland Parkway, at E Sahara Avenue, East Las Vegas (732 4453). Bus 109, 204. **Open** 9am-8pm Mon-Sat. **Credit** Disc, MC, V. **Map** p311 Y2.

Every magazine known to man (and woman) is sold at Readmore, though the selection of books is scanty. It's your best bet in Las Vegas for those obscure, hard-to-find publications, scientific journals, plus an abundance of smut.
Branches: throughout the city.

Cameras & film processing

Beware photo processing and film developing services on the Strip, which often charge three times the going rate. Instead, use the photo centres at large drugstores, such as Walgreens (*see p178*) or Sav-On – or try one of the specialist shops listed below.

Allen Photographic Services

3223 S Industrial Road, between Desert Inn Road & Spring Mountain Road, West of Strip (735 2222). Bus 105. **Open** 9am-5.30pm Mon-Fri; 9am-3pm Sat. **Credit** MC, V. **Map** p315 A5.

This professional developing and digital processing centre behind the Fashion Show Mall offers its services to the public as well as to professional photographers. The prices are reasonable, even if time is of the essence, especially for black and white film and speciality processing.

Sahara Camera Center

Albertson Shopping Center, 2305 E Sahara Avenue, at Eastern Avenue, East Las Vegas (457 3333). Bus 110, 204. **Open** 9am-6pm Mon-Fri; 9am-5pm Sat. **Credit** AmEx, Disc, MC, V. **Map** p311 Z2.

Claiming to be 'Nevada's largest full-service camera store', the Sahara Camera Center pretty much has, and does, it all. In business for close to 30 years, it offers rental and repair services, quality new and used equipment, very knowledgeable staff and one-hour photo processing. Prices are fair and many items are discounted.

Wolf Camera & Video

Belz Factory Outlet World, 7400 Las Vegas Boulevard South, at Warm Springs Road (896 4271/www.wolfcamera.com). Bus 303. **Open** 10am-9pm Mon-Sat; 10am-6pm Sun. **Credit** AmEx, Disc, MC, V.

A welcome escape from the electronics superstores, Wolf Camera & Video has friendly, well-informed staff, an excellent selection of still and video cameras and one-hour photo processing. Bargain-hunting Brits should take note: Wolf also stocks UK-compatible PAL camcorders.
Branches: throughout the city.

Electronics

Bang & Olufsen

Fashion Show Mall, 3200 Las Vegas Boulevard South, between Desert Inn & Spring Mountain Roads (731 9200). Bus 301, 302, 203. **Open** 10am-9pm Mon-Fri; 10am-7pm Sat; noon-6pm Sun. **Credit** AmEx, Disc, MC, V. **Map** p316 A/B6.

This exclusive store features its own signature line of home entertainment wares, BEO. It will cost you. But isn't the coolest, best-quality home audio and visual hardware worth a little extra dough?

Circuit City

4860 Eastern Avenue, at Tropicana Avenue, University District (898 0500/www.circuitcity.com). Bus 110, 201. **Open** 10am-9pm daily. **Credit** AmEx, Disc, MC, V. **Map** p311 Z3.

Electronics and home appliances galore. If, after making a purchase here, you find the identical merchandise sold cheaper anywhere in town, Circuit City will refund the difference.
Branches: 5055 W Sahara Avenue, South-west Las Vegas (367 9700); 561 Stephanie Street, between Sunset Road & Warm Springs Road, Green Valley (451 7111).

The Good Guys

4580 W Sahara Avenue, at Decatur Boulevard, South-west Las Vegas (364 2500/www.thegood guys.com). Bus 103, 204. **Open** 9am-midnight daily. **Credit** AmEx, Disc, MC, V.

Good Guys offers competitive prices, a decent selection (especially in computers and related equipment) and non-commissioned sales staff. That means no one overwhelming you with a barrage of slick sales talk and useless information. Plus, there's a Tower Records (*see p178*) and a small café on site.
Branches: 3778 S Maryland Parkway, East Las Vegas (892 9200).

Fashion

Las Vegas has become a major fashion mecca for those with the stamina and wherewithal to navigate the area's massive retail scene. The casino malls (surprise, surprise) are the places to start: spend the rent at the **Via Bellagio** on Gucci, Prada, Chanel and Hermès. Blow the bank at the **Forum Shops** bagging Versace, Armani, Ferragamo, Louis Vuitton and Dior. And polish off those last few dollars buying Burberry in the **Grand Canal Shoppes** or Hervé Lèger in the **Desert Passage**. (*See also p168* **Shopping by design**.)

The better deparment stores are also worth a look (*see p163*) and you'll have no trouble finding fashionable and cheaper chainstores: **Gap, Abercrombie & Fitch** and **Victoria's Secret** all occupy space in most shopping malls. Other slightly more upmarket chains, such as **Banana Republic** and **Guess**, can be found scattered among the big-dollar boutiques at the Forum Shops and the Grand Canal Shoppes. For cut-price fashion, try the discount outlet stores (see p164).

Bebe

Forum Shops, Caesars Palace, 3500 Las Vegas Boulevard South, at Flamingo Road (735 8885/ www.bebe.com). Bus 202, 301, 302. **Open** 10am-11pm Mon-Thur, Sun; 10am-12am Fri, Sat. **Credit** AmEx, DC, Disc, MC, V. **Map** p316 A7.

This hip, funky chainstore outfits those trendy young things who want to look like fashionistas without having to pay super-hefty price tags – though Bebe's clothes are still not cheap. Most of the tempting merchandise is high quality and was clearly inspired by top designers and the latest catwalk trends.

Branches: Fashion Show Mall, 3200 Las Vegas Boulevard South (892 8083).

Betsey Johnson

Desert Passage, Aladdin, 3663 Las Vegas Boulevard South, at Harmon Avenue (731 0286/www.betsey johnson.com). Bus 301, 302. **Open** 10am-11pm Mon-Thur, Sun; 10am-midnight Fri, Sat. **Credit** AmEx, DC, Disc, MC, V. **Map** p316 A7.

Betsey Johnson, the wild woman of fashion, has stayed true to her wacky ways over the years with her signature line of clothing, and now that the 1980s are back in fashion, Betsey is at her best. Many of her current covetable pieces have a 1940s and 1950s vintage quality too.

Branches: Fashion Show Mall, 3200 Las Vegas Boulevard South (735 3388).

Detour

Fashion Show Mall, 3200 Las Vegas Boulevard South, between Desert Inn & Spring Mountain Roads (894 5030). Bus 203, 301, 302. **Open** 10am-9pm Mon-Fri; 10am-7pm Sat; noon-6pm Sun. **Credit** AmEx, MC, V. **Map** p316 A/B6.

Fun and funky fashions for the Hollywood starlet copycat. Prices are as large as the attitude of the staff, but it does have a great selection from the trendiest street designers around.

Diesel USA

Forum Shops, Caesars Palace, 3500 Las Vegas Boulevard South, at Flamingo Road (791 5927/ www.diesel.com). Bus 202, 301, 302. **Open** 10am-11pm Mon-Thur, Sun; 10am-midnight Fri, Sat. **Credit** AmEx, DC, Disc, MC, V. **Map** p316 A7.

Diesel USA carries the latest in denim and denim lifestyle-inspired clothing for those who aspire to Euro-style street cred.

Musette

Village Square Shopping Center, 9420 W Sahara Avenue, at Fort Apache Drive, South-west Las Vegas (309 6873). Bus 204. **Open** 10am-8pm Mon-Fri, 10am-7pm Sat, noon-6pm Sun. **Credit** AmEx, Disc, MC, V.

Owner Gary Ghonik – and trusted canine companion Molly – offer this advice in the form of a shop motto: 'Explore your inner princess'. And, with the latest from Earl Jean, Three Dot, Diane Von Furstenberg and other trendy designers on offer among the clothing and accessories, it's easy to follow such a directive.

Pacific Sunwear of California

Suite 2653, the Galleria at Sunset Mall, 1300 W Sunset Road, at Stephanie Street, Green Valley (433 0003/www.pacsun.com). Bus 212, 217. **Open** 10am-9pm Mon-Sat; 11am-6pm Sun. **Credit** AmEx, Disc, MC, V.

Surf's up, dude, even in the desert. Most of the merchandise here is Pacific Sunwear's own label, but surfing brands, including O'Neill and Quicksilver, are also available.

Branch: Meadows Mall, 4300 Meadows Lane, North-west Las Vegas (878 3250); Belz Factory Outlet World, 7400 Las Vegas Boulevard South (897 1723).

Shopping by design

Where to find the big fashion names.

Alfred Dunhill Forum Shops. **A/X Armani** Forum Shops. **Boss/Hugo Boss** Desert Passage; Forum Shops. **Bulgari** Forum Shops. **Burberry** Grand Canal Shoppes. **Chanel** Forum Shops, Via Bellagio. **Christian Dior** Forum Shops. **DKNY** Forum Shops. **Emporio Armani** Forum Shops. **Escada** Forum Shops. **Fendi** Forum Shops. **For Joseph** Grand Canal Shoppes. **Fred Leighton** Via Bellagio. **Giorgio Armani** Via Bellagio. **Gianni Versace** Forum Shops. **Gucci** Forum Shops; Via Bellagio. **Hermès** Via Bellagio. **Hervé Lèger** Desert Passage. **Jhane Barnes** Desert Passage.

Jimmy Choo Grand Canal Shoppes. **Judith Leiber** Forum Shops. **LaCoste** Forum Shops. **Louis Vuitton** Forum Shops. **MaxMara** Forum Shops. **Moschino** Via Bellagio. **Movado** Grand Canal Shoppes. **Polo/Ralph Lauren** Forum Shops. **Prada** Via Bellagio. **St John** Forum Shops. **Salvatore Ferragamo** Forum Shops. **Simayof** Grand Canal Shoppes. **Stuart Weitzman** Forum Shops. **Tiffany & Co** Via Bellagio. **Tommy Bahama** Desert Passage. **Versace Jeans Couture** Forum Shops. For details of the casino shopping malls listed here, *see pp162-3*.

Poise

7581 W Lake Mead Boulevard, at Buffalo Drive,
Summerlin, North-west Las Vegas (341 8090).
Bus 210. **Open** 11am-7pm Mon-Sat. **Credit** AmEx,
Disc, MC, V.

Nestled next to one of Summerlin's most popular
salon and day spas, this boutique sells a wide variety of clothes for working women and more casual,
athletics-inspired clothes for the soccer moms who
live in the area. Good accessories, too.

Stash

Village Square Shopping Center, 9410 W Sahara
Avenue, at Fort Apache Road, South-west Las Vegas
(804 1640). Bus 204. **Open** 10am-7pm Mon-Thur;
10am-8pm Fri, Sat; noon-6pm Sun. **Credit** AmEx,
Disc, MC, V.

Holding steady as one of the first off-Strip boutiques
to offer trend-ware for both men and women, Stash
is a favourite with silver spoon-fed locals, trans-
plants and tourists alike. You'll find designer jeans
by Lucky Brand and Big Star, plus labels from
Betsey Johnson, Bisou Bisou and Ann Ferriday.
Branch: 8876 Eastern Avenue, just north of I-215,
East Las Vegas (933 4567).

White House, Black Market

Desert Passage, Aladdin, 3663 Las Vegas Boulevard
South, at Harmon Avenue (732 2562). Bus 301,
302. **Open** 10am-11pm Mon-Thur, Sun; 10am-
midnight Fri, Sat. **Map** p316 A7.

Nearly everything in this store is either black or
white, but the variety of fabrics and styles make it
anything but boring. There's monochrome clothing
and accessories for all occasions, plus a peppering
of colour to brighten things up.

Accessories & jewellery

If you've hit the jackpot, you'll no doubt want
to celebrate in style: head to Bellagio to pick
up a tip-top tiara at **Tiffany & Company**
(697 5400) or some bodacious baubles at **Fred
Leighton** (693 7050). Rock hounds will also
love **Paradis Jewels** at Mandalay Bay (632
6133) and **Simayof** in the Venetian (731 1037).
Smaller spenders might prefer the **Jewelers
of Las Vegas** (www.thejewelers.com), a real
pirate's chest of affordable treasures, including
a selection of watches. There are 12 branches
in Vegas: try the ones at the Tropicana, the
Las Vegas Hilton and the Flamingo.

The Hat Company

Belz Factory Outlet World, 7400 Las Vegas
Boulevard South, at Warm Springs Road (897
1666). Bus 303. **Open** 10am-9pm Mon-Sat; 10am-
6pm Sun. **Credit** AmEx, Disc, MC, V.

From Indiana Jones hats to Easter bonnets, the Hat
Company has them all. The variety is overwhelming:
from plumed, flowered and ribboned to felt, cloth
and straw, plus name brands such as Stetson,
Kangol and Panama.

Jaqueline Jarrot

Desert Passage, Aladdin, 3663 Las Vegas Boulevard
South, at Harmon Avenue (731 3200). Bus 301,
302. **Open** 10am-11pm daily. **Credit** AmEx, DC,
MC, V. **Map** p316 A7.

Probably the ideal spot for casual accessories, with
products from about 300 noteworthy designers
displayed in one convenient location. You'll find
handbags, toe rings and other trendy pieces.

John Fish Jewelers

Commercial Center, 953 E Sahara Avenue, between
Paradise Road & Maryland Parkway, East Las
Vegas (731 1323). Bus 204. **Open** 9.30am-5.30pm
Mon-Sat. **Credit** AmEx, Disc, MC, V. **Map** p311 Y2.

A hole-in-the-wall that hides some mind-blowing
finds with price tags that will put a smile on your
face. There's a little of everything: antiques, one-off
pieces from estate sales and custom-made designs.

Judith Leiber Boutique

Forum Shops, Caesars Palace, 3500 Las Vegas
Boulevard South, between W Spring Mountain &
Flamingo Roads (792 0661). Bus 301, 302. **Open**
10am-11pm Mon-Thur, Sun; 10am-midnight Fri, Sat.
Credit AmEx, Disc, MC, V. **Map** p316 A7.

A Judith Leiber handbag whispers 'great taste!' and
'you must be loaded!'. But when that $2,550 purse is
shaped like a Valentine and emblazoned with 13,000
Austrian rhinestones depicting the queen of hearts,
it can only scream out 'Las Vegas!'.

Serges Showgirl Wigs

953 E Sahara Avenue, at Maryland Parkway, East
Las Vegas (732 1015). Bus 109, 204. **Open** 10am-
5.30pm Mon-Sat. **Credit** AmEx, Disc, MC, V.
Map p311 Y2.

Wigs were big in the 1960s, but in Las Vegas they
never went out of style. Serges is the world's largest
wig retailer and offers thousands of natural and
synthetic hairpieces in hundreds of styles and
colours. It sells mainly to showgirls, but anyone can
browse and buy.

Children

You'll find branches of **Gap Kids** in the
Fashion Show Mall (796 0010) and the Desert
Passage (866 0703); check the phone book for
other locations.

Brats

Fashion Show Mall, 3200 Las Vegas Boulevard
South, at W Spring Mountain Road (735 2728). Bus
203, 301, 302. **Open** 10am-9pm Mon-Fri; 10am-7pm
Sat; noon-6pm Sun. **Credit** AmEx, DC, Disc, MC, V.
Map p316 A/B6.

A kid's fashion boutique for your little prince or
princess, with brands including Hollywood Babe,
Sarah Sarah, San Francisco Blues, Flapdoodles,
Cach-cach, Princess Kids, Guess and DKNY. Sizes
are from infant to age 14.
Branch: Monte Carlo, 3770 Las Vegas Boulevard
South (795 8350).

Eat, Drink, Shop

Stars, stripes, sequins and feathers: kit yourself out at **Bare Essentials Fantasy Fashions**.

Cleaning & repairs

Al Phillips dry-cleaning chain has 15 drive-through locations in Vegas. Eight are open 24 hours a day, seven days a week, and all provide dry-cleaning, laundry, alterations, shoe repairs plus men's formal wear hire. Check the phone book for your nearest branch.

Cora's Coin Laundry
1097 E Tropicana Avenue, at Maryland Parkway, University District (736 6181). Bus 108, 201. **Open** 8am-9pm daily. **No credit cards. Map** p311 Y3.
Located just two miles off the Strip, Cora's is popular with UNLV folk. It's clean, open seven days a week and offers self-service or drop-off laundry, dry-cleaning and, yes, there are video poker machines.

Frame Fixer
3961 W Charleston Boulevard, at Valley View Boulevard, North-west Las Vegas (735 7879). Bus 206. **Open** 10am-5.30pm Mon-Fri; 10am-4pm Sat. **Credit** AmEx, Disc, MC, V. **Map** p311 X2.
Sometimes it's cheaper to repair the eyewear than replace it, and this fast, friendly place is a good bet.

Silver Needle
2550 S Rainbow Boulevard, at W Sahara Avenue, South-west Las Vegas (365 6693). Bus 204. **Open** 8am-5pm Mon-Fri, 9am-2pm Sat. **No credit cards.**
This one-man show is by far the best tailor in the area. Vegas's best-dressed locals take their clothes to the Silver Needle for a perfect job every time.

Sparkle Cleaners
326 W Sahara Avenue, between Las Vegas Boulevard & Industrial Road, West of Strip (382 8161). Bus 301, 302, 204. **Open** 7am-5.30pm Mon-Fri, 9am-4pm Sat. **No credit cards. Map** p315 B4.
Many of the Strip's top hotels send their guests' soiled finery to this dry-cleaner.

Eyewear

Davante
Forum Shops, Caesars Palace, 3500 Las Vegas Boulevard South, between W Spring Mountain & Flamingo Roads (737 8585). Bus 301, 302. **Open** 10am-11pm Mon-Thur, Sun; 10am-midnight Fri, Sat. **Credit** AmEx, DC, Disc, MC, V. **Map** p316 A7.
Find your favourite eyewear among more than 50 of the world's top designers in this beautiful boutique setting. An optician is on site to assist with your prescription. For those with 20/20 vision, non-prescription eyewear is also available.
Branches: see the phone book.

Oculus
Caesars Palace, 3570 Las Vegas Boulevard South, between Tropicana & Harmon Avenues (731 4850). Bus 301, 302. **Open** 10am-10pm daily. **Credit** AmEx, DC, Disc, MC, V. **Map** p316 A7.
Located in the Appian Way shops at Caesars Palace, Oculus is a Strip-convenient outpost of Ed Malik's stylish eyewear boutique, Eyes & Optics. You'll find an excellent selection of frames from trendy designers such as Oliver Peoples and Alain Mikli, plus eye examinations and repairs.

Lingerie

Bare Essentials Fantasy Fashions
4029 W Sahara Avenue, at Valley View Boulevard, West of Strip (247 4711). Bus 104, 204. **Open** 10am-7pm Mon-Sat; noon-5pm Sun. **Credit** AmEx, Disc, MC, V. **Map** p311 X2.
Whatever your fantasy, the friendly boys at Bare Essentials will outfit you the right way with lingerie, bikinis, G-strings, sky-high platforms and even feather boas. The campy gay owners are right when they say that women feel at ease shopping in their fabulous store.

Frederick's of Hollywood

3725 S Maryland Parkway, at Twain Avenue, East of Strip (734 2070/www.fredericks.com). Bus 108, 203. **Open** 10am-9pm Mon-Fri; 10am-6pm Sat; noon-5pm Sun. **Credit** AmEx, Disc, MC, V. **Map** p311 Y3.
The old stand-by for wild lingerie, although it's actually somewhat closer to mild these days. A recent campaign saw Frederick's trying to be a more couple-friendly store by offering 'classier' lingerie for men and women. Did it succeed? Does it matter?

Le Boudoir Boutique

2600 W Sahara Avenue, at Palace Street. South-west Las Vegas (395 6363). Bus 204. **Open** noon-8pm Tue-Sat. **Credit** AmEx, MC, V.
This hidden gem is an amazing lingerie and loungewear shop. Look forward to a wonderful selection of top-quality pretty and playful underthings for all outfits and occasions at reasonable and not-so-reasonable prices.

Shoes

You'll find **Salvatore Ferragamo** in the Forum Shops and the Fashion Show Mall, **Steve Madden** in the Desert Passage, and **Kenneth Cole** in the Forum Shops and the Grand Canal Shoppes. Many of the major Strip casino-hotels can arrange shoe repairs.

Hot Foot Shoes

9420 W Sahara Avenue, at Fort Apache Road, South-west Las Vegas (579 9672). Bus 105, 204. **Open** 10am-6pm Mon-Thur; 10am-7pm Fri, Sat; noon-5pm Sun. **Credit** AmEx, Disc, MC, V.
A trek out to this shoe and accessory shop could save you hours of trudging through casino malls. Hot Foot Shoes carries the best of the regular department store lot, including Kenneth Cole, Via Spiga, Charles David, DKNY and Cole Haan. Seasonal clearances and frequent sales.

Just For Feet

Forum Shops, Caesars Palace, 3500 Las Vegas Boulevard South, between W Spring Mountain & Flamingo Roads (791 3482). Bus 301, 302. **Open** 10am-11pm Mon-Thur, Sun; 10am-midnight Fri, Sat. **Credit** AmEx, Disc, MC, V. **Map** p316 A7.
Every kind of athletic shoe, with styles by New Balance, Nike, Reebok, Converse, Adidas and more, plus a fair selection of hiking boots and Doc Martens. The Caesars store is a huge, multi-level beast, with a place for shooting hoops upstairs and a giant video screen. Staff are often overworked and under-interested, but if you know what you want, you'll do fine.
Branch: 4500 W Sahara Avenue, South-west Las Vegas (878 7463).

Stiletto

Fashion Show Mall, 3200 Las Vegas Boulevard South (791 0505). Bus 203, 301, 302. **Open** 10am-9pm Mon-Fri, 10am-7pm Sat, noon-6pm Sun. **Credit** AmEx, Disc, MC, V. **Map** p316 A/B6.

Hot shoes and a hot location at the centre of one of the better shopping malls. Look for a strong selection from Guess, Charles David, Natalie M, Via Spiga, Donald Pliner and Aquatella. You'll find the same offerings at Shooz in the Forum Shops and Rococo in the Desert Passage.

Vintage & second-hand

The Attic

1018 S Main Street, just north of Charleston Boulevard, Downtown (388 4088/www.atticvintage.com). Bus 105, 206. **Open** 9am-6pm daily. **Credit** DC, Disc, MC, V. **Map** p312 C3.
Probably the most popular in the Vegas vintage category, thanks to an eye-catching, colourful store and some savvy advertising. At ground level there's furniture, appliances and the like, while one level up you'll find clothing, shoes, oddities, accessories and Café Neon (open 10am-4pm daily). Admission (really!) costs $1, refundable on purchase.

Bricktop & Boris

Commercial Center, 900 E Karen Avenue, between Paradise Road & Maryland Parkway, East Las Vegas (735 3007). Bus 204. **Open** 10am-7pm Mon-Sat. **Credit** AmEx, Disc, MC, V. **Map** p311 Y2.
Picture the estate sale of a rich, eccentric woman and you'll have an idea of the contents of this tiny boutique. A thorough search will often net you a find, if you're into feathers, rhinestones and fake fur.

Buffalo Exchange

Suite 18, Pioneer Center, 4110 S Maryland Parkway, at Flamingo Road, University District (791 3960/ www.buffaloexchange.com). Bus 109, 202, 213. **Open** 11am-7pm Mon-Sat; noon-6pm Sun. **Credit** MC, V. **Map** p311 Y3.
One of Vegas's most popular student shops, Buffalo Exchange has price tags somewhere between budget and mid-level. The clothing is mainly second-hand, with some items from shop clearances.

Retro Vintage Couture

Valley View Plaza, 906 S Valley View Road, at Charleston Boulevard, North-west Las Vegas (877 8989). Bus 104. **Open** 11am-7pm Tue-Fri; 11am-6pm Sat. **Credit** AmEx, Disc, MC, V. **Map** p311 X2.
Owner Melina Crisostomo makes shopping at this tiny boutique a pleasure. This stuff is vintage, not thrift, so prices are higher than at a charity shop, but the calibre of the clothing is vastly different, too: beautiful, classically tailored suits and dresses and a good selection of shoes and accessories. There's a jam-packed rack of sale clothing in front of the shop.

Wedding outfits & costume hire

The chapels try to control all the wedding paraphernalia, so you won't be allowed to arrange your own flowers, photographer or Elvis. But no one can stop you turning up in a frock or frock coat you've rented elsewhere.

Eat, Drink, Shop

I&M Formalwear

3345 S Decatur Boulevard, between W Desert Inn & Spring Mountain Roads, South-west Las Vegas (1-800 249 5075/364 4696). Bus 103. **Open** 9am-7pm Mon-Fri; 9am-5pm Sat; 11am-3pm Sun. **Credit** MC, V.

This outfit claims to have the biggest selection of famous-name wedding gowns and dresses in town. Prices for a three-day rental range from $135 to $375, including any alterations and cleaning.

Renta-Dress & Tux Shop

Sahara Paradise Plaza, 2240 Paradise Road, at Sahara Avenue, East of Strip (796 6444/ www.weddinginvegas.com). Bus 108, 204. **Open** 10am-4pm Sun. **Credit** AmEx, Disc, MC, V. **Map** p315 C4.

Whether you're in search of an elegant evening gown, a flashy cocktail dress, bridal wear or a standard tux, you'll find it in the racks of this diverse store. There's a seamstress on the premises for alterations and adjustments. It also has shoes.

Tuxedo Palace

Suite 21, Renaissance Center West, 4001 S Decatur Boulevard, at W Flamingo Road, South-west Las Vegas (1-800 777 1884/367 4433). Bus 103, 104, 202. **Open** 9am-6pm Mon-Thur; 9am-7pm Fri; 9am-5pm Sat; 11am-4pm Sun. **Credit** AmEx, Disc, MC, V.

You'll find a huge selection of tuxes here, with prices from $50 to $109.95 for a two-day rental, including trousers, waistcoat and all accessories except shoes ($10-$15). For the full get-up, the in-house Bridal Salon offers bridesmaids' dresses from $65 and wedding dresses from $99 to $450.

Williams Costume Company

1226 S Third Street, between Colorado Avenue & Charleston Boulevard, Stratosphere Area (384 1384). Bus 206, 301, 302. **Open** 10am-5pm Mon-Sat. **Credit** AmEx, Disc, MC, V. **Map** p315 C3.

With more than 10,000 frocks in stock, Williams is the only place in town that carries enough ancient Egyptians, Elvises and Pioneers (the latest trend) to dress the bride, groom and guests, too. Rental costs between $50 and $100 per night, plus a hefty deposit.

Food & drink

Bakeries & pâtisseries

Byblos Café

Mediterranean Restaurant & Bakery, 4825 W Flamingo Road, at Decatur Boulevard, South-west Las Vegas (222 1801). Bus 103, 202. **Open** 10am-10pm Mon-Sat. **Credit** AmEx, DC, Disc, MC, V.

From the delicious maamohl (rose water and cream pie with pistachios) to the decadent shibeeb (filo-wrapped, honey-dipped cream), and the scrumptious namora (lightly fried dough, dipped in honey), the possibilities for pleasure are endless.

Diamond Bakery

Chinatown Mall, 4255 W Spring Mountain Road, at Wynn Road, South-west Las Vegas (368 1886). Bus 203. **Open** 9am-9pm daily. **Credit** AmEx, MC, V.

Chicken cookies, apple turnovers, ham and cheese rolls, steamed cream buns, fresh fruitcakes and, of course, mile-high wedding cakes and children's birthday cakes. Staff are patient and knowledgeable.

Williams Costume Company is a dressing-up box gone wild. Enjoy.

Freeds Bakery
4780 S Eastern Avenue at E Tropicana Avenue,
University District (456 7762). Bus 110, 201. **Open**
7am-6pm daily. **Credit** AmEx, MC, V. **Map** p311 Z3.
Freeds doesn't mess around. For 40 years, it has
been baking rye breads, challa breads, all kinds of
speciality cakes and cookies for Las Vegas's most
discerning eaters. It gets busy, so be patient.

Great Harvest Bread Company
Suite A, Sunset Mountain Vista Plaza, 4650 Sunset
Road, at Mountain Vista Street, Green Valley
(547 1555). Bus 212. **Open** 7am-7pm Mon-Sat.
Credit MC, V.
Banana walnut, white cheddar garlic, cranberry
orange, spinach feta, apple crumble: freshly baked
breads fill this shop with a truly mouth-watering
aroma. Free sample slices are offered daily.

Krispy Kreme Doughnuts
Excalibur, 3850 Las Vegas Boulevard South
(736 1306). Bus 201, 301, 302. **Open** 24hrs daily.
No credit cards. Map p316 A8.
Discover the doughnut that has taken the US by
storm. Wait for the neon 'Hot doughnuts now' sign
to light up and indulge in a tasty treat.

Lenôtre
Paris Shoppes, Paris Las Vegas, 3655 Las Vegas
Boulevard South, between Harmon Avenue & E
Flamingo Road (946 4341). Bus 202, 301, 302.
Open 11am-11pm daily. **Credit** AmEx, DC, Disc,
MC, V. **Map** p316 A7.
Less crowded than the other boulangerie at Paris
and a bit gentler on the nerves, Lenôtre is loaded
with luscious éclairs, cakes, cookies and croissants.
You still have to order cafeteria-style, but it's bright
and spacious and there's plenty to keep the eyes
happy while you wait.

Toscano's Baking Co
Rio, 3700 W Flamingo Road, at Valley View
Boulevard, West of Strip (364 8724). Bus 202.
Open 7am-8pm daily. **Credit** AmEx, Disc, MC, V.
Map p311 X3.
Giant cinnamon rolls and massive muffins, special-
ity breads, pies and cheesecakes are all freshly
baked daily. Not a bargain bakery by any means,
but the expenditure will be worth it.

Beer & wine
Cost Plus (*see p175*) has one of the best
priced, most varied wine and beer selections in
town (and no porno mags at the checkout).

La Cave
Paris Shoppes, Paris Las Vegas, 3655 Las Vegas
Boulevard South, between Harmon Avenue & E
Flamingo Road (946 4339). Bus 202, 301, 302.
Open 11am-11pm daily. **Credit** AmEx, Disc, DC,
MC, V. **Map** p316 A7.
La Cave may disappoint real wine enthusiasts and
if you're looking for a moderately priced bottle,

you'll be disappointed, too; the price of some labels
seems very high. However, the champagne and
sparkling wine are handy for impromptu celebrations, and there are some interesting pâtés, cheeses,
cookies and truffles, too.

Lee's Discount Liquor
3480 E Flamingo Road, at Pecos Road, East Las
Vegas (458 5700). Bus 111, 202. **Open** 9am-10pm
Mon-Thur; 9am-11pm Fri, Sat; 9am-9pm Sun. **Credit**
AmEx, Disc, MC, V. **Map** p311 Z3.
Old favourites, hard-to-find European wines and dirt-
cheap prices make Lee's the best liquor store in town.
Refrigerators offer a surprising sampling of beers
from around the planet, and a few ciders as well.
Branches: throughout the city.

Marché Bacchus
2620 Regatta Drive, at Mariner Way, Summerlin,
North-west Las Vegas (804 8008). No bus. **Open**
10am-10pm daily. **Credit** MC, V.
This fabulous little French store stocks fine wines,
champagnes, pâtés and cheeses. It also has tasting
kits for sale, monthly wine-tasting parties and a
small menu of salads and sandwiches. What's more,
there's outdoor seating on the edge of the lake.

Nevada Wine Cellar & Spirits
8664 W Flamingo Road, at Durango Drive, South-
west Las Vegas (222 9463). Bus 202. **Open** 10am-
10pm Mon-Sat, 10am-6pm Sun. **Credit** AmEx, Disc,
MC, V.
Opened in autumn 1999 by a trio of former wine
stewards from the Riviera, this is a connoisseur's
dream store. It specialises in hard-to-find cult wines.
Every Friday, it receives a shipment of fresh cheeses,
caviar, pâtés and mousses from France.

The Wine Cellar
Rio, 3700 W Flamingo Road, at Valley View
Boulevard, West of Strip (247 7962). Bus 202.
Open 11am-midnight Mon-Thur; 10am-2am Fri, Sat;
10am-midnight Sun. **Credit** AmEx, DC, Disc, MC, V.
Map p311 X3.
By far the finest selection of wine in Las Vegas, the
retail arm of the Rio's impressive cellars has about
150 kinds of wine on sale, ranging in price from $8
to astronomical. A vast selection is available by the
glass in 'tastings' for $6-$60. Any questions are
answered by two resident sommeliers.

Chocolate
Chocolate fiends shouldn't miss the **Ethel M**
Chocolates factory in Henderson (*see p126*).

Godiva
Forum Shops, Caesars Palace, 3570 Las Vegas
Boulevard South (734 8855). Bus 202, 301, 302.
Open 10am-11pm daily. **Credit** AmEx, DC, Disc,
MC, V. **Map** p316 A7.
The Belgian chocolatier decided to remember the
most famous tax rebel/nudist of all time in the most
delicious way – so why don't you, too?

Teuscher

Desert Passage, Aladdin, 3663 Las Vegas Boulevard South, (866 6624). Bus 301, 302. **Open** 9am-11pm Sun-Thur, 9am-midnight Fri-Sat. **Credit** AmEx, DC, Disc, MC, V. **Map** p316 A7.

There are 28 Tuescher shops around the world and one is in Las Vegas. Once you've tried these Swiss-made delights you'll never go back to Hershey.

Ethnic

Eliseevsky Russian-European Food

4825 W Flamingo Road, at Decatur Boulevard, South-west Las Vegas (247 8766). Bus 103, 202. **Open** 10am-8pm Mon-Sat; noon-6pm Sun. **Credit** MC, V.

This family-owned Russian deli and grocer is a find. The shelves are filled with cryptically labelled delicacies in fantastic wrappings, while drinks, rich cakes and cream cheeses fill the cooler. The deli case houses salads, pirojki, caviar, fish and salami.

Gee's Oriental Market

4109 W Sahara Avenue, at Valley View Boulevard, West of Strip (362 5287). Bus 104, 204. **Open** 8am-8pm daily. **Credit** Disc, MC, V. **Map** p311 X2.

The place for Chinese, Thai, Vietnamese and Filipino groceries, with first-rate fresh produce and seafood. Gee's claim to fame is that it's the only place in Las Vegas to carry meang da na, a cockroach-like insect that is considered an oriental delicacy.

India Sweets & Spices

Commercial Center, 953 E Sahara Avenue, between Paradise Road & Maryland Parkway, East Las Vegas (892 0720). Bus 204. **Open** 11am-8pm daily. **Credit** AmEx, Disc, MC, V. **Map** p315 C4.

Come here for curry spices, a small array of Indian and Pakistani groceries and a weekend deli offering samosas and the like.

International Marketplace

5000 S Decatur Boulevard, at Reno Street, south of W Tropicana Avenue, South-west Las Vegas (889 2888). Bus 103, 201. **Open** 9am-8pm Mon-Fri; 9am-6pm Sat, Sun. **Credit** AmEx, MC, V.

Hard to miss, this huge building is a warehouse of imported edibles, goodies and gadgetry of every kind. Prices are on the serious side of cheap.

Italcream

3871 Valley View Boulevard, at W Spring Mountain Road, West of Strip (873 2214). Bus 104, 203. **Open** 8am-4pm Mon-Fri. **No credit cards.** **Map** p311 X3.

Magnifico! Giovanni Parente and his family have a secret recipe for the best gelato we've ever tasted.

Mediterranean Café & Market

Tiffany Square, 4147 S Maryland Parkway, at E Flamingo Road, University District (731 6030). Bus 109, 202. **Open** *Café* 11am-8pm daily. *Market* 9.30am-8pm Mon-Fri; 9.30am-5pm Sat. **Credit** AmEx, Disc, MC, V. **Map** p311 Y3.

Shop at this excellent grocery/deli for a wide variety of Arabic, Armenian, Greek and Iranian groceries, then visit the relaxed next-door café for the best baklava in town (*see p149*). Warning: you may be distracted by a belly dancer undulating nearby.

Siena Deli

Renaissance Plaza, 2250 E Tropicana Avenue, at Eastern Avenue, University District (736 8424). Bus 110, 201. **Open** 10am-6pm Mon-Sat; 10am-4pm Sun. **Credit** AmEx, DC, Disc, MC, V. **Map** p311 Z3.

The Italian owner of this deli/restaurant has brought Italy's finest cuisine to Vegas. Prices may be steep ($144 for aged balsamic vinegar), but the quality and authenticity are impeccable. Siena also carries Italian cooking hardware, such as pasta machines. **Branch:** 5755 Spring Mountain Road, at Duneville Street, South-west Las Vegas (871 8616).

Health food & vitamins

Rainbow's End Natural Foods

1100 E Sahara Avenue, at Maryland Parkway, East Las Vegas (737 7282). Bus 109, 204. **Open** 9am-9pm Mon-Fri; 9am-8pm Sat; 11am-6pm Sun. **Credit** AmEx, Disc, MC, V. **Map** p311 Y2.

Offers a broad choice of herbs, vitamins and body-care products, but limited produce and food. A café full of veggie delights makes up half the store and is a good place for lunch.

Wild Oats Community Market

3455 E Flamingo Road, at Pecos Road, East Las Vegas (434 8115/www.wildoats.com). Bus 111, 202. **Open** 8am-9pm daily. **Credit** MC, V. **Map** p311 Z3.

Wild Oats monopolises the Vegas health food industry, and for good reason. Prices are a bit steep, but its stock of organic produce, health foods, natural body-care products, homeopathic medicines and macrobiotic supplies is exemplary. The adjacent café offers fab juices and healthy snacks. **Branch:** 6720 W Sahara Avenue, South-west Las Vegas (253 7050).

Supermarkets & grocery shops

There are four main supermarket chains in Las Vegas – **Albertson's**, **Smith's**, **Vons** and **Raley's** – but you'll have to get off the Strip to find one; consult the Yellow Pages for locations.

British Grocery Store

Pioneer Square, 3375 S Decatur Boulevard, at Desert Inn Road, South-west Las Vegas (579 7777/www.britishgrocers.com). Bus 103. **Open** 10am-8pm Mon-Fri; 10am-6pm Sat. **Credit** MC, V.

Reportedly, more than 40,000 Brits now call Las Vegas home. To dispel any lingering homesickness, this shop offers copies of the *Sunday Times*, plus marmalade, teas, sweets and fruit squash. The freezers are stocked with steak and kidney pies, sausage rolls, black pudding and scones, and the dairy case holds clotted cream and Red Leicester cheese.

British Grocery Store. *See p174.*

Trader Joe's

*2101 S Decatur Boulevard, at O'Bannon Drive,
north of Sahara Avenue, North-west Las Vegas (367
0227/www.traderjoes.com). Bus 103, 105, 204.*
Open 9am-9pm daily. **Credit** Disc, MC, V.
Trader Joe's emulates the old-time grocery with a
twist: the products are all tested to ensure they are
'the best' (it claims) of their kind. The ambience is
New Agey, but there's plenty of hedonism to be
found: delicious chocolate and cookies and decadent
party foods. High quality and highish prices.
Branch: 2716 N Green Valley Parkway, Henderson
(433 6773); 7585 West Washington Drive, Summerlin,
North-west Las Vegas (242 8240)

Gifts & collectibles

Amon Wardy Home Store

*Forum Shops, Caesars Palace, 3570 Las Vegas
Boulevard South (734 0480). Bus 202, 301, 302.*
Open 10am-11pm daily. **Credit** AmEx, DC, Disc,
MC, V. **Map** p316 A7.
Aspen-based decorator extraordinaire Amon
Wardy's wildly successful boutique at the Forum
Shops has great and sometimes humorous home
accessories. His latest showroom features the bulk
of his eclectic and wild furniture line, as well as some
McKenzie Child furniture.

Ca'd'Oro

*Grand Canal Shoppes, Venetian, 3355 Las Vegas
Boulevard South, at Sands Avenue (696 0080/
www.thecadoro.com). Bus 301, 302.* **Open** 10am-
11pm Mon-Thur, Sun; 10am-midnight Fri, Sat.
Credit AmEx, Disc, MC, V. **Map** p316 A6.
This gorgeous gallery is named after one of the
finest façades in Venice, the Palace of Gold. From
the delicate hand-blown Murano glass light fittings
to the beautiful hand-made custom tiles, it's a gem.
You'll find contemporary creations as well as some
classic timepieces from the likes of Omega, Tag
Heuer and Bertolucci.

The Chihuly Store

*Via Bellagio, Bellagio, 3600 Las Vegas Boulevard
South, at Flamingo Road (693 7995).* **Open** 9am-
midnight daily. **Credit** AmEx, Disc, MC, V.
Map p316 A7.

It seems fitting that glass sculptor Dale Chihuly
should open his first signature gallery inside the
Bellagio, since his largest sculpture – with over 2,000
pieces of glass – adorns the ceiling of the hotel lobby.
The store focuses mainly on affordable Chihuly
glass editions, plus some more elaborate pieces.

Cost Plus World Market

*3840 S Maryland Parkway, at E Flamingo Road,
University District (794 2070). Bus 109, 202, 213.*
Open 9am-9pm Mon-Sat; 10am-7pm Sun. **Credit**
AmEx, Disc, MC, V. **Map** p311 Y3.
An arty superstore of imported furnishings and dec-
orations with a neo-natural feel. Cost Plus also has
good imported vino, pastas, sauces, curries, candies
and such like. The perfect place to pick up a couple
of glasses and a bargain-priced bottle of red.
Branch: 2151 S Rainbow Boulevard, between Oakey
Boulevard & Sahara Avenue, North-west Las Vegas
(638 8844).

The Museum Company

*Forum Shops, Caesars Palace, 3500 Las Vegas
Boulevard South, between W Spring Mountain &
Flamingo Roads (792 9220/www.museumcompany.
com). Bus 301, 302.* **Open** 10am-11pm Mon-Thur,
Sun; 10am-midnight Fri, Sat. **Credit** AmEx, Disc,
MC, V. **Map** p316 A7.
This chainstore is a good place to find interesting
arty gifts for kids and adults, including cards, books,
calendars, music, toys and oddities. There's a branch
at McCarran Airport for last-minute gifts.
Branch: Desert Passage, Aladdin, 3663 Las Vegas
Boulevard South, at Harmon Avenue (836 0808).

Re Gallerie

*Paris Shoppes, Paris Las Vegas, 3655 Las Vegas
Boulevard South, between Harmon Avenue & E
Flamingo Road (792 2278). Bus 202, 301, 302.*
Open 9am-11pm daily. **Credit** AmEx, DC, Disc, MC,
V. **Map** p316 A7.
This lovely shop specialises in vintage French
posters and prints re-created on its 100-year-old
press, on display in the adjoining room. Designs
include the art nouveau goddesses of Alphonse
Mucha, the bold geometric designs of art deco and
Hollywood classics such as King Kong and Charlie
Chaplin. Prices from $100 (small) or $300 (large).

Seven Rings Gallery

*9350 W Sahara Avenue, at S Fort Apache Road,
South-west Las Vegas (363 7727). Bus 204.* **Open**
10am-8pm Mon-Sat; 10am-7pm Sun. **Credit** AmEx,
Disc, MC, V.
Distinctive desert-themed gifts, including miniature
fountains, jewellery and 3D sculptures pepper this
gallery, frame shop and gift boutique.

Smoking

Smokers with style will be glad to find a branch
of **Davidoff**, Switzerland's finest cigar maker,
located in the Grand Canal Shoppes at the
Venetian (733 5999).

Eat, Drink, Shop

Las Vegas Cigar Co

3755 Las Vegas Boulevard South, between E Tropicana & Harmon Avenues (262 6140). Bus 301, 302. **Open** 8am-9.30pm daily. **Credit** AmEx, Disc, MC, V. **Map** p316 A8.

All cigars here are 100% hand-rolled using imported tobaccos blended by Cuban masters and cigar makers. Sweet, natural or maduro wraps are available, plus pipe tobacco and imported cigarettes such as clove and beedies.

Paiute Tribal Smoke Shop

1225 N Main Street, between Washington & Owens Avenues, North Las Vegas (387 6433). Bus 208, 214. **Open** 7am-8pm Mon-Sat; 8am-7pm Sun. **Credit** Disc, MC, V. **Map** p311 Y1.

This is one of Nevada's finest tobacco collections. You pay taxes to the Paiute nation rather than the state of Nevada, and prices end up pretty competitive. There's a cigarette shop (some non-domestic brands) and a cigar and pipe tobacco room.

Vegas souvenirs

Of course, Las Vegas has supermarkets, department stores, auto parts suppliers, chi-chi boutiques and all those other boring, normal retail outlets. But who cares? This city is all about image, and in this instance, image means 'Vegas, bay-bee!'. While the monied hordes are schlepping through the upmarket resort malls, dropping dosh on stuff they can find in any other global city, you will have the inside track on items that really say 'Las Vegas'. And don't think that means cheap, tacky souvenirs. Then again, don't think it doesn't.

Bonanza: The World's Largest Gift Shop

2460 Las Vegas Boulevard South, at Sahara Avenue (385 7359). Bus 204, 301, 302. **Open** 8am-midnight daily. **Credit** AmEx, Disc, MC, V. **Map** p315 C4.

If it is Las Vegas-related kitsch you want, behold the jackpot. Roulette-wheel ashtrays, Elvis sunglasses-sideburn combos, slot machine salt-and-pepper sets, coin-filled toilet seats, used playing cards and dice clocks galore fill aisle after aisle.

The Bud Jones Company

3640 S Valley View Boulevard, between Spring Mountain Road & Twain Avenue, West of Strip (876 2782). Bus 104. **Open** 8am-4pm Mon-Fri. **Credit** MC, V. **Map** p311 X3.

A set of custom-made casino-quality chips in their very own storage and carrying case can be yours. How can you resist?

Gamblers General Store

800 S Main Street, at Hoover Avenue, Downtown (382 9903). Bus 108, 204. **Open** 9am-5pm daily. **Credit** AmEx, Disc, MC, V. **Map** p312 C2.

If you desperately want to live la vida Vegas when you get home, this is the place for you. All manner

What more can we say?

of gaming hardware – craps tables, roulette wheels, gaming layouts, poker chips, slot machines – are available, and they'll even ship it for you.

Las Vegas Harley-Davidson

2605 S Eastern Avenue, at Sahara Avenue, East Las Vegas (431 8500). Bus 110. **Open** 9am-7pm Mon-Fri; 9am-6pm Sat; 10am-5pm Sun. **Credit** AmEx, MC, V. **Map** p311 Z2.

The world's largest Harley-Davidson outlet, where Harley junkies can pick up their own Las Vegas T-shirt souvenirs.

Paul Son Gaming Supplies Inc

1700 S Industrial Road, at New York Avenue, West of Strip (384 2425). Bus 105. **Open** 10am-6pm Mon-Fri. **Credit** AmEx, MC, V. **Map** p316 A8.

Ever pondered where casinos buy all the gambling tables and accessories? Visit this shop and all your casino supply questions will be answered.

Siegfried & Roy Boutique

Mirage, 3400 Las Vegas Boulevard South, between Spring Mountain & W Flamingo Roads (791 7111). Bus 203, 301, 302. **Open** *Summer* 10am-7pm daily; *Winter* 11am-6pm Mon-Fri; 10am-6pm Sat, Sun. **Credit** AmEx, DC, Disc, MC, V. **Map** p316 A6.

In the '50s it was Louis Prima and Keely Smith; in the '70s, Tom Jones and Elvis Presley. Today, it is magicians Siegfried and Roy. This shop specialises in all the S&R merchandise you could want: stuffed tigers, CDs, pyjamas, even boxer shorts.

Health & beauty

Many of the casinos have lavish full-service spas and beauty salons; for details of some of the best, *see p235.*

Complementary therapies

Body Works Massage Therapy
5025 S Eastern Avenue, just south of E Tropicana Avenue, East Las Vegas (736 8887). Bus 110, 201. **Open** 10am-6pm daily. **Credit** MC, V. **Map** p311 Z4.
All the usual treatments, including Swedish deep tissue and Chinese Mix, as well as muds and salts.

Healthy Alternatives
Suite 20, 820 Rancho Lane, between Tonopah Avenue & Charleston Boulevard, North-west Las Vegas (382 5717). Bus 106, 206, 215. **Open** 10am-6pm Tue-Sat. **Credit** AmEx, MC, V. **Map** p315 A2.
Here you'll find consultation, therapy and training all in one place. Therapies include Ayurvedics, massage and energy work. Training is available in meditation, yoga and t'ai chi. Note that it's on a small inlet of Rancho Lane, off the main drag.

T&T Ginseng
Chinatown Mall, 4215 W Spring Mountain Road, at Wynn Road, South-west Las Vegas (368 3898). Bus 203. **Open** 10am-8.30pm daily. **Credit** MC, V.
A fascinating store and Chinese herbal pharmacy. Diagnosis and treatment are handled with ancient wisdom and extreme care. An oriental medical doctor and herbalist are on duty daily.

Worton's Palmistry Studios
1441 Las Vegas Boulevard South, at Convention Center Drive (386 0121). Bus 301, 302. **Open** by appointment. **No credit cards**. **Map** p315 B5.
Holding hands with Las Vegas since 1958, this wonderful place offers professional palmistry and astrology and then some. It's located at the northern, more eclectic, end of the Strip.

Cosmetics & perfume shops

Perfume Depot
5725 Pecos Road, between Russell Road & Patrick Lane, East Las Vegas (454 5059). Bus 111. **Open** 10am-7pm Mon-Fri; 10am-6pm Sat; 11am-5pm Sun. **Credit** AmEx, Disc, MC, V. **Map** p311 Z4.
As you might expect, the Perfume Depot offers huge quantities of cut-price designer fragrances.

Sephora
3311 Las Vegas Boulevard South, just south of Sands Avenue (735 3896/www.sephora.com). Bus 203, 301, 302. **Open** 10am-11pm Mon-Thur, Sun; 10am-midnight Fri, Sat. **Credit** AmEx, Disc, MC, V. **Map** p316 A6.
This French cosmetics and perfume emporium is the largest and most comprehensive in Las Vegas. Packed with products ranging from Dior and Yves

St Laurent to the latest hip offerings from Stila, Anna Sui and Urban Decay. Use the make-up application areas, or let a pro apply the goods. You can also create your own scent.

Ulta3
3776 S Maryland Parkway, at Twain Avenue, East Las Vegas (735 4744/www.ulta3.com). Bus 109, 203, 213. **Open** 10am-9pm Mon-Sat; 11am-6pm Sun. **Credit** AmEx, DC, Disc, MC, V. **Map** p311 Y3.
If you can pump it, dab it, spray it, squirt it, squeeze it or otherwise apply it, Ulta3 has got it. Another plus: it's located inside a full-service beauty salon.
Branches: 2120 N Rainbow Boulevard, North-west Las Vegas (631 3556); 543 N Stephanie Street, between Sunset Road & Warm Springs Road, Green Valley (451 6211).

Hair & beauty salons

Beauty Center & Salon
6160 W Tropicana Avenue, at Jones Boulevard, South-west Las Vegas (891 8895). Bus 102, 201. **Open** 9am-8pm Mon-Fri; 9am-7pm Sat; 9am-5pm Sun. **Credit** AmEx, MC, V.
A great source of high-end hair-care products, cosmetics and nails. It's not quite as wide-ranging as Ulta3 (*see above*), but brands include Sebastian, Joico, Aveda, Redken and Matrix Essentials. The salon area at the back offers professional cuts and colour at reasonable prices.
Branches: throughout the city.

Diva Studio
3159 W Tompkins Avenue, between Polaris Avenue & Industrial Road, West of Strip (736 2011). Bus 201. **Open** 9am-7pm Mon-Sat. **Credit** MC, V. **Map** p311 X3.
Ideal for the down-to-earth diva (or dude) wanting great service at reasonable prices in a trendy, neoclassical atmosphere. Treatments include massage, facials, reflexology, waxing, body sculpture and manicures and pedicures. Great haircuts, too.

Dolphin Court
7581 W Lake Mead, at Buffalo Road, North-west Las Vegas (432 9772/ www.dolphincourt.com). Bus 210. **Open** 8am-9pm Mon-Sat; 9am-6pm Sun. **Credit** AmEx, DC, Disc, MC, V.
One of numerous 'day spa' chains, Dolphin Court seems hell-bent on taking over the city. Hair care is offered, but spa services are the real strength.
Branch: 3455 S Durango Drive, South-west Las Vegas (949 9999).

Globe Salon
Suite 130, 1121 South Decatur Boulevard, at Charleston Boulevard, North-west Las Vegas (938 4247/www.globesalon.com). Bus 103, 206. **Open** 10am-7pm Mon-Fri; 9am-6pm Sat. **Credit** AmEx, MC, V.
Las Vegas native Staci Linklater, who made a name for herself as the 'Hairstylist to the Hip' in the 1990s, has taken her success to the next level with Globe

Ultra-hip snips at **Globe Salon**. See p177.

Salon. This fashion-forward, full-service hair and skincare boutique has on its staff ten hairstylists (including the 2001 Las Vegas Hairdresser of the Year) and a skincare professional.

A Little Off the Top

3140 S Valley View Boulevard, between Desert Inn Road & Sahara Avenue, West of Strip (222 3599/ www.alittleoffthetop.com). Bus 104. **Open** 10am-6pm Tue-Fri; 10am-5pm Sat. **Credit** MC, V. **Map** p311 X2.

Lovely, lingerie-clad ladies will wash, trim and blow-dry your hair, and even throw in a shoulder and neck massage for a price that'll make you blush. This tiny joint tends to be popular with male clients. We can't think why...

Pharmacies

You'll find drugstores with pharmacy services all over Las Vegas. On the Strip, try **Walgreen Drug Store** (at Charleston Boulevard; 471 6844) and **White Cross Drugs** (at Oakey Boulevard; 382 1733). Both are open 24 hours, although pharmacy services at White Cross are only available from 7.30am to 1am daily.

Tattoos

Absolute Ink

1141 Las Vegas Boulevard South, just south of Charleston Boulevard, Stratosphere Area (383 8282). Bus 301, 302. **Open** noon-10pm Mon-Thur, Sun; noon-midnight Fri, Sat. **Credit** AmEx, Disc, MC, V. **Map** p315 C3.

If you want a permanent souvenir of Las Vegas, visit this attitude-free tattoo parlour near Downtown. The staff are serious about their art, and you should be too if you choose to book their time. Piercings start at $20 and tattoo prices claim to be the lowest in town. Ask for Iron Mike.

Music & video

With 30 locations in Vegas, **Blockbuster** (www.blockbuster.com) is the most widespread video shop, though not the cheapest. Call 1-800 800 6767 to find your nearest branch. Or try **Hollywood Video** (www.hollywoodvideo. com), which has a dizzying selection, especially of kids' movies, and a new-release policy.

Big B's CDs & Records

4761 S Maryland Parkway, just south of Tropicana Avenue, East of Strip (732 4433/www.bigbsmusic. com). Bus 108, 201. **Open** 11am-9pm Mon-Sat; noon-6pm Sun. **Credit** AmEx, Disc, MC, V. **Map** p311 Y4.

Big B's buys used CDs and vinyl or offers a trade-in from among its inventory of new and used music. Staff are knowledgeable and friendly, and high turnover keeps the stock current. Recommended.

Odyssey Records

1600 Las Vegas Boulevard South, at Wyoming Avenue, Stratosphere Area (384 4040). Bus 301, 302. **Open** 24hrs daily. **Credit** AmEx, Disc, MC, V. **Map** p315 C3.

This excellent rap and R&B headquarters has occupied the same location for more than 25 years on a once prominent stretch of Las Vegas Boulevard that is now considered seedy. We prefer to think of it as colourful.

Tower Records, Video & Books

4580 Decatur Boulevard, at W Sahara Avenue, South-west Las Vegas (364 2500/www.tower records.com). Bus 103, 204. **Open** 9am-midnight daily. **Credit** AmEx, Disc, MC, V.

Located in the vast Tower-Good Guys-Wow! super-store, this branch of Tower Records wins the prize for variety: it has videos (for sale and rent, with a refreshingly strong foreign selection), books, maga-zines and, of course, a vast array of CDs, cassettes and vinyl. Pop/rock consumes the majority of space, but the generous selection of world beat, jazz vocal-ists and classical keeps things balanced. If it all becomes too much, have a rest in the café. **Branch:** 4110 Maryland Parkway, at Flamingo Road, University District (371 0800).

Virgin Megastore

Forum Shops, Caesars Palace, 3500 Las Vegas Boulevard South, between W Spring Mountain & Flamingo Roads (696 7100/www.virginmega.com). Bus 202, 301, 302. **Open** 10am-midnight Mon-Thur, Sun; 10am-1am Fri, Sat. **Credit** AmEx, DC, Disc, MC, V. **Map** p316 A7.

This vast place has everything, and lots of it. On your way to the indie racks, you'll be pulled towards the huge electronica section, and if you're heading for funk, you may be swayed by a movie sound-track. Prices are steep, but promotions on new releases and some 'nice price' older material can be found. Staff are youthful and perky, and seem genuinely happy to help.

Wax Trax Records

2909 S Decatur Boulevard, between Sahara Avenue & Desert Inn Road, South-west Las Vegas (362 4300). Bus 103, 204. **Open** 10am-5pm daily. **Credit** AmEx, MC, V.

Wax Trax offers two storeys of vinyl and memorabilia – bins busting at the seams, fat with old soul and R&B, jazz, doo-wop and rock 'n' roll – plus a mixed selection of used CDs. Walls are covered with signed photos of the greats, givin' up love and thanks to owner Rich Rosen. Be prepared for some boisterous East Coast conversation, a friendly house pup and an ear- and eyeful of music history.

Sex & erotica

For details of the raunchy **Showgirl Video** store, *see p209.*

Adult Superstore

3850 W Tropicana Avenue, at Valley View Road, West of Strip (798 0144). Bus 201. **Open** 24hrs daily. **Credit** AmEx, Disc, MC, V. **Map** p311 X3.

There are four branches of this locals' favourite, but this is the one to visit. The 'mega-superstore' has magazine and video sections devoted to every fetish and fantasy legal in Nevada, plus an unequalled selection of toys, fetish gear and sexy food items. There are private movie-viewing booths, too, and it's the only place in Vegas where you can view adult films on the big screen.

(SPL-516)
$39.95

Ball Vice
(NC15052)
$29.95

7 Ring Gates of Hell
(SPL-511)
$14.95
(SPR-5)
5 Ring Gates of Hell

Paradise Electro Stimulations: Ouch!

Paradise Electro Stimulations

1509 W Oakey Boulevard, at Western Avenue, Stratosphere Area (474 2991/www.peselectro.com). Bus 105. **Open** 9am-6pm Mon-Fri. **Credit** AmEx, Disc, MC, V. **Map** p315 B3.

Discard any preconceptions of adult playthings before entering: PES (aka the Studio) is known for electric muscle stimulation devices. That's right, folks – dildos, plugs, sheaths, you name it – all composed of striking crystal-clear plastic, and all attachable to an electrical impulse control unit that purportedly stimulates the user from the inside out. PES is an experience for the sexually adventurous; call ahead for a private viewing.

Rancho Adult Entertainment Center

4820 N Rancho Drive, at Lone Mountain Road, North-west Las Vegas (645 6104). Bus 106. **Open** 24hrs daily. **Credit** AmEx, MC, V, Disc.

The best of the small adult bookstores has something for everyone: a large variety of new videos, magazines and vibrating toys, S&M gear, leather and vinyl, massage oils and more. If you can't find what you want, the friendly staff – including several women – will help or order it for you. All this contributes to a comfortable atmosphere.

Sport & outdoor

Callaway Center Pro Shop

6730 Las Vegas Boulevard South, at Sunset Road (896 4100). Bus 301, 302. **Open** 6.30am-9pm daily. **Credit** AmEx, Disc, MC, V. **Map** p311 X4.

Golfing fanatics will be glad to find Callaway's. Not only is it located on the Strip's best three-par golf course, but it also has golfing gear galore.

Copelands Sports

2178 North Rainbow Boulevard, at Lake Mead Boulevard, Summerlin, North-west Las Vegas (631 7497). Bus 101. **Open** 10am-9pm Mon-Sat; 11am-7pm Sun. **Credit** AmEx, Disc, MC, V.

A clean, huge, well-lit superstore of sporting equipment and clothing. There's gear and gadgets for everything from weightlifting to tennis, camping and golf, neatly organised into sporting sections. There's even a boarding section for surfers and skateboarders, or those who just like the look. **Branch**: 579 North Stephanie St, at Sunset Way, Green Valley (436 3089).

Desert Rock Sports

8201 W Charleston Boulevard, at Cimarron Road, North-west Las Vegas (254 1143/www.desertrock sports.com). Bus 206. **Open** 9am-7pm Mon-Fri; 9am-6pm Sat; 10am-6pm Sun. **Credit** AmEx, Disc, MC, V.

All kinds of climbing and hiking equipment, including a large selection of backpacking and camping stuff. Rent the necessary gear (including shoes) and try the wall at the climbing centre next door before buying (*see p233*). Well-known names are available at highish prices, and staff are well informed. There's great gear for children and the pooch, too.

Eat, Drink, Shop

McGhie's

*4503 W Sahara Avenue, between Arville Street
& Decatur Boulevard, South-west Las Vegas
(252 8077) Bus 204.* **Open** 10am-7pm daily.
Credit Disc, MC, V.

McGhie's was smart enough to embrace the snow-boarding craze in the early 1990s, and also to add mountain biking to its water/snow ski goods. This wise decision probably saved one of Las Vegas's oldest and more respected outdoor outfitters from demise. Rentals, plus advice on the area's better recreation areas, are available.

Nevada Bob's

*3999 Las Vegas Boulevard South, at Russell Road
(451 3333). Bus 301, 302.* **Open** 9am-9pm Mon-Fri;
9am-9pm Sat; 10am-9pm Sun. **Credit** AmEx, Disc,
MC, V. **Map** p316 A9.

The world's largest chain of pro golf shops has several stores in Vegas. Choose from brands such as Callaway, McGregor and Arnold Palmer – and keep an eye out for Vegas local, Tiger Woods.
Branches: throughout the city.

Pro Cyclery

*7034 W Charleston Boulevard, at Vincent Way,
Summerlin, North-west Las Vegas (228 9460).
Bus 206.* **Open** 10am-7pm Mon-Fri; 10am-5pm Sat.
Credit AmEx, MC, V.

This long-time Las Vegas bicycling fixture is a great source of gear for both hire and purchase.

The Sports Authority

*Sahara Pavilion, 2620 S Decatur Boulevard, at
Sahara Avenue, South-west Las Vegas (368 3335).
Bus 103, 204.* **Open** 10am-9pm Mon-Fri; 9am-8pm
Sat; 10am-6pm Sun. **Credit** AmEx, Disc, MC, V.

This chain store is definitely the authority on selection and price, though staff assistance could do with a bit of fine tuning. It offers a wide assortment of athletic fashions, plus equipment for every sport in the book, from canoeing to hunting.
Branch: 1431 W Sunset Road, West of Strip
(433 2676).

Subskates

*3736 E Flamingo Avenue, at Sandhill Road, East
Las Vegas (435 1978/www.subskates.com). Bus 202.*
Open 10am-7pm Mon-Sat; 11am-5pm Sun. **Credit**
AmEx, Disc, MC, V. **Map** p311 Z3.

Snowboarders, bladers, skaters and anyone with a fetish for balancing on a board congregate here to purchase their equipment, plus plenty of cool clothing – size XXXL, of course.
Branch: 840 N Rainbow Boulevard, North-west
Las Vegas (258 3635).

Toys

You will find branches of the **Disney Store** all over Las Vegas, including in the Forum Shops at Caesars Palace and at the Boulevard, Fashion Show and Galleria Malls. For more individual toys, try some of the following:

Build-A-Bear

*Desert Passage, Aladdin, 3663 Las Vegas Boulevard
South, at Harmon Avenue (836 0899/www.builda
bear.com). Bus 301, 302.* **Open** 10am-11pm Mon-Thur, Sun; 10am-midnight Fri, Sat. **Credit** AmEx,
Disc, MC, V. **Map** p316 A7.

Try your hand at creating that special stuffed bear for yourself or someone you love. Or better yet, take the kids there for a real treat. Customers pick everything, including fur colour, eye colour, costume and stuffing type, and watch as it is all assembled.

The Discovery Store

*Fashion Show Mall, 3200 Las Vegas Boulevard
South, at W Spring Mountain Road (792 2121/
www.discoverystore.com). Bus 203, 301, 302.* **Open**
10am-9pm Mon-Fri; 10am-7pm Sat; noon-6pm Sun.
Credit AmEx, DC, Disc, MC, V. **Map** p316 A/B6.

Part of the nature-driven Discovery Channel TV network, this is a paradise of learning and thinking toys and games for knowledge-seekers of any age.
Branches: Forum Shops, 3500 Las Vegas Boulevard
South (733 0787).

FAO Schwarz

*Forum Shops, Caesars Palace, 3500 Las Vegas
Boulevard South, between W Spring Mountain &
Flamingo Roads (796 6500/www.faoschwartz.com).
Bus 301, 302.* **Open** 10am-11pm Mon-Thur, Sun;
10am-midnight Fri, Sat. **Credit** AmEx, DC, Disc,
MC, V. **Map** p316 A7.

FAO Schwarz is right up there with Willie Wonka's Chocolate Factory in terms of a child's dream come true. Three storeys of playthings make this one of the largest toyshops in the US. Serious collectors should visit the private room.

Toys of Yesteryear

*2028 E Charleston Boulevard, at Eastern Avenue,
East Las Vegas (598 4030). Bus 110, 206.*
Open 11am-4pm Sat. **Credit** AmEx, Disc, MC, V.
Map p311 Z2.

Forget the dice clocks and take home a prized piece of Americana. This tiny shop has all sorts of old-fashioned toys and collectibles – including Kewpie dolls, *Star Wars* toys, cars and books. Check out the great collection of cast-metal toys.

Travel agents

Most of the larger hotels have a travel desk that will help guests change flights or book their next Vegas vacation. The service is often available for non-guests with ID, too.

Prestige Travel

*6175 W Spring Mountain Road, at Jones Boulevard,
South-west Las Vegas (251 5552). Bus 203.* **Open**
7.30am-6pm Mon-Fri. **Credit** AmEx, Disc, MC, V.

If you're tired of long waits on the phone listening to elevator music, let someone else do the dirty work. Prestige has 22 locations and will book your airline tickets, rental cars, cruises, tours and packages.
Branches: throughout the city.

Arts & Entertainment

By Season

Whatever the occasion, you can always expect a big blow-out in a city that claims to be the Entertainment Capital of the World.

Las Vegas may lack the high-profile arts festivals found in other more seriously 'cultural' destinations, but it has more than enough unique events to pack out the calendar. From poker tournaments, marathons and rodeos to outdoor food festivals and some spectacular celebrity shows, the city's party spirit means there always some kind of celebration in town.

New Year's Eve is always explosive and 2001 was no exception. Millennial fears had quelled the 2000 crowds a bit, but for 2001 they turned up in force to witness the largest pyrotechnic display in the world. Fourteen casinos along the Strip participated in a choreographed fireworks show entitled the 'Big Bang' that cost more than half a million dollars and drew an estimated 300,000 visitors to the city.

However, Vegas doesn't restrict itself to one party a year. The city's role as the nation's wedding capital means that on **Valentine's Day**, the city is packed with loving couples trying to get hitched in wacky ways – at quickie wedding chapels, drive-through wedding windows or in lavish surroundings fit for royalty.

Nevada Day (31 October), which commemorates the day Nevada officially joined the Union in 1864, is a state holiday. And, since it coincides with Hallowe'en, there's even more of an excuse for a celebration. In addition to numerous parties held in casinos and bars around town, there are two super-glitzy charity balls that put anything most other cities have to offer to shame. Many people have the day off work, and all city, county and state offices are closed (federal offices remain open). *See p184* **What a scream!**

For details of major conventions held in Las Vegas and tips on when to visit, *see chapter* **Resources A-Z: When to go.**

Spring

Big League Weekend
Cashman Field, 850 Las Vegas Boulevard North, at Washington Avenue, North Las Vegas (386 7184). Bus 106, 113. **Tickets** $27.50-$40 for 2 days. **Credit** AmEx, DC, MC, V. **Date** early Mar.

Las Vegas is without a major league baseball team, so fans take advantage of this chance to watch professional teams in these pre-season exhibition games.

Las Vegas 400 NASCAR Winston Cup Race
Las Vegas Motor Speedway, 7000 Las Vegas Boulevard North, North Las Vegas (information 644 4444/tickets 1-800 644 4444). Bus 113A. **Tickets** $50-$110. **Credit** AmEx, Disc, MC, V. **Date** mid-Mar.

Motor-racing fans can get their fill of excitement during this stop on the NASCAR circuit. The Sam's Town 300 Busch Series Grand National Division race precedes the big event. Reserve tickets early.

St Patrick's Day
Date 17 Mar.

If you're looking for a good *craic*, Irish pubs Houlihan's (1951 N Rainbow Avenue; 648 0300) and JC Wooloughan's (*see p160*) will give you a taste of the old country. Head Downtown to watch the Sons of Erin's lively parade, and retire to Fitzgerald's to sip green beer with O'Lucky the Leprechaun.

Clark County Fair
Clark County Fairgrounds, I-15, Logandale, Nevada (398 3247/www.ccfair.com). No bus. **Date** early Apr.

Southern Nevada's old-time county fair offers four days of food, rides, rodeo events and entertainment.

NHRA Drag Racing
Las Vegas Motor Speedway, 7000 Las Vegas Boulevard North, North Las Vegas (information 644

The best | Events

Las Vegas 400 NASCAR Winston Cup Race March; *see above.*

Binion's World Series of Poker April-May; *see p183.*

Andre Agassi's Grand Slam for Children late September; *see p185.*

Art in The Park October; *see p185.*

National Finals Rodeo December; *see p186.*

Billboard Music Awards December; *see p186.*

New Year's Eve 31 Dec; *see p186.*

Speed down to the **NASCAR**. See p182.

4444/tickets 1-800 644 4444). Bus 113A. **Tickets** $50-$110. **Credit** AmEx, Disc, MC, V. **Date** Apr.
The oldest and most prestigious straight-line racing organisation in the world, the NHRA sanctions ¼-mile stand-offs in cars ranging from street-legal sedans to jet-powered dragsters.

Great Duck Derby
Monte Carlo, 3770 Las Vegas Boulevard South, between Harmon Avenue & Tropicana Avenue (262 0037). Bus 301, 302. **Map** p316 A8. **Date** 3rd Sat in Apr.
Adopt a rubber duck ($5) and then watch it race against thousands of others in aid of local disability charity, Positively Kids. It's a pretty weird but wonderful sight.

Eco Jam
Las Vegas Silver Bowl Park, 6800 E Russell Road, at Boulder Highway, Henderson (455 8271). **Date** Sat near the end of Apr.
Vegas may not be known for its environmental awareness, but this annual Earth festival still manages to attract more than 50,000 people. They flock to Silver Bowl Park to check out the displays of electric cars and cool science projects – or to get their hands on some free trees and plant seedlings.

UNLVino
Paris, 3655 Las Vegas Boulevard South, between Harmon Avenue & E Flamingo Road (876 4500). Bus 202, 301, 302. **Admission** $35 in advance or $50 at the door. **No credit cards.** **Map** p316 A7. **Date** late Apr.

Sponsored by the University of Nevada, Las Vegas, this wine-tasting event brings around 100 of California's best wine-growers to town. It gets rowdier by the hour, so go early for the least hassle.

Professional Bowling Association (PBA) National & Senior Tour
Orleans, 4500 W Tropicana Avenue, at Arville Street, South-west Las Vegas (365 7400/1-303 836 5568). **Date** end Apr.
Nine championship rounds of bowling and other events for big prize money. Spectators get in free.

Las Vegas Gay Pride Festival & Parade
Festival picnic: Silver Bowl Park, Sam Boyd Stadium, 7000 E Russell Road, at Boulder Highway, Henderson (information 733 9800/225 3389/www. lasvegaspride.org). Bus 201. **Date** late Apr or May.
Come out and support the gay and lesbian community at their annual festival. In 2001, the parade, now regarded as one of the best in the West, was held on in the evening in Downtown, with Mayor Oscar Goodman acting as Grand Marshall. The parade is followed by the Pridefest picnic at Sam Boyd Stadium, with food booths, games, workshops and entertainers. Check the website for details.

World Series of Poker
Binion's Horseshoe, 128 Fremont Street, at Second Street, Downtown (382 1600). Bus 107, 301. **Map** p312 D1. **Date** Apr-May (finals in May).
The best poker players in the world get down to serious business during this three-week event with more prize money ($100 million) up for grabs than any other major sporting event. The final can be watched for free from small stands around the game itself or on numerous TV screens.

Cinco de Mayo
Lorenzi Park, 3333 W Washington Avenue, at Rancho Road, North-west Las Vegas (649 8553). **Admission** $5; free under-12s. **No credit cards.** **Map** p311 X1. **Date** Sun closest to 5 May.
In Las Vegas this traditional Mexican holiday is an excuse to hold a huge free party in Lorenzi Park. The festivities, including mariachi bands and a fireworks display, begin at 10am and last all day. Celebrations continue at the three-day fiesta on Fremont Street.

Craft Fair, Rib Burn-Off & Car Show
Sunset Park, 2601 Sunset Road, at S Eastern Avenue, East Las Vegas (455 8206). Bus 110, 212. **Date** May.
This two-day weekend event spreads itself over the sprawling grounds of Sunset Park, offering live music, a classic car show and acres of vendors hawking everything from freshly sizzled ribs to jewellery.

Liberace Birthday Celebration & Play-Alike Contest
Liberace Museum, 1775 E Tropicana Avenue, at Spencer Street, University District (798 5595). Bus 201. **Admission** $6.95; $2-$4.50 concessions. **Credit** AmEx, Disc, MC, V. **Map** p311 Y3. **Date** mid-May.

To commemorate Mr Showmanship's birthday, the Liberace Museum sponsors an impersonation contest for amateurs and professionals, who are judged on their technique, costume and presentation by a panel of celebrity judges.

EAT'M Festival

Mirage, 3400 Las Vegas Boulevard South, between Spring Mountain & W Flamingo Roads (792 9430/ www.eat-m.com). **Admission** free-$10.

Credit AmEx, Disc, MC, V. **Map** p316 A6.
Date late May or early June.
The Emerging Artists & Talent in Music festival is a four-day event that gives up-and-coming bands the opportunity to display their skills and make their mark in front of recording executives, talent developers and fans. The Mirage hosts the event, with other showcase stages around the city at the Hard Rock, Gilley's, Imperial Palace, Tommy Rocker's and Treasure Island.

What a scream!

Expect the unexpected on 31 October: it's sure to be a wicked night.

HALLOWE'EN FOR KIDS

As elsewhere in the States, it's traditional in Vegas for children to go around the neighbourhood in costumes, knocking on every door for a 'trick or treat'. But today, in the era of real bogeymen, many families opt to go to one of the official 'safehouse' trick-or-treating events instead, held in the local shopping malls. If you're in town with little ones on 31 October, try the **Boulevard Mall** (3528 S Maryland Parkway; 732 8949), the **Hallowe'en Bash** at the Galleria at Sunset Mall (1300 W Sunset Road, Henderson; 434 0202), or the **Spooktacular Halloweekend** at the Trails Village Center (1900 Village Center Drive, Summerlin; 341 5500) .

There's more family-oriented fare to be enjoyed at casinos such as **Boulder**, **Sunset** and **Texas Stations** (*see pp100-1*), which have carnivals in their parking lots, haunted houses, sideshows, free entertainment and food. Also visit **Screamfest** at the Las Vegas Mini Grand Prix (1401 N Rainbow Boulevard, at Vegas Drive; 259 7000) for a haunted house, a Castle of Carnage in horrorvision 3-D and all the regular go-kart rides.

Freaking Brothers' haunted houses will test your nerve at the **Black Box Haunted House** (corner of Rainbow Boulevard and Smoke Ranch Road) and the **Dungeon** (corner of Bonanza Road and Nellis Road). For a real horror show, however, visit the **Hauntridge Theatre of Terror** at the Huntridge Theatre (1208 E Charleston Boulevard; 386 4868). Only for the truly brave, this vast, spooky place promises 10,000 square feet of fear.

HALLOWE'EN FOR ADULTS

Once you've recovered from the kids' stuff, it's time for some grown-up fun. The annual **Las Vegas Fetish & Fantasy Hallowe'en Ball**, usually held in the Tiffany Theatre at the Tropicana (739 2645; *see p87*), is a truly 'adult' party, and to gain admittance, you have to be dressed for it. The tame might come in tuxedos and evening gowns, but the more adventurous strut their stuff in lingerie, leather, lace or latex. If your wardrobe's a bit short of fetish fashion, you can buy a suitably shocking ensemble once you get there; note that those who choose otherwise suffer the humiliation of a $40 party-pooper fine.

If that's not enough sexy, scary fun for you, check out the **Pimp & Ho Ball** and the **Saints & Sinners Ball**, both usually held at Mandalay Bay (*see p78*) for more utterly outrageous costumes and a unique party vibe.

Club fiends can dance the night away at the annual **Dr Superfreakinstein's Mad Halloween Bash** at the Rio, or at the hip Hallowe'en happenings at Studio 54 (MGM), Baby's and the Joint (Hard Rock Hotel), Jack's Velvet Lounge (Venetian) and Ra Nightclub (Luxor). For details of these venues, *see chapter* **Nightlife**.

The biggest bash of the lot, though, is the annual **Beaux Arts Hallowe'en Ball**, held at a different glamorous location each year. A big hit with the drag community, it features the city's most elaborate costumes and a humorous crowning of the king and queen of the ball. What's more, the proceeds go to charity. In previous years AFAN (Aid for AIDS in Nevada) has benefited, but a new recipient is to be announced for 2002. Call 382 2326 for further details.

And, finally, those in love at Hallowe'en can tie the knot in freakish fashion. The **Viva Las Vegas Wedding Chapel** (1205 Las Vegas Boulevard South; 384 0771) offers a Graveyard Wedding for $475 and a Gothic Wedding for $750.

The street heat of **New Year's Eve**. See p186.

Summer

Junefest

Silver Bowl Park, Sam Boyd Stadium, 7000 E Russell Road, at Boulder Highway, Henderson (895 3900/ 739 9600). Bus 201. **Tickets** $15-$30. **Credit** AmEx, Disc, MC, V. **Date** 1st Sat in June.

This day-long concert has a festival atmosphere and features classic rock 'n' roll groups. As the temperature rises, the crowd gets hosed off.

Independence Day & Damboree Days Festival

Bicentennial Park, at Colorado Street & Nevada Highway, Boulder City (293 2034). Bus 116. **Date** 4 July weekend.

Damboree Days is the best Independence Day celebration in the area, packed with outdoor contests, dancing and fireworks. Some of the local casinos host barbecues and small fireworks shows in Vegas itself, but the biggest extravaganza of all is presented by the Firemen's Benefit Association at Sam Boyd Stadium.

Autumn

Las Vegas International Mariachi Festival

Mandalay Bay, 3950 Las Vegas Boulevard South, between W Tropicana Avenue & Russell Road (632 7777). Bus 301, 302. **Tickets** $35-$100. **Credit** AmEx, Disc, MC, V. **Map** p316 A9. **Date** early Sept.

The annual Mariachi Festival at Mandalay Bay will set your ears on fire with passionate Latin rhythms. Jose Luis Rodriguez has been the director of the festival since 1999 and frequently stars in the shows.

Grand Slam for Children

MGM Grand, 3799 Las Vegas Boulevard South, at E Tropicana Avenue (information 227 5700/tickets from TicketMaster 474 4000). Bus 201, 301, 302. **Tickets** *Concert* $35, $50, $75. **Credit** AmEx, Disc, MC, V. **Map** p316 A9. **Date** late Sept.

Much-beloved tennis star and Vegas resident Andre Agassi invites a group of his closest celebrity friends

to town for a huge auction and dinner event followed by a stadium-seated concert at the MGM Grand Garden, which is open to the general public.

Shakespeare in the Park

Foxridge Park, Valle Verde Drive, off Warm Springs Road, Henderson (799 1042). Bus 217. **Admission** free-$25. **Credit** Disc, MC, V. **Date** end Sept.

The best outdoor theatre event in town: a travelling troupe presents a Shakespeare play (usually a comedy one year, a tragedy the next). Mimes, madrigal singers and jugglers complete the spectacle. A fine spot to make a full day of – bring a picnic and arrive early for a good seat.

Greek Food Festival

St John the Baptist Greek Orthodox Church, 5300 El Camino Road, at Hacienda Road, Southwest Las Vegas (221 8245). No bus. **Tickets** $5. **No credit cards.** **Date** late Sept/early Oct.

Started in 1972 to raise money to build the St John the Baptist Church, this weekend festival is now the longest continuously running festival in Las Vegas, attended by nearly 20,000 people annually. Enjoy authentic Greek food, plus bands, bouzouki players and folk dancing.

Art in the Park

Bicentennial Park, at Colorado Street & Nevada Highway, Boulder City (294 1611). Bus 116. **Date** 1st weekend in Oct.

Hundreds of artists and craftmakers from throughout the South-west set up shop for this strolling art show in the park. It is one of the largest events of the year in Boulder City.

King of the Beach Invitational Volleyball Tournament

Hard Rock, 4455 Paradise Road, at Harmon Avenue, East of Strip (693 5000). Bus 108. **Tickets** $10-$15. **Credit** AmEx, Disc, MC, V. **Map** p316 7C. **Date** Oct.

Tons of fine beach sand cover the car park of this Miami-styled hotel, as players from the pro volleyball circuit dig deep and spike hard for more than $200,000 in prize money.

Arts & Entertainment

Las Vegas Jaycees State Fair

Cashman Field, 850 Las Vegas Boulevard North, at E Washington Avenue, North Las Vegas (457 8832). Bus 113. **Date** early Oct.

Enjoy live music, contests, carnival rides, exhibits, delicious food and a host of other activities at this six-day fair, which draws a crowd of about 60,000. Old-fashioned fun for all the family.

Italian Festival

Rio, 3700 W Flamingo Road, at Valley View Boulevard, West of Strip (252 7777). Bus 202. **Tickets** $5. **Credit** AmEx, Disc, MC, V. **Map** p311 X3. **Date** 2nd weekend in Oct.

Authentic Italian food from some of the city's best restaurants will damage everyone's waistlines. Pile on the pounds and inches at the spaghetti-eating contest and then try to work them off again at the grape-stomping competition.

Professional Bull Riders Tour

Thomas & Mack Center, 4505 S Maryland Parkway, at E Tropicana Avenue, University District (information 1-719 471 3008/tickets from Ticket Master 474 4000). Bus 201. **Tickets** $20-$50. **Credit** AmEx, Disc, MC, V. **Date** mid-Oct.

If you can't wait for the rodeo in December, check out this event sponsored by Caesars Palace. The top 45 bull riders in the world arrive in Las Vegas to compete over three days for $1 million and the title of World Champion Bull Rider.

Las Vegas Balloon Classic

Las Vegas Silver Bowl Park, 6800 E Russell Road, at Boulder Highway, Henderson (452 8066). **Date** 3rd weekend in Oct.

Hot-air balloons fill the sky during a weekend of flying competitions. The Saturday sundown 'balloon glow' demonstration is a must-see.

PGA Invesys Classic

Information 242 3000. **Tickets** $15-$20. **Credit** AmEx, Disc, MC, V. **Date** late Oct.

This four-day golf tournament, held at three area courses, is one of the most exciting events on the PGA Tour. It brought Tiger Woods his first PGA victory in 1996.

Turkey Trot

Information 367 1626. **Date** early Nov.

Nevada's largest charity run (usually about 900 people take part) features a 3-mile fun walk and a competitive 10km run. Call for details of the route.

Winter

Nutcracker Holiday Market

Convention Center, Riviera, 2901 Las Vegas Boulevard South, at Riviera Boulevard (732 1638). Bus 301, 302. **Map** p315 B5. **Date** late Nov.

This market provides a shopping extravaganza in a village setting, plus there are performances by local ballet company Nevada Dance Theater (*see* chapter **Performing Arts**).

The Magical Forest

Opportunity Village, 6300 W Oakey Boulevard, between Jones & Rainbow Boulevards, South-west Las Vegas (259 3741). Bus 102, 205. **Date** late Nov-late Dec.

A Christmas display with two million lights and a castle complete with Santa, giant candy canes and a forest of decorated trees.

Billboard Music Awards

MGM Grand Garden, 3799 Las Vegas Boulevard South, at E Tropicana Avenue (information 891 7777/tickets from TicketMaster 474 4000). Bus 201, 301, 302. **Credit** AmEx, Disc, MC, V. **Map** p316 A8. **Date** early Dec.

Music celebrities gather to honour the number-one performers of the year as determined by record charts and radio play. A great night for star-gazing.

National Finals Rodeo

Thomas & Mack Center, 4505 S Maryland Parkway, at E Tropicana Avenue, University District (information 895 3900/Professional Rodeo Cowboys Association 1-719 593 8840). Bus 201. **Tickets** $24-$38. **Credit** AmEx, Disc, MC, V. **Date** early Dec.

Top cowboys and girls set Vegas ablaze with country-oriented entertainment. For nine days the city goes rodeo mad and tickets are hard to come by. Buy western duds at the Cowboy Christmas Gift Show (260 8605) at the Las Vegas Convention Center and party all night at Dylan's (451 4006) and Sam's Town (456 7777). For details of the competition, *see* p229.

Parade of Lights

Lake Mead Marina, Lake Mead National Recreation Area (293 2034). No bus. **Date** mid-Dec.

Boats covered with lights sail around Lake Mead. A good viewing spot is near Boulder Beach.

Winter Wonderland

Sunset Park, 2601 Sunset Road, at S Eastern Avenue, East Las Vegas (455 8206). Bus 110, 212. **Date** late Dec.

The winter holiday season is celebrated with a day of reindeer games, ice-carving demonstrations, snow play (it's usually shipped in from Mount Charleston) and live entertainment.

New Year's Eve

Date 31 Dec.

The Strip and Fremont Street in Downtown turn into a couple of big street parties as more than a quarter of a million visitors arrive to celebrate the New Year. Expect headline performers, a party at every casino, fireworks and a shortage of hotel rooms. Don't attempt to get anywhere by car. Check local publications for details.

Las Vegas International Marathon

Information 876 3870/459 8314. **Date** 2nd weekend in Feb.

Some 6,000 runners participate in this 5km run and half-marathon along the old Los Angeles Highway. It starts in Jean, south of Vegas, and ends at the Vacation Village hotel at the south end of the Strip.

Children

Little ones will love the bright lights and eye-popping attractions – just keep 'em away from the gambling.

Las Vegas is known for many things – gambling, drinking, topless showgirls and adult entertainment among them – but it's also a 'family destination'. Many of the city's advertising campaigns in the 1990s promoted Las Vegas as a place for family fun, and even though there have been moves recently to reinstate adult entertainment at the centre of the Vegas experience, there is still a lot for kids to do here. Most of the larger resorts have games arcades and child-friendly attractions – though adult supervision is usually required and always advisable – and some even have enclosed and supervised activity areas where children can play in safety while parents gamble, shop or visit a show nearby. What's more, there plenty to entice you away from the casinos.

THE LAW

State law forbids those under 21 from being on a casino floor. Children are allowed to pass through the casino area when accompanied by an adult, but they cannot linger by any of the gaming tables or machines. A security guard is likely to ask them – albeit politely – to move outside the casino. Parents are also not allowed to wager when they have youngsters in tow.

A Clark County curfew dictates that unaccompanied under-18s are not allowed on the streets after 10pm (Mon-Thur, Sun) and after midnight on weekends (Fri, Sat) and during school holidays. Teenagers probably have the roughest time, because until you're 21, you can't drink or gain admission to the city's bars, and most of the clubs and showrooms.

Accommodation

The price of most hotel rooms in Las Vegas is reasonable – or at least as reasonable as you'll find in any big city. The hotel-casinos that are most family-friendly are **Circus Circus**, **Excalibur**, the **Luxor** and **Mandalay Bay** (all owned by Mandalay Resort Group), as well as the **MGM Grand** and **Treasure Island**. Circus Circus, Excalibur and Treasure Island have always appealed to families and are the most affordably priced; Luxor and Mandalay Bay weren't initially positioned as family properties, but have attractions that rank high

with kids and some enjoyably decorated rooms – though they are more expensive. The MGM Grand recently closed its theme park, but still has a great childcare programme, which makes it ideal for parents with young kids.

Other reasonably priced hotel-casinos that offer childcare or other family attractions include the **Rio, Stratosphere**, **Boulder Station** and **Sunset Station**, though their location – they're all off the Strip – might not be so appealing. **Caesars Palace** is expensive, but popular with kids. And, ironically, one of the most lavish, adult-oriented hotels, the prestigious non-gaming **Four Seasons**, has some special incentives for kids. Milk and cookies are sent to all young guests on arrival and staff provide special T-shirts and packages filled with beach goodies for use by the pool. Hotels that are not suitable for children include **Bellagio**, the **Hard Rock**, the **Stardust** and the **Riviera**. For further information, *see chapter* **Accommodation**.

Sights & attractions

Arcades

Most of the major casinos have games arcades. In some, this amounts to little more than a midsize room with a few video games, but there are also some superlative arcades that include fairground entertainment. These can be found at the **Excalibur** (on the Fantasy Faire level), **Circus Circus** (where the games surround a central ring featuring free circus acts), the **Las Vegas Hilton**, the **MGM Grand**, **Sunset Station** and **Texas Station**. The very best arcades of all, however, are the **Coney Island Emporium** at New York-New York (*see p103*), the **Games of the Gods** arcade at Luxor and **GameWorks** (*see p105*).

Note that a Clark County ordinance prohibits under-18s from being in arcades after 10pm on weekdays or after midnight at the weekend unless accompanied by an adult.

Attractions

Height restrictions are in force for many thrill rides and other attractions in Vegas; phone ahead to avoid having to console a disappointed child.

Arts & Entertainment

The **Adventuredome** (*see p110*) at Circus Circus is a wacky indoor theme park that will keep big and small kids happy for hours, with a variety of thrill rides and calmer attractions. Further south, the **Forum Shops** (*see p162*) at Caesars Palace have a lot in store: in addition to the free animatronic shows in the mall, kids can exploring mega toy shop **FAO Schwarz** (*see p180*) and try out the IMAX **Race for Atlantis** (*see p108*) and the **Cinema Ride** (*see p107*). Sci-fi lovers may prefer the interactive fun at **Star Trek: The Experience** (*see p113*) in the Las Vegas Hilton. The motion simulator here gives riders a view of the action not only in front of their simulated shuttlecraft, but above and on its sides, too.

The Showcase Mall is another family hotspot. Older kids and teens can spend hours in **Game Works** (*see p105*) trying out 300 interactive video games and the world's tallest indoor rock climbing structure, while sweet-toothed kids get stuck into **M&M World** (*see p105*) and **Ethel M Chocolates**.

At New York-New York, the **Coney Island Emporium** (*see p103*) offers a mix of old-fashioned carnival games and high-tech gadgetry, while the very popular **Manhattan Express** rollercoaster (*see p104*) twists and loops inside and outside the hotel.

The **High Roller** rollercoaster and the **Big Shot** (for both, *see p111*) at the Stratosphere offer heart-stopping thrills more than 1,000 feet (300 metres) above the earth. For little ones, however, the recently opened **Strat-O-Fair** (380 7777) inside the casino is more appropriate, featuring a bucking bronco, a restored 1958 Ferris wheel and a child-sized Little Shot.

Indoor attractions, such as these are perfect at any time of the year, but during the summer, don't miss the excellent **Wet 'n Wild** water theme park (*see p236*) for 'splashtacular' fun.

Museums

Although the educational value of some of Vegas's 'attraction' museums may be doubtful, they are great fun for children. The **Guinness World of Records Museum** (*see p110*) brings the *Guinness Book of Records* to life with videos, hands-on displays and replicas of assorted oddities. The **Liberace Museum** (*see p120*) is a sparkling tribute to the eccentric Las Vegas entertainer and **Madame Tussaud's Celebrity Encounter** (*see p108*) at the Venetian, allows tots to get up close and personal with lifelike renditions of their favourite stars.

For something a little more edifying, try the **Las Vegas Natural History Museum** and the excellent **Lied Discovery Children's**

Museum, both located just north of Downtown (*see p123*). With dozens of interactive exhibits, the Lied is entertaining and educational for kids, and fun for parents, too.

Parks, animals & zoos

Numerous parks and recreational areas dot the Las Vegas Valley. **Sunset Park** (at E Sunset Road and Eastern Avenue) and **Lorenzi Park** (at W Washington Avenue and N Rancho Drive) are two large parks with rolling grass, lakes and volleyball, tennis and baseball facilities. Kids can feed the ducks, too, so don't forget to bring a loaf of bread. Call 455 8200 for details.

Children will also appreciate the animal habitats that have popped up in several casinos. At the Mirage, they can check out Siegfried and Roy's royal white tigers and other jungle cats in the **Tiger Habitat** and the **Secret Garden**, or play with bottlenose dolphins in the **Dolphin Habitat** (for all, *see p107*), while at the MGM Grand, a glass tunnel will lead them to a view of the beasts in the **Lion Habitat** (*see p104*).

The reconstructed Wildlife Walk at the **Tropicana** (*see p87*) is home to a menagerie of unusual creatures, including pygmy marmosets and toucans – not to mention Joe Krathwohl, 'the Birdman of Las Vegas', who puts on a free show with his trained birds in the Tropics Lounge most afternoons. Call 739 2222 for details.

The **Flamingo** (*see p76*) has a beautifully landscaped pool area (open to non guests) where you'll find pink flamingos and penguins along with other tropical birds and fish (it's closed in winter). And Mandalay Bay recently

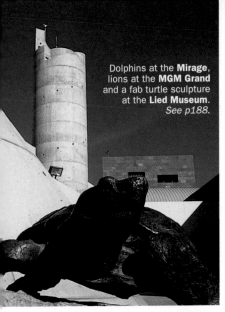

Dolphins at the **Mirage**, lions at the **MGM Grand** and a fab turtle sculpture at the **Lied Museum**. See p188.

opened the **Shark Reef** (*see p104*), which features more than 75 species of fish and reptiles, including golden crocodiles.

If you're in the mood for a real zoo, then the **Southern Nevada Zoological Park** (*see p124*) houses a collection of endangered species including apes and eagles, plus every species of venomous reptile native to southern Nevada.

Eating & drinking

The best restaurants for families in Las Vegas are usually themed and often a lot of fun.

The **Rainforest Café** (891 8580; open 8am-11pm Mon-Thur, Sun; 8am-midnight Fri, Sat) in the MGM Grand is filled with fake foliage and real fish, plus life-size, robotic animals and a huge aquarium. There's even an occasional 'thunderstorm' to cool things off. Sports fans will find something to inspire them at the Sahara's **NASCAR Café** (734 7223; open 11am-10pm daily), which has an exciting thrill ride, an auto-racing theme, an all-American menu and live entertainment at the weekends. Most fun of all, perhaps, is **Quark's Bar & Restaurant** in Star Trek: The Experience (*see p113*) at the Las Vegas Hilton (697 8725; open 11am-11pm daily). Characters from the TV series serve food from the 24th-century menu, including Isolinear chips, Talaxian turkey wraps and Final Frontier desserts.

For a more down-to-earth meal that will still rank high with kids, try **Tony Roma's** (*see p147*), **Battista's Hole in the Wall** (*see p143*) or New York-New York's **America** (*see p130*). As for the buffets, the Rio's **Carnival World**

Buffet (*see p152*) is an overwhelming hit with families. The desserts are especially indulgent, and the festive carnival decor is loud and fun.

Services

Babysitters

There are several reliable babysitting agencies in Las Vegas offering licensed and bonded babysitters who have been cleared through the sheriff's department and the FBI. The sitters, often equipped with toys, games, books and videos, will come directly to your hotel room and are available around the clock, but you usually have to give advance notice. Another option is to drop your child off at **Grandma Thompson's** homely nursery.

A1 Babysitting Service

1201 Las Vegas Boulevard South, at Charleston Boulevard, Stratosphere Area (382 0432). **Open** 24hrs daily. **Rates** $40 for 4hrs ($8 per additional hr). **Credit** AmEx, MC, V. **Map** p315 C3.

Four Seasons Babysitting Service

Information 384 5848. **Open** 24hrs daily. **Rates** $30-$40 for 4hrs ($7-$9 per additional hr). **No credit cards**.

Grandma Thompson's Romp 'n' Play

1804 Weldon Place, at St Louis Street, Stratosphere Area (735 0176). **Bus** 301, 302. **Open** 24hrs daily. **Rates** (minimum 5hrs) $4-$5 per hr. **No credit cards**. **Map** p315 C4.

Children's supplies

Baby's Away

Rentals 1-800 560 9141/458 1019/www.babys away.com). **Open** 24hrs daily. **Rates** $10 delivery, plus rental cost. **Credit** AmEx, Disc, MC, V. Baby's Away will rent, deliver and pick up baby supplies, including strollers, cribs, car seats and even VCRs and Nintendo games.

Nurseries & activity centres

Many of the largest resorts – even those with family attractions – don't have childcare facilities, but a few of the neighbourhood hotel-casinos do. They usually require written consent from the parents and some may ask you to leave a valid ID with them. They also may insist the child is potty-trained and not in nappies. Most have a maximum three-hour time limit, and only the person who drops off the child may pick them up. You don't have to be staying at the hotel, but you do have to be on the premises while your child is in the nursery.

In addition to the Kids Quest and MGM facilities, try the free nursery at the **Gold**

Arts & Entertainment

Coast (*see p99*), the Kids Fun facility at the Orleans (*see p99*), or the Playroom in **Sam's Town** (*see p100*), all of which feature movies, toys, crafts and licensed supervisors. Stays are limited to three hours.

Kids Quest

Boulder Station, 4111 Boulder Highway, at E Desert Inn Road, East Las Vegas (432 7777). Bus 107, 112. **Open** 9am-11pm Mon-Thur, Sun; 9am-1am Fri, Sat. **Rates** $5.50 per hr Mon-Thur; $6.50 per hr Fri-Sun. **Credit** Disc, MC, V.
Located at three of the Station Casinos properties, Kids Quest has everything from a Barbie area to computer games. The big cliff and the jungle area are very popular. Children (six weeks to 12 years) can be dropped off for up to five hours (3.5 hours at Boulder). Parents must remain on the premises.
Branches: Sunset Station and Texas Station (for both, *see p101*).

MGM Grand Youth Activity Centre

MGM Grand, 3799 Las Vegas Boulevard South, at E Tropicana Avenue (891 3200). Bus 201, 301, 302. **Open** 9am-midnight daily. **Rates** $8.50 MGM guests; $10.50 non-MGM guests. **Credit** AmEx, Disc, MC, V. **Map** p316 A8.
Youngsters aged 3-12 can check in for up to five hours at a time. The centre has crafts, toys, Super Nintendo, air hockey, a pool and close supervision by enthusiastic staff. It also serves meals.

Arts & entertainment

Shows

Casino showrooms will specify the minimum age for admission to a particular show (ask before booking tickets). Parents will find this useful, since many shows feature topless performers and sexually-charged material. Tickets to most shows are in great demand, which means the casinos usually charge full price, even when a child is occupying the seat.

The best shows – such as Cirque du Soleil's **Mystère** and **O**, and **EFX Alive!** – can cost over $100 a ticket, so this can be an expensive family outing. However, **Tournament of Kings** and **Lance Burton: Master**

Magician are both reasonably priced shows suitable for the whole family. **Caesars Magical Empire** charges half-price for ages five to ten for its dinner and magic show.

Small-scale magic shows include comedy juggler **Michael Holly** at the Sahara and **Rick Thomas** at the Tropicana. Thomas performs at 2pm and 4pm daily, except Fridays, and tickets cost $16.95 to $21.95. For further details of these and other casino production shows, *see chapter* **Casino Entertainment**.

Away from the Strip resorts, the **Rainbow Company Children's Theatre** (*see p227*) stages high-calibre performances for the over-fours in the Reed Whipple Cultural Center. Tickets are a bargain compared to the casino shows; well worth a visit.

Sport

For other family-friendly suggestions, including ice-skating and bowling alleys, *see chapter* **Sport & Fitness**.

Scandia

2900 Sirius Avenue, just south of Sahara Avenue, between Rancho Drive & Valley View Boulevard, West of Strip (364 0070). Bus 401. **Open** *June-Sept* 24hrs daily. *Oct-May* 10am-10pm Mon-Thur, Sun; 10am-11pm Fri, Sat. **Rates** $3.95-$5.95 per game; $15.95 all games. **Credit** MC, V. **Map** p315 A5.
The video arcade is so-so, but the whole family will enjoy the batting cages, three miniature golf courses, bumper boats and Indy go-karts.

Trips out of town

For a rewarding day out, don't miss the natural and man-made attractions just outside Las Vegas. Red Rock Canyon, the Hoover Dam and Bonnie Springs/Old Nevada are all great for exploring with children. (For details, *see chapter* **Day Trips**.) Further afield, **Primm** (on the California state line) has a trio of resorts created by the Primm family empire: Buffalo Bill's, Whiskey Pete's and Primm Valley. Kids will love the Desperado rollercoaster and other rides at Buffalo Bill's (*see p271*).

Fun in the sun at **Scandia**.

Casino Entertainment

The glut of entertainment on offer in Vegas proves that, in this town at least, there's no business like showbusiness.

As the self-proclaimed 'Entertainment Capital of the World', Las Vegas offers something for every night crawler – from piano bars to discos to rock concerts to comedy clubs to showroom extravaganzas – it's all here, basking in neon and blinking until dawn. Inevitably, most of the city's nightlife is focused on the casinos and their lavish stage productions, celebrity concerts, topless revues, comedy shops and free lounge shows. On any given night you can choose from about 70 different stage shows and headliners, plus a similar number of lounge acts.

INFORMATION

Although the information given here is as accurate as possible, unsuccessful shows do close, and new ones open. To check what's on and who's appearing in town, look at the entertainment supplement 'Neon' in the Friday edition of the *Review-Journal*. You'll find the same information in visitor magazines such as *Showbiz* and *What's On*, and the free weeklies, such as *Las Vegas Weekly, Las Vegas Mercury* and *CityLife*. If you're out of town, call the **Las Vegas Convention & Visitors Authority** (892 0711) for a free copy of its 'Showguide' or check its website (www.vegasfreedom.com).

TICKETS AND PRICES

You can buy tickets at the box office where the show is being staged or through ticket agencies such as **TicketMaster** (474 4000) and **Allstate Ticketing** (597 5970). There are ticket brokers in nearly every casino, but, like the agencies, they often charge a commission (sometimes called an entertainment tax) on top of the face value of the tickets. It's best to deal with the show's own box office because you can sometimes pick up free two-for-one coupons or other discounts. If you book by phone, pick up the tickets at the 'will call' window.

Admission prices for production shows range from about $32 for the campy drag show *An Evening at La Cage* at the Riviera to as much as $121 for Cirque du Soleil's water spectacular *O* at Bellagio. Celebrity concerts usually fall somewhere in between – you can pay $35 for Neil Sedaka and $75 for Earth, Wind & Fire. Comedy clubs charge from $13 to $45 for a one-hour show, and prices usually include one or two drinks. Sometimes ticket prices include tax;

sometimes it goes on top. Expect to pay higher prices on holidays and during conventions. Reduced-price kids' tickets are rare, although children over five (sometimes three) are allowed in to most shows (if nudity is involved, the limit is 18 or 21). Only the really big shows (*EFX Alive, Mystère, O, Siegfried & Roy*) sell out early – it's best to book two to six weeks ahead for these. But it's always worth calling the box office, especially midweek, and you can queue for last-minute cancellations.

Following a trend that started in the early 1990s, most tickets are for specific seats, thus all but eliminating the worn-out practice of greasing the captain's palm for a better seat. At the few showrooms that still use maitre d' seating, you'll have to arrive early and stand in line if you want a good seat. If you're not satisfied with your seat's location, discreetly tip the maitre d' or the captain, from $10 to $20. For information on how to get discounted or

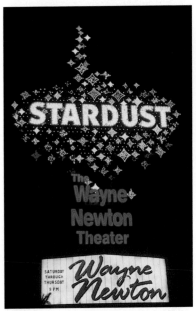

All that glitters: **Wayne Newton**. *See p199.*

comped tickets, *see below* **Vegas on the cheap: Entertainment**. For rock and pop music venues, nightclubs and other entertainment options, *see chapter* **Nightlife**.

Shows

Las Vegas's first stage productions were called 'floor shows'. When Sophie Tucker performed at El Rancho and Jimmy Durante played the Flamingo in the 1940s and 1950s, they were preceded by a line of girls, a comedian or a magician, and a speciality act like a juggler or ventriloquist. In 1958, the specs for the Vegas floor show changed radically with the introduction of the spectacular production show *Lido de Paris* at the Stardust. It was all production and no headliner. In this case, the show itself was the star.

With its big spectacle and topless showgirls, the Stardust packed them in and set the stage for other productions: *Folies Bergère, Jubilee!*, *City Lites, Splash!* and others followed. Soon other genres were developed. Shows with a magic theme are popular (*Siegfried & Roy* still leads the pack in this category), as are so-called 'tribute' or celebrity impersonator shows (*Legends in Concert, American Superstars*), which feature lookalike impressionists who perform live or lip-sync to recordings of their more famous alter-egos.

A few casinos have experimented with new-wave shows. Cirque du Soleil's surreal *Mystère* and *O* are often sold out, the Luxor has done very well with its New York-based *Blue Man Group*, and in 2001, Mandalay Bay debuted a new show, *Storm*, geared towards the Gen-X crowd. The most innovative show in recent times, however, has been the anarchic and energetic *De La Guarda* show staged by an Argentine circus troupe at the Rio. This wild and booming interactive show exploded all notions of what works in Vegas by blending bungee-jumping performance art with a dance club vibe. Sadly the troupe returned to Buenos Aires in summer 2001.

Casinos also book touring Broadway shows. In 2001, the Aladdin brought *Les Misérables* and *Forever Yours* to its Theater for the Performing Arts, and the Orleans will debut its new Best of Broadway Series with *Mame* (December 2001), to be followed by *Dream Girls* (February 2002) and *Damn Yankees* (April 2002). Such shows don't always last: Andrew Lloyd Webber's *Starlight Express* ended its run at the Las Vegas Hilton after a couple of years; similarly, *Chicago* at Mandalay Bay and *Notre Dame* at Paris were over in less than 12 months.

As an alternative to the stage extravaganza, some casinos continue the Las Vegas tradition of booking celebrity headliners, such as Natalie Cole, George Carlin, Johnny Mathis, country singer Reba McEntire, Tony Bennett, Ricky Martin, Huey Lewis & the News – the list eventually includes anyone in mainstream show business, past or present. The goal, of course, is to pack the showroom and, thus, pack the casino. The practice was kickstarted during the early days of the Rat Pack – that ultra-hip symbol of Las Vegas in 1960. The Rat Pack would ad lib and clown around, often until the showroom closed, then carry on in the lounges. Their routine was simple: Davis played the 'kid' to Sinatra's 'swinger' and Martin's 'drunk' (*see p196* **Las Vegas legends: Frank Sinatra**).

Despite the cornucopia of entertainment choices, the traditional production show, with its schlocky themes, feeble storylines, contemporary music, special effects, dancers, jugglers, parlour magicians and brigades of statuesque showgirls, continues to carry the banner of Las Vegas entertainment. A typical

Vegas on the cheap Entertainment

The best entertainment value among all the casino venues remains the lounges, where you can listen to contemporary singers and musicians for the nominal cost of one or two drinks. However, if you're after the spectacle and glitz of the large-scale casino production shows, you'll find discount coupons or two-for-one specials in all the visitor magazines. It's also possible to get discounted tickets through funbooks and slot club membership, and if you're a regular gambler, your casino host or slot club rep should be able to get you a free show ticket. In fact, many of the shows in town have fewer paying customers in the audience than comped guests.

If you're in town when a new casino is opened, look out for special launch parties with free entertainment, refreshments and firework displays. Outside the casinos, there are dozens of community events, openings, sports events, craft fairs, parades and mixers that are free and worth attending. *See chapter* **By Season** for details. The *Review-Journal*'s Friday supplement, 'Neon', and the free local tabloids (*Las Vegas Weekly* and *CityLife*) give listings of special events.

A little paint, a few pipes, a marshmallow or two: meet the **Blue Man Group**. *See p197.*

example is Bally's *Jubilee!,* which opened in 1981 and continues in updated incarnations. The latest rendition features, in the first few minutes alone, the destruction of a temple and the sinking of a giant model of the *Titanic,* complete with pyrotechnics, cascading water, fire-spewing blast furnaces and 80 topless dancers who drop from the ceiling, ascend from elevators or stroll in from the wings.

Most production shows have at least some topless numbers (typically in the later of the two evening shows), and in the past couple of years, the casinos have launched four new adult revue shows, including *La Femme* at the MGM Grand. So much for the family tourist market.

Adult revues

Crazy Girls Fantasy Review

Riviera, 2901 Las Vegas Boulevard South, at Riviera Boulevard (794 9433). Bus 301, 302. **Shows** 8.30pm, 10.30pm Tue-Fri, Sun; 8.30pm, 10.30pm, midnight Sat. **Tickets** $24.78-$33.03; no under-18s. **Credit** AmEx, DC, Disc, MC, V. **Map** p315 B5.

The Riviera's long-running topless show was launched in 1985 and continues to jiggle twice nightly. It features eight girls who dance to canned music and act out silly skits on a small stage. As might be expected, the clientele consists primarily of high-testosterone frat boys and Asian businessmen.

La Femme

MGM Grand, 3799 Las Vegas Boulevard South, at Tropicana Avenue (891 7777). Bus 201, 301, 302. **Shows** 8pm, 10.30pm Mon, Wed-Sun. **Tickets** $49; no under-21s. **Credit** AmEx, DC, Disc, MC, V. **Map** p316 A8.

Opened in 2001, La Femme traces its artistic roots to the *Crazy Horse* revue in Paris. In fact, the dancers are all French imports and members of the original *Crazy Horse* cast. This is by far the most artistic of all the adult shows: the choreography, lighting and natural women (don't expect any silicone here) create a superb spectacle.

Midnight Fantasy

Luxor, 3900 Las Vegas Boulevard South, between W Tropicana Avenue & Russell Road (262 4400). Bus 301, 302. **Shows** 8.30pm, 10.30pm Tue, Thur-Sat; 10.30pm Wed; 8.30pm Sun. **Tickets** $29.95; no under-21s. **Credit** AmEx, Disc, MC, V. **Map** p316 A9.

This topless show at the Pharoah's Theatre is actually a pretty tame affair that relies on colourful costumes and interesting choreography rather than acres of flesh to entertain the punters.

Showgirls of Magic

San Remo, 115 E Tropicana Avenue, between Island Drive & Duke Ellington Way, East of Strip (597 6028). Bus 201, 301, 302. **Shows** 8pm, 10.30pm Tue-Sun. **Tickets** (incl 1 drink) $25.99; no under-18s for late show. **Credit** AmEx, DC, Disc, MC, V. **Map** p316 B8.

Harkening back to the burlesque days (albeit with a modern twist) this place offers an unusual blend of comedy, cockatoos and cleavage. Comedian Joe Trammel provides the jokes, while Clint Carvalho supplies the parrots and other feathered friends in a fast-paced bird act. The stars of the show, however, are the topless magicians, who sing, dance and show off their illusions as well as their physical attributes.

Skintight

Harrah's, 3475 Las Vegas Boulevard South, between Sands Avenue & E Flamingo Road (369 5111). Bus 301, 302. **Shows** 10.30pm Mon-Wed; 10pm, midnight Fri; midnight Sat; 7.30pm, 10.30pm Sun. **Tickets** $39.95; no under-18s. **Credit** AmEx, Disc, MC, V. **Map** p316 A6.

The casino bills this as a 'musical adult revue', which is correct if you count the singing Playboy Playmate. She's not bad, in fact, so it's a shame that nobody is listening.

Celebrity impersonators

American Superstars

Stratosphere, 2000 Las Vegas Boulevard South, at St Louis Avenue, between Oakey Boulevard & E Sahara Avenue, Stratosphere Area (380 7711). Bus 301, 302. **Shows** 7pm Mon, Tue, Sun; 7pm, 10pm Wed, Fri, Sat. **Tickets** $29.95; $22.95 5-12s. **Credit** AmEx, DC, Disc, MC, V. **Map** p315 C3/4.

Stars in their eyes, indeed. This rock 'n' roll celebrity tribute treats you to impersonations of Madonna, Ricky Martin, Michael Jackson and Christine Aguilera, with support from a live band and dancers. Kids' tickets are available.

An Evening at La Cage

Riviera, 2901 Las Vegas Boulevard South, at Riviera Boulevard (794 9433). Bus 301, 302. **Shows** 7.30pm, 9.30pm Mon, Wed-Sun. **Tickets** $32.90-$49.40. **Credit** AmEx, DC, Disc, MC, V. **Map** p315 B5.

The city's most popular drag show stars Frank Marino as a catty Joan Rivers and also features lip-sync impersonations of Liza Minnelli, Dionne Warwick, Madonna, Diana Ross and others. A great moment is the 'Sister Act', when a dozen hip-hopping 'nuns' bound on and off the stage. The show is superbly choreographed (the supporting female dancers are great) and the taped music and lighting tastefully enhance the show.

Bill Acosta's Lasting Impressions

Flamingo, 3555 Las Vegas Boulevard South, at E Flamingo Road (733 3333). Bus 202, 301, 302. **Shows** 10pm Mon, Wed, Thur; 7.30pm (non-topless), 10pm Tue. **Tickets** $49.95-$69.95. **Credit** AmEx, Disc, MC, V. **Map** p316 A7.

Bill Acosta's show is reminiscent of the variety acts that used to appear on the Ed Sullivan Show. There's an old-school air to his tributes to late, great celebs

Forget all that avant-garde nonsense; showgirls are still the stars in **Jubilee!** *See p197.*

such as Frank Sinatra, Sammy Davis Jr, Nat King Cole and George Burns that's almost sweet, and is certainly familiar. His act is supported by dance impressionist Jay Fagan, as well as the inevitable bevy of showgirls.

Danny Gans: The Ultimate Variety Performer

Mirage, 3400 Las Vegas Boulevard South, between Spring Mountain & W Flamingo Roads (791 7111). Bus 301, 302. **Shows** 8pm Tue-Thur, Sat, Sun. **Tickets** $77-$99; no under-5s. **Credit** AmEx, DC, Disc, MC, V. **Map** p316 A6.

Installed in his very own 1,250-seater theatre at the Mirage, Danny Gans continues to stage one of the hottest shows in town. His show contains many favourites from his long stint at the Rio, but here he is supported by a multimillion-dollar sound-and-light system and an expanded band. Once called the man with a thousand voices, Gans does remarkable singing impressions from a repertoire of some 200 voices. He's also adept at mimicking celebs and has a spontaneous comedy style that audiences love.

The Kenny Kerr Show

The Regent, 221 N Rampart Avenue, at Summerlin Parkway, Summerlin, North-west Las Vegas (869 7777). Bus 207. **Shows** 8.30pm Wed-Sat. **Tickets** $27.45; no under-21s. **Credit** AmEx, Disc, MC, V.

Long-time female impersonator Kenny Kerr presents his slightly sinful drag show that pays tribute to the likes of Barbra Streisand, Cher, Diana Ross and Marilyn Monroe. Kerr's flair for comedy sets up his 'boys-will-be-girls' cast as they celebrate their favourite female stars in inimitable style.

Legends in Concert

Imperial Palace, 3535 Las Vegas Boulevard South, between Sands Avenue & E Flamingo Road (794 3261). Bus 301, 302. **Shows** 7.30pm, 10.30pm Mon-Sat. **Tickets** $34.50. **Credit** AmEx, DC, Disc, MC, V. **Map** p316 A6.

More stars in their eyes, Vegas-style: this venerable revue has been cloning entertainer lookalikes since the mid-1980s. The secret to its success is the astonishingly believable performers, who spookily re-create the likes of Elvis, Roy Orbison, Buddy Holly, Liberace, Madonna, the Blues Brothers and the recently added James Brown. Unlike some shows, the impersonators sing live – rather than lip-sync – and are backed by a live band. Adding sparkle are the obligatory showgirl dancers, back-up singers and a red laser and projection system that creates mystifying patterns and special effects.

Dinner shows

Caesars Magical Empire

Caesars Palace, 3570 Las Vegas Boulevard South, at W Flamingo Road (731 7333). Bus 202, 301, 302. **Shows** 4.30pm, 9.30pm Tue-Sat. **Tickets** $75.50; $37.75 5-10s. **Credit** AmEx, DC, Disc, MC, V. **Map** p316 A7.

Breaking from the format of traditional stage shows, this is a multi-chambered magical mystery tour that blends fine dining with the world of illusion. It begins with an intimate supper show, where a magician performs for a small group of about 15 diners. After feasting, the audience is guided through subterranean catacombs to a seven-storey Sanctum Secorum, where you can explore the Forbidden Crypt of Rameses, watch a brief Lumineria show or quench your palate in the Sanctum bars. You then move on to one of two theatres where magicians perform on rotating schedules. The price includes a three-course dinner, and just as well – this is as much hokum as magic. Construction of the new Colosseum Arena means the future of the Magical Empire is uncertain, so call in advance for details.

Tournament of Kings

Excalibur, 3850 Las Vegas Boulevard South, at W Tropicana Avenue (597 7600). Bus 201, 301, 302. **Shows** 6pm, 8.30pm daily. **Tickets** $39.95. **Credit** AmEx, DC, Disc, MC, V. **Map** p316 A8.

The Tournament of Kings is a medieval-themed dinner show in a multi-tiered theatre, with magic acts, singers and laser special effects. There's even jousting, as armour-clad knights thunder across the stage on huge steeds before doing battle with axes and swords. It's all, of course, irredeemably Las Vegas and therefore terribly cheesy – maidens dance in Broadway-style formation while a courtly king suddenly bursts into a version of *Viva Las Vegas*. However, on the plus side, the medieval theme does mean you can eat with your fingers.

Magicians & magic shows

Lance Burton: Master Magician

Monte Carlo, 3770 Las Vegas Boulevard South, at Rue de Monte Carlo, between W Flamingo Road & W Tropicana Avenue (730 7777). Bus 201, 301, 302. **Shows** 7.30pm, 10.30pm Tue-Sat. **Tickets** $54.95-$59.95. **Credit** AmEx, DC, Disc, MC, V. **Map** p316 A8.

Although magicians are now commonplace in Vegas, Lance Burton remains the city's premier illusionist. His show is an entertaining blend of intimate cabaret and high-powered extravaganza. There are usually 17 illusions in the show: highlights include a levitating and disappearing white Corvette, and Burton's 'off to the gallows' stunt, in which he somehow escapes the noose and ends up in the middle of the audience. A winsome sextet of dancers helps out.

Melinda: The First Lady of Magic

Venetian, 3355 Las Vegas Boulevard South, at Sands Avenue (948 3007). Bus 203, 301, 302. **Shows** 6.30pm, 8.30pm, Mon, Tue, Thur, Sun; 6.30pm Fri, Sat. **Tickets** $34.95-$69.95; $19.95 under-12s. **Credit** AmEx, DC, Disc, MC, V. **Map** p316 A6.

Native Las Vegan Melinda Saxe returned to the Vegas stage in 2000 with this show that relies more heavily on her ditsy California-girl charm rather than

Arts & Entertainment

Las Vegas legends Frank Sinatra

It's best to set this straight right away: his marriage at the old Aladdin and his long run at the International Hotel (now the Las Vegas Hilton) notwithstanding, Elvis Presley is not the true iconic singer of Las Vegas. Forget the Flying Elvi, the legion of impersonators, the Elvis weddings: they're about as Vegas-like as a slot machine offering a 100 per cent payback. Elvis never lived here, in fact he spent most of his time holed up in his hotel room with a shotgun and a TV. The performer who really put Vegas, and its entertainment, on the map, was Frank Sinatra.

By the late 1950s, Sinatra, who first played the Desert Inn in 1952 at the nadir of his career, had established the free-wheeling, 'booze and broads' image that defined the Vegas lounge aesthetic to the world for decades to come. Along with his court of drinking buddies – Dean Martin, Sammy Davis Jr, Peter Lawford, Joey Bishop – Sinatra swung hard every night at the Copa Room at the Sands (which is now re-created in the WB Stage 16 restaurant at the Venetian; see p132), to the delight of packed crowds. The shows were filled with songs, risqué jokes and plenty of juvenile high jinks: the spectacle of such talents wallowing in good-natured debauchery was irresistible.

Sinatra became so heavily identified with the Sands that he even bought a share in the casino itself (a nine per cent share by 1961). It wasn't until 1967, when Howard Hughes bought the property and an argument ensued over Sinatra's very liberal casino credit, that Ol' Blue Eyes switched allegiance to the hotels with which he would be associated in the twilight of his long career: Caesars Palace and the Golden Nugget.

But such an image cuts both ways: while being a part of what made Vegas Vegas, it also became a licence to succeeding generations, who thought that being an obnoxious, sexist, cigar-chomping, Martini-swilling ass was all the Rat Pack was about. Of course, what the Rat Pack represented, first and foremost, was entertainment and music. Those who want to access the Vegas Sinatra should pop a copy of *Sinatra at the Sands* into their CD player. Backed by the Count Basie Orchestra, Sinatra swings hard and beautifully (his shticky monologue aside). Long after the iconic image fades away, the music will continue to represent the soundtrack of Vegas in its first glory days.

on the performer's more obvious physical attributes (Melinda used to do a topless magic show). It's not a very big act, and the small stage doesn't allow for making Greyhound buses disappear, but her patter is amusing and her illusions are entertaining, if not awe-inspiring.

Siegfried & Roy

Mirage, 3400 Las Vegas Boulevard South, between Spring Mountain & W Flamingo Roads (791 7777). Bus 301, 302. **Shows** *7.30pm, 11pm Mon, Tue, Fri-Sun.* **Tickets** *$100.50.* **Credit** *AmEx, DC, Disc, MC, V.* **Map** *p316 A8.*

The hottest ticket in town is also, at $100, one of the most expensive. But then S&R is an institution par excellence – think about it: where else can you catch a fire-breathing dragon, white tigers, a vanishing (and reappearing) elephant and any number of eye-rubbing illusions? While some are simply variations of time-tested tricks (men get levitated, women are sawn in half), they are performed with great flair. The magicians (imagine, if you dare, a hybrid of Liberace, Marlin Perkins, David Copperfield and Arnold Schwarzenegger) are supported by a large-scale production company of dancers and acrobats, as well as impressive state-of-the-art sound, lighting and special effects.

Steve Wyrick: World Class Magician

Sahara, 2535 Las Vegas Boulevard South, at E Sahara Avenue (737 2111). Bus 204, 301, 302. **Shows** *7pm Mon, Sun; 7pm, 10pm Wed-Sat.* **Tickets** *$34.95.* **Credit** *AmEx, Disc, MC, V.* **Map** *p315 C4.*

Steve finally landed on the Strip in 2000 after moving from the Lady Luck in Downtown. His tightly knit magic show may be something of an economy version of Lance Burton, but many of his illusions are dramatic enough that they keep audience members on the edge of their seats. Wyrick performs some big-time illusions, usually along the lines of cutting himself in half, or moving an aeroplane from the stage to the lobby.

Production shows & headliners

Blue Man Group

Luxor, 3900 Las Vegas Boulevard South, between W Tropicana Avenue & Russell Road (262 4400). Bus 301, 302. **Shows** *7pm, 10pm daily.* **Tickets** *$59.50-$69.50.* **Credit** *AmEx, DC, Disc, MC, V.* **Map** *p316 A9.*

The New York-based Blue Man Group came west in 2000 and since then it has steadily become one of the city's more popular shows. Whether they're banging on home-made instruments constructed from PVC pipe or shooting marshmallows into each other's mouths, the talented blue-skinned trio gently but thoroughly mock the absurdities of performance art while at the same time engaging in some highly funny and innovative performance art of their own.

Clint Holmes: Takin' It Uptown

Harrah's, 3475 Las Vegas Boulevard South, between Sands Avenue & E Flamingo Road (369 5222). Bus 301, 302. **Shows** *7.30pm, 10pm Mon, Tue, Thur, Sat; 9pm Wed, Fri.* **Tickets** *$44.95.* **Credit** *AmEx, DC, Disc, MC, V.* **Map** *p316 A6.*

Holmes' show, *Takin' It Uptown* blends classical music, jazz and even samba, backed by a live band. The concert-like approach means that no two shows are alike. Holmes enjoys lively dialogue with the audience and frequently invites guest celebrities onto the stage for impromptu duets or skits.

EFX Alive!

MGM Grand, 3799 Las Vegas Boulevard South, at E Tropicana Avenue (891 7777). Bus 201, 301, 302. **Shows** *7.30pm, 10.30pm Tue-Sat.* **Tickets** *$49.50-$70; $35 5-12s.* **Credit** *AmEx, DC, Disc, MC, V.* **Map** *p316 A8.*

Now starring 1980s heartthrob Rick Springfield, *EFX Alive!* has taken on a heavy rock feel. In a high-tech musical odyssey through time and space, Springfield discovers surreal worlds and encounters such diverse characters as Harry Houdini, Merlin the Magician and HG Wells (as you do). Despite the hokey storyline, the show's special effects, which are derived from film and theme park technology, are undeniably spectacular.

Folies Bergere

Tropicana, 3801 Las Vegas Boulevard South, at E Tropicana Avenue (739 2411). Bus 201, 301, 302. **Shows** *8pm, 10.30pm Mon-Wed, Fri-Sun.* **Tickets** *$44.95-$54.95; no under-16s.* **Credit** *AmEx, DC, Disc, MC, V.* **Map** *p316 A8.*

Vegas's longest-running production show was revamped in 1997 with new numbers, costumes and sets, but has kept the city's most exquisite showgirls. The show is a tribute to the Parisian music hall as well as a romp through 100 years of French fashion, music and social mores: there's a royal ballroom sequence, a 1920s beach scene, a jazzy 1950s number and a 'Contemporarily Yours' finale that then catapults the show into the present day. Other highlights include a 1940s jukebox number with jitterbugs and flying acrobats, a Hollywood glamour scene from the 1930s and, of course, a signature can-can routine from turn-of-the-20th-century Paris.

Jubilee!

Bally's, 3645 Las Vegas Boulevard South, at E Flamingo Road (967 4567). Bus 202, 301, 302. **Shows** *7.30pm, 10.30pm Mon, Wed-Sun.* **Tickets** *$49.50-$66.* **Credit** *AmEx, DC, Disc, MC, V.* **Map** *p316 A7.*

This long-running show is a musical extravaganza with a huge cast of dancers and dizzying stage effects ranging from the sinking of the *Titanic* to an aerial dogfight to Samson destroying the Temple of the Philistines. The 16-minute opening number, based on Jerry Herman's *Hundreds of Girls*, sets the pace with dozens of dancers and singers in beaded costumes and feathered headdresses. This is turned-on-tacky at its best.

Arts & Entertainment

It floats, she sings, you drink. Welcome to **Cleopatra's Barge**. *See p201.*

Michael Flatley's Lord of the Dance

New York-New York, 3790 Las Vegas Boulevard South, at W Tropicana Avenue (740 6815). **Bus 201, 301, 302. Shows** 7.30pm, 10.30pm Tue, Wed; 9pm Thur, Fri; 3pm, 7.30pm, 10.30pm Sat. **Tickets** $50 3pm Sat; $59 Mon-Thur, Sun; $68 Fri, 7.30pm, 10.30pm Sat; no under-5s. **Credit** AmEx, DC, Disc, MC, V. **Map** p316 A8.

This high-energy *Riverdance* clone is performed by a troupe of talented young dancers – without Michael Flatley. The uninspiring storyline follows a Celtic version of *West Side Story*, but the rousing dance numbers are more than enough to keep the audience's attention from straying, even though the show's signature tap-dancing sounds are enhanced with recordings.

Mystère

Treasure Island, 3300 Las Vegas Boulevard South, at Spring Mountain Road (894 7111). **Bus 203, 301, 302. Shows** 7.30pm, 10.30pm Wed-Sun. **Tickets** $88. **Credit** AmEx, DC, Disc, MC, V. **Map** p316 A6.

The genre-stretching Cirque du Soleil take audiences on a metaphorical journey starting at the beginning of time – symbolised by a blast of Japanese Taiko drums sent from the heavens. The show is a surreal celebration of music, dance, acrobatics, gymnastics, mime and comedy. Show-stopping moments include the mesmerising aerial bungee ballet, the dazzling Korean plank, the precision Chinese poles performance and some awesome trapeze artists. Spectacular stuff.

O

Bellagio, 3600 Las Vegas Boulevard South, at W Flamingo Road (1-888 488 7111/693 7111). **Bus 202, 301, 302. Shows** 7.30pm, 10.30pm Wed-Sun. **Tickets** $93.50-$121. **Credit** AmEx, DC, Disc, MC, V. **Map** p316 A7.

It's hard to imagine Cirque du Soleil outdoing itself, but its production of *O* comes close. This stunning spectacular has a cast of 74 trapeze artists, contortionists, divers, synchronised swimmers and others, who navigate an unbelievable stage that transforms from the Arctic Ocean to an African watering hole practically instantaneously. Like *Mystère*, *O* is performed in a specially built theatre. The use of water – as a character in its own right and not just a theatrical prop – gives fluidity to this Fellini-esque show. Watching the performance unfold is rather like climbing inside a Salvador Dalí painting.

The Scintas

Rio, 3700 W Flamingo Road, at Valley View Boulevard, West of Strip (1-888 746 7784/252 7777). **Bus 202. Shows** 8pm Mon, Fri-Sun; 8pm, 10.30pm Tue. **Tickets** $35. **Credit** AmEx, DC, Disc, MC, V. **Map** p311 X3.

New for 2001, the Rio lured the Scintas from their digs inside the Las Vegas Hilton and the seduction has paid off. Audiences love this family band/comedy team show, which relies on lashings of Las Vegas nostalgia and sentimentality, plus fairly decent impressions of old rock 'n' rollers like Mick Jagger and Joe Cocker.

Splash!

Riviera, 2901 Las Vegas Boulevard South, at Riviera Boulevard (794 9433). Bus 301, 302. **Shows** 7.30pm, 10.30pm daily. **Tickets** $42.40-$51.50; no under-18s. **Credit** AmEx, DC, Disc, MC, V. **Map** p315 B5.

Splash! was the original aquatic revue, staged around a 20,000-gallon aquarium complete with mermaids, high divers and synchronised swimmers. But, after 15 years it was beginning to look waterlogged, so the producers scrapped the water tank, installed an ice-rink, updated the production numbers and introduced a new *Splash!* at the end of 1999. The gravity-defying motorcyclists who ride around inside a 16ft (5m) steel globe continue to thrill audiences. Also popular is the juggler and talented contortionist Underarmaa Darihuu.

Storm

Mandalay Bay, 3950 Las Vegas Boulevard South, between W Tropicana Avenue & Russell Road (632 7580). Bus 301, 302. **Shows** 7.30pm Mon, Wed, Sun; 7.30pm, 10.30pm Thur, Sat; 10.30pm Fri. **Tickets** $55-$65. **Credit** AmEx, Disc, MC, V. **Map** p316 A9.

The Strip's newest production show is a high-octane, mixed-media extravaganza, featuring cutting-edge music and dance that takes on the powers of the universe by incorporating elements of earth, wind, fire and water (expect to get misted if you sit in the front row). Artistic direction is by Ricky Martin's creative team (Martin sunk some money into the show), and the music and choreography follow the basic MTV formula of pulsating rhythms and forceful images, but the numbers are best when taken as short bursts; the show tries just a little too hard to seduce the new, hip, young Vegas visitor.

Wayne Newton

Stardust, 3000 Las Vegas Boulevard South, at Stardust Drive, between W Sahara Avenue & Desert Inn Road (732 6325). Bus 301, 302. **Shows** 9pm Mon-Thur, Sun; 8pm, 11pm Sat. **Tickets** $49.95. **Credit** AmEx, DC, Disc, MC, V. **Map** p315 B5.

Yes, he's still here. Newton is as much a part of Vegas as the Strip itself. He's been playing here for as long as many Las Vegas visitors have been alive. Since January 2000, he's taken over the Stardust's showroom (and he reputedly signed the most lucrative contract in Vegas history).

Showrooms

Nearly every casino has a showroom or theatre in which productions, concerts and special events are staged. They range from intimate rooms such as the **Cabaret Theatre** at New York-New York to massive arenas such as the **MGM Grand Garden** (*see p221*).

A recent trend has been for showrooms to host celebrity headliners when the in-house production show is dark. The Mirage, for instance, often books an artist like Paul Anka

into either its Siegfried & Roy or Danny Gans Theatres. Caesars Palace, meanwhile, is in the process of building a 4,000-seat Colosseum Arena, which will open in 2003 with Celine Dion as the headline performer. For venues that host big-name concerts and other one-off events, *see chapter* **Nightlife: Music**.

Congo Room

Sahara, 2535 Las Vegas Boulevard South, at E Sahara Avenue (737 2111). Bus 204, 301, 302. **Shows** usually 8.30pm daily. **Tickets** from $30; no under-18s. **Credit** AmEx, DC, Disc, MC, V. **Map** p315 C4.

The Sahara's Congo Room has showcased four decades of Las Vegas entertainers, from Mae West, George Burns and Judy Garland to Tina Turner – even the Beatles played here in 1964. Today, it stages the popular tribute show *The Rat Pack Is Back* – which is scheduled to close in early 2002 – as well as headliners such as Judy Tenuta, Rich Little and Jackie Mason.

Hilton Theater

Las Vegas Hilton, 3000 Paradise Road, between Karen Avenue & E Desert Inn Road, East of Strip (732 5111). Bus 108, 112. **Shows** daily; times vary. **Tickets** $45-$100. **Credit** AmEx, DC, Disc, MC, V. **Map** p315 C5.

The room that Elvis built is one of the best concert venues in town. None of the 1,700 seats is more than 87ft (26m) from the stage, and the crystal-clear sound and lighting systems are state of the art. The casino's continuing *Hilton Nights Live* concert series features celebs such as Kenny Roger, Hall & Oates, Trisha Yearwood, Johnny Mathis, Olivia Newton John and Smokey Robinson.

Hollywood Theatre

MGM Grand, 3799 Las Vegas Boulevard South, at E Tropicana Avenue (891 7777). Bus 201, 301, 302. **Shows** daily; times vary. **Tickets** $37-$70. **Credit** AmEx, DC, Disc, MC, V. **Map** p316 A8.

This theatre has an old-fashioned movie house entrance and 630 seats arranged in a tiered horseshoe around the stage. It's one of the city's top spaces, and stars ranging from country singer Randy Travis to Sheena Easton, Smokey Robinson, Rita Rudner and the Go-Gos have all played here, and it's also home to Jay Leno's *Tonight Show* for its fairly regular Las Vegas tapings. Performers are usually booked for a two-week run.

The Nightclub

Las Vegas Hilton, 3000 Paradise Road, between Karen Avenue & E Desert Inn Road, East of Strip (732 5111). Bus 108, 112. **Shows** times vary. **Tickets** $35-$70. **Credit** AmEx, DC, Disc, MC, V. **Map** p315 C5.

Since the Scintas (*see p198*) emigrated to the Rio, the 450-seat Nightclub has hosted 1980s pop star Sheena Easton, who signed a contract that will cover most of 2001. The showroom features steeply tiered seating and an excellent light and sound system.

Sam's Town Live

Sam's Town, 5111 Boulder Highway, at Flamingo Road, East Las Vegas (456 7777). Bus 107, 201, 202. **Shows** vary; call for details. **Tickets** from $15. **Credit** AmEx, Disc, MC, V.

In 2000, Sam's Town gained a 1,100-seat multi-use concert hall. This is the only large-scale entertainment venue on the Boulder Strip and it showcases pop, country and rock stars such as Kenny Loggins, Boyz II Men and Tracy Lawrence.

Lounges

The glory days of the fabulous casino lounge entertainers (Shecky Greene, Don Rickles, Wayne Newton, Louis Prima and Keely Smith) ended in the 1970s, when casinos began to book the better lounge acts into the main showrooms (where they could charge real money), and customers began to find other interests (sleeping?) to occupy them until five in the morning.

Although lounges have made a comeback, they are no longer mini-showroom-type venues. Instead, they are smaller and open to the casino, and typically feature homogenous acts that serve best as background noise or a respite from the tables. The kind of act varies, from your basic sloppy ventriloquist to one-woman bands to polished groups like the Fortunes and the Coasters. Many lounges are used as a testing ground for up-and-coming musicians and singers, so it's possible you could stumble on the next Tom Jones in a dimly lit corner of some off-Strip hotel. There are even a few lounges dedicated to showing you a good time; for extraordinary people-watching and a great view, you shouldn't miss the **VooDoo Lounge** at the Rio (*see p158*).

Admission to the casino lounges is free unless otherwise stated. Dress codes have been given where applicable.

Armadillo

Texas Station, 2101 Texas Star Lane, at N Rancho Drive, between Lake Mead Boulevard & Vegas Drive, North Las Vegas (631 1000). Bus 106, 208. **Open** 24hrs daily. **Credit** AmEx, DC, Disc, MC, V. **Map** p311 X1.

This saloon-style lounge features the retro sounds of cover band Love Shack (Fridays and Saturdays) and swing-era pianist Jerry Tiffe (Sunday).

The Bar at Times Square

New York-New York, 3790 Las Vegas Boulevard South, at W Tropicana Avenue (740 6400). Bus 201, 301, 302. **Open** 4pm-2am daily. **Credit** AmEx, Disc, MC, V. **Map** p316 A8.

Sing along with the 'duelling piano' show, which takes place in a Western-style bar with hardwood floors, Tiffany art and oak furniture. Dress code: jackets required; no jeans or T-shirts.

Get wet at **Storm**. *See p199.*

Bourbon Street Cabaret

Orleans, 4500 W Tropicana Avenue, at Arville Street, South-west Las Vegas (365 7111). Bus 201. **Open** 24hrs daily; live music from 6.30pm. **Admission** 2-drink minimum. **Credit** AmEx, DC, Disc, MC, V.

With the quiet feel of a courtyard club in New Orleans's French Quarter, the Bourbon Street Cabaret, located a few blocks west of the Strip, is a nice spot for a drink and some classic jazz, blues and zydeco. The club's decor includes replicas of grand and baby grand pianos suspended from the ceiling.

Coral Reef Lounge

Mandalay Bay, 3950 Las Vegas Boulevard South, between W Tropicana Avenue & Russell Road (632 7777). Bus 201, 301, 302. **Open** 24hrs daily. **Credit** AmEx, DC, Disc, MC, V. **Map** p316 A9.

Although this comfortable lounge's location – at the intersection of Mandalay Bay's 'Restaurant Row' and the casino floor – may be distracting to some, it is perfectly aligned with the traditional lounges of Las Vegas's past, offering a quick, but not permanent diversion from the gambling action. It has a secluded, tropical feel, a large and often crowded dancefloor and live bands (usually from 9pm-3am) playing everything from pop to salsa. It's a bit like wandering back in time.

Cleopatra's Barge

Caesars Palace, 3570 Las Vegas Boulevard South, at W Flamingo Road (731 7110). Bus 202, 301, 302. **Open** 9pm-4am Tue-Sun. **Admission** 2-drink minimum Fri, Sat. **Credit** AmEx, DC, Disc, MC, V. **Map** p316 A7.

For one-on-one encounters, climb aboard Cleopatra's Barge and dance to live bands, usually playing rock or R&B. This lively lounge is a crayon-coloured Viking boat, complete with oars, furled sails and a buxom mermaid figurehead; it floats in real water and bobs up and down when the dancefloor action heats up. Be careful when crossing the gangplank: inebriated revellers have been known to take a dive into the drink. Dress code: smart casual; no jeans.

Fontana Lounge

Bellagio, 3600 Las Vegas Boulevard South, at W Flamingo Road (693 7722). Bus 202, 301, 302. **Open** 10pm-2am Tue-Sat. **Credit** AmEx, Disc, MC, V. **Map** p316 A7.

This is one of the best places in Vegas to knock back a gin and lime and listen to some top-notch performers. A seductive, high-class establishment in the centre of the Bellagio, it harks back to the classy, Rat Pack days when drinks were expensive and lounge shows were free. Late at night, check out Vargas, a sexy crooner, or Jimmy Hopper and his band, who crank out a set list that is all over the map, from Neil Diamond to David Bowie. You'll find nothing but top-shelf liquor and classic cocktails on the menu, so be sure to sip that Sidecar with someone special.

Lagoon Saloon

Mirage, 3400 Las Vegas Boulevard South, between Spring Mountain & W Flamingo Roads (791 7111). Bus 301, 302. **Open** 10am-4am daily. **Admission** 2-drink minimum. **Credit** AmEx, Disc, MC, V. **Map** p316 A6.

There might not be a lagoon, but this tropically themed lounge is set amid flowing waterfalls and lush foliage from the casino's rainforest atrium. But it doesn't stop there, as it also comes with parrot-style chairs and a seashell-studded bar top. Just like they have in Jamaica. Or not. The music is usually of the easy listening variety, and, interestingly, is nearly always accompanied by the incessant screech of parrots. What are they trying to tell us? Dress code: no tank tops.

Le Bistro Lounge

Riviera, 2901 Las Vegas Boulevard South, at Riviera Boulevard (734 5110). Bus 301, 302. **Open** 6pm-1am Tue-Fri, Sun; 6pm-3am Mon, Sat. **Admission** 2-drink minimum. **Credit** AmEx, Disc, MC, V. **Map** p315 B5.

The lounge, slightly elevated above the casino, has a New York-style ambience with ribbons of red neon, chrome columns and brass accents. If you like jazz, stop by on Monday nights for Don Menza's jam session, which often includes well-known guest artists. Another regular performer is singer Susan McDonald, who blends country and western hits with Top 40 numbers.

La Playa

Harrah's, 3475 Las Vegas Boulevard South, between Sands Avenue & E Flamingo Road (369 5000). Bus 301, 302. **Open** 8.30pm-2.30am daily. **Credit** AmEx, Disc, MC, V. **Map** p316 A6.

La Playa's tropical flavour is a good complement to Harrah's carnival motif. The indoor-outdoor lounge has multi-coloured palm trees, a nine-screen video wall and festive fibre-optic lighting throughout. Live music – everything from salsa to rock – plays every day, without fail.

Naughty Ladies Saloon

Arizona Charlie's, 740 S Decatur Boulevard, at Alta Drive, South-west Las Vegas (258 5200). Bus 103, 207. **Open** 9.15pm-1.30am Tue-Sun. **Credit** AmEx, Disc, MC, V.

Old West hospitality is the fare at this saloon that looks like it's straight from a *Gunsmoke* set. There's no Miss Kitty tending the bar, and the Naughty Ladies no longer perform, but live, old-style music – from Beatles tribute bands to big band swing – is still a regular feature. Attire is mostly jeans and boots; the place is friendly and the drinks are cold.

The Railhead

Boulder Station, 4111 Boulder Highway, at E Desert Inn Road, East Las Vegas (432 7777). Bus 107, 112. **Open** 24hrs daily; live music from 7pm. **Credit** AmEx, Disc, MC, V.

There's always something happening in this cabaret-style lounge on the Boulder Strip. The booking agent shows no favouritism when choosing his acts, which have included retro rock stars like Chubby Checker, R&B's Sonny Turner and country and western's Charlie Daniels. When headliners aren't lighting up the stage, customers come under the spotlight themselves during the frequent karaoke nights.

Royal Street Theater

Jerry's Nugget, 1821 Las Vegas Boulevard North, at Main Street, North Las Vegas (399 3000). Bus 113. **Open** 8pm-2am daily. **Credit** AmEx, DC, Disc, MC, V.

This intimate lounge and dance hall has split-level seating and space-age lighting, and frequently hosts live entertainment such as Magaly and the Vamps – when it isn't staging a Latin dance party, that is.

Starlight Lounge

Stardust, 3000 Las Vegas Boulevard South, at Stardust Drive, between W Sahara Avenue & Desert Inn Road (732 6213). Bus 301, 302. **Open** 24hrs daily; shows usually 11pm. **Admission** free-$10. **Credit** AmEx, Disc, MC, V. **Map** p315 B5.

Even though the lounge lizard has become an endangered species in recent years, you may spot one or two here, crouching in the corner, cigarette in one hand, Martini in the other. The Starlight is a throwback to the old-time Vegas lounge – dark, smoky and lacking all political correctness. The entertainment is quite good, though, and often includes the Maxx and Chuy's Company.

Arts & Entertainment

Comedy clubs

The city's comedy clubs are a by-product of the cable TV and Comedy Store craze that swept the nation in the 1980s. Before gaining their own venue, comedians in Las Vegas generally worked in lounges or as opening acts for the headliners in the main showroom, where they functioned as a kind of high colonic, loosening up the audience for the marquee attraction that followed.

Today's comedy clubs follow the same format: two or three stand-up comics deliver their jokes, then the featured comedian closes out the show. Headliners are often known for their work on TV or movies (Chris Rock, Robert Schimmel, Jimmie Walker and Willie Tyler & Lester), while many of the country's biggest comedians (Jerry Seinfeld, Drew Carey, Don Rickles), who once played the Vegas comedy shops, now return for the large audiences (and pay cheques) of the casinos' showrooms. In addition to the clubs reviewed here, check out the **Golden Nugget** (*see p95*) in Downtown where David Brenner performs nightly.

Bourbon Street Comedy Theater

Bourbon Street, 120 E Flamingo Road, just east of Las Vegas Boulevard South, East of Strip (228 7591). Bus 202, 301, 302. **Shows** 10.15pm Mon-Sat. **Tickets** (incl 2 drinks) $45; no under-18s. **Credit** AmEx, Disc, MC, V. **Map** p316 B7.
The ongoing show in this intimate club is Dr Naughty, the X-rated comedy hypnotist. Selecting subjects (victims?) from the audience, Dr Naughty induces people to say and do bawdy things, either by themselves or in tandem with fellow volunteers. Oh, the hilarity.

Catch a Rising Star

Excalibur, 3850 Las Vegas Boulevard South, at W Tropicana Avenue. Bus 201, 301, 302. **Shows** 7.30pm, 10pm daily. **Tickets** $16.95; no under-21s. **Credit** AmEx, Disc, MC, V. **Map** p316 A8.
Stand-up comedy in King Arthur's Court. *Catch* returned to Las Vegas in 2001 after a two-year hiatus and features two nationally known comics doing their schtick in an intimate showroom.

Comedy Stop

Tropicana, 3801 Las Vegas Boulevard South, at E Tropicana Avenue (739 2714). Bus 201, 301, 302. **Shows** 8pm, 10.30pm daily. **Tickets** (incl 2 drinks) $17.50. **Credit** AmEx, DC, Disc, MC, V. **Map** p316 A8.
One of the oldest venues for comedy in Las Vegas, the Comedy Stop is also one of the largest, with more than 400 seats. Seating is at large tables, which creates a convivial atmosphere but makes it hard to see the stage clearly from the back of the room. Typically, three comedians are presented at the Comedy Stop twice nightly.

The Improv

Harrah's, 3475 Las Vegas Boulevard South, between Sands Avenue & E Flamingo Road (369 5111). Bus 301, 302. **Shows** 8pm, 10pm Tue-Sun. **Tickets** $24.95; no under-18s. **Credit** AmEx, DC, Disc, MC, V. **Map** p316 A6.
The Budd Friedman-owned club, part of a nationwide chain, traces its roots to the old cellar comedy stores of New York and Chicago. The Improv usually presents three or four comedians twice nightly except on Mondays.

Laugh Trax

Palace Station, 2411 W Sahara Avenue, at Rancho Drive, West of the Strip (367 2411). Bus 204, 401. **Shows** 7.30pm, 10pm Wed-Sun. **Tickets** $12.95. **Credit** AmEx, Disc, MC, V. **Map** p311 X2.
Palace Station's lounge/nightclub turns into an intimate comedy club, with two stand-up comedians doing the honours. Expect plenty of banter from the comedians with the up-close-and-personal audience. The comedians are funny, but you won't find many big names here.

Michael Holly's Off-The-Wall Comedy Hour

Sahara, 2535 Las Vegas Boulevard South, at E Sahara Avenue (737 2515). Bus 204, 301, 302. **Shows** 1pm, 3pm Tue-Sat. **Tickets** $12.95; no under-5s. **Credit** AmEx, Disc, MC, V. **Map** p315 C4.
This irresistible show in the Sahara's Congo Room takes the people-pleasing art of juggling and adds a manic twist – to hilarious effect. Michael Holly also does some wire-walking and other stunts, and he always manages to get the crowd going with plenty of audience participation. It's a fun way to kill some time in the afternoon.

Riviera Comedy Club

Riviera, 2901 Las Vegas Boulevard South, at Riviera Boulevard (794 9433). Bus 301, 302. **Shows** 8pm, 10pm daily. **Tickets** (incl 2 drinks) $21.95; $32.95 VIP seats. **Credit** AmEx, DC, Disc, MC, V. **Map** p315 B5.
The Riviera Comedy Club presents three or four comics twice nightly. The acts include all-gay comedy revues and XXXtreme Comedy – mostly shock comedians who talk nasty about bodily functions and social diseases.

Second City

Flamingo, 3555 Las Vegas Boulevard South, at E Flamingo Road (733 3333). Bus 202, 301, 302. **Shows** 8pm, 10.30pm Tue-Sun. **Tickets** $24.95. **Credit** AmEx, DC, Disc, MC, V. **Map** p316 A7.
The famous Chicago-based comedy troupe has successfully brought its penetrating humour out west, performing two shows nightly in the intimate Bugsy's Celebrity Theater. The troupe is known for its cutting-edge work, and the Las Vegas show is no exception, transcending the typical three stand-up routine with topical skits, songs and hilarious set pieces. The Second City comedians even take a humorous swipe at the Vegas scene.

Film

Las Vegas is a cinematographer's dream – and there are plenty of multiplexes for viewing the finished product.

Las Vegas must surely vie with New York as one of cinema's most popular locations. Hollywood never tires of using the city: it is conjured up in the cinematic imagination again and again, and the list of movies that have mined Vegas's iconography grows with each passing year. One of the drawbacks of being the world's most colourful soundstage, however, is that many of the complexities and hidden stories that make Vegas so fascinating never make it on to the screen.

Every so often a film comes along with some insights into what makes Vegas tick – such as Martin Scorsese's *Casino* or Albert Brooks' *Lost in America* – but the city still awaits its apotheosis à la Robert Altman's *Nashville*. For the moment, though, no one is complaining. As long as studios pump millions of dollars into the economy, and stars such as Ben Affleck (a routine visitor) leave several thousands behind at the Hard Rock's blackjack tables, Vegas seems happy to provide a ready-made set for Hollywood's latest blockbuster.

Film fans, meanwhile, have numerous options for places to enjoy movies in Las Vegas, with well-equipped multiplexes popping up everywhere. A hotel-casino project doesn't feel complete these days without a cinema attached to it, and movies may also return to the Downtown area as part of the Neonopolis mall project now under construction.

For a brief period, there were even two international film festivals: the Las Vegas International Film Festival and CineVegas, both of which drew decent crowds and some media attention. Sadly, the LVIFF is defunct and CineVegas is on an indefinite hiatus.

In addition to the Hollywood blockbusters, foreign, independent and art films routinely play in town, albeit for only a week at a time (unless it's a surprise hit, like *Croupier* or *Memento*). Most are shown at the **Regal Village Square**, at the Valley's far west end, or at the **Century Suncoast 16**.

The **Charleston Heights Arts Center** (*see page 122*) hosts a varied and inexpensive series of documentaries and foreign films every spring and autumn, while the **Winchester Community Center** (3130 S McCleod Drive, 455 7340; tickets $2) in East Las Vegas presents the liveliest rep series in town with foreign

films, series devoted to individual directors and an annual film noir series. In addition, the **UNLV International Film Series** (895 3547) has quietly been screening foreign films every autumn in a small auditorium on the UNLV campus. Films are usually subtitled and a couple of years old, and attended by students and academics – though all are welcome and admission is free.

For film listings information, check the *Las Vegas Sun*, the *Review-Journal*'s 'Neon' supplement or the free weeklies, *Las Vegas Weekly* and *CityLife*. Alternatively, you can phone MovieFone on 222 3456 for listings, but note that this service uses zip codes to direct callers to their nearest cinema.

Cinemas

These are the best and most interesting movie houses in town.

Century Orleans 12
Orleans, 4500 W Tropicana Avenue, at Arville Street, South-west Las Vegas (227 3456). Bus 201. **Admission** $5-$8; $5 concessions. **No credit cards.**
The Orleans' 12-screen cineplex features full THX on all screens and was the first to have stadium-style staggered seating – many other cinemas soon followed suit. The sound and projection is the best in town, and the Orleans' proximity to the Strip makes it the best bet for visiting film buffs.

Century Suncoast 16
Suncoast, 9090 Alta Drive, at Rampart, Summerlin (341 5555). **Admission** $5-$8; $5 concessions. **No credit cards.**
The new Suncoast multiplex offers first-rate sound and projection – and is one of few valley spots to include non-Hollywood fare. Its proximity to the golf courses of Summerlin makes it a perfect afternoon option for golf widows. Plus, the theatres are narrow and quite steeply raked, so there's nary a bad seat in the house.

Las Vegas Drive-In
4150 Smoke Ranch Road, at Rancho Drive, North Las Vegas (646 3565). Bus 106. **Open** 6-10pm Mon-Thur; 6-10.30pm Fri, Sat. **Admission** $5.50; free under-13s. **No credit cards.**
In the 1960s, Las Vegas hosted half-a-dozen drive-ins, virtually all of them long gone since the era of open-air moviegoing faded. Surprisingly, however, one

Arts & Entertainment

Celluloid city

Using Vegas as a backdrop for a motion picture can be a risky manoeuvre, owing to the city's proclivity for upstaging nearly everything put in front of it. The Julia Roberts/Brad Pitt comedy *The Mexican* only comes alive when Roberts and James Gandolfini goof about to 'The Safety Dance' in their hotel room at the Plaza, the lights of Fremont Street twinkling behind them. *3000 Miles to Graceland* suffers a similar fate: shortly after Kurt Russell and Kevin Costner rob the Riviera in full Elvis garb, the movie sinks like a brick greased with pomade.

Some films hold their own, however. The last of the Sean Connery Bond films, *Diamonds are Forever*, bends locations at the Riviera, Circus Circus and the Las Vegas Hilton to its bidding. *Casino* (*pictured*) and *Go* also made good use of the Riv. In *Casino* it stars as the fictional Tangiers Hotel & Casino, with real-life, late-night gamblers providing

authentic background action. In *Go*, Desmond Askew seduces two stoned bridesmaids, sets fire to their room at the Riviera and then tears around the casino's underground parking garage at high speeds. And naturally, the Terry Gilliam film of Hunter S Thompson's *Fear and Loathing in Las Vegas* (*pictured*) made the most of shooting at Binion's Horseshoe – formerly the Mint casino, where Thompson's misadventures originally took place.

Then there's the films that have tried to make Vegas look phony, ridiculous – before the city showed them who's boss. Paul Verhoeven's *Showgirls* didn't even begin to tell the truth about Vegas's exotic dancers, even though Cheetah's Topless Lounge (*see p207*) allowed itself to be portrayed in an unflattering light in the movie. *Con Air* crashed a plane into the late Sands (the Venetian now stands on its grounds) and pitted John Malkovich against Nicolas Cage

drive-in remains in Vegas. Located just north of Rancho Drive (aka US 95), its six screens provide an authentic drive-in movie experience, though it's marred by the intense light from the towering sign of the nearby Fiesta casino.

Regal Cinemas

All venues: Information 221 2283. **Admission** $5-$8; $5 concessions. **No credit cards.**
Boulder Station 11 *Boulder Station, 4111 Boulder Highway, at Desert Inn Road, East Las Vegas. Bus 107.*

Colonnade 14 *8880 S Eastern Avenue, at Pebble Road, Green Valley. No bus.*
Sunset Station 13 *Sunset Station, 1301 W Sunset Road, at Stephanie Street, Green Valley. Bus 212, 217.*
Texas Station 18 *Texas Station, 2101 Texas Star Lane, at Rancho Drive, North Las Vegas. Bus 106, 208.*
Village Square 18 *9400 W Sahara Avenue, at S Fort Apache Road, North-west Las Vegas. Bus 105.*
Although three of these are located in the neighbourhood Station casinos, the Regal Cinemas have

in a motorcycle-mounted joust on Fremont Street; but their characters duck into a tunnel that doesn't exist in the real world.

The interaction of cinema and real life can cut both ways. The Flying Elvi who perform a heroic parachute drop in front of Bally's in *Honeymoon in Vegas* didn't exist when the movie was released; a Las Vegas producer named Dick Feeney formed the actual Elvis skydiving troupe later to capitalise on the film's popularity.

Finally, there are a number of 'Vegas' films that weren't shot in town at all: *Leaving Las Vegas* was filmed in Laughlin; the sets of *Bugsy* were built in California's Mojave Desert, and Francis Ford Coppola's *One From the Heart*, while set entirely in Vegas, was shot entirely on a sound stage in Hollywood. Oh, well – at least there were some good Tom Waits songs on the soundtrack.

Which brings us, indirectly, to the old master: *Ocean's 11*. Nearly all the locations used in the filming of the famed Rat Pack picture are gone, or look so radically different that recreating them in your mind is nearly impossible. However, while you won't be able to follow in the footsteps of Frank Sinatra, George Clooney's are easy to track: the Steven Soderbergh remake of *Ocean's 11* was shot at several Vegas casino-hotels, all of which are still open for business.

As you stroll through Bellagio, trying to get that Clooney feeling, give a thought to the reels and reels of celluloid wrapped around this strange, but photogenic town. Vegas may not have always looked friendly on film, but it's almost always looked good.

For further details of these and other films featuring Las Vegas, *see pp298-9* **Further Reference**.

Arts & Entertainment

a touch of the old movie palace in their design: the Boulder cinema evokes an art deco train station with its enormous lobby clock, while the Sunset takes its inspiration from the tilework of Barcelona architect Antonio Gaudí.

The Regal Cinemas may involve a bit of a trek, but they're worth the effort for the film purist who demands wide screens and good prints. Note that the Village Square is one of only two cinemas in the rapidly growing Summerlin neighbourhood, and is surrounded by a collection of low- to mid-priced restaurants, so weekends can get very busy.

United Artists Showcase

Showcase Mall, 3785 Las Vegas Boulevard South, between E Tropicana & Harmon Avenues (740 4911). Bus 301, 302. **Admission** $7.75; $4.75 children & all matinées. **No credit cards**. **Map** p316 A8.

The UA Showcase is the only cinema on the Strip, tucked into a side alley next to the MGM Grand's parking garage. Its location is definitely an advantage, although the sound and projection are merely competent. Filmgoers can park for free, with validation, in the Showcase garage.

Nightlife

Mega dance clubs are the new tip in after-hours Vegas, but if you want to see
sexy strippers or bawdy burlesque, you can can.

Adult

It's been a long time coming, but the Las Vegas
of the 21st century is once again a relaxed place
when it comes to sexy entertainment. Probably
because the power players took notice when
other states successfully experimented with
the legalised vices Las Vegas has depended
upon for so long.

Mayor Oscar Goodman can be at least
partially credited with Las Vegas embracing
its sexy past; since being elected in June 1999,
he has taken a pragmatic approach to the
city's sins – even half-heartedly suggesting
the legalisation of prostitution.

Prostitution remains illegal in Clark County
(in which Las Vegas sits), and street hustling is
prevented by law enforcement. The lure of legal
prostitution is just an hour's drive south-west –
across the Nye County line in Pahrump – but its
advertisement is prohibited in Clark County.

Those nearly naked girls in the pamphlets
that seem to be shoved in your face every time
you walk the Strip are merely 'entertainers',
who will gladly come to your hotel room and
dance for you. Naked. And nothing else. Or
if they do, you will get busted. That's the
official line, anyway.

Today, adult entertainment spreads beyond
the obvious lapdance venues and into the
casinos themselves. In mid-2001 there were
11 adult-oriented production shows in Vegas,
featuring sexy topless showgirls – a nearly
four fold increase over the late 1990s.

Elsewhere, live adult entertainment is
principally geared towards the heterosexual
male (and his experimenting girlfriend, as
long as they arrive together); women are
prohibited by strict house rules from entering
strip clubs without a male escort, purportedly
to discourage prostitution and jealous outrage.

There are more than 35 places where nude
or nearly nude ladies dance for dollars, but
just two where women can see men do the
same (the **Olympic Garden**'s male revue,
and the New Frontier's playfully named
Aussie revue, 'Thunder From Down Under').
Gay men, meanwhile, must resort to slipping
tips in the G-strings of the muscled go-go
boys at disco **Gipsy** (*see p216*).

Adult entertainment in 21st-century Las
Vegas falls into four categories: casino revues;
topless or nude clubs; adult book/toy stores;
and swingers' clubs.

Casino revues

As Las Vegas has rediscovered its naughty
netherlands, sexy hotel entertainment has
made a dramatic comeback. These shows
range from the campy burlesque of *Crazy
Girls* (an old standby at the Riviera) to
Bally's *Jubilee!*, a traditional Vegas feather-
and-sequin show, similar to the Tropicana's
Folies Bergere. Smaller shows featuring
comedy and magic also offer a bit of skin.
Bill Acosta's impressionist show at the
Flamingo features topless dancers, as does
Naked Angels, a downtown show at the
Plaza which showcases long-time Vegas
comedian Pete Barbutti, along with a cast
of are-they-nude-or-not dancers. Perhaps
the most impressive newcomer is *La Femme*,
a troupe of classically trained dancers, straight
from the Crazy Horse in Paris, that boasts
all-natural, silicone-free women. For full
details on these and other shows, *see chapter*
Casino Entertainment.

Topless bars

Topless bars are dark, loud and crowded –
especially on Friday and Saturday and during
conventions. A non-stop parade of entertainers
shimmies to the music, stripping down to a
G-string, a pair of six-inch platform shoes and,
if you're lucky, a smile.

The dancers are more chatty than those
in nude clubs, and the bars all serve alcohol
and are open to those aged 21 and above.
There are many more clubs than the ones
listed below, but these offer the best
atmosphere and dancers.

A word of warning: most of these clubs
are located in dark, industrial areas, so you're
better off catching a cab than walking. Be sure
to specify which club you want to visit; cabbies
are often paid kickbacks to drop tourists at
certain clubs, regardless of their quality.
For more information, see ads in free local
weeklies *Las Vegas Weekly* and *CityLife*.

High-kickin' Vegas Vickie lures the punters into the **Girls of Glitter Gulch**.

Cheetahs Topless Club

2112 Western Avenue, between W Oakey Boulevard & Sahara Avenue, Stratosphere Area (384 0074/ www.cheetahstoplessclub.com). Bus 105, 204, 205. **Open** 24hrs daily. **Admission** $10 8pm-5am daily. **Credit** AmEx, Disc, MC, V. **Map** p315 B4.

This is Vegas's most relaxed topless bar, and offers the best overall experience. Large enough to have five intimate stages working at once, yet as homey as a neighbourhood sports bar, Cheetahs has a reputation as the locals' hangout. The place is packed during American football season, when Monday Night Football parties offer $10 'touchdown dances'. The gals are varied in style and there is less silicone here than at other clubs. Bouncers and bartenders are friendly. Dress: casual.

Club Paradise

4416 Paradise Road, between Flamingo Road & Harmon Avenue, University District (734 7990). Bus 108, 202. **Open** 4pm-6am Mon-Fri; 6pm-6am Sat, Sun. **Admission** $10. **Credit** AmEx, DC, Disc, MC, V. **Map** p316 C7.

A hyperbolic exercise in the popular 'gentlemen's club' genre, Paradise has all the trappings (classy exterior, plush carpeting, pampering seating and no dancer poles) and high-dollar luxuries (expensive champagnes, cigars and even dinner service) you might expect. All the dancers must wear similarly styled long evening gowns. This is clearly an effort to maintain the classy atmosphere, but instead results in dozens of lookalike gals doing lookalike moves on stage.

Crazy Horse Too Gentlemen's Club

2476 Industrial Road, at Sahara Avenue, Stratosphere Area (382 8003/www.crazyhorsetoo. com). Bus 105, 204. **Open** 24hrs daily. **Admission** $10 6.30pm-4.30am daily. **Credit** AmEx, DC, MC, V. **Map** p315 B4.

Following a much-needed face-lift and expansion, the Crazy Horse Too remains a frustrating experience. The two large main rooms have only one stage each, in the centre of each room, making the place look more like an illegal card room than a strip club. It's nearly impossible to get a stageside seat, the rest of the seats offer bad-to-worse views, and with only one stage per room, if you don't like what you see, you'll have to wait for a change of dancer. We can only guess that the party gets better in the VIP Emperor's Room, where a pricey two-drink, four-dance minimum is in effect.

Girls of Glitter Gulch

20 Fremont Street, between Casino Center & Main Street, Downtown (385 4774). Bus 107, 108, 301, 302. **Open** noon-4am Mon-Thur, Sun; noon-6am Fri, Sat. **Admission** 2-drink minimum. **Credit** AmEx, MC, V. **Map** p312 C1.

In the security-sanitised area beneath the Fremont Street Experience canopy, this hold-out from the old days still draws in the punters. After watching the FSE's free light and music show, you can stroll inside for a performance with a different kind of sizzle. Glitter Gulch features average-looking women with enormous breasts lap-dancing for men with enormous wallets. It draws a touristy crowd.

Olympic Garden Cabaret

1531 Las Vegas Boulevard South, at Wyoming Avenue, Stratosphere Area (385 8987). Bus 301, 302. **Open** 24hrs daily. **Admission** (incl 2 drinks) $20. **Credit** AmEx, DC, MC, V. **Map** p315 C3.
This is the largest and most visible of Las Vegas's adult entertainment venues, and can perhaps best be described as a warehouse of sexuality. The main room has large, pole-less circular stages surrounded by stageside seating, couches, booths, the DJ stall and the main bar. Opposite is a darker, more intimate and luxurious room with a catwalk and two circular stages. Upstairs, a VIP room awaits, where Vegas's longest-running male exotic dance revue is presented to the delighted shrieks of women gone wild. The atmosphere is comfortable, though the incessant strobe lights and loud sound system can be overwhelming. The number of physical enhancements have earned Olympic Garden the nickname 'Silicone Valley' among local dancers, but the sheer number of performers on the roster should keep the visitor happy. Dress: no tank tops.

Spearmint Rhino

3340 Highland Drive, at W Desert Inn Road (access via Spring Mountain Road), West of Strip (734 7336). Bus 105. **Open** 24hrs daily. **Admission** $10. **No credit cards. Map** p315 A5.
Part of a renowned California chain, Spearmint Rhino boasts one of the most chic, comfortable, modern interiors of any adult club. The DJ also plays more electronica and industrial music than at any other adult club in town. Opened as a totally nude juice bar, Spearmint Rhino eventually gave in, went topless and now offers a full alcohol bar and even a small menu of food. Though Rhino has the expected stage and lap-dancing, what makes this place unique is that it tends to draw the most diverse crowd, being a haven for young couples out for a good time.

Homey: **Cheetahs Topless Club.** *See p207.*

Nude clubs

Nude clubs, in which the girls go bare-assed naked, are similar to topless bars with an important difference – they're prohibited from serving alcohol. This results in a strange twist: most nude clubs are open to patrons 18 and older (except the **Palomino**, the only nude bar in town permitted a liquor licence and therefore restricted to over-21s). As a result, nude clubs attract a different type of patron (younger and less affluent) and a different kind of dancer (younger and more money-hungry) – a combo that leads to an annoying, anxious synergy.

For some reason, nude dancers try to take their 'art' more seriously than topless dancers, when most patrons just want to see them wiggle, spread and show some personality. Aside from the Palomino, all nude clubs lack atmosphere compared to the topless clubs.

Déjà Vu Showgirls

3247 Industrial Road, between Spring Mountain Road & Sahara Avenue, West of Strip (894 4167). Bus 105, 203. **Open** 11am-6am Mon-Sat; 6pm-4am Sun. **Admission** before 6pm $10; bar minimum after 6pm $10. **No credit cards. Map** p316 A5.
'Hundreds of beautiful girls and three ugly ones, coast-to-coast' is this national chain's slogan. The dancers here lean towards the pretty end of the scale, with a uniqueness that is difficult to come by in the land of silicone sameness. Déjà Vu's claim to fame is a series of theme nights – from amateur nights to oil and Jell-O wrestling to shower parties and more – lending them a kind of frat-house-party-with-strippers ambience. Dress: no tank tops.

Little Darlings

1514 Western Avenue, just north of Wyoming Avenue, Stratosphere Area (366 1141/www.showgirl. com). Bus 105. **Open** 11am-6am Mon-Sat; 6am-4am Sun. **Admission** $20 men; free women. **Credit** MC, V. **Map** p315 B3.
Stark lighting, annoying DJs and plastic drink cups are immediate challenges to the success of Little Darlings. Add that most patrons are high-school

grads in backwards baseball caps and you're wondering why we've listed the place. It's simple: most of the girls are gorgeous. Body piercings – in the most inaccessible of places – and wax jobs are all the rage. Stage dancers pick their own music, so you'll get a hint of their personalities before committing to a private lap-dance. The dances can get pretty wild, but the performers are not at all chatty; either cough up for a lap-dance or they move on. Dress: no tank tops.

Palomino Club

1814 Las Vegas Boulevard North, just north of Main Street, North Las Vegas (642 2984). Bus 113. **Open** 2pm-4am daily. **Admission** $15. **No credit cards.**
The granddaddy of Las Vegas clubs may not be as 'world-famous' as the advertising slogans suggest, but has nevertheless earned its reputation as the most atmospheric nude club in the city (it's amazing what liquor profits can do). The Palomino is no mere strip joint; instead, it offers a true cabaret atmosphere. Upstairs, dancers work a small round stage with a pole, while downstairs, a catwalk stage juts into the audience and an MC performs his comedy act between floor shows. The catwalk showcases only uniformly beautiful 'feature dancers' (adult-film actresses, centrefolds, published models), who all have fully fledged fantasy costumes (cowgirl, cheerleader, nurse and so on): every stitch is gracefully and sexily removed until they are completely naked.

Adult book & toy stores

Typically, adult bookstores are seedy locales with porn mags, adult videos for rent or sale and rubber and leather novelties lined up in rows of dirty-floored aisles. There are, however, a few that are clean, nicer or notable in some way – *see p179* for details.

Showgirl Video

631 Las Vegas Boulevard South, at Bonneville Avenue, Downtown (385 4554). Bus 206, 301. **Open** 24hrs daily. **Credit** AmEx, MC, V. **Map** p312 C2.
This otherwise unappealing adult bookstore is notable for its live dancer fantasy booths. While the one-on-one booths are always big on action, feature dancers (adult-film and magazine starlets) rule the place during the trade convention season. A few blocks south of Showgirl is its sister store, Talk of the Town, a similar operation, though slightly larger and more accommodating to couples. If you enjoy adult videos, the live shows viewed from the booths make for an interesting heavy-breather.
Branch: **Talk of the Town** 1238 Las Vegas Boulevard South, Stratosphere Area (385 1800).

Swingers' clubs

Swingers' clubs are legal adult gathering spots where consenting adults of all sexual proclivities and relationship arrangements

have the opportunity to mix, mingle and more. The clubs do not offer gambling or alcohol (though you can bring your own), but they do have dance floors and music. You pay an entrance fee (or 'donation') only.

Hide 'n' Seek

3084 S Highland Drive, between Desert Inn Road & Sahara Avenue, West of Strip (650 2747/www.hnslv. com). Bus 105. **Open** 7pm-4am daily. **Credit** MC, V. **Map** p315 A5.
Billed as a fully licensed, right-in-the-city 'alternative nightclub', Hide 'n' Seek has a dancefloor and an entertainment area. Looking for couples, singles, bisexuals? You'll find them all here, enjoying a little partying, playing and perhaps petting, if the vibe is right. Theme nights are offered and admittance is limited to couples or single women, though a few single men can get in, depending on the crowd mix. Staff 'hostesses' will dance for you for a fee.

The Red Rooster

Information 451 6666/www.vegasredrooster.com.
The city's oldest swingers club. Located in the huge home of hosts Mike and Chris out in a remote area of old Henderson, the Rooster is a bizarre mix of private nightclub and sex extravaganza. It's not unusual to see a crowd of 100 boogying on the dancefloor, a small group of men playing on one of the many pool tables or couples relaxing around the straight-from-the-1970s sunken fire pit. It's also not unusual to see people giving and getting oral sex at the bar. There are several hot tubs, a pool, private play rooms and an upstairs area for 'committed couples' only. Sodas and snacks are provided, but BYOB.

Dance Clubs

It doesn't seem all that long ago that you could count off all of Las Vegas's nightclubs on the fingers of one hand. If you got a sudden craving for the big-city club experience, then you could go to any disco you wanted – as long as it was the Shark Club, the Palladium or the Metz, three establishments that offered a surfeit of attitude, but little fun. If you're going to suffer a thick-headed doorman, criminally expensive drinks and an arrogant crowd, shouldn't there be at least one or two compensations? A good DJ? An unsolicited grope as you bend to tie your shoes?

The opening of **Club Utopia** in the mid-1990s single-handedly changed the tide. When the two-storey techno and rave club took over the old Metz space on the Strip, Sin City found out what it had been missing. The vibe at Utopia was easygoing, the music as current as the latest issue of *Mixmag* and the crowd attractive and ready for anything. Before long, Vegas's hotels and casinos were running to catch up with Utopia, as large numbers of their guests fled to the wildly successful nightclub.

King of clubs – **Utopia** sparked a music and nightclubbing revolution in Vegas. *See p212.*

Arts & Entertainment

The MGM Grand resurrected New York's infamous **Studio 54**; Luxor went *Stargate* with the future-Egyptian **Ra**; the Hard Rock opened a true underground club, **Baby's**, far below street level. And after-hours clubs – for Vegas, that's 3am to well past breakfast – sprang up almost as quickly as the casino dance clubs did.

Today, Vegas is one of the hottest nightclub cities in the world, owing to the town's refusal to do anything by halves. Superstar DJs stop by on a weekly basis, playing in clubs that are as unique as they are enormous, and independent promoters work the town like pimps, setting up distinctive – though often short-lived – clubs in various restaurants, lounges and bars.

The club vibe isn't restricted to the large-scale dance venues either. 'Destination' bars, such as **V Bar** (*see p157*) and **Jack's Velvet Lounge** (*see p156*), feature live DJs and attract a ultra-hip, club-savvy crowd. The new Palms, opening in late 2001, will not only sport a 1,200 seat nightclub, but also the **Little Buddha Café**, an outpost of Paris's noted Buddha Bar. Although not yet established on the city's nightlife scene, this and other recent openings – **Seven** on the Strip and **Kahunaville** at Treasure Island – are apparently trying to blur the boundaries between club, restaurant and bar, by offering a mix of neo-trendy food, a happening bar scene and cutting-edge DJ music.

Gay dance club **Gipsy** (*see p216*) remains hugely popular with non-gays; many long-time locals maintain it is the best disco in town, period. Even concert venues get in on the act: Mandalay Bay's **House of Blues** (*see p219*) and the Hard Rock's **Joint** showroom (*see p219*) have been known to offer after-hours dancing on weekend nights, as well as gigs by international DJs. It would seem, then, that no resort can afford to miss out on the young, club-going market: in 2002, the Aladdin plans to join the fray with **Tatou**, a huge, hyper-designed entertainment and nightclub venue, featuring a four-storey glass entrance and a 110-foot waterfall to entice clubbers inside.

Nearly all clubs admit only 21s and over, except for (very rare) special events. Some clubs have no fixed closing time; they just run until the last body drops from exhaustion. It's wise to call before setting out as times and prices may change. Women with local ID often get in free.

Baby's
Hard Rock, 4455 Paradise Road, at Harmon Avenue, East of Strip (693 5000/www.hardrock. com). Bus 108, 213. **Open** 10pm-5am daily. **Admission** $7-$15. **Credit** AmEx, DC, Disc, MC, V. **Map** p316 C7.
Sin City's celebrated nightlife got a lot hipper in 1999 with the addition of Baby's, where *Austin Powers* meets *Logan's Run* beneath the Hard Rock Hotel. This secluded, subterranean hideaway – through a

nondescript doorway and down two flights of stairs – encourages the frolicking friskiness of today's Mod Squad. Far more retro than rave, dark wood panelling and velveteen upholstery greet clubsters in the small aquarium room, where acid jazz sets the mood. The main room is all done up in retro-futurist fancy with illuminated walls and a glowing moat. DJs spin techno, trance, house and garage, and the waitresses burst forth from barely zipped vinyl.

The Beach
365 Convention Center Drive, at Paradise Road, East of Strip (731 1925/www.beachlv.com). Bus 108. **Open** *Cabana & sports bar* 24hrs daily. *Dance club* 10pm-4am Mon-Thur, Sun; 10pm-6am Fri, Sat. **Admission** $5-$15. **Credit** AmEx, Disc, MC, V. **Map** p315 C5.
Described by one observer as 'Gidget Goes to Studio 54' (a reference to the series of campy American beach movies of the 1960s), the Beach is a two-storey fun stop playing heavily on the sun 'n' surf theme. This 'meet market' features a surfboard and grass hut decor, with bartenders and waitresses in beachwear and bikinis, who sometimes get up on the bar to do suggestive dances. Thanks to its location across from the Convention Center, the Beach also has a cabana and sports bar that is open during the day, and has hosted special performances, including the one Pink Floyd is reputed to have given Microsoft chairman Bill Gates. Dress: smart casual.

C2K
Venetian, 3355 Las Vegas Boulevard South, at Sands Avenue (948 3007/www.clubc2k.com). Bus 203, 301, 302. **Open** 11pm-dawn Wed-Sun. **Admission** $10 men; $5 women. **Credit** AmEx, Disc, MC, V. **Map** p316 A6.
This multifaceted entertainment venue – a showroom in the early evening, a modest dance party after hours – has space for 1,400 seated patrons and who knows how many grooving on the dancefloor. Narrow but tall, C2K's two upper storeys (including private skyboxes) offer nice views of the party below. Despite drawbacks, such as bars foolishly placed on the dancefloor and drinks priced on the gold standard, C2K does offer a good time – largely dependent on who's working the DJ booth. Dress: no athletic shoes, baggy trousers, jeans, beach attire or hats.

Club Rio
Rio, 3700 W Flamingo Road, at Valley View Boulevard, West of Strip (252 7727/252 7777/www.playrio.com). Bus 202. **Open** from 10.30pm Wed-Sat. **Admission** $10 men; $5 women. **Credit** AmEx, DC, Disc, MC, V. **Map** p311 X3.
Las Vegas's original casino nightclub operates in the Copa showroom after the headliners pack up for the evening. The surroundings are wide open and plush, with plenty of booths and seating under the high ceilings. The crowd is decidedly older for a nightclub, consisting mostly of tourists, single conventioneers and middle-aged couples. Dress: smart casual; no shorts, collarless shirts, tennis shoes, flip-flops or excessively baggy or ripped clothing.

Club Utopia

The Epicenter, 3765 Las Vegas Boulevard South, between Harmon & E Tropicana Avenues (740 4646/www.clubutopia.com). Bus 301, 302. **Open** 9pm-10am Thur-Sat. **Admission** from $10 Thur, Fri; $15 Sat. **Credit** AmEx, MC, V. **Map** p316 A8.

The innovator when Vegas dance clubs were still stuck in pop-land, Utopia sparked a music and nightclubbing revolution. The recently remodelled Miami-style club plays host to every travelling techno and big-beat outfit that rolls through Sin City. BT, Electric Skychurch, Juno Reactor, Sasha, Paul Oakenfold and Moby have all taken the large circular stage, and Vegas's native sons Crystal Method shot their Busy Child video inside the enormous discotheque. The club is rave-friendly music from techno and house to breakbeat and more – with the tunes spun by both local and name DJs. There are three rooms, two levels, a huge dancefloor, an upstairs outdoor patio and a great sound system. The vibe has softened since the early days, but it's still the king of Vegas clubs.

The Dragon

Mandalay Bay, 3950 Las Vegas Boulevard South, between W Tropicana Avenue & Russell Road (893 3388/www.reddragonlounge.com). Bus 301, 302. **Open** 10am-4pm Wed. **Admission** $10. **Credit** AmEx, DC, Disc, MC, V. **Map** p316 A9.

Currently being staged in the China Grill (*see p132*), a funky modernist restaurant that looks like it's straight out of the pages of *Wallpaper** magazine, this midweek neo-Asian affair is the product of veteran Vegas club scenesters. An instant hit with those in the know, the Dragon has that hard-to-find, big-city-underground vibe – and boasts the city's only marble dancefloor. Deep-lounge DJs are flown in weekly to complement the house guests. The crowd dresses to kill: best get out those high heels, and put on the more attractive of your tongue studs. Dress: smart casual; no tank tops, cut-offs or excessively baggy clothing.

Drai's After Hours

Barbary Coast, 3595 Las Vegas Boulevard South, at Flamingo Road (737 0555). Bus 310, 302. **Open** 3-10am Wed-Sat; from 2am 1st Sun of month. **Admission** $10. **Credit** AmEx, Disc, MC, V. **Map** p316 A7.

Though it adjoins a French restaurant and looks like it (*see p133*), Drai's works admirably as an after-hours club, picking up those who've had enough of the big discos up the street, but not quite enough to retire to the hotel room and grab even one hour's sleep. On its own, Drai's kitschy chic – animal prints, a faux library, overstuffed couches – succeeds in making you forget that the sun actually does rise in the morning, and a succession of deep house and techno DJs enhance the illusion. The Drai's crowd gets a bit wild, so be ready for anything – and you should definitely expect to stand in a long line to enter. Dress: smart casual; no tank tops, cut-offs or excessively baggy clothing.

Glo at the Hop

1650 E Tropicana Avenue, between Maryland Parkway & Spencer Street, University District (310 5060/736 0042). Bus 201. **Open** from 7pm Wed-Sat. **Admission** $5 Wed, Fri; $10 Thur, Sat. **Credit** AmEx, Disc, MC, V. **Map** p311 Y3.

Like a hybrid of something from *Casablanca* and *Ocean's 11*, Glo is a classic speakeasy in the Vegas style. Low ceilings mask the spacious interior: a multi-tiered room filled with plush velvet booths and unltra-comfortable chairs. All seats face the stage, and the stage fronts the dancefloor. Dancing to live music, ranging from old-school funk to trance, happens several nights a week, with each night promoted by a different group. Dress: smart casual; no blue jeans, athletic wear or excessively baggy clothing.

Pink E's

3695 W Flamingo Road, at Valley View Boulevard, West of Strip (252 4666). Bus 202. **Open** 24hrs daily. **Admission** free Mon; $1-$3 Tue-Fri, Sun; $6-$8 Sat; free women Thur. **Credit** MC, V. **Map** p311 X3.

Is it a nightclub? Is it a pool bar? Is it a video arcade? Whatever it is, Pink E's is the most popular weekend gathering spot for the local rock 'n' roll crowd. Dozens of pink-felt pool tables (free on Sundays) are available for that eight-ball fix, plus more than a fistful of pinball machines and electronic games. All of this, plus a constant blast of rock music, keeps the tight-pants girls happy, and that keeps the biker guys smiling, too. Watch out for occasional live gigs by local and national bands, and don't miss the 'artwork' in the toilets. Dress: casual; no cut-offs, biker and gang wear, or excessively baggy trousers.

Ra

Luxor, 3900 Las Vegas Boulevard South, between W Tropicana Avenue & Russell Road (262 4000/www.rathenightclub.com). Bus 301, 302. **Open** 10pm-6am Wed-Sat. **Admission** $10 men; $5 women. **Credit** AmEx, DC, Disc, MC, V. **Map** p316 A9.

Ra is intimate in comparison with some of the more excessive spaces in town, but the elaborate Egyptian theming is seamless and impressive. Now one of the 'oldest' of the new clubs (it opened in 1997), Ra is still one of the best in terms of atmosphere, packing 'em in with excellent lighting and sound and a furious promotions schedule. A variety of special theme nights keep things interesting; call ahead to find out what's on. Cage dancers get their groove on to keep the crowd moving, and there are some concerts, with big-name spinners such as ATB and DJ Rap making guest stops. Dress: no tank tops, baggy trousers, shorts, sport wear, jeans, T-shirts or hats.

rumjungle

Mandalay Bay, 3950 Las Vegas Boulevard South, between W Tropicana Avenue & Russell Road (632 7777/www.mandalaybay.com). Bus 301, 302. **Open** 10.30pm-2am Mon-Thur, Sun; 10.30pm-4am Fri, Sat. **Admission** $10 Mon-Wed, Sun; $15 Thur; $20 Fri, Sat. **Credit** AmEx, DC, Disc, MC, V. **Map** p316 A9.

Live and let dance – **Gipsy** gyrators get down at the oldest gay disco in town. *See p216.*

Not since the Shark Club has the raging-hormones crowd had such a jumping nightspot in which to get jiggy. By day, rumjungle is a pleasantly hip restaurant and bar with a world-friendly menu and pocket-friendly pricing. By night, it morphs into one of Vegas's hottest clubs. A DJ spins music heavy on Latin house and techno, and thundering bass pours from the entrance as a long line of partygoers waits to be admitted. Once past the velvet ropes and the steaming 50ft (15m) high fire-and-water wall, you'll swear you landed in Rio de Janiero. The dancefloor is tiny compared with the rest of the club, but this does little to quell the spirits of the young and beautiful. Dress code: smart casual. No shorts, tank tops, flip flops.

Studio 54

MGM Grand, 3799 Las Vegas Boulevard South, at E Tropicana Avenue (891 1111/www.mgmgrand.com). Bus 201, 301, 302. **Open** 10pm-3am Tue-Sat. **Admission** *Men* $10 Tue-Thur; $20 Fri, Sat. *Women* free. **Credit** AmEx, DC, Disc, MC, V. **Map** p316 A8.

With everyone from teenage technoids to new grandmas dancing to disco, re-creating the famed Studio 54 was an obvious move. The warehouse-styled club has four levels, each of them featuring its own dancefloor, seating and a bar tended by the prettiest boys this side of *An Evening at La Cage.* There's also great lighting and sound, sexy go-go dancers (men and women) and a fun, high-energy mix of music from the 1970s to the present. Though its initially strict 'are you hip enough?' admission policy has been relaxed a bit, the high cover charge and chi-chi VIP lounges still result in an odd mix of club kids and high-rollers sharing dancing space with baby boomers reliving their glory days. MGM hotel guests get in for free Tuesdays to Thursdays. Dress: smart casual. Men: collared shirts, sports jackets, no baggy jeans or tennis shoes.

Vamp

Napoleon's, Paris-Las Vegas, 3655 Las Vegas Boulevard South, between Flamingo Road & Harmon Avenue (946 4567). Bus 301, 302. **Open** 10pm-4am Fri, Sat. **Admission** $15. **Credit** AmEx, DC, Disc, MC, V. **Map** p316 A7.

Nightclub impresario John D Guzman (producer of the notorious Naked Hollywood club nights) turns cigar bar Napoleon's into an alluring bump-and-grind lounge every Friday night. The room is small, the beats are loud, and the prevailing attitude one of highly developed self-love. The crowd is pretty to look at, but doesn't move much: this is a place to be seen, not to make a scene. Vamp is a great place to end up, but if you plan to do any serious dancing, you may want to go somewhere else beforehand. Dress code: smart casual; no shorts.

Gay & Lesbian

Las Vegas works hard at being all things to all people. However, while the city has experienced a tremendous growth spurt in the past decade, it has remained quite a small town when it comes to gay culture. But fear not, queer tourist: there's a burgeoning GLBT community in Las Vegas that's ready to welcome you. Resist the temptation to compare Vegas's tiny 'Fruit Loop' with San Francisco's famous Castro district, and venture out to party with the straight folk the way the locals do, and your sojourn in this sparkling desert gem is guaranteed to delight every one of your senses.

Currently, the only way the GLBT community can experience the glitz and glamour of Vegas is to go mainstream. The city's nightlife scene is experiencing the joys and tribulations of its own accelerated growth, and while some of the casino dance clubs are almost comparable to those in LA or New York, the gay scene hasn't caught up yet. So have some patience, enjoy the small-town qualities that Vegas bars still offer and make the most of the fabulous array of restaurants, clubs, bars and entertainment inside the casinos: they'll provide a veritable buffet of cruising opportunities.

And finally, the **Gay Pride Festival** in spring (*see p183*) is a flamboyant opportunity for the city to come out and celebrate GLBT culture. A major event on the local calendar, the festival attracts party people of every persuasion from all across the Southwest, proving it's hip to be gay now, even in Vegas.

WHERE TO GO

Commercially, Las Vegas has two gay areas: the ever popular Gay Triangle – or Fruit Loop, as it is affectionately called – and the Commercial Center on Sahara Avenue.

The Fruit Loop is easily reached from the Strip. Its epicentre is the corner of Naples Drive and Paradise Road, just south of the Hard Rock Café. There you'll find **Get Booked** (*see p166*), which stocks local GLBT publications and plenty of other books; a host of gay bars; **Gipsy**, the oldest and most popular gay disco in Las Vegas; and a New York/European-style gay-owned restaurant, **Café Luna** (4647 Paradise Road; 735 5858).

The Commercial Center on Sahara Avenue, just east of the Strip, boasts the **Spotlight**, **Badlands Saloon** and the **Apollo Health Spa**. You'll also find several new hotspots, including **Cobalt**, an industrial-style video cruise bar; the **Las Vegas Lounge**, the city's only transgender bar; and **Wet Lizard**, for something a little steamier. The **Gay & Lesbian Center of Las Vegas** is opposite and **Key's Piano Bar & Restaurant** is just across the street.

Many of the city's cafés and coffeehouses are either gay-operated, or gay- and lesbian-friendly. Of those listed in this guide, **Café Espresso Roma** and the **Mermaid Café** (for both, *see p222*) have particular gay appeal. Guppies (Gay Urban Professionals) can always be found hanging out in packs at **Starbucks**.

For other socialising, check out events at the Gay & Lesbian Center. It has a film night every Saturday at 8pm and sponsors a gay skate night on the third Monday of each month at the **Crystal Palace Skating Center** (4680 Boulder Highway, East Las Vegas; 458 7107). Entrance (including skate hire) is $6 in advance, $8 on the door. A youthful crowd of around 50 to 100 skaters attend, but all are welcome.

LESBIAN LAS VEGAS

A note to female readers: don't be discouraged by the apparent lack of lesbian bars and activities geared towards women. Most of the gay bars have a healthy mix of men and women at the weekends; **FreeZone** has a ladies' night on Tuesdays and attracts a primarily female crowd on Saturdays; and the **Backstreet Bar & Grill** has an unofficial ladies' night on Thursdays.

Vegas also has a women's social group called **Betty's Outrageous Adventures** (BOA), which organises movie nights, hiking and camping excursions, sporting events, pool parties and other non bar-related fun. All ages, sexual orientations and male friends (unless it's a specifically women-only function) are welcome to attend. For details, check out its website (www.bettysout.com).

For details of gay support groups and other useful organisations, *see chapter* **Resources A-Z: Gay & lesbian**.

Bars

There are about a dozen or so gay bars in the city, plus a few that identify themselves as 'alternative' and therefore gay-friendly.

Backdoor Lounge

1415 E Charleston Boulevard, at 15th Street, Downtown (385 2018). Bus 206. **Open** 24hrs daily. **Admission** $3 Fri. **No credit cards. Map** p312 E3. A haven for local gay men, the Backdoor boasts 'the friendliest bartenders in town', some occasional slot and video poker tournaments and, best of all, regular drink specials.

Backstreet Bar & Grill

5012 Arville Street, between W Flamingo Road & Tropicana Avenue, South-west Las Vegas (876 1844). Bus 104, 201, 202. **Open** 24hrs daily. **No credit cards.** A favourite haunt for all the cowboys and cowgirls of Las Vegas (of which there are quite a few) and also the home of the Nevada Gay Rodeo Association, Backstreet has the busiest Sunday afternoon beer bust in town. Attention, ladies: if you want to meet women of all ages and interests, git yerself down to the Backstreet every Thursday night at 7pm for some line dancing lessons. Non-dancers are welcome, too, of course.

Badlands Saloon

Commercial Center, 953 E Sahara Avenue, unit 22B, between Sixth Street & Maryland Parkway, East of Strip (792 9262). Bus 204. **Open** 24hrs daily. **No credit cards. Map** p311 Y2.

Located in the Commercial Center, Badlands Saloon is a popular bar on the local circuit. It's nothing out-of-the-ordinary, and features the usual combination of country music, pool tables and nary a woman in the place.

The Buffalo

Paradise Plaza, 4640 Paradise Road, at Naples Drive, between Harmon & Tropicana Avenues, East of Strip (733 8355). Bus 108, 213. **Open** 24hrs daily. **No credit cards. Map** p316 C8.

Las Vegas's legendary Levi-leather bar is a place where only the boldest of lesbians dares to cross the threshold. Once in, however, you'll find the usual pool-playing, recipe-swapping, friendly crowd of guys (and a few gals) dressed to look meaner than they really are.

Cobalt

Suite 102, Commercial Center, 900 East Karen Suite, East of Strip (693 6567). Bus 204. **Open** 24hrs daily. **Credit** MC, V. **Map** p311 Y2.

The city's hottest new video cruise bar has an extreme industrial party atmosphere.

Key's Piano Bar & Restaurant

1000 E Sahara Avenue, at Maryland Parkway, East Las Vegas (731 2200/www.keys-lv.com). Bus 204. **Open** *Bar* 10am-4am daily. *Restaurant* 6-11pm Mon-Thur, Sun; 6pm-midnight Fri, Sat. **Credit** AmEx, Disc, MC, V. **Map** p311 Y2.

Key's bills itself as 'the hottest little piano bar in town' and is busy with a largely professional, over-30s crowd. Reservations are recommended for the popular live entertainment night – Dining with the Divas – on Wednesdays at 8pm. Key's also houses a good-value restaurant offering pizza, buffalo wings, steak and the like, for around $10 a head. On Sundays (10.30am-2.30pm), enjoy a champagne brunch buffet for $7.95.

Hey boy, hey girl: **Las Vegas Lounge**.
See p216.

Las Vegas Eagle

Tropicana Plaza, 3430 E Tropicana Avenue, at Pecos Road, East Las Vegas (458 8662). Bus 111, 201. **Open** 24hrs daily. **No credit cards.** **Map** p312 Z3.

Famous for its Underwear Nights (Wednesdays and Fridays), this is primarily a men's Levi-leather bar, with busts twice a week and nightly drink specials.

Las Vegas Lounge

900 E Karen Avenue, between Paradise Road & Maryland Parkway, East of Strip (737 9350). Bus 108, 109. **Open** 24hrs daily. **No credit cards.** **Map** p312 Y3.

A mixed venue: mostly queens, transsexuals, cross-dressers and their friends, fans and appreciators. There are regular live shows and drinks promotions.

Phoenix

40 North Nellis, Charleston Boulevard, East Las Vegas (438 3050). Bus 206. **Open** 24hrs daily. **No credit cards.**

The most recent addition to Las Vegas' GLBT party scene, the Phoenix hosts nightly shows, drink specials, karaoke on Tuesday, ladies' night with the gorgeous Go-Go Grrlz on Thursday, and a beer bust for boys on Mondays. There's also a great outdoor party yard and patio, with a sand volleyball court.

Snick's Place

1402 S Third Street, between E Charleston Boulevard & Wyoming Street, Stratosphere Area (385 9298). Bus 301, 302. **Open** 24hrs daily. **No credit cards.** **Map** p311 Y2.

Las Vegas's oldest gay men's bar is a historic must-see neighbourhood landmark.

Spotlight

957 E Sahara Avenue, at Commercial Center, East Las Vegas (696 0202). Bus 204. **Open** 24hrs daily. **No credit cards.** **Map** p311 Y2.

Very much a locals' hangout, Spotlight aims to be the 'friendliest gay bar in Las Vegas'. It hosts regular liquor/beer busts, free dinners at the weekend and Jock Night on Saturdays.

Casino entertainment

While many of the big production shows are worth a visit, the Riviera's **An Evening at La Cage** (*see p194*) probably has the most consistent gay following. This classic female impersonation review stars Frank Marino as Joan Rivers and features the most amazing array of evening gowns this side of Chicago.

The **Kenny Kerr Show** (*see p195*) is also a must-see. Flanked by gorgeous, scantily clad male dancers and flawless female impersonators, Kenny's live singing and hilarious stand-up comedy has made him the Queen of Queens in Las Vegas. The show has moved several times, most recently to the Regent in Summerlin; call ahead to confirm its current location.

Clubs

The newer, glitzier, more entertainment-oriented casinos house the most popular nightclubs in the city, and all boast a 'mixed' or 'alternative' dance crowd. Some have even developed special gay nights in an attempt to enhance their existing GLBT clientele. For details of the top spots, *see pp209-13*.

Angles/Club Lace

4633 Paradise Road, at Naples Drive, between Harmon & Tropicana Avenues, East of Strip (791 0100). Bus 108, 213. **Open** 3pm-6am daily. **Admission** $2-$5. **No credit cards. Map** p316 C8.

This was at one time the city's sole women's bar. It's now a mixed dance bar, with ladies' nights (for 'Womyn Only') on Thursdays and Fridays. Saturday nights are dominated by a male African-American crowd grooving to house and hip hop music.

Flex Lounge

4371 W Charleston Boulevard, at Arville Street, North-west Las Vegas (385 3539). Bus 206. **Open** 24hrs daily. **Admission** $2 Fri, Sat; $5 Sun. **No credit cards.**

One of Las Vegas's few truly mixed clubs, the Flex Lounge on Charleston Boulevard is a favourite because of its drink specials and great dancing. There are karaoke nights on Mondays, go-go boys and DJs from Wednesday to Saturday, and a Latino drag show on Sundays.

FreeZone

610 E Naples Drive, at Paradise Road, between Harmon & Tropicana Avenues, East of Strip (794 2300/2310). Bus 108, 213. **Open** 24hrs daily. **Admission** varies. **No credit cards. Map** p316 C8.

A relatively recent addition to the Fruit Loop scene, FreeZone (opposite Gipsy) caters for women on Tuesday nights, men on Thursdays, mixed karaoke fans on Sundays and Mondays, and has some of the best drag shows in town on Fridays and Saturdays. It's also home to Celebrations! restaurant.

Gipsy

4605 Paradise Road, between Harmon & Tropicana Avenues, East of Strip (731 5171). Bus 108, 213. **Open** from 10pm daily. **Admission** $5 Mon, Tue, Thur, Fri, Sun; $6 Sat. **No credit cards.** **Map** p316 C8.

Until the Strip's nightclub explosion, Gipsy was the only place to go for a taste of the live-and-let-dance attitude prevalent in most metropolitan nightclubs, and it still draws more than just gays. Though it is small (tiny, even) by most standards, the club sports a video wall and some seating, and by 2am on a Saturday night, it's a heaving wall-to-wall sweatfest with no room to move. Music ranges from techno to R&B to the gay-friendly neo-disco heard around the globe, while scantily clad go-go boys work the corners of the dancefloor. Don't miss the incredible Toni James Lip Sync Contest on Thursday nights.

Las Vegas legends Liberace

A famous 1956 Las Vegas publicity photograph shows Elvis Presley and Liberace together, Elvis smiling at a piano, Liberace struggling with a guitar, and each sporting the other's jacket. (Even then, Liberace's over-the-top overcoat was fabulously sparkly.) Years later, Elvis and Liberace (each of whom had a twin brother die at birth) would emerge as two of the most enduring symbols of Las Vegas, although at opposite ends of the spectrum of excess. While Elvis's sexually powerful gyrations and 'man's man' attitude melted young ladies into puddles, Liberace's refined foppishness attracted the attention of the older set, and he became an unexpected sex symbol for romance-starved women over 50.

A classically trained child prodigy, Liberace found, at an early age, that sneakily playing racy burlesque clubs earned him much more money than the same work at conservative concert halls. In addition, the environment was far more accommodating to his emerging personality, one that eventually set the standard for gay flamboyance for decades to come.

Perhaps chasing an elusive freedom that he never found, Liberace made his way to Las Vegas. Never mind the proliferation of steamy strip and drag queen shows along the Strip, sexual orientation was (and often still is) a taboo subject in Las Vegas, and Liberace discovered a Sin City with a persona as deeply conflicted as his own. Perhaps this was why he loved the city so much. In any case, and despite the obvious outward clues, Liberace's homosexuality remained the unspoken, dark element in his life, denied until after his death from an AIDS-related illness in 1987. His fan base – right up to the end – was comprised of swooning, heavily made-up older ladies, proving the cliché that once they get past child-rearing age, every woman wants a gay man around the house.

Today, Liberace's diamond and dazzle persona lives on at the **Liberace Museum** (*see p120*), which he opened in 1979 as a funding arm for his Foundation for the Performing and Creative Arts. Not surprisingly, the topic of Liberace's sexuality is taboo among the museum staff, who approach their jobs with a reverence usually reserved for fallen kings. Sombre, teary-eyed visitors wander through two separate buildings of Liberace history: rhinestone-encrusted pianos, candelabras, fur coats, sparkly hotpants, even a pink convertible Volkswagen Beetle. Framed show posters and tickets adorn the walls, and a video montage runs continuously. In any other context, such a display would be bizarre, but in Las Vegas the celebration of excess is what it's all about.

GoodTimes Bar & Nightclub

*Liberace Plaza, suite 1, 1775 E Tropicana Avenue,
at Spencer Street, University District (736 9494).
Bus 201.* **Open** 24hrs daily. **No credit cards.**
Map p311 Y3.

Although it's open throughout the week, GoodTimes
is the only place to be on a Monday night, when a
lively mixed crowd and plenty of younger party
goers take advantage of the best liquor bust in town
before dancing into the morning on the only stainless steel dancefloor in Las Vegas.

Cruising

In addition to the sites listed below, Vegas
boasts a plethora of adult bookstores, theatres
and video arcades, which are prime spots for
cruising. The **Adult Superstore** at Tropicana
and Valley View (*see p179*) is the largest adult-
oriented enterprise on the West Coast, offering
a 200-channel arcade and a two-screen theatre.

Apollo Health Spa

*Suite A19, Commercial Center, 953 E Sahara
Avenue, between Sixth Street & Maryland Parkway,
East Las Vegas (650 9191/www.apollospa.com). Bus
109, 204.* **Open** 24hrs daily. **Admission** $21-$30.
Credit MC, V. **Map** p311 Y2.

The Apollo is known worldwide – not for its lavish
pamperings, mind, but for the notoriety of its former
co-owner, Doc Ruehl. Doc owned the houseboat in
Miami where gay serial killer Andrew Cunanan took
his own life. Nevertheless, the spa enjoys a healthy
crowd most nights, many of them tourists. It has a
heated pool, Jacuzzi, steam room, sauna, video room,
a gym and a maze (darkroom) area.

Desert Books

*4350 N Las Vegas Boulevard, at Craig Road, North
Las Vegas (643 7982). Bus 113, 115.* **Open** 24hrs
daily. **Credit** MC, V.

If you like a man in uniform, then try hanging out
at Desert Books, which is located near the Nellis Air
Force Base. This adult bookshop has been open
since the 1980s and attracts an older gay clientele
during the day, while in the evenings couples come
in for a browse.

Gay beach

This 'clothing optional' gay men's beach is located
just outside the city at Lake Mead. Even though the
site falls under federal jurisdiction, there is a state
law against nudity 'with sexual intent' – so cruise
with caution. To reach the beach, head east on Lake
Mead Boulevard (Highway 147) until you hit the
lakeside road: turn left (north) towards Calville and
Overton Bays. At the eight-mile marker, turn right
on to a dirt road; stay left at all forks, making all
left turns. Park where it seems obvious, then head
left over the hills and continue along the path: gays
to the left, straights to the right. Beware: park
rangers are on the lookout for people engaging in
sexual activity.

Wet Lizard

*Suite B-20, Commercial Center, 953 E Sahara
Avenue, between Sixth Street & Maryland Parkway,
East Las Vegas (732 2587).* **Open** 1pm-5am Mon-
Thur, Sun; 1pm-7am Fri, Sat. **Admission** $20.
Credit AmEx, Disc, MC, V. **Map** p311 Y2.

Las Vegas's newest playpen has group rooms, a
customer dance stage, an interactive playground,
showers, a Jacuzzi, private areas and a fetish store.

Music

Las Vegas is so rich in live music that it's
almost impossible to avoid. It pours from
every casino lounge, fills every showroom
and theatre – and, sometimes, bands even play
on the Strip itself. Despite some production
shows moving to recorded music in the 1980s,
many of the newer shows boast a live band –
whether it's an eclectic art-rock ensemble for
Blue Man Group, a kickin' big band for *The
Rat Pack is Back* or new-age enterprise for
Cirque du Soleil's *O* and *Mystère*. (For details,
see chapter **Casino Entertainment**). Many
of these musicians – such as Uberschall, an
unofficial *Blue Man Group* spin-off – also
play side gigs in local clubs.

Needless to say, Vegas regularly pulls in
international talents, too. Nearly every major
touring musician in the world has either played
Las Vegas already or will soon enough. Recent
visitors include Madonna, Tom Petty, Paul
Oakenfold, Dave Matthews Band and far too
many others to mention. Considering the
number of world-class venues in Vegas, finding
a number of amazing shows during your visit
is almost guaranteed. What's more, there are
scores of local bands, each trying to attract an
audience with their own distinct groove.

INFORMATION AND TICKETS

To find a band or venue that suits your
taste, pick up one of Vegas's many free arts
and entertainment publications. The free
'alternative' weekly newspapers, *Las Vegas
Weekly*, *Las Vegas Mercury* and *CityLife*, all
feature live music and event calendars, as does
tourist publication *Showbiz*. Online, check out
www.vegas. com and www.lvlocalmusicscene.
com for daily updated calendars of live music
and special events.

The strict licensing laws mean that under-21s
are limited in their choice of venue. However,
they are welcome at the Huntridge, the Joint
(depending on the performer), the House of
Blues (also conditional – call ahead), the major
arenas and all the coffeehouses and cafés;
we've indicated age restrictions for each place.
Admission prices throughout the venues vary

depending on the act: there may be no charge in bars and cafés, while prices at the major arenas range from around $20 for a local show at the House of Blues to $40-plus at the MGM Grand Garden. Tickets for the larger venues can be bought through **TicketMaster** (474 4000) for a fee. Unless otherwise stated, venues do not accept credit cards.

Rock, punk, hip hop, pop & rave

The number of popular songs *about* Las Vegas far outnumbers any popular songs recorded by native acts. And there's little hope that the scales will balance: songwriters have had years to immortalise the town (and everyone from Bruce Springsteen to Nina Hagen has done so), but a homegrown music scene has tried in vain to punch through a solid foundation of imported entertainment for two decades.

Las Vegas's best known pop music exports are defunct punk band MIA, 1980s pop diva (and *Grease* choreographer) Toni Basil, techno/breakbeat outfit Crystal Method, gay disco favourite Kristine W and hair-rock band Slaughter. Many of the popular artists associated with this town – Tom Jones, Frank Sinatra, Ann-Margaret, Louis Prima, the inescapable Elvis Presley – were not Las Vegans per se; but many kept residences here and were considered natives whenever they were in town. *See p220* **Las Vegas legends: Elvis Presley.**

Meanwhile, the local talent keeps working, in the hope it'll be able to contribute to Vegas's too-short homegrown history, and perhaps even add its own Vegas-themed tune to the pop culture vernacular. Local acts are patient, knowing they still have to compete with international names. And most of them are painfully aware that they may have to relocate in order to gain the full attention of the major record labels, as Crystal Method did in 1991 when the band moved to Los Angeles.

A few local rock bands are on the cusp. Inside Scarlet, 12 Volt Sex, Phatter Than Albert and many others have drawn major label interest of late. Vegas's vastly underrated punk scene isn't fading away either, with Vermin and 2 Cents Worth rocking the bars on a regular basis. And despite the lack of an established indigenous musical culture, there are a variety of eclectic groups in town – the Nines, Mama Zeus, Automatic Taxi Star, the Watson Family and Native Tongue come to mind – that draw inspiration from an array of influences, ranging from Tom Waits to classic flamenco.

The local music scene takes on the look of a lost cause sometimes, but the musicians never falter. They play in local bars, support national bands, perform at varied local festivals, put music on MP3.com, gradually gaining popularity and looking for an opening. They continue playing to crowds that may be as apathetic as the band is eager, in venues that may close a week hence. And they play in defiance of a town that, despite its self-declared title as the 'Entertainment Capital of the World', often refuses to acknowledge there's any homegrown talent at all.

Major venues

Aladdin Theater for the Performing Arts
Aladdin, 3667 Las Vegas Boulevard South, at Harmon Avenue (736 0111) Bus 301, 302. **Open** *Box office* 10am-midnight. **Tickets** from $15. **Credit** AmEx, Disc, MC, V. **Map** p316 A7.
Fresh from a recent remodelling, the Aladdin Theater remains one of Vegas's best midsize venues. With a large proscenium-arch stage (reportedly America's biggest) and the crispest acoustics you'll hear outside your living room, it continues to be a fine place to see and hear everyone from Whitney Houston to Pearl Jam.

House of Blues
Mandalay Bay, 3950 Las Vegas Boulevard South, between W Tropicana Avenue & Russell Road (632 7600/tickets 632 7666/www.hob.com). Bus 301, 302. **Open** *Box office* 8am-11pm. **Tickets** from $12. **Credit** AmEx, Disc, JCB, MC, V. **Map** p316 A9.
Just like every other House of Blues venue in the US? Not really. This 1,900-capacity, three-level room, is such a thoughtfully planned and richly soulful venue that it feels as if it's been part of the Strip since the beginning (it opened in March 1999). There's not a surface in the HOB that's not painted or otherwise covered with striking 'outsider' folk art and, odd as it may seem, the look of the room somehow improves the quality of the experience. It's a pretty high-quality affair to begin with: the sound system is state of the art, and there are very few bad seats in the house (beware the pillars on the main floor). Recent visitors have included the Keb Mo, the Cult and Moby.

The Joint
Hard Rock, 4455 Paradise Road, at Harmon Avenue, University District (693 5000/www.hard rock.com). Bus 213. **Open** *Box office* noon-7pm. **Tickets** from $15. **Credit** AmEx, DC, Disc, MC, V. **Map** p316 C7.
This 1,400-capacity, two-level room has become widely recognised as the most prestigious rock venue in town, thanks to its sterling sound, swanky ambience and location inside 'the world's first rock 'n' roll casino'. Playing the Joint has now become a

Arts & Entertainment

Las Vegas legends Elvis Presley

Las Vegas incarnate – and embedded himself so deeply in the city's folklore that you can scarcely mention one without the other.

Today, some two decades after his death, Elvis is still lighting up Las Vegas. The **Elvis-A-Rama Museum** (*see p113*) houses the largest private collection of Elvis memorabila west of Graceland, including his cars, his clothes, his horoscopes, his tax returns – even a dirty letter he wrote to a pre-Priscilla girlfriend. Best of all, a tribute artist performs his hits, with all due reverence, every few hours.

And it's not just in the museum that the King still reigns supreme: throughout town, murals, sidewalk stars, even buses bear his likeness. Two of his jumpsuits are on display at the Hard Rock Hotel and the Las Vegas Hilton; and you can't swing your pelvis

In Las Vegas, Elvis is an iconic, inescapable part of the scenery – but it's not always been that way. Presley played his first Vegas show in April 1956, in the Venus Room of the New Frontier Hotel, and he didn't go down particularly well. The audience gave him only polite applause and local critics savaged him: 'For the teenagers, the long, tall Memphis lad is a whizz; for the average Vegas spender or showgoer, a bore,' said Bill Williard of the *Las Vegas Sun*.

By the time the King returned, at the International Hotel in July 1969, the tide had turned. Fans packed the International night after night to hear Elvis sing his hits, banter with his band and watch him 'take care of business in a flash' with his gemstudded jumpsuits and karate kicks. For the next seven years, Elvis went about becoming

without knocking over jump-suited 'tribute artists' – no-one calls them 'impersonators' here – performing everywhere from the Riviera to Fitzgeralds. Periodically, a mob of skydiving Elvises – the Flying Elvi – fall from the sky. And needless to say, a King, in any one of several downtown wedding chapels, can marry you to your teddy bear.

It's not a bad legacy for a performer whose first appearance in Las Vegas, by many accounts, was a flop – upstaged by comedian Shecky Greene. Elvis never forgot that first impression of Vegas, even going so far as to open his 1969 shows with 'Welcome to the New Frontier'.

Elvis Presley is now regarded as the Vegas entertainer *par excellence* – all it took to win over the crowd was a couple of chords, some white blues and a few chop-socky kicks.

mark of stature, one that countless bands – from the Pet Shop Boys to Garbage to Sting – have felt compelled to claim. The venue's biggest drawbacks are its high ticket prices (seldom under $30) and the management's annoying habit of overloading the room. Not that these caveats matter in the slightest when the drink is flowing and the beats hit you.

Mandalay Bay Events Center

Mandalay Bay, 3950 Las Vegas Boulevard South (632 7777/www.mandalaybay.com). Bus 301, 302. **Open** *Box office* 10am-11pm. **Tickets** from $15. **Credit** AmEx, Disc, MC, V. **Map** p316 A9.

This 12,000-seat arena is the second-best large venue in Las Vegas (MGM's Grand Garden beats it). It has hosted everyone from the Three Tenors to Christina Aguilera, and the acoustics are as good as whoever's working the soundboard. Getting in and out is terribly easy – far better than at the Grand Garden – since the Events Center is located at the end of Mandalay Bay's sedate Restaurant Row. It makes all the difference when you and 12,000 other enthusiasts are filing out all at once, all keen on getting a cab, food or a much-needed cocktail.

MGM Grand Garden Arena

MGM Grand, 3799 Las Vegas Boulevard South, at E Tropicana Avenue (891 1111/www.mgmgrand.com). Bus 201, 301, 302. **Open** *Box office* 10am-11pm. **Tickets** from $40. **Credit** AmEx, DC, Disc, MC, V. **Map** p316 A8.

Modelled after New York City's Madison Square Garden, the MGM Grand's 17,000-seat Grand Garden is the best arena-sized venue in Vegas in terms of sound, sightlines and comfort. Its crisp acoustics have served the likes of N'Sync, the Who and Janet Jackson very well indeed.

Thomas & Mack Center

4505 Maryland Parkway, at E Tropicana Avenue, University District (895 2787). Bus 108, 109, 201. **Open** *Box office* 10am-6pm Mon-Fri; 10am-4pm Sat, Sun. **Tickets** from $30. **Credit** AmEx, Disc, MC, V. **Map** p311 Y3.

The Thomas & Mack is primarily a sports venue, built for UNLV's win-some, lose-more basketball team. A recent refitting corrected some acoustic problems, and not a minute too soon. It shouldn't be the first choice of venue to see anyone play, but you rarely have a choice in the matter.

Clubs & smaller venues

The **Sanctuary**, one of the best small venues, closed down in summer 2001. **Pink E's** pool hall and club (*see p212*) sometimes hosts local and national rock acts.

Boston Grill & Bar

Mountain View Center, 3411 S Jones Boulevard, at Spring Mountain Road, South-west Las Vegas (368 0750). Bus 102, 203. **Open** 24hrs daily. *Shows* 9pm Mon-Thur, Sun; 10pm Fri, Sat. **Admission** free. **No credit cards.**

If you're searching for the elusive 'Vegas Sound', this is the place to find it. The Boston features live local music seven nights a week. Though its surroundings and ambience could politely be called dank, local rockers and funksters play the Boston by the busload – from quirky jazz-rockabilly performer Chris King to earnest singer-songwriter Mark Huff.

Huntridge Performing Arts Theatre

1208 E Charleston Boulevard, at Maryland Parkway, Downtown (477 7703/information 471 6700). Bus 109, 206. **Open** *Box office* 10am-2pm daily. **Admission** from $6. **No credit cards.** **Map** p312 D3.

Las Vegas's oldest venue, built at the height of World War II, began life as a movie house where Frank Sinatra and Judy Garland once performed. Today, the Huntridge Theatre hosts so many punk, hardcore, rap and metal bands that locals have tagged it 'the Punktridge'. The sound mix is good and loud, the beer good and cold and if you avoid the 'orchestra' pit (where a number of teenage boys are beating the living daylights out of each other), you should have a good evening's worth of entertainment. Tickets for national acts here are available from TicketMaster.

Legends Lounge

Lamb Square, 865 N Lamb Boulevard, at Washington Drive, North Las Vegas (437 9674). Bus 112, 208. **Open** 24hrs daily. *Shows* 9pm Wed-Sat. **Admission** $3. **No credit cards.**

The Grateful Dead paraphernalia on the walls is a bit misleading. Sure, you'll find Dead or Phish fans listening to old bootlegged tapes, but when performers are featured, the programme is deliciously varied. It could be the earthy funk of locals Mama Zeus, the folk-rock explorations of Mark Huff or travelling 'jam' bands such as the Disco Biscuits and String Cheese Incident. Too far out of town to pop in for casual drinks, but a fine destination if one of Las Vegas's better local bands is rocking the house.

Money Plays

Flamingo Center, 4755 W Flamingo Road, between Cameron Street & Decatur Boulevard, South-west Las Vegas (368 1828). Bus 103, 202. **Open** 24hrs daily. *Shows* 10pm Sat. **Admission** free. **No credit cards.**

The typical sports bar decor is not much to look at, but Money Plays draws a huge party crowd of drunken college kids. Local rock bands play in the back almost every weekend, squeezed behind the pool tables. Anybody and everybody is welcome, wearing whatever the hell they want.

Blues, country & folk

Blues

The infamous **Double Down Saloon** (*see p157*) hosts a live blues jam on Wednesday nights; call ahead for times.

Arts & Entertainment

Sand Dollar Blues Lounge

3355 Spring Mountain Road, at Polaris Street, West of Strip (871 6651). Bus 203. **Open** 24hrs daily. *Shows* 10pm daily. **Admission** $3 Mon-Thur, Sun; $5 Fri, Sat. **No credit cards. Map** p311 X3.

Hosts at least one band, sometimes two, a night. The room runs thick with smoke and atmosphere, the cover charge never exceeds $5 and an active fan base supports, with fervour, shows by local heroes Charlie Tuna Band, the Ruffnecks, the Smokin' Crawdads, the Moanin' Blacksnakes and more.

Country & western

Las Vegas's country and western scene is like a bear – it hibernates most of the year, only waking up for the National Finals Rodeo in early December (*see p186*). Around that time, nearly every popular country artist that's not nailed down or currently serving time comes to Vegas to roost.

Otherwise, when country artists play Vegas, they tend to gravitate toward the **Silverton** hotel-casino (3333 Blue Diamond Road, Southwest Las Vegas; 263 7777/1-888 588 7711), the **House of Blues** (*see p219*) and the **Star of the Desert Arena** (box office 386 7867 ext 7145) at Buffalo Bill's casino in Primm, on the California border (*see p271*).

Larry's Hideaway

3369 Thom Boulevard, at Rancho Drive, North Las Vegas (645 1899). Bus 106. **Open** 11am-2am Mon-Sun; 11am-5am Fri, Sat. *Shows* 8.30 pm daily. **Admission** free. **No credit cards.**

This modest establishment features live bands every night, playing country classics to a packed dancefloor. Expect excellent service, friendly staff and some serious honky-tonkin'.

Folk

Café Espresso Roma

The Promenade, 4440 S Maryland Parkway, at Harmon Avenue, University District (369 1540). Bus 109, 213. **Open** 7am-10pm Mon, Tue, Thur; 7am-2am Wed; 8am-11pm Fri, Sat; 8am-10pm Sun. *Shows* Fri, Sat. **Admission** free; donations $3-$5 are welcome. **No credit cards. Map** p311 Y3.

Café Espresso Roma was once the only place folk performers could truly call home; now that the town has grown and venues aren't as hard to come by, a wide variety of bands takes the café's tiny stage. Most are local rock outfits, but you can catch a hardcore troubadour every now and again, and the odd open-mic poetry evening; call for a schedule. *See also p140* **Caffeine fix.**

Mermaid Café

2910 Lake East Drive, at Sahara Avenue, South-west Las Vegas (240 6002). Bus 204. **Open** noon-11am Mon-Thu, Sun; noon-1am Fri-Sat. *Shows* 8.30pm Fri. **Admission** free; donations $3-$5 are welcome. **Credit** AmEx, MC, V.

Mermaid features folk/acoustic performers on Friday nights; quite a few of Las Vegas's up-and-coming folk voices have made it a home away from home. Call ahead to find out who's baring their soul.

Jazz & swing

Las Vegas's jazz scene has improved markedly in recent years, but is still a few years away from consolidating its position. Big-name jazz musicians such as Branford Marsalis and Nicholas Payton have been known to play one-night stands, but if you walk into a casino lounge hoping for a shot of the real stuff, be prepared to hear the art form set back some 15 years. Most of the live jazz on the Strip is of the saccharine variety; expect to hear Miles Davis standards mangled seven ways for Sunday.

Good swing bands are somewhat easier to find. Several venues feature live big bands – you haven't lived until you've heard Art Vargas at the Bellagio's **Fontana Lounge** (*see p201*) – but on a basis that could kindly be called irregular. Sometimes the town is packed with swing bands; at other times, you won't find one for miles, but the Fontana Lounge and New York-New York's **Empire Bar** (740 6969) are always worth a try. Check local calendars for details.

Blue Note Jazz Club

Suite A41, 3663 Las Vegas Boulevard, at Harmon Avenue (862 8307). Bus 301, 302. **Open** *Box office* noon-11pm daily. **Tickets** up to $30. **Credit** AmEx, MC, V. **Map** p316 A7.

Cool, dark and blessed with a cabaret-like air, Blue Note Jazz Club endeavours to bring its namesake musical form to the Strip. Lou Rawls, Pat Metheny and Cassandra Wilson have all taken the club's tiny stage, and non-jazz acts such as the Godfather of Soul himself, James Brown, have graced the room. Check local calendars or call ahead to see who's keeping time that night.

Pogo's Tavern

2103 N Decatur Boulevard, between Smoke Ranch Road & Lake Mead Boulevard, North-west Las Vegas (646 9735). Bus 103. **Open** 9am-3am daily. *Shows* 8pm Fri. **Admission** free. **No credit cards.**

This tiny dive bar is the perfect place to escape the gaudy neon overkill of Las Vegas, yet still enjoy its charm, plus it hosts the town's only weekly swing night. The nameless band is made up of old-timers, veterans of a dozen or so big bands that shook Sin City when swing was the undisputed king of the Strip. Hearing the stories they have to tell is reason enough to make a night of it and, unlike almost every other band in town, these fine gentlemen will honour every request.

Performing Arts

Big money may lure artists to the Strip, but elsewhere in the city local dance and theatre companies keep the cultural fires burning.

Las Vegas may make grandiose claims to being the 'entertainment capital of the world', but when it comes to performing arts off the Strip, the city continues to struggle. This is not surprising when you consider that local theatre and dance companies must battle with the resort industry juggernaut for the hearts and minds of both locals and tourists. While Vegas attracts excellent international talent to its performing arts centres and hosts an ever-shifting but vibrant theatre scene, it's hard to see this cultural variety in the glare of the hotels' efforts to make sure everybody spends as much time as possible on their property.

The good news is that, over the past few years, entertainment options on the Strip have blossomed into areas once unthinkable, from the performance art parodies of the *Blue Man Group* show at the Luxor (*see p197*) to the avant-garde theatrics of Argentina's *De La Guarda* troupe at the Rio. It is to be hoped that the mainstream acceptance of such offbeat performances might pave the way for more attention (and funding) for the city's non-resort theatre arts. Meanwhile, artists of all disciplines continue to pursue their vocations with as much dedication and vision as those in more culturally hospitable climes. Las Vegas boasts some truly great talents, if the visitor has the patience to dig a little deeper to discover them.

Classical music

After many years of union strife and a lack of artistic direction on the part of the now-defunct Nevada Symphony Orchestra (formerly the city's principal classical organisation), the classical music scene has been re-energised by the emergence of the new **Las Vegas Philharmonic** (895 2728). The Philharmonic had its first full season in 1999 and, under the leadership of director Harold Weller, has established itself as the city's leading orchestra. The **Nevada Chamber Symphony** (433 9280) has also made great strides in presenting programmes that are distinctive and adventurous, and offers far more concerts than the Philharmonic, many with a populist flair (such as their outdoor and children's concerts).

UNLV's annual **Charles Vanda Master Series** (895 2787), held from autumn to spring, has brought numerous classical solo and ensemble performers, along with dance productions, to the city. Performers have included the Iceland Symphony Orchestra and the Moscow Festival Ballet. Visitors to Las Vegas in summer can enjoy the **Las Vegas Music Festival** (895 3949). For 11 seasons, this event, founded by conductor Evan Christ, has brought together top professional and student talent from around the city and the nation for concerts at various venues, under the direction of the UNLV music department.

Artemus W Ham Concert Hall

University of Nevada Las Vegas, 4505 S Maryland Parkway, between Flamingo Road & Tropicana Avenue, University District (895 2787). Bus 213. **Tickets** from $15. **Credit** AmEx, Disc, MC, V. **Map** p311 Y3.
Part of UNLV's Performing Arts Center, this is the main venue for both local and national artists. Designed specifically for acoustic music, it has hosted everything from the Bolshoi Ballet to national and international orchestras. When Itzahk Perlman plays Vegas, he plays here. It's also the home of the LV Philharmonic.

Arts & Entertainment

Las Vegas Philharmonic.

Culture shock

When visitors ask where the cultural centre of Las Vegas is, most residents will probably scratch their heads. This is because Vegas has a good half dozen of them, thanks to the vision of former Las Vegas-Clark County Library District director Charles Hunsberger. He realised that, with the rise of the Internet, libraries needed to broaden the range of services they provided in order to stay relevant. He conceived libraries as more than warehouses of books: they could house theatres, concert halls, galleries, museums and more. Thanks to a voter-approved funding bond, Las Vegas boasts some of the newest and most architecturally significant libraries in the region, all of them a testament to this vision.

The **Summerlin Library & Performing Arts Center**, the **Whitney Library & Recital Hall**, the **Rainbow Library & Amphitheater** and the **Sahara West Library & Fine Arts Museum** were all built in the past ten years. While some of these structures' potential as cultural centres for the Valley has yet to be fully realised, it's only a matter of time (and

a few changes in shortsighted policy) before they take up the slack caused by the absence of a traditionally central performing arts centre. Currently, if you attend a performing arts event off the Strip, it will probably be held in one of these libraries.

Beyond providing a venue for the city's cultural events, the libraries' greatest attraction is their design: they represent some of the best modern architecture in the city. The most interesting are Santa Fe architect Antoine Predock's 1989 **Las Vegas Library & Lied Discovery Children's Museum** (*see p123*), a striking combo of stark, sculptural volumes (more effective from outside than in), and the pompous but curious neo-classical **Clark County Library & Performing Arts Center**, built in 1994 by internationally renowned New York architect Michael Graves; its striking, postmodern, neo-classical labyrinth has been dubbed 'the pastel mausoleum'. The dramatic, monolithic entrance to the **West Charleston Library** resembles a cock-eyed Stonehenge: a series of columns that look as though they have had their tops sliced off at an angle by a giant butter knife. The **Sahara West Library & Museum** (*pictured; see also p122*), by local architects Meyer, Scherer & Rockcastle, is undoubtedly the finest of all; a grand marriage of form and function, complete with a simulated grotto (although the effect has been lessened by the removal of the water feature) and vast, airy galleries that put one in mind of an elegant ocean liner stranded upon the high desert seas.

If Las Vegas is a paradigm for the modern American city – a vast monument, for better or worse, of suburban sprawl that flies in the face of a word such as 'centre' – then perhaps it's appropriate that Hunsberger's vision has created this many cultural centres, each serving its own neighbourhood and linking the Vegas cultural scene in a way that no other government agency could.

For library contact details and opening times, *see p291*.

Arts & Entertainment

Theatre & dance

Thanks to the sudden and swift success of Broadway shows such as *Chicago* and *Rent* on the Strip, the Las Vegas theatrical landscape is shifting away from hackneyed production shows and into the brave new world of legitimate theatre. Travelling productions of *Fosse*, *Fame* and *Les Miserables* now stop off at the **Aladdin Theatre for the Performing Arts** (*see p219*), and many hotels are scrambling to feature Broadway-style entertainment. But for those hungering for non-musical dramas and comedies, the city's off-Strip theatre companies remain the best option.

Both amateur and professional theatre are thriving, with several new (and, amazingly enough, competent) theatre companies taking to the boards all over town. The success of UNLV's MFA stage-writing programme has energised not only the university theatre department, but feeds such companies as **The Asylum** – a readers' theatre devoted to works by local playwrights. While the perennial Neil Simon play performed by a small community group still makes its appearance, the Vegas theatre scene has many gems for the adventurous theatre-goer. One of the best and most well-attended theatre events in town is the annual **Shakespeare in the Park** – three nights of free performances by the Henderson Arts Council (765 9800) held in late September/early October (*see p185*).

The number of local dance performances has diminished somewhat in recent years, which is odd considering the number of professionals drawn to Las Vegas in search of employment in hotel-casino productions. Dance companies include a mix of former and current Strip performers moonlighting for the love of their art, along with a handful of ballet dancers who resist the lure of big showroom pay cheques.

For an inside scoop on all current dance and theatre productions, pick up a copy of the free newspapers *Las Vegas Weekly*, *Las Vegas Mercury* or *CityLife*, or phone the individual companies.

Venues

Most theatre and dance companies operate out of a hodgepodge of facilities. Three come under the banner of the local library district: the **Summerlin Library & Performing Arts Center Theater** (1771 Inner Circle Drive, North-west Las Vegas; 256 5111), the **West Las Vegas Library Theater** (951 W Lake Mead Boulevard, North Las Vegas; 647 2118) – both of which seat around 300 and have proscenium stages – and the **Clark County Library Theater** (1401 E Flamingo Road, East Las Vegas; 733 7810) – a 500-seater with a thrust stage. These are the newest venues in town, with excellent sightlines and acoustics. *See also p224* **Culture shock**.

UNLV has three venues: the 550-seat **Judy Bayley Theater** for major shows, the smaller **Paul C Harris Theater** and the **Black Box** for intimate, workshop-style shows. Companies also use the more limited facilities offered by city-run spaces at the **Charleston Heights Arts Center Theater** (800 S Brush Street, North-west Las Vegas; 229 6388) and the **Winchester Community Center Theater** (3130 S McCleod Drive, East Las Vegas; 455 7340).

Theatre companies

Actors' Repertory Theater

Information 1824 Palo Alto Circle, Las Vegas, NV 89108 (647 7469). **Tickets** $12-$25.
Credit AmEx, Disc, MC, V.
Now in its 15th season, ART is the only professional Equity company in Las Vegas. With an audience weighted toward the retirees of nearby Sun City Summerlin, the productions tend to be highly populist. Seasons are divided between mainstream musicals (*Oliver*, *The King and I*), comedies (*The Importance of Being Earnest*, *Run for Your Wife*) and topical dramas such as Tom Stoppard's *Rough Crossing* and Tony Kushner's controversial *Angels in America: Millennium Approaches*. Usually staged in the Summerlin Library & Performing Arts Center, ART's productions are always well mounted and show a particular talent for farce.

The Asylum

Winchester Community Center Theater, 3130 S McCleod Drive, just north of E Desert Inn Road, East Las Vegas (455 7340). Bus 108, 111.
Tickets up to $10. **No credit cards.**
Run by local actress and theatre maven Maggie Winn-Jones, this is one of the newer companies in town and focuses on bringing the work of local playwrights to a wider audience. It also features PlayPen, a staged reading series that encourages feedback from the audience.

Las Vegas Little Theater

Schiff City, 3850 Schiff Drive, at Spring Mountain Road & Valley View Boulevard, South-west Las Vegas (362 7996). Bus 104, 203. **Tickets** around $12. **No credit cards.**
The pre-eminent amateur company in town, the LVLT has the distinct advantage over other companies of having its own theatre. It's also notable for tackling less-than-sure-fire crowd-pleasers, dramas such as *Ordinary People* and plays by Athol Fugard and Wendy Wasserman (along with the usual Noel Coward comedies). LVLT makes a virtue of its modest production values by presenting straightforward, serious shows.

Arts & Entertainment

Casino shows

O

Cirque du Soleil's *O* (a pun on the French *eau*) is simply amazing. The multi-talented circus troupe creates a surreal world where water itself is one of the performers. The show is a must-see, and worth the high ticket prices – but book early. *See p198.*

Mystère

Mystère is another step on the ladder of Cirque du Soleil's total reinvention of the circus. If you can't get tickets to see *O*, *Mystère* is the one to see; the show would be first choice in any other circumstance. *See p198.*

Blue Man Group

This blue-skinned trinity of holy fools is truly like nothing else on the Strip. The famous New York-based group's weird and delightful East Coast antics have proved a refreshing antidote to the usual Vegas shows. *See p197.*

The Second City

The newest outpost of Chicago's famous improvisational theatre company brings a new level of comedy sophistication to the Strip. *See p202.*

Nevada Theatre Company

Lakes Business Center, 2928 Lake East Drive, at W Sahara Avenue, South-west Las Vegas (873 0191). **Tickets** up to $10. **Credit** AmEx, Disc, MC, V.

The newest and strongest company on the scene, the Nevada Theatre Company, founded in 1998, has drawn positive notices for its recent productions of *The Illusion* by Corneille, collective, multi-media piece *And Then They Came for Me: Remembering the World of Anne Frank,* and *Twelfth Night.* Led by artistic director Deanna Dupelchain, the company has created quite a buzz among theatre fans, winning several local 'Best Theatre Company' polls. It recently moved into its own space in the Lakes neighbourhood.

Rainbow Company Children's Theatre

Reed Whipple Cultural Center, 821 Las Vegas Boulevard North, between Washington Street & Bonanza Road, North Las Vegas (229 6211). Bus 113. **Tickets** $5; $2-$3 concessions. **No credit cards. Map** p312 D1.

Las Vegas's oldest theatre company (it's been going strong for 25 years) is, to some minds, also its best.

Housed in its own space in the Reed Whipple, its consistent high quality has brought it a reputation as the place for young actors and directors to hone their craft. The company prides itself on creating children's theatre that doesn't insult young people's intelligence, and its productions are always highly creative and well designed. Shows are usually aimed at kids aged four and up.

UNLV Department of Theater Arts

4505 S Maryland Parkway, between E Flamingo Road & Tropicana Avenue, University District (895 3666). Bus 109, 201, 202. **Tickets** from $20. **Credit** AmEx, DC, Disc, MC, V. **Map** p311 Y3.

UNLV presents classic drama and recent musicals during spring and autumn in its unappealing Judy Bayley Theater, but its most lively and interesting productions are often found in the Black Box, where the MFA stage-writing programme runs workshops on one-act plays by students and the faculty. The annual series of student one-acts, held in the Black Box in spring and autumn, is usually good for a gem or two; the quality of acting and directing can be surprisingly accomplished.

Dance companies

Las Vegas Civic Ballet

Reed Whipple Cultural Center, 821 Las Vegas Boulevard North, between Washington Street & Bonanza Road, North Las Vegas (229 6211). Bus 113. **Tickets** $5; $2-$3 concessions. **No credit cards. Map** p312 D1.

The city's ballet company has its own space at the Reed Whipple and remains one of the primary training grounds for aspiring young dancers before the lure of employment on the Strip becomes too strong to resist. Although the quality of productions varies, the LVCB takes risks and provides a valuable showcase for local choreographers.

Nevada Ballet Theater

Information 1651 Inner Circle Drive, Town Center Parkway, Summerlin (243 2623). **Tickets** up to $48. **Credit** AmEx, Disc, MC, V.

Associated with UNLV, the NBT is the city's only fully professional ballet company and tends towards classical works and certified crowd-pleasers, such as its recent hit adaptation of Bram Stoker's *Dracula* and its annual version of *The Nutcracker.* Shows are held at UNLV's Judy Bayley Theater.

UNLV Dance Theater

4505 S Maryland Parkway, between E Flamingo Road & Tropicana Avenue, University District (895 3827). Bus 109, 201, 202. **Tickets** $10; $8 concessions. **Credit** varies. **Map** p311 Y3.

Many devotees of dance consider the UNLV student dance department to be the best in town, particularly because of the many fine guest artists who come here from around the world. Both classical ballet and modern work are well represented in its productions, usually mounted at the Artemus W Ham Concert Hall or the Judy Bayley Theater.

Sport & Fitness

Step outside the casino for a different kind of gaming.

Las Vegas has made significant strides as a sporting destination, though the games inside the casinos will always be a bigger draw than anything with racquets and balls. The arrival of acclaimed new courses means Las Vegas rivals Arizona as the Southwest's top golf destination; there's a variety of watersports on Lake Mead, and plenty of hiking and biking trails in the beautiful landscapes surrounding the city. There are even winter games like skiing and snowboarding to be enjoyed on the slopes of nearby Mount Charleston.

Moreover, the newest casino-resorts have accentuated their role as elite holiday destinations with the creation of upmarket fitness facilities and luxury spas. They're ideal places to unwind, whether you're recovering from a long workout on the tennis court or the baccarat pit.

COPING WITH THE HEAT

Las Vegans say, 'It's a dry heat.' Tourists just say, 'Damn, it's hot!' During summer, the temperature outside will top 90°F (32°C) before breakfast and climb into triple digits by the afternoon. Even the locals stay inside between June and August, but that's no reason to limit your outdoor activities, as long as you take the proper precautions: wear a cap or some protection for your head, use sunblock (at least factor 15) and carry plenty of water.

Spectator sports

Las Vegas Mayor Oscar Goodman has set his sights on bringing a major professional sports team to the city before 2005. The locals are eager, but the owners of the basketball, football and baseball teams have expressed concern that players might be tempted to bet on (or against) their own team. The recent decision to allow wagering on UNLV basketball games may be a sign that things are changing. Still, all of the most prominent American sports are represented locally, through exhibition games, minor league teams and college teams.

And two or three times a year, the focus of the entire sporting world centres on Las Vegas for championship boxing (see p233 **Ringside**). With the rich and famous amassed in the first few rows, the audience is sometimes more interesting than the action in the ring.

American football

The **UNLV football** team plays at the **Sam Boyd Stadium** on Boulder Highway and Russell Road (895 3900), and in the shadow of the college's more prominent basketball team. However, the hiring of former National Football League coach John Robinson has re-energised the programme and support is picking up. The season runs from September to December. Tickets cost $12 to $20; there are usually plenty of good seats available.

Monday night pro football on network television is also an institution in a town built on betting. Nearly every drinking establishment – casino, neighbourhood pub, topless bar – offers big-screen viewing of the games.

Baseball

The **Las Vegas 51s** (formerly the Las Vegas Stars), the AAA farm team of the major league Los Angeles Dodgers, play their home games at **Cashman Field** (850 Las Vegas Boulevard North, at Washington Avenue) from April to September. The 12,000-seat stadium is rarely full, though the 51s have ranked among the most consistently successful teams in the Pacific Coast League. Try to go on a promotion night, when you might receive free merchandise or see a concert after the game. Call 386 7200 for tickets ($4-$7).

Basketball

From 1977, when they first made it to the Final Four, through to 1990, when they captured the national collegiate championship, the **UNLV Runnin' Rebels** men's basketball team were the hottest ticket in town. Since then, the team's fortunes have fluctuated wildly, a result of NCAA sanctions and the difficulty of keeping a head coach. Games are played at the **Thomas & Mack Center** on the UNLV campus (4505 Maryland Parkway; 895 3900/www.thomasand mack.com) from November to May. In October, NBA teams sometimes play exhibition games at the Thomas & Mack as well, but the tickets ($10-$25) disappear quickly.

UNLV's women's basketball team, the **Lady Rebels**, play at the new **Cox Pavilion** (895 0992/www.coxpavilion.com), which opened in

The rodeo hits town every December.

May 2001 next door to the Thomas & Mack Center. The team has been posting as many wins as the men in the past few seasons. Tickets are just $4; one of the cheapest ways in town to spend two hours.

Motor racing

Las Vegas Motor Speedway

7000 Las Vegas Boulevard North, North Las Vegas (644 4444/www.lvms.com). No bus. **Tickets** $50-$110. **Credit** AmEx, Disc, MC, V.
This 1,500-acre (607ha) motorsports entertainment complex holds up to 107,000 spectators and presents drag races, NASCAR events, short track races, motocross and a variety of other contests. The highlights of the local racing calendar are the annual Las Vegas 400, a Winston Cup event held in March and the NHRA's two drag racing events in April and October (for both, *see p182*).

Rodeo

Held every December, the **National Finals Rodeo** (*see p186*) is the sport's most prestigious event. Finalists compete in seven different events during the nine-day competition at the UNLV's **Thomas & Mack Center** (895 3900). Tickets cost $24 to $38, but they are hard to come by and can cost more from ticket touts. Cowboys from all over the United States converge on Las Vegas to attend, and to watch the superstars of country music perform on the Strip after the ridin' and ropin' is done.

Wrestling

Every year, Las Vegas hosts half a dozen or so **World Wrestling Federation** and **World Championship Wrestling** events. WCW's 'Halloween Havoc' is held every October at the MGM Grand; other event schedules vary: for details, you should check the local newspapers or the websites of the WWF (www.wwf.com) or WCW (www.wcwwrestling.com).

Active sports

The **All-American SportPark** (121 E Sunset Road, at Las Vegas Boulevard South, East of Strip; 369 9595) has all the sporting facilities imaginable for the wannabe jock: baseball batting cages, indoor rock climbing, putting green, go-kart race track, rollerskating and plenty of room to jog.
    At press time, however, the park was closed after a change of ownership; phone for up-to-date information.

Bowling

A number of neighbourhood casinos have good bowling alleys. Try **Castaways** (2800 Fremont Street; 385 9153), which has 106 lanes with automatic scoring and is open 24 hours. The 56-lane bowling facility at **Sam's Town** (5111 Boulder Highway; 454 8022) is also open all night. The 60 lanes at **Santa Fe Station** (4949 N Rancho Drive; 658 4995) feature Bowlervision, a system that tracks the speed and path of the ball from release until it strikes the pins. There are also 72 lanes at the **Gold Coast** (4000 W Flamingo Road; 367 4700) and 70 at the **Orleans** (4500 W Tropicana Avenue; 365 7400).

Bungee jumping

AJ Hackett Bungy

Circus Circus, 810 Circus Circus Drive, between Las Vegas Boulevard South & Industrial Road, West of Strip (385 4321). Bus 301, 302. **Open** 11am-8.30pm Mon-Fri; 11am-10.30pm Sat, Sun. **Rates** *First jump* $54-$79. **Credit** AmEx, Disc, MC, V. **Map** p315 B5.
Bungee jumpers leap from a steel tower 210ft (64m) above the Strip and drop with heart-stopping speed towards a sparkling pool. For your trouble, you get a T-shirt and certificate with your first jump.

Arts & Entertainment

Badlands golf course. *See p231.*

Cycling

Sure, you can ride a bike down the Strip, but it's not recommended. Distracted drivers in rented cars are a potential hazard to pedestrians and anyone using two-wheeled transport. Instead, head west on Charleston Boulevard to **Escape the City Streets** to rent a bike and then pedal on to the scenic drive through the **Red Rock Canyon National Conservation Area** (*see p249*). Also within reach are the wide, marked bike lanes of the sparkly new corporate-planned town of **Summerlin**; Pueblo Park at the north end of Rampart Boulevard has several miles of paved paths that are separated from the traffic.

Other popular routes include the eight-mile (13-kilometre) off-road **Cottonwood Valley Loop** near Red Rock: head west from town on Highway 160 and look for a dirt road 5.9 miles (9.5 kilometres) past the junction with Highway 159. The **River Mountain Peak** is a ten-mile (16-kilometre) route between Vegas and Henderson. To get to the head of the trail, drive along I-93/95 to Equestrian Drive, turning east.

An unofficial mountain bike trail exists at the north-west corner of Tropicana Avenue and Decatur Boulevard. This challenging and well-worn trail runs through one of the few undeveloped parcels of land in the urban area – power your bike up and down steep standstone formations and across a natural wash. Though used often by local gearheads, it is unsanctioned, so bike safely.

Escape the City Streets

Unit 101, 8221 W Charleston Boulevard, between Buffalo & Durango Drives, North-west Las Vegas (596 2953/www.escapeadventures.com). Bus 205, 206. **Open** 10am-6pm Mon-Fri; 9am-5pm Sat, Sun. **Rates** *Bike hire* from $26 per day. **Credit** AmEx, Disc, MC, V.

Located en route to Red Rock Canyon, this outfit conducts various road and off-road tours in Red Rock or will provide bikes, maps and supplies if you'd rather go it alone. Items for rent include road bikes, mountain bikes, tandems and children's trailers, and it also offers guided bike tours to the national parks of Utah, Arizona and California.

Disc golf

Disc golf is golf played with a flying disc a little smaller than a traditional Frisbee and made from a softer, heavier rubber. Players must toss the disc into 'holes' – actually above-ground containers on poles. The valley's best disc golf course, located in **Sunset Park** (2601 E Sunset Road, at Eastern Avenue, East Las Vegas; 455 8200), has 18 holes and is open from 7am to 11pm daily. Admission is free, but the park gets very crowded, so try to play during the week.

Fishing

There's superb fishing year round at **Lake Mead** (*see p247*). The lake is stocked with half a million rainbow trout every year, and there are also excellent stocks of black and striped bass, some as big as 50 pounds (23 kilograms). Head for the upper Overton Arm of the lake for crappie, blue gill, green sunfish and catfish. To fish from the Nevada shore, you'll need a Nevada fishing licence ($15, plus $4 per extra day); to fish from a boat, you'll need a licence from Nevada and a special-use stamp from Arizona (the two states share jurisdiction over the lake); note that you can't fish within harbour areas.

Lake Mohave, further to the south (*see p253*), is a good spot for rainbow trout, especially in its upper reaches in Black Canyon and at the Willow Beach just south of the Hoover Dam. (Note that an extra stamp is required for trout fishing.) Katharine Landing, a couple of miles north of Davis Dam on the Arizona side is the best place from which to plunder the lake's huge striped bass.

You can also fish within the city at **Lorenzi Park** (Rancho Road, at Washington Avenue, North-west Las Vegas) at **Sunset Park** (Sunset Road, at Eastern Avenue, East Las Vegas) and at pretty **Floyd Lamb State Park** (*see p252*). For more information contact the **Nevada Division of Wildlife**

(4747 Vegas Drive, Las Vegas, NV89108; 486 5127/www.state.nv.us/cnr/nvwildlife), check at a ranger station for the current hot fishing spots or consult **Fish-Inc** (1500 Palomino Drive, Henderson; 565 8396) or **Karen Jones Fishing Guide Service** (1018 Cutter Street, Henderson; 566 5775).

Golf

Las Vegas has about half the golf courses it needs to meet the demand, but the addition of several new courses in the past few years have improved visitors' odds of getting a tee time without booking months in advance. You'd still be advised to call up to two weeks before your visit and you should expect to pay $100 or more per round on any of the better courses. If you can stand the desert heat, some places offer discounts on July and August afternoons. **Las Vegas Preferred Tee-Times** (1-888 368 7833) will make reservations for you at a number of courses in the area, most of which are open from 7am to dusk.

Further afield, try the two courses surrounded by unspoilt desert scenery at the **Las Vegas Paiute Resort**, north-west of the city (10325 Nu-Wav Kaiv Boulevard, at US 95; 658 1400/www.lvpaiutegolf.com). The Pete Dye-designed courses have earned rave reviews from *Golf Digest*. Rates are $145 during the week, $160 at weekends. Golfers heading south into California can stop off at the challenging Lakes Course at **Primm Valley** (I-15 south, exit Yates Well Road; 679 5510). Rates are $130 during the week, $160 at the weekends, with discounts for guests of Primm Properties, MGM Grand and New York-New York.

For information on the PGA Invesys Classic tournament, *see p186*.

Badlands

9119 Alta Drive, at Rampart Drive, South-west Las Vegas (363 0754/www.americangolf.com). Bus 211. **Rates** $140 Mon-Thur; $205 Fri-Sun. **Credit** AmEx, Disc, MC, V.

This target layout designed by Johnny Miller is one of the most unforgiving tracks in Las Vegas. Failure to hit the ball straight will lead to an up-close-and-personal experience with one of many washes, arroyos and canyons. Championship; 6,926yds; par 72.

Bali Hai Golf Club

5160 Las Vegas Boulevard South, adjacent to Mandalay Bay (450 8000). Bus 301, 302. **Rates** $250 Mon-Thur; $295 Fri-Sun. **Credit** AmEx, Disc, MC, V. **Map** p316 A9.

Designed by Lee Schmidt and Brian Curley as a South Pacific-style hideaway, this challenging track features seven acres of water, 2,500 palm trees, Augusta white sand and more than 100,000

tropical plants and flowers. Black volcanic rock outcroppings endanger any shot that strays from the fairway. Championship; 7,015yds; par 72.

Desert Pines Golf Club

3415 E Bonanza Road, at Pecos Road, North Las Vegas (366 1616). Bus 111, 215. **Rates** $135 Mon-Thur; $165 Fri-Sun. **Credit** AmEx, MC, V. **Map** p311 Z1.

Voted one of the best public courses in the US by *Golf Digest* magazine, Desert Pines' tight, challenging layout has narrow, tree-lined fairways and nine holes on water. The practice facility is the best in Las Vegas. Championship; 6,810yds; par 71.

Highland Falls

10201 Sun City Boulevard, at Lake Mead Boulevard, North-west Las Vegas (254 7010). Bus 210. **Rates** *Winter* $101 before 1pm; $59 after 1pm. *Summer* rates vary. **Credit** AmEx, Disc, MC, V.

A narrow layout that favours the sand player. Large, imposing traps mean that a bit of wedge wizardry might be the difference between par and double bogie. A well-maintained, reasonably priced 18-hole course that hasn't been discovered by most locals... yet. Championship; 6,512yds; par 72.

Las Vegas Golf Club

4300 W Washington Avenue, between Valley View & Decatur Boulevards, North Las Vegas (646 3003). Bus 103, 208. **Rates** $16.75; $25.75 with cart. **Credit** AmEx, DC, Disc, MC, V.

The 'Municipal' is a bargain, with extra discounts for seniors. It's a good beginners' course, with wide fairways and large greens and it's well maintained considering how much play it receives. Pack a lunch, as it's busy from sunrise to sunset and you may be there all day. Championship; 6,631yds; par 72.

Rhodes Ranch

9020 Rhodes Ranch Parkway, at Durango Drive, South-west Las Vegas (740 4114). No Bus. **Rates** $130 Mon-Thur; $160 Fri-Sun. **Credit** AmEx, MC, V.

One of the better and more scenic courses built around a residential community, Rhodes Ranch provides a challenge to players of every skill level. Ted Robinson design features mounding fairways, waterfalls and numerous bunkers. Championship; 6,860yds; par 72.

Royal Links Golf Club

5995 E Vegas Valley Drive, East Las Vegas (450 8123). **Rates** $225 Mon-Thur; $275 Fri-Sun. **Credit** AmEx, Disc, MC, V.

This unique, one-of-a-kind layout re-creates the best of the links-style holes from the British Open courses. It ranked among *Golf Magazine*'s top ten new courses in 1999, but it's an expensive place to play. Championship; 7,029yds; par 72.

Hiking

For information on the best hiking areas near Las Vegas, *see chapter* **Day Trips**.

Arts & Entertainment

Desert Rock Sports. *See p233.*

Sierra Club

PO Box 19777, Las Vegas, NV 89132 (recorded information 363 3267/membership 735 9144/ www.sierraclub.org).
The grandaddy of environmental outfits, the Sierra Club organises regular guided hikes (open to non-members) in Red Rock Canyon, Mount Charleston and the Lake Mead area. Call for information on upcoming hikes, monthly meetings and membership.

Horse riding

Cowboy Trail Rides

Suite 204, 800 N Rainbow Boulevard, North-west Las Vegas, NV 89107 (387 2457/www.cowboytrail rides.com). No bus. **Open** 9am-5pm daily. **Credit** AmEx, Disc, MC, V.
Ride a genuine mustang on rustic mountain trails through Red Rock Canyon. The most popular rides are the Sunset BBQ ride ($139 per person) and the two-hour Rim Canyon Ride ($89). All rides are accompanied by a cowboy guide, and first-time riders are welcome. Booking is advisable.

Hunting & shooting

Call the **Nevada Department of Wildlife** (486 5127/www.state.nv.us/cnr/nvwildlife) for information on hunting dove and quail, and waterfowl in the Lake Mead area. Limited deer hunting is also available. Special seasons are scheduled for elk, antelope and bighorn sheep. The **American Shooters Supply & Gun Club** (3440 Arville Street, between W Desert Inn & Spring Mountain Roads; 362 1223) has the only 50-yard (45-metre) indoor shooting range in Las Vegas. A hunting licence for non-residents is $111. The **Las Vegas Gun Club** (9200 Tule Springs Road, behind Floyd Lamb State Park; 645 5606) has an outdoor range, where scenes from *Viva Las Vegas* were filmed.

Ice-skating

Santa Fe Station Ice Arena

Santa Fe Station, 4949 N Rancho Drive, at Lone Mountain Road, North-west Las Vegas (658 4991). Bus 106. **Open** noon-2pm Mon, Wed; 3-5pm Tue, Thur; noon-2pm, 8pm-midnight Fri; 2-4pm, 8pm-midnight Sat; 2-4pm Sun. **Admission** $5; $4 concessions; $1.50 skate rental. **Credit** AmEx, DC, Disc, MC, V.
Chill out at Las Vegas's refreshing ice arena, which offers rentals for public ice-skating throughout the year as well as hockey leagues and lessons for kids.

Pool & billiards

Pink E's

3695 W Flamingo Road, at Valley View Boulevard, West of Strip (252 4666). Bus 202. **Open** 24hrs daily. **Cost** free-$3. **Credit** AmEx, MC, V.
Map p311 X3.
A bright, colourful spot with a café, dancing and 50 pool tables (with pink playing surfaces). No under-21s are allowed.

Rafting

Black Canyon River Raft Tours

1-800 696 7238/293 3776/www.rafts.com. **Rates** *River tour* $69.95 per person or $94.95 with hotel pick-up. **Credit** Disc, MC, V.
One-day guided raft trips along the Colorado River, from just below the Hoover Dam to Willow Beach, through a waterfall and hot springs. There are a few splashes along the way, but no rapids. Based in Boulder City, the company will pick up groups from most Las Vegas hotels, and lunch is usually included. Similar trips are offered by **Down River Outfitters** (1-800 748 3702/293 1190).

Rock climbing

The outstanding rock climbing opportunities around Las Vegas are one of the area's most under-publicised attractions. In particular, **Red Rock Canyon** (*see p249*) offers some of the best year-round climbing in the States. The best guide to routes is *Red Rock Select* by Todd Swain (Chockstone Press; $25). Call the visitor centre (363 1921) for information on climbing regulations and stop off at **Desert Rock Sports** (*see p179*) en route to the park, for climbing, backpacking and camping equipment, and some practice on the excellent huge indoor climbing wall. There are a number of other indoor climbing walls in the city itself, including one at **GameWorks** (*see p105*).

Sky's the Limit

1270 Calico Drive, off W Charleston Boulevard, Red Rock Canyon National Conservation Area (1-800 733 7597/363 4533/www.skysthelimit.com). No bus. **Open** *Office 9am-5pm Mon-Fri.* **Rates** from $189. **Credit** AmEx, Disc, MC, V.
This is the best outfit for beginners' climbing courses as well as guided scrambles, technical climbs and advanced alpine courses. Transport from the city can be arranged.

Sky's the Limit Climbing Center

Suite 4, 3065 E Patrick Lane, at McLeod Drive, East Las Vegas (363 4533/www.skysthelimit.com). Bus 111, 212. **Open** noon-10pm Mon-Fri; 11am-10pm Sat; 11am-8pm Sun. **Rates** $12 per day; equipment $8; lesson $25-$55. **Credit** Disc, MC, V. **Map** p311 Z4.
Indoor training facility with specially designed climbing walls and professional instructors.

Scuba & skin diving

Scuba divers should head to **Lake Mead** (*see p247*), where visibility averages 30 feet (nine metres) and can reach up to 60 feet (18 metres) in winter. There are some unusual underwater sights, including plenty of boat wrecks and Hoover Dam's asphalt factory. The most popular diving area is **Scuba Park**, adjacent to Lake Mead marina.

American Cactus Divers

Annie Oakley Plaza, 3985B E Sunset Road, at Annie Oakley Drive, Henderson (433 3483). Bus 114, 212. **Open** 9am-6pm Mon-Fri; 9am-4pm Sat, Sun. **Rates** *Beach dives $35. Equipment rental $37 per day.* **Credit** AmEx, Disc, MC, V.

Ringside

No other city in the world is more closely associated with boxing than Las Vegas, and it's a relationship that makes perfect sense: both the sport and the city embrace winners and detest losers; both have ardent followings among the richest of the rich and the poorest of the poor, and both present action that is exciting and dangerous, while trying to shake off a seedy reputation.

Las Vegas evolved into a boxing mecca primarily because fight fans like to bet on who's going to win, and for years Vegas was the only place they could do that (legally, anyway). Since 1960, the city has played host to some of the most celebrated – not to mention the most bizarre – boxing events in the sport's history.

Muhammad Ali held numerous title defences at Caesars Palace, which for decades was to boxing what St Andrews or Pebble Beach is to golf. The legendary battles between Sugar Ray Leonard and both Thomas Hearns and 'Marvellous' Marvin Hagler took place at Caesars and the Mirage; fans may recall the fight in which a man in a home-made glider crash-landed into the centre of the ring. And it was in Las Vegas that Mike Tyson rose to prominence as the most dominant heavyweight since Ali. His most difficult challenger proved to be the Nevada Boxing Commission, which got rather upset when the boxer began dining on his opponent Evander Holyfield's ear during that infamous fight in 1997 (*pictured*).

Heavyweight and middleweight boxing championship bouts are usually held at Caesars Palace, the MGM Grand or Mandalay Bay. Ringside seats can cost as much as $1,500; the 'cheap' seats fall into the $100 to $200 range, depending on the event and venue. Order well in advance through the hotel or from TicketMaster (474 4000).

Non-title fights, and title bouts in the flyweight, bantamweight and other divisions, also take place in Las Vegas, at smaller venues such as Texas Station. The tickets are a little cheaper, but not much. Some boxers also open their workout and training sessions to the public free of charge; for information you should contact the hotel that is hosting the fight.

Blue Seas Scuba Center

4661 Spring Mountain Road, between Arville Street & Decatur Boulevard, South-west Las Vegas (1-800 245 2036/367 2822). Bus 203. **Open** 11am-7pm Mon-Fri; 9am-5pm Sat; noon-5pm Sun. **Rates** *Equipment rental* $35-$70 per day. **Credit** AmEx, Disc, MC, V.

Desert Divers Supply

5720 E Charleston Boulevard, at Nellis Boulevard, East Las Vegas (438 1000). Bus 115, 206. **Open** 10am-7pm Mon-Fri; 8am-6pm Sat, Sun. **Rates** *Equipment rental* $35 per day. **Credit** AmEx, Disc, MC, V.

Snow sports

Visitors might feel odd packing their skis for the desert, but there are two first-class skiing areas within day-trip distance of the city. The ski season is usually from November to April.

Just 47 miles (75km) from downtown Las Vegas, the **Las Vegas Ski & Snowboard Resort** (645 2754/snow conditions 593 9500/www.skilasvegas.com) at Mount Charleston's Lee Canyon offers slope action for all abilities – including a half-pipe and terrain park – and snow-making equipment in case nothing falls the old-fashioned way. Lift passes cost $28 per day. Sledding, snowmobiling and cross-country skiing are available further down the mountain. There's a free bus from town and the day lodge (open 7am-4pm daily) has a ski school, rental shop, coffeeshop and cocktail lounge. Night skiing is available on Saturdays (4-10pm). For more on Mount Charleston, *see p250*.

A three-hour drive from Vegas on the I-15 and Highway 145 is the **Brian Head Ski Resort** in Utah (454 7669/www.brianhead.com). The resort offers terrific skiing on two peaks – a total of 53 trails in all – and plenty of accommodation if you want to stay the night. Lift passes are $38. **Escape the City Streets** (*see p230*) runs buses from Las Vegas to Brian Head on Wednesdays and Saturdays.

Swimming

In summer, overheated visitors and locals flock to **Wet 'n Wild**, one of the best water parks in the US. In addition, almost every hotel and motel in Las Vegas has a swimming pool, which is fortunate, since most of the city's public pools are located in neighbourhoods that tourists would prefer not to visit. Despite the balmy evening temperatures between April and October, the majority of resort pools close at twilight; casino bosses would rather have their guests in the casino than lounging poolside. The pools are for hotel guests only: although you can sometimes just wander in, you'll need

Splash out at **Wet 'n Wild**.

to show a room key to receive a towel and a cushion for the lounge chairs. Many are worth a peek even if you've left your cossie at home: the **Caesars Palace** pool area is as opulent as a Roman villa; the **MGM Grand**'s pools look big enough to float an ocean liner; and the **Rio**'s pool has a sandy beach for volleyball. **Mandalay Bay**'s fantastic pool complex comes complete with fake beach, wave machine, lazy river and zillions of palm trees.

Wet 'n Wild

2601 Las Vegas Boulevard South, between Sahara Avenue & Convention Center Drive (737 3819). Bus 204, 301, 302. **Open** *June, July* 10am-8pm daily. *May, Aug, Sept* 10am-6pm daily. Closed Oct-Apr. **Admission** $25.95 visitors over 4ft (1.22m); $19.95 visitors under 4ft (1.22m); free under-2s. **Credit** AmEx, MC, V. **Map** p315 C4.
In summer, this 26-acre (10.5ha) water park is the coolest place on the Strip. There are thrilling water flumes and hydrotubes for the X-treme generation, a water play area for young kids and wave pools for everyone. Challenge the monster wave-making machine, take a plunge down the world's tallest waterslide or just try to cope with the hordes of teenagers, who inevitably overrun the place during school holidays. Or spread a blanket on the picnic area at the rear and escape the crowds.

Tennis

Some hotels have tennis courts that are open to the public, though hotel guests receive priority. These include **Bally's** (ten courts, six lighted), the **Flamingo** (four lighted courts), and the **Monte Carlo** (four lighted courts). You can also play for $5 on **UNLV**'s 12 lighted courts (4505 S Maryland Parkway; 895 4489), or for free at **Paradise Park** (4770 S Harrison Drive; 455 7513) and **Sunset Park** (2601 E Sunset Road, at Eastern Avenue; 260 9803). Other tennis facilites are available at the city's sport centres – *see p235*.

Water-skiing

Expansive **Lake Mead** (*see p247*) offers great water-skiing opportunities. You can hire boats and equipment from most marinas or join a charter trip.

Tom's Water Sports

Information 400 Sebastian Avenue, Henderson,
NV 89015 (558 0678/www.tomswatersports.com).
Rates (for groups of 2-6) $445 for 4hrs; $695 for 7hrs.
Credit Disc, MC, V.
From April to October, Tom's Water Sports rents
equipment, organises trips to Lake Mead and offers
lessons in water-skiing, wakeboarding and tubing.
Trips are arranged on demand in winter.

Health & fitness

Gyms & sports centres

24 Hour Fitness

2605 S Eastern Avenue, at E Sahara Avenue, East
Las Vegas (641 2222). Bus 110, 204. **Open** 24hrs
daily. **Rates** $10 day; $25 week. **Credit** AmEx, MC,
V. **Map** p311 Z2.
Feel the urge to pump some iron at 2am? Then 24
Hour Fitness is the place.
Branches: throughout the city.

Gold's Gym

Gold's Plaza, 3750 E Flamingo Road, at Sandhill
Road, East Las Vegas (451 4222). Bus 202. **Open**
24hrs daily. **Rates** $10 day; $35 week; $50 month.
Credit AmEx, MC, V. **Map** p311 Z3.
Touted as a no-frills gym, Gold's offers all the aero-
bics classes, free weights, weight machines and
cardio equipment an exercise buff could handle.
Branches: throughout the city.

Las Vegas Athletic Club

2655 Maryland Parkway, at Karen Avenue, East
Las Vegas (734 5822). Bus 109. **Open** 24hrs daily.
Rates $10 day; $25 week. **Credit** AmEx, Disc, MC,
V. **Map** p311 Y2.
Five locations throughout Las Vegas, each with
swimming pools, saunas, jacuzzis, racquetball
courts, Nautilus, free weights and more than 200
weekly aerobics classes, including dance, step and
cardio. This is the only 24-hour branch.
Branches: throughout the city.

Las Vegas Sporting House

3025 S Industrial Road, between Circus Circus Drive
& Stardust Drive, West of Strip (733 8999). Bus
105. **Open** 24hrs daily. **Rates** $15 day; $50 week.
Credit AmEx, Disc, MC, V. **Map** p315 A5.
Located just west of the Strip, directly behind the
Stardust, the Sporting House offers aerobics, ten
racquetball courts, two tennis courts, indoor and
outdoor swimming pools, basketball, personal
training, yoga, t'ai chi and a restaurant.

Spas & health clubs

A few hours at a health spa can seem like a
vacation within a vacation. Many hotels,
including Bally's, Caesars Palace, the MGM
Grand, the Tropicana and the Mirage, have
health club facilities that are free to guests and

open to the public for a fee. Others, such as the
Venetian, have on-site independent spas that
can be enjoyed separately to the resort. Several
of the facilities rival the best in Palm Springs
and Scottsdale, and offer a variety of massage
therapies (Swedish, shiatsu, aromatherapy) and
skin-care programmes (loofah, exfoliation), plus
a sauna, steam room, whirlpool and fitness
rooms. The spas listed below have mixed
fitness facilities and beauty salons, but single-
sex steam rooms, saunas and jacuzzis.
Reservations are advised.

Bellagio Spa

Bellagio, 3600 Las Vegas Boulevard South, at
W Flamingo Road (693 8080). Bus 202, 301, 302.
Open 6am-8pm daily. **Rates** $25. **Credit** AmEx,
Disc, MC, V. **Map** p316 A7.
This classy spa offers personal training and pam-
pering delights (massages, facials and body wraps)
in a deluxe Mediterranean-style environment – but
it's open only to guests of MGM-Mirage Resorts.

Canyon Ranch Spa Club

Venetian, 3355 Las Vegas Boulevard South, at
Sands Avenue (414 3600). Bus 203, 301, 302.
Open 5.30am-10pm daily. **Rates** $25. **Credit** AmEx,
Disc, MC, V. **Map** p316 A6.
At 64,000sq ft (5,950sq m), Canyon Ranch is one of
the largest spa and fitness centres in the city, with
24 treatment rooms, classes and a climbing wall.
Aromatherapy treatments are a speciality.

Four Seasons Health Club & Spa

Four Seasons, 3950 Las Vegas Boulevard South,
at Russell Road (632 5000). Bus 301, 302. **Open**
6am-9pm daily. **Rates** free guests; free with
treatment non-guests. **Credit** AmEx, Disc, MC, V.
Map p316 A9.
Like the small but exclusively intimate Four Seasons
Hotel itself, this spa offers its guests personal attention and expert service. The best part: staff leave a
15-minute interlude between every appointment so
you won't be rushed off after your relaxing massage.

Grand Spa

MGM Grand, 3799 Las Vegas Boulevard South, at
E Tropicana Avenue (891 3077). Bus 201, 301, 302.
Open 6am-8pm daily. **Rates** $20 guests; $25 non-
guests (Mon-Thur only). **Credit** AmEx, Disc, MC, V.
Map p316 A8.
Renovated in 1998, this 30,000sq ft (2,790sq m) spa
features state-of-the-art equipment, 30 massage
treatment rooms and two suites for couples.

Paris Spa by Mandara

Paris, 3655 Las Vegas Boulevard South, between
Harmon Avenue & E Flamingo Road (946 7000).
Bus 202, 301, 302. **Open** 6am-9pm daily. **Rates**
free guests; free with treatment non-guests. **Credit**
AmEx, Disc, MC, V. **Map** p316 A7.
The European-style Paris Spa creates a tranquil
environment for its guests. Massage therapies, inno-
vative skin-care and body treatments are available.

Arts & Entertainment

Weddings

Elvis-impersonators, singing gondoliers and bungee-jumping brides: anything is possible when you tie the knot in Vegas.

For impetuous couples or those who scoff at tradition, Las Vegas is the perfect place for a quick and easy wedding. In fact, recent statistics show that 116,000 marriages took place in Las Vegas in 2000; that's an average of about 2,230 a week. And each year on Valentine's Day alone, nearly 3,000 couples choose to tie the knot in the city.

Nevada's role as the 'State of Matrimony' dates back to about 1912. That was the year California passed its Gin Law, which required couples to wait a whopping three days after obtaining a marriage licence before exchanging vows. It was designed to prevent inebriated couples from marrying under the influence. Nevada, however, decided to be more lenient, and drunken lovey-dovey couples could come to the state and get married almost instantly.

In the 1920s and '30s, a lot of out-of-staters drove into Nevada to take advantage of the state's relaxed laws, which also extended to divorce. In 1931, an unhappy spouse could get a divorce after residing in Nevada for just six weeks and then marry someone else right away – sometimes ten minutes after the divorce had been finalised.

The marriage industry truly came of age in the early 1940s, however, when large numbers of GIs wanted speedy, no-fuss weddings before being sent abroad – that's when the idea of the dedicated wedding chapel was born. Since then, the Las Vegas marriage business has never looked back. As more and more people flock to the city to get hitched, so the number of chapels has increased from around a dozen in the 1970s, to more than 50 today.

YOU'VE GAMBLED ONCE...

The big casinos provided another boost to the business by jumping on the wedding bandwagon. Initially, casinos were rather sniffy about the marriage game (where's the sense in taking out 50 slots to make room for a chapel?), but, since the late 1980s, they got wise. What's the most popular post-nuptial activity in Vegas? You've guessed it – gambling. And if you marry in a casino, you'll probably gamble away your honeymoon in the same casino. So, in came the chapels, often more elaborate than the little stand-alones, but rarely more tasteful (and always more expensive).

A Roman wedding at **Caesars Palace**.

Getting spliced in a casino chapel gives couples the chance to taste the sort of luxury that usually only serious high-rollers enjoy. Many casinos provide elaborate honeymoon suites, while the newer mega-resorts capitalise on their meticulously detailed theme elements to customise the wedding ceremony (it's a uniquely Las Vegas mix of the classy and the offbeat to be married in a gondola on the Venetian's faux Grand Canal). Few things are as surreal as seeing a bride, clad in white lace and a veil, trying her luck at a video poker machine, high-heeled shoes in hand.

REQUIREMENTS

The straightforward, liberal marriage laws in Nevada are the main reason for the popularity of Las Vegan weddings: the requirements are the same for US and non-US citizens; no blood tests are needed and there's no waiting period between obtaining the licence and exchanging vows. All that is necessary is for both parties to present themselves at the **Clark County Marriage License Bureau** at first floor, 200 S Third Street (455 3156/outside office hours 455 4415; open 8am-midnight Mon-Thur, Sun; 24hrs Fri, Sat and holidays) with some form of picture ID (a passport, for instance) and $35 in cash for the marriage licence. The bureau will even accept traveller's cheques. No appointment is necessary and the whole process shouldn't take longer than ten minutes. However, if you want to think it over first, the licence is good for up to one year and can be used to be married anywhere in the state.

Couples from outside the United States who are married in Las Vegas may have to contend with extra paperwork to ensure the marriage is acknowledged in their home countries. Most countries want a certified copy of your marriage certificate ($7) and an Apostille ($20) from the Nevada Secretary of State, which can be sent directly to your government.

TRAD OR TRASH?

Anything goes in Vegas – if you've got the money to pay for it. Want Elvis to serenade you in the chapel? Fancy dressing like an ancient Roman to get spliced? Want to bungee jump to your destiny? You got it. The terminally lazy can even get married without setting foot outside their car at a drive-up wedding, courtesy of **A Special Memory Wedding Chapel** (384 3332/www.aspecialmemory.com). Or, to really start your married life on a high, **Las Vegas Helicopters** (736 0013/www.lv helicopters.com) charges $249-$449 plus $50 minister's fees for a wedding above the Strip.

Yet here is one of Vegas's many paradoxes. More and more couples are rejecting the wacky and tacky, and wearing white wedding dresses rather than purple togas; walking down the aisle to Pachelbel rather than Billy Idol. Most brides and grooms want to buy into the Vegas dream only up to a point; to get a whiff of the glitz without losing all touch with middle-American reality. As one wedding co-ordinator notes, the words 'Las Vegas' alone are often enough to impart the needed nuptial pizzazz.

And here's a second paradox: easy, cheap and fast as a Nevadan marriage is, relatively few Las Vegas weddings are what-the-hell, on-a-whim affairs. The great majority of couples are from other states or abroad; they plan their weddings in advance and shell out large sums for air fares and accommodation. Few of their weddings end up either cheap or quick. Again, it's that vicarious Vegas vibe that pulls them in – the thrill of following famous couples such as Priscilla and Elvis, Demi and Bruce, Cindy and Richard (*see p239* **Celebrity splicings**); the feeling of getting married in Disneyland.

WHAT WILL IT COST?

Getting married in Las Vegas is not only easy and fast, but it can be relatively cheap, too, as long as you don't want all the trimmings. If a

quick service with the **Commissioner of Civil Marriages** suffices, $35 is all you need fork out. It's a one-block walk from the Clark County Marriage License Bureau to reach the Commissioner at the Clark County Court House, 309 S Third Street (open 8am-midnight Mon-Thur, Sun and 24 hours Fri, Sat and holidays) for an instant civil ceremony.

Chapel services cost more. The most basic ten-minute, in-and-out ceremony will cost upwards of $125 including the licence. Legally, all weddings must be witnessed, but chapels will normally supply a witness without charge.

Most chapels offer various levels of inclusive package (subject to a number of extra costs), and may also obtain the licence, if necessary. At the most basic end, expect to pay $50-$60 for use of the chapel, pre-recorded music (you can usually bring your own if you object to Mendelssohn) and, perhaps, a wedding scroll. Add in photographs (typically, six to 12 prints), a bouquet and a buttonhole, and the cost rises to $100-$200; a video recording and a limo will bump it up to at least $250. At the pricier end of the scale, it pays to shop around – there's a lot of variation between chapels. Extras are also available à la carte: expect to pay a minimum of $99 for gown hire, $55 for tuxedo hire, $25 for a bouquet, $5 for a buttonhole. Be warned: most chapels reserve the right to provide all professional services themselves (including photos, flowers and video recording).

HIDDEN EXTRAS

Only qualified ministers can officiate at wedding chapel services and, because they are rarely employees of the chapel, a 'donation' of at least $50 will be expected (to be handed over discreetly after the service) on top of the chapel fee. If you want the minister to come to you, then expect to pay more. If you splash out on a limo, it's usual to tip the driver upwards of $25. Read between the lines when comparing the deals offered by chapels. For instance, all will provide a professional photographer on request, but few will let you take the negatives away; the idea being that you come back to the chapel (and pay extra) for further prints. In fact, you will likely receive a letter at your first anniversary with forms for ordering more photos and then, in a couple of years, you'll get a notice offering you a chance to buy your negatives before they are destroyed. All chapel packages are also subject to sales tax.

BREAKING UP IS EASY TO DO

And if it does all turn out to have been a horrible mistake, the flip side is that divorce couldn't be easier: minimal costs, a six-week

Arts & Entertainment

residency – easy come, easy go. An uncontested divorce can cost as little as $147, which is a good job, since you've got six weeks to gamble away the rest of the divorce settlement.

The rest of the US, while getting a guilty kick out of Nevadan naughtiness, has never really been comfortable with such basically un-American values. Many states are now considering legislation to introduce 'covenant marriages' whereby couples agree to have pre-marital counselling to assess whether they really are doing the right thing. It's highly unlikely that Nevada, the land of immediate gratification and to hell with the consequences, will follow suit, particularly since a decent chunk of the state's tourism revenue is generated by the marriage business.

Where to wed

Las Vegas is the wedding chapel capital of the world. It's not the only place in the US where you'll find these nuptial equivalents of fast-food joints (seems like a great idea beforehand, leaves you feeling queasy afterwards), but nowhere has spawned chapels in such number and nowhere has that special glitzy Vegas cachet. Yet, while a few, like the **Little Church of the West** (built in 1942 and the oldest building on the Strip), are picturesque, most are small, tacky and decidedly unromantic, with all the atmosphere of a tarted-up garden shed.

The experience also tends to be on the impersonal side, with the minister – who has already officiated at a dozen hitchings before yours – pausing to glance at his script every time the service requires him to mention your name. And most chapels are located in the less than salubrious section of the Strip between Circus Circus and Fremont Street, amid pawn and porn shops. Perhaps their biggest advantage, then, is the relatively low cost; if your budget is tight, you'll be able to get hitched for as little $100.

Las Vegas's wedding business has learned to market itself as aggressively as any other industry. Look in the Yellow Pages in Pigswill, Iowa, and most of the wedding chapels listed will be located in Las Vegas. Scour the Internet and you'll find most chapels have their own websites: some of them even offer a live Internet broadcast of your ceremony so family and friends who are unable to attend can still watch the special moment. And it's not only naive first-timers who want a piece of the action; Las Vegas's quickie wedding chapels have become such a big attraction that many married couples return to the city to renew their vows. In fact, renewals now account for nearly a quarter of the ceremonies performed.

Casino weddings

Bellagio Wedding Chapels

Bellagio, 3600 Las Vegas Boulevard South, at W Flamingo Road, NV 89117 (1-888 987 3344/693 7700/www.bellagio.com). Bus 202, 301, 302. **Open** 8am-7pm daily. **Credit** AmEx, DC, Disc, MC, V. **Map** p316 A7.

There are no Elvis impersonators at this elegant resort; instead, Bellagio promises a lavish $30,000 wedding at a fraction of the price (although at $1,500 and $2,500, they're still among the most costly in the business). The wedding area is done up in peach, with antiques, draperies and chandeliers, and the co-ordinator can supply all the flowers, photography and special touches you need.

The Chapel

Monte Carlo, 3770 Las Vegas Boulevard South, at Rue de Monte Carlo, between W Flamingo Road & W Tropicana Avenue, NV 89109 (1-800 822 8651/ 730 7575/www.monte-carlo.com). Bus 201, 301, 302. **Open** 10.30am-7.30pm Mon-Fri, or by appointment. **Credit** AmEx, Disc, MC, V. **Map** p316 A8.

The Monte Carlo's four reasonably priced wedding packages ($220-$995) entitle the lucky couple to a pleasant ceremony, with all the trimmings, in a French-Victorian chapel complete with hand-painted murals. This isn't Bellagio, with its $1.6 billion in appointments, but for those without Bellagio-style dollars, it's a fine substitute.

Graceland: for Elvis fans. *See p239.*

Celebrity splicings

Celebrities have eloped to Las Vegas for decades because of the ease and privacy of a wedding there. Some of the most famous unions have included Paul Newman and Joanne Woodward (El Rancho, 1958), Errol Flynn and Beverley Adland (Silver Bell Chapel, 1962), Jane Fonda and Roger Vadim (Dunes, 1965), Elvis Presley and Priscilla Beaulieu (Aladdin, 1967), Joan Collins and Peter Holm (Little White Chapel, 1985), Bruce Willis and Demi Moore (Little White Chapel, 1987), Cindy Crawford and Richard Gere (Little Church of the West, 1992), Noel Gallagher and Meg Matthews (Little Church of the West, 1997), Dennis Rodman and Carmen Electra (Little Chapel of the Flowers, 1999), Billy Bob Thornton and Angelina Jolie (Little Church of the West, 2000) and Chris Evans and Billie Piper (Little Church of the West, 2001).

Mickey Rooney has, perhaps, enjoyed the chapels a little too much. He married Ava Gardner at Little Church of the West in 1942, and proceeded to visit the church on seven more occasions, each time with a different blushing bride: Betty Jane Rase (1944), Martha Vickers (1948), Elaine Mahnken (1952), Barbara Ann Thompson (1958), Marge Lane (1967), Carolyn Hockett (1969) and January Chamberlin (1978).

Chapelle du Jardin/ Chapelle du Paradis

Paris-Las Vegas, 3655 Las Vegas Boulevard South, between Harmon Avenue & E Flamingo Road, NV 89109 (1-877 796 2096/946 4060/www.paris lasvegas.com). Bus 202, 301, 302. **Open** 9am-7pm daily. **Credit** AmEx, Disc, MC, V. **Map** p316 A7.
Paris offers a number of wedding packages in its attractive chapels, and those with a head for heights can even say their vows on the outdoor observation deck at the top of the resort's Eiffel Tower. You should expect to pay between $2,000 to $3,000 for the experience.

Star Trek: The Experience at the Las Vegas Hilton

Las Vegas Hilton, 3000 Paradise Road, between Karen Avenue & E Desert Inn Road, East of Strip, NV 89109 (1-888 732 7117/697 8752/www.ds9 promenade.com/startrek). **Open** phone for an appointment. **Credit** AmEx, Disc, MC, V. **Map** p315 C5.
How about a Vulcan wedding on the Starship Enterprise? The 24th-century wedding packages ($2,000-$3,000) include a ceremony on the bridge, all wedding photography, an intergalactic floral bouquet, and Starfleet officers as guests. The reception is held at Quark's Bar & Restaurant.

Venetian Wedding Services

Venetian, 3355 Las Vegas Boulevard South, at Sands Avenue, NV 89109 (1-877 883 6423/ 414 4242/www.venetian.com). Bus 203, 301, 302. **Open** by appointment. **Credit** AmEx, Disc, MC, V. **Map** p316 A6.
This is the only wedding service in Las Vegas (so far, at least) that offers singing gondoliers, with the faux Grand Canal inside the Venetian as a backdrop. Depending on the cost of the package ($399-$1,450), you can be married on the mock Rialto Bridge or in a gondola.

Independent chapels

Divine Madness Fantasy Wedding Chapel

111 Las Vegas Boulevard South, at Fremont Street & Bridger Avenue, Downtown, NV 89101 (1-800 717 4734/384 5660/www.fantasychapel.com). Bus 107, 301, 302. **Open** 10am-7.30pm Mon-Thur, Sun; 10am-10pm Fri, Sat. **Credit** DC, Disc, MC, V. **Map** p312 D2.
What this chapel lacks in tradition, it makes up for in outrageous cheek. Weddings cost $175 or $275, including costumes for the bridal couple ranging from virginal white lace to raunchy black leather. Fancy yourself as Cleopatra? Step this way. Themed rooms provide a suitably flamboyant backdrop.

Graceland Wedding Chapel

619 Las Vegas Boulevard South, between Charleston Boulevard & Bonneville Avenue, Downtown, NV 89101 (1-800 824 5732/382 0091/www.graceland chapel.com). Bus 206, 301, 302. **Open** 9am-9pm Mon-Thur, Sun; 9am-midnight Fri, Sat. **Credit** AmEx, DC, Disc, MC, V. **Map** p312 C2.
A favourite with rockers (such as Jon Bon Jovi) and their chicks. Should you so wish, Elvis impersonator Norm Jones will walk the bride down the aisle, strum a little light background music during the ceremony and then perform a moving 15-minute mini-concert. Prices are $50-$200 plus minister's fees.

Little White Chapel

PO Box 15229, 1301 Las Vegas Boulevard South, between E Charleston & Oakey Boulevards, Stratosphere Area, NV 89104 (1-800 545 8111/ 382 6134/www.littlewhitechapel.com). Bus 206, 301, 302. **Open** 24hrs daily. **Credit** AmEx, Disc, MC, V. **Map** p312 C3.
The flagship of Charolette Richards' three-strong chapel chain (plus one hot-air balloon – 'my little white chapel in the sky', from $650) is famed for its

Arts & Entertainment

Drive up, get hitched, drive off: the **Little White Chapel** makes it so easy. *See p239*.

friendliness and unique drive-by wedding window, the 'Tunnel of Love' ($60-$100). In close to 40 years, Charolette has married more than 300,000 couples, but swears she is still touched by each pairing – and the strange thing is, we believe her.

Viva Las Vegas Wedding Chapel

1205 Las Vegas Boulevard South, between E Charleston & Oakey Boulevards, Stratosphere Area, NV 89104 (1-800 574 4450/384 0771/ www.vivalasvegasweddings.com). **Credit** AmEx, Disc, MC, V. **Map** p315 C3.

The most popular wedding is the Elvis Blue Hawaii package ($700) set in lush tropical surroundings with theatrical fog and lighting effects. Elvis (Ron de Car) performs the ceremony and sings the songs, surrounded by a bevy of dancing hula girls.

Outdoor specialist services

AJ Hackett Bungy

801 Circus Circus Drive, between Las Vegas Boulevard South & Industrial Road (385 4321). Bus 301, 302. **Open** 10am-8.30pm Mon-Thur, Sun; 10am-11pm Fri, Sat. **Credit** AmEx, Disc, MC, V. **Map** p315 B5.

For $300, including a video and minister's fees, you can say your vows at the top of a bungee tower and then take the plunge, quite literally.

Cowboy Trail Rides

Suite 204, 800 N Rainbow Boulevard, North-west Las Vegas, NV 89107 (249 6681/387 2457/www. cowboytrailrides.com). No bus. **Open** 9am-5pm daily. **Credit** AmEx, Disc, MC, V.

Wannabe cowboys and girls can get hitched against the russet desert of Red Rock Canyon or the majestic mountains scenery of Mount Charleston. Make your vows from atop your trusty steeds or from the back of a wagon. Prices start at $500 including free transportation, but vary depending on the location.

Lake Mead Cruises

Information: PO Box 62465, Boulder City, NV 89006 (293 6180/www.lakemeadcruises.com). **Credit** AmEx, Disc, MC, V.

For a nautical wedding, charter the *Desert Princess* paddlewheeler. It holds 300 passengers and is climate-controlled (very important in summer). A cheaper option is a top-deck marriage before the ship leaves port followed by the regular dinner cruise (*see p248*).

Wedding consultants

For details of fancy-dress shops and wedding outfitters, *see p171*.

American Theme Weddings

390 W Sahara Avenue, at Industrial Road, West of Strip, NV 89102 (671 0116/www.americancostumes. com/weddings). **Credit** AmEx, MC, V. **Map** p315 B4.

ATW can organise Roaring '20s, Scarlett and Rhett, Elvis and Priscilla, Wild West, and Renaissance weddings, complete with costumes ($65-$125) and the hire of a wedding chapel to suit your theme.

Andrea's Wedding Consultants

Information 367 7799. **Open** usually 9am-5pm Mon-Fri. **Credit** MC, V.

This outfit charges from $189 to arrange ceremonies with celebrity impersonators, as well as in the spectacular outdoor settings around Las Vegas, such as Red Rock Canyon and the Valley of Fire.

Wedding Dreams of Las Vegas

3412 Kidd Street, north of W Cheyenne Avenue, North Las Vegas, NV 89032 (432 1077/www. weddingdreams.com). **Rates** from $150. **Credit** AmEx, MC, V.

Along with the use of a private chapel, Wedding Dreams offers to plan a customised wedding for you (from $150). Get married in a limo, hot air balloon or helicopter, or even in your hotel room.

Trips Out of Town

Getting Started

All you need to know to make the most of the stunning desert scenery of the south-western United States.

For all Las Vegas's many attractions, it is quite likely that after a few days among the slot machines you'll be yearning for sunlight rather than neon, and for the clear skies of the Nevadan desert rather than the painted skies of the Forum Shops. Luckily, Las Vegas's location means it is remarkably easy to leave the city behind and explore the unspoilt wilderness on its doorstep. The options for day trips are plentiful; within 50 miles (80 kilometres) of the city you'll find peaceful desert parks (**Red Rock Canyon**, **Valley of Fire**), boating and fishing (on **Lake Mead**), man-made marvels (**Hoover Dam**) and even somewhere to ski (**Mount Charleston**).

Further afield lie more possibilities. Las Vegas's position in the southernmost tip of Nevada means it has access to four states packed with interesting destinations: to the north is the rest of Nevada, to the north-east Utah, to the east is Arizona and to the south and west lies California. Some of the best-known natural sights in the US, including the **Grand Canyon**, **Death Valley** and **Zion National Park**, are all within easy reach.

GETTING AROUND

This is the land of the automobile, so the easiest – usually the only – way to get anywhere is by car. Fortunately, road connections are good, with interstates and federal highways leading off at all points of the compass. The I-15 takes you south-west (towards Los Angeles) and north-east (towards Salt Lake City); US 93 and US 95 head north into Nevada and south into Arizona and California, respectively. The I-40, which leads to the Grand Canyon and points west, is also nearby. The I-15 can be unpleasantly crowded, especially heading into California, but, in general, you'll be travelling roads that are fast, empty and surrounded by spectacular desert scenery.

If you can't drive, then **Greyhound** (1-800 231 2222/www.greyhound.com) runs bus services to major destinations, including Los Angeles, Reno and Phoenix. However, you'll miss out on the pleasure of the drive itself, which on most trips is as much of an experience as the destination.

Desert survival

The desert is a dangerous place, especially in high summer when temperatures rocket and frazzled skin and dehydration are real possibilities. Don't be fooled into thinking that an air-conditioned automobile will keep you safe: cars break down. Treat the desert with the respect it deserves; here are a few tips for your journey.

● **Clothing** Always wear suitable clothing, including a broad-brimmed hat, sunglasses and a light-coloured cotton shirt. Wear long trousers and tough walking boots to protect you from the sun, spiky plants, snakes and uneven terrain; sandals are not adequate for most desert trails. Temperatures can plummet at night, even in summer, so carry warm clothing if necessary.

● **Dehydration** If you feel dizzy, nauseous or develop a headache, get out of the sun immediately and drink plenty of water. Dampen your clothing to lower your body temperature.

● **Equipment** Take a compass and a good topographic map if you're heading off-trail into remote areas or exploring back roads. Distances are deceptive and it's easy to get lost. Carrying a torch is also a good idea.

● **Environment** The desert is a fragile place. Stick to marked trails if possible and don't trample vegetation, soil crusts or animal burrows. Don't place your hands or feet where you can't see them: snakes and scorpions may be lurking.

● **Road conditions** Check with a park ranger or visitor centre before you set out, especially if you're planning to drive on any unpaved roads. If you break down, stay with your car; striking out on foot can be highly dangerous.

● **Sun** In summer, it's most comfortable to hike in the early morning or late afternoon. Carry sunscreen – and use it.

● **Vehicles** Turn off air-conditioning on uphill grades to lessen engine strain and, if the engine overheats, slowly pour water over the surface of the radiator to cool it – do not open the radiator. Leave a window slightly open if you park the car for any length of time in the heat, and use a fold-up windscreen shield to keep interior temperatures down. Never park or camp in washes (dry creek beds).

● **Water** Carry plenty of drinking water in your car and with you when hiking. In summer, allow at least one gallon (four litres) per person per day.

● **Weather** Look out for changes in the weather, especially in the summer, when storms and flash floods are common.

THE DESERT

Desert lovers are drawn to the very starkness and nakedness that others find so repellent. Compared to wetter, greener areas, deserts are very easy to read: the 'bones' of mountains are laid bare before you; views are long and unobscured; plants are sparse in form and coverage; the cloudless skies and intense sunlight can bleach out colours, but also create fabulous shadows and vivid hues, especially towards dusk.

And Las Vegas is one of the best places in the US from which to explore the country's dramatic desertscapes. It lies slap bang in the middle of one – the **Mojave** – and close to two others – the **Great Basin** and the **Sonoran** (also known as the Colorado desert).

The usual definition of a desert is that it receives less than ten inches (25 centimetres) of precipitation a year and has high evaporation (curiously, temperature doesn't come into it, although deserts are usually thought of as hot), but this is a pretty wide definition, allowing much room for variation. Lack of cloud cover is also important, because it causes heat to

reradiate – go back into the sky – very rapidly at night, hence the often high variation between day and night temperatures. Other determining factors are how and when precipitation occurs, and elevation. All three of the deserts near Las Vegas share characteristics, but they also exhibit great differences in landscape, vegetation and wildlife.

The **Mojave** is the smallest, covering the lower quarter of Nevada and part of Southern California, a total of 54,000 square miles (140,000 square kilometres). It is deemed a 'hot' desert, with low average elevations (Las Vegas is at 2,200 feet/670 metres) and precipitation falling as rain, usually in winter. It includes some of the most dramatic landscapes to be found in the North American deserts and also the lowest absolute elevation and highest maximum temperature recorded in the US (both in Death Valley, California). Unless you venture far from Las Vegas, most of your driving will be in the Mojave desert and you'll soon learn to recognise characteristic plants: the spidery creosote bush predominates, but its signature plant is the bizarre **Joshua tree**, a yucca and member of the lily family. Many think the Joshua ugly – explorer John C Fremont considered it 'the most repulsive tree in the vegetable kingdom' – though rock group U2 liked it enough to name an album after it. Early Mormon pioneers named it after the Biblical character Joshua as its branches resembled upstretched arms beckoning them to the promised land.

Joshuas grow very slowly and live up to 900 years, with an average height of 20 to 30 feet (six to nine metres). In the spring, the tips of the branches carry large clusters of creamy flowers, which open for one night only and smell like mushrooms. After blossoming, the branch forks, eventually giving the Joshua its many-limbed form. Though not exclusive to the Mojave, it is abundant there, at elevations between 2,000 and 4,500 feet (600 to 1,370 metres). However, the most extensive forests are found in Joshua Tree National Park and the East Mojave National Preserve (see p275).

The **Great Basin**, which covers the northern three-quarters of Nevada plus the western half of Utah, is the largest desert in the USA, covering more than 158,000 square miles (409,000 square kilometres). It is described as a 'cold' desert because more than half its annual precipitation occurs in winter in the form of snow, and its northern position and high base elevations mean it experiences lower average temperatures than areas to the south. It was named by 19th-century explorer John C Fremont because its rivers lack outlets to the sea – although it is not shaped like a basin. It doesn't look much like a desert, either: silvery green sagebrush (Nevada's state plant) blankets vast areas, and many desert plants of popular imagination – such as large cacti, agaves and yuccas – are conspicuous by their absence.

The transition between the Great Basin and the Mojave deserts occurs north-west of Las Vegas, roughly between Beatty and Caliente; the transition zone is marked by the existence of blackbrush, a small, dark, round shrub.

The **Sonoran** desert extends over part of southern California and the south-western quarter of Arizona. Like the Mojave, it is both lower and hotter than the Great Basin, and rain falls in both summer and winter. Unless you drive as far south as Joshua Tree National Park, you won't cross into the Sonoran.

There's also the **Colorado Plateau**, an area of semi-desert that includes the canyon country of south-eastern Utah and the north-eastern portion of Arizona. Geologically, it is different from the nearby desert, its landscape made up of colourful layers of sedimentary rock that erosion has carved into dramatic rock formations and stunning canyons – of which the Grand Canyon

is the most magnificent. It includes many of the plants found in true desert areas as well as grassland and woodland species.

Useful information

Driving & transportation

Driving in the South-west frequently involves crossing from one state to another and back again, so remember that speed limits and time zones may change from state to state. Call the following hotlines for up-to-date information on road conditions: **California** 1-916 445 1534; **Nevada** 486 3116; **Utah** 1-801 964 6000.

For details of vehicle rental companies, the **Automobile Association** and **Greyhound** services, *see chapter* **Getting Around**. For details of outfits offering tours to sights outside Las Vegas, *see p66* **Trips and tours**.

Tourist information

Call the following offices for visitor information, maps and accommodation advice in each state. The Nevada office is good, sending out a comprehensive – and free – information pack.

Arizona Office of Tourism
In the USA 1-888 520 3433/1-602 230 7733/in the UK 01426 946334/www.arizonaguide.com.

California Division of Tourism
In the USA 1-800 862 2543/overseas 1-916 322 2881/www.gocalif.ca.gov.

Nevada Commission of Tourism
1-800 638 2328/www.travelnevada.com.

Utah Travel Council
1-800 200 1160/1-801 538 1030/www.utah.com.

Trip planning

Bureau of Land Management
4765 Vegas Drive, Las Vegas, NV 89108 (647 5000/www.nv.blm.gov). **Open** *Telephone enquiries* 7.30am-4.15pm Mon-Fri.

Lake Mead Recreational Service/ National Park Service
601 Nevada Highway, Boulder City, NV 89005 (293 8906/www.nps.gov). **Open** *Telephone enquiries* 8.30am-4pm Mon-Fri.

Nevada State Parks
District VI headquarters, 4747 W Vegas Drive, Las Vegas, NV 89108 (486 5126/www.state.nv.us). **Open** *Telephone enquiries* 8am-5pm Mon-Fri.

US Forest Service
2881 S Valley View Boulevard, Suite 16, Las Vegas, NV 89102 (873 8800/www.fs.fed.us/htnf). **Open** 8am-4.30pm Mon-Fri.

Trips Out of Town

Day Trips

A different world awaits a short drive from the bright lights of the Strip.

Heading East

Hoover Dam

Half an hour's drive south-east of Las Vegas lies the engineering marvel that ensured the city's survival and made possible its phenomenal growth. The Hoover Dam, built at the height of the Depression, is a mind-boggling structure. Without it, much of the Southwest would not exist. Constructed and still run by the Bureau of Reclamation, it controls the flood-prone Colorado River, providing electricity and water to more than 18 million people in California, Nevada and Arizona, and makes it possible for huge cities and rich farmland to flourish in one of the driest, hottest and most inhospitable regions of the world.

The bare facts are impressive enough: it's big, very big – 726 feet (221 metres) high, 660 feet (200 metres) thick at its base, 40 feet (12 metres) at the top, 1,244 feet (379 metres) wide at its crest. Its reservoir, the 110-mile (177-kilometre) long and 500-foot (152-metre) deep Lake Mead, is the largest man-made lake in the US and can hold enough water to cover the entire state of Nevada, six inches (15 centimetres) deep. The dam used up enough concrete to pave a highway between San Francisco and New York. Its two flood-control spillways, used only once in 1983, can each handle the equivalent of the Niagara Falls.

Building it was an equally mammoth task. First the mighty Colorado had to be temporarily diverted, so the dam wall could be constructed. The concrete would have taken 100 years to set if left under normal conditions, so the cooling

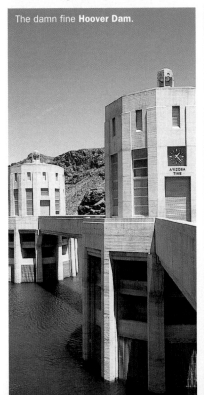

The damn fine **Hoover Dam**.

Visit man-made **Lake Mead** for fishing, boating and other watery pleasures. *See p247.*

process was speeded up by pouring ice-cold water through a network of pipes laid into each block of concrete. Next, vast 30-foot (nine-metre) diameter pipes (known as penstocks) were lowered from an overhead cableway 800 feet (244 metres) above the canyon floor and squeezed into tunnels blasted out of the side walls. An army of workers, 16,400-strong, laboured for four years, night and day, finishing in February 1935 – an amazing two years ahead of schedule.

Named after US president Herbert Hoover, the dam straddles the border between Arizona and Nevada: two clocks on the intake towers show the time in each state. The busy US 93 passes over the top of the dam (though a bypass bridge is being planned); on the Nevada side are the main, multi-storey car park ($3) and escalators leading to the subterranean visitor centre; there's free parking (and stunning views of the whole structure) on the Arizona side. You can walk around at the top of the dam, but be careful when crossing busy US 93.

Don't miss the sculptures (by Norwegian-born artist Oskar Hansen) on the Nevada side. A bronze bas-relief commemorates the 96 workers who died during the dam's construction and two huge, bronze-winged figures flank a flagpole above a terrazzo floor inlaid with a celestial map, marking Franklin D Roosevelt's dedication of the dam in September 1935. The white mark on the shoreline indicates the flood level in 1983 when Lake Mead rose to within seven feet (two metres) of the top.

The visitor centre, which opened in 1995, cost a stonking $123 million – although you wouldn't know it from the exhibits upstairs, which are badly laid out and uninformative. The theatre shows three films in succession (about 35 minutes in total), one of which is a short 1930s film on the building of the dam with great footage and gung-ho narration. There's a top-floor observation deck and, across the road, a snack bar and poorly stocked gift shop. But, of course, the highlight of any visit is getting down into the dam itself.

There are two tours, a regular tour and two 'hard hat' tours (so-called because everyone gets to don a hard hat). The dam receives more than a million visitors a year, so expect to queue for tickets and then to queue for your tour; go early in the morning or late in the afternoon to avoid the worst of the rush. Tour times vary during the year, and space is limited on the hard hat tours, so it's a good idea to book. In fact, reservations for all tours are recommended between May and September.

The 35-minute regular tour (which starts about every ten minutes) takes a group of about 80 visitors in an elevator 560 feet (170 metres) down through the volcanic canyon wall to the power plants housing the gargantuan turbines, through the central office building and to the base of the dam, where the tamed Colorado bubbles out green and furious.

The hard hat tour (leaving every half-hour) is pricey, but more detailed (it takes an hour) and is for smaller groups of 20 people. You see the original staircase (982 steps) and also get to peek out of a ventilation inlet halfway up the dam face. The art deco detailing is fabulous: look for abstract Indian symbols inlaid in the black and white terrazzo floor in the office building and the huge fluted brass doors to the toilets at the top of the dam. If you really want to find out exactly how the dam was built and works, it's worth the extra dosh; and, hey, you get to keep your hard hat.

Hoover Dam Visitor Center

1-866 291 8687/294 3523/www.hooverdam.usbr. com. **Open** 8am-3pm daily. *Tours* times vary; phone for details. **Admission** *Exhibits only* $4. *Regular tour* $8; $2-$7 concessions. *Exhibits plus hard hat tour* $25; free under-5s. **Credit** AmEx, Disc, MC, V.

Getting there

To reach the Hoover Dam from Las Vegas, take US 93 south for 32 miles (51 kilometres). You will pass through Boulder City en route.

Boulder City

A few miles from the Hoover Dam is the green and pleasant town of Boulder City, built from scratch in 1931 to house the dam workers. Triangular in shape, it was the first 'model city' in the US, built according to progressive planning theories. The Bureau of Reclamation, government buildings and a park sit at the apex of the triangle, with the workers' houses radiating down from there. It was not intended as a permanent settlement, but though the population dropped after the dam was finished, it recovered during World War II and the town is now flourishing, with a population of 14,500.

Driving down US 93, you pass some small, old-fashioned motels and stalls selling Mexican pottery and other handicrafts. Only slowly do you realise that something's missing: there are no casinos. Boulder City is the only town in Nevada where gambling is illegal – maybe the reason for its quiet and civilised atmosphere.

Take a detour through the US 93 business loop to view the historic district, full of tree-lined streets and grassy parks. Visitors can stay at the historic **Boulder Dam Hotel** (turn right at Arizona Street), a white and green building with tall cypresses outside. Recently reopened after a $2-million renovation, it counts the Duchess of Westminster, James Cagney and Howard Hughes among its former guests. The hotel houses a gift shop, two art galleries, a restaurant and the **Chamber of Commerce** (293 2034, closed Sat, Sun), where you can pick up a map and a guide to walking tours of the district. It is also home to the recently renovated **Hoover Dam/Boulder City Museum** (294 1988, closed am Sun, admission $2), which has social history exhibits and shows a film on the building of Boulder City and the dam.

On US 93, try **Jitters** (1045 Nevada Highway, 293 0099, open 6am-6pm daily) for excellent, freshly made sandwiches, desserts and coffee (all under $5), or **Two Gals** (1632 Nevada Highway, 293 1793, open 7am-2pm daily, main courses $5-$10) for light lunches and a wide selection of tasty vegetarian sandwiches. The **Happy Days Diner** (512 Nevada Highway, 293 4637, open 7am-8pm daily, main courses $5-$10) is one of the city's oldest restaurants. It is decorated in 1950s diner style and serves classic diner food.

If you're heading from Boulder City towards the dam, you'll get a clear view of Lake Mead as you rejoin US 93. After that the road starts descending through twisty canyons covered with pylons and power lines.

Getting there

Boulder City is seven miles (11 kilometres) west of the dam on US 93. To see Boulder City's historic district, turn off at the business loop, which rejoins US 93 on the far side of the town.

Lake Mead

Lake Mead is the second most popular recreation spot (after Las Vegas, of course) in Nevada: 9.6 million visitors (the vast majority of them locals) come to its 550 miles (885 kilometres) of shoreline every year to sail, fish, swim, water-ski, camp, picnic and generally enjoy watery pleasures in the middle of the desert. It's completely artificial, created when the natural flow of the Colorado River was blocked by the Hoover Dam, and is certainly an incongruous sight: a large blue splodge surrounded by barren mountains, with the very tops of canyons peeking above the water. It's the centrepiece of the huge **Lake Mead National Recreation Area** (administered by the National Park services), which also includes Lake Mohave to the south (created when the Colorado River was stemmed again in 1953 by the Davis Dam; *see p253*) and the desert east to the edge of Grand Canyon National Park (*see p262*) and north to Overton, from where you are within easy reach of the Valley of Fire State Park (*see p249*). There is a $5 permit fee per car (or $3 per person), which grants five days' access to the whole Lake Mead area.

Lakeside Scenic Drive (Highway 146) and **Northshore Scenic Drive** (Highway 167) skirt the western and northern sides of Lake Mead for nearly 60 miles (96 kilometres). The route is not particularly scenic and you rarely see the lake, but it's the access road for the five concession-operated marinas along the Nevada shoreline. Planted with palms, eucalyptus and (very poisonous) oleander, these are green havens in the stark landscape. **Lake Mead Resort** on Boulder Beach (293 3484) and **Las Vegas Bay Marina** (565 9111/www.boating lakemead.com) are the largest and closest marinas to Las Vegas – and the busiest; further north are **Callville Bay Resort** (565 8958), **Echo Bay** (1-800 752 9669/394 4000) and **Overton Beach Resort** (394 4040), while **Temple Bar Resort** (1-800 752 9669/1-520 767 3211) is a less accessible and quieter marina on the Arizona side of the lake. There are a couple of other boat landings and many small dirt roads leading to the lake edge.

All the marinas have small ranger stations (which are not always open), grocery stores and some form of restaurant or bar; some marinas have additional facilities such as swimming beaches (without lifeguards), picnic sites, motels, showers, laundries and petrol stations.

On the water

The best way to explore the lake is, of course, by boat. There are numerous secluded coves, sandy beaches and narrow canyons accessible only by water, and the warm, clear lake is ideal for swimming: the water temperature averages 78°F (26°C) in spring, summer and autumn. If you have time to spare, consider renting a houseboat (*see below*). Otherwise you can hire a range of boats for daily use from the marinas

around the lake; the choice, rates and rental conditions will vary, but are likely to include: large ski boats ($100 for two hours/$300 per day, plus $20 for waterskiing gear); patio boats ($40-$70 two hours/$120-$210 per day); small fishing boats ($20-$40 two hours/$60-$120 per day) and Sea-Doos ($50 per hour/$270 per day).

If you don't want to pilot your own craft, you can take a cruise on Lake Mead on the three-deck paddlewheeler *Desert Princess*. The paddlewheeler, run by **Lake Mead Cruises** (PO Box 62465, Boulder City, NV 89006; 293 6180/www.lakemeadcruises.com), offers breakfast and dinner-dance cruises, as well as tours from Lake Mead Cruises Landing (between Boulder Beach and Las Vegas Bay) to the Hoover Dam (an hour-and-a-half round trip).

Lake Mead offers some of the best year-round sport fishing in the country – *see p230*. The clarity and warmth of the water make the lake ideal for scuba diving, and although you can't hire equipment at the lake, dive shops in Las Vegas rent gear and run courses (*see p233*).

Where to stay & eat

For decent food, try the family-run eaterie on the water at **Las Vegas Bay** (565 9111, open 7am-8pm daily, main courses $10-$25) or the grander **Tail O' The Whale** restaurant at Echo Bay (394 4000, open 8am-10pm daily, main courses $14-$30).

Seven Crown Resorts (1-800 752 9669) runs motels (rates $85-$300) at Echo Bay (394 4000), Boulder Beach (293 2074) and Temple Bar (1-520 767 3211), or there are campgrounds ($10 per night) at all marinas except Overton and Willow Beach.

Alternatively, you can rent a houseboat from **Seven Crown Resorts Houseboats** at Echo Bay Marina (1-800 752 9669/394 4000/ www.sevencrown.com) or from **Forever Resorts Houseboats** at Callville Bay Marina (1-800 255 5561/565 4813/www.foreverresorts. com). Prices vary according to the season. Book well in advance during the summer.

Getting there

The **Alan Bible Visitor Center** is 27 miles (43 kilometres) south of Las Vegas on US 93, at the junction with Lakeshore Scenic Drive (Highway 146). Alternatively, to reach Las Vegas Bay, Boulder Beach and Lake Mead marinas without going to the visitor centre, take Boulder Highway south from Las Vegas and turn left at Lake Mead Drive (Highway 146), or take I-15/US 93 north to exit 45 in North Las Vegas and turn on to Lake Mead Boulevard east (Highway 147). Both routes join the shore road.

Tourist information

Consult the **NPS website** (ww.nps.gov/lame) for detailed information about the Lake Mead Recreation Area. The **Alan Bible Visitor Center** (293 8990, open 8.30am-4.30pm daily) on US 93 is rather basic, but has a useful map and information on fishing and other activities there. Information stations are also located around Lake Mead at Overton Beach, Echo Bay, Callville Bay, Las Vegas Bay and Temple Bar.

Valley of Fire

Bored of the man-made wonders of Las Vegas? Head north-east for 50 miles (80 kilometres) to discover a natural marvel whose eroded red sandstone formations are just as spectacular as the neon-clad casinos on the Strip. The **Valley of Fire State Park** is bounded by the grey limestone Muddy Mountains to the south and west and was Nevada's first state park (entrance is $5). It's easily explored in a day.

Summer highs top 110°F (43°C); as such, the best times to visit are (as is usual in the desert) spring and autumn. The cactus and wildflower blooms are usually at their peak in mid-April. If you're lucky you may catch a glimpse of a desert tortoise (Nevada's state reptile) and you're sure to see antelope ground squirrels (aka chipmunks), which are a nuisance if you're camping or picnicking. Don't feed or pet them: they may be carrying bubonic plague.

Marked trails are few and very short, but hiking is permitted throughout the park; ask for advice at the visitor centre. The main attractions are the fiery Aztec sandstone formations, created from sand dunes deposited 135-150 million years ago and sculpted by wind and water into bizarre, often anthropomorphic shapes: look for the **Beehives**, **Elephant Rock** and **Seven Sisters** along Highway 169, the main east–west road through the park. Short walks lead to some ancient petrified logs and three stone cabins, constructed by the Civilian Conservation Corps in the 1930s to provide primitive shelter for travellers. A two-mile (five-kilometre) scenic loop road takes you past some of the park's most dramatic rock formations. Nestled in among them are two campgrounds; campsite B has the best sites. Back country camping isn't allowed.

Set halfway along Highway 169, the **visitor centre** is a gem, with superb displays on the area's geology, ecology, flora and fauna and human history, all of which compensate for a feeble bookshop. The road north from the centre offers a panoramic view of multicoloured sandstone at Rainbow Vista and ends at the White Domes picnic area. An easy three-mile

(seven-kilometre) trail from Rainbow Vista leads to yet more spectacular and colourful rocks at **Fire Canyon**, from where you can see the spot where Captain Kirk met his doom in the movie *Star Trek: Generations*. A popular movie location, the Valley of Fire provided a backdrop for the classic *One Million Years BC* as well as numerous Westerns.

Humans have lived in the area for about 4,000 years and Indian rock writings are common throughout the park. **Atlatl Rock** on the scenic loop road has an impressive number of petroglyphs, while others are visible on the short trail to **Mouse's Tank**, a natural water basin used in the 1890s as a hideout by a renegade Indian known as Mouse. Visit the **Lost City Museum** in Overton, eight miles (13 kilometres) north of the park, to learn more about the Indian inhabitants, from the ancient Basketmaker people and the Puebloans (Anasazi) to the Paiute, whose present-day descendants still live in Southern Nevada.

Lost City Museum

721 South Moapa Valley Boulevard, Overton (1-702 397 2193). **Open** 8.30am-4.30pm daily. **Admission** $2. **Credit** MC, V.

Valley of Fire Visitor Center

Information 1-702 397 2088/www.desertusa.com/ nvval). **Open** 8.30am-4.30pm daily.

Getting there

Head north on the I-15 for 33 miles (53 kilometres) to Highway 169: it's 17 miles (27 kilometres) to the park's western entrance. You can also enter the park from Lake Mead, off Northshore Scenic Drive (*see p248*).

Heading West

Red Rock Canyon

A mere 20 miles (32 kilometres) from the gaming tables of Vegas is one of Nevada's most popular and beautiful outdoor areas. The cool, deep-cut canyons of the Red Rock Canyon National Conservation Area make it a popular hiking spot all year round, while climbers come here from all over the world to enjoy some of the best rock climbing in the US (*see p232*).

Red Rock Canyon is part of the Spring Mountains and has as its centrepiece a nearly sheer escarpment of Aztec sandstone, the remnant of ancient sand dunes that covered this area some 180 million years ago. About 65 million years ago, the Keystone Thrust Fault pushed older grey limestone over younger sandstone, reversing the normal layering and resulting in today's dramatic – and unique – landscape. The red and cream Calico Hills to the east are more rounded, as they are not protected from erosion by a higher limestone layer.

Because of the availability of water in the area – there are more than 40 springs and many natural catchment basins (known as *tinajas* or tanks) – Native Americans have used Red Rock Canyon since about 3,500 BC: evidence remains in the form of rock art (etched petroglyphs and painted pictographs), as well as occasional artefacts such as arrowheads and ceramics. Roasting pits – circular areas of piled-up limestone that were used as ovens – are common and distinctive landmarks, some being several yards high.

More than 45 mammal species, attracted by the area's water, also inhabit the park, among them mountain lions, kit foxes, coyotes, kangaroo rats, mule deer and the near-mythical desert bighorn sheep – but you'll be lucky to spot any. The most visible animals are probably the non-native burros (donkeys). About 50 live around Red Rock Canyon, and they're often seen along the roadside. Remember that these are wild animals that can bite and kick: observe from a distance and never try to feed them (it's illegal and dangerous). Humans are also a danger to burros; if they are encouraged to gather at roadsides, some will inevitably be injured by vehicles.

Though much of the Red Rock Canyon has free access, entrance to the federal park itself costs $5 for vehicles. Stop first at the **Bureau of Land Management Visitor Center** (363 1921, open 8.30am-4.30pm daily) for information and a map, before exploring the one-way, 13-mile (21-kilometre) scenic drive through the canyon. There are picnic sites at Willow Spring, Red Spring and Red Rock Vista. The drive is popular with cyclists (*see p230*) and gives access to numerous hiking trails. Many trails are not clearly marked and involve scrambling over rocks, so it's a good idea to take a topographic map (available from the visitor centre) and a compass.

A good introduction to the Calico Hills that line the start of the scenic drive is the two-and-a-half mile (four-kilometre) **Calico Tank** trail from Sandstone Quarry. Just above the tank is a fine view (smog permitting) of the valley and the Strip's casino monoliths. Other good short summer hikes include **Ice Box Canyon** and **Pine Creek Canyon**. For further details of the scores of other trails, pick up a copy of the BLM's trail leaflet, or Branch Whitney's *Hiking Las Vegas*, which also covers Mount Charleston. Guided hikes are led by park staff

at the weekends and some weekdays (ask at the visitor centre) and by the Sierra Club (363 3267).

Around Red Rock Canyon

If you'd prefer something less physical, head further west on Highway 159 to the green and pretty oasis of **Spring Mountain State Park**, situated at the base of the dramatic Wilson Cliffs. Admission to the park includes entrance to the New England-style ranch house. You can also stroll around the historic buildings in the white fenced grounds (look for the old fig tree by the blacksmith's shop) and picnic on a grassy meadow under shady trees. There are regular guided walking tours (not available Tuesday to Thursday), open-air theatre performances and live jazz during the summer and 'living history' programmes in the autumn.

A few miles south on Highway 159 is **Bonnie Springs/Old Nevada**, a mock Wild West town with a melodrama, gunfight and hanging staged daily (usually 11.30am, 2pm and 4pm). It's rather dilapidated, but good fun, and there's also a free petting zoo, restaurant and bar (open 8am-11pm daily, main courses $8-$18), horse rides ($25 per person) and a motel (875 4400, rates $60-$70) on site.

Bonnie Springs/Old Nevada
1 Gun Fighter Lane, off Highway 159, south of Red Rock Canyon (875 4191). No bus. **Open** *May-Oct* 10.30am-6pm daily. *Nov-Apr* 10.30am-5pm daily. **Admission** $6.50; $4 concessions; free under-5s. **Credit** MC, V.

Spring Mountain State Park
Information 875 4141. **Open** *Park* 8am-dusk. *Ranch house* noon-4pm Mon-Fri; 10am-4pm Sat, Sun. **Admission** $5. **No credit cards.**

Getting there

To reach the visitor centre and the start of the scenic drive, head west on Charleston Boulevard (Highway 159) for 20 miles (32 kilometres). Alternatively, if you're staying near the southern end of the Strip, drive south on the I-15, take Highway 160 (towards Pahrump) and then turn right on to Highway 159, passing Bonnie Springs and Spring Mountain State Park en route to Red Rock Canyon.

Mount Charleston

It's true: you can jet-ski near Las Vegas in the morning and snow ski in the afternoon. Forty-five minutes north-west of the city lies the **Spring Mountain Recreation Area**, more commonly known as Mount Charleston. It's part of the massive Spring Mountain range,

You can hike and climb in **Red Rock Canyon**, but don't feed the burros. *See p249.*

which is dominated by Charleston Peak, the highest point in Southern Nevada at 11,918 feet (3,633 metres). In the winter, you can ski and snowboard at Lee Canyon; in the summer, you can hike around the forested slopes, which are substantially cooler than the city. There are also picnic sites and several campgrounds ($10, open mid-May to mid-Oct) in the area.

Watch the vegetation change as you climb into the mountains, moving from creosote, bursage and Joshua trees on the lower slopes to piñon and Utah juniper, through ponderosa pine and mountain mahogany, and finally to gnarled bristlecone pines where the tree-line peters out at 10,000 feet (3,000 metres). Due to the isolation of the Spring Mountain Range, about 27 species of flora and fauna are unique to this 'sky island'.

Exploring by car

There are two roads into the area, both off US 95. Nearest to Las Vegas is Highway 157 (Kyle Canyon Road), which ascends through winding canyons and wooded slopes – very pretty in autumn – to **Mount Charleston Hotel**, a rustic-style lodge with a huge green lobby warmed by an open fireplace (*see also p252*). The road continues west for another few miles,

past a small **park information office** (872 5486, closed Mon, Tue in winter), terminating at **Mount Charleston Lodge**. Here, you'll find a 24-hour bar, restaurant, riding stables and expensive log cabins (*see p252*).

From the Mount Charleston Hotel, Highway 158 (Deer Creek Highway), heads north to the junction with Highway 156 (Lee Canyon Road). Seven miles (11 kilometres) along Highway 158, the short **Desert View Trail** leads to a spectacular view of the valley below and the mountains in the distance. In the 1950s, when the atomic era was at its height, locals came here to view the mushroom clouds billowing up from the Nevada Test Site (*see p256*).

At the junction with Highway 156, turn left for the ski area, which is open between Thanksgiving and Easter. The elevation here is 8,500 feet (2,600 metres), with three chairlifts leading up another 1,000 feet (300 metres) to 13 slopes. (For further details of skiing in the area, *see p234*). Drive back to US 95 on Highway 158 for a fine view of the desert below.

Hiking

The US Forest Service prefers hikers to stick to its designated trails, but there are numerous unmarked hikes, too (take a compass and a trail guidebook). The six-mile (ten-kilometre) **Bristlecone Trail** provides views of limestone cliffs and bristlecone pines. The short trail to **Mary Jane Falls** is more strenuous, with hikers climbing 900 feet (274 metres) towards a waterfall. The mother of all hikes, though, is the 18-mile (29-kilometre) round-trip to Mount Charleston Peak: best attempted by experienced walkers, it's a difficult and demanding trail that's not clear of snow until July. From the summit you can enjoy a stunning view of southern Nevada, eastern California and southern Utah. For all hikes, you'll need warm clothing and water.

Around Mount Charleston

On your way to Mount Charleston stop off at **Floyd Lamb State Park**, former site of Tule Springs Ranch. Located 15 miles (24 kilometres) from the city, its lush lawns, shady cottonwoods and four lakes make it a popular, year-round picnicking and fishing spot, although it's best to avoid weekends and Easter Sunday if you don't like crowds. It's serene during the week, though, with peacocks wandering around the white ranch buildings built by Jacob Goumond in the 1940s. As well as raising cattle and growing alfalfa, Goumond catered for prospective divorcees waiting out the six-week residency required to get a divorce in Nevada. You can hire horses from the old stables (rides cost $20 per hour, $15 per half-hour), and the Las Vegas Gun Club (*see p232*) is next door.

Further to the north is the **Desert National Wildlife Refuge** (information 646 3401), established in 1936 to protect the desert bighorn sheep and its habitat. A gravel road leads to a self-service information centre, where you can pick up a leaflet on the refuge and stroll around the ponds of Corn Creek Springs. The refuge occupies 1.3 million acres (526,500 hectares) and receives only about 20,000 visitors a year. The western half is used by the Nellis Air Force Range as a bombing area and is closed to the public, while the rest is a nature reserve, accessible by two unmaintained dirt roads: you'll need a high clearance or 4WD vehicle. Summer is the best time to spot the elusive bighorn sheep and the wildflowers are usually in bloom from March to May.

Floyd Lamb State Park

9200 Tule Springs Road, off US 95 (486 5413). **Open** 8am-sunset daily. **Admission** $5. **No credit cards**.

Where to stay & eat

The pleasant **Mount Charleston Hotel** (1-800 794 6456/872 5500/www.mtcharleston

hotel.com) has a cavernous dining room and 63 rooms (rates $60-$350). **Mount Charleston Lodge** (1-800 955 1314/872 5408/www.mt charlestonlodge.com) offers accommodation in upmarket cabins (rates $95-$200) and rather bland, overpriced meals (main courses $10-$25) in its restaurant.

Getting there

Take US 95 north from Downtown for about 35 miles (56 kilometres) to reach Highway 157; Highway 156 is about 12 miles (19 kilometres) further on. In winter, you'll need snow chains on the mountain roads.

Heading South

Laughlin & around

Wedged into the far southern tip of the Nevadan portion of Tristate (the Nevada/ Arizona/California border region), Laughlin has no right to exist, even by Nevadan standards. This is one of the hottest spots in one of the hottest states in the Union, with midsummer temperatures that can sizzle all the way up to 120°F (47°C). Yet, when Don Laughlin, a Las Vegas club owner, bought the failing bait shop, bar and motel that stood here in 1969, he had a vision of a mini-Vegas by the Colorado River. In the last two decades, that dream has become reality: nine major casino-hotels line the two-mile strip, Casino Drive, making Laughlin Nevada's third biggest gambling centre.

The sophisticates of Las Vegas may sniff at Laughlin's (not entirely justified) reputation as a hick, low-roller resort, but it's a relaxed, friendly place and enjoys two major advantages over its flashier neighbour to the north-west: extremely cheap hotel rooms (book ahead), and a riverside location. Stressed-out gamblers can cruise or jet-ski on the Colorado, stroll along the riverside walk, relax on the public beach or gaze at the monster carp outside the **Edgewater** casino (1-800 677 4837/1-702 298 2453). And if you fancy a casino crawl, hop on the water taxi, which costs a mere $2 per journey. Every April, thousands of motorcycle fans converge on the city for the **Laughlin River Run** (www.laughlinriverrun.com).

With the exception of the **Colorado Belle** (1-800 477 4837/1-702 298 4000), a faux Mississippi paddlesteamer, the casinos lack the architectural chutzpah found in Vegas, although each one has its own charms. Nostalgic gamblers pack out Don Laughlin's

For messing about in boats

Hire everything from a jetski to a houseboat on **Lake Mead** (see p247) or **Lake Mohave** (see p253). Or cruise around on the Colorado River in **Laughlin** (see p252).

For getting your rocks off

Be amazed by the extraordinary Aztec sandstone in the **Valley of Fire** (see p249) and **Red Rock Canyon** (see p249).

For counting sheep

The elusive bighorn sheep hides out in the **Desert National Wildlife Reserve** (see p252).

For taking a hike

Lose yourself (not literally, we hope) in the spectacular desert scenery of **Red Rock Canyon** (see p249) or among the forested splendour of **Mount Charleston** (see p250).

For low-rolling casino action

Don't laugh at **Laughlin**: it's fun, friendly and cheap (see p252).

Riverside (1-800 227 3849/1-702 298 2535), with its gold, glass and wood decor, vintage car collection and a six-screen cinema; floor-to-ceiling windows ensure fine views from the **Hilton Flamingo** (1-800 352 6464); while effective theming characterises low-rise **Wild West Pioneer** (1-800 634 3469/1-702 298 2442), south-of-the-border **Harrah's** (1-800 427 7247/1-702 298 2442) and the turn-of-the-century railroad **Ramada Express** (1-800 243 6846/1-702 298 4200).

Laughlin's boom times are under threat from an audacious plan conceived by the Fort Mojave Tribe, which owns 33,000 acres (13,300 hectares) of land along the Colorado River in Arizona. A planned community of 40,000 people to be called **Aha Macav** will include 11 casinos that threaten to siphon off some of Laughlin's five million annual visitors. At the time of writing, however, Aha Macav consists of one casino, **Avi** (1-800 284 2946/1-702 535 5555), and lots of empty space.

Something of the history of the Fort Mojave Tribe can be gleaned from the delightfully eclectic displays in the **Colorado River Museum**, which is located half a mile north of the Laughlin bridge on the Arizona side of the river. The museum also contains information on the petroglyphs to be found in **Grapevine Canyon** across the river, which can be reached by heading a couple of miles up a dirt road (follow the signposts to Christmas Tree Pass) off Highway 163.

The **Davis Dam**, a mile to the north of Laughlin, was completed in 1953, spawning the Arizonan settlement of Bullhead City and creating long, thin **Lake Mohave**, part of the Lake Mead National Recreation Area (see p247). Lake Mohave is narrower than Lake Mead, inaccessible by road for most of its length and attracts far fewer visitors. However, it does have a limited service harbour at the north end of the lake at **Willow Beach** (1-520 767 4747), two marinas offering boat rentals and other facilities at **Cottonwood Cove** (297 1464) and **Katharine Landing** (1-520 754 3245), and some excellent fishing (see p230). A ranger station (1-520 754 3272) is open 8am to 4pm daily.

Colorado River Museum

2201 Highway 68 (1-520 754 3399). **Open** 10am-4pm daily. **Admission** $1. **No credit cards**.

Where to stay & eat

Laughlin, to be polite, is not renowned for its food. Stuff-your-face bargain buffets, surf'n'turf combos and steak deals dominate the scene. If you're prepared to pay for a little more class, then the **Lodge** at Gold River (1-702 298 2242, open 5-10pm daily, main courses $9-$20) and **William Fisk's Steakhouse** at Harrah's (1-702 298 4600, open 4.30-11pm daily, main courses $10-$25) both offer good fare in tranquil surroundings. The pick of the pack, however, is probably Colorado Belle's **Boiler Room** (1-702 298 4000, open 4-10pm daily, main courses $7-$15), which is impressively decked out and is Laughlin's only brew pub.

Laughlin's casinos offer good-value accommodation, but book in advance. For details of lodging on Lake Mohave, contact **Forever Resorts** (1-800 255 5561) and **Seven Crown Resorts** (1-800 752 9669).

Getting there

To reach Laughlin from Las Vegas, head south on US 95 for about 70 miles (113 kilometres), then take Highway 163 east for about 100 miles (160 kilometres). To reach Cottonwood Cove on Lake Mohave, turn east off US 95 at Searchlight onto Highway 164. Katharine's Landing is best approached from Laughlin via Highway 98.

Tourist information

Laughlin Visitor Center

1555 Casino Drive, Laughlin, NV 89029 (1-800 452 8445/1-702 298 3321). **Open** 8am-4.30pm daily.

Trips Out of Town

Into Nevada

If there's more to Las Vegas than gambling, then there's certainly more to Nevada than just Las Vegas.

Las Vegas, in case you hadn't realised, is not typical of anywhere, least of all Nevada. The state is the seventh largest in the Union but has a population of only 2.06 million, of which nearly 1.42 million live within 40 miles (64 kilometres) of Las Vegas. Take away the population (265,000) of the other main urban area, Reno/Sparks, and that leaves very few people scattered across a large and empty state.

Reno itself, 440 miles (700 kilometres) to the north-west, is smaller, greener and less brash than its loud southern cousin, but still has enough glitzy casinos to entertain even the most dedicated gambler. En route to Reno, you'll pass numerous north–south mountain ranges and sagebrush-covered valleys, typical of the Great Basin desert. You'll also come across once-prosperous mining towns such as **Goldfield** and **Tonopah**, and evidence of Nevada's other great money-maker, the US military. The massive **Nellis Air Force Range** stretches from just north of Las Vegas all the way to Tonopah. In the 1950s, curious onlookers came to watch the nuclear tests that were conducted there (*see p256* **The big bang**); nowadays, visitors are drawn in droves to the (literally) other-worldly sights and delights of the **Extraterrestrial Highway**, and by the many extraordinary tales of UFO sightings and other sinister goings-on at the base's infamous **Area 51**.

The road to Reno

Driving north to Reno on US 95 takes you almost entirely through classic Nevada scenery: Mojave and Great Basin desertscapes, boom-and-bust mining towns and huge, off-limits military bases. Leaving Las Vegas, US 95 passes the high peaks of Mount Charleston to the west and, for nearly 200 miles (321 kilometres), skirts the edge of the vast Nellis Air Force Range to the east. You pass **Amargosa Valley, Beatty** (watch your driving speed here; this is a notorious speed trap) and **Scotty's Junction**, all gateways to Death Valley National Park just over the California border (*see p277*). Near Beatty (on the Nevada side) lies the photogenic ghost town of **Rhyolite**. Established in 1905 after gold and silver were discovered in the Bullfrog Hills, its

population peaked at 10,000, but by 1912 the town was deserted. Now you can wander past ghost sculptures and various crumbling brick buildings, including the town jail, train depot and school, and the famous bottle house, constructed when building materials were scarce, but there was no shortage of empty beer bottles from the town's 50 saloons. The **Friends of Rhyolite** (PO Box 85, Amargosa Valley, NV 89020) was set up to protect and preserve the town and presents 'living history' events at the annual Rhyolite Resurrection Festival, held in March.

About 30 miles (48 kilometres) north of Scotty's Junction is **Goldfield**, a classic example of Nevada's once-grand mining towns. Gold was discovered here in 1902: by 1907 the population had passed 10,000. At the height of the boom in 1910, it was easily the largest town in the state, with a population of 20,000, but the gold ran out and a fire in 1923 destroyed 53 square blocks; now there are less than 500 inhabitants. Several grand stone buildings, including the abandoned Goldfield Hotel, the high school and the occupied county courthouse, are poignant reminders of the town's heyday. Drop into the **Santa Fe Saloon** (turn right at Fifth Avenue) for a taste of the past: it's a rickety structure with a long wooden bar and signed photos of boxer and ex-miner Jack Dempsey.

About 200 miles (321 kilometres) from Las Vegas is **Tonopah**. Prospector Jim Butler discovered silver here in 1900 and for the next 15 years (until the lode ran out) almost $150 million of ore was dug out of the small mines that still dot the surrounding area. Tonopah survives mainly as a convenient crossroads town, at the junction of US 95 and US 6, and through the jobs provided by the **Tonopah Test Range**, where top-secret military planes are test-flown (listen for the sonic booms). At the southern end of town is the **Central Nevada Museum**. It is a fascinating, if haphazardly arranged place: photos of Tonopah and Goldfield in their glory days line the walls, clothing, household goods and other artefacts are crammed into glass cases, and there's a 'purple glass' collection (manganese used in early glass turns purple in sunlight). Rusting mining equipment sits outside.

The 'original' Las Vegas: welcome to downtown **Reno**. *See p256.*

From Tonopah there's 100 miles (161 kilometres) of gloriously empty road until **Hawthorne**, the next town of any size. As you approach the town, you see one, then two, then thousands of strange, half-buried, oblong structures jutting out of the desert floor, looking like they belong in a *Mad Max*-style movie. Since the 1930s, Hawthorne has been home to one of the US Army's largest ammunition depots, and these half-buried bunkers are in fact full of bullets, bombs and weapons.

Just north of Hawthorne, the road skirts the western edge of the 30-mile (48-kilometre) long **Walker Lake**, a remnant of an ancient lake that once covered most of western Nevada (and a small portion of eastern California). The lake has dropped 100 feet (30 metres) since 1930, and its fish are slowly dying because the Walker River has been diverted for irrigation, but it's still a popular spot for swimming, boating and fishing: there are picnic sites and one campground (Sportsmans Beach) off US 95. At the northern end of the lake is the **Walker River Indian Reservation**, which belongs to a tribe of the Northern Paiute.

About 30 miles (48 kilometres) north of Hawthorne, you have the choice of taking the 'alternate' US 95 north-west to Fernley, where it joins the I-80, or continuing on the main US 95 north to Fallon to join the US 50. Take main US 95 if you plan to head back east into Nevada on US 50 or I-80; otherwise, alternate US 95 provides a useful shortcut to Carson City or Reno and is the more interesting route. It takes you through the attractive oasis of **Yerington**, surrounded by big trees in the fertile Mason Valley; rest your eyes on all that green after miles of scrubby desert. You can visit **Fort Churchill Historic State Park**, which

houses the ruins of an 1860s US army outpost, a visitor centre, picnic sites and a campground. At I-80, head west: it's a fast 30 miles (48 kilometres) into Reno.

Central Nevada Museum

1900 Logan Field Road, Tonopah (1-775 482 9676). **Open** *Summer* 9am-5pm daily. *Winter* 11am-5pm Mon-Sat. **Admission** free.

Fort Churchill Historic State Park

Silver Springs (1-775 577 2345). **Open** 8am-5pm daily. **Admission** free.

Where to stay, eat & drink

In Tonopah, choose from numerous motels along the main street. The large **Station House** casino (1100 Erie Main Street, 1-775 482 9777) next to the Central Nevada Museum has a dark, cramped gaming area, rooms ($95 for two people), a restaurant and a wonderful collection of old chrome slot machines in the basement next to the toilets. The **El Marques** restaurant (1-775 482 3885) serves decent, good-value Mexican food (main courses $6-$12).

Hawthorne has a number of motels and one casino, the **El Capitan** (540 F Street, 1-775 945 3321). **Maggie's Restaurant** (on US 95 at E Street, 1-775 945 3908/www.maggie's restaurant.com) is a clean, pink, but rather soulless place serving reasonable steak, burgers, salads and sandwiches.

Tourist information

For more information about Tonopah, contact the **Chamber of Commerce** at 301 Brougher Avenue (1-775 482 3859).

The big bang

An hour's drive outside Las Vegas to the north-west is a vast tract of uninhabited desert, covering nearly 5,500 square miles (14,250 square kilometres). A reminder of the stark grandeur of nature on the doorstep of one of the world's most artificial cities? Yes, but also one of the largest secured areas of government-owned land in the United States, and since 1951 the location of more than 1,200 nuclear blasts. Welcome to the Nevada Test Site.

In 1940, the US Army Air Corps was gearing up for possible participation in World War II. Searching for a practice range for fighter pilots and gunners, the Army selected Western Air Field, the small airport on the edge of tiny Las Vegas and to the south of a huge area of unpopulated desert. When the US entered the war in late 1941, the airfield, now called the Las Vegas Bombing & Gunnery Range, went into full operation. At the height of the war build-up, classes of 4,000 bombers and gunners were graduating every six weeks and the practice range had grown to cover 5,156 square miles (13,360 square kilometres) of south-central Nevada.

After the war, the base and range shut down – but not for long. In the late 1940s,

after blowing off a few A-bombs over the Marshall Islands, the Atomic Energy Commission needed a more convenient location to conduct its tests, and the Rhode Island-sized plot of desert at the heart of the old Las Vegas bombing range seemed perfect for its nuclear purposes.

The first test, in January 1951, was a relatively small one-kiloton bomb dropped from an aeroplane roughly 90 miles (145 kilometres) north of Vegas on what is now known as Frenchman Flat. Over the next 11 years, 126 atomic weapons were detonated above ground, until the first Limited Nuclear Test Ban Treaty prohibited atmospheric explosions. For 30 years after that, another 1,100 warheads, including the so-called hydrogen or fusion bomb, were detonated deep underground in the same area. By the early 1990s, the tests had slowed to one or two a year, and in 1996 President Clinton signed the Comprehensive Test Ban Treaty, which ended all nuclear testing in the US.

But the Feds aren't through with the Nevada Test Site. Not by a long shot. An area near the centre of the site, known as **Yucca Mountain**, is earmarked to become the only permanent repository for nearly

Reno

Though few people outside the American West are aware of it, Las Vegas isn't the only large gambling city in Nevada. Reno is the 'original' Las Vegas; Las Vegas could never have become Las Vegas if Reno hadn't been Reno first. But in the 1950s, Reno took one look at what was happening to Las Vegas and made a deliberate decision to limit the spread of gambling to the downtown core along Virginia Street. This 'redline' remained in effect till 1978; even today, only a handful of casinos are found outside downtown.

You could comfortably fit four Renos inside Las Vegas. It's not only smaller, it's also slower and prettier. The Truckee River runs right through the middle of downtown, giving the

city a more natural and rural flavour. Along the riverfront is a two-block plaza that leads to two downtown parks: **Wingfield**, on an island in the middle of a bulge in the river, connected to the mainland by pedestrian bridges; and **Riverside**, three acres of grass, with tennis and basketball courts and a playground. Also unlike Las Vegas, Reno experiences four distinct seasons: in winter, skiers jam the slopes of more than 20 ski resorts within an hour of town; summers are balmy and every weekend some special event closes off Virginia Street for a block party.

Look out for **Hot August Nights**, the classic-car equivalent of a Grateful Dead gig. Up to 60,000 people come to town to join in the fun: cruisin', drag races, cool car contests and live music. **Street Vibrations**, in

70,000 metric tons of high-level radioactive waste. Not surprisingly, it's a controversial subject: many Nevadans are unhappy about the prospect of tons of spent radioactive fuel travelling by rail and road past their front doors, to be dumped in their backyard. A 'study' of the area has been going on for years; its cost runs into billions of dollars, as opposing factions (the Feds versus the state, the nuclear power industry versus environmentalists) battle it out in Congress, the courts, scientific journals and the mainstream media. It would seem that the Nevada Test Site is as explosive now as at any period in its eventful past.

If you're interested in visiting the area without facing possible arrest, consider taking one of the Department of Energy's guided tours, either to the bomb-cratered test site or to the Yucca Mountain depository. Both tours are free, but be sure to apply for your place weeks in advance.

Nevada Test Site Tour

US Department of Energy, Nevada Operations Office, Office of Public Affairs & Information, Visit Coordination Staff, PO Box 98518, Las Vegas, NV 89193 (295 0944/fax 295 0943/ www.nv.doe.gov). **Tours** once a month.
The Test Site Tour, though very informative, is also more than a little sinister. The site is massive – miles and miles of uninhabited desert, pock-marked by vast subsidence craters formed by the underground nuclear explosions. An atmosphere of Big Brother surveillance and secrecy pervades the whole experience: from the initial bus search to the bizarre, 1950s-style printed propaganda. Tour buses are sometimes surrounded by workers

in protective suits toting Geiger-counters, and woe betide any hapless tourist found with binoculars or a camera – both are forbidden. The tour visits Mercury, the operations centre of the Test Site, then Frenchman Flat, site of the first tests – where visitors used to be allowed to gather glass, formed as the heat of the nuclear blasts melted the exposed sand. Other points of interest include News Nob, where journalists would gather to watch the mushroom clouds.

Due to the popularity of the tour, at least six weeks' advance booking is required. There are 270 places on each tour, which are allocated on a first-come, first-served basis.

Yucca Mountain Tour

Information 295 5555. **Tours** *Sept-Nov, Mar-May once a month, on Sat.*
Tour groups have the chance to walk into the underground repository, talk to experts at the site and see the huge drilling equipment used to bore the storage tunnels. To join a tour, contact the Department of Energy's Yucca Mountain Science Center (*see below*) well in advance – applications by non-nationals can take up to 70 days to be processed. All visitors require photo ID, and both cameras and recording equipment are forbidden on the tour.

Yucca Mountain Science Center

4101B Meadows Lane, at Valley View Boulevard, North-west Las Vegas, NV 89107 (1-800 225 6972/Science Center 295 1312/ www.ymp.gov). Bus 104. **Open** 10am-6pm Tue-Sat.
The centre has interactive exhibits on the geology, culture, volcanics and storage technology of the Yucca Mountain Project.

mid-September, is the Harley-Davidson version, attracting thousands of bikers on their 'hawgs'.

Compared to brazen Las Vegas, sedate Reno is one of the best-kept secrets in the West.

Sights & attractions

The venerable **Reno Arch** spans Virginia Street in the heart of downtown and proudly proclaims Reno the 'Biggest Little City in the World', as opposed to Las Vegas, which is one of the littlest big cities in the world. This is the fourth such arch: the first was erected in 1926 to celebrate the completion of a transcontinental highway that passed through Reno, while the second, built in 1938, stands outside the **National Automobile Museum** at Lake and Mill Streets a few blocks away. Housed in a

$10-million building reminiscent of a sleek 1950s Chrysler, the museum has nearly 200 classic and unique cars, from an 1890 Philion to one of Elvis's custom Cadillacs.

For a few blocks on either side of the current 13-year-old arch there are souvenir shops, pawn shops and old hotels, as well as some major hotel-casinos. Choose between the Irish green of **Fitzgeralds** (255 N Virginia Street, at W Second Street, 1-800 535 5825/1-775 785 3300/ www.fitzgeralds.com/reno) or the garish pink of the **Flamingo Reno** (255 N Sierra Street, at W Second Street, 1-800 648 4882/1-775 322 1111/ www.flamingoreno.com), which has a rockin' casino, a large show lounge and dining with a view in the Top of the Flamingo restaurant on the 21st floor. More upscale eateries can be found at **Eldorado** (345 N Virginia Street, at E Fourth Street, 1-800 648 5966/1-775 786 5700/www.eldoradoreno.com), while **Harrah's Reno** (219 N Center Street, at E Second Street, Reno, 1-800 427 7247/1-775 786 3232/www.harrahs.com) boasts one of the best buffets in town.

Hard-core gamblers head for the sprawling **Cal-Neva Virginian** (140 N Virginia Street, at E Second Street, 1-877 777 7303/1-775 323 1046) for its 24-hour 99¢ breakfast and rammin' jammin' gaming action, while large crowds of low-rollers, gawkers and kids flock to the carnival-themed **Circus Circus** (500 N Sierra Street, at W Fifth Street, 1-800 648 5010/1-775 329 0711/www.circusreno. com). Most impressive is perhaps the **Silver Legacy** (407 N Virginia Street, at W Fourth Street, 1-800 687 8733/1-775 329 4777/www.silverlegacyreno. com), which opened in June 1995 and is one of Reno's two Las Vegas-style mega-resorts. The casino boasts a lobby filled with treasures from Tiffany's and the world's largest composite dome. A 120-foot (37-metre) high mining rig inside the dome mints silver dollars.

The railroad tracks bisect Virginia Street and every day two passenger and several freight trains still close the street to traffic, as they have for the past 132 years. Stop off at the **Liberty Belle Saloon** (4250 S Virginia Street, at Peckham Lane, 1-775 825 1776) to see its outstanding exhibit on the development of slot machines. Owners Marshall and Frank Fey are the grandsons of Charlie Fey, who invented the first slot machines in 1898.

Also in downtown is the purpose-built **National Bowling Stadium** (see p260), a unique $35-million arena that has single-handedly turned Reno into the Bowling Capital of the World and draws tens of thousands of bowlers to the city for several months at a time. The stadium has 80 lanes with seating for up to 2,000 spectators, plus pro shops, repair facilities, snack bars, a 100-seat geodesic-domed Omnimax cinema and the downtown visitor centre. The stadium is reserved for national tournaments, but the public can tour the building for free when there's no action, or for a small charge when a tournament is on.

In addition to those around Virginia Street, there are five major hotel-casinos scattered throughout the valley in which Reno sits. Located a couple of miles south of downtown, the monstrous **Reno Hilton** (2500 E Second Street, at Manuel Street, 1-800 648 5080/1-775 789 2000/www.renohilton.com) is visible for miles around and is the largest hotel-casino in Nevada (outside Vegas). Nearby are the tropically themed **Atlantis** (3800 S Virginia Street, at Peckham Lane, 1-800 723 6500/1-775 825 4700/www.atlantiscasino.com) and the

glam **Peppermill** (2707 S Virginia Street, at Grove Street, 1-800 282 2444/www.peppermill. com), while in Reno's sister city of Sparks, you'll find low-roller haven the **Silver Club** (1040 Victorian Avenue, at Dickerson Street, 1-800 905 7779) and the more upmarket **Nugget** (1100 Nugget Avenue, at Victorian Square & I-80 east, Sparks, 1-800 648 1177/ www.janugget.com), which boasts a very good oyster bar.

National Automobile Museum

10 Lake Street South, at Mill Street (1-775 333 9300/www.automuseum.com). **Open** 9.30am-5.30pm Mon-Sat; 10am-4pm Sun. **Admission** $7.50; $6.50 concessions; $2.50 6-18s; free under-5s. **Credit** AmEx, Disc, MC, V.

Around Reno

From Reno you can head east into the hills to **Virginia City** (south on US 395 for eight miles/13 kilometres, then east on Highway 341 for another eight miles/13 kilometres), one of the most authentic (albeit touristy) historic mining towns in the American West, where the famous Comstock Lode was unearthed. Visit museums, saloons and gift shops, tour two underground mines and take a ride on a railway powered by a steam engine, or seek out a historic mansion tour for a more authentic, less touristy experience.

An hour north of Reno is the turquoise expanse of **Pyramid Lake**, a large and beautiful natural desert lake. A remnant of ancient Lake Lahontan, which once covered much of north-western Nevada, it's the only home of the prehistoric cui-ui (pronounced 'kwee-wee') sucker fish, and is considered to be sacred by the Native American Paiute who look after it.

Fifty miles (80 kilometres) to the north is the small town of Gerlach, gateway to the large and very flat **Black Rock Desert**. This was the site of Richard Noble's 1997 successful bid to set a new land speed record of 764 mph (1,230 kmph), which broke the sound barrier on land for the first time in history. The Black Rock Desert is also the home of the annual and infamous **Burning Man Festival**, now the largest outdoor art extravaganza in the world, attracting 30,000 celebrants in 2000 (see p259 **The Burning Man Festival**).

If you still have time, take a drive into the mountains to the west of Reno to **Lake Tahoe** (drive south on US 395 for eight miles/13 kilometres, then take Highway 431 west for 25 miles/40 kilometres). The beautiful Lake Tahoe is one of the greatest alpine lakes in the world and the undisputed crown jewel of western Nevada.

The Burning Man Festival

Every year in the first week of September, 25,000 to 30,000 people gather in the Black Rock Desert in a remote north-western corner of Nevada to build a temporary city. The physical, spiritual and symbolic centre of this city is a 50-foot (15-metre) tall Man made of wood, neon and fireworks, surrounded by installations of outrageous art – some sublime, some ridiculous. At the end of the week, when the Man is burned, his flaming, exploding skeleton triggers one of the most remarkable and mind-boggling all-night celebrations anywhere on Earth. Burning Man is not your average outdoor art festival.

To spend three or five or seven days in Black Rock City is about as close as you'll ever get to passing time on a different planet. The Black Rock Desert is a vast expanse of cracked clay where absolutely nothing grows. The terrain is so flat that if you look out towards the horizon, you can actually see the foxy curvature of our Mother Earth.

Treeless hills, some swathed with outlandish swirls of colour, rise up on all sides of the flats. And above you is a giant dome of the purest blue sky; at night it pulses with the cool fire of nine million stars. The setting, in short, is unnerving and surreal.

In the middle of this rugged bizarre locale, artists, engineers, hipsters, tripsters, cosmic comedians and even some ordinary people build the most unabashed and unflinchingly psychedelic city that ever existed. Black Rock City, which has two newspapers, a post office, at least two dozen radio stations, and an airstrip, exists to astonish, to expose, to make sacred, to make fun, to unsettle and to

undress (it's perfectly acceptable to be naked). It's a place where the ancient (Ur, Egypt, Atlantis) merges with the future (ultra-wired cyber-cynicism), where the creation of community takes precedence over crass commerce (once you get there, your money is basically worthless). Burning Man is where reality dares to dream of ways to somehow do better – then sets itself on fire.

One thing's for sure: this is no lark in the desert. The festival is not only a showcase for radical self-expression, it's also an exercise in radical self-survival. Participants are expected to stay for five to seven days, and to bring with them everything they might need to remain comfortable in awesome thunderstorms, tent-ruffling winds and temperatures ranging from 0°C to 40°C (32-104°F).

If you're serious about attending Burning Man, your first stop should be the website www. burningman.com. Click straight through to the Survival Guide, which drives home the absolute necessity of proper preparation. The site also answers just about every question you could ever think to ask about Burning Man, and includes an extensive archive of photos illustrating some of the more colourful participants and artwork of years past. Ticket info is also available online; figure on paying $150 to $200 per ticket, depending on how early in the year you buy your admission.

You may be enthralled or irritated, delighted or revolted, charmed or repulsed, but even the most been-there, done-that, fast-lane world traveller will never, ever be bored at Burning Man.

About 30 miles (48 kilometres) south of Reno on US 365 lies **Carson City**, a picturesque and quaint historical town that also happens to be the Nevada state capital. Historically home to many of the state's politically powerful families, Carson is also site of the state legislature building, the governor's mansion, the state supreme court and the **Nevada State Museum** (600 North Carson Street, 1-775 687 4810, open 8.30am-4pm daily, admission $3), housed in the old mint building.

Where to eat & drink

Until 1999, the family-value, family-style, family-run Santa Fe topped the list of places to eat in Reno. This traditional Basque restaurant stood on the same spot for more than 50 years, until an unexplained family feud closed it down. All that remains is **Louie's Basque Corner** (301 E Fourth Street, at Evans Avenue, 1-775 323 7203). Louie's continues to serve the Santa Fe's signature Picon Punch cocktail and food (main courses $7-$15) but, all in all, the place is no substitute for the original.

The best casino food is available at the **Eldorado**, the **Peppermill**, **Harrah's**, the **Nugget** and the **Reno Hilton**, but you should check out the city's other dining options, too. For good food, beer and great coffee, head for the **Pneumatic Diner** (second floor, Truckee River Lodge, 501 W First Street, 1-775 786 8888 ext 106, main courses $4-$7) and **Deux Gros Nez** (628 Gordon Avenue, 1-775 786 9400, main courses $3-$7). Also worth a try is the **Silver Peak Restaurant & Brewery** (124 Wonder Street, at Holcomb Avenue, 1-775 324 1864), which offers eight in-house draught beers and a hearty menu that ranges from gourmet pizza ($7-$11) to steaks and chops ($10-$18).

Reno's bar scene is limited, but check out **Reno Live**, on the lower level of Eddie's Fabulous Fifties club in downtown (45 W Second Street, 1-775 329 1950), where you'll find 'Reno's hottest party' from Thursday to Sunday, with perpetual promotions and discounts. **Big Ed's Alley Inn** (1036 E Fourth Street, 1-775 322 4180) is a local institution, now owned by Reno's most popular DJ, Bruce Van Dyke (the morning jock at KTHX, 100.1 FM). Big Ed's offers raucous weekend concerts, good beer and great pizza.

There's also fun to be had at the 24-hour **Little Waldorf Saloon** (1661 N Virginia Street, 1-775 323 3682), a barbaric college bar across from the university. The **Great Basin Brewing Co** in Sparks (846 Victorian Avenue, 1-775 355 7711) is within walking distance of a host of other bars.

Where to stay

Roughly 25,000 rooms are available in Reno, running the gamut from dirt-cheap to sky-high. The hotel-casinos (see p257-8) fall into the medium price range – call each property for details of its current rates and discounts. Prices peak in August but can be rock-bottom during winter. Contact the **Reno/Sparks Convention & Visitors Authority** hotel reservation service (1-800 367 7366/www.rscva. com) for further information.

Getting there

By air

If you haven't enough time to drive, a round trip to Reno from McCarran International Airport on American (1-800 433 7300/www.im.aa.com), Southwest (1-800 435 9792/www.southwest. com) and America West (1-800 235 9292/www.americawest. com) costs $88-$184 depending on the time of year.

Tourist information

Call or visit the visitor centre inside the **National Bowling Stadium** or phone the automated information line at the **Reno/Sparks Convention & Visitors Authority** (1-800 367 7366/www.rscva. com).

National Bowling Stadium

300 N Center Street, at E Fourth Street (1-775 334 2695/334 2600). **Open** 8am-5pm daily.

ET Highway

If you think Las Vegas is strange, just wait until you drive along the 87 miles (140 kilometres) of Highway 375, also known as the Extraterrestrial Highway and a mecca for UFO freaks and tourists. It's a beautiful, lonely desert road, typical of Nevada's range and basin landscape, that cuts across mountains and through 20-mile (32-kilometre) valleys. The real reason for its fame, though, is that it skirts the north-eastern edge of **Nellis Air Force Range**, the vast and sinister military complex that covers a big swathe of south-central Nevada. This area of government-controlled land is not only the location of the Nevada Test Site (where numerous atomic bombs were exploded above ground in the 1950s and below ground through the early 1990s; see p256 **The big bang**) and the Tonopah Test Range (testing ground for the B-2 Stealth bomber in the 1980s), it is also the site of **Area 51**, the top-secret R&D facility, whose existence the US government still refuses to acknowledge.

Mystery surrounds and rumours abound about Area 51, specifically concerning the dry beds of Groom Lake and Papoose Lake. The US military is said to be experimenting with new-tech aircraft including a hypersonic spy plane dubbed Aurora and, if you believe the more outrageous claims, also conducting tests on alien spaceships and holding at least a couple of aliens in cold storage, some say the self-same aliens that dropped in on Roswell, New Mexico, in 1947.

Speculation reached fever pitch in 1989, when physicist Bob Lazar appeared on a Las Vegas news show, claiming he had worked at Papoose Lake and seen nine flying saucers in camouflaged hangars: he even said he'd seen one briefly in flight. Numerous UFO sightings have since been reported along Highway 375, notably near the 'black mailbox' (much to the disgust of the mailbox's owner). The latest rumour is that the military has effectively closed down Area 51 and moved testing to locations in Utah and Colorado.

The road was officially designated ET Highway in 1996 to coincide with the launch of the movie *Independence Day*. All but one of the official state 'Extraterrestrial Highway' signs along the route have since been stolen.

The only settlement on the highway is **Rachel** (population 80), a straggly collection of mobile homes, called **The Little A'Le'Inn** – geddit?. You can't miss it: there's a bug-eyed alien painted on the side and a parking sign on the roof with a picture of a flying saucer. It's the only motel on the road, and also serves food (an Alien Burger costs $3). There's alien-related literature and UFO photos on the walls, as well as a pool table, video poker machines (this is Nevada, after all) and a bar area bedecked with Republican posters: don't get into a conversation about gun control unless you're against it.

At the other end of Rachel, fill your tank at the highway's only petrol station and visit the **Area 51 Research Center**, set up by Glenn Campbell to highlight the government's shenanigans around Area 51 rather than to attract alien enthusiasts. The black mailbox is now painted white and located south of Rachel, between mileposts 29 and 30.

Whatever the truth about Area 51, there is certainly no end to alleged bizarre goings-on in the skies above the ET Highway. But whether the reports of strange lights, odd-shaped craft and unconventional flying patterns are due to visitors from outer space or wishful thinking is open to debate.

Given the number of military planes, commercial jets, flares, weather balloons, satellites and general airborne activity in the region, you would expect to see something unusual overhead. Rachel attracts plane spotters, obsessed with the latest military hardware, as well as UFO geeks.

Novice sky-gazers should note that the B-2 stealth plane looks like a classic flying saucer when viewed from the front or rear, and at night even a car's headlights in the distance can look spooky. Sadly, the closest (and potentially most dangerous) encounter you're likely to experience is with a cow wandering into the middle of the road while you're feverishly scanning the sky for spaceships.

Since 1995, when the military annexed more land, the only view of Area 51 is from **Tikaboo Peak**, 26 miles (42 kilometres) from the base. You get superb views of the desert, but all you'll see of the base is a few distant buildings. It's a strenuous, high-altitude hike, best done in summer (snow can last until April) and early in the morning, before heat haze distorts the view. Make sure you and your vehicle are properly equipped; conditions are harsh and there are no park rangers out here. Take binoculars. The best route (usually accessible by a non-4WD vehicle) is via a dirt road off US 93 at milepost 32.2, south of Alamo. It's just over 22 miles (35 kilometres) to Badger Spring and then a two-hour hike to the summit, but it's easy to get lost. For a detailed description, read Chuck Clark's *Area 51 Viewer's Guide* ($15), available from the Area 51 Research Center.

Take care when approaching Area 51. Armed guards patrol the border, and you can be sure someone is watching your movements. Do not, repeat, *do not* cross the boundary into the military zone: you will be arrested, questioned and fined at least $600. The guards are also authorised to use 'deadly force' on trespassers. The border is not accurately marked on maps and often hard to detect: it's defined by orange posts, some topped with silver globes, and occasional 'restricted area' signs, but no fence.

Area 51 Research Center

Rachel (1-775 729 2648/www.area51researchcenter. com). **Open** 9am-5pm daily. **Admission** free.

Where to stay

The Little A'Le'Inn

HCR 61 Box 45, Rachel, NV 89001 (1-775 729 2515). **Rates** double $42.50.
Seven rooms located in cosy, if dilapidated trailers: you get a shared bathroom, a communal kitchen-cum-living room and yet more UFO photos.

Getting there

By car

Take US 93 north for 107 miles (172 kilometres) to the junction with ET Highway (Highway 375). Rachel is 36 miles (58 kilometres) to the north-west of the junction.

Trips Out of Town

Into Arizona

Make a trip to the beautiful, awe-inspiring Grand Canyon – there's no place on earth quite like it.

Although Phoenix and Tucson are too far to visit comfortably in a couple of days, parts of north and west Arizona are easily reached from Las Vegas. What's more, the **Grand Canyon**, the undisputed jewel in Arizona's crown, is only a few hours' drive or a short flight away.

Grand Canyon National Park

Everything you've heard about the Grand Canyon is true: it's stunning; overwhelming; mind-blowing; one of the great natural wonders of the world. The national park is 277 miles (446 kilometres) long, most of which is difficult to reach and rarely visited; just a tiny portion of it is accessible from the South Rim, where most visitors congregate. The canyon is also misnamed: it's not just one rip in the earth, but rather a series of canyons surrounding the central gorge cut by the Colorado River – a staggering 5,000 feet (1,524 metres) from top to bottom. At an average elevation of 7,000 feet (2,134 metres), the South Rim is not unbearably hot in summer, but the canyon bottom, a mile down, can push 110°F (43°C). April, May, September and October are probably the best months to visit; most of the rainfall occurs in summer, and from December to March, the upper canyon is usually snowbound and temperatures plummet.

Entrance to the park costs $20 per car ($10 per person for pedestrians and cyclists) and is valid for seven days; you'll need to stay at least two nights to give yourself enough time to explore the village, rim drives and various lookout points and to venture into the canyon itself – and drive back to Vegas. If you want to take a mule trip, air tour or hike to the bottom of the canyon, you'll need longer.

TOURIST INFORMATION

For general information, call the National Park Service on 1-520 638 7888, or check out the Grand Canyon's excellent website at www.nps. gov/grca/grandcanyon. It has information on accommodation, hiking, backcountry permits, maps of the area and so on – all you need to know, in fact, to plan your trip.

En route to the South Rim

One hundred and fifty miles west of the South Rim, the Grand Canyon forms the northern boundary of the **Hualapai Indian Reservation**, a 1,563-square-mile (4,048-square-kilometre) Wildlife Conservation Area. Although not as spectacular as the South Rim, the western canyon is much closer to Las Vegas and will give you a taste of the grandeur further east. Turn off the I-40 on to old Route 66 to reach **Peach Springs**, the gateway to the area and the location of the Hualapai tribal headquarters (1-520 769 2216). Permits for sightseeing, fishing and camping in the western canyon are available from **Hualapai Lodge** (PO Box 358, Peach Springs, AZ 86434, 1-888 255 9550/fax 1-520 769 2372). The lodge also provides accommodation and dining facilities, and is the place to find out general information about sightseeing tours. One-day white-water trips on the Colorado River starting at Diamond Creek are offered by **Hualapai River Runners** (1-800 622 4409/1-520 769 2210).

Continuing along I-40 will bring you to the small and friendly town of **Williams**, located just sixty miles (97 kilometres) south of the National Park. Named after legendary mountain man 'Old' Bill Williams, whose huge statue can be found at the west end of town, it has the distinction of being the last town on Route 66 to be bypassed by the freeway system (in 1984). Williams is still a mecca for Route 66 fans, lured by numerous souvenir shops and regular classic car rallies. The centre of town is lined with early-20th century buildings, old-style concrete street lamps and some fab retro signs; don't miss the shop and headquarters of *Route 66 Magazine* (323 W Route 66, 1-520 635 4322) for some great memorabilia. For details on lodging, restaurants and other facilities, stop at the **visitor centre** in the old Santa Fe Freight Depot (200 W Railroad Avenue, 1-520 635 4061, open 8am-5pm daily).

Flagstaff, 35 miles (56 kilometres) east of Williams, is also a good jumping-off point for the Canyon via Highway 180 and Highway 64. Situated at the base of the San Francisco Peaks (the highest mountains in Arizona), this pleasant railroad and university town has motels, good restaurants and brewpubs, interesting museums, and the **Lowell Observatory** (from

On the edge: the **Lookout Studio**.

where the planet Pluto was first spotted in 1930). The atmosphere is laid-back and the historic downtown area is full of small coffee-houses, shops and restaurants. Route 66 runs right through the centre of town. More information is available from the **Chamber of Commerce** (101 E Route 66, 1-520 774 4505).

South Rim

Most of the park's annual five million visitors head for the **South Rim** and the restaurants, accommodation, shops and sights of **Grand Canyon Village**, perched on the edge of the canyon lip. Inevitably, it's crowded, but remains remarkably untouristy. It is also closer to the Colorado River than the North Rim and has much better views into the canyon.

If you have the patience to not drive straight to the rim, park your car and take a free shuttle bus to the new **Canyon View Information Plaza**, where you will find a well equipped visitors' centre and bookstore (open 8am-5pm daily). Pick up a map of the National Park and a copy of *The Guide*, the park's newspaper, which has comprehensive information on sights, transportation, facilities and activities, before strolling to **Mather Point** for your first gob-smacking view of the Canyon. The **Village Route** shuttle bus will take you from the Information Plaza into Grand Canyon Village.

Grand Canyon Village

Travellers have been coming to gawp at the Grand Canyon since the 19th century and the village is dotted with historic buildings. Many of the most interesting were built by pioneering female architect Mary Colter for the Fred Harvey Travel Company.

A leaflet describes a self-guided walking tour around the village's historic district, starting at the **Santa Fe Railway Station** (1909), the terminus for the Grand Canyon Railway (*see p266*). Across the road on the canyon edge is the luxurious **El Tovar Hotel**, a large wooden building in hunting lodge style, which cost a cool quarter of a million dollars when it was built in 1905. Next to it is the **Hopi House** (open 8am-8pm daily summer, 9am-5pm daily winter), which was designed by Mary Colter in 1904 as a showroom and salesroom for Indian handicrafts. Colter modelled the building on a terraced Hopi dwelling, using local stone and wood and employing Hopi builders. Nearby is **Verkamps Curios** (1906), one of the canyon's oldest continuously operating stores.

Walking west from the hotel along the Rim Trail, you will pass the modern Kachina and Thunderbird lodges and the pioneer-style stone and log **Bright Angel Lodge**, designed by Mary Colter in 1935. If you happen to be at the Canyon in winter, warm your hands at the fabulous 'geological' fireplace. The design mimics the layers of rock in the Grand Canyon, from the hearth, which is made from stone from the bed of the Colorado River, right up to a layer of Kaibab limestone at the top of the chimney breast.

Beyond Bright Angel Lodge is **Bucky O'Neill's cabin**, which dates from the 1890s and is the oldest surviving building on the rim, and the **Lookout Studio** (Colter, 1914), which now houses a gift shop (open 8am-7pm daily summer, 9am-5pm daily winter). Perched on the edge of the precipice, the studio was designed as an observation building, from where visitors could view the canyon. Colter did not want the building to detract from the natural beauty of the Grand Canyon itself, so created a stone structure that merges almost completely with the surrounding rock; from a distance, the Lookout Studio is almost invisible.

The **Kolb Studio** was built by pioneering photographers Ellsworth and Emery Kolb, who started snapping mule riders venturing into the canyon in 1902. The lack of water on the rim meant the brothers had to hike halfway down the canyon to their developing tent at Indian Gardens, process the photos and get back to the top before the mules returned. (All water at the South Rim is still pumped up from inside the canyon; look out for the transcanyon pipeline on the Bright Angel trail.) The Kolbs were also the first to film a boat trip down the Colorado in 1912. The studio houses a bookstore and gallery (open 8am-6pm daily), and has displays on the Kolb brothers' work. Just beyond here is the head of the **Bright Angel Trail** into the Canyon (*see p267*).

The ever-changing colours of the
Grand Canyon.

Along the South Rim

Two roads lead west and east out from the
village along the canyon rim. Both are worth
exploring because each provides very different
views into the canyon. You can also walk along
the very edge of the rim, on the 11-mile (18-
kilometre), pedestrian-only **Rim Trail**. The
village section of the trail is paved; elsewhere
it can get rocky.

The eight-mile (13-kilometre) **West Rim
Drive** along Hermit Road is closed to private
vehicles from March to November. Instead,
visitors are encouraged to take the shuttle
bus from the western edge of the village to
Hermit's Rest, built by Mary Colter as a
refreshment stop for visitors in 1914. The
building (now a gift shop), is deliberately
primitive in style so that it blends with its
natural surroundings (fortunately, a Swiss
chalet design was rejected). The **Hermit Trail**
into the Canyon starts from here (*see p267*).

The shuttle bus stops at various observation
points on its way out, including the spectacular
Abyss, where the Great Mohave Wall drops
3,000 feet (915 metres) to the Tonto Platform
above the Colorado River. However, it only
stops at Mohave Point and Hopi Point on its
return. If you're planning to watch the sunset,
make sure you check the time of the last bus
before you leave to avoid a long, dark walk
back to the village.

The **East Rim Drive** goes 23 miles
(37 kilometres) in the opposite direction along
Desert View Drive as far as the park's eastern
entrance. On the way, the road passes several
excellent lookout points, with access to the
South Kaibab and **Grand View Trails**
(*see p267*). (Note that the side road to the South
Kaibab Trailhead and Yaki Point is closed to
private vehicles from March to November.)
Near the end of the drive, there's an 800-year-
old ruin of an Anasazi pueblo and the **Tusayan
Museum**, which provides rather scanty
information on the history and culture of the
canyon's Native American inhabitants.

The drive finishes at **Desert View**, which
offers the clearest views of the Colorado River.
This is also the location of the amazing
Watchtower, a circular, 70-foot (21-metre)
tower, regarded as Mary Colter's masterpiece.
A re-creation of the ancient Indian towers Colter
had seen at Mesa Verde and Canyon de Chelly,
it is a remarkable structure, as striking now as
when it was first unveiled. The exterior is
deliberately ruined in appearance, while the
interiors are a tribute to Colter's life-long love of
Native American culture and art. The ground-
floor room is modelled after a *kiva* or sacred
ceremonial chamber, while the roof provides a
panoramic view of the Grand Canyon, the
Painted Desert and the San Francisco Peaks,
40 miles (64 kilometres) to the south. It is fitted
with black-mirror reflectoscopes, which

condense and simplify the views of the canyon, while also intensifying the colours. The centrepiece, however, is the Hopi Room, which is decorated with vivid Hopi designs depicting various gods and legends including the famous Snake Dance.

To learn more about the geology, history and archaeology of the South Rim, join one of the Park Service's ranger-guided walks and activities. Call 1-520 638 7888 for details, or check *The Guide* for a programme schedule.

Where to eat

There are three restaurants, two self-service cafés and a takeaway snack bar in the Grand Canyon Village, all open daily. The splendid, dark wooden dining room with its large Indian murals at the **El Tovar Hotel** is very popular – you have to take your chances at breakfast (6.30-11am) and lunch (11.30am-2pm), but must book for dinner (5-10pm); hotel guests take priority over non-guests.

Nearby are the less formal **Bright Angel Lodge** dining room (6.30am-10pm) and the **Arizona Steakhouse** (from 5.30pm daily). **Maswik Lodge** has a friendly sports bar and inexpensive, but rather institutional cafeteria (6am-10pm) and there's a larger cafeteria at **Yavapai Lodge** (6am-10pm). Wherever you dine, have a drink in the cocktail lounge at the El Tovar; it was decorated by Mary Colter.

There are also snack bars at **Hermit's Rest** (open summer 8am-6.30pm daily, winter 9am-5pm daily) and at **Desert View** (open summer 8am-6pm daily, winter 9am-5pm daily).

Where to stay

There's plenty of accommodation in Grand Canyon Village, but rooms are often reserved 23 months in advance, so book as far ahead as you can. That said, there is often accommodation available for walk-in visitors at Yavapai and Maswik Lodges, even in high season. Bookings are made through **Amfac** (1-303 297 2757/ same-day reservations 1-520 638 2631/fax 1-303 297 3175/www.grandcanyonlodges.com).

The **El Tovar Hotel** ($118-$286), with its grand lobby adorned with stuffed animal heads, offers the most splendid lodging in the village. The 78 rooms have recently been refurbished to a high standard; try to get one with a spacious private balcony overlooking the rim. Less expensive are the 1930s **Bright Angel Lodge** ($48-$236) and more modern, motel-style **Kachina** and **Thunderbird Lodges** ($114-$142), also on the edge of the canyon. **Maswik** ($73-$136) and **Yavapai Lodges** ($88-$120) are located in pine forest a short walk away.

Also within the village are **Mather Campground**, run by the Park Service (1-800 365 2267), with 320 pitches ($15-$20) and a trailer village for RVs ($25). **Desert View**

Campground, 25 miles (40 kilometres) east of Grand Canyon Village, is open from May to October and operates on a first-come, first-served basis ($10 per site).

A few miles south of the village, just outside the park, is **Tusayan**, where you'll find the **Grand Canyon IMAX Theater** (if the real thing's not good enough for you; call 1-520 638 2203 for details) and a number of motels, including **Moqui Lodge**, also run by Amfac (closed Nov-Mar, rates $94). Other choices are **Red Feather Lodge** (1-800 538 2345/1-520 638 2414), **Best Western** (1-800 528 1234/1-520 638 2681), **Holiday Inn** (1-800 465 4329/1-520 638 3000) and **Quality Inn** (1-800 221 2222/1-520 638 2673). A free shuttle-bus service runs between Tusayan and the village.

There are also plenty of motels in Williams, where the friendly, British-run **Norris Motel** (1-800 341 8000/1-520 635 2202, rates from $55) is easy to spot: look out for the Union Jack flying from the roof.

Getting there

By air

Several companies offer scheduled flights from North Las Vegas airport to Grand Canyon airport at Tusayan: try **Scenic Flights** (1-800 634 6801/1-702 638 3300). The flight takes 1hr 15mins and a return ticket costs $160-$200. For details of aeroplane and helicopter sightseeing flights over the Grand Canyon, *see p267*.

By bus

Buses from Flagstaff to the South Rim are run by **Nava-Hopi Bus Lines** (1-520 774 5003) and **South Rim Travel** (1-888 291 9116/1-520 638 2748). **Greyhound** provides a bus service to Flagstaff from Las Vegas. The ride takes around 10hrs and the fare is $77 single, $154 return.

By car

To reach the South Rim, head south on US 93 to the I-40, then turn left on to Highway 64. It's 290 miles (467 kilometres) from Vegas and the journey takes about 5½hrs. For information on road conditions in the park, call 1-520 638 7888. Alternatively, drive as far as Williams and board the Grand Canyon Railway (*see below*).

By rail

The **Grand Canyon Railway** (1-800 843 8724/international calls 1-520 773 1976/www.thetrain.com) runs train services from the depot in Williams (9.30am daily) to the old Santa Fe Railway station in the heart of Grand Canyon Village, returning at 3.15pm. In summer the train is pulled by a turn-of-the-19th-century steam locomotive. There are various 'classes' of service in an assortment of historic carriages, and musicians and characters in Western costume entertain passengers on the journey. The trip takes 3hrs and tickets, which do not include the park entrance fee, are $54.95-$139.95 per person ($24.95-$94.95 concessions).

Getting around

The park service has limited private-vehicle access in some areas to encourage use of the free shuttle buses, and is currently expanding bicycle and pedestrian routes around the South Rim. Long-term plans are for a light rail service to take visitors from Tusayan to Canyon View Information Plaza, but for the moment private cars and buses are still the main form of transport into the park.

By bus

A free shuttle bus service operates on three interconnecting loops around the South Rim: the **Village Route** (from Canyon View Information Plaza to Bright Angel Trailhead); **Hermit's Rest Route** (from the Bright Angel Trailhead to Hermits Rest; Mar-Nov only) and **Kaibab Trail Route** (from Yavapai Observation Station to Yaki Point).

By car

The following areas are *not* accessible to private vehicles: Canyon View Information Plaza; Mather Point; Yaki Point Road (Mar-Nov); West Rim Drive (Mar-Nov).

By coach

Choose from various sightseeing trips around the Canyon rim run by Amfac, including the **Hermits Rest Tour** ($14.50 per person), **Desert View Tour** ($26.50), and a popular 90min trip to watch the sunset from **Mohave Point** ($11). Call 1-303 297 2757 for reservations or visit the desks at Bright Angel, Maswik and Yavapai Lodges and Canyon View Information Plaza to book your place.

By taxi

A 24hr taxi service runs between the village and the airport, trailheads and other destinations (for more information, call 1-520 638 2631).

Exploring the canyon

Hiking in the canyon

However limited your time, try to hike at least part-way into the canyon. As jaw-dropping as the views are from the rim, it's almost too huge to take in the full extent of this unique environment: you need to get closer to appreciate the stunning colours of the cliffs; to identify the different geological layers of rock; to watch the vegetation gradually change from pine trees to cacti as you descend, and finally to see the turbulent brown waters and hear the roar of the Colorado River.

Hikers should note that mule riders have priority on the **Bright Angel**, **South Kaibab** and **North Kaibab** trails. Stop walking when the mules approach, and follow the instructions of the rider leading the tour. For details of mule rides, *see p268* **Ride 'em cowboy**.

Tips for the trail

To prevent yourself becoming one of the statistics of dehydrated or exhausted hikers picked up by rangers (the number of search and rescue missions each year regularly tops the 400 mark), take note of the following hiking advice:

● Know your limitations and choose a hike that is suited to both your ability and your fitness.

● Allow twice as much time to walk up as down. A three-hour canyon hike means one hour down, two hours up.

● Never attempt to hike from the rim to the river and back in one day.

● There is little shade in the inner canyon, so avoid hiking in the hottest part of the day; start early in the morning or delay your hike until after 4pm.

● Water supplies below the rim are very limited, so carry plenty (allow one gallon per person per day in summer).

● Eat high-energy food. A few granola bars or a bag of trail mix is not enough for a day's arduous hiking.

● Wear proper hiking boots and take a ten-minute rest every hour; if you begin to feel faint, raising your legs above the level of your heart will aid recovery.

Bright Angel Trail

Grand Canyon Village to Phantom Ranch. **Round trip** 19.2 miles (31km). **Duration** 2 days.
This popular, maintained trail follows the line of a wide geological fault, which shifted the layering of the rock strata; as you descend you can see that the layers on the left are much higher than those on the right. Water is usually available (May-Sept) at the **resthouses** 1.5 miles (2.4km) and 3 miles (5km) from the trailhead (the first one also has toilet facilities). These are good day-hike destinations, but can get crowded; more experienced hikers could head for the campground at **Indian Gardens** (4.5 miles/ 7.2km), whose tall cottonwoods, planted in the early 1900s, can be seen from the rim. From here you can take a detour to **Plateau Point** (6.1 miles/9.8km) for a dramatic view into the river gorge, or continue on the River Trail to the east, crossing the **Bright Angel Suspension Bridge** to reach Phantom Ranch.

Grandview Trail

Grandview Point to Horseshoe Mesa. **Round trip** 6 miles (9.6km). **Duration** 1 day.
This unmaintained trail is steep and should only be attempted by experienced hikers. There's no water en route, but toilet facilities are available at **Horseshoe Mesa**, the site of an abandoned mining works.

Hermit Trail

Hermit's Rest to Colorado River. **Round trip** 17 miles (27.3km). **Duration** 2-3 days.
This difficult trail passes Hermit Gorge, Santa Maria Spring and the Redwall Formation en route to the Colorado River and is recommended for experienced desert hikers only. A precipitous side trail leads for 1.5 miles (2.4km) to **Dripping Springs**. Note that there is no drinking water on this trail; spring water must be treated.

North Kaibab Trail

North Rim to Colorado River Bridge. **Round trip** 29.2 miles (47km). **Duration** 3-4 days.
The North Kaibab trail starts about 1.5 miles (2.5km) from Grand Canyon Lodge on the North Rim and begins with a beautiful but steep hike through the trees. The **Supai Tunnel** (1.8 miles/3km) is an ideal day hike with a great view of the canyon, plus water and toilet facilities. There is little shade beyond this point. More experienced hikers might make it to **Roaring Springs**, but should not attempt to go further than this and back in one day. Beyond Roaring Springs the trail continues to **Phantom Ranch** (13.8 miles/22km) and the **Colorado River Bridge** (14.6 miles/23.5km).

South Kaibab Trail

Yaki Point to Phantom Ranch. **Round trip** 12.6 miles (20km). **Duration** 2 days.
The trail, which starts 5 miles (8km) east of Grand Canyon Village, is shorter but steeper than Bright Angel trail, dropping 5,000ft (1,525m) in little over six miles. The route follows a series of ridge lines, eventually crossing the Colorado at the Kaibab Suspension Bridge on its way to Phantom Ranch. There is no campground or water en route; hike to the tree-dotted plateau of **Cedar Ridge** (1.5 miles/ 2.4km) if you're short of time.

Plane & helicopter rides

Plane and helicopter rides over the the rim are a major cause of air and noise pollution in the canyon, reducing visibility and disturbing the area's natural tranquility. In fact, there has recently been talk of greatly restricting flights in the Canyon. However, if you're determined to get a bird's eye view of the canyon, various outfits operating out of Grand Canyon Airport in Tusayan will oblige.

Try **Air Grand Canyon** (1-800 247 4726/1-520 638 2686); **Grand Canyon Airlines** (1-800 528 2413/1-520 638 2407); **Papillon Grand Canyon Helicopters** (1-800 528 2418/1-520 638 2419); **Airstar Helicopters** (1-800 962 3869/1-520 638 2622) or **Kenai Helicopters** (1-800 541 4537/1-520 638 2412/638 2764). Plane rides cost $75 to $180 per person; helicopter rides are $90 to $165. For details of sightseeing flights departing direct from Las Vegas, *see p66* **Trips and tours**.

Ride 'em cowboy

Riding into the canyon perched on the back of a mule may be less strenuous than hiking, but it's not really a soft option. Easier on the legs, perhaps, but not on your backside, it brings a whole new meaning to the term 'Rawhide'. Don't let this put you off, however: with mule trips booked up to 11 months in advance, wannabe cowboys and girls have been known to lie, cheat and sell their grannies down the Colorado River in order to get on the back of one of these critters – and you should too.

Mules are the (usually sterile) offspring of a male donkey and a female horse and take characteristics from both their parents: they are similar to a horse in size and muscle, but have many of the features of a donkey, including long, pointed ears and short, spiky manes. As you stare down the precipitous Bright Angel Trail, you should be grateful that mules have also inherited the donkey's straight legs and compact, upright hooves, which make them extremely sure-footed; round-hooved horses could not cope with the steep inclines and uneven surfaces on the Grand Canyon trails.

A mule ride into the Canyon is a truly unforgettable experience, allowing you simultaneously to see the inner canyon in all its geological glory, pretend you're starring in a Western and smirk smugly down on the out-of-breath hikers trudging wearily up the trail. The day trip ($111.25 per person) takes you 3,200 feet (975 metres) down the Bright Angel trail to Plateau Point where you enjoy a cowboy-sized picnic lunch overlooking the inner canyon and the Colorado River. Sit back, gaze at the scenery and thank your lucky stars you're not getting drenched/drowned on the scarily tiny raft you can see making its precarious way over the rapids below. On the two-day trip ($314.25 one person, $563.50 two people) you'll go into the canyon on the Bright Angel trail, overnight in a cabin in the magical setting of Phantom Ranch and return on the shorter South Kaibab trail, allowing you to see the canyon from a different perspective. From mid-November to mid-March there are also three-day trips, with meals and two nights'

accommodation at Phantom Ranch ($428.75 one person, $727.50 two people).

If you turn up at the South Rim without a reservation, you can put your name on the waiting list at the Bright Angel transportation desk. Cancellations are rare, but you never know: riders with reservations have been known to come to a sticky end at the edge of the canyon...

Grand Canyon Mule Trips

Reservations: Grand Canyon National Park Lodges, South Rim, Grand Canyon, AZ 86023 (1-303 297 2757/fax 1-303 297 3175/ www.amfac.com).

Grand Canyon Trail Rides

Reservations: PO Box 128, Tropic, UT 84776 (1-435 679 8665/www.canyonrides.com/ pkgrandcanyon.html).
Organises half-day and full-day mule rides from the North Rim to Roaring Springs.

River rafting

You can follow in the wake of one-armed explorer Major John Wesley Powell, the first man to navigate the length of the Colorado River by boat (in 1869), by taking a river trip through the rapids of the Grand Canyon.

You'll need at least eight days to travel the entire distance – 277 miles (446 kilometres) downriver from Lees Ferry at the far eastern end of the Grand Canyon to Pearce Ferry on Lake Mead – and you'll have to book months in advance. Numerous commercial river runners offer trips in a range of vessels, but the season is short, and the number of boats is strictly controlled, so they're often full. Operators include: **Arizona Raft Adventures** (1-800 786 7238/1-520 526 8200); **Canyon Explorations** (1-800 654 0723/1-520 774 4559); and **Grand Canyon Expeditions** (1-800 544 2691/1-435 644 2691). Consult *The Guide* or the Grand Canyon website (www.nps.gov/grca/grandcanyon) for a list of companies.

Some companies, including **Canyoneers** (1-800 525 0924/1-520 526 0924) also offer shorter trips that start or finish at Bright Angel Beach, near Phantom Ranch. Although these trips mean less time on the river, remember you'll also have to hike in or out of the canyon at the beginning or end of your trip.

East of the park, you can book smooth-water raft trips from Glen Canyon Dam to Lees Ferry through Amfac desks in Grand Canyon Village (1-303 297 2757) and also make arrangements for transportation from the South Rim. For details of whitewater trips from Diamond Creek in Grand Canyon West (roughly a four-hour drive from the South Rim), *see p262*.

Staying in the canyon

Phantom Ranch at the bottom of the canyon was designed by Mary Colter in 1922 and is a welcome oasis after the rigours of a strenuous hike. Hikers who stay at Phantom Ranch do not need backcountry permits, but will need to book their accommodation months in advance; the rustic log and stone cabins ($85) and more modern dorms ($30 per person) are usually filled to capacity. Non-guests can eat at the ranch, but must book meals in advance ($10-$15 breakfast, $12-$20 lunch, $19-$28 dinner).

There are campsites at **Indian Gardens**, **Bright Angel** (next to Phantom Ranch) and **Cottonwood Springs** (open May to October, accessible from the North Rim on the North Kaibab trail). If you want to camp overnight anywhere below the rim, you'll need a **backcountry permit**, available for a fee by mail, fax or in person from the Backcountry Information Center (no permits are issued by phone). The number of permits is limited and most applications should be made well in advance; however, you can also join the waiting list for next-day cancellations.

Backcountry Information Center

Grand Canyon National Park, PO Box 129, Grand Canyon, AZ 86023 (information 1-520 638 7875/fax 1-520 638 2125). **Open** 1-5pm Mon-Fri. **Rates** *Backcountry permit* $10, plus $5 per person per night. **No credit cards**.

The North Rim

From the South Rim you can see lightning forks hit the **North Rim** ten miles (16 kilometres) away across the canyon, but to reach it you'll have to hike down to the bottom and up again, drive 200 miles (322 kilometres) or catch the rim-to-rim bus. The North Rim is 1,000 feet (305 metres) higher and only open mid-May to mid-October; it has fewer facilities and is less accessible than the South Rim, so doesn't get as many visitors. Many seasoned visitors prefer the North Rim for this very reason; its tranquil atmosphere can still evoke what it may have been like to visit the canyon in the early days. That said, it can still get pretty crowded and you should book ahead for lodging.

Facilities on the North Rim include a National Park Visitor Centre, a grocery and camping-supplies shops and a post office.

Where to stay & eat

Grand Canyon Lodge (also run by Amfac; reservations 1-303 297 2757/same-day reservations 1-520 638 2631) has rooms and cabins ($65-$105 double) and a spectacular dining room. There's also a campsite (1-800 365 2267, $15-$20 per night). Reservations are recommended. Outside the park, there are accommodation and restaurant facilities at **Kaibab Lodge**, 18 miles (29 kilometres) north (1-520 638 2389) and **Jacob Lake Inn**, 45 miles (72 kilometres) north (1-520 643 7232).

Getting there

By car

From Las Vegas, head north on the I-15, then east on Hwy 9, Hwy 59 and US 89A to Jacob Lake. The park entrance is 30 miles (48km) south of Jacob Lake on Hwy 67; the canyon rim is another 14 miles (22.5km) further south. At a distance of 263 miles (423km), the North Rim is nearer to Las Vegas than the South Rim, but the journey will take longer.

By bus

The only public transport to the North Rim is the **Trans Canyon Shuttle** bus service between the two rims; the journey takes about 5hrs. Call 1-520 638 2820 for details.

Into California

A day's travel will take you through the desert to the Californian coast.

The vast, empty expanses of the
Mojave National Preserve. *See p275.*

It used to be that Las Vegas was where Angelenos went for a sizzling weekend away from the growing metropolis of Los Angeles. But now that Las Vegas is an established international destination, LA has become a trip out of town for hordes of Vegas visitors. And it's a trip that's well worth making. Not only will the drive take you from the glitz of Vegas to the glam of LA, but it will also take you through some spectacular desert scenery.

The main road from Las Vegas to Southern California is I-15, 270 miles (435 kilometres) of divided four-lane asphalt that can take you from the desert to the beach in a little under four hours (a good day), or more then eight hours (after a holiday weekend). Driving the Interstate, you enter a world of subtly hued barren mountains and sloping valleys with only creosote bushes and Joshua trees to provide relief from the alienating aridity.

This is pioneer country, traversed in the 19th century by weary migrants travelling westwards, celebrated in the 20th century in Hollywood Westerns, and now offering 21st-century trippers a dramatic landscape dotted with other-worldly frontier towns. Just across the Nevada-California border lies the vast, empty expanse of the **Mojave National Preserve** and, less than 100 miles (160 kilometres) further south, is **Joshua Tree National Park**, where the Mojave desert joins the Sonoran desert. Alternatively, head west on Highway 160 from Las Vegas to America's most infamous desert area, the starkly beautiful **Death Valley National Park**, beloved by some mad tourists in high summer, but best visited in spring after the rains have left a light gauze of desert flowers.

Of course, you can just drive through the desert without stopping; plenty of regular gamblers do. Breakfast in Las Vegas, sup on Venice Beach, and drink to the chutzpah of the entrepreneurs who made wonderlands out of two such infertile places.

Note that much of south-western California is remote, largely uninhabited and sometimes scorching, so take precautions for desert driving and hiking (*see p243* **Desert survival**).

Along I-15

You can throw the dice one last time at the mini-gambling resorts of **Jean**, a few miles from the Californian border, and tiny **Primm**, situated on the border itself. **Jean** is the older of the two, and feels like it. Its two casinos, **Gold Strike** (1-800 634 1359/477 5000) and **Nevada Landing** (1-800 628 6682/387 5000) have an agreeably old-time aura; small by Las Vegas standards, and kitted out in red, gold and glittering glass. **Primm** is a three-resort cluster of an altogether more modern aspect, making the most of its prime location on the Nevada/California state line to get first dibs on those desperate inbound gamblers. The success of the Primm family's first casino-hotel here, **Whiskey Pete's**, was so great that they followed it with **Primadonna** and **Buffalo Bill's** (reservations for all three resorts on 1-800 386 7867). Buffalo Bill's is the most impressive of the three, with its silo-like exterior ringed by the Desperado, one of the world's tallest and fastest rollercoasters.

The **visitor centre** (874 1360) behind the Gold Strike in Jean provides information on Jean, Primm and other Southern Nevadan attractions, such as the nearby ghost town of **Goodsprings**. Founded in the 1860s, the town hit the headlines in 1942 when Clark Gable stayed there awaiting news of the plane crash that killed his wife Carole Lombard. It is currently enjoying something of a revival, with a population of more than 100. The **Pioneer Saloon** (off I-15; 874 9362), with its walls and ceiling made of pressed tin, has been in business here since 1913.

Continuing south, the I-15 passes through some stunning scenery along the northern boundary of the **Mojave National Preserve** (for details about exploring the preserve; *see p275*). The small town of **Baker**, 90 miles (145 kilometres) south of Las Vegas, makes a convenient gateway to this vast swathe of wilderness. Baker's only other claim to fame is as the home of the tallest thermometer in the world, which towers 134 feet (40 metres) above the desert floor and is visible from miles away.

West of Baker, the I-15 continues through stark desert terrain until it reaches **Barstow**, 63 miles (101 kilometres) further on, an unattractive and sprawling town notable primarily for its vast factory mall and railroad depot. (You may want to turn south off the I-15 at Barstow onto Highway 247 in order to reach Palm Springs, a Hollywood hangout that has experienced a super-cool renaissance in recent years.) Hot on Barstow's heels is the high desert hick-town of **Hesperia**, forgettable were it not for the **Deep Creek Hot Springs** to be found nearby.

Located in a river valley, deep in the San Bernardino Mountains, the springs are a series of bath-temperature rock pools, perfect for a soothing dip; clothing is optional. From the centre of Hesperia, it's a 45-minute drive and a two-and-a-half-mile hike to reach the springs; ask in town for directions.

Beyond Hesperia, I-15 takes you through the pine-capped wilderness country of the San Bernardino Mountains until it hits the Los Angeles sprawl.

Los Angeles

If you haven't been to Los Angeles before, the first thing you need to know is that it doesn't really exist as an identifiable place. Los Angeles is a city, a county and a region; the county contains 88 cities merged into a single vast agglomeration over more than 100 miles (160 kilometres) wide, of which the City of Los Angeles is the nominal heart. LA's sights are spread throughout the region and the essential LA experience – driving the freeways – has no precise location. If you only have a short time, however, you should focus on the area between Downtown and the ocean, known as the LA basin, which includes the best-known beach areas, and the fabulous burgs of the rich and famous, Hollywood and Sunset Strip.

BEVERLY HILLS, BEL AIR AND RODEO DRIVE

Whether you're a hard-core shopper or a sociologist, don't miss a walk or drive down **Rodeo Drive**. In the very heart of **Beverly Hills**, these few blocks, where some of the superswanky shops require appointments for entrance, embody conspicuous consumption at its best or worse. Trinkets sell for thousands, and men, women and children don furs, silks and giant gemstones for a regular afternoon outing. It attracts a mix of tourists and very wealthy Angelenos, many of them residents of Beverly Hills' mansions. Beverly Hills became a city in 1880, before which it was known chiefly for its crops of robust lima beans. The houses are big, as expected, with perfectly manicured gardens and built in every style imaginable. Drive off the main drag and explore the tree-lined side streets to get the full effect. But beware of the zealous Beverly Hills police, who sometimes stop strangers to check why they might be walking in the area.

Bel Air, also home to the rich and famous, is a posh hillside community that lies west of Beverly Hills. Known for their privacy and pretty views, the gated houses in this neighbourhood are visual feasts, but, unfortunately, visitors driving along the meandering roads won't see much save the

Trips Out of Town

names written on the mailboxes, as the best houses are hidden from sight. To get a closer look, stop in for breakfast or tea at the ultra-exclusive, vintage **Hotel Bel-Air** at 701 Stone Canyon Road (1-800 648 4097).

DOWNTOWN

Downtown LA is an odd stew of old and new, vibrant and stagnant, beautiful and ugly. Circumscribed by a vast moat of freeways, it's a hotchpotch of areas including the skyscraper-studded financial district, El Pueblo de Los Angeles – the site of the original settlement, now a buzzing pedestrian area based around Olvera Street – the civic centre, the garment district, Chinatown and Little Tokyo. It is vibrant by day (the best time to explore on foot) and desolate at night but for the hundreds of homeless people who congregate in the Skid Row area to the east. It's currently undergoing a revival, however, with a burgeoning downtown art scene in Chinatown and east of Little Tokyo, and the regeneration of office buildings and warehouses into lofts in the historic buildings on Broadway and to the east.

Some of LA's most stunning architecture is also to be found downtown, like the romantic **Union Station**, where you almost expect to see Bogie and Bergman kissing a star-crossed goodbye. Other landmarks in the area are the **Bradbury Building** (304 South Broadway), as featured in *Blade Runner*, and the space-age **Westin Bonaventure Hotel** (404 South Figueroa Street). Of note are the **Performing Arts Center**, the **Museum of Contemporary Art** (MOCA; *see p273*), the **Angels Flight** funicular railway (Hill Street, between Third and Fourth Streets) and **Broadway**, a thriving Mexican shopping street. Under construction near MOCA are Frank Gehry's **Walt Disney Concert Hall** and a new cathedral by Spanish architect Rafael Moneo.

In the 1940s, the Redevelopment Agency developed **Little Tokyo** and **Chinatown** to the east, which have since blossomed into thriving, bustling communities, great spots for Asian cuisine, shops and religious shrines. A new addition to downtown is the vast **Staples** arena, at 1111 Figueroa Street (on the corner of Figueroa and 11th Streets), home to ice-hockey, basketball, pop concerts, and events like the Democratic Convention in 2000. It's worth driving by at night when the arena is bathed in a lurid purple glow.

HOLLYWOOD BOULEVARD

Gone are the days of fur-wrapped starlets and tuxedoed leading men. Over the past few decades, Hollywood Boulevard has descended into a sink of X-rated cinemas, tacky tourist

Find your way around **Los Angeles**.

shops, vagrants and unrealised dreams. To say it's become anticlimactic would be an understatement, but there are nevertheless a few places on this long street well worth a stop: the historic **Mann's Chinese** and **El Capitan Theaters**, the old **Roosevelt Hotel**, the beautifully designed **Pantages Theater**, **Musso & Frank's Grill** and **Frederick's of Hollywood** lingerie store among them. Furthermore, the strip is now undergoing a facelift. The street has been cleaned up: an open-air mall and purpose-designed theatre for the Oscar ceremony are being built above a new subway at the corner of Hollywood and Highland; grand old cinemas, such as the Egyptian, have been restored, as well as the neighbouring Pig 'n' Whistle, a classic bar, and restaurants and cafés have opened in the area.

The **Walk of Fame**, with bronze stars embedded in the pavement paying tribute to more than 2,500 Hollywood greats (and not-so-greats, as long as they had a good publicist and some spare cash), extends in all directions from the junction of Vine Street and Hollywood Boulevard, with the longest stretch running westwards to La Brea Avenue.

MELROSE AVENUE AND LOS FELIZ

It's less cutting-edge than it used to be, but Melrose Avenue is still a mecca of LA trendiness. Locals and tourists throng to it, especially the stretch between La Brea and Fairfax Avenues. Lined with funky restaurants, art galleries, theatres, comedy clubs and shops selling everything from vintage clothes and used Levi's, it attracts mainly young trendoids and the punk-grunge hippies with its adrenalin pulse. A few happenin' highlights: **Aardvark** for vintage clothing, **Caffe Luna** for espresso and mouth-watering tiramisu, the **Wound & Wound Toy Company** for wind-up toys and music boxes, and the **Groundlings Improv Theatre**, where many of the *Saturday Night Live* greats served their apprenticeship.

Melrose Avenue suffers from a lack of parking, a fact that may have contributed to the emergence in recent years of other trendy shopping streets that are a bit more accessible: try **Robertson Boulevard** in Beverly Hills for upmarket clothing stores, and **La Brea Avenue** between Beverly and Sixth for modernist furniture and clothing. In particular, **Los Feliz**, the stretch of Vermont Avenue between Hollywood and Franklin Boulevards, has become a rival to Melrose; it even boasts **Wacko**, a famous goofy games and cards store that left its long-time home on Melrose and is now on Hollywood at Rodney. **Sunset Boulevard**, east of Hillhurst, is also a magnet for the would-be bohemian denizens of East Hollywood and Silverlake.

SANTA MONICA

Beautifully framed by mountains and sea, affluent Santa Monica is the jewel of LA's Westside. Known locally as 'the people's republic of Santa Monica', it is the heart of bourgeois liberalism, noted for its environmental causes, rent control, relative tolerance of the homeless – and great shopping and restaurants. At its heart is **Third Street Promenade**. Created in the late 1980s for pedestrians only, its four blocks are at their busiest on weekend nights, when hordes of Angelenos mill around the high-street stores, entertained by regulated street performers and street vendors selling everything from organic cotton clothes to bonsai trees. Don't let this put you off, though: Third Street Promenade also has some decent cafés, bars, restaurants, late-opening shops and several good multiplexes. Perhaps the most pleasant times to visit are Wednesday and Saturday mornings, when a large farmers' market, selling glorious organic produce, takes over the street.

Third Street Promenade is also handy for the beach and the pier (see p276 **Which way's the beach?**), with ample parking on Second and Fourth Streets. You'll also find good shopping and food to the south on Main Street between Edgemar and Rose Avenue.

SUNSET STRIP

The famous Sunset Strip is the section of Sunset Boulevard that runs from Doheny Drive to Laurel Canyon in West Hollywood. Studded with billboards and bright lights, it has been the centre of LA nightlife since the 1920s. Along its length are such landmarks as the **Whisky A-Go-Go** and **House of Blues** music clubs, the **Comedy Store** and the **Viper Room** nightclub, as well as swinging hotels such as the **Mondrian**, the **Standard** and the perennially glamorous **Chateau Marmont**. Lots of restaurants and shops, too.

VENICE

At the turn of the century, builders, the government and, most notably, tobacco magnate Abbot Kinney transformed this area into the 'Venice of America', complete with canals, bridges, imported gondolas, meandering streets and a bohemian spirit. The canals were condemned in 1940 and some were filled with concrete, but those that remain have since been restored and gentrified into an idyllic residential neighbourhood, complete with quacking ducks. These days, only those with relatively robust wallets can live along the quaint waterways, but everyone is free to wander among them. Enter the network by turning south off Venice Boulevard on to Dell Avenue, about a quarter of a mile back from the beach. Venice as a whole is a mixed and magnetic community of post-1960s hippies, the elderly, artistic and free-spirited, with a bit of gang territory thrown in (watch yourself and your car in inland areas, especially after dark). **Abbot Kinney Boulevard** is a good place to window-shop and eat well. And then, of course, there's **Venice Beach** (see p276 **Which way's the beach?**).

Sights & attractions

There are a million things to see and do in LA; if you have limited time, try the following.

Disneyland Resort

1313 Harbor Boulevard, Anaheim, Orange County (1-714 999 4565/1-714 781 4560/recorded information 1-714 781 4565/www.disneyland.com). I-5, exit Harbor Boulevard. **Open** hours vary; phone for details. **Admission** $43; $33 3-11s. **Credit** AmEx, Disc, MC, V.

Disneyland has now been joined by Disney's California Adventure (a new theme park) and Downtown Disney (a themed shopping experience) to create the Disneyland Resort. 'The happiest place on earth' is all it's cracked up to be – if you like that kind of thing, but get there early to beat the crowds, be prepared to queue and pace yourself – the new Resort is more exhausting than ever before.

Getty Center

1200 Getty Center Drive, at the I-405, Brentwood (1-310 440 7300/www.getty.edu). I-405, exit Getty Center Drive. **Open** 11am-7pm Tue, Wed; 11am-9pm Thur, Fri; 10am-6pm Sat, Sun. **Admission** free. **Credit** AmEx, MC, V.

The much-fêted Getty museum gave Los Angeles the cultural kudos it had long desired. It cost over $1 billion to build and stock, and it shows, with fabulous art and artefacts from antiquities to modern masters and world-class archives. The stunning architecture by Richard Meier is complemented by beautiful views over the city.

Museum of Contemporary Art

California Plaza *250 S Grand Avenue, at Third Street, Downtown. Metro Pershing Square/37, 76, 78, 96, DASH B bus/I-10, exit Fourth Street east.*

Geffen Company *152 N Central Avenue, at First Street, Downtown. Bus 30, 31, 40, 42, DASH A/US 101, exit Alameda Street south.*
General information 1-213 626 6222/visitor services 1-213 621 1741/www.moca-la.org. **Open** 11am-5pm Tue, Wed, Fri-Sun; 11am-8pm Thur. **Admission** $6; $4 concessions; free under-12s. Free to all 5-8pm Thur. **Credit** AmEx, MC, V.
The MOCA is the city's – and perhaps the American West's – premier showcase for late-20th-century art. Upwards of a dozen shows are held at any one time, divided between the building on California Plaza (designed by Arata Isozaki) and the Geffen Company building, a former warehouse converted by Frank Gehry. A free shuttle bus runs roughly every hour between the two sites.

Six Flags California

Magic Mountain Parkway, off the I-5, Valencia (1-661 255 4100/recorded information 1-661 255 4111/www.sixflags.com). I-5, exit Magic Mountain Parkway. **Open** 10am-7pm Mon-Thur; 10am-8pm Fri-Sun. Hurricane Harbor closed in winter.
Admission *Magic Mountain* $43; $21.50 over-55s, children under 4f5 (1.2m). *Hurricane Harbor* $22; $15 children, seniors. **Credit** AmEx, Disc, MC, V.
Set scenically in the San Fernando Mountains, the theme park comprises Six Flags Magic Mountain and Six Flags Hurricane Harbor Water Park. Unlike Disneyland, there's not much theming at either park, rather attention is focused firmly on rides, rides and more rides. Fun with a screamingly huge capital F.

Universal Studios Hollywood & CityWalk

100 Universal City Plaza, Universal City (1-818 508 9600/www.universalstudios.com). US 101, exit Universal Center Drive. **Open** 11am-11pm Mon-Thur, Sun; 11am-midnight Fri, Sat. **Admission** $43; $33 3-11s. **Credit** AmEx, DC, Disc, MC, V.
You can stroll round the Lucille Ball museum, experience the *Back to the Future* flight simulator, watch scripted shows inspired by recent TV programmes, but the best way to see Universal is to take the tram. Passing through the backlot of the working studio, you'll see King Kong, the shark from *Jaws*, the parting of the Red Sea and the *Psycho* house, plus glimpses of studio life. The complex also houses Universal CityWalk, a Los Angeles-themed shopping and eating 'street', at its glitzy best at night.

Where to stay, eat & drink

Los Angeles was once a gastronomic wasteland, lagging far behind the rest of California. But in the 1980s, a string of high-concept restaurants appeared, characterised by inventive decor, food and presentation, which won the city a place on the culinary map. My, how things have changed. Now, superchefs have become big business in the city and foodie mania is rife. It can be a bit dizzying for visitors, so, for details, consult the *Time Out Los Angeles Guide*, which lists

The famous **Hollywood** sign. *See p272.*

everything from branches of fast-food chains to seriously upscale restaurants, as well as numerous coffeehouses and ethnic eateries.
For a list of places to stay in LA, contact the **Los Angeles Convention & Visitors Bureau** (*see p275*) or **Preferred Hotels & Resorts** (10877 Wilshire Boulevard, suite 403, LA, CA 90024; 1-888 755 9876/fax 1-310 374 7025). Contact numbers for the main US chain hotels are given on *p54* **Chain gang**.

Getting there

By car

Los Angeles is 293 miles (471km) from Las Vegas; the journey can take 4-8hrs, plus stops, depending on the traffic.

By bus

Greyhound operates a frequent service (every 30min-1hr during the day) between Las Vegas and LA, costing $37 one-way, $72 return.

By air

Numerous airlines, including **United** (1-800 241 6522/www.united.com), **Northwest** (1-800 225 2525/www.nwa.com) and **America West** (1-800 235 9292/www.americawest.com), ply the oversubscribed LA route. Fares vary tremendously ($80-$200 return) according to availability and time of year, but in general, the earlier you book, the better the price. Night flights are usually cheaper.

Tourist information

For extensive insider information on the city, get hold of a copy of the *Time Out Los Angeles Guide*, published by Penguin ($14.95/£11.99). For useful Internet-based information try www.at-la.com, which has links to a vast array of sites.

Los Angeles Visitor & Convention Bureau

685 S Figueroa Street, between Seventh Street & Wilshire Boulevard, Downtown, LA, CA 90017 (1-213 689 8822/www.lacvb.com). I-110, exit Ninth Street east. **Open** 8am-5pm Mon-Fri; 8.30am-5pm Sat.

This helpful tourist office will mail out a visitor information pack on request.
Branch: The Janes House, Janes Square, 6541 Hollywood Boulevard, at Hudson Avenue, Hollywood (1-213 689 8822).

Mojave National Preserve

Covering a wedge-shaped area bordered by two interstates (the I-15 to the north and the I-40 to the south), the 2,500 square miles (6,477 square kilometres) of the Mojave National Preserve are sparsely inhabited – you can drive for miles without seeing another car – but conveniently close to Las Vegas for exploration in a day. Good paved roads and myriad dirt roads (some of which can only be driven in a 4WD vehicle) criss-cross the area, and the weird Joshua tree, with its toilet-brush like branches, is abundant at higher elevations.

Although mines and ranches still operate in the area (obey all 'no trespassing' signs) and hunting is allowed, half the preserve is designated as wilderness. Signs of human habitation, past and present, are scattered about in isolated pockets, serving to emphasise how vast and empty the desert can be. The best times to visit are either in the spring or the autumn; it's brutally hot between mid-May and mid-September, when temperatures spiral well over 110°F (43°C). Try to be there in the late afternoon, when the shadows are long and the mountains are at their most beautiful.

A good starting point for exploring the Mojave is the small town of **Baker**. The **Desert Information Center** (*see p277*), located under the thermometer in the town, has good maps, books and updates on road conditions. Don't forget to fill up on petrol and drinking water while you're in Baker: there are no services in the preserve. If you have only a few hours, a 67-mile (107-kilometre) triangular drive from Baker, via the Kelbaker Road, Kelso–Cima Road and Cima Road to rejoin I-15 at the end of the trek, acts as a good

introduction to the preserve's sights, both natural and man-made. And these sights are myriad and fascinating.

You pass the reddish humps of over 30 young volcanic cones before reaching **Kelso**, which used to be a major passenger stop on the Union Pacific Railroad; now only freight trains, looking like long silver caterpillars, pass through. The grand, Spanish Mission-style depot, built in 1924 and finally closed in 1985, is in the process of being turned into a visitor centre. At Kelso, turn left towards Cima, passing the 7,000-foot-high (2,130-metre) Providence Mountains en route. At **Cima**, little more than a collection of wooden shacks, take the Cima Road back towards the I-15: you'll head past the gently swelling Cima Dome, which has the largest stand of Joshua trees anywhere in the world. The variety here (*Yucca brevifolia jaegeriana*) is shorter and has more branches than the one found in the Joshua Tree National Park (*see p276*).

If you want to detour to the 500-foot (150-metre) Kelso sand dunes, continue south from Kelso on the Kelbaker Road and turn right after about seven miles (11 kilometres) on to a signed dirt road. Formed between 10,000 and 20,000 years ago, the dunes support a remarkable variety of plant and animal life, including the rarely seen desert tortoise. You may hear the dunes 'booming' when dry sand grains slide down the steep upper slopes.

If you have more time, and particularly if you're in the area during the blistering summer, head east from Kelso to the **Providence Mountains State Recreation Area**, which is significantly cooler than the desert floor. Multi-branched cholla, spiky Mojave yucca, round barrel cactus, spindly Mormon tea and the flat pads of prickly pears share the upland slopes with juniper and piñon trees, creating a stunning geometric display. There are great views south from the visitor centre. The park also houses the dramatic limestone **Mitchell Caverns**, which remain a cool 65°F (18°C) year round. There are guided tours of the caves ($4 adults, $2 children) daily from Labor Day to Memorial Day, and on Saturday and Sunday only the rest of the year; call 1-760 928 2586 for tour times and reservations.

Also worth visiting is the tiny settlement of **Nipton** (population 40), located just outside the northern edge of the preserve. Here you'll find a railroad crossing, an old-fashioned country store selling souvenirs, books and some groceries, a town hall and the charming Hotel Nipton (*see p276*). If you head back towards Las Vegas from Nipton via Searchlight, you pass an impressively huge forest of Joshua trees. Other sights in the preserve include unpronounceable **Zzyzx**, also known as Soda Springs, located

Trips Out of Town

Which way's the beach?

Locals will tell you two things about LA's beaches: one, just because it's the Pacific, don't expect the ocean to be warm, and, two, the further away you are from Santa Monica Bay, where waste is pumped into the water, the cleaner the water. The public beaches are usually open from dawn to sunset. Most have parking (though spaces are at a premium in high season), showers, restrooms, volleyball courts and rental stands for inline skates and bicycles. Dogs are off-limits.

Venice Beach is the place to go for people-watching – every category of life is represented among the throngs that descend here. Ocean Front Walk (popularly known as the Boardwalk) offers restaurants, shops, food stands and Muscle Beach, the outdoor gym where you can watch exhibitionist, would-be Arnies tone up. **Santa Monica Beach** is often crowded and has a summer-holiday feel to it, enhanced by its pier, three blocks in length and packed with engagingly low-tech diversions, including the famous carousel – fun, but not the main

attraction. The best beaches in **Malibu**, to the north, are private. The public stretches may not quite live up to the Malibu of the popular imagination, but they're still well liked, especially by surfers. Further north still are **Zuma Beach** – quintessential California sun and sand – and **El Matador**, small, beautiful and dominated by rocky outcrops, hence the steep walk down. Beaches also extend to the south of the city; the best are **Manhattan** (*pictured*), **Huntington** and **Hermosa**.

---

on the edge of the white expanse of Soda Dry Lake (60 miles east of Barstow and eight miles south-west of Baker). It has been used as an Indian campsite, a military outpost, and a health resort by early radio evangelist Curtis Howe Springer, and is now a study centre for the California State University. Note that Zzyzx Road is unpaved for most of its length.

If you're still thirsting for more parched land, head south-east to **Joshua Tree National Park** (entrance fee $10 per vehicle), which occupies a transitional zone between two desert ecosystems. The western half is in the Mojave, and has large Joshua-tree forests and jumbled piles of massive granite boulders, which are popular with climbers. The eastern half is in the Colorado desert, and is lower, drier, hotter and dominated by creosote; you'll also see numerous types of cholla and the distinctive 20- to 30-foot (six- to nine-metre) ocotillo, which is most striking when in bloom (usually in March).

There are two entrances into the park from the north and one from the south; and the main visitor centre is off Highway 62, near the military town of **Twentynine Palms**. A scenic drive through the park will pass conveniently close to viewpoints, a few marked trails, campgrounds and picnic sites.

Where to stay & eat

In Baker contact the **Chamber of Commerce** (*see p277*) for details of motels and restaurants, but don't miss the fabulous **Mad Greek Diner** for houmous and spanakopita (1-760 733 4354, main courses $5-$10). In Nipton, the place to stay is the very pleasant **Hotel Nipton** (107335, Nipton, CA 92364, 1-760 856 2335/ www.nipton.com, rates $60). Fronted by a large cactus garden, it has four rooms, a jacuzzi and a large verandah with views across the Ivanpah Valley. One of the hotel's rooms is named after silent film star Clara Bow, whose husband owned a ranch nearby and who used to stop by to entertain Hollywood guests at the hotel. Rates include continental breakfast and reservations are recommended.

Inside the preserve are two campgrounds ($10), with a limited water supply. Set among juniper and piñon woodland, the **Mid-Hills** campground is usually significantly cooler than **Hole-in-the-Wall** – and much prettier. Sites are allocated on a first-come, first-served basis (call 1-760 733 4040 for more information).

For access to the Joshua Tree National Park the best place to stay is **Twentynine Palms**

Inn (73950 Inn Avenue, Twentynine Palms, CA 92277, 1-760 367 3505/www.29palmsinn.com, rates $75-$115). This is a real oasis in the desert, with blooming trees (including 29 palms), adobe cottages, a pool and a homely restaurant (main courses $8-$17).

Getting there

By car

Baker is 90 miles (145km) south of Las Vegas on the I-15. **Nipton** is located on Hwy 164, accessible via the I-15 or Hwy 95, 63 miles (101km) south of Las Vegas. To reach **Joshua Tree National Park**, take the Kelbaker Road through the Mojave National Preserve and continue south via Amboy until you reach Twentynine Palms; it's about 130 miles (210km) from Baker to the park entrance.

Tourist information

Chamber of Commerce

PO Box 241, Baker, CA 92309 (1-760 733 4469). **Open** 9am-5pm daily.

Desert Information Center

72157 Baker Boulevard, Baker, CA 92509 (1-760 733 4040). **Open** 9am-5pm daily.

Joshua Tree National Park Visitor Center

74485 National Park Drive (1-760 367 5500/www. nps.gov/jotr). **Open** 8am-5pm daily.

Death Valley National Park

The near-naked mountains, vast, white salt lakes and blistering climate of Death Valley National Park are other-worldly, but then that's the point. This is a land of extremes. It is one of the hottest and driest places on earth: precipitation averages less than two inches (five centimetres) a year and the highest temperature in the US (and the world, for several years) – a mind-numbing 134°F (57°C) – was recorded here in 1913. The lowest point in the western hemisphere is here – near Badwater, at 282 feet (86 metres) below sea level – only 85 miles (137 kilometres) from the highest point in the US, the 14,494-foot (4,420-metre) high peak of Mount Whitney in the Sierra Nevada. An annual bicycle race takes place between the two.

Enlarged and redesignated as a national park under the 1994 Desert Protection Act, Death Valley is now the largest national park outside Alaska, covering more than 5,156 square miles (13,355 square kilometres). Usually it's only Europeans that are mad enough to venture out here in the height of summer, when it can be hot enough to literally take your breath away and walking 20 yards from the air-conditioned

safety of your car can become a major ordeal. The air temperature in July and August often tops 120°F (49°C) – the ground temperature can be 50 per cent higher – and lows average 90°F (32°C); now you know why Furnace Creek got its name. The best months to visit are October to March, though it can approach freezing at night in December and January.

Although only one pioneer actually died while trying to cross Death Valley, its reputation as a savage and life-threatening place is well deserved. It is reassuring to know that all the major car manufacturers test their vehicles in the extreme conditions here, but keep an eye on gauges and make sure you have enough petrol (available at Furnace Creek, Stovepipe Wells, Scotty's Castle and Panamint Springs). Roadside storage tanks hold radiator water. Check road conditions at the visitor centre, especially if you plan to drive any unpaved roads. Always carry plenty of water and take desert survival very seriously. Entrance to the park is $10 per car.

The visitor centre, with its 1950s exhibits and great bookshop, is at **Furnace Creek**, near the park's main accommodation and many of its best-known sights. A short drive east, you can walk around the ruins of **Harmony Borax Works**, from where the famous 20-mule teams used to haul wagons 165 miles (266 kilometres) across the desert to the nearest railroad. The eroded golden hills of nearby **Zabriskie Point** (named, rather prosaically, after a borax mine superintendent, but immortalised in a movie of the same name by Michelangelo Antonioni) are best seen at sunrise. Further south is the white expanse of **Badwater** (the mountainside sign marking sea level shows how low you are) and the road to the cool heights of **Dante's View**, which provides a spectacular view across blindingly white salt lakes to the Panamint Mountains.

Fifty miles (80 kilometres) north of Furnace Creek is the extravagant mansion of **Scotty's Castle** (1-760 786 2392), built in the 1920s as a winter retreat for Chicago millionaire Albert Johnson. The castle is named after Johnson's eccentric and flamboyant friend Walter Scott, more commonly known as 'Death Valley Scotty'. Costumed rangers give highly popular 50-minute tours of the interior from 9am to 5pm, usually every hour (admission $8 for adults; $4 concessions). While you wait your turn, you can explore the landscaped grounds containing Scotty's grave. Nearby is the 500-foot (152-metre) deep volcanic **Ubehebe Crater**. Other sights include the 700-foot (213-metre) high **Eureka sand dunes**, the **Wildrose charcoal kilns** and **Racetrack Valley**, a dry mud flat covered in faint trails left by large, probably wind-blown, boulders.

Baking **Death Valley**. *See p277.*

Although it's often too hot to hike in Death Valley, there are plenty of trails, short and long. The question, in the end, is just how brave are you? And, perhaps even more important, are you in really good shape? Among the possible hikes is the strenuous 14-mile (23-kilometre) round-trip to the 11,000-foot (3,353-metre) summit of **Telescope Peak**. This is a good summer hike (remember the higher you climb, the cooler it gets), which starts at Mahogany Flat campground and climbs 3,000 feet (914 metres) for spectacular views of Mount Whitney. In winter it should only be attempted by experienced climbers equipped with ice axes and crampons.

The Death Valley area is also littered with ghost towns and abandoned mines (watch your step). If you're heading into California on Highway 178, be sure to drop in on the tiny ghost town of **Ballarat**, set on the edge of the beautiful Panamint Valley.

Where to eat

Pickings are a bit slim in these parts, but the **Furnace Creek Inn**'s dining room is open to non-guests for breakfast ($7-$14), lunch ($9-$18) and dinner ($10-$27; and reservations are recommended). Complimentary afternoon tea and coffee is available daily in the lobby. There are also restaurants at Furnace Creek Ranch, Stovepipe Wells Village and Panamint Springs.

Where to stay

Set into the hillside above Furnace Creek Wash, the 1930s **Furnace Creek Inn** is the most luxurious place to stay in Death Valley, with 66 rooms, a swimming pool surrounded by date palms, a grand dining room and four tennis courts. Non-guests can use some of the facilities. Rates ($155-$350) are cheapest from mid-May to mid-October. Down the road, the more rustic **Furnace Creek Ranch** has nearly 200 rooms (rates $130-$175) and 28 cabins ($105-$120), an 18-hole golf course (the lowest in the world), a pool, stables (open Oct-May), tennis courts, a bar, restaurant and shop. Details of both properties are available from PO Box 1, Death Valley, CA 92328 (1-760 786 2361/www.furnacecreek resort.com).

Further north, **Stovepipe Wells Village** has 83 rooms (1-760 786 2837, rates $65-$85), while at Death Valley Junction you can stay at the atmospheric if shabby **Amargosa Opera House** (1-760 852 4441/www.amargosaopera house.com, rates $50-$60) and watch ballet performances by eccentric owner Marta Becket.

There are also nine campgrounds in the park (some are accessible only by 4WD). Most cost $10 per night; Furnace Creek, Mesquite Spring and Wildrose are open all year. Check with the Death Valley visitor centre for rules about backcountry camping.

Getting there

By car

From Las Vegas, the shortest route into Death Valley is via Pahrump on Hwy 60. Drive south on I-15 towards LA, exit onto Blue Diamond Road (at Silverton), then head west on Hwy 160 up and over the Spring Mountains (affectionately known as the 'hump to Pahrump'). A few miles after Pahrump take State Line Road to Death Valley Junction and Highway 190 into the park (120 miles/193km).

Alternatively, head out of Vegas on US 95, entering the southern end of the park from Amargosa Valley (via Hwy 373 and Death Valley Junction), the centre of the park from Beatty (via Hwy 374), or the north from Scotty's Junction (via Hwy 267). From the Mojave National Preserve, head north from Baker on Hwy 127.

Tourist information

Death Valley Visitor Center

Furnace Creek, Death Valley National Park, CA 92328 (1-760 786 2331/www.nps.gov/deva). **Open** 8am-6pm daily.

Into Utah

Follow in the footsteps of the Mormon pioneers to Zion National Park.

Utah, home to the Mormons and Little Jimmy Osmond, is an enormous state, with its capital, Salt Lake City, and upriver canyon country too far away to contemplate as reasonable side-trips from Las Vegas. However, **Zion National Park** in the south of the state offers enough awe-inspiring landscapes to make even the most jaded traveller pause for thought, and for visitors with more time, it is the perfect starting point for an exploration of the natural wonders of southern Utah and northern Arizona.

Also within easy reach of Vegas is **Brian Head**, a mountain resort popular with mountain bikers in the summer and snow sports fanatics in the winter. For further details, contact the Chamber of Commerce (1-435 677 2810/www.brianheadutah.com) and *see p234*.

Enjoy **Zion**'s awe-inspiring scenery.

Zion National Park

A few hours north from Las Vegas on the I-15 lies Zion National Park, a glorious introduction to the spectacular canyon country of south-east Utah. Zion's 2,000-foot (610-metre) high cliffs and towering rock formations were discovered by early Mormon travellers in the 1880s. The area was originally called Mukuntuweap (loosely meaning 'like a quiver', a description of the shape of Zion Canyon), its name was changed to Zion in 1919 when it became a national park. With more than 2.5 million visitors a year, most travelling in private cars, Zion is crowded all year round, but can become unbearable in summer, when you don't so much hike as queue along the more popular trails. Spring and autumn are ideal times to visit; the wild flowers are usually at their peak in May. In July and August, daytime temperatures can exceed 110°F (43°C) and brief thunderstorms are common in the afternoon. Winters are usually mild, with snow falling at higher elevations but rarely in Zion Canyon itself.

The main entrance to the park is in the south, near the small, pretty town of **Springdale**. Admission costs $20 per car, and the park's two campgrounds, visitor centre and administrative offices lie just beyond the entrance. **Kolob Canyons**, in the north-western corner of the park, has its own entrance (at exit 40 off the I-15) and visitor centre, from where a stunning five-mile (eight-kilometre) drive leads into the sheer, red-rock **Finger Canyons**. There are

also two hiking trails in this part of the park; the longer of the two culminates at **Kolob Arch**, possibly the world's largest natural arch at 310 feet (94.5 metres).

Most other sights and trails are accessible or visible from the six-mile (ten-kilometre), dead-end **scenic drive**, starting at the south entrance of park through the Virgin River gorge of **Zion Canyon** itself. The names of the vividly coloured Navajo sandstone monoliths along the drive echo the religious sensibilities of the area's first visitors: look out for the **Great White Throne**, the **Three Patriarchs**, **Angel's Landing**, the **Pulpit** and the **Temple of Sinawava**. Scan the rock faces and you may see tiny, ant-like figures clinging to the sheer cliffs: Zion is popular with climbers. Climbing routes are detailed in Eric Bjourstad's *Desert Rock – Rock Climbs in the National Parks* (Chockstone Press).

East from Springdale and the scenic drive, you will travel along the twisting **Zion-Mount Carmel Highway**, an engineering miracle when it was built in 1930. The impressive route leads through two long, narrow tunnels, passing scenery that is completely different from the landscapes of Zion Canyon. This is slickrock country: vast white, orange and pink rock formations, eroded into domes and buttes and marked with criss-cross patterns, loom next to the road. You can't miss the huge white monolith of **Checkerboard Mesa**.

Beyond the eastern entrance to the park, Highway 9 joins up with US 89 for access to the rest of Utah and Arizona; head north to reach **Bryce Canyon National Park**, east to **Lake Powell** and **Glen Canyon** or south to the North Rim of the **Grand Canyon** (*see p269*).

Where to eat

Springdale has plenty of cafés and restaurants, but a shortage of bars (this is Utah, after all). The closest you'll find is **Bit & Spur** (1212 Zion Park Boulevard, 1-435 772 3498, closed winter), a smart Mexican restaurant with covered, outdoor seating. **Oscar's Café & Deli** (612 Zion Park Boulevard, 1-435 772 3232), just off the main drag, does pizzas, pastries, good coffee and six types of breakfast burrito ($5.50-$6.50). **Zion Lodge** (*see below*) is open to non-guests for dinner (main courses $11-$20; reservations needed).

Where to stay

There are numerous places to stay in Springdale, ranging from cheap to top-dollar. Contact the **Zion Chamber of Commerce** (PO Box 331, Springdale, UT 84767, 1-888 518 7070) for details. Its website (www.zionpark.com) provides useful information on sightseeing, dining and other activities, as well as a list of accommodation options.

Accommodation inside the park consists of two campgrounds ($16) and **Zion Lodge** (1-303 297 2757/front desk 1-435 772 3213/www.zionlodge.com, rates lodge suite $127) a rustic-style lodge, built in 1925 by the Union Pacific Railroad. There are also 40 cabins ($107) and a motel ($97) on the Zion Lodge site, but you'll still have to book about five months ahead for a room between April and October.

An alternative at the top-end is **Cliffrose Lodge & Gardens** (281 Zion Park Boulevard, 1-800 243 8824/1-435 772 3234, rates May-Oct $119-$145), a pricey but pretty place, with gardens stretching down to the Virgin River and a large swimming pool. It's child-friendly and rates are 50 per cent cheaper in winter. Less expensive is **El Rio Lodge** (995 Zion Park Boulevard, 1-888 772 3205/1-435 772 3205, rates May-Oct $47-$52, Nov-Apr $35-$39), a ten-room, two-storey motel with great views run by a friendly local couple. **O'Toole's Under the Eaves** (980 Zion Park Boulevard, 1-435 772 3457, rates Mar-Oct $60-$125, Nov-Feb $55-$95) is a cute, clean B&B with six rooms, including a splendid en suite studio attic and a cabin in the back garden. Rates include breakfast.

Getting there

To reach the main entrance to the park (164 miles/264 kilometres from Vegas), take the I-15 north (watching your speed once you leave Nevada) through the pleasant Mormon town of St George and turn right at exit 16 on to Highway 9 to Springdale. To visit the Kolob Canyons area of the park, continue for 25 miles (40 kilometres) on the I-15 to exit 40.

Getting around

By car & bus

To cope with the volume of visitors, half of whom spend less than 4hrs in the park, and to minimise their environmental impact, a transport plan was implemented in May 2000. From April to October, the **Zion Canyon scenic drive** is closed to private vehicles. Visitors have to leave vehicles at the south entrance or in Springdale, and then catch a (free) shuttle bus into the park. (Guests of Zion Lodge are permitted to drive as far as the lodge.) The rest of the park is open to private cars, but note that vehicles wider than 7ft 10in (2m 39cm) or higher than 10ft 4in (3m 15cm) must be escorted through the **Zion-Mount Carmel tunnel** ($10 per vehicle), which can lead to delays on this stretch of road.

By bike

The **Pa'rus Trail**, a short cycle path along the Virgin River, connects Zion Canyon to the visitor centre and the campgrounds. You can rent bikes in Springdale – try **Bike Zion** (1458 Zion Park Boulevard, 1-435 772 3929/www.bikezion.com, $23-$35 per day). Explore the off-road trails and the nearby ghost town of **Grafton**, which was used in the movie *Butch Cassidy & the Sundance Kid*.

Hiking

There are plenty of maintained hiking trails off the scenic drive; the short easy routes along the valley floor (such as **Weeping Rock** and the **Riverside Walk**) are the busiest; head upwards to get away from the crowds, but be prepared for tough climbs and steep drop-offs. You get a fine view of lower Zion Canyon and Springdale at the end of the 2mile (3.2km) **Watchman** trail, but shade is minimal. Don't attempt the 5mile (8km) trail to **Angel's Landing** if you're afraid of heights; the last half mile follows a steep, narrow ridge fitted with chains – but the view is worth the heart palpitations. The most spectacular hike is perhaps through the 16mile (26km) **Narrows**, a section of the Virgin River where the canyon walls are up to 2,000ft (610m) high and at times only 20-30ft (2-8m) apart. Be prepared to wade (or even swim) through cold water and always check conditions at the visitor centre first; there can be dangerous flash floods in summer. Permits are required for all-day or overnight hikes.

Tourist information

Kolob Canyon Visitor Center

3752 E Kolob Canyon Road, New Harmony, UT 84757 (1-435 586 9548/www.nps.gov/zion). **Open** *Summer* 7am-7pm daily. *Winter* 8am-4.30pm daily.

Zion Canyon Visitor Center

Springdale, UT 84767 (recorded information 1-435 772 3256/www.nps.gov/zion). **Open** *Summer* 8am-7pm daily; closes earlier in winter.

Directory

Directory

Getting Around

By air

Las Vegas has grown so quickly that **McCarran International Airport** (261 5211/www.mccarran.com) now finds itself in the centre of town, just five minutes from the south end of the Strip. This makes arriving in Las Vegas relatively free of the usual headaches of getting from airport to hotel. Clean, modern and well designed, McCarran takes first (and last) tilt at the tourist dollar with halls full of slot machines and video poker.

Direct international flight service into Las Vegas is limited. There are five direct weekly flights from Tokyo to Las Vegas aboard Japan Air, while Virgin Atlantic has three flights a week (Tuesday, Thursday and Sunday) from the UK's Gatwick Airport. Most flights from Europe require passengers to change at an East Coast airport or in Los Angeles. Southwest Airlines is the busiest domestic carrier at McCarran, with 43 non-stop flights from destinations around the US. The airline uses 19 gates and occupies the whole of the C terminal.

Public bus routes 108 and 109 run north from the airport, but neither go up the Strip: the 108 heads north up Swenson Street and stops at the Las Vegas Hilton; the 109 goes along Maryland Parkway. Private shuttle buses run by **Bell Trans** (739 7990) or **Gray Line** (739 5700) to the Strip and Downtown hotels are available outside the arrivals terminal 24 hours daily.

Reservations are advised for the trip from the airport (just pick up the appropriate courtesy phone on arrival) and required for the trip back. Fares are less than $5 each way to the Strip and slightly more to Downtown. Bell Trans also runs a limo service.

Taxis can be found right outside the arrivals terminal: expect to pay $9-$12 to get to most hotels on the Strip, about $15 to Downtown (plus tip).

Airlines

Air Canada 1-800 247 2262
American Airlines domestic 1-800 433 7300
America West 1-800 235 9292
British Airways 1-800 247 9297
Canadian Airlines International 1-800 661 1505
Continental Airlines domestic 1-800 523 3273 international 1-800 231 0856
Delta Airlines domestic 1-800 221 1212 international 1-800 241 4141
Northwest Airlines domestic 1-800 225 2525 international 1-800 447 4747
Southwest Airlines 1-800 435 9792
TWA 1-800 221 2000
United Airlines 1-800 241 6522
US Airways 1-800 428 4322
Virgin Atlantic Airways 1-800 862 8621

By road

Almost half of visitors to Las Vegas drive their own cars into town, but it's also possible to catch the bus.

Greyhound

200 S Main Street, at Carson Street, Downtown (384 9561/information 1-800 231 2222). Bus 113, 207. **Open** 24hrs daily. **Credit** AmEx, Disc, MC, V. **Map** p312 C1/2. Greyhound covers 2,000 destinations nationwide, including Los Angeles ($32 one-way, $59 round-trip; 5-7hrs) and Reno ($72 one-way, $136.80 round-trip; 9hrs). Reservations are not required.

Car hire is relatively cheap and is likely to be the most convenient means of getting around for visitors without their own transport. Both self- and valet parking are free and, outside rush hour, you can get from one end of town to the other in 30 minutes. Having a vehicle is certainly advisable in the summer when walking even a short distance can be very uncomfortable. Car hire is also recommended if you are staying away from the Strip, and becomes essential if you plan to visit any out-of-town destinations, as few are served by public transport. On the other hand, if you're based on the Strip, a combination of walking, buses, taxis, shuttles and monorail services will get you around cheaply and relatively efficiently.

Information

The bus system is run by Citizens Area Transit (CAT), with 45 scheduled routes throughout the Las Vegas valley and the outlying cities of Laughlin and Mesquite. For a bus route map, *see p313*.

Downtown Transportation Center

Stewart Avenue, at Casino Center Boulevard, Downtown (228 7433/ www.rtc.co.clark.nv.us/cat/cat.htm). **Open** 6am-10pm Mon-Fri; 6am-6pm Sat, Sun. **Map** p312 D1. The DTC is the main transfer point for most bus routes.

Fares & tickets

Most CAT routes cost $1.25 for adults and 60¢ for seniors, juniors aged six to17 and disabled passengers. The exact change is required, and you must have a photocard to obtain a concessionary fare (available from the DTC with the appropriate certification). The 301/302 routes along the Strip costs $2 for all passengers. Transfers are free, but you must ask for one when you pay the fare. An exact fare of $1.50 is required for the Strip Trolley.

A 30-day reduced fare pass costs $30 either in person from the DTC or by mail (processing takes seven to ten days, money order only). Tokens are a better bet for short-term visitors: they're sold in bags of 40 for $20; you need two tokens for an adult fare (four on the 301 or 302 buses) and one for children, a saving of about 25 per cent.

Bus routes

CAT buses run 24 hours between Downtown and the Strip, and from about 5.30am to 1.30am on other routes. The buses are safe and relatively comprehensive in their coverage of the city. All can take both bicycles and wheelchairs.

The CAT bus network is scrambling to keep pace with the growth of the city, and services are continually being revised. Bus stops are marked by white, green and purple signs with the feline CAT logo; most have shelters to provide relief from the summer sun, though they're often full.

Bus 301, 302

The most useful bus for tourists is the 24-hour 301, which travels the length of Las Vegas Boulevard from the DTC in the north to Vacation Village hotel at Sunset Road in the south, stopping in front of all major casinos (every 10min, 5.30am-midnight; every 15min thereafter). 301s are often overcrowded, especially in the late afternoon and early evening. The 302 evening express service (every 15min, 6pm-1am) follows the same route along the Strip but makes fewer stops.

Strip trolley

A more colourful alternative is the privately run Strip Trolley, which runs every 20min 9.30am-2.30am along the Strip, stopping at all major hotels, the Fashion Show Mall, Wet 'n' Wild water park and the Las Vegas Hilton (just east of the Strip). Unlike the CAT buses, the trolley picks up and drops off passengers at the front door of some hotels, instead of on the street outside. The trolleys are no less crowded than the city buses, but the experience has a more congenial feel. Ask your hotel front desk if it's on the trolley route or call 382 1404 for information.

Shuttle buses & monorails

You can travel around for free on the numerous hotel shuttle buses and the four monorails. If they don't take you direct to the casino you want, they'll take you within walking distance.

Monorails

The most useful monorail links Bally's and the MGM Grand (9am-1am daily) for access to the cluster of major mid- and south-Strip resorts. The other monorails operate 24hrs and link Monte Carlo and Bellagio; the Mirage and Treasure Island; and the Excalibur, Luxor and Mandalay Bay – but in all cases, it's often quicker to walk.

Shuttle buses

The Barbary Coast runs a shuttle bus to the Gold Coast on Flamingo Road (also useful for the Rio and the Palms), and to the Orleans in South-west Las Vegas. The Rio's own shuttle runs from a small building on the east side of the Strip, just south of the Aladdin. The Stratosphere runs a shuttle to and from the Strip, while the Hard Rock's shuttle travels in a loop to the Stardust, Fashion Show Mall, Forum Shops, Tropicana and back to the Hard Rock. The Sam's Town shuttle bus is the most efficient of all and gives you access to just about every other shuttle in town. Useful places to pick up shuttles are the Fashion Show Mall and the Tropicana.

Taxis & limos

There are taxi ranks outside most hotels and throughout tourist areas, and restaurants and bars will be happy to call a cab for you. Note that taxis are tougher to find when there's a major convention in town and on New Year's Eve and holiday weekends. Technically, you are not allowed to hail a taxi from the street, although it's usually acceptable to approach an empty cab with its light on if it's stopped in traffic. Meters start at $2.20, and increase by $1.50 per subsequent mile. If you have a complaint about a registered taxi, note the cab number and contact the Nevada Taxicab Authority (486 6532; open 24hrs daily). For lost property, see p291.

Limousines are a flash and popular way of getting around Las Vegas. The rides vary from the basic black stretch at about $40 an hour to flamboyant party-venues-on-wheels, with hot tubs, disco balls and the like ($100 an hour). Many limos are available for hire outside hotels and the airport; if you are in a large group on a busy night, the cost is worth it to avoid the long taxi queue. In order to protect the taxicab trade, limo drivers are not allowed to solicit passengers, but you are perfectly at liberty to approach them for a ride.

Cab companies

Checker/Star/Yellow Cab 873 2000
Whittlesea Blue 384 6111

Limousine companies

Bell Trans 385 5466
CT&T Transportation 731 0900
Las Vegas Limo 739 8414
Presidential 731 5577

Driving

Though many streets in Las Vegas are smoother and wider than in most urban centres, growth rates mean you'll have to navigate construction zones in every corner of the city. Streets get very congested in the morning and evening rush hours (7-9am, 4-7pm), and at weekends, when the number of

Directory

visitors increases dramatically and traffic is much heavier in tourist areas after 4pm. The Strip is slow-going most of the time and turns into a virtual car park when the town is crowded: avoid it if possible after 6pm at the weekend.

The nearby parallel streets – Industrial Road to the west and Paradise Road to the east – move a bit faster, and provide access to the back entrances of several casinos. For north–south journeys that are longer than a block or so, it's often worth getting on the I-15, which runs parallel to the Strip. If you're trying to get east–west across town, aim for the fast-moving Desert Inn arterial, a mini-expressway that runs under Las Vegas Boulevard and over the I-15 (no junctions at either).

The north–south I-15 intersects with the east–west US 95 just to the north-west of Downtown at the ever-congested and confusing 'Spaghetti Bowl' (though major improvements are currently under way). US 95 connects to the 53-mile (80-kilometre) beltway under construction, which will eventually (by 2003) transport commuters around the entire Las Vegas valley. Portions of the beltway, such as the I-215 airport connector and the section running north-west to Summerlin, are already in use. For up-to-the-minute local road conditions, call 486 3116 or log on to the City of Las Vegas website (www.ci.las-vegas.nv.us).

Speed limits vary through-out Nevada. Generally the speed limit on freeways is 65mph (104kph), while on the highway, it is either 70mph (112kph) or 65mph. Major urban thoroughfares, such as Tropicana Avenue and Flamingo Road are 45mph, but otherwise, speed limits throughout town are 35mph (56kph), with residential neighbourhoods limited to 25mph (40kph). Note that these are general guidelines only; always follow the roadside speed limit signs. School and construction zones, marked by signs and sometimes flashing lights, are strictly enforced and fines are doubled. Unless otherwise specified, you can turn right on a red light after stopping, if the street is clear. U-turns are not only legal (unless otherwise specified) but often a positive necessity given the length of the blocks, particularly on the Strip.

In case of a car accident, call 911; do not move the cars involved in the accident until the police ask you do so.

In Nevada, you can be arrested for driving under the influence if your blood alcohol level is 0.08 or higher. If you are pulled over, the police are legally within their rights to submit you to a drink-driving test, which they will administer on the spot. If you refuse, you will be taken to jail immediately and your blood will be taken by force if necessary.

Breakdown services

American Automobile Association (AAA)

3312 W Charleston Boulevard, just west of Valley View Boulevard, North-west Las Vegas (870 9171/ emergency service 1 800 222 4357). **Open** 8.30am-5.30pm Mon-Fri. The Triple A provides excellent maps, guidebooks and campsite listings – and they won't cost you a penny if you're a member or belong to an affiliated organisation, such as the British AA. Many motels offer discounts to AAA members. **Branches**: 601 Whitney Ranch Drive, Henderson (458 2323); 8440 W Lake Mead Boulevard, Summerlin (360 3151)

Fuel stations

Petrol prices are far cheaper than in Europe, but among the most expensive in the US. Drivers will be hard-pressed to find service stations on the central Strip, but there are a few at the far north and south ends (*see below*). Travel off the Strip, and convenience stores and self-service fuel stations abound. For mechanics and full-service gas stations, look under 'Automobile repair' in the Yellow Pages. The following are open 24 hours.

AM-PM/Arco *3858 Las Vegas Boulevard North, at Bonanza Road, Downtown (736 3397).* **Credit** AmEx, Disc, MC, V. **Map** p312 D1.
7-11/CitGo *1100 Las Vegas Boulevard South, at Charleston Boulevard (366 9025).* **Credit** AmEx, Disc, MC, V. **Map** p315 C3.
Terrible's/Chevron *6176 Las Vegas Boulevard South, at Russell Road (361 5174).* **Credit** AmEx, Disc, MC, V. **Map** p316 A9.

Insurance

Nevada law requires drivers to carry vehicle insurance supplied by a state-licensed insurance agent. The minimum coverage is $15,000 for bodily injury, $30,000 for personal accident and $10,000 for property damage. You must keep a proof of insurance card in your vehicle at all times, otherwise you risk a fine of up to $500. If you hire a car, make certain your agency provides you with proof of registration and insurance. Additional insurance may also be necessary or advisable.

Parking

Most hotel-casinos have valet parking, which is convenient, safe and free (apart from the $1-$2 tip to the valet on your way out). If you see a sign saying valet parking is full, and you're driving a luxury car, stay put: chances are they'll find an empty spot. If you're a guest of the hotel, you will also get preferential treatment. Alternatively, flashing your cash – a $5 or $10 bill (sometimes a bit more if the resort is very busy) – will usually get you a spot no matter what the sign says. Valeting is usually the best option if time is a factor; but bear in mind that you'll have to wait in line to have your car returned (advance tips will help here, too). Self-parking is plentiful and free at every Vegas resort and attraction (Downtown casinos require a validation stamp), but the lots vary in their convenience.

Vehicle hire

Most of the major car hire agencies are located at or near McCarran Airport, with other branches around town. Call around to find the best rate, and book well in advance if you're planning to visit over a holiday weekend or to attend a major convention. Conversely, at times when business renters are scarce, you should get a good rate – and it's worth asking for an upgrade. If your hotel has a car-rental desk, start there; if not, ask the concierge for advice.

Almost every rental agency will require a credit card and a matching driver's licence, and few will rent to anyone under 25. The price quoted will not include tax, liability insurance or collision damage waiver (CDW), which could double the daily rental rate. Ask about discounts, available to members of the AAA (and British AA), AARP and other organisations. Travel agents often get a worthwhile discount. Also keep an eye out for coupons. Motorcycle rental companies offer unlimited mileage, insurance, helmets and anything else you need to get your motor runnin'.

Car rental: local companies

Some local companies have more flexible policies than their national counterparts, and sometimes offer better rates. **A-Fairway Rent-A-Car** (369 8533) and **X-Press International** (795 4008) accept cash deposits instead of a credit card, and have no age restriction beyond the Federal requirement. And for those who want to make their Vegas

entrance in appropriately flashy style, **Rent-A-Vette** (736 2592) rents Corvettes, Porsches, Vipers, Ferraris and the like. Well reputed local company **Allstate** (736 6147) is strong on heavy-duty off-road vehicles and pick-up trucks. The Las Vegas franchise of **Rent-A-Wreck** (474 0037) has year-old models at great prices, and offers the cheapest insurance we found. **Sav-More Rent-A-Car** has standard cars for those on a budget (736 1234).

Car rental: national companies

Alamo 263 8411/1-800 327 9633/ www.freeways.com
Avis 261 5595/1-800 331 1212/ www.avis.com
Budget 736 1212/1-800 527 0700/ www.budgetrentacar.com
Dollar 739 8408/1-800 800 4000/www.dollarcar.com
Enterprise 1-800 736 8222/ www.pickenterprise.com
Hertz 220 9700/1-800 704 4473/ www.hertz.com
National 261 5391/1-800 227 7368/ www.nationalcar.com
Thrifty 896 7600/1-800 367 2277/ www.thrifty.com

Motorcycle rental

Eaglerider 876 8687
Easyriders 368 7808
Harley-Davidson of Southern Nevada 431 8500
North American Motorcycle Tours 434 0200

RV rental

Renting a recreational vehicle (camper van) will cost about $400 for three days and between $800 and $1,000 for a week, depending on the vehicle. **Cruise America** (456 6666/ 1-800 327 7799) has everything from 18ft (5.5m) camper homes to 30ft (9m) RVs. Call ahead for a brochure, which comes with a 10% money-off coupon. **RVN4Fun** (254 0770/1-800 717 6960/www.rvn4 fun.com) has 125 US and Canada branches.

Cycling

In 1999, Las Vegas was named one of the 'Top 10 Worst Bicycling Cities in the Nation'. The road system (except in Summerlin) is designed solely for the car driver, and bikes are such a rarity that drivers forget to check for their existence. The only people who cycle in Las Vegas are security guards and people with a death wish.

Bike rental outlets are aimed at leisure riders planning out-of-town excursions – there are some great desert rides in the vicinity (*see p230*).

Walking

No one would call Las Vegas a foot-friendly city. Pedestrians are rarely seen off the Strip, and even there they face considerable dangers, resulting in some unpleasant accident statistics: 37 pedestrians, many of them tourists, were killed in Clark County in 2000. The intersection bridges on the Strip are helping, but now the Flamingo Road area near the Rio and Gold Coast is becoming dangerous.

Even if you stick to one side of Las Vegas Boulevard you will constantly be crossing entrance and exit roads. And if you want to traverse the Strip, you have the choice of a long walk to the next cross street or a dangerous dash across ten lanes of traffic; the practice is so deadly that police issue jaywalking citations on a regular basis. It is vital that pedestrians remember that the laws favour the driver: never put yourself in the path of cars that have the green light.

The safest places to cross are via the three pedestrian bridges at the Strip/Tropicana Avenue intersection – which (of course) guide you past the entrances of the four casinos on each corner – and via the pedestrian bridge between Bellagio and Bally's. A further bridge is planned between the Venetian and the Mirage.

It's possible to take short-cuts from one Strip hotel to the next, but you are likely to get trapped in a maze of service roads. Use the maps at the back of this book to guide you (*see pp307-316*) and don't underestimate distances: it's a four-mile (6.4-kilometre) trek from one end of the Strip to the other.

Directory

Resources A-Z

Addresses

Written addresses in Las Vegas follow the standard US format. The room and/or suite number usually appears after the street address (where applicable), followed by the city name and the zip code. Note that Las Vegas Boulevard South is the official name of the Strip and is the designation that is used in the addresses of all Strip properties.

For information on street-numbering and orientation, *see p64.*

Age restrictions

Las Vegas may be a carefree city of hedonism and wild abandon, but only if you're old enough:
Admission to nude clubs 18
Admission to topless clubs 21
Buying alcohol 21
Drinking alcohol 21
Driving 16
Gambling 21
Marriage with parental consent 16 (younger in special circumstances)
Marriage without parental consent 18
Sex (heterosexual couples) 16
Sex (homosexual couples) 18

Attitude & etiquette

Despite a glamorous past, Las Vegas the tourist city is as formal or informal as you want it to be, and universally friendly. During the warmer months, shorts and T-shirts are accepted wear along the Strip and in most casinos, though in recent years, dressing up to a minimum of smart-casual has become the norm for a night out. Some lounges, nightclubs and restaurants have dress codes (sports shoes, T-shirts and baggy jeans may be prohibited), and dining can be quite formal.

Business

Gambling and tourism remain the city's most prominent enterprises, in terms of both revenue and employment. However, though tourism has been thriving for more than a decade, the Las Vegas business community has recognised the need for economic diversification. Its efforts have been successful, particularly in manufacturing – wood, plastic and rubber products and gambling equipment – trade and distribution. The climate and favourable tax structure have helped the state's economic development authorities attract hundreds of companies to the city.

Business travellers are well served in Las Vegas: most major Strip resorts have business centres that offer a variety of services, including faxing, photocopying, shipping (via US postal service or special carriers such as Federal Express and United Parcel Service), computer, digital pager and mobile phone hire and private conference rooms.

Conventions & conferences

Several cities have claimed to be the 'Convention Capital of the World', but when judged by sheer volume of convention business, Las Vegas has no competition. The numbers speak for themselves: in 2000, the city played host to nearly 4,000 trade shows, attended by 3.8 million delegates. Most of the largest conventions in existence are held in Las Vegas, including the Consumer Electronics Show (100,000 delegates), the National Association of Broadcasters (90,000 delegates), the Sporting Good Manufacturers

Association (80,000) and the huge computer industry show Comdex (225,000 delegates). Most conventions and trade fairs are held at the following three locations:

Cashman Field Center
850 Las Vegas Boulevard North, at Washington Avenue, North Las Vegas (386 7100). Bus 113.
Located just north of Downtown, Cashman Field is used only for smaller events.

Las Vegas Convention Center
3150 Paradise Road, opposite Convention Center Drive, East of Strip (892 0711/www.lasvegas 24hours.com). Bus 108.
Map p315 C5.
The largest convention and meeting facility in the US is still growing every few years. The most recent expansion project, scheduled for completion in December 2001, will bring the total meeting and exhibit space to 2 million sq ft. There are 91 meeting rooms, with seating capacities ranging from 200 to 2,000. The on-site business centre provides access to computers, fax machines, telephones and courier services. Parking is limited, so walk if you're staying in the area, or use hotel shuttle buses.

Sands Expo & Convention Center
210 Sands Avenue, at Koval Lane, East of Strip (733 5556). Bus 203.
Map p316 B6.
Second in size to the Las Vegas Convention Center, this facility offers the same state-of-the-art amenities, with even worse parking frustrations.

Convention dates
A complete list of upcoming conventions can be found on the LVCVA website (*see p296*).
Consumer Electronics Show 8-11 Jan 2002 (125,000 delegates).
Men's Apparel Guild in California 27-30 Aug 2001; 19-22 Feb 2001, 26-29 Aug 2002 (95,000).
National Association of Broadcasters 6-11 Apr 2002, 5-10 Apr 2003 (90,000). A good time for star-gazing.
Specialty Equipment Market Association/APAA/ASIA/ MEMA 30 Oct-2 Nov 2001, 5-8 Nov, 2002 (65,000). Check out automobile

Resources A-Z

accessories and hundreds of flashy custom cars.

Comdex 12-16 Nov 2001, 18-22 Nov 2002 (225,000).

Sporting Goods Manufacturers Association 20-23 Jan 2002, 19-22 Jan 2003 (80,000)

World Gaming Congress & Expo Oct 2001, Oct 2002. An annual showcase for all the new-generation slot and video poker machines, table games and casino paraphernalia.

Couriers & shippers

The courier services listed below all offer worldwide delivery. Each service has drop-off points throughout the city. If you're attending a convention, there will probably be a drop-off box on site, and many of the big hotels have business centres with courier services.

Airborne Express *1-800 247 2676.* **Open** 8am-5pm Mon-Fri; 8am-noon Sat. **No credit cards.**

Federal Express (FedEx) *1-800 463 3339.* **Open** 9am-5.30pm Mon-Sat. **Credit** AmEx, DC, Disc, MC, V.

United Parcel Service (UPS) *1-800 742 5877.* **Open** 8.30am-5.30pm Mon-Fri. **Credit** AmEx, MC, V.

Office equipment & services

Accurate Communications

Suite 21, 2101 S Decatur Boulevard, between W Sahara Avenue & Oakey Boulevard, North-west Las Vegas (259 1520). **Open** *Office* 8am-5pm Mon-Fri. **No credit cards.**

Users can call in and receive messages from a secretary or voicemail box. AC will also fax messages to a specified location, or relay them to a pager.

Bit-by-bit

3400 Desert Inn Road, at Polaris Avenue, West of Strip (474 6311/ www.bit-by-bit.com). Bus 105. **Open** 9am-5pm Mon-Fri. **Credit** AmEx, MC, V. **Map** p311 X2/3.

Bit-by-bit offers computers and other equipment for hire.

Kinko's

Howard Hughes Center, 395 Hughes Center Drive, at Paradise Road, just north of Flamingo Road, East of Strip (951 2400/1-800 546 5674/ www.kinkos.com). Bus 108, 202.

Open 24hrs daily. **Credit** AmEx, Disc, MC, V. **Map** p316 C7.

America's most prominent chain of copy shops has seven branches in Las Vegas, all open 24 hours – except the Fourth Street branch in Downtown (open 6am-11pm daily). Services include on-site use of computers, typesetting, printing, fax and phone facilities, as well as courier service via FedEx.

Branches: throughout the city.

Officemax

Sahara Pavilion South, 2640 S Decatur Boulevard, at Sahara Avenue, South-west Las Vegas (221 0471/1-800 788 8080/www. office.com). Bus 103, 204. **Open** 7am-9pm Mon-Fri; 9am-9pm Sat; 10am-6pm Sun. **Credit** AmEx, Disc, MC, V.

Each store carries a full line of office supplies, computers, furniture and business machines.

Branches: throughout the city.

Useful organisations

For details of the **Las Vegas Chamber of Commerce** and the **Las Vegas Convention & Visitors Authority**, *see p296* **Tourist information**.

Nevada Development Authority

Hughes Center, 3773 Howard Hughes Parkway South, between Sands Avenue & E Flamingo Road, East of Strip (791 0000/www. nevadadevelopment.org). Bus 108, 203. **Open** 8am-5pm Mon-Fri. **Map** p316 B/C 6/7.

Consumer

For complaints against casinos, contact the Enforcement Department of the **Gaming Control Board** (555 E Washington Avenue, Las Vegas, NV 89101; 486 2000). For general consumer enquiries and complaints contact the following:

Better Business Bureau *5595 Spring Mountain Road, Las Vegas, NV 89104 (320 4500).* Private agency that can report on the background of businesses and review written complaints.

Nevada Department of Business and Industry, *Consumer Affairs Division 1805 E Sahara Avenue, Las Vegas, NV 89104 (486 7355).* The state division overseeing correct business practices.

Customs

The lack of direct international flights to Las Vegas means that most non-US visitors usually have to change at another US city and go through Immigration and Customs there. This involves reclaiming your baggage at the transfer airport, taking it through Customs and then checking it in again. The airlines try to make this a painless process by having a transfer check-in desk just outside Customs at most major airports; however, you will have to make your own way to the domestic departures terminal. Connection times take account of this – and the fact that you may have to queue at Immigration – but we suggest you go through the transfer process and check in for your Las Vegas flight before you take any time to relax at the airport.

On a flight to the US, non-US citizens are given two forms, one for Immigration, one for Customs, which must be filled in accurately and in full, and handed in at the appropriate desk on landing.

US customs regulations allow foreign visitors to import the following items duty-free: 200 cigarettes or 50 cigars (not Cuban; over-18s only) or 2kg of smoking tobacco; one litre (1.05 US quart) of wine or spirits (over-21s only); and up to $100 in gifts ($400 for returning Americans). You can take up to $10,000 in cash, travellers' cheques or endorsed bank drafts in or out of the country tax-free. Anything above that must be declared, or you risk forfeiting the lot. Depending on the state in which you land, you may also need to declare any foodstuffs or plants you have with you. Many food and plants are prohibited entirely, while canned or processed items are permitted with restriction.

Time Out Las Vegas Guide **287**

Directory

Check with **US Customs** (www.customs.gov/travel/travel.htm) to be sure.

UK Customs & Excise allows returning travellers to bring in £145 worth of gifts and goods and an unlimited amount of money, as long as you can prove it's yours. Other nationalities should check the rules in their country.

Disabled travellers

Las Vegas is a disabled-friendly city. The casinos have always relied on luring a sizeable elderly clientele, and they complied swiftly with the Americans with Disabilities Act for fear of losing their gaming licences. Hence all Strip casino resorts are fully wheelchair-accessible, from their pools, spas and toilets through to their gambling and parking facilities (things are a little harder in the older properties Downtown). A handful, notably Caesars Palace, also offer games designed for sight- and hearing-impaired players. Disabled parking is ubiquitous and buses and many taxis are adapted to take wheelchairs (specify when you book).

The **Society for the Advancement of Travel for the Handicapped** (1-212 447 7284/fax 1-212 725 8253) can offer advice for disabled people planning trips to all parts of the United States.

Southern Nevada Center for Independent Living

6200 W Oakey Boulevard, at Jones Avenue, North-west Las Vegas (870 7050 inc TDD). Bus 205. **Open** 8am-5pm Mon-Fri.
Services include advice, information, transport and equipment loan (including wheelchairs). It can refer you to other disabled organisations.

Drugs

Illegal drugs, including designer club drugs such as Ecstasy, are quite prevalent in Sin City. Dealers will approach you all over town, but you should ignore them. In addition, watch your drink at all times: illicit, hard-to-trace drugs are sometimes slipped into unattended drinks.

In stark contrast to the seemingly lax policies towards the sex industry and other morally questionable behaviour, the local authorities have a strict zero-tolerance policy when it comes to illegal drug use and trafficking. If you are implicated in a drug sale or purchase, you will be arrested and subject to trial. If convicted you can receive the maximum sentence of five to ten years in prison. Jails in the United States are full of first-time drug offenders: it's best not to mess around.

Electricity & appliances

Rather than the 220-240V, 50-cycle AC used in Europe, the United States uses a 110-120V, 60-cycle AC voltage. Except for dual-voltage, flat-pin plug shavers, most foreign visitors will need to run their own appliances via an adaptor, available at airport shops. Bear in mind most US videos and TVs use a different frequency from those in Europe.

Embassies & consulates

Most foreign embassies in the US are based in Washington, DC (contact directory assistance in Washington to get the appropriate number; 1-202 555 1212). The only countries with a consulate in Las Vegas are **Ecuador** (735 8193), **Germany** (734 9700) and **Italy** (385 6843). Nationals of other countries should contact their consulate or consulate general in Los Angeles or San Francisco.

Australia *19th Floor, Century Plaza Towers, 2049 Century Park East, Los Angeles, CA 90067 (general 1-310 229 4800/consular 229 4865/passports 229 4828/fax 277 2258).* **Open** *Office* 9am-5pm Mon-Fri.
Canada *9th Floor, 550 South Hope Street, Los Angeles, CA 90071 (1-213 346 2700/fax 620 88270).* **Open** 9am-5pm Mon-Fri.
New Zealand *Suite 1150, 12400 Wilshire Boulevard, Los Angeles, CA 90025 (1-310 207 1605/207 3605).* **Open** 9am-5.30pm Mon-Fri
Republic of Ireland *Suite 3830, 44 Montgomery Street, San Francisco, CA 94104 (1-415 392 4214).* **Open** 9am-5pm Mon-Fri.
South Africa *6300 Wilshire Boulevard, Suite 600, Los Angeles, CA 90048 (1-323 651 0902/fax 651 5969).* **Open** *Office* 8am-4.30pm Mon-Fri. *Consulate* 9am-noon Mon-Fri.
United Kingdom *Suite 400, 11766 Wilshire Boulevard, Los Angeles, CA 90025 (1-310 477 3322/24hr emergency number 1-213 856 3755/fax 1-310 575 1450).* **Open** 8.30am-5pm Mon-Fri.

Emergencies

In case of emergency dial 911 (free from public phones) and calmly state the nature of the emergency; the operator will connect you to the appropriate authority. For further details of what to do in a medical emergency, *see p289* **Health**.

Gay & lesbian

Help & information

For information on bars and special events, local and national news, local gossip and personal ads, pick up *Out Las Vegas*, and its sister publication, *Lesbian Voice*. These monthlies are the leading resources for the Las Vegas GLBT community, and are available at all gay bars, bookstores, coffeehouses, libraries, in several casinos, and at most businesses included in the Gay & Lesbian section of this guide, starting on page 214. The *Las Vegas Bugle* may also come in handy. Online, check out information on the gay events website www.gayvegas.com.

Gay & Lesbian Center of Las Vegas

912 E Sahara Avenue, between Sixth Street & Maryland Parkway, East Las Vegas (733 9800/fax 733 9075/ www.thecenter-lasvegas.com). Bus 204. **Open** 11am-7pm Mon-Fri; 10am-9pm Sat. **Map** p311 Y2.
A support organisation for gay men and lesbians. The centre organises social events (*see p214*) and is a meeting place for a variety of groups, including a gay men's discussion group, a lesbian group and a youth group. There are also free and confidential HIV tests. Call ahead to check the schedule. Note that the centre can be tricky to find: it's on a little cul-de-sac off Sahara Avenue, opposite the Commercial Center.

Accommodation

Chapman Guesthouse

1904 Chapman Drive, off Sahara Avenue, just east of Maryland Parkway, East Las Vegas (312 4625/ www.chapmanguesthouse.com). Bus 204. **Rates** (incl breakfast) $69-$79. **Credit** AmEx, MC, V.
An exclusively gay male guesthouse. The mailing address is 2961 Industrial Road, Suite 104, Las Vegas, NV 89109, and advance booking is recommended.

The Ranch

1110 Ralston Drive, near Martin Luther King Boulevard & Washington Avenue, North Las Vegas (631 7013/fax 631 7723). Bus 105, 208. **Rates** (per person) $75 summer; $150 winter; phone for weekend and weekly rates. **No credit cards**.
The one lesbian-owned B&B in town.

Other groups & organisations

Las Vegas Metropolitan Community Church

Suite 301, 1140 Almond Tree Lane, at Maryland Parkway, East Las Vegas (369 4380). **Open** *Services* 6pm Wed; 10am Sun.
The city's only gay church.

Health

Health services in Las Vegas are comparable to those in other US cities. Doctors are available around the clock in emergency rooms and at some UMC Quick Care locations, and by appointment during regular business hours. Most hospitals accept major insurance plans, but, unless it's an emergency, you should call ahead to check. The large hotels can help guests reach on-call doctors who will come to you in case of emergency. Of course, you may have to pay cash for this service. Try to find out the hotel and the doctor's policy on this in advance.

Accident & emergency

In case of an accident or medical emergency, call 911 immediately. If you have an emergency while in a major resort, call 911, then call security, although the chances are that security will have already been alerted by the eye-in-the-sky. Never move a person who has been hurt.

Ambulances

Several ambulance companies operate in Las Vegas. If you are injured and conscious, you can choose which ambulance company you would like to service you. If you are not conscious, the first ambulance on the scene will take you to the closest hospital emergency room available.

Complementary medicine

The few practitioners of complementary medicine, and especially holistic chiropractors, enjoy a healthy business in Las Vegas, as do aromatherapists and herbal healers. In fact, all of the major hotel spas include some form of aromatherapy among their treatments. The city even has its very own popular purveyor of Chinese medicine, **T&T Ginseng**.

For this, and other suppliers of alternative therapies, *see p177.*

Contraception & abortion

Planned Parenthood

3220 W Charleston Boulevard, between Rancho Drive & Valley View Boulevard, North-west Las Vegas (878 7776). Bus 206. **Open** (by appointment only) 9am-6pm Mon; 9am-5pm Tue; 10am-6pm Wed; 9am-4pm Thur, Fri; 9am-2pm Sat.
This non-profit organisation can supply contraception (including the morning-after pill), treat STDs, perform abortions and test for AIDS (results take a week). You'll need an appointment for everything except a pregnancy test.

Doctors & dentists

Clark County Medical Society (739 9989) provides information on and referrals to local doctors, including Medicaid and Medicare practitioners. The **Southern Nevada Dental Society** (733 8700) will make referrals to registered local dentists, including Medicaid and Medicare practitioners.

Hospitals

All the hospitals listed below have 24-hour emergency rooms, although only the **Sunrise Medical Center** and the **University Medical Center** have out-and-out trauma centres that are able to handle every type of medical emergency on the spot.
Desert Springs Hospital *2075 E Flamingo Road, at Burnham Street, East Las Vegas (733 8800). Bus 202.*
Lake Mead Hospital Medical Center *1409 E Lake Mead Boulevard, between Las Vegas Boulevard, North & Eastern Avenues, North Las Vegas (649 7711). Bus 113, 210.*
St Rose Dominican Hospital *102 E Lake Mead Drive, at Boulder Highway, Henderson (564 2622). Bus 107, 212.* A non-profit hospital that never turns patients away. No trauma unit.
Summerlin Hospital Medical Center *657 Town Center Drive, at Hualapai Way, North-west Las Vegas (233 7000). No bus.* Las Vegas's newest hospital has excellent maternity care.

Directory

Sunrise Hospital & Medical Center *3186 S Maryland Parkway, between Sahara Avenue & Desert Inn Road, East Las Vegas (731 8000). Bus 109.* Nevada's largest hospital has a poison control centre and a children's hospital.
University Medical Center *1800 W Charleston Boulevard, at Shadow Lane (383 2000). Bus 206.* The only hospital in Las Vegas that by law must treat all applicants. It's a good one, too. The ER entrance is on the corner of Hasting and Rose Streets.
Valley Hospital Medical Center *620 Shadow Lane, off Charleston Boulevard, between Rancho Drive & Martin Luther King Boulevard (388 4000). Bus 206.*

Pharmacies

Both over-the-counter and prescription drugs are readily available all over Las Vegas. Most hotel gift shops carry a variety of non-prescription pain-killers for the most common ailments such as headache and upset stomach, although you are likely to be charged outrageous prices for these items. It's best, therefore to use specialist drugstores and licensed pharmacies.

All-night pharmacies are plentiful in Las Vegas: they're listed in the Yellow Pages under 'Pharmacies' and include all branches of **Sav-on**, which are open 24 hours daily. The closest branches to the Strip are at 2300 E Tropicana Avenue (736 4174) and 1360 E Flamingo Road (731 5373). For details of other pharmacies, *see p178*.

Prescriptions

In order to get a prescription drug, you must have a written prescription from a practising physician. Doctors in Las Vegas will generally insist on giving you a physical examination before they will write out a prescription. Take the prescription to a licensed pharmacist, who will usually be able to provide you with the medication within a few minutes.

STDs, HIV & AIDS

At the risk of stating the obvious, Nevada is a unique state with legalised gaming and limited legalised prostitution in some counties. It ranks 12th in the nation for AIDS cases per capita and second for alcohol consumption. Combine these sobering statistics with the fact that Las Vegas's thriving tourist industry attracts more than 35 million visitors a year, and it soon becomes obvious that Las Vegas is not only a pleasure zone but a danger zone, too. To restate the obvious, always practise safe sex.

For more specific information on HIV/AIDS, local resources and various support groups and free, confidential tests, contact **Aid for AIDS of Nevada**, the state's largest and most comprehensive AIDS service provider. Information is also available from the **Nevada AIDS Hotline** (474 2437/1-800 842 2437) and the AIDS information line at the **Clark County Health District**. For treatment of STDs and free AIDS tests, visit **Planned Parenthood** (*see p289* **Contraception & abortion**).

Aid for AIDS of Nevada (AFAN)

Suite 211, Sahara Rancho Medical Center, 2300 S Rancho Drive, between Sahara Avenue & Oakey Boulevard, West of Strip (382 2326/hotline 474 2437/ www.wizard.com/afan). Bus 201. **Open** 8am-5pm Mon-Fri.
In addition to offering free advice and testing, this support group raises money and awareness through big-scale annual events, including the lavish Black & White Party at the Hard Rock Hotel in September, and an annual benefit walk along the Strip, which attracted 3,500 participants in 2001.

AIDS Information Line

Clark County Health District, Annexe A, 625 Shadow Lane, just north of Charleston Boulevard, North-west Las Vegas (383 1393). Bus 206, 401. **Open** 8am-4.30pm Mon-Fri.

For AIDS helplines, *see above*. For information on what to do in an emergency, *see p288* **Emergencies**.

Helplines

Alcoholics Anonymous 598 1888.
Gamblers Anonymous 385 7732.
Narcotics Anonymous 369 3362.
Poison Control Center 732 4989.
Rape Crisis 366 1640.
Suicide Prevention 731 2990.

ID

While travelling in and around Las Vegas, you will need to have your identification at the ready. You will need it to prove your age for tobacco and alcohol purchases, to gamble and get into nightclubs and adult strip clubs. Occasionally, you may also need it when you are using a credit card or travellers' cheque.

Legal identification includes the following: a government-issued passport, a state-issued driver's licence or state-issued identification card.

Insurance

Non-nationals should arrange comprehensive baggage, trip-cancellation and medical insurance before they leave home. Medical centres will ask for details of your insurance company and your policy number if you require treatment; keep the details with you at all times.

Internet

Though slow to connect at first, the Internet has started to take hold in Las Vegas. The newest hotels and casinos provide guests with in-room connections and the older resorts have Internet access in their business centres.

Local Internet Service Providers are rapidly being taken over by the cable

Directory

television and telephone service companies. Try **Cox Communications** (598 2100) or **Sprint** (244 7400). Las Vegas lone Internet café provides a place to get connected on the Strip in a pleasant environment. In addition, the public libraries (*see below*) offer free time-limited Internet access and Kinko's will grant you access all day long for $15 per hour.

For a selection of useful websites, *see p299*.

Coffeemani@ Las Vegas
2417 Las Vegas Boulevard South, at Sahara Avenue, Stratosphere Area (737 5241). **Open** 9am-10pm Mon-Sat; noon-8pm Sun. **Rates** $6 for 30min. **Credit** AmEx, Disc, MC, V. **Map** p315 C4.
Friendly staff, cosy surroundings and excellent coffee.

Left luggage

Left-luggage lockers in two sizes are available inside terminal one at McCarran International Airport. Exact change in quarters is required. You may also leave luggage at the Greyhound Terminal. Most major hotels will let you leave luggage with the bellmen for a nominal fee (a tip of $5 per bag in most cases).

Certified Airline Passenger Services or CAPS (5757 Wayne Newton Boulevard, McCarran International Airport, East of Strip; 736 2605) will pick up your luggage on arrival and deliver it to your hotel. It can also collect the luggage from your hotel at the end of your stay and check it through to your final destination. CAPS is one hundred per cent certified and meets FAA requirements; phone for rates.

Legal help

If you are arrested, use your phone call to contact either your insurance company's emergency number, your

consulate or the referral service listed below. If you do not have a lawyer, the court will appoint one for you.

Lawyer Referral Service
State Bar of Nevada 382 0504. **Open** *Telephone enquiries* 9am-4pm Mon-Fri. **Rates** $45 referral fee. You will be referred to an attorney who specialises in the specific field.

Libraries

For details of Las Vegas's most significant library buildings, *see p224* **Culture shock**.

Las Vegas Library District
Open 9am-9pm Mon-Thur; 9am-5pm Fri, Sat; 1-5pm Sun.
Clark County Library *1401 E Flamingo Road, University District (733 7810).* **Map** p311 Y3.
Las Vegas Library *833 Las Vegas Boulevard North, between Washington Avenue & Bonanza Road, North Las Vegas (382 3493).* **Map** p312 D1.
Rainbow Library *3150 N Buffalo Drive, North-west Las Vegas (243 7323).*
Sahara West Library *9600 W Sahara Avenue, between S Fort Apache Road & Grand Canyon Drive, North-west Las Vegas (360 8000).*
Summerlin Library *1771 Inner Circle Drive, North-west Las Vegas (256 5111).*
West Charleston Library *6301 W Charleston Boulevard, South-west Las Vegas (878 3682).*
Whitney Library & Recital Hall *5175 E Tropicana Avenue, East Las Vegas (454 4575).*

Lied Library
4505 S Maryland Parkway, between E Flamingo Road & Tropicana Avenue, University District (895 3531/ www.library.nevada.edu). Bus 109, 201, 202. **Open** 7am-midnight Mon-Thur; 7am-6pm Fri; 9am-9pm Sat; 10am-midnight Sun. **Map** p311 Y3.
Opened in 2000, UNLV's $40-million Lied Library is the most expensive public building project in Nevada's history. The facility houses 1.8 million volumes, and is serviced by an automatic book retrieval system. It's the best library in Las Vegas, but call first to make sure it's open – hours vary with UNLV's class schedule. Chances are you'll find everything you need here, except for a place to park: most of the spaces are reserved for students or faculty members.

Lost property

Airport
Lost & Found, 2nd level above ticketing, McCarran International Airport, East of Strip (261 5134). Bus 108, 109. **Open** 6.30am-1.30am daily. **Map** p316 B/C9.

Public transport
600 Grand Central Parkway, at Alta Drive, Downtown (228 7433). Bus 207, 801. **Open** 8am-5pm Mon-Fri. **Map** p312 C1.

Taxis
Checker/Star/Yellow Cab *3950 W Tompkins Avenue, at Arville Street, South-west Las Vegas (873 8012).* **Open** 8.30am-5pm daily.
Whittlesea *2030 Industrial Road, between Sahara Avenue & Oakey Boulevard, Stratosphere Area (384 6111).* **Open** 10am-4pm daily. **Map** p315 B4.

Media

Newspapers
Two daily newspapers are based in Las Vegas, the *Las Vegas Review-Journal* and the *Las Vegas Sun*. The *Los Angeles Times* (50¢) is also widely available throughout the valley and sells out quickly. Most large Strip hotels will carry the *Wall Street Journal* (75¢) and *New York Times* ($1); international newspapers and magazines are harder to find.

Las Vegas Review Journal
The *Review-Journal* (50¢, $2.50 on Sunday) offers bland but serviceable coverage of local and national stories. John L Smith's column is must-reading for local politicos, and new arrival Norm Clarke writes a fun celebrity people-watching feature. The Friday 'Neon' section is the *R-J*'s entertainment guide, where you'll find listings for movies, shows and restaurants. Entertainment critic Mike Weatherford provides honest, balanced coverage.

Las Vegas Sun
The *Las Vegas Sun* (50¢, Mon-Fri) used to offer a populist alternative to the conservative *R-J*, reflecting the shoot-from-the-hip style of its maverick founder and editor, Hank Greenspun. The newspaper has steadily declined since Hank's death in 1989, though most of his family is

still on the payroll. The *R-J* outsells the *Sun* more than five to one – perhaps another reason why the paper took on John Ralston's wacky political column.

CityLife

A huge restaurant guide, a calendar of workshops for local clubs and organisations and all the sleazy classifieds that one expects from a free tabloid. It has also scooped the town's mainstream press on occasion, though the quality has suffered of late – particularly since editor Geoff Schumacher left to launch *The Mercury* (*see below*). You'll find *CityLife* at most bookshops, cafés and bars.

The Mercury

In 2001, the publishers of the *Las Vegas Review-Journal*, decided to tackle the alternative arena with *The Mercury*, a free weekly publication dedicated to humorous and satirical coverage of local politics and events. It's available at most grocery stores, bookshops, some cafés, and in racks along the Strip; the Strip copies also include the *RJ*'s extensive 'Neon' section. At press time, *The Mercury* was considering becoming a full-blown alternative newsweekly with more news and less humour.

Las Vegas Weekly

Established in 1992 as *SCOPE*, the *Weekly* is the city's oldest weekly newspaper. Though some say it has been diluted, it remains the city's leading newsweekly and Las Vegas's answer to the Reader publications found in other US cities: counter-culture journalism surrounded by ads for coffeehouses and tattoo parlours. The calendar is an excellent guide to the music and nightlife scene.

Free weeklies

Numerous freebie mags – including *The Vegas Visitor*, *Today in Las Vegas* and *What's On in Las Vegas* – are distributed at hotels and other tourist spots. The editorial is uncritical and not always comprehensive, depending on who's buying adverts that week, but each contains a cornucopia of handy tourist facts and phone numbers, plus coupons.

Magazines

City-wide magazines

Three city magazines constitute overkill for a town the size of Las Vegas. *Las Vegas Magazine* (bi-monthly ($3.95) emphasises upscale fashion and shopping, blended with chi-chi adverts and eclectic articles. The *Las Vegan* (monthly, $2.95) is a

serviceable glossy, but can be hard to find. *Las Vegas Life* (monthly, $3.50) is the best of the bunch, and has distinguished itself from its competitors with feature stories that are both fun and useful. It's also the first city magazine to show signs of a sense of humour.

Statewide magazines

Nevada Magazine (bi-monthly, $3.95) contains an events calendar for Las Vegas, Reno and the rural areas in between; most articles focus on Nevada's pioneer history. The bi-monthly *Nevada Woman* ($3.95), contains exactly the type of articles you'd expect, though its integrity has recently been called into question.

Business magazines

Business news is covered by the *Nevada Business Journal* (monthly, $5), the *Las Vegas Business Press* (weekly, $1.25) and the latest addition to the scene, the Greenspun Media Group's *In Business Las Vegas* (weekly, $1.25). All provide coverage of Nevada's business scene with an emphasis on non-gaming industries. *Las Vegas Business Press* is by far the most comprehensive. For gaming news, check out *Casino Journal* (quarterly, $10) and *Gaming Today* (weekly, $1.95).

Television

The Las Vegas affiliates of the four major American networks are **KVBC 3** (NBC), **KVVU 5** (Fox), **KLAS 8** (CBS) and **KTNV 13** (ABC). The two new would-be networks UPN and WB are represented by channels **KTUD 25** and **KVWB 21**. The Greenspun Media Group and **KLAS 8** also operate Las Vegas **ONE** cable channels 1 and 38, with lots of Las Vegas-oriented news and programming. Las Vegas's public broadcasting affiliate is **KLVX 10**, where you'll find 20-year-old British comedies and the *Teletubbies*.

Every hotel TV will get these stations, and most will also carry some of the more popular cable networks, such as **CNN** (news), **ESPN** (sport) and **HBO** (movies).

Daily TV listings can be found in the *Sun* and *Review-Journal*, *Showbiz*, *What's On* and the *TV Guide* ($1.79).

News programmes

Las Vegas's good reporters and anchors are usually quickly promoted to bigger cities, while the merely adequate stay forever. If you're interested in what's happening in town, KTNV's 11pm news presents the top stories in just 11 minutes, while KLAS's nightly news features the city's most popular anchors, Gary Waddell and Paula Francis, plus the quirky investigative reporting of UFO reporter George Knapp. Local public affairs shows are of value only as a cure for insomnia. But if you must and if you're up early enough, there's 'Good Morning Las Vegas' (KTNV; 5am Mon-Fri).

Radio

With a rather limited local music scene to draw upon, Las Vegas radio is reduced to the same formats available in any American city. Music radio is a magnet for advertisers; commercials hype 'fabulous' shows, 'delicious' buffets and 'discount' hotel rates.

In talk radio, Las Vegas presents no homegrown talent to speak of, but all the most popular national hosts are syndicated on one of the local stations. These include right-wing rabble-rouser Rush Limbaugh (KXNT, 840 AM; 9am-noon Mon-Fri), veteran New York renegade Don Imus (KVBC, 105.5 FM; 7-10am Mon-Fri) and Howard Stern on KXTE (*see below*). Sports talk enthusiasts will enjoy the humour and insight of Dan Patrick (KBAD, 920 AM; 10am-1pm Mon-Fri).

Traffic reports are played every few minutes on many stations during morning and evening rush hours. Catch one before deciding whether to take the I-15 or a surface street.

Radio stations

KCEP (88.1 FM) Slow grooves and urban contemporary tunes.
KNPR (89.5 FM; affiliate of National Public Radio) Classical music plus in-depth news shows 'Morning Edition' (7-9am Mon-Fri) and 'All Things Considered' (4-6pm Mon-Fri).
KUNV (91.5 FM; affiliate of National Public Radio) jazz music round the clock, plus hourly NPR news.

KOMP (92.3 FM) Mainstream rock.
KMXB (94.1 FM) Contemporary music and '80s hits.
KWNR (95.5 FM) Country and western 'hat' acts: Clint Black, Garth Brooks, Alan Jackson.
KKLZ (96.3 FM) Classic rock; lots of Led Zeppelin.
KLUC (98.5 FM) Top 40 hits with an emphasis on dance tracks.
KMZQ (100.5 FM) Light pop of the Mariah and Celine variety.
KJUL (104 FM) Ballad after ballad by Johnny Mathis, Frank Sinatra and Barbra Streisand; popular with the over-60s.
KSNE (106.5 FM) Light rock and pop; beware the occasional Michael Bolton bombast.
KXTE (107.5 FM) Aggro-rock, plus the crude but often hilarious Howard Stern (7-10am Mon-Fri).

Money

The US dollar ($) is divided into 100 cents (¢). Coin denominations run from the copper penny (1¢), to the silver nickle (5¢), dime (10¢), quarter (25¢) and the less-common half-dollar (50¢). There are also two $1 coin – the silver Susan B Anthony and the gold Sacagawea coin. Confusingly, notes or 'bills' are all the same green colour and size; they come in denominations of $1, $5, $10, $20, $50 and $100. You will find both old-style and new-style notes in circulation.

Though Las Vegas has a reputation for being cheaper than most resort cities, recent changes mean that the difference has been cut to about 20 per cent. Hotels remain good value, but in the end you get what you pay for; the top restaurants and shows aren't much cheaper than they would be in New York.

What's more, you may spend a substantial amount of money on gambling, so it's essential that you set, and stick to, a budget. (The average visitor's gambling budget is about $600.) You should never gamble more than you can afford to lose, but if you do find yourself broke, the best thing you can do is call **Western Union** on 1-800 325 6000 and arrange for someone to wire some money to you. Numerous pawnbrokers, especially in Downtown, can convert your goods to cash. **Superpawn** has 12 branches, the closest to the Strip at 1611 Las Vegas Boulevard North (642 1133) and 2300 E Charleston Boulevard (477 3040). For information on buying or cashing casino chips and for tips on sensible gaming, *see chapter* **Gambling**.

ATM/Cash machines

Automated Teller Machines are ubiquitous in Las Vegas – we doubt that any city in the US has as many. Casinos are so keen for you to have a ready supply of cash that pretty much all of them have ATMs in every corner.

ATMs are undoubtedly the most convenient way for visitors to top up their funds. You can use your credit card (and PIN) to withdraw money or make the most of the international networks such as Cirrus and Plus, which allow you to withdraw money directly from your account (using your PIN) from any machine that bears the appropriate symbol. (Call 1-800 424 7787 to locate your nearest Cirrus machine, or 1-800 843 7587 for the nearest Plus.)

Follow the usual safety procedures when using an ATM – don't let anyone see your PIN and stick to brightly lit, populated locations.

Banks

Given the casinos' willingness to supply you with your own money, you are unlikely ever to need to visit a bank (unless, perhaps, you forget your PIN and need to get cash on your credit card; casinos do this but charge more). Banks are not hard to find, but few are close to the Strip. In addition to the main branches, usually only open 9am to 6pm Monday to Friday, there are (full-service) branches in selected stores that are open up to 7pm or 8pm during the week, and a good chunk of Sunday. **Wells Fargo** (1-800 869 3557) has branches in Lucky; **Bank of America** (1-800 388 2265) in Vons; and **Nevada State Bank** (1-800 727 4743) in Smiths Food & Drug. Contact the banks directly for branch locations and opening hours.

Credit & debit cards

Credit cards are almost a necessity. You won't be able to rent a car without one, for a start (except at the agencies noted on p285). They are accepted (with few exceptions) in hotels, restaurants and shops, but keep a bit of cash on hand just in case (and for tips). The cash card networks explained above are also linked to Maestro (Cirrus) and Delta (Plus), which allow the card function to be used as a debit card for paying for goods and services and getting cash back in foreign countries. Note, however, that only Visa and MasterCard debit cards are acceptable for car hire.

Currency exchange

You will never have trouble getting hold of the green stuff, day or night. Now that ATMs are rife, cashing standard cheques is seldom necessary.

Some casinos have their own bank or bureau de change and all have a 24-hour, seven-days-a-week cashier's cage where you can cash most bank (US only) and travellers' cheques, and exchange most major currencies on the spot – the good news is that they don't usually charge commission, just the bank rate. The casinos tend to offer better rates on currency than **American Express** desks. If you're staying at a non-casino hotel, you should be able to cash travellers' cheques at the front desk. There's also a **Travelex** bureau at the airport. You may require picture ID in order to cash travellers' cheques.

American Express

MGM Grand, 3799 Las Vegas Boulevard South, at E Tropicana Avenue (739 8474). Bus 201, 301, 302. **Open** 8am-6pm daily. **Map** p316 A8.

The only specialist AmEx office in town is located in the main lobby of the MGM Grand. It offers the full range of services, including cheque-cashing, poste restante, currency exchange and the buying and selling of travellers' cheques. If you lose your card (*see below*) ask for the replacement to be issued here, as it will be faster.

Lost & stolen cards

American Express cards 1-800 528 4800
travellers' cheques 1-800 221 7282
Diners Club 1-800 234 6377
Discover 1-800 347 2683
MasterCard 1-800 307 7309
Thomas Cook travellers' cheques 1-800 223 7373
Visa 1-800 336 8472

Tax

Sales tax is currently 7.25 per cent; food (groceries) purchased in stores is exempt. Accommodation tax is nine per cent in most of the city's hotels, but stands at 11 per cent in Downtown, until the hotels there have paid for the Fremont Street Experience.

Natural hazards

The most obvious hazards are the heat and intense sunshine (*see p297*), which can be enervating and potentially dangerous. Visitors who come in the summer should be prepared for other severe weather conditions, too. Las Vegas receives the majority of its annual rainfall in July and August, which is wonderful for the flora and fauna of the Mojave Desert, but also causes severe flooding, leading to drownings as well as a great deal of property damage.

Opening hours

The casinos, their cashiers' cages, bars and at least one restaurant/coffeeshop are open all day, every day (other tourist attractions also keep long hours) and require thousands of workers on three eight-hour shifts. As a result, grocery stores, dry-cleaners and gas stations are open 24 hours to accommodate the workers who have to do their chores in the middle of the night.

On a more local level, Las Vegas still keeps to small-town hours: many restaurants take last orders before 10pm and may not open for lunch or on certain days; non-chain shops may shut at 6pm and won't open on Sundays. Standard and government office hours are 9am to 5pm, give or take half an hour, but public institutions such as libraries and museums are open slightly longer and at weekends.

Police stations

Police (non-emergency)

400 Stewart Avenue, at Las Vegas Boulevard, Downtown (795 3111). Bus 113. **Open** 24hrs daily. **Map** p312 D1.

For general police enquiries only.

Postal services

US mailboxes are red, white and blue with the US Mail bald eagle logo on the front and side. There is usually a timetable of collections and a list of restrictions inside the lid. Due to increases in terrorism, post exceeding a maximum weight must be taken directly to a post-office counter (*see below*). For details of couriers and shipping companies, *see p287*.

Stamps are on sale in shops and from machines (for a nominal charge). Contract stations (there's one at Allstate Ticketing in the Forum Shops) can send international mail, but they will charge a supplement. Domestic mail costs 34¢ per piece or 21¢ for a postcard. To send a postcard abroad costs 50¢ to Canada and Mexico and 70¢ to all other international destinations. Airmail letters cost 60¢ per ounce to Canada and Mexico and 70¢ per ounce to all other countries.

Post offices

For most transactions the **Post Office Express** counters (open 10.30am-7.30pm Mon-Sat; 11am-7pm Sun) in several Lucky grocery stores should suffice. However, general delivery/poste restante mail can only be collected from the Downtown Station. Ask correspondents to send it to: General Delivery, Las Vegas, NV 89125. You will need to show picture ID when you pick it up. For the location of your nearest post office, call 1-800 275 7777 and quote the Las Vegas zip code.

Main Post Office *1001 E Sunset Road, between Paradise Road & Maryland Parkway, East Las Vegas (1-800 275 8777). Bus 212.* **Open** 7.30am-9pm Mon-Fri; 8am-4pm Sat.

Strip Station *3100 S Industrial Road, at Stardust Way, West of Strip (1-800 275 8777). Bus 301, 302.* **Open** 8.30am-5pm Mon-Fri; 10am-2pm Sat. **Map** p315 A5.

Religion

There are over 500 places of worship in Vegas, serving 65 denominations. To find your nearest Lutheran church, call 456 2001, Episcopal 737 9190 and Methodist 369 7055. For others, consult the phone book.

Congregation Ner Tamid *2761 Emerson Avenue, at Eastern Avenue & Desert Inn Road, East Las Vegas (733 6292). Bus 112.* **Map** p311 Z3. Jewish Reform.

First Baptist Church *300 Ninth Street, at Bridger Street, Downtown (382 6177). Bus 301.* **Map** p312 D2.

First Presbyterian Church *1515 W Charleston Boulevard, just west of I-15, West of Strip (384 4554). Bus 206.* **Map** p315 B3.

Latter-Day Saints Las Vegas Temple *827 N Temple View Drive, off Bonanza Drive, East Las Vegas* *(452 5011/information 435 8545).* Bus 208. Members of the Church of Jesus Christ of Latter-Day Saints (Mormons) only.

Guardian Angel Cathedral *336 Cathedral Way, next to E Desert Inn Road, at Las Vegas Boulevard South (735 5241).* Bus 301, 302. **Map** p315 C5. The cathedral church of the Catholic diocese of Reno-Las Vegas.

Hindu Temple & Cultural Center *1702 Sageberry Drive, Summerlin (304 9207).* No bus. The only Hindu worship centre for hundreds of miles opened in 2001.

Islamic Center of Las Vegas *3799 Edwards Avenue, North-west Las Vegas (395 7013).* Bus 106. Services 1pm Friday.

St Joan of Arc *315 S Casino Center Boulevard, at Bridger Avenue, Downtown (382 9909).* Bus 301. **Map** p312 C2. The city's oldest Catholic church.

Temple Beth Sholom *9700 Hillpointe Road, off Hills Center Drive, Summerlin, North-west Las Vegas (804 1333).* Bus 211. The city's oldest Jewish congregation.

Safety & security

Considering that Las Vegas contains so many wide-eyed tourists wandering around carrying large amounts of cash, crime is relatively low. But pickpocketing, theft and muggings do happen, and more frequently than the tourist industry would like.

Casinos have such elaborate security systems that few serious offences take place within their confines. But on the streets, especially outside the well-lit, busy tourist areas, Las Vegas has the same crime problems as any large town. Be particularly careful in the seedier-looking areas of Downtown. The Strip is generally safe, but don't venture into the Naked City area behind the Stratosphere at any time of day.

● Only take out with you what you need for that trip: leave the bulk of your money and travellers' cheques in your room safe or in a safety deposit box at the front desk.

● Keep a separate note of the numbers and details of your passport, driving licence, travellers'

cheque numbers, travel/health insurance policy and cards, along with the phone numbers you'll need to report their loss (*see p294* **Lost & stolen credit cards**). Leave the same list with somebody at home.

● Take the usual precautions with your wallet or handbag, especially on buses and at bus stops; don't keep valuables in your pockets; and try not to let the excitement of gambling make you forget about them.

● If you are threatened with a weapon, give your assailants what they want, with no fuss. When they've gone, go to the nearest phone and call the police (911 toll-free).

Smoking

Feel free to puff away while in Las Vegas – a place many consider to be one of the few pro-smoking strongholds left in the US. Casinos provide free cigarettes (and in some cases even cigars) to gamblers and every convenience store in town sells tobacco products. The majority of restaurants have smoking sections, and in bars and nightclubs, smoking something seems to be practically a requirement.

Study

The most successful local colleges feed some part of the service and gaming industry. The University of Nevada Las Vegas has established one of the top hotel and hospitality degree programmes in the United States and there is a strong community college programme for service industry workers who want to learn new skills. Those looking to learn how to become a casino dealer or croupier must attend one of the city's specialist dealer schools.

Community College of Southern Nevada *3200 E Cheyenne Avenue, North Las Vegas, NV 89030 (651 4000).*

Dealers Training Center *3330 E Tropicana Avenue, East Las Vegas, NV 89121 (547 1171).* **Map** p311 Z3.

PCI Dealers School *920 Valley View Boulevard, West of Strip, Las Vegas, NV 89102 (877 4724).* **Map** p311 X2.

University of Nevada Las Vegas *4505 Las Vegas Boulevard South, University District, Las Vegas, NV 89109 (895 3011).* **Map** p311 Y3.

Telephones

Dialling & codes

There are two area codes for Nevada: 702 for Clark County (including Las Vegas) and 775 for the rest of the state. Within the Las Vegas area, calls are local and there is no need to use the area code (just dial the seven-figure number). Outside this area, calls are long distance (and charged as such): you need to dial 1, then the area code, then the number. Numbers prefaced by 1-800, 1-888 and 1-877 are toll-free within the US; many are available from outside the country, too, but you will be charged for the call.

Making a call

Local calls are free, but most hotels nevertheless charge a flat fee of between 50¢ and $1 for them – which can quickly mount up. This charge also applies to toll-free numbers. You can get round this at some hotels by using a house phone and asking the operator to connect you to your number. Alternatively, you will usually find payphones in the lobby or near the restrooms (local and toll-free calls cost 35¢).

If you want to make long-distance and international calls, you will often have to leave a credit card or cash deposit with the hotel desk. The rates will be high, so you are better off using a US phone card, whether tied to your domestic account or bought on a one-off basis. Supermarkets, drugstores and convenience stores sell them in various denominations, which you can 'charge up' with a credit card. Shop around to find a deal that offers the longest talk-time for the lowest price.

Directory

AT&T (1-800 225 5288)
allows you to make calls on a
Visa credit card. Most foreign
visitors will find it cheaper to
use this service to call abroad
than to use a phone chargecard
issued in their home country.

Public phones

To use a public phone, pick up
the receiver, listen for a dialling
tone and feed it change (35¢ for
a local call); some phones ask
you to dial first and then assess
the cost. Operator, directory
and emergency calls are free.
Avoid using a payphone for
long-distance or international
calls; a quarter is the highest
denomination a payphone will
accept, so you'll need stacks of
change. (A recorded voice will
tell you how much you need
to put in.) Payphones at the
airport and at the bigger
casinos accept credit cards.

If you encounter voicemail,
note that the 'pound' key is
marked # and the 'star' key *.
On automated answering
systems, 0 often gets you
straight to an operator.

Operator services & directory enquiries

Collect (reverse charge) calls 0.
Local enquiries 411.
National enquiries 1 + [area code]
+ 555 1212 (if you don't know the
area code, dial 0 for the operator).
International calls 011 + [country
code] + [area code] + [number].
International country codes UK
44; New Zealand 64; Australia 61;
Germany 49; Japan 81.
**Police, fire, or medical
emergencies** 911.

Mobile phones

Mobile phone service has
traditionally been a problem
in Las Vegas's casinos, but
in 2001 the Venetian made
wireless communication
possible throughout its
property for users of AT&T,
Cingular, Nextel, Sprint PCS
and Verizon. The Forum Shops
soon followed suit.

Cellular City *4720 S Polaris
Avenue, at Tompkins Avenue, West
of Strip (873 2489). Bus 203.* **Open**
Office 8.30am-5pm Mon-Fri. *Phone
lines* 24hrs daily. **Credit** AmEx, DC,
Disc, MC, V. **Map** p311 X3. Rents
mobile phones by the day or week.

Time

Nevada operates on Pacific
Standard Time, which is eight
hours behind Greenwich Mean
Time (London), one hour
behind Mountain Time
(Denver), two hours behind
Central Time (Chicago) and
three hours behind Eastern
Standard Time (New York).
Clocks go forward by an hour
in late April, and back again in
late October. Note that Arizona
has no daylight saving time,
and so in summer is one hour
behind Nevada.

Tipping

Limo drivers ($10 to $25 per
ride), valet parking attendants
($1 to $2), cocktail waitresses
(50¢ to $1), housekeepers ($1 a
night), even front desk clerks
($10 to $20 if you're looking
for a better room): all ride the
tip gravy train. For detailed
information on tipping in
the casino, *see p30*.

Toilets

Toilets are available to all
guests and visitors in every
major casino and public place
in Las Vegas. Casino toilets are
always well marked and easy
to find, though they may be far
away from the main entrance
to encourage business.

Tourist information

You will see many self-styled
tourist offices on the Strip,
but only those listed below
are official. The others are
primarily tour and booking
agents. For contact details for
the **Nevada Commission of
Tourism**, *see p244*.

Las Vegas Chamber of Commerce

*Hughes Center, 3720 Howard
Hughes Parkway, between Sands
Avenue & E Flamingo Road,
East of Strip, Las Vegas, NV 89109
(735 1616/www.lvchamber.com).
Bus 108, 203.* **Open** 8am-5pm Mon-
Fri. **Map** p316 C6.
Advice, brochures, maps and a few
coupons available in person; there's
also a good phone information
service, and you can write in advance
for a visitor pack.

Las Vegas Convention & Visitors Authority

*3150 Paradise Road, opposite
Convention Center Drive, East of
Strip, Las Vegas, NV 89109 (892
0711/fax 892 2824/www.vegas
freedom.com). Bus 108.* **Open** 8am-
5pm Mon-Fri. **Map** p316 C6.
A comprehensive and helpful office.
Write to the CVA for a visitor pack
that includes lists of hotels, a
brochure, a map and the regularly
updated *Showguide*.

In the UK

*Cellet Travel Services 47 High Street,
Henley-in-Arden, Warwickshire B95
5AA (brochure line 0870 523 8832/
fax 01564 795 333).*
The British outpost of the LVCVA.

Visas & immigration

Citizens of the UK, Japan,
Australia, New Zealand and
west European countries
(except for Portugal, Greece
and the Vatican City) do not
need a visa for stays in the US
of less than 90 days (business
or pleasure) if they have a
passport that is valid for the
full 90-day period and a return
(or open standby) ticket.

Canadians and Mexicans do
not need visas but must have
legal proof of their residency.
All other travellers must have
visas. Full information and
visa application forms can
be obtained from your nearest
US embassy or consulate.
Generally, you should send
in your application at least
three weeks before you plan
to travel. Visas required more
urgently should be applied
for through the travel agent
booking your ticket.

Climate chart

Month	High	Low
January	58°F (14.4°C)	34°F (1°C)
February	63°F (17.2°C)	39°F (3.8°C)
March	69°F (20.5°C)	44°F (6.6°C)
April	78°F (25.5°C)	51°F (10.5°C)
May	88°F (31°C)	60°F (15.5°C)
June	100°F (37.7°C)	69°F (20.5°C)
July	106°F (41.1°C)	74°F (23°C)
August	103°F (39.4°C)	74°F (23°C)
September	95°F (35°C)	66°F (19°C)
October	82°F (27.7°C)	54°F (12.2°C)
November	67°F 19.4°C)	43°F (6°C)
December	58°F (14.4°C)	34°F (1°C)

Average rainfall 4.13 inches per year
Average sunshine 294 days per year
(211 clear, 83 partly cloudy)

US Embassy Visa Information (UK only) *Recorded information 0891 200 290 (50p per minute)/ advice & appointments 0991 500 590 (£1.50 per minute)/fax 0171 495 5012.*

Weights & measures

The USA uses the imperial system for all weights and measures. Note, however, that liquid measures in the US are slightly different from their UK equivalents.

When to go

Though there is no real off-season in Las Vegas, there are times when it's slightly quieter and hotel prices are lower. These are between Thanksgiving (fourth Thursday in November) and Christmas, and during the extreme heat of July and August. Public holidays are always busy, especially the New Year. If you're planning a short visit, try to avoid the weekend crowds (and higher accommodation prices).

Las Vegas's hectic convention schedule also has a major effect on visitor numbers: when over 125,000 delegates hit town at once, hotel and car prices and availability naturally suffer. *See p286* **Conventions & conferences**.

Public holidays

1 Jan New Year's Day; **3rd Mon in Jan** Martin Luther King, Jr Holiday; **3rd Mon in Feb** President's Day; **late Mar/early Apr** Easter Sunday; **last Mon in May** Memorial Day; **4 July** Independence Day; **1st Mon in Sept** Labor Day; **last Fri in Oct** Nevada Day; **2nd Mon in Nov** Veterans' Day; **4th Thur in Nov** Thanksgiving; **25 Dec** Christmas Day.

Climate

Las Vegas has blue skies and little rain, year round (the percentage of sunny daylight hours runs from 77 per cent in December and January to 92 per cent in June). Daytime temperatures vary from burning hot – afternoon temperatures can reach 110°F (43°C) in July and August, remaining above 90°F (32°C) at midnight – to pretty chilly – and can approach freezing in December and January, though 50-60°F (10-15°C) is more usual during the day.

Don't plan on doing too much exercise in summer, drink lots of water and wear a hat, sunglasses and sunscreen. Note that hotel swimming pools close from roughly October to March – the same time you may need to wear a sweater or jacket.

For local weather, call 248 4800; for national weather, call the Weather Channel (1-900 932 8437; 95¢ per minute)

Women

Las Vegas presents an interesting contradiction in feminist politics. On the one hand, women are continually objectified in the entertainment industry, but on the other hand, they fare well in the job market, often occupying positions of power, and they are well represented in politics. Albeit for dubious reasons, most Las Vegas bars and clubs offer free/discounted admission to women. There is no no single woman's centre but the **UNLV Women's Studies Office** (895 0837) is a good first contact. Also try the **National Organisation of Women for Southern Nevada** (382 7552).

Working in Las Vegas

To work anywhere in the US, non-nationals must be sponsored by a US company and obtain an H-1 visa (five years' work entitlement). They will also have to convince the US immigration department that no American is qualified to do the job. Contact the US embassy for full details.

The Chamber of Commerce (*see p296*) and the Post Office (*see p294*) offer useful leaflets for people moving to Las Vegas, and some of the major websites (lasvegas.com, in particular) can be especially helpful. The CoC will send a relocation package, for $20.

Directory

Further Reference

Books

Non-fiction

Anderton, Frances & Chase, John *The Success of Excess* Gorgeous large-format photo book on Vegas's theme park architecture.

Bass, Thomas *The Newtonian Casino* Can the casinos be beaten? Yes, according to these Reservoir Dogs of computer geekery.

Basten, Fred E & Phoenix, Charles, with Smith, Keely *Fabulous Las Vegas in the 50s* A nostalgic full-colour collection of photographs, menus and postcards from the lost glory days of Vegas.

Berman, Susan *Lady Las Vegas: The Inside Story Behind America's Neon Oasis* By the daughter of a Mob insider, this view of Vegas is made all the more creepy by the author's recent murder. Out-of-print, but still available with a bit of searching.

Denton, Sally & Morris, Roger *The Money and the Power: The Making of Las Vegas and Its Hold on America* Investigative history of Vegas: learn how money and power shaped and corrupted the city, and, subsequently, the nation.

German, Jeff *Murder in Sin City: The Death of a Las Vegas Casino Boss* Reporter German explores the details of the recent Vegas murder of Ted Binion, of the casino family.

Gottdiener, Mark, Collins, Claudia C & Dickens, David R *Las Vegas: The Social Production of an All-American City* A fascinating look at the social phenomenon of Vegas, from how a city grows in the desert to what it means to live off the tourist dollar and a created image.

Hopkins, AD & Evans, KJ (eds) *The First 100: Portraits of the Men and Women Who Shaped Las Vegas* A thought-provoking, well-written encyclopaedia.

Levy, Shaun *Rat Pack Confidential* A modern, funky appraisal of the Rat Pack years and beyond.

Littlejohn, David (ed) *The Real Las Vegas* A group of Berkeley grad students look down their noses at the Las Vegas underbelly.

Martinez, Andrés *24/7: Living It Up and Doubling Down in the New Las Vegas* Attorney and journalist Martinez spends his $50,000 advance in this modern-day *Fear and Loathing*.

McCracken, Robert D *Las Vegas: The Great American Playground* History, biting commentary and a great read.

Odessky, Dick *Fly on the Wall* Amusing anecdotes and insider accounts told by long-time Vegas reporter and publicity man Odessky.

Roemer, William F *The Enforcer: Spilotro – The Chicago Mob's Man over Las Vegas* Vegas attorney Oscar Goodman kept Tony 'The Ant' Spilotro out of jail for over a decade. Now, Goodman is mayor of Vegas and Spilotro is dead, beaten to death and buried in an Indiana cornfield.

Shaner, Lora *Madam: Chronicles of a Nevada Cathouse* Check out a legal Nevada brothel. The author is a full-time madam (brothel-greeter, hostess, shift boss, den mother).

Smith, John L *No Limit – The Rise and Fall of Bob Stupak & Las Vegas' Stratosphere Tower; Running Scared: The Life and Treacherous Times of Las Vegas Casino King Steve Wynn* Savvy *Review-Journal* columnist and de facto modern Vegas historian Smith dishes the dirt on two major players in the casino business.

Stuart, Lyle *Howard Hughes in Las Vegas* It's out of print, but if you can get hold of a copy, this history of an original Vegas maverick gets behind the privacy of the recluse.

Thompson, David *Into Nevada* Musings on Nevada – its mining, nuclear and gambling history – by an expat Brit-Californian.

Tosches, Nick *Dino* Scorching biography of the Rat Pack principal.

Tronnes, Mike (ed) *Literary Las Vegas* An excellent anthology of journalism from 1952 to the present, with Tom Wolfe, Noel Coward, Joan Didion and Hunter S Thompson.

Venturi, Robert, Izenour, Steven & Scott Brown, Denise *Learning from Las Vegas: The Forgotten Symbolism of Architectural Form* Fascinating study of the auto-driven architecture of the Strip.

Weatherford, Mike *Cult Vegas: The Weirdest! The Wildest! The Swingin'est Town on Earth* Informal, kitschy history. Offbeat movies, ornery characters, unforgettable trivia – all explained in gossipy detail by a *Review-Journal* columnist.

Whitney, Branch *Hiking Las Vegas: 60 Hikes Within 60 Minutes of the Strip* Clear instructions, good detail, a locals' favourite. *Hiking Southern Nevada* came out in 2000.

Wilkerson, WR III *The Man Who Invented Las Vegas* Think Bugsy Siegel moved Las Vegas into the big time? Learn about Billy Wilkerson – from whom Siegel stole the Flamingo – and stand corrected. Penned by Wilkerson's son.

Fiction

McMurtry, Larry *Desert Rose* The *Terms of Endearment* writer turns his attentions to a portrayal of a washed-up showgirl.

O'Brien, John *Leaving Las Vegas* Love, loneliness and alcoholism in the city of fun. Better than the film.

Perriam, Wendy *Sin City* Personal drama played out against an impersonal city.

Pileggi, Nicholas *Casino: Love and Honour in Las Vegas* Book of the film: a cracking read.

Powers, Tim *Last Call* A fantasia on the Las Vegas myth, in which Bugsy Siegel is the Fisher King and Tarot cards the deck of choice at the Flamingo's poker tables. Don't come here looking for facts.

Puzo, Mario *Fool's Die* The *Godfather* author with another 'sweeping epic' with lots of casino colour and semi-autobiographical detail.

Thompson, Hunter S *Fear and Loathing in Las Vegas* The drug-crazed classic is always worth re-reading, even if this ain't the '60s any more.

Ventura, Michael *The Death of Frank Sinatra* Cracking private-eye story set among the implosions of the early 1990s.

Gambling

Gambling books are ubiquitous, but many are poorly researched and dangerously misleading. We recommend ordering material direct from **Huntington Press** (1-800 244 2224/www.huntingtonpress.com) – such as the titles below:

Anderson, Ian *Burning the Tables in Las Vegas* One of the world's most successful high-stakes blackjack players reveals how he gets away with it.

Dancer, Bob *Bob Dancer Presents WinPoker* Software tutor (PC only) on proper strategies for video poker. An absolute must for anyone who plays these machines.

Rubin, Max *Comp City: A Guide to Free Gambling Vacations* Classic text on the casino comps system. A hilarious read.

Vancura, Olaf & Fuchs, Ken *Knock-Out Blackjack: The Easiest Card-Counting System Ever Devised* Revolutionary 'unbalanced' count eliminates most of the mental gymnastics of all the other count systems. Still not easy, but doable.

Film

Bugsy (1991) Witty script (James Toback), classy direction (Barry Levinson) and terrific performances (Beatty, Bening, Keitel) make this a Vegas movie not to miss.

Casino (1995) Martin Scorsese's three-hour mishmash of gambling and the Mob, voiceovered to death.

Diamonds Are Forever (1971) Bond in Vegas. Silly gadgets abound.

Fear and Loathing in Las Vegas (1998) Whoa… is Terry Gilliam on something? This relentless, bizarre adaptation of the Thompson classic was a cult movie before it was even released.

Go (1999) Doug Liman's follow-up to *Swingers* seems a little forced, but there are some good bits of business.

Honeymoon in Vegas (1992) Nicolas Cage in oddball comedy mode, contrasting with his later, very different turn in *Leaving Las Vegas*.

Leaving Las Vegas (1995) Nicolas Cage, as a self-destructive alcoholic, won an Oscar for his performance in this Mike Figgis masterpiece.

Meet Me in Las Vegas (1956) Problem gambler hooks up with Strip dancer in a familiar plot, this time brightened by Cyd Charisse as the dancer. Musical.

Ocean's 11 (1960) Eleven military buddies plan a robbery. With all of the Rat Pack present, this kitschy, corny film has become the de facto video history of a romantic Vegas era. It remains to be seen whether the 2001 remake with George Clooney et al, can live up to the original.

Rain Man (1988) Dustin Hoffman's autistic Raymond finds his ability to remember numbers comes in handy in Vegas. Or rather, brother Charlie (Tom Cruise) finds it comes in handy.

Showgirls (1995) Some films that are universally panned on release benefit from a later reappraisal. Paul Verhoeven's Vegas misadventure is unlikely to be one of them.

Swingers (1996) First feature by Doug Liman: 90 minutes spent learning how not to pick up girls.

Viva Las Vegas (1964) Fun film for those nostalgic for the old, swanky Vegas and the young, svelte Elvis. Stars Ann-Margret as a Strip dancer.

Music

B-52s 'Queen of Las Vegas' The B-52s have played Vegas more often than any other campy new wave artist, and they always seem to pull this one from their repertoire. Wonder why?

Cocteau Twins *Heaven or Las Vegas* Doesn't really have much to do with Vegas, but works like a dream.

Crow, Sheryl 'Leaving Las Vegas' Her lyrics move with ease from the Sunset Strip to the Vegas Strip; her melancholy voice does both justice.

Crystal Method *Vegas* An entire album of big beat techno that has nothing directly to do with Las Vegas – except for the fact that both Ken Jordan and Scotty Kirkland honed their DJ skills here, and that Vegas is itself one massive, blazing, big beat techno party.

Death in Vegas *The Contino Sessions* Dot Allison, Jim Reid, Iggy Pop and the London Community Gospel Choir join the Death in Vegas crew for this rousing, raunchy set.

Everly Brothers 'I'm Tired of Singing My Song in Las Vegas' Surprisingly bitter piece of spleen-venting from Don Everly against the oldies circuit on which he was forced to ply his trade.

Gomez 'Las Vegas Dealer' From the excellent *Liquid Skin* album, this is Nevada via Southport.

Parsons, Gram 'Ooh Las Vegas' Ex-Byrd loses big in the crystal city.

Presley, Elvis 'Viva Las Vegas' Made famous by the King, but the song has also been covered by ZZ Top, Nine Inch Nails, the Dead Kennedys and the Flintstones.

Presley, Elvis *Live in Las Vegas* As Elvis got fatter, his shows got glammier. This box set is all the fat Elvis you'll ever need, and then some.

Sinatra, Frank *Sinatra at the Sands* Classic recording of Frank backed by the Count Basie Orchestra.

Various Artists *Las Vegas Grind Parts 1-6* Vegas strippers' music and grimy, lost rock 'n' roll gems.

Websites

http://art.inlasvegas.com Listing of galleries and museums, plus creative community information.

www.crecon.com/vintagevegas/matches.htm Nothing here but images of classic Vegas casino matchbooks, postcards and gambling chips, but isn't that enough?

www.gayvegas.com Gay-friendly establishments, from nightclubs to restaurants, plus a list of community resources and an events calendar.

www.hiddenvegas.com A trip through the Vegas no one knows. Homepages for wild art-terrorists the LaserVida arts collective, the UNLV Arboretum and local artist/unofficial Vegas historian Anthony Bondi.

www.knpr.org Run by the local National Public Radio affiliate, KNPR (89.5 FM), this site has a great local programming archive that includes transcripts as well as Real Audio files of informative restaurant reviews, cultural calendars and essays about life in Las Vegas.

www.lasvegas.com Operated by the *Review-Journal*, this focuses on local news, events and resources. Hosts *CityLife*, an alternative Vegas weekly, and lists lots of community links. Excellent for those relocating.

www.lasvegastaxi.com/index.html (The Las Vegas Hack Attack) Who knows a city better than its cab drivers? These cabbies share everything from adult entertainment info to tips on avoiding being ripped off by other cabbies.

www.lvlocalmusicscene.com Every local band, music venue and musician has a space in this locally produced, grassroots music site.

www.lvstriphistory.com Both the design and the editing illustrate that this is a small, homespun effort, but the information is invaluable.

www.nitewalk.com A former local journalist uncovers the other side of Vegas, from hip coffeehouses to gay bathhouses, and more.

www.prairienet.org/~scruffy/homepage.html From *Fear and Loathing* to *Bugsy*: if any part of it was filmed in Las Vegas, you'll find it on Scruffy's Las Vegas Movie List. The site also features a map of the historical Strip, pre-implosions.

www.sincity.com Official website for Vegas's unofficial emissaries and full-time madmen, Penn & Teller – all you might expect from two guys whose idea of a good time is shooting at each other on stage.

www.stripclubreview.com/vegas.html The webmaster isn't updating like he shoud, but still loaded with info.

www.unlv.edu/Tourism/lvmisc.html Interesting and informative links assembled by the tourism department of UNLV's college of Hotel Administration.

www.vegas.com All-encompassing Vegas portal site for visitors. Book hotels, search for restaurants. Includes the *Las Vegas Sun*, the alternative *Las Vegas Weekly*, *Vegas Golfer*, *Las Vegas Life* and *Showbiz*; great calendar, wedding and nightlife sections; plus column 'Tourists for Breakfast' by Vegaphile Geoff Carter.

www.vegasfreedom.com The official and useful (if badly designed) website of the Las Vegas Convention & Visitors Authority. Has a section on how to play nearly every casino game, from bingo to Pai Gow poker, plus a convention calendar.

www.weddinginvegas.com Planning to get hitched in Vegas? This may help.

Directory

Index

Advertisers' Index

Please refer to the relevant sections for
addresses/telephone numbers

Interstate	══
Interstate under construction	▓ ▓
Casino hotels	▢
Places of interest	▢
Non casino hotels	▢
One way street	→

Maps

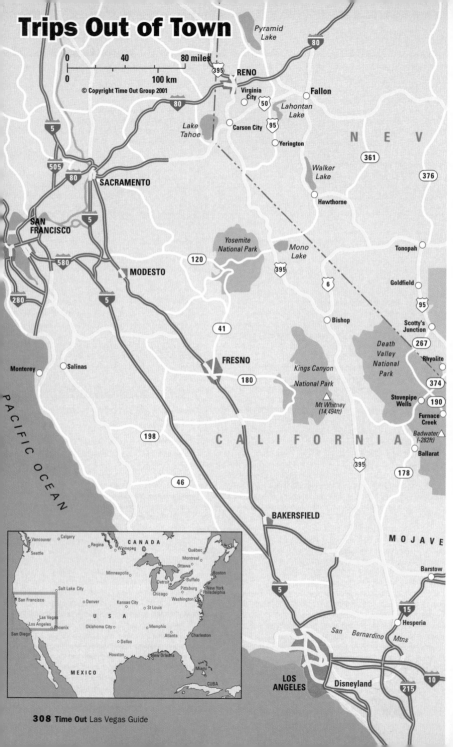

Trips Out of Town

0 | 40 | 80 miles
0 | 100 km
© Copyright Time Out Group 2001

Pyramid Lake

RENO

Virginia City (50)
Fallon
Lahontan Lake
Carson City (95)
Lake Tahoe
Yerington

N E V

(361)
(376)

Walker Lake

Hawthorne

SACRAMENTO

SAN FRANCISCO

Yosemite National Park
Mono Lake
Tonopah
(120)
(395)
(6)
Goldfield
(95)

MODESTO

(41)
Bishop
Scotty's Junction
(267)

Death Valley National Park
Rhyolite
(374)

FRESNO
(180)
Kings Canyon National Park
Stovepipe Wells (190)
Monterey
Salinas

Mt Whitney (14,494ft)
Furnace Creek
Badwater (-282ft)
Ballarat

(198)

C A L I F O R N I A
(395)
(178)

(46)

BAKERSFIELD

M O J A V E

Barstow

P A C I F I C   O C E A N

CANADA
Vancouver
Calgary
Regina
Winnipeg
Seattle
Québec
Minneapolis
Montreal
Ottawa
Buffalo
Boston
Salt Lake City
Detroit
Pittsburg
New York
San Francisco
Denver
Kansas City
Chicago
Washington Philadelphia
Las Vegas
U S A
St Louis
Los Angeles
Phoenix
Oklahoma City
Memphis
San Diego
Dallas
Atlanta
Charleston
Houston
New Orleans
M E X I C O
Miami
CUBA

Hesperia
(15)
San Bernardino Mtns
(5)
(215)
(10)
LOS ANGELES
Disneyland

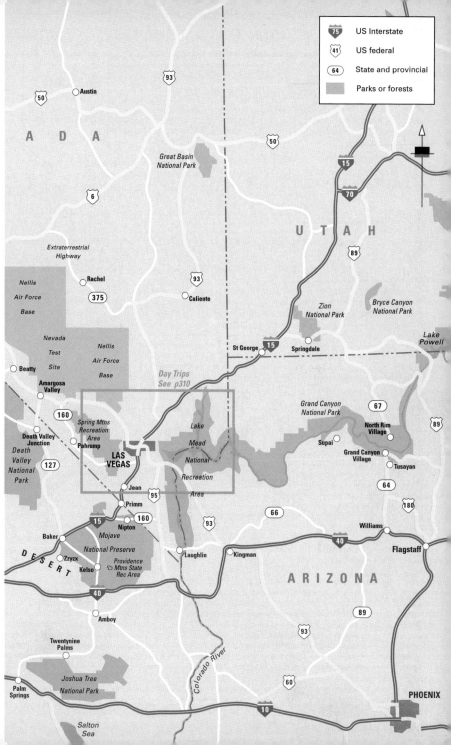

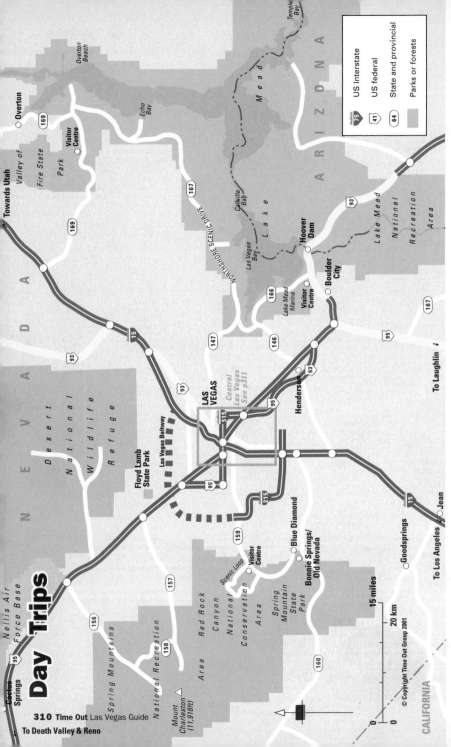

Day Trips

To Death Valley & Reno

Towards Utah

NEVADA

ARIZONA

Overton

Valley of Fire State Park

Overton Beach

Echo Bay

Temple Bay

Lake Mead

Northshore Scenic Drive

Visitor Centre

Callville Bay

Las Vegas Bay

Hoover Dam

Lake Mead National Recreation Area

Boulder City

Lake Mead Marina

Visitor Centre

Nellis Air Force Base

Cactus Springs

Desert National Wildlife Refuge

Floyd Lamb State Park

Las Vegas Beltway

LAS VEGAS

Central Las Vegas See p311

Henderson

To Laughlin

Spring Mountains

Mount Charleston (11,918ft)

Red Rock Canyon National Conservation Area

Scenic Loop

Visitor Centre

Spring Mountain State Park

Bonnie Springs/ Old Nevada

Blue Diamond

Goodsprings

Jean

To Los Angeles

CALIFORNIA

15 miles

20 km

© Copyright Time Out Group 2001

Key

75 — US Interstate
41 — US federal
64 — State and provincial
Parks or forests

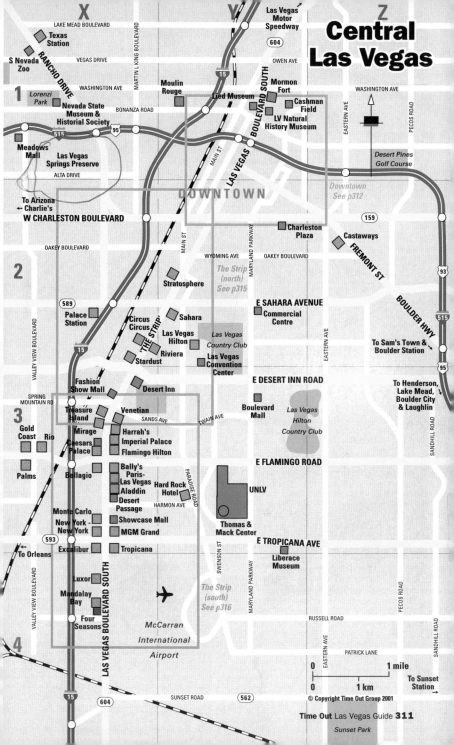

Central
Las Vegas

Sunset Park

© Copyright Time Out Group 2001

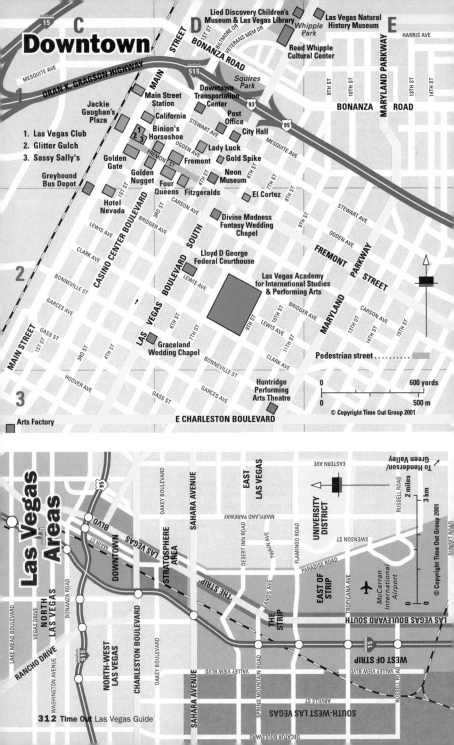

Downtown

1. Las Vegas Club
2. Glitter Gulch
3. Sassy Sally's

C

MESQUITE AVE

15

ORAN K. GRAGSON HIGHWAY

D

STREET

BONANZA ROAD

BILTMORE DR

1ST ST

VETERANS MEM DR

515

MAIN

Main Street
Station

California

Binion's
Horseshoe

Jackie
Gaughan's
Plaza

Golden
Gate

Golden
Nugget

Four
Queens

Fremont

Fitzgerals

Hotel
Nevada

Greyhound
Bus Depot

CASINO CENTER BOULEVARD

1ST ST

2ND ST

3RD ST

FREMONT ST

OGDEN AVE

CARSON AVE

BRIDGER AVE

LEWIS AVE

CLARK AVE

BONNEVILLE ST

GARCES AVE

MAIN STREET

GASS ST

1ST ST

3RD ST

4TH ST

HOOVER AVE

GASS ST

GARCES AVE

BONNEVILLE ST

LAS VEGAS BOULEVARD SOUTH

6TH ST

7TH ST

Graceland
Wedding Chapel

Arts Factory

Downtown
Transportation
Center

Post
Office

City Hall

Lady Luck

Gold Spike

Neon
Museum

El Cortez

Divine Madness
Fantasy Wedding
Chapel

Lloyd D George
Federal Courthouse

Las Vegas Academy
for International Studies
& Performing Arts

STEWART AVE

OGDEN AVE

4TH ST

CARSON AVE

LEWIS AVE

9TH ST

LEWIS AVE

11TH ST

BONNEVILLE ST

CLARK AVE

GARCES AVE

E CHARLESTON BOULEVARD

Huntridge
Performing
Arts Theatre

Squires
Park

Whipple
Park

Lied Discovery Children's
Museum & Las Vegas Library

Reed Whipple
Cultural Center

BONANZA ROAD

93

95

STEWART AVE

MESQUITE AVE

5TH ST

6TH ST

7TH ST

8TH ST

9TH ST

OGDEN AVE

STEWART AVE

FREMONT

PARKWAY

STREET

MARYLAND

CARSON AVE

13TH ST

14TH ST

15TH ST

E

Las Vegas Natural
History Museum

HARRIS AVE

MARYLAND PARKWAY

9TH ST

10TH ST

BONANZA ROAD

13TH ST

14TH ST

1

2

3

Pedestrian street . . . .

0   600 yards

0   500 m

© Copyright Time Out Group 2001

Las Vegas Areas

95

LAKE MEAD BOULEVARD

VEGAS DRIVE

RANCHO DRIVE

WASHINGTON AVENUE

NORTH LAS VEGAS

BONANZA ROAD

515

DOWNTOWN

LAS VEGAS BLVD

MAIN ST

NORTH-WEST
LAS VEGAS

CHARLESTON BOULEVARD

OAKEY BOULEVARD

SAHARA AVENUE

STRATOSPHERE
AREA

THE STRIP

SAHARA AVENUE

OAKEY BOULEVARD

VALLEY VIEW BLVD

SPRING MOUNTAIN ROAD

SOUTH-WEST LAS VEGAS

DECATUR BOULEVARD

DESERT INN ROAD

TWAIN AVE

SANDS AVE

THE STRIP

FLAMINGO ROAD

MARYLAND PARKWAY

EAST
LAS VEGAS

EASTERN AVE

To Henderson/
Green Valley

UNIVERSITY
DISTRICT

SWENSON ST

PARADISE ROAD

EAST OF
STRIP

TROPICANA AVE

McCarran
International
Airport

LAS VEGAS BOULEVARD SOUTH

15

WEST OF STRIP

VALLEY VIEW BLVD

ARVILLE ST

RUSSELL ROAD

RUSSELL ROAD

SUNSET ROAD

2 miles

3 km

0

© Copyright Time Out Group 2001

CAT Bus Routes

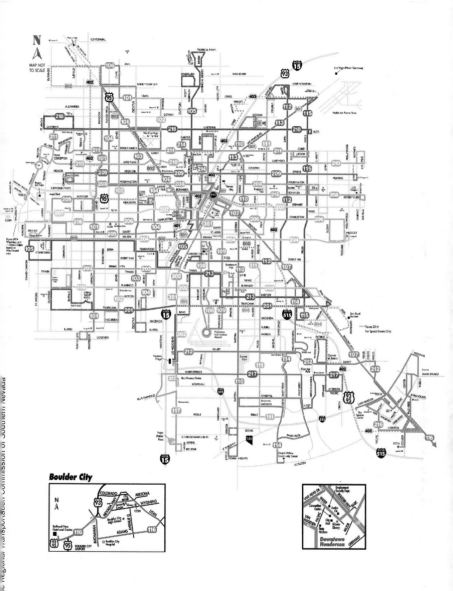

Street Index

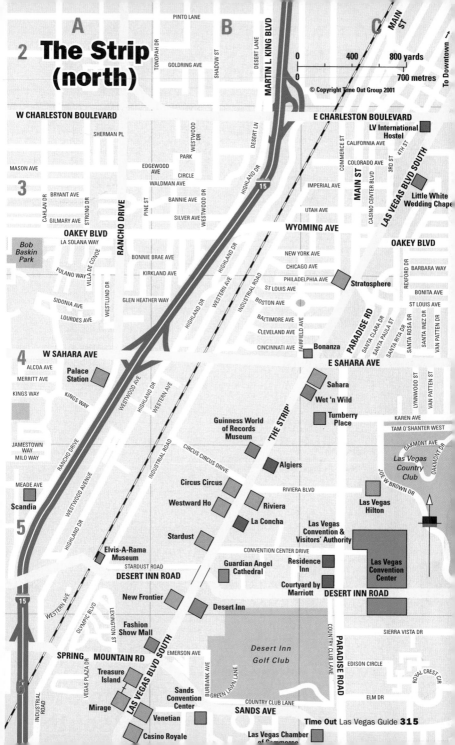

A | B | C

PINTO LANE

MAIN ST

To Downtown

0 — 400 — 800 yards
0 — 700 metres
© Copyright Time Out Group 2001

TONOPAH DR
GOLDRING AVE
SHADOW ST
DESERT LANE
MARTIN L. KING BLVD

W CHARLESTON BOULEVARD

E CHARLESTON BOULEVARD

LV International Hostel

SHERMAN PL
CALIFORNIA AVE
COMMERCE ST
4TH ST

MASON AVE
WESTWOOD DR
PARK
EDGEWOOD AVE
CIRCLE
WALDMAN AVE
COLORADO AVE
CASINO CENTER BLVD
3RD ST
LAS VEGAS BLVD SOUTH

Little White Wedding Chapel

IMPERIAL AVE

CAHLAN DR
BRYANT AVE
STRONG DR
PINE ST
WESTWOOD DR
BANNIE AVE
SILVER AVE
HIGHLAND DR
UTAH AVE
MAIN ST

GILMARY AVE
OAKEY BLVD
LA SOLANA WAY
WYOMING AVE

OAKEY BLVD

Bob Baskin Park

RANCHO DRIVE
VILLA DE CONDE
BONNIE BRAE AVE
KIRKLAND AVE
GLEN HEATHER WAY
WESTERN AVE
INDUSTRIAL ROAD
HIGHLAND DR

NEW YORK AVE
CHICAGO AVE
PHILADELPHIA AVE
ST LOUIS AVE
BOSTON AVE
BALTIMORE AVE
CLEVELAND AVE
CINCINNATI AVE

Stratosphere

REXFORD DR
BARBARA WAY
BONITA AVE
ST LOUIS AVE

FULANO WAY
SIDONIA AVE
LOURDES AVE
WESTLUND DR

PARADISE RD
SANTA CLARA DR
SANTA PAULA ST
SANTA ROSA ST
SANTA RITA DR
SANTA INEZ DR
VAN PATTEN DR

FAIRFIELD AVE

Bonanza

E SAHARA AVE

W SAHARA AVE

ALCOA AVE
MERRITT AVE
KINGS WAY
Palace Station
KINGS WAY

Sahara
Wet 'n Wild
Turnberry Place

LYNNWOOD ST
VAN PATTEN ST

KAREN AVE
TAM O'SHANTER WEST

JAMESTOWN WAY
MILO WAY
WESTWOOD AVE
HIGHLAND DR
WESTERN AVE
INDUSTRIAL ROAD

Guinness World of Records Museum

'THE STRIP'

Las Vegas Country Club

OAKMONT AVE
OAKMONT AVE
JOE W BROWN DR

MEADE AVE
Scandia

CIRCUS CIRCUS DRIVE

Algiers

RIVIERA BLVD

Circus Circus
Westward Ho
Riviera
La Concha
Stardust

Las Vegas Hilton

RANCHO DRIVE
WESTWOOD AVENUE
HIGHLAND DR
WESTERN AVE

Elvis-A-Rama Museum
STARDUST ROAD
DESERT INN ROAD

CONVENTION CENTER DRIVE
Guardian Angel Cathedral

Las Vegas Convention & Visitors' Authority

Residence Inn

Las Vegas Convention Center

SIERRA VISTA DR

New Frontier
Desert Inn

Courtyard by Marriott
DESERT INN ROAD

PARADISE ROAD
EDISON CIRCLE

LEXINGTON ST
OLYMPIC BLVD
Fashion Show Mall

Desert Inn Golf Club

COUNTRY CLUB LANE

ROYAL CREST CIR

SPRING MOUNTAIN RD
EMERSON AVE
Treasure Island
Sands Convention Center
Mirage
Venetian
Casino Royale

BURBANK AVE
GREEN VALLEY LANE
SANDS AVE
Las Vegas Chamber of Commerce

ELM DR

VEGAS PLAZA DR
INDUSTRIAL ROAD
LAS VEGAS BLVD SOUTH

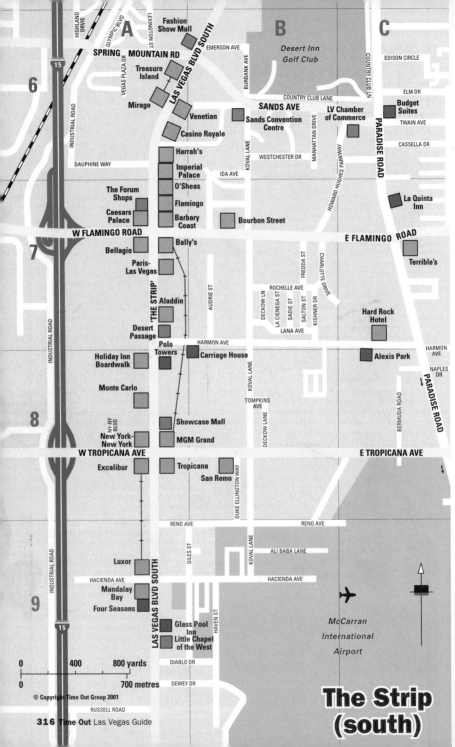

The Strip (south)

TimeOut Las Vegas Please let us know what you think

About this guide...

1. How useful did you find the following sections?

	Very	Fairly	Not very
In Context	☐	☐	☐
Accommodation	☐	☐	☐
Sightseeing	☐	☐	☐
Eat, Drink, Shop	☐	☐	☐
Arts & Entertainment	☐	☐	☐
Trips Out of Town	☐	☐	☐
Directory	☐	☐	☐
Maps	☐	☐	☐

2. Did you travel to Las Vegas...?

Alone ☐	With children ☐		
As part of a group ☐	On vacation ☐		
On business ☐	To study ☐		
With a partner ☐	I live here ☐		

3. How long was your trip to Las Vegas?
(write in) _____ days

4. Where did you book your trip?
Time Out Classifieds ☐
On the Internet ☐
With a travel agent ☐
Other (write in) ☐
_____

5. Where did you first hear about this guide?
Advertising in *Time Out* magazine ☐
On the Internet ☐
From a travel agent ☐
Other (write in) ☐
_____

6. Is there anything you'd like us to cover in greater depth?
_____
_____
_____

7. Are there any places that should/ should not * be included in the guide?
(*delete as necessary)
_____
_____
_____
_____

8. How many other people have used this guide?
none ☐ 1 ☐ 2 ☐ 3 ☐ 4 ☐ 5+ ☐

9. What city or country would you like to visit next? (write in)
_____
_____

About other Time Out publications...

10. Have you ever bought/used *Time Out* magazine?
Yes ☐   No ☐

11. Have you ever bought/used any other Time Out City Guides?
Yes ☐   No ☐
If yes, which ones?
_____

12. Have you ever bought/used other Time Out publications?
Yes ☐   No ☐
If yes, which ones?
_____

About you...

13. Title (Mr, Ms etc): _____
First name: _____
Surname: _____
Address: _____
_____ P/code: _____
Email: _____
Nationality: _____

14. Date of birth: ☐☐/☐☐/☐☐

15. Sex: male ☐ female ☐

16. Are you...?
Single ☐
Married/Living with partner ☐

17. What is your occupation? ☐☐☐☐☐

18. At the moment do you earn...?
under £15,000 ☐
over £15,000 and up to £19,999 ☐
over £20,000 and up to £24,999 ☐
over £25,000 and up to £39,999 ☐
over £40,000 and up to £49,999 ☐
over £50,000 ☐

☐ Please tick here if you do not wish to receive information about other Time Out products.
☐ Please tick here if you do not wish to receive mailings from third parties.

Time Out Guides

FREEPOST 20 (WC3187)
LONDON
W1E 0DQ